10TH EDITION

MICROECONOMICS *for* Today

Irvin B. Tucker
University of North Carolina at Charlotte

CENGAGE

Australia • Brazil • Mexico • Singapore • United Kingdom • United States

CENGAGE

Microeconomics for Today, Tenth Edition

Irvin B. Tucker

Contributing Authors: Douglas W. Copeland, Johnson County Community College and Joseph P. McGarrity, University of Central Arkansas

Senior Vice President, Higher Ed Product, Content, and Market Development: Erin Joyner

Product Director: Jason Fremder

Sr. Product Manager: Michael Parthenakis

Sr. Content Developer: Julia Chase

Executive Marketing Manager: John Carey

Sr. Content Project Manager: Colleen Farmer

Production Service: Lumina Datamatics, Inc.

Sr. Art Director: Michelle Kunkler

Cover and Internal Designer: Red Hangar Design

Cover Image: Andrew Koturanov/ Shutterstock.com

Intellectual Property

　Analyst: Diane Garrity

　Project Manager: Sarah Shainwald

Internal Image Credit Lines: dencg/Shutterstock.com; Andrii Symonenko/Shutterstock.com; mkos83/Shutterstock.com; Nelson Marques/Shutterstock.com; Intrepix/Shutterstock.com; Jezper/Shutterstock.com

Library of Congress Control Number: 2017963568

ISBN: 978-1-337-61306-4

Cengage
20 Channel Center Street
Boston, MA 02210
USA

Cengage is a leading provider of customized learning solutions with employees residing in nearly 40 different countries and sales in more than 125 countries around the world. Find your local representative at **www.cengage.com.**

Cengage products are represented in Canada by Nelson Education, Ltd.

To learn more about Cengage platforms and services, visit **www.cengage.com**

To register or access your online learning solution or purchase materials for your course, visit **www.cengagebrain.com**

Printed in the United States of America
Print Number: 01　　Print Year: 2018

IRVIN B. TUCKER

IRVIN B. TUCKER was a longtime leader in economic education with over 30 years of experience teaching introductory economics at the University of North Carolina at Charlotte. He earned his B.S. in economics at N.C. State University and his M.A. and Ph.D. in economics from the University of South Carolina. Dr. Tucker served as executive director of the S.C. Council of Education and director of the Center for Economic Education at the University of North Carolina at Charlotte. Dr. Tucker is recognized for his ability to relate basic principles to economic issues and public policy. His work has received national recognition by being awarded the Meritorious Levy Award for Excellence in Private Enterprise Education, the Federation of Independent Business Award for Postsecondary Educator of the Year in Entrepreneurship and Economic Education, and the Freedom Foundation's George Washington Medal for Excellence in Economic Education. In addition, his research has been published in numerous professional economics journals on a wide range of topics including industrial organization, entrepreneurship, and economics of education. Dr. Tucker is also the author of the highly successful *Survey of Economics*, tenth edition, a text for the one-semester principles of economics courses, published by Cengage Learning.

BRIEF CONTENTS

CONTENTS

AVAILABLE VERSIONS

The Four Versions of This Book

Economics for Today	Economics for Today	Microeconomics for Today	Macroeconomics for Today	Survey of Economics
1 Introducing the Economic Way of Thinking	X	X	X	X
2 Production Possibilities, Opportunity Cost, and Economic Growth	X	X	X	X
3 Market Demand and Supply	X	X	X	X
4 Markets in Action	X	X	X	X
5 Price Elasticity of Demand and Supply	X	X		X
6 Consumer Choice Theory	X	X		
7 Production Costs	X	X		X
8 Perfect Competition	X	X		X
9 Monopoly	X	X		X
10 Monopolistic Competition and Oligopoly	X	X		X
11 Labor Markets	X	X		X
12 Income Distribution, Poverty, and Discrimination	X	X		X
13 Antitrust and Regulation	X	X		
14 Environmental Economics	X	X		
15 Gross Domestic Product	X		X	X
16 Business Cycles and Unemployment	X		X	X
17 Inflation	X		X	X
18 The Keynesian Model	X		X	
19 The Keynesian Model in Action	X		X	
20 Aggregate Demand and Supply	X		X	X
21 Fiscal Policy	X		X	X
22 The Public Sector	X		X	X
23 Federal Deficits, Surpluses, and the National Debt	X		X	X
24 Money and the Federal Reserve System	X		X	X
25 Money Creation	X		X	X
26 Monetary Policy	X		X	X
27 The Phillips Curve and Expectations Theory	X		X	
28 International Trade and Finance	X	X	X	X
29 Economies in Transition	X	X	X	X
30 Growth and the Less-Developed Countries	X	X	X	X

Note: Chapter numbers refer to the complete book, *Economics for Today*.

PREFACE

TEXT WITH A MISSION

The purpose of *Economics for Today*, tenth edition, is to teach, in an engaging style, the basic operations of the U.S. economy to students who will take a two-term economics course. Rather than taking an encyclopedic approach to economic concepts, *Economics for Today* focuses on the most important tools in economics and applies these concepts to clearly explain real-world economic issues and events.

Every effort has been made to make *Economics for Today* the most student-friendly text on the market. This text was written because so many others expose students to a confusing array of economic analyses that force students to simply memorize in order to pass the course. Instead, *Economics for Today* presents a straightforward and unbiased approach that effectively teaches the application of basic economic principles. After reading this text, the student should be able to say, "Now that economics stuff in the news makes sense."

HOW IT FITS TOGETHER

This text presents the core principles of microeconomics, macroeconomics, and international economics. The first 14 chapters introduce the logic of economic analysis and develop the core of microeconomic analysis. Here, students learn the role of demand and supply in determining prices in competitive markets versus monopolistic markets. Within these chapters, the book explores such issues as minimum wage laws, rent control, and pollution. The next 13 chapters develop the macroeconomics part of the text. Using the modern yet simple aggregate demand and aggregate supply model, the text explains measurement of and changes in the price level, national output, and employment in the economy. The study of macroeconomics also includes how the supply of and the demand for money influences the economy. Finally, this text concludes with three chapters devoted entirely to global issues. For example, students will learn how the supply of and demand for currencies determine exchange rates and what the implications are for a strong or a weak dollar on our nation's economy.

TEXT FLEXIBILITY

The full version of *Economics for Today* is easily adapted to an instructor's preference for the sequencing of microeconomics and macroeconomics topics. This text can be used in a macroeconomic–microeconomic sequence by teaching the first four chapters and then Parts 5 through 7. Next, microeconomics is covered in Parts 2 through 4. Finally, the course can be completed with Part 8, consisting of three chapters devoted to international economics.

An important design of this text is that it accommodates the two major approaches for teaching principles of macroeconomics: those who cover both the Keynesian Cross and AD/AS models, and those who skip the Keynesian model and cover only the AD/AS model. For instructors who prefer the former, *Economics for Today* moves smoothly in Chapters 18–19 (*Macroeconomics for Today* Chapters 8–9) from the Keynesian model (based on the Great Depression) to the AD/AS model in Chapter 20 (*Macroeconomics for Today* Chapter 10). For instructors using the latter approach, this text is written so that instructors can skip the Keynesian model in Chapters 18–19 (*Macroeconomics for Today* Chapters 8–9) and proceed from Chapter 17 (*Macroeconomics for Today* Chapter 7) to Chapter 20 (*Macroeconomics for Today* Chapter 10) without losing anything. For example, the spending multiplier is completely covered both in the Keynesian and AD/AS model chapters.

For instructors who want to teach the self-correcting AD/AS model, emphasis can be placed on the appendixes to Chapters 20 (*Macroeconomics for Today* Chapter 10) and 26 (*Macroeconomics for Today* Chapter 16). Instructors who choose not to cover this model can simply skip these appendixes. In short, *Economics for Today* provides more comprehensive and flexible coverage of macroeconomics models than is available in other texts. Also, a customized text might meet your needs. If so, contact your Cengage learning consultant for information.

HOW NOT TO STUDY ECONOMICS

To some students, studying economics is a little frightening because many chapters are full of graphs. Students often make the mistake of preparing for tests by trying to memorize the lines of graphs. When their graded tests are returned, the students using this strategy will probably exclaim, "What happened?" The answer to this question is that the students should have learned the economic concepts *first;* then they would understand the graphs as *illustrations* of these underlying concepts. Stated simply, superficial cramming for economics quizzes does not work.

For students who are anxious about using graphs, the Appendix to Chapter 1 provides a brief review of graphical analysis. In addition, Graph Builder in the Tucker MindTap product contains step-by-step features on how to construct and interpret graphs. Moreover, and new to this edition, Videos entitled "GuideMe Videos" (A Graphing Tutorial for Students) are found in the Tucker MindTap product that explain numerous key graphs throughout the textbook.

CHANGES TO THE TENTH EDITION

The basic layout of the tenth edition remains the same. The following are changes:

- Chapter 1, Introducing the Economic Way of Thinking, recognizes that students taking introductory, college-level economics courses are considering their major. One reason to select economics is that the average starting salary for an undergraduate economics major is higher compared to many other majors. To aid their decision, current average starting salary figures for selected majors have been updated. In addition, the *You're the Economist* feature on the Minimum Wage has been updated with the positive and normative arguments both for and against the minimum wage.

- Chapter 2, Production Possibilities, Opportunity Cost, and Economic Growth has an updated discussion on how public investment in infrastructure can promote economic growth and enhance the average absolute standard of living for a nation.

- Chapter 4, Markets in Action, has updated the *You're the Economist* feature entitled "Rigging the Market for Milk" to reflect the latest changes in government's attempts at supporting farm incomes.

- Chapter 9, Monopoly, has an example of the "sharing economy" that has been updated in the *You're the Economist* on New York Taxicabs. This feature now concludes with a discussion of the unregulated rideshares market with companies like Uber and Lyft.

- Chapter 11, Labor Markets, has a new *Checkpoint* that asks students to consider a business' location decision based on union membership.

- Chapter 12, Income Distribution, Poverty, and Discrimination, has been updated with the latest figures on family income distribution and poverty rates. In addition, Chapter 12 also has a new *You're the Economist* feature that focuses on the growing income and wealth inequality in the United States. The other *You're the Economist* that addresses fair pay for females has been updated. These features generate great interest for students.

- Chapter 14, Environmental Economics, has an updated *You're the Economist* on climate change that incorporates the Paris Climate Agreement.

- Chapter 15, International Trade and Finance, has updated data for international balance of payments and trade.

- Chapter 16, Economies in Transition, has greater clarification on the differences between capitalism and socialism and why all real-world economies are mixed economies. This chapter also features a new *You're the Economist* entitled "The unrealistic path to communism." In addition, there is a new *Global Economics* section that points to a satellite photo of North Korea as perhaps a compelling testimony to the long-run failure of undemocratic command economies. Students should find this interesting.

- Chapter 17, Growth and the Less-Developed Countries, presents updated data ranking countries by their GDP per capita. It also presents updated data comparing regions of the world by their average GDP per capita. Here, updated data is used to explain the link between economic freedom and quality-of-life indicators. There is a new *You're the Economist* section entitled "India and China's Economic Growth: An Updated Version of Aesop's Tale" that probes the ingredients for sustained economic growth.

ALTERNATIVE VERSIONS OF THE BOOK

For instructors who want to spend various amounts of time for their courses and offer different topics of this text:

- *Economics for Today.* This complete version of the book contains all 30 chapters. It is designed for two-semester introductory courses that cover both microeconomics and macroeconomics.

- *Microeconomics for Today.* This version contains 17 chapters and is designed for one-semester courses in introductory microeconomics.
- *Macroeconomics for Today.* This version contains 20 chapters and is designed for one-semester courses in introductory macroeconomics.
- *Survey of Economics.* This version of the book contains 23 chapters. It is designed for one-semester courses that cover the basics of both microeconomics and macroeconomics.

The Available Versions accompanying table on page xxi shows precisely which chapters are included in each book. Instructors who want more information about these alternative versions should contact their local Cengage learning consultant.

MOTIVATIONAL PEDAGOGICAL FEATURES

Economics for Today strives to motivate and advance the boundaries of pedagogy with the following features:

Part Openers

Each part begins with a statement of the overall mission of the chapters in the part. In addition, there is a nutshell introduction of each chapter in relation to the part's learning objective.

Chapter Previews

Each chapter begins with a preview designed to pique the student's interest and reinforce how the chapter fits into the overall scheme of the book. Each preview appeals to students' "Sherlock Holmes" impulses by posing several economics puzzles that can be solved by understanding the material presented in the chapter.

Margin Definitions and Flashcards

Key concepts introduced in the chapter are highlighted in bold type and then defined with the definitions again in the margins. This feature therefore serves as a quick reference. Key terms are also defined on the Tucker MindTap product with a flashcard feature that is great for learning terms.

You're the Economist

Each chapter includes boxed inserts that provide the acid test of "relevance to everyday life." This feature gives the student an opportunity to encounter timely, real-world extensions of economic theory. For example, students read about Fred Smith as he writes an economics term paper explaining his plan to create FedEx. To ensure that the student wastes no time figuring out which concepts apply to the article, applicable concepts are listed after each title. Several of these boxed features include quotes from newspaper articles over a period of years demonstrating that economic concepts remain relevant over time. Many of these boxed features have been updated or changed in the tenth edition to reflect the latest issues, developments, and relevant applications of economics for students today.

Conclusion Statements

Throughout the chapters, highlighted conclusion statements of key concepts appear at the ends of sections and tie together the material just presented. Students will be able to see quickly if they have understood the main points of the section. A summary of these conclusion statements is provided at the end of each chapter.

Global Economics

Today's economic environment is global. *Economics for Today* carefully integrates international topics throughout the text and presents the material using a highly readable and accessible approach designed for students with no training in international economics. All sections of the text that present global economics are identified by a special global icon in the text margin and in the *Global Economics* boxes. In addition, the final three chapters of the book are devoted entirely to international economics.

Analyze the Issue

This feature follows each *You're the Economist* and *Global Economics* feature and asks specific questions that require students to test their knowledge of how the material in the boxed insert is relevant to the applicable concept. To allow these questions to be used in classroom discussions or homework assignments, answers are provided in the Instructor's Manual rather than in the text.

Checkpoint

Watch for these! Who said learning economics can't be fun? This feature is a unique approach to generating interest and critical thinking. These questions spark students to check their progress by asking challenging economics puzzles in game-like style. Students enjoy thinking through and answering the questions, and then checking the answers at the end of the chapter. Students who answer correctly earn the satisfaction of knowing they have mastered the concepts. Many of these have been updated for the tenth edition to pique interest and to apply to the experiences of students today.

Exhibits

Attractive large graphical presentations with grid lines and real-world numbers are essential for any successful economics textbook. Each exhibit has been carefully analyzed to ensure that the key concepts being represented stand out clearly. Brief descriptions are included with graphs to provide guidance for students as they study the graph. The MindTap course brings these exhibits to life:

- Students can interact with selected exhibits via Graph Builder.
- Students can watch detailed explanations of selected exhibits via GuideMe Videos (A graphing tutorial for students.)

Causation Chain Game

This will be one of your favorites. The highly successful causation chains are included under many graphs throughout the text. This pedagogical device helps students visualize complex economic relationships in terms of simple box diagrams that illustrate how one change causes another change. Each exhibit has a causation chain in the text, and a correlating in the animated causation chain game exercise in the Tucker MindTap product. Arrange the blocks correctly to win the game.

Key Concepts

Key concepts introduced in the chapter are listed at the end of each chapter and defined in the margins. Visit the Tucker MindTap to access for interactive flashcards.

Visual Summaries

Each chapter ends with a brief point-by-point summary of the key concepts. Many of these summarized points include miniaturized versions of the important graphs and causation chains that illustrate many of the key concepts. These are intended to serve as visual reminders for students as they finish the chapters and are also useful in reviewing and studying for quizzes and exams.

Study Questions and Problems

These end-of-chapter questions and problems offer a variety of levels ranging from straightforward recall to deeply thought-provoking applications. The answers to odd-numbered questions and problems are found in Appendix A in the back of the text. This feature gives students immediate feedback without requiring the instructor to check their work. The even-numbered answers are found in the Instructor's Manual.

End-of-Chapter Sample Quizzes

These particular assessments are a great help before quizzes. Many instructors test students using multiple-choice questions. For this reason, the final section of each chapter provides the type of multiple-choice questions given in the test bank. The answers are readily available to students to help them learn the material and are found in Appendix B at the end of the textbook. In addition to the end-of-chapter sample quizzes, each section quiz appears in the Tucker MindTap product. Each quiz contains multiple questions like those found on a typical exam. Feedback is included for each answer so that you may know instantly why you have answered correctly or incorrectly. Between this feature and the end-of-chapter sample quizzes, students are well prepared for tests. Finally, the Instructor's Manual also contains four to five multiple choice questions per chapter that can also be used to engage students with the material.

Road Maps

This feature concludes each sectioned part with review questions listed by chapter from the particular part. To reinforce the concepts, each set of questions relates to the interactive causation chain game that is available in the Tucker MindTap product. This makes learning fun. Answers to the questions are also found in Appendix C in the back of the text.

A SUPPLEMENTS PACKAGE DESIGNED FOR SUCCESS

Tucker is known for its unequaled resources for instructors and students. To access additional course material for *Economics for Today,* visit www.cengagebrain.com. At the CengageBrain.com home page, search for "Tucker" using the search box on the page. This will take you to the product page where these resources can be found. For additional information, contact your Cengage learning consultant.

INSTRUCTORS RESOURCES

Tucker Companion Site

The Tucker website at www.cengagebrain.com provides open access to PowerPoint chapter review slides; an instructor's manual prepared by Douglas Copeland of Johnson County Community College, available in various formats; updates to the text, describing key concepts relevant to the current states of economics and the world today; PowerPoint lecture tools elaborating on key concepts and exhibits, which can be used as supplies or can be customized for instructor intentions; and test banks in various downloadable formats.

STUDENT RESOURCES

MindTap for Tucker

MindTap engages students and aids them in consistently producing their best work. By seamlessly integrating course material with interactive media, step-by-step graphing, activities, apps, and much more, MindTap creates a unique learning path for courses that foster increased comprehension and efficiency of material.

- MindTap delivers real-world relevance with activities, assignments, homework, media, and study tools that help students build critical thinking and analytic skills that will carry over to their professional lives.
- MindTap helps students stay organized and efficient with a single destination that reflects what's important to the instructor and the tools to master that content. MindTap empowers students to get their "game face on" by motivating them with competitive benchmarks in performance.
- Relevant readings, multimedia, and activities are designed to take students up the levels of learning from basic knowledge to analysis and application.
- Graph Builder exercises enable students to practice building their own graphs and honing the skills to do so for application both in the course and real-life situations.

- Students can watch detailed explanations of selected exhibits via GuideMe Videos (A Graphing Tutorial for Students) that explain numerous key graphs throughout the textbook.
- Analytics and reports provide a snapshot of class progress, time in course, engagement and completion rates.
- Homework and the Math & Graphing Tutorial, both powered by Aplia, as well as videos that explain key graphs round out the student learning experience within MindTap that enable students to master course content.

Acknowledgments

A deep debt of gratitude is owed to the reviewers of all ten editions for their expert assistance. All comments and suggestions were carefully evaluated and served to improve the final product.

Special Thanks

Much appreciation goes to Michael Parthenakis, Senior Product Manager. Thanks also to Clara Goosman, Content Development Manager, Julia Chase, Content Developer, Colleen Farmer, Senior Content Project Manager; Michelle Kunkler, Senior Art Director; Derek Drifmeyer, Senior Digital Project Manager; Drew Gaither, Media Producer; and Denisse Zavala-Rosalez, Product Assistant. I am also grateful to John Carey for his skillful marketing. Finally, I give my sincere thanks for a job well done to the entire team at Cengage.

A Tribute to Irvin B. Tucker

The contributing authors and the entire Cengage team want to express our heartfelt gratitude for the opportunity and the privilege to have been able to work with Irvin Tucker and this textbook over all these years. Some of us have had the honor of working with Irvin from the beginning, when this book was just a manuscript. We know of few, if any, other authors who have consistently demonstrated such a firm commitment and tireless dedication to teaching and learning. Irvin has always believed that knowledge of economics can enhance people's lives and should therefore be made accessible to everyone. And Irvin has displayed the rare ability to translate complex concepts into easily understood principles that have enriched the lives of countless numbers of students across the globe. He has made economics not only accessible but fun to learn. For this, he has distinguished himself among the very best economists of our time! He is a true complement to the profession of economics and to the noble cause of education. Beyond having earned our respect as a superb economist and author, Irvin has also been such a joy to work with. He has always been kind to everyone, willing to listen to any new ideas or suggestions, and has consistently made everyone feel needed and appreciated.

We would be remiss if we did not also make a tribute to Irvin's wife, Nonie. Nonie also possesses the traits of those you feel blessed to work with. She has also made countless meaningful contributions to this title from the very beginning. Irvin and Nonie have always been known to be "quite the team!" Thank you Irvin, and thank you Nonie! You have made the world a better place!

This edition is dedicated to Irvin B. Tucker.

Microeconomics *for* Today

PART 1

Introduction to Economics

The first two chapters introduce you to a foundation of economic knowledge vital to understanding the other chapters in the text. In these introductory chapters, you will begin to learn a valuable reasoning approach to solving economics puzzles that economists call "the economic way of thinking." Part 1 develops the cornerstone of this type of logical analysis by presenting basic economic models that explain such important topics as scarcity, opportunity cost, production possibilities, and economic growth.

CHAPTER 1

Introducing the Economic Way of Thinking

CHAPTER PREVIEW

You and I know that navigating the complex social environment in which we live as we strive to be successful and happy is not easy. However, understanding the important economic, social (cultural), and political (legal) elements at play and how they interact can certainly help. In fact, all headline-grabbing issues of our times can be viewed from these three perspectives. Perhaps all too often the economic perspective is the least understood. So, what is this *economic perspective*? What is the economic way of thinking?

In this text, you will learn what it means to think economically. You will discover that the world is full of economics problems requiring more powerful tools than just common sense. Just to give a sneak preview, in later chapters, you will discover the shortcomings of government price fixing for gasoline and health care. You will also find out why colleges and universities charge students different tuitions for the same education. You

will investigate whether you should worry if the federal government fails to balance its budget. You will learn that the island of Yap uses large stones with holes in the center as money. In the final chapter, you will study why some countries grow rich while others remain poor and less developed. And the list of fascinating and relevant topics continues throughout each chapter. As you read these pages, your efforts will be rewarded by an understanding of just how much economic theories and policies affect our daily lives past, present, and future.

Chapter 1 acquaints you with the foundation of the economic way of thinking. The first building blocks joined are the concepts of scarcity and choice. The next building blocks are the steps in the model-building process that economists use to study the choices people make. Then we look at some pitfalls of economic reasoning and explain why economists might disagree with one another. The chapter concludes with a discussion of why you may want to be an economics major.

IN THIS CHAPTER, YOU WILL LEARN TO SOLVE THESE ECONOMICS PUZZLES:

- Can you prove there is no person worth a trillion dollars?
- Why would you purchase more Coca-Cola when its price increases?
- How can the relationship between the Super Bowl winner and changes in the stock market be explained?

1-1 THE PROBLEM OF SCARCITY

At the heart of the economic way of thinking is the fact that we live in a world of scarcity. **Scarcity** is the condition in which human wants are forever greater than the available supply of time, goods, and resources. Because of scarcity, we are unable to have as much as we would like. It is impossible to satisfy every desire. Pause for a moment to list some of your unsatisfied wants. Perhaps you would like a big home, gourmet meals, designer clothes, clean air, better health care, shelter for the homeless, more leisure time, and so on. Unfortunately, nature does not offer the Garden of Eden, where every desire is fulfilled. Instead, there are always limits on the economy's ability to satisfy unlimited wants. Alas, scarcity is pervasive, so "you can't have it all."

You may think your scarcity problem would disappear if you were rich, but wealth does not solve the problem. No matter how affluent an individual is, the wish list continues to grow. We are familiar with the "rich and famous" who never seem to have enough. Although they live well, they still desire finer homes, faster planes, and larger yachts. In short, the condition of scarcity means all individuals, whether rich or poor, are dissatisfied with their material well-being and would like more. What is true for individuals also applies to society. Even Uncle Sam can't escape the problem of scarcity because the federal government never has enough money to spend for education, highways, police, national defense, Social Security, and all the other programs it wants to fund.

Scarcity is a fact of life throughout the world. In much of South America, Africa, and Asia, the problem of scarcity is often life-threatening. On the other hand, North America, Western Europe, and some parts of Asia have achieved substantial economic growth and development. Although life is much less "gruelling" in the more developed countries, the problem of scarcity still exists because individuals and countries never have as much of all the goods and services as they would like to have. As a result of scarcity, every nation must decide what combination of products to produce, how much to produce, and who is going to get those goods and services. These economic choices have profound social and political implications.

Scarcity
The condition in which human wants are forever greater than the available supply of time, goods, and resources.

> The problems of scarcity and choice are basic economic problems faced by every society.

CONCLUSION

1-2 SCARCE RESOURCES AND PRODUCTION

Because of the economic problem of scarcity, no society has enough resources to produce all the goods and services necessary to satisfy all human wants. **Resources** are the basic categories of inputs used to produce goods and services. Resources are also called *factors of production*. Economists divide resources into three categories: *land, labor,* and *capital* (see Exhibit 1).

1-2a Land

Land is a shorthand expression for any natural resource provided by nature that is used to produce a good or service. *Land* includes those resources or raw materials that are gifts of

Resources
The basic categories of inputs used to produce goods and services. Resources are also called *factors of production*. Economists divide resources into three categories: *land, labor,* and *capital.*

Land
Any natural resource provided by nature that is used to produce a good or service.

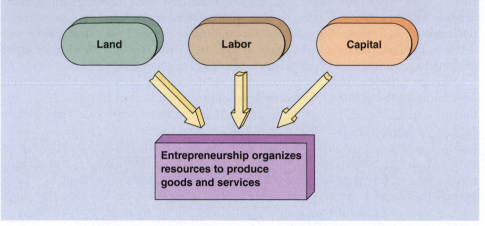

EXHIBIT 1 Three Categories of Resources

Resources are the basic categories of inputs organized by entrepreneurship (a special type of labor) to produce goods and services. Economists divide resources into the three categories of land, labor, and capital.

Land   Labor   Capital

Entrepreneurship organizes resources to produce goods and services

nature available for use in the production process. Farming, building factories, and constructing oil refineries would be impossible without land. Land includes anything natural above or below the ground, such as forests, gold, diamonds, oil, coal, wind, and the ocean. Two broad categories of natural resources are *renewable resources* and *nonrenewable resources*. Renewable resources are basic inputs that nature can automatically replace. Examples include crops, clean air, and the water and fish in lakes. Nonrenewable resources are basic inputs that nature cannot automatically replace. There is only so much coal, oil, and natural gas in the world. If these fossil fuels disappear, we must use substitutes.

1-2b Labor

Labor is the mental and physical capacity of workers to produce goods and services. The services of farmers, assembly-line workers, lawyers, professional football players, and economists are all *labor*. The labor resource is measured both by the number of people available for work and by the skills or quality of workers. One reason nations differ in their ability to produce is that human characteristics, such as the education, experience, health, and motivation of workers, differ among nations.

Entrepreneurship is a special type of labor. **Entrepreneurship** is the creative ability of individuals to seek profits by taking risks and combining resources to produce innovative products. An *entrepreneur* is a motivated person who seeks profits by undertaking risky activities such as starting new businesses, creating new products, or inventing new ways of accomplishing tasks. Entrepreneurs are often successful when they embrace new or existing technologies (using their "know-how") in creative ways. For example, consider all of the amazing apps created for use with Androids and the iPhone. Entrepreneurship is a scarce human resource because relatively few people are willing or able to innovate and make decisions involving a high likelihood of failure. An important benefit of entrepreneurship is that it creates a growing economy.

Labor
The mental and physical capacity of workers to produce goods and services.

Entrepreneurship
The creative ability of individuals to seek profits by taking risks and combining resources to produce innovative products.

Entrepreneurs are the agents of change who bring material progress to society. The birth of the Levi Strauss Company is a classic entrepreneurial success story. In 1853, at the age of 24, Levi Strauss, who was born in Bavaria, sailed from New York to join the California Gold Rush. His intent was not to dig for gold but to sell cloth. By the time he arrived in San Francisco, he had sold most of his cloth to other people on the ship. The only cloth he had left was a roll of canvas for tents and covered wagons. On the dock, he met a miner who wanted sturdy pants that would last while digging for gold, so Levi made a pair from the canvas. Later, a customer gave Levi the idea of using little copper rivets to strengthen the seams. Presto! Strauss knew a good thing when he saw it, so he hired workers, built factories, and became one of the largest pants makers in the world. As a reward for taking business risks, organizing production, and introducing a product, the Levi Strauss Company earned profits, and Strauss became rich and famous.

1-2c **Capital**

Capital can be defined as a human-made good used to produce other goods and services; for example, capital includes the physical plants, machinery, and equipment used to produce other goods. Capital can be privately or publicly owned. Private capital is owned by private companies and consists of factories, office buildings, warehouses, robots, trucks, and distribution facilities. Public (or social) capital, also known as *infrastructure*, is provided by government through taxes and is collectively owned. It consists of roads, bridges, dams, airports, harbors, and public universities and other government buildings. The term *capital*, as it is used in the study of economics, can be confusing. Economists know that capital in everyday conversations means money or the money value of paper assets, such as stocks, bonds, or a deed to a house. This is actually *financial* capital. In the study of economics, capital does not refer to money assets. Capital in economics means a factor of production, such as a factory or machinery. Stated simply, you must pay special attention to this point: Money is not capital and is, therefore, not a resource. Instead, money is used to purchase land, labor, or capital, as well as many consumer goods and services.

Capital
A human-made good used to produce other goods and services.

> Money by itself does not produce goods and services; instead, it is only a means to facilitate the purchase and sale of resources and consumer products.

CONCLUSION

1-3 ECONOMICS: THE STUDY OF SCARCITY AND CHOICE

The perpetual problem of scarcity forcing people to make choices is the basis for the definition of economics. **Economics** is the study of how society chooses to allocate its scarce resources to satisfy unlimited wants. You may be surprised by this definition. People often think economics means studying supply and demand, the stock market, money, and banking. Well, those are certainly parts, but economics is more all-encompassing. It is the study of the choices we make because we are faced with scarcity—because we are unable to have as much as we would like.

Society makes two broad levels of choices: economy-wide, or macro choices, and individual, or micro choices. The prefixes *macro* and *micro* come from the Greek words

Economics
The study of how society chooses to allocate its scarce resources to the production of goods and services to satisfy unlimited wants.

meaning "large" and "small," respectively. Reflecting the macro and micro perspectives, economics consists of two main branches: *macroeconomics* and *microeconomics*.

1-3a Macroeconomics

Macroeconomics
The branch of economics that studies decision making for the economy as a whole.

The old saying "Looking at the forest rather than the trees" describes **macroeconomics**, which is the branch of economics that studies decision making for the economy as a whole. Macroeconomics applies an overview perspective to an economy by examining economy-wide variables, such as inflation, unemployment, economic growth, the money supply, and the national incomes of different countries. Macroeconomic decision making considers such "big picture" policies as the effect that federal tax cuts will have on unemployment and the effect that a change in the money supply will have on inflation.

1-3b Microeconomics

Microeconomics
The branch of economics that studies decision making by a single individual, household, firm, industry, or level of government.

Examining individual trees, leaves, and pieces of bark, rather than surveying the forest, illustrates microeconomics. **Microeconomics** is the branch of economics that studies decision making by a single individual, household, firm, industry, or level of government. It applies a microscope to study specific parts of an economy, as one would examine cells in the body. The focus is on small economic units, such as economic decisions of particular groups of consumers and businesses. An example of microeconomic analysis would be to study economic units involved in the market for ostrich eggs. Will suppliers decide to supply more, less, or the same quantity of ostrich eggs to the market in response to price changes? Will individual consumers of these eggs decide to buy more, less, or the same quantity at a new price?

We have described macroeconomics and microeconomics as two separate branches, but they are related. Because the overall economy is the sum, or aggregation, of its parts, micro changes affect the macro economy, and macro changes produce micro changes.

1-4 THE METHODOLOGY OF ECONOMICS

As used by other disciplines, such as criminology, biology, chemistry, and physics, economists employ a step-by-step procedure for solving problems by identifying the problem, developing a model, gathering data, and testing whether the data are consistent with the theory. Based on this analysis, economists formulate a conclusion. Exhibit 2 summarizes the model-building process.

1-4a Problem Identification

The first step in applying the economic method is to define the issue. Suppose an economist wishes to investigate the microeconomic problem of why U.S. motorists cut back on gasoline consumption in a given year from, for example, 400 million gallons per day in May to 300 million gallons per day in December.

Model
A simplified description of reality used to understand and predict the relationship between variables.

1-4b Model Development

The second step in our hypothetical example toward finding an explanation is for the economist to build a model. A **model** is a simplified description of reality used to

EXHIBIT 2 The Steps in the Model-Building Process

The first step in developing a model is to identify the problem. The second step is to select the critical variables necessary to formulate a model that explains the problem under study. Eliminating other variables that complicate the analysis requires simplifying assumptions. In the third step, the researcher collects data and tests the model. If the evidence supports the model, the conclusion is to accept the model. If the evidence doesn't support the model, the model is rejected.

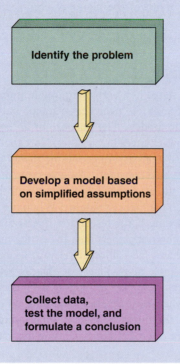

understand and predict the relationship between variables. The terms *model* and *theory* are interchangeable. A model emphasizes only those variables that are most important to explaining an event. As Albert Einstein said, "Theories should be as simple as possible, but not more so." The purpose of a model is to construct an abstraction from real-world complexities and make events understandable. Consider a model airplane that is placed in a wind tunnel to test the aerodynamics of a new design. For this purpose, the model must represent only the shapes of the wings and fuselage, but it does not need to include tiny seats, electrical wiring, or other interior design details. A highway map is another example. To find the best route to drive between two distant cities, you do not want extraneous information on the location of all roads, streets, potholes, telephone lines, trees, stoplights, schools, hospitals, and firehouses. This would be too much detail, and the complexity would make it difficult to choose the best route.

A map is a model because it is an abstraction from reality.

To be useful, a model requires simplified assumptions. Someone must decide, for example, whether a map will include only symbols for the major highways or the details of hiking trails through mountains. In our gasoline consumption example, several variables might be related to the quantity of gasoline consumed, including the price of gasoline, consumer incomes, the fuel economy of cars, and weather conditions. Because a theory focuses only on the main or critical variables, the economist must be a "Sherlock Holmes" and use a keen sense of observation to form a model. Using his or her expertise, the economist must select the variables that are related to gasoline consumption and reject variables that have only a slight or no relationship to gasoline consumption. In this simple case, the economist removes the cloud of complexity by formulating a theory, which states that increases in the price of gasoline *cause* the quantity of gasoline consumed to decrease during the time period.

1-4c Testing a Theory

An economic model can be stated as a verbal argument, numerical table, graph, or mathematical equation. You will soon discover that a major part of this book is devoted to building and using economic models. The purpose of an economic model is to *forecast* or *predict* the results of various changes in variables. Note that the appendix to this chapter provides a review of graphical analysis. An economic theory can be expressed in the form "If X, then Y, all other things held constant." An economic model is useful only if it yields accurate predictions. When the evidence is consistent with the theory that X causes outcome Y, there is confidence in the theory's validity. When the evidence is inconsistent with the theory that X causes outcome Y, the researcher rejects this theory.

In this third step, the economist gathers data to test the theory that if the price of gasoline *rises*, then gasoline purchases *fall*—all other relevant factors held constant. Suppose the investigation reveals that the price of gasoline rose sharply between May and December of the given year. The data, therefore, appear to support the theory that the quantity of gasoline consumed per month falls when its price rises, assuming no other relevant factors change. Thus, the conclusion is that the theory is valid if, for example, consumer incomes or the fuel economy of cars does not change at the same time that gasoline prices rise.

CHECKPOINT

Can You Prove There Is No Trillion-Dollar Person?
Suppose a theory says that no U.S. citizen is worth $1 trillion. You decide to test this theory and send researchers to all corners of the nation to check financial records to see whether someone qualifies by owning assets valued at $1 trillion or more. After years of checking, the researchers return and report that not a single person is worth at least $1 trillion. Do you conclude that the evidence proves the theory? Explain.

1-5 HAZARDS OF THE ECONOMIC WAY OF THINKING

Models help us understand and predict the impact of changes in economic variables. A model is an important tool in the economist's toolkit, but it must be handled with care. The economic way of thinking seeks to avoid reasoning mistakes. Two of the most common pitfalls to clear thinking are

1. failing to understand the *ceteris paribus assumption.*
2. confusing *association* and *causation.*

1-5a The Ceteris Paribus Assumption

As you work through a model, try to think of a host of relevant variables assumed to be "standing still," or "held constant." **Ceteris paribus** is a Latin phrase that means while certain variables change, "all other things remain unchanged." In short, the ceteris paribus assumption allows us to isolate or focus attention on selected variables. In the gasoline example discussed earlier, a key simplifying assumption of the model is that changes in consumer incomes and certain other variables do not occur and complicate the analysis. The ceteris paribus assumption holds everything else constant and therefore allows us to concentrate on the relationship between two key variables: changes in the price of gasoline and the quantity of gasoline purchased per month.

Now suppose an economist examines a model explaining the relationship between the price and quantity purchased of Coca-Cola. The theory is "If the price increases, then the quantity of Coca-Cola purchased decreases, ceteris paribus." Now assume you observe that the price of Coca-Cola increased one summer and some people actually bought more, not less. Based on this real-world observation, you might declare that the theory is incorrect. Think again! Perhaps the reason the model appeared flawed is because another factor—for example a sharp rise in the temperature—*caused* people to buy more Coca-Cola in spite of its higher price. However, if the temperature and all other factors were held constant, and the ceteris paribus assumption is satisfied, we would find that as the price of Coca-Cola rises, people will indeed buy less Coca-Cola, as the model predicts.

Ceteris paribus
A Latin phrase that means while certain variables change, "all other things remain unchanged."

A theory cannot be tested legitimately unless its ceteris paribus assumption is satisfied.

CONCLUSION

1-5b Association versus Causation

Another common error in reasoning is confusing *association* (or correlation) and *causation* between variables. Stated differently, you err when you read more into a relationship between variables than is actually there. A model is valid only when a cause-and-effect relationship is stable or dependable over time, rather than being an association that occurs by chance and eventually disappears. Suppose a witch doctor performs a voodoo dance during three different months and stock market prices skyrocket during each of these months. The voodoo dance is *associated* with the increase in stock prices, but this does not mean the dance *caused* the event. Even though there is a statistical relationship between these two variables in a number of observations, eventually the voodoo dance will be performed, and stock prices will fall or remain unchanged. The reason is that there is no true systematic economic relationship between voodoo dances and stock prices.

Further investigation may reveal that stock prices actually responded to changes in interest rates during the months that the voodoo dances were performed. Changes in interest rates affect borrowing and spending, which in turn impacts corporate profits and stock prices. In contrast, there is no real economic relationship between voodoo dances and stock prices, and therefore, the voodoo model is not valid.

CONCLUSION   The fact that one event follows another does not necessarily mean that the first event caused the second event.

CHECKPOINT

Should Nebraska State Join a Big-Time Athletic Conference?
Nebraska State (a mythical university) stood by while Penn State, Florida State, the University of Miami, and the University of South Carolina joined big-time athletic conferences. Now Nebraska State officials are pondering whether to remain independent or to pursue membership in a conference noted for high-quality football and basketball programs. An editorial in the newspaper advocates joining and cites a study showing that universities belonging to major athletic conferences have higher graduation rates than nonmembers. Because educating its students is the number one goal of Nebraska State, will this evidence persuade Nebraska State officials to join a big-time conference? Why or why not?

Throughout this book, you will study economic models or theories that include variables linked by stable cause-and-effect relationships. For example, the theory that a change in the price of a good *causes* a change in the quantity purchased is a valid microeconomic model. The theory that a change in the money supply *causes* a change in interest rates is an example of a valid macroeconomic model. The You're the Economist gives some amusing examples of the "association means causation" reasoning pitfall.

1-6 WHY DO ECONOMISTS DISAGREE?

Why might one economist say a clean environment should be our most important priority and another economist say economic growth should be our most important goal? If economists share the economic way of thinking and carefully avoid reasoning pitfalls, then why do they disagree? Why are economists known for giving advice by saying, "On the one hand, if you do this, then *A* results, and, on the other hand, doing this causes result *B*?" In fact, President Harry Truman once jokingly exclaimed, "Find me an economist with only one hand." George Bernard Shaw offered another famous line in the same vein: "If you took all the economists in the world and laid them end to end, they would never reach a conclusion." These famous quotes imply that economists should agree, but the quotes ignore the fact that physicists, doctors, business executives, lawyers, and other professionals often disagree as well.

Economists may appear to disagree more than other professionals partly because it is more interesting to report disagreements than agreements. Actually, economists agree

YOU'RE THE ECONOMIST

Mops and Brooms, the Boston Snow Index, the Super Bowl, and Other Economic Indicators

Although the Commerce Department, the Wharton School, the Federal Reserve Board, and other organizations publish economic forecasts and data on key economic indicators, they are not without armchair competition. For example, the chief executive of Standex International Corporation, Daniel E. Hogan, reported that his company can predict economic downturns and recoveries from sales reports of its National Metal Industries subsidiary in Springfield, Massachusetts. National makes metal parts for about 300 U.S. manufacturers of mops and brooms. A drop in National's sales always precedes a proportional fall in consumer spending. The company's sales always pick up slightly before consumer spending does.[1]

The Boston Snow Index (BSI) is the brainchild of a vice president of a New York securities firm. It predicts a rising economy for the next year if there is snow on the ground in Boston on Christmas Day. The BSI predicted correctly about 73 percent of the time over a 30-year period. However, its creator, David L. Upshaw, did not take it too seriously and views it as a spoof of other forecasters' methods.

Greeting card sales are another tried and true indicator, according to a vice president of American Greetings. Before a recession sets in, sales of higher-priced greeting cards rise. It seems that people substitute the cards for gifts, and since there is no gift, the card must be fancier.

A Super Bowl win by a National Football Conference (NFC) team predicts that in the following December the stock market will be higher than the year before. A win by an old American Football League (AFL) team predicts a dip in the stock market.

Several other less well-known indicators have also been proposed. For example, one economist suggested that the surliness of servers is a countercyclical indicator. If they are nice, expect that bad times are coming, but if they are rude, expect an upturn. Servers on the other hand, counter that a fall in the average tip usually precedes a downturn in the economy.

Finally, Anthony Chan, chief economist for Bank One Investment Advisors, studied marriage trends over a 34-year period. He discovered that when the number of marriages increases, the economy rises significantly, and a slowdown in marriages is followed by a decline in the economy. Chan explains that there is usually about a one-year lag between a change in the marriage rate and the economy.[2]

TIMOTHY A. CLARY/Getty Images

ANALYZE THE ISSUE

Which of the above indicators are examples of causation? Explain.

1. "Economic Indicators, Turtles, Butterflies, Monks, and Waiters," *The Wall Street Journal*, August 27, 1979, pp. 1, 16.
2. Sandra Block, "Worried? Look at Wedding Bell Indicator," *The Charlotte Observer*, April 15, 1995, p. 8A.

on a wide range of issues. Many economists, for example, agree that the benefits from free trade outweigh the costs, that a market-driven healthcare delivery system has many flaws, and that government deficit spending (which adds to the national debt) can be a good thing if we want to recover more quickly from a recession. When disagreements do exist, the reason can often be explained by the difference between *positive economics* and *normative economics*.

1-6a Positive Economics

Positive economics
An analysis limited to statements that are verifiable.

Positive economics deals with facts and therefore addresses "what is" true or false about how the economy really works. **Positive economics** is an analysis limited to statements that are verifiable. Positive statements can be proven either true or false. Often a positive statement is expressed: "If *X*, then *Y*." For example, if the national unemployment rate rises to 9 percent, then teenage unemployment exceeds 80 percent. This is a positive "if-then" prediction, which may or may not be correct. Accuracy is not the criterion for a statement to be positive. The key consideration is whether the statement is *testable* and not whether it is true or false. Suppose the data show that when the nation's overall unemployment rate is close to 9 percent, the unemployment rate for teenagers never reaches 80 percent. For example, the overall unemployment rate was 9.6 percent in 2010, and the rate for teenagers was 25.9 percent—far short of 80 percent. Based on the facts, we would conclude that this positive statement is false.

Now we can explain one reason why economists' forecasts can diverge. The statement "If event *X* occurs, then event *Y* follows" can be thought of as a *conditional* positive statement. For example, two economists may agree that if the federal government cuts spending by 10 percent this year, prices will fall about 2 percent next year. However, their predictions about the fall in prices may differ because one economist assumes Congress will not cut spending, while the other economist assumes Congress will cut spending by 10 percent.

CONCLUSION   Economists' forecasts can differ because using the same methodology; economists can agree that event *X* causes event *Y*, but disagree over the assumption that event *X* will occur.

1-6b Normative Economics

Normative economics
An analysis based on subjective value judgments.

Instead of using objective statements, an argument can be phrased subjectively. Normative economics attempts to determine "what should be." **Normative economics** is an analysis based on subjective value judgments. Normative statements express an individual or collective opinion on a subject and cannot be proven by facts to be true or false. Certain words or phrases, such as *good*, *bad*, *need*, *should*, and *ought to*, tell us clearly that we have entered the realm of normative economics.

The point here is that these subjective value judgments are the result of ever-present social and political influences that shape our opinions. An animal rights activist says that no one *should* purchase a fur coat. Someone else may argue that government *ought to* take steps to ensure a more *fair* distribution of income and wealth. Others argue that health care is a basic human right that *needs* to be made available to all regardless of their ability to pay.

CONCLUSION   When opinions or points of view are not based on facts, they are scientifically untestable.

YOU'RE THE ECONOMIST

Applicable Concepts: Positive and Normative Analyses

Does the Minimum Wage Really Help the Working Poor?

Minimum wages exist in more than 100 countries. In 1938, Congress enacted the federal Fair Labor Standards Act, commonly known as the "minimum-wage law." Today, a minimum wage worker who works full-time still earns a deplorably low annual income. One approach to help the working poor earn a living wage might be to raise the minimum wage.

The dilemma for Congress is that a higher minimum wage for the employed is enacted at the expense of jobs for unskilled workers. Opponents forecast that the increased labor cost from a large minimum wage hike would jeopardize hundreds of thousands of unskilled jobs. For example, employers may opt to purchase more capital and less expensive labor. Restaurants can use iPads instead of servers to take orders and install robotic burger flippers. The fear of such sizable job losses forces Congress to perform a difficult balancing act to ensure that a minimum wage increase is large enough to help the working poor, but not so large as to threaten their jobs.

Some politicians claim that raising the minimum wage is a way to help the working poor without cost to taxpayers. Others believe the cost is hidden in inflation and lost employment opportunities for marginal workers, such as teenagers, the elderly, and minorities. One study by economists, for example, examined 60 years of data and concluded that minimum wage increases resulted in reduced employment and hours of work for low-skilled workers.[1]

Another problem with raising the minimum wage to aid the working poor is that the minimum wage is a blunt weapon for redistributing wealth. Some studies show that only a small percentage of minimum wage earners are full-time workers whose family income falls below the poverty line. This means that most increases in the minimum wage go to workers who are not poor. For example, many minimum wage workers are students living at home or workers whose spouse earns a much higher income. To help only the working poor, some economists argue that the government should target only those who need assistance, rather than using the "shotgun" approach of raising the minimum wage.

Supporters of raising the minimum wage are not convinced by these arguments. They say it just isn't right that a worker who works full-time should live in poverty. They point to the fact that the minimum wage has not kept pace with the typical worker's wage or with the cost of living. As a result, a growing underclass has to rely on some form of public assistance, like food stamps. And this, they argue, only adds to income inequality as taxpayers end up subsidizing profitable companies who don't pay their workers a living wage.

Tony Stock/Shutterstock.com

Moreover, people on this side of the debate believe that opponents exaggerate many of their claims, especially the extent to which unemployment and higher prices result from a higher minimum wage. They provide evidence that the benefits from a higher minimum wage may more than offset these costs.[2] For example, when earning a higher wage, workers will spend more money, generating a need for companies to expand production and to hire even more workers. In addition, the gain from these higher incomes far exceed the cost of higher prices, leaving workers better off. To proponents, increasing the minimum wage is a win-win proposition. We return to this issue in Chapter 4 as an application of supply and demand analysis.

ANALYZE THE ISSUE

1. Identify two positive and two normative statements given above concerning raising the minimum wage. List other minimum wage arguments not discussed in this You're the Economist and classify them as either positive or normative economics.
2. Give a positive and a normative argument why a business leader would oppose raising the minimum wage. Give a positive and a normative argument why a labor leader would favor raising the minimum wage.
3. Explain your position on this issue. Identify positive and normative reasons for your decision. Are there alternative ways to aid the working poor? Explain.

---

1. David Neumark and William Wascher, *Minimum Wages*, Cambridge, MA, The MIT Press, 2008.
2. Economic Policy Institute, "The impact of raising the federal minimum wage to $12 by 2020 on workers, businesses, and the economy." Testimony before the U.S. House Committee on Education and the Workforce Member Forum. April 27, 2016, found at http://www.epi.org/publication/the-impact-of-raising-the-federal-minimum-wage-to-12-by-2020-on-workers-businesses-and-the-economy-testimony-before-the-u-s-house-committee-on-education-and-the-workforce-member-forum/.

When considering a debate, make sure to separate the arguments into their positive and normative components. This distinction allows you to determine whether you are choosing a course of action based on factual evidence or on opinion. The material presented in this textbook, like most of economics, takes pains to stay within the boundaries of positive economic analysis. In our everyday lives, however, politicians, business executives, relatives, and friends use mostly normative statements to discuss economic issues. Economists may also associate themselves with a political position and use normative arguments for or against some economic policy. When using value judgments, an economist's normative arguments may have no greater validity than those of other people. Biases or preconceptions can cloud an economist's thinking about deficit spending or whether to increase taxes on gasoline. Like beginning economics students, economists are human.

1-7 CAREERS IN ECONOMICS

The author of this text entered college more years ago than I would like to admit. In those days, economics was not taught in high school, so I knew nothing of the subject. Like many students taking this course, I was uncertain about which major to pursue, but selected electrical engineering because I was an amateur radio operator and enjoyed building radio receivers and transmitters. My engineering curriculum required a course in economics. I signed up thinking that "econ is boring." Instead, it was an eye-opening experience that inspired me to change my major to economics and pursue an economics teaching career.

The study of economics has attracted a number of well-known people. For example, The Rolling Stones' Mick Jagger attended the London School of Economics, and other famous people who majored in economics include four presidents—George H. W. Bush, Ronald Reagan, Gerald Ford, and Donald Trump.

An economics major can choose many career paths. Most economics majors work for business firms. Because economists are trained in analyzing financial matters, they find good jobs in management, sales, or as a market analyst interpreting economic conditions relevant to a firm's market. For those with an undergraduate degree, private-sector job opportunities exist in banking, securities brokering, management consulting, computer and data processing firms, the power industry, market research, finance, health care, and many other industries. Other economics majors work for government agencies and in colleges and universities.

Government economists work for federal, state, and local governments. For example, a government economist might compile and report national statistics for economic growth or work on projects such as how to improve indexes to measure trends in consumer prices. Economists in academe not only enjoy the challenge of teaching economics but also have great freedom in selecting research projects.

Studying economics is also an essential preparation for other careers. Those preparing for law school, for example, find economics an excellent major because of its emphasis on a logical approach to problem solving. Economics is also great preparation for an MBA. In fact, students majoring in any field will benefit throughout their lives from learning how to apply the economic way of thinking to analyze real-world economic issues.

Finally, economics majors shine in salary offers upon graduation. Exhibit 3 shows average yearly salaries for some bachelor's degrees with 0–5 years of experience for 2016–2017.

EXHIBIT 3 Average Yearly Salary for Selected Bachelor Majors with 0–5 Years of Experience

Bachelor's major	Median salary with 0–5 years of experience, 2016–2017
Petroleum engineering	96,700
Nuclear engineering	68,500
Computer science	65,300
Nursing	57,500
Economics	53,900
Finance	53,300
International business	48,800
Accounting	48,300
Business administration	46,100
Chemistry	45,700
Marketing	45,300
Philosophy	44,700
Communications	42,100
Human resources	41,900
Journalism	41,200
Biology	40,800
Sociology	40,400
Psychology	37,800
Criminal justice	37,000
Animal science	35,800
Early childhood education	30,700

SOURCE: www.payScale.com/college-salary-report.

Key Concepts

Scarcity	Entrepreneurship	Macroeconomics	Ceteris paribus
Resources	Capital	Microeconomics	Positive economics
Land	Economics	Model	Normative economics
Labor			

Summary

- **Scarcity** is the fundamental economic problem that human wants exceed the availability of time, goods, and resources. Individuals and society therefore can never have everything they desire.

- **Resources** are factors of production classified as land, labor, and capital. Entrepreneurship is a special type of labor. An entrepreneur seeks profits by taking risks and combining resources to produce innovative products.

- **Economics** is the study of how individuals and society choose to allocate scarce resources to satisfy unlimited wants. Faced with unlimited wants and scarce resources, we must make choices among alternatives.

- **Macroeconomics** applies an economy-wide perspective that focuses on such issues as inflation, unemployment, and the growth rate of the economy.

- **Microeconomics** examines individual decision-making units within an economy, such as a consumer's response to changes in the price of coffee and the reasons for changes in the market price of personal computers.

- **Models** are simplified descriptions of reality used to understand and predict economic events. An economic model can be stated verbally or in a table, a graph, or an equation. If the event is not consistent with the model, the model is rejected.

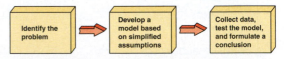

- **Ceteris paribus** holds "all other factors unchanged" that might affect a particular relationship. If this assumption is violated, a model cannot be tested. Another reasoning pitfall is to think that *association* means *causation*.

- Use of positive versus normative economic analysis is a major reason for disagreements among economists. **Positive economics** uses testable statements. Often a positive argument is expressed as an *if-then* statement. **Normative economics** is based on value judgments or opinions and uses words such as *good, bad, ought to,* and *should.*

Summary of Conclusion Statements

- The problems of scarcity and choice are basic economic problems faced by every society.

- Money by itself does not produce goods and services; instead, it is only a means to facilitate the purchase and sale of resources and consumer products.

- A theory cannot be tested legitimately unless its ceteris paribus assumption is satisfied.

- The fact that one event follows another does not necessarily mean that the first event caused the second event.

- Economists' forecasts can differ because using the same methodology, economists can agree that event *X* causes event *Y*, but disagree over the assumption that event *X* will occur.

- When opinions or points of view are not based on facts, they are scientifically untestable.

Study Questions and Problems

Please see Appendix A for answers to the odd-numbered questions. Your instructor has access to the answers for even-numbered questions.

1. Explain why both nations with high living standards and nations with low living standards face the problem of scarcity. If you won $1 million in a lottery, would you escape the scarcity problem?

2. Why isn't money considered capital in economics?

3. Explain the difference between macroeconomics and microeconomics. Give examples of the areas of concern to each branch of economics.

4. Which of the following are microeconomic issues? Which are macroeconomic issues?
   a. How will an increase in the price of Coca-Cola affect the quantity of Pepsi Cola sold?
   b. What will cause the nation's inflation rate to fall?
   c. How does a quota on textile imports affect the textile industry?
   d. Does a large federal budget deficit reduce the rate of unemployment in the economy?

5. Explain why it is important for an economic model to be an abstraction from the real world.

6. Explain the importance of the ceteris paribus assumption for an economic model.

7. Suppose Congress cuts spending for the military, and then unemployment rises in the U.S. defense industry. Is there causation in this situation, or are we observing an association between events?

8. Analyze the positive versus normative arguments in the following case. What statements of positive economics are used to support requiring air bags? What normative reasoning is used?

Should the Government Require Air Bags?
Technological advances continuously provide new high-tech options to save lives that add to the price of cars, such as cameras, radar, and airbags. Air bag advocates say air bags will save lives and the government should require them in all cars. Air bags add an estimated $600 to the cost of a car, compared to about $100 for a set of regular seat belts. Opponents argue that air bags are electronic devices subject to failure and have produced injuries and death. For example, air bags have killed both adults and children whose heads were within the inflation zone at the time of deployment. Opponents therefore believe the government should leave the decision of whether to spend an extra $600 or so for an air bag to the consumer. The role of the government should be limited to providing information on the risks of having versus not having air bags.

✔ **CHECKPOINT ANSWERS**

Can You Prove There Is No Trillion-Dollar Person?
How can researchers ever be certain they have found all the rich people in the United States? There is always the possibility that somewhere there is a person who qualifies. If the researchers had found one, you could have rejected the theory. Because they did not, you cannot reject the theory. If you said that the evidence can support but never prove the theory, **YOU ARE CORRECT**.

Should Nebraska State Join a Big-Time Athletic Conference?
Suppose universities that belong to big-time athletic conferences do indeed have higher graduation rates than nonmembers. This is not the only possible explanation for the statistical correlation (or association) between the graduation rate and membership in a big-time athletic conference. A more plausible explanation is that improving academic variables, such as tuition, quality of faculty, and student-faculty ratios, and not athletic conference membership, increase the graduation rate. If you said correlation, does not mean causation, and therefore Nebraska State officials will not necessarily accept the graduation rate evidence, **YOU ARE CORRECT**.

Sample Quiz

Please see Appendix B for answers to Sample Quiz questions.

1. Which of the following illustrates the concept of scarcity?
   a. More clean air is wanted than is available in large polluted metropolitan areas such as Mexico City.
   b. There is usually more than one use of your "free" time in the evening.
   c. There are many competing uses for the annual budget of your city, county, or state.
   d. All of the above are correct.

2. Which of the following are factors of production?
   a. The outputs generated by the production process transforming land, labor, and capital into goods and services
   b. Resources restricted to the land, such as natural resources that are unimproved by human economic activity
   c. Land (natural resources), labor (human capital, entrepreneurship), and capital (constructed inputs such as factories)
   d. Just labor and capital in industrialized countries, where natural resources are no longer used to produce goods and services

3. Which of the following is *not* an example of a capital input?
   a. A person's skills and abilities, which can be employed to produce valuable goods and services
   b. Factories and offices where goods and services are produced
   c. Tools and equipment
   d. Computers used by a company to record inventory, sales, and payroll

4. Which of the following is the best definition of economics?
   a. Economics is the study of how to manage corporations to generate the greatest return on shareholder investment.
   b. Economics is the study of how to manage city and county government to generate the greatest good to its citizens.
   c. Economics is the study of how society chooses to allocate its scarce resources.
   d. Economics is the study of how to track revenues and costs in a business.

5. Which of the following *best* illustrates the application of the model-building process to economics?
   a. On a Sunday morning talk show, two economists with differing political agendas argue about the best way to solve the Social Security problem.
   b. A labor economist notices that unemployment tends to be higher among teenagers than more experienced workers, develops a model, and gathers data to test the hypotheses in the model.
   c. A Ph.D. student in economics makes up data on the lumber market and develops a model for his dissertation that seems to be consistent with the data.
   d. Economists come to believe that some economic models are true simply because prominent leading economists say they are true.

6. Which of the following represents causality rather than association?
   a. In years that fashion dictates wider lapels on men's jackets, the stock market grows by at least 5 percent.
   b. Interest rates are higher in years ending with a 1 or a 6.
   c. Unemployment falls when the AFC champion wins the Super Bowl.
   d. Quantity demanded goes up when price falls because lower prices increase consumer purchasing power and because some consumers of substitute goods switch.

7. Which of the following describes the ceteris paribus assumption?
   a. If we increase the price of a good, reduce consumer income, and lower the price of substitutes and if quantity demanded is

observed to fall, we know that the price increase caused the decline in quantity demanded.

b. If the federal government increases government spending and the Federal Reserve Bank lowers interest rates, we know that the increase in government spending caused unemployment to fall.

c. If a company reduces its labor costs, negotiates lower materials costs from its vendors, and advertises, we know that the reduced labor costs are why the company's profits are higher.

d. If we decrease the price of a good and observe that there is an increase in the quantity demanded, holding all other factors that influence this relationship constant.

8. The condition of scarcity
   a. cannot be eliminated.
   b. prevails in poor economies.
   c. prevails in rich economies.
   d. all of the above are correct.

9. Which of the following *best* describes an entrepreneur?
   a. A person who works as an office clerk at a major corporation
   b. A person who combines the factors of production to produce innovative products
   c. A special type of capital
   d. Wealthy individuals who provide savings that stimulates the economy

10. Which of the following is *true* about renewable natural resources?
    a. They are a type of land resource (for example, oil, coal, and natural gas) that has a fixed stock.
    b. They are a type of capital resource (for example, irrigation networks and wastewater treatment plants) that utilize water.
    c. They are a type of capital resource (for example, air filtration systems in buildings) that renew and refresh polluted air from the outside.
    d. They are a type of land resource (for example, forests, rangelands, and marine fisheries) that naturally regenerate and thus can tolerate a sustained harvest but can be depleted from excessive harvest.

11. Because of scarcity,
    a. it is impossible to satisfy every desire and choices must be made.
    b. the available supply of time, goods, and resources is greater than human wants.
    c. every desire is fulfilled.
    d. there are no limits on the economy's ability to satisfy unlimited wants.

12. Which of the following represents positive economics?
    a. Policy X is fair.
    b. Outcome Y is the best objective to achieve.
    c. If policy X is followed, then outcome Y results.
    d. All of the above are positive economic analyses.

13. Which of the following is the last step in the model-building process?
    a. Collect data and test the model.
    b. Develop a model based on simplified assumptions.
    c. Identify the problem.
    d. Formulate an assumption.

14. Which of the following is *not* a type of economic analysis?
    a. Positive
    b. Resources
    c. Normative
    d. None of the above

15. Which word indicates that an economist is using positive economics?
    a. Good
    b. Bad
    c. If-then
    d. Should

16. Which of the following would eliminate scarcity as an economic problem?
    a. Moderation of people's competitive instincts
    b. Discovery of new, sufficiently large energy reserves
    c. Resumption of steady productivity growth
    d. None of the above is correct

17. Which resource is *not* an example of capital?
    a. Equipment
    b. Machinery
    c. Physical plants
    d. Stocks and bonds

18. Which of the following is the second step in the model-building process?
    a. Collect data and test the model.
    b. Develop a model based on simplified assumptions.
    c. Identify the problem.
    d. Include all possible variables that affect the model.

19. Which of the following is a type of economic analysis?
    a. Positive
    b. Resources
    c. Association
    d. None of the above is correct.

20. Which of the following careers could result from majoring in economics?
    a. Management
    b. Banking
    c. Government
    d. All of the above is correct.

Applying Graphs to Economics

Economists are famous for their use of graphs. The reason is "a picture is worth a thousand words." Graphs are used throughout this text to present economics models. By drawing a line, you can use a two-dimensional illustration to analyze the effects of a change in one variable on another. You could describe the same information using other model forms, such as verbal statements, tables, or equations, but a graph is the simplest way to present and understand the relationship between economic variables.

Don't be worried that graphs will "throw you for a loop." Relax! This appendix explains all the basic graphical language you will need. The following illustrates the simplest use of graphs for economic analysis.

A-1 A DIRECT RELATIONSHIP

Basic economic analysis typically concerns the relationship between two variables, both having positive values. Hence, we can confine our graphs to the upper-right (northeast) quadrant of the coordinate number system. In Exhibit A-1, notice that the scales on the horizontal axis (*x*-axis) and the vertical axis (*y*-axis) do not necessarily measure the same numerical values.

The horizontal axis in Exhibit A-1 measures annual income, and the vertical axis shows the amount spent per year for a personal computer (PC). The intersection of the horizontal and vertical axes is the *origin* and the point at which both income and expenditure are zero. In Exhibit A-1, each point is a coordinate that matches the dollar value of income and the corresponding expenditure for a PC. For example, point *A* on the graph shows that people with an annual income of $10,000 spent $1,000 per year for a PC. Other incomes are associated with different expenditure levels. For example, at $30,000 per year (point *C*), $3,000 will be spent annually for a PC.

The straight line in Exhibit A-1 allows us to determine the direction of change in PC expenditure as annual income changes. This relationship is *positive* because PC expenditure, measured along the vertical axis, and annual income, measured along the horizontal axis, move in the same direction. PC expenditure increases as annual income increases. As income declines, so does the amount spent on a PC. Thus, the straight line representing the relationship between income and PC expenditure is a direct relationship. A **direct relationship** is a positive association between two variables. When one variable increases, the other variable increases, and when one variable decreases, the other variable decreases. In short, both variables change in the *same* direction.

Finally, an important point to remember: A two-variable graph, like any model, isolates the relationship between two variables and holds all other variables constant under the

Direct relationship
A positive association between two variables. When one variable increases, the other variable increases, and when one variable decreases, the other variable decreases.

EXHIBIT **A-1** Direct Relationship between Variables

The line with a positive slope shows that the expenditure per year for a personal computer has a direct relationship to annual income, ceteris paribus. As annual income increases along the horizontal axis, the amount spent on a PC also increases, as measured by the vertical axis. Along the line, each 10-unit increase in annual income results in a 1-unit increase in expenditure for a PC. Because the slope is constant along a straight line, we can measure the same slope between any two points. Between points A and D, the slope $= \Delta Y / \Delta X = +3 / +30 = +1 / +10 = 1/10$.

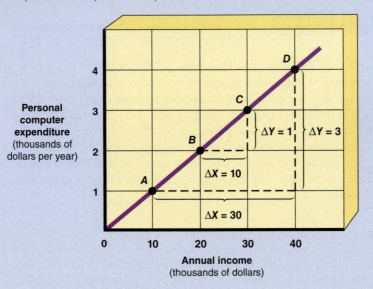

Expenditure for a Personal Computer at Different Annual Incomes		
Point	Personal computer expenditure (thousands of dollars per year)	Annual income (thousands of dollars)
A	$1	$10
B	2	20
C	3	30
D	4	40

ceteris paribus assumption. In Exhibit A-1, for example, factors such as the prices of PCs and education are held constant by assumption. In Chapter 3, you will learn that allowing variables not shown in the graph to change can shift the position of the line or curve.

A-2 AN INVERSE RELATIONSHIP

Now consider the relationship between the price of compact discs (CDs) and the quantity consumers will buy per year, shown in Exhibit A-2. These data indicate an *inverse* (or *negative*) relationship between the price and quantity variables. When the price is low, consumers purchase a greater quantity of CDs than when the price is high.

In Exhibit A-2, there is an inverse relationship between the price per CD and the quantity consumers buy. An **inverse relationship** is a negative association between two variables. When one variable increases, the other variable decreases, and when one variable decreases, the other variable increases. Stated simply, the variables move in *opposite* directions.

The line drawn in Exhibit A-2 is an inverse relationship. By long-established tradition, economists put price on the vertical axis and quantity on the horizontal axis. In Chapter 3, we will study in more detail the relationship between the price and the quantity demanded called the *law of demand*.

Inverse relationship
A negative association between two variables. When one variable increases, the other variable decreases, and when one variable decreases, the other variable increases.

EXHIBIT A-2 An Inverse Relationship between Variables

The line with a negative slope shows an inverse relationship between the price per compact disc and the quantity of CDs consumers purchase, ceteris paribus. As the price of a CD rises, the quantity of CDs purchased falls. A lower price for CDs is associated with more CDs purchased by consumers. Along the line, with each $5 decrease in the price of CDs, consumers increase the quantity purchased by 25 units. The slope $= \Delta Y / \Delta X = -5 / +25 = -1/5$.

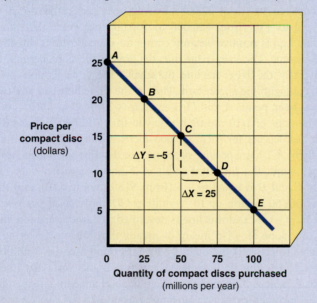

The Quantity of Compact Discs Consumers Purchase at Different Prices		
Point	Price per compact disc	Quantity of compact discs purchased (millions per year)
A	$25	0
B	20	25
C	15	50
D	10	75
E	5	100

In addition to observing the inverse relationship (negative slope), you must interpret the *intercept* at point *A* in the exhibit. The intercept in this case means that at a price of $25 no consumer is willing to buy a single CD.

A-3 THE SLOPE OF A STRAIGHT LINE

Slope
The ratio of the change in the variable on the vertical axis (the rise or fall) to the change in the variable on the horizontal axis (the run).

Plotting numbers provides a clear visual expression of the relationship between two variables, but it is also important to know how much one variable changes as another variable changes. To find out, we calculate the slope. The **slope** is the ratio of the change in the variable on the vertical axis (the rise or fall) to the change in the variable on the horizontal axis (the run). Algebraically, if *Y* is on the vertical axis and *X* is on the horizontal axis, the slope is expressed as follows (the delta symbol, Δ, means "change in"):

$$\text{Slope} = \frac{\text{rise}}{\text{run}} = \frac{\text{change in vertical axis}}{\text{change in horizontal axis}} = \frac{\Delta Y}{\Delta X}$$

Consider the slope between points *B* and *C* in Exhibit A-1. The change in expenditure for a PC, *Y*, is equal to +1 (from $2,000 to $3,000 per year), and the change in annual income, *X*, is equal to +10 (from $20,000 to $30,000 per year). The slope is therefore +1/+10 = 0.10. The sign is positive because computer expenditure is directly, or positively, related to annual income. The steeper the line, the greater the slope because the ratio of ΔY to ΔX rises. Conversely, the flatter the line, the smaller the slope. Exhibit A-1 also illustrates that the slope of a straight line is constant. That is, the slope between any two points along the line, such as between points *A* and *D*, is equal to +3/ + 30 = 1/10 = 0.10

What does the slope of 1/10 mean? It tells you that a $1,000 increase (decrease) in PC expenditure each year occurs for each $10,000 increase (decrease) in annual income. The line plotted in Exhibit A-1 has a *positive slope,* and we describe the line as "upward-sloping."

On the other hand, the line in Exhibit A-2 has a *negative slope*. The change in *Y* between points *C* and *D* is equal to −5 (from $15 down to $10), and the change in *X* is equal to +25 (from 50 million up to 75 million CDs purchased per year). The slope is therefore −5/ + 25 = −1/5, and this line is described as "downward-sloping."

What does this slope of −1/5 mean? It means that raising (lowering) the price per CD by $1 decreases (increases) the quantity of CDs purchased by 5 million per year.

Suppose we calculate the slope between any two points on a flat line—for example, points *B* and *C* in Exhibit A-3. In this case, there is no change in *Y* (expenditure for toothpaste) as *X* (annual income) increases. Consumers spend $20 per year on toothpaste regardless of annual income. It follows that $\Delta Y = 0$ for any ΔX, so the slope is equal to 0. The two variables along a flat line (horizontal or vertical) have an independent relationship. An **independent relationship** is a zero association between two variables. When one variable changes, the other variable remains unchanged.

Independent relationship
A zero association between two variables. When one variable changes, the other variable remains unchanged.

A-4 A THREE-VARIABLE RELATIONSHIP IN ONE GRAPH

The two-variable relationships drawn so far conform to a two-dimensional flat piece of paper. For example, the vertical axis measures the price per CD variable, and the horizontal axis measures the quantity of CDs purchased variable. All other factors, such as

EXHIBIT A-3 An Independent Relationship between Variables

The flat line with a zero slope shows that the expenditure per year for toothpaste is unrelated to annual income. As annual income increases along the horizontal axis, the amount spent each year for toothpaste remains unchanged at 20 units. If annual income increases 10 units, the corresponding change in expenditure is zero. The Slope $= \Delta Y/\Delta X = 0/ + 10 = 0$

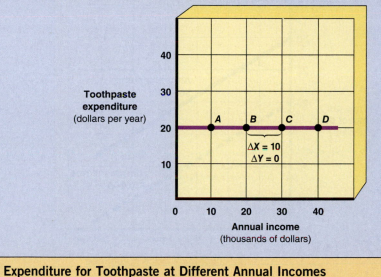

Expenditure for Toothpaste at Different Annual Incomes		
Point	Toothpaste expenditure (dollars per year)	Annual income (thousands of dollars)
A	$20	$10
B	20	20
C	20	30
D	20	40

consumer income, that may affect the relationship between the price and quantity variables are held constant by the ceteris paribus assumption. But reality is frequently not so accommodating. Often a model must take into account the impact of changes in a third variable (consumer income) drawn on a two-dimensional piece of paper.

Economists' favorite method of depicting a three-variable relationship is shown in Exhibit A-4. As explained earlier, the cause-and-effect relationship between price and quantity of CDs determines the downward-sloping curve. A change in the price per CD causes a movement downward along either of the two separate curves. As the price falls, consumers increase the quantity of CDs demanded. The location of each curve on the graph, however, depends on the annual income of consumers. As the annual income variable increases from $30,000 to $60,000 and consumers can afford to purchase more at any price, or pay more at any quantity, the price–quantity demanded curve shifts rightward. Conversely, as the annual income variable decreases and consumers have less to spend, the price–quantity demanded curve shifts leftward.

EXHIBIT A-4 Changes in Price, Quantity, and Income in Two Dimensions

Economists use a multicurve graph to represent a three-variable relationship in a two-dimensional graph. A decrease in the price per CD causes a movement downward along each curve. As the annual income of consumers rises, there is a shift rightward in the position of the demand curve.

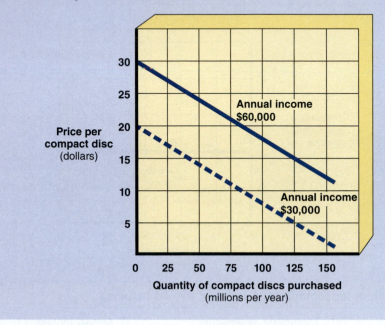

This is an extremely important concept that you must understand: Throughout this text, you must distinguish between *movements along* and *shifts in* a curve. Here's how to tell the difference. A change in one of the variables shown on either of the coordinate axes of the graph causes *movement along* a curve. On the other hand, a change in a variable not shown on one of the coordinate axes of the graph causes a *shift* in a curve's position on the graph.

CONCLUSION   A shift in a curve occurs only when the ceteris paribus assumption is relaxed and a third variable not shown on either axis of the graph is allowed to change.

A-5 A HELPFUL STUDY HINT FOR USING GRAPHS

To some students, studying economics is a little frightening because many chapters are full of graphs. Just remember that a graph is simply a visual aid that illustrates the relationship between economic variables. Noting these relationships is the ticket to understanding how the economy really works. So, keep in mind that all inverse (negative) relationships are expressed as downward sloping curves (or lines), and all direct (positive) relationships are expressed as upward sloping curves (or lines). This will help you to do well on tests!

Key Concepts

Direct relationship
Inverse relationship

Slope
Independent relationship

Summary

- **Graphs** provide a means to clearly show economic relationships in two-dimensional space. Economic analysis is often concerned with two variables confined to the upper-right (northeast) quadrant of the coordinate number system.

- A **direct relationship** occurs when two variables change in the *same* direction.

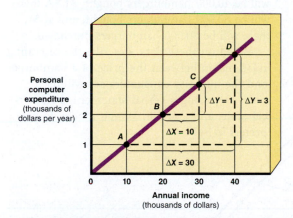

- An **inverse relationship** occurs when two variables change in *opposite* directions.

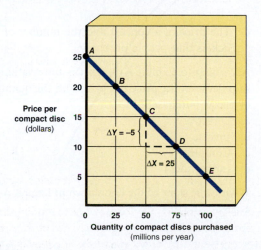

- An **independent relationship** occurs when two variables are unrelated.

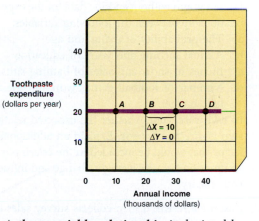

- A **three-variable relationship** is depicted by a graph showing a shift in a curve when the ceteris paribus assumption is relaxed and a third variable (such as annual income) not on either axis of the graph is allowed to change.

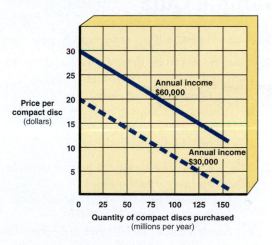

Summary of Conclusion Statement

• A shift in a curve occurs only when the ceteris paribus assumption is relaxed and a third variable not shown on either axis of the graph is allowed to change.

Study Questions and Problems

Please see Appendix A for answers to the odd-numbered questions. Your instructor has access to the answers for even-numbered questions.

1. Draw a graph without specific data for the expected relationship between the following variables:
   a. The probability of living and age
   b. Annual income and years of education
   c. Inches of snow and sales of bathing suits
   d. Number of football games won and the athletic budget

   In each case, state whether the expected relationship is *direct* or *inverse*. Explain an additional factor that would be included in the *ceteris paribus* assumption because it might change and influence your theory.

2. Assume a research firm collects survey sales data that reveal the relationship between the possible selling prices of hamburgers and the quantity of hamburgers consumers would purchase per year at alternative prices. The report states that if the price of a hamburger is $4, then 20,000 will be bought. However, at a price of $3, there will be 40,000 hamburgers bought. At $2, there will be 60,000 hamburgers bought, and at $1, there will be 80,000 hamburgers purchased.

   Based on these data, describe the relevant relationship between the price of a hamburger and the quantity consumers are willing to purchase, using a verbal statement, a numerical table, and a graph. Which model do you prefer? Why?

Sample Quiz

Please see Appendix B for answers to Sample Quiz questions.

1. What is used to illustrate an independent relationship between two variables?
   a. An upward-sloping curve
   b. A downward-sloping curve
   c. A hill-shaped curve
   d. A horizontal or vertical line

2. Which of the following pairs is *most* likely to exhibit an inverse relationship?
   a. The amount of time you study and your grade point average
   b. People's annual income and their expenditure on personal computers
   c. Baseball players' salaries and their batting averages
   d. The price of a concert and the number of tickets that people purchase

3. According to Exhibit A-5, what is the relationship between the price per pizza and the quantity of pizzas purchased?
   a. Direct
   b. Inverse
   c. Complex
   d. Independent

4. What is the slope of the line shown in Exhibit A-5?
   a. −1
   b. −1/2
   c. −1/4
   d. 0

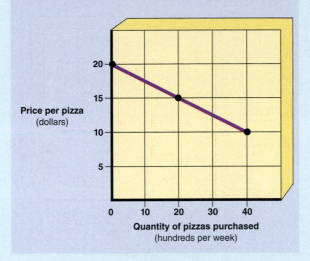

EXHIBIT A-5 Straight Line Relationship

Price per pizza (dollars)

Quantity of pizzas purchased (hundreds per week)

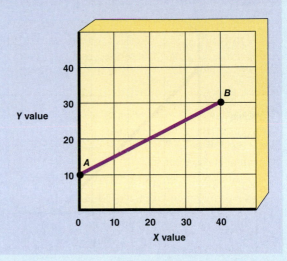

EXHIBIT A-6 Straight Line Relationship

Y value

X value

5. Which of the following would cause a leftward shift in the relationship shown in Exhibit A-5?
   a. A fall in household incomes
   b. A fall in the price of pizza
   c. A fall in the quantity of pizza that people want to purchase
   d. All of the above would shift the line in the graph

6. Suppose two variables are directly related. If one variable rises, the other variable
   a. also rises.
   b. falls.
   c. remains unchanged.
   d. reacts unpredictably.

7. When an inverse relationship is graphed, the resulting line or curve is
   a. horizontal.
   b. vertical.
   c. upward-sloping.
   d. downward-sloping.

8. Straight line AB in Exhibit A-6 shows that
   a. increasing values for X decreases the values of Y.
   b. decreasing values for X increases the values of Y.

   c. there is a direct relationship between X and Y.
   d. all of the above are true.

9. In Exhibit A-6, what is the slope of straight line AB?
   a. Positive
   b. Zero
   c. Negative
   d. Variable

10. In Exhibit A-6, what is the slope of straight line AB?
    a. 1
    b. 5
    c. 1/2
    d. −1

11. As shown in Exhibit A-6, the slope of straight line AB
    a. decreases with increases in X.
    b. increases with increases in X.
    c. increases with decreases in X.
    d. remains constant with changes in X.

12. In Exhibit A-6, as X increases along the horizontal axis, the Y values increase. What is the relationship between the X and Y variables?
    a. Direct
    b. Inverse

EXHIBIT A-7 Straight Line Relationship

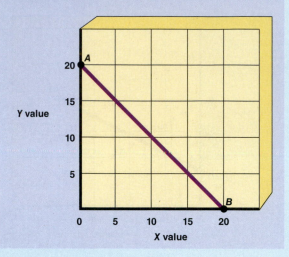

EXHIBIT A-8 Straight Line Relationship

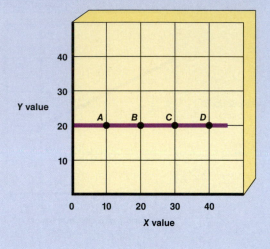

c. Independent

d. Variable

13. In Exhibit A-7, as X increases along the horizontal axis, the Y values decrease. What is the relationship between the X and Y variables?
    a. Direct
    b. Inverse
    c. Independent
    d. Variable

14. Straight line AB in Exhibit A-7 shows that
    a. increasing values for X reduces the value of Y.
    b. decreasing values for X increases the value of Y.
    c. there is an inverse relationship between X and Y.
    d. all of the above are true.

15. As shown in Exhibit A-7, the slope of straight line AB
    a. decreases with increases in X.
    b. increases with increases in X.
    c. increases with decreases in X.
    d. remains constant with changes in X.

16. In Exhibit A-7, what is the slope for straight line AB?
    a. 3
    b. 1

c. −1

d. −5

17. In Exhibit A-7, what is the slope of straight line AB?
    a. Positive
    b. Zero
    c. Negative
    d. Variable

18. In Exhibit A-8, as X increases along the horizontal axis, corresponding to points A–D on the line, the Y values remain unchanged at 20 units. What is the relationship between the X and Y variables?
    a. Direct
    b. Inverse
    c. Independent
    d. Undefined

19. In Exhibit A-8, what is the slope of straight line A–D?
    a. Greater than 1
    b. Equal to 1
    c. Less than 1
    d. Zero

20. Exhibit A-9 represents a three-variable relationship. As the annual income of consumers falls from $50,000 (line A) to $30,000 (line B), the result is a(n)
    a. upward movement along each curve.
    b. downward movement along each curve.
    c. leftward shift in curve A to curve B.
    d. rightward shift in curve A to curve B.

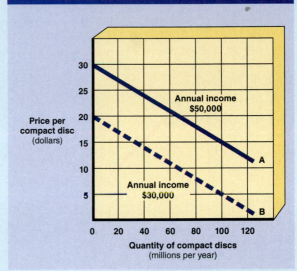

EXHIBIT **A-9** Multicurve Graph

CHAPTER 2

Production Possibilities, Opportunity Cost, and Economic Growth

CHAPTER PREVIEW

This chapter continues building on the foundation laid in the preceding chapter. Having learned that *scarcity* forces *choices*, here you will study the choices people make in more detail. This chapter begins by examining the three basic choices: *What*, *How*, and *For Whom* to produce. The process of answering these basic questions introduces two other key building blocks in the economic way of thinking—*opportunity cost* and *marginal analysis*. Once you understand these important concepts stated in words, it will be easier to interpret our first formal economic model, the *production possibilities curve*. This model illustrates how economists use graphs as a powerful tool to supplement words and develop an understanding of basic economic principles. You will discover that the production possibilities model teaches many of the most important concepts in economics, including scarcity, the law of increasing opportunity costs, efficiency, investment, and economic growth. For example, this chapter applies the production possibilities curve to explain why developing countries find it difficult to achieve economic growth and thereby reach a higher standard of living for their people.

IN THIS CHAPTER, YOU WILL LEARN TO SOLVE THESE ECONOMICS PUZZLES:

- Why do so few rock stars and movie stars go to college?

- Why would you spend an extra hour reading this text rather than going to a movie or sleeping?

- Why are investment and economic growth so important?

- What does a war on terrorism really mean?

2-1 THREE FUNDAMENTAL ECONOMIC QUESTIONS

Because of the problem of scarcity, whether rich or poor, every nation must answer the same three fundamental economic questions:

1. *What* products will be produced?
2. *How* will they be produced? and
3. *For Whom* will they be produced?

Later, the chapter on economies in transition introduces various types of economic systems and describes how each deals with these three economic choices.

2-1a What to Produce?

The *What* question requires an economy to decide the mix and quantity of goods and services it will produce. Should society devote more of its limited resources to producing more health care and fewer military goods? Should society produce more iPods and fewer Blu-rays? Should more capital goods be produced instead of consumer goods, or should more small hybrid cars and fewer SUVs be produced? The problem of scarcity restricts our ability to produce everything we want during a given period, so the choice to produce "more" of one good requires producing "less" of another good. In the United States, consumer sovereignty answers the *What* question. In Cuba and North Korea, for example, the government and not the consumer answers this question.

2-1b How to Produce?

After deciding *what* products to make, the second question for society to decide is *how* to mix technology and scarce resources in order to produce these goods. For instance, a towel can be sewn primarily by hand (labor), partially by hand and partially by machine (labor and capital), or primarily by machine (capital). In short, the *How* question asks whether a production technique will be more or less capital-intensive. The *How* question also concerns choices among resources for production. Should electricity be produced from oil, solar power, or nuclear power?

Education plays an important role in answering the *How* question. Education improves the ability of workers to perform their work. Variation in the quality and quantity of education among nations is one reason economies differ in their capacities to apply resources and technology to answer the *How* question. For example, the United States is striving to catch up with Japan in the use of robotics. Answering the question *How do we improve our robotics?* requires engineers and employees with the proper training in the installation and operation of robots.

2-1c For Whom to Produce?

After the *What* and *How* questions are resolved, the third question is *For Whom*. Among all those desiring the produced goods, who actually receives them? This question concerns how the economic pie is divided. Who is fed well? Who drives a Mercedes? Who receives organ transplants? Should economics professors earn a salary of $1 million a year and others pay higher taxes to support economists? The *For Whom* question means that society must have a method to decide who will be "rich and famous" and who will be "poor and unknown." Chapter 12 returns to the *For Whom* question and discusses it in more detail.

2-2 OPPORTUNITY COST

Because of scarcity, the three basic questions cannot be answered without sacrifice or cost. But what does the term *cost* really mean? The common response would be to say that the purchase price is the cost. A movie ticket *costs* $8, or a shirt *costs* $50. Applying the economic way of thinking, however, *cost* is defined differently. A well-known phrase from Nobel Prize–winning economist Milton Friedman says, *There is no such thing as a free lunch.* This expression captures the links among the concepts of scarcity, choice, and cost. Because of scarcity, people must make choices, and each choice incurs a cost (sacrifice). Once one option is chosen, another option is given up. The money you spend on a movie ticket cannot also buy a Blu-ray. A business may purchase a new textile machine to manufacture towels, but this same money cannot be used to buy a new recreation facility for employees.

The Blu-ray and recreation facility examples illustrate that the true cost of these decisions is the opportunity cost of a choice, not the purchase price. **Opportunity cost** is the best alternative sacrificed for a chosen alternative. Stated differently, it is the cost of not choosing the next best alternative. This principle states that some highly valued opportunity must be forgone in all economic decisions. The highest-valued good or use of time given up for the chosen good or use of time measures the opportunity cost. We may omit the *opportunity* before the word *cost,* but the concept remains the same. Exhibit 1 illustrates the causation chain linking scarcity, choice, and opportunity cost.

Examples are endless, but let's consider a few. Suppose your economics professor decides to become a rock star in the Rolling in Dough band. Now all his or her working hours are devoted to creating hit music, and the opportunity cost is the educational services no longer provided. Now a personal example: The opportunity cost of dating a famous model or movie star (name your favorite) might be the loss of your current girlfriend or boyfriend. Opportunity cost also applies to national economic decisions. Suppose the federal government decides to spend tax revenues on a space station. The opportunity cost depends on the next best program *not* funded. Assume roads and bridges are the highest-valued projects not built as a result of the decision to construct the space station. Then the opportunity cost of the decision to devote resources to the space station is the forgone roads and bridges and not the money actually spent to build the space station.

Opportunity cost
The best alternative sacrificed for a chosen alternative.

EXHIBIT 1 The Links between Scarcity, Choice, and Opportunity Cost

Scarcity means that no society has enough resources to produce all the goods and services necessary to satisfy all human wants. As a result, society is always confronted with the problem of making choices. This concept is captured in Milton Friedman's famous phrase, "There is no such thing as a free lunch." This means that each decision has a sacrifice in terms of an alternative choice that has to be foregone.

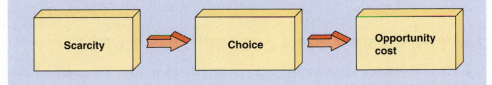

To personalize the relationship between time and opportunity cost, ask yourself what you would be doing if you were not reading this text. Your answer might be watching television or sleeping. If sleeping is your choice, the opportunity cost of studying this text is the sleep you sacrifice. Rock stars and movie stars, on the other hand, must forfeit a large amount of income to attend college. Now you know why you see so few of these stars in class.

Decisions often involve sacrifice of *both* goods and time. Suppose you decide to see a movie at a theater located 15 minutes from campus. If you had not spent the money at the movie theater, you could have purchased a Blu-ray and watched a movie at home. And the time spent traveling to and from the movie and sitting through it could have been devoted to studying for your economics exam. The opportunity cost of the movie consists of giving up a Blu-ray as well as the study time needed to score higher on the economics exam.

2-3 MARGINAL ANALYSIS

Marginal analysis
An examination of the effects of additions to or subtractions from a current situation.

At the heart of all rational decision-making is marginal analysis. **Marginal analysis** examines the effects of additions to or subtractions from a current situation. This is a very valuable tool in the economic way of thinking toolkit because it considers the "marginal" effects of change. The rational decision maker decides on an option only if the marginal benefit exceeds the marginal cost. For example, you must decide how to use your scarce time. Should you devote an extra hour to reading this text, going to a movie, watching television, texting, or sleeping? Which of your many options do you choose? The answer depends on marginal analysis. If you decide the benefit of a higher grade in economics exceeds the opportunity cost of, say sleep, then you allocate the extra hour to studying economics. Excellent choice!

Businesses use marginal analysis. Hotels, for example, rent space to student groups for dances and other events. Assume you are the hotel manager, and a student group offers to pay $400 to use the ballroom for a party. To decide whether to accept the offer requires marginal analysis. The marginal benefit of renting otherwise vacant space is $400, and the marginal cost is $300 for extra electricity and cleaning services. Since the marginal benefit exceeds the marginal cost, the manager sensibly accepts the offer.

Similarly, farmers use marginal analysis. For example, a farmer must decide whether to add more fertilizer when growing corn. Using marginal analysis, the farmer estimates that the corn revenue yield will be about $75 per acre with the current amount of fertilizer usage and about $100 per acre using one more application of fertilizer. If the cost of fertilizer is $20 per acre, marginal analysis tells the farmer to add one more application of fertilizer. The addition of fertilizer will increase profit by $5 per acre because fertilizing adds $25 to the value of each acre at a cost of $20 per acre.

Marginal analysis is an important concept when the government considers changes in various programs. For example, as demonstrated in the next section, it is useful to know that an increase in the production of military goods will result in an opportunity cost of fewer consumer goods produced.

2-4 THE PRODUCTION POSSIBILITIES CURVE

The economic problem of scarcity means that society's capacity to produce combinations of goods is constrained by its limited resources. This condition can be represented in a model called the production possibilities curve (*PPC*). The **production possibilities curve** shows the maximum combinations of two outputs that an economy can produce in a given period of time with its available resources and technology. Three basic assumptions underlie the production possibilities curve model:

1. **Fixed Resources.** The quantities and qualities of all resource inputs remain unchanged during the time period. But the "rules of the game" do allow an economy to shift any resource from the production of one output to the production of another output. For example, an economy might shift workers from producing consumer goods to producing capital goods. Although the number of workers remains unchanged, this transfer of labor will produce fewer consumer goods and more capital goods.

2. **Fully Employed Resources.** The economy operates with all its factors of production fully employed and producing the greatest output possible without waste or mismanagement.

3. **Technology Unchanged.** Holding existing technology fixed creates limits, or constraints, on the amounts and types of goods any economy can produce. **Technology** is the body of knowledge applied to how goods are produced.

Exhibit 2 shows a hypothetical economy that has the capacity to manufacture any combination of military goods (guns) and consumer goods (butter) per year along its production possibilities curve (*PPC*), including points *A*, *B*, *C*, and *D*. For example, if this economy uses all its resources to make military goods, it can produce a *maximum* of 160 billion units of military goods and zero units of consumer goods (combination *A*). Another possibility is for the economy to use all its resources to produce a *maximum* of 100 billion units of consumer goods and zero units of military goods (point *D*). Between the extremes of points *A* and *D* lie other production possibilities for combinations of military and consumer goods. If combination *B* is chosen, the economy will produce 140 billion units of military goods and 40 billion units of consumer goods. Another possibility (point *C*) is to produce 80 billion units of military goods and 80 billion units of consumer goods.

What happens if the economy does not use all its resources to their capacity? For example, some workers may not find work, or plants and equipment may be idle for any number of reasons. The result is that our hypothetical economy fails to reach any of the combinations along the *PPC*. In Exhibit 2, point *U* illustrates an *inefficient* output level for any economy operating without all its resources fully employed. At point *U*, our model economy is producing 80 billion units of military goods and 40 billion units of consumer goods per year. Such an economy is underproducing because it could satisfy more of society's wants if it were producing at some point along the *PPC*.

Even if an economy fully employs all its resources, it is impossible to produce certain output quantities. Any point outside the production possibilities curve is *currently unattainable* because it is beyond the economy's present production capabilities. Point *Z*, for example, represents an unattainable output of 140 billion units of military goods and 80 billion units of consumer goods. Society would prefer this combination to any combination along, or inside, the *PPC*, but the economy cannot reach this point with its existing resources and technology.

Scarcity limits an economy to points on or below its production possibilities curve.

CONCLUSION

Production possibilities curve
A curve that shows the maximum combinations of two outputs an economy can produce in a given period of time with its available resources and technology.

Technology
The body of knowledge applied to how goods are produced.

Because all the points along the curve are *maximum* output levels with the given resources and technology, they are all called *efficient* points. A movement between any two efficient points on the curve means that *more* of one product is produced only by producing *less* of the other product. In Exhibit 2, moving from point *A* to point *B* produces

---

EXHIBIT 2 The Production Possibilities Curve for Military Goods and Consumer Goods

All points along the production possibilities curve (*PPC*) are maximum possible combinations of military goods and consumer goods. One possibility, point *A*, would be to produce 160 billion units of military goods and zero units of consumer goods each year. At the other extreme, point *D*, the economy uses all its resources to produce 100 billion units of consumer goods and zero units of military goods each year. Points *B* and *C* are obtained by using some resources to produce each of the two outputs. If the economy fails to utilize its resources fully and has some unemployment, the result is an inefficient combination given by a point inside the *PPC*, like point *U*. Any point outside the *PPC*, like point *Z*, lies beyond the economy's present production capabilities and is currently unattainable.

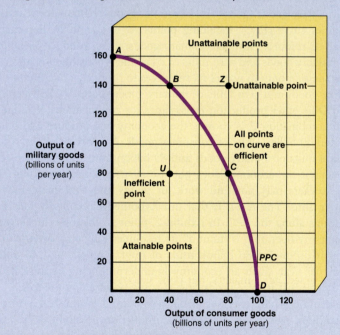

Production Possibilities Schedule for Military and Consumer Goods per Year				
Output	**Production possibilities**			
(billions of units per year)	**A**	**B**	**C**	**D**
Military goods	160	140	80	0
Consumer goods	0	40	80	100

40 billion additional units of consumer goods per year, but only at a cost of sacrificing 20 billion units of military goods. Thus, a movement between any two efficient points graphically illustrates opportunity cost and that "There is no such thing as a free lunch."

The production possibilities curve consists of all efficient output combinations at which an economy can produce more of one good only by producing less of the other good.

2-5   THE LAW OF INCREASING OPPORTUNITY COSTS

Why is the production possibilities curve shaped the way it is? Exhibit 3 will help us answer this question. It presents a production possibilities curve for a hypothetical economy that must choose between producing tanks and producing sailboats. Consider expanding the production of sailboats in 20,000-unit increments. Moving from point *A* to point *B*, the *opportunity cost* is 10,000 tanks; between points *B* and *C*, the *opportunity cost* is 20,000 tanks; and the *opportunity cost* of producing at point *D*, rather than point *C*, is 50,000 tanks.

Exhibit 3 illustrates the **law of increasing opportunity costs**, which states that the opportunity cost increases as production of one output expands. Holding the stock of resources and technology constant (ceteris paribus), the law of increasing opportunity costs causes the production possibilities curve to display a *bowed-out* shape.

Why must our hypothetical economy sacrifice larger and larger amounts of tank output in order to produce each additional 20,000 sailboats? The reason is that resources, like workers, are not equally suited to producing one good compared to another good. For example, expanding the output of sailboats requires the use of more resources, like workers who may be less suited to producing sailboats than producing tanks. Suppose our hypothetical economy produces no sailboats (point *A*) and then decides to produce them. At first, the least-skilled tank workers are transferred to making sailboats, and 10,000 tanks are sacrificed at point *B*. As the economy moves from point *B* to point *C*, more highly skilled tank makers become sailboat makers, and the opportunity cost rises to 20,000 tanks. Finally, the economy can decide to move from point *C* to point *D*, and the opportunity cost increases even more—to 50,000 tanks. Now the remaining tank workers, who are superb tank makers, but poor sailboat makers, must adapt to the techniques of sailboat production.

Finally, it should be noted that the production possibilities curve model could assume that resources are equally well-suited to producing all goods and the opportunity cost remains constant. In this case, the production possibilities curve would be a straight line, which is the model employed in the chapter on international trade and finance.

Law of increasing opportunity costs
The principle that the opportunity cost increases as production of one output expands.

Because resources are not equally well-suited to producing all products, it's common to experience increasing opportunity costs and a bowed-out production possibilities curve.

EXHIBIT 3 The Law of Increasing Opportunity Costs

A hypothetical economy produces equal increments of 20,000 sailboats per year as we move from point A through point D on the production possibilities curve (PPC). If the economy moves from point A to point B, the opportunity cost of 20,000 sailboats is a reduction in tank output of 10,000 per year. This opportunity cost rises to 20,000 tanks if the economy moves from point B to point C. Finally, production at point D, rather than point C, results in an opportunity cost of 50,000 tanks per year. The opportunity cost rises because workers are not equally suited to making tanks and sailboats.

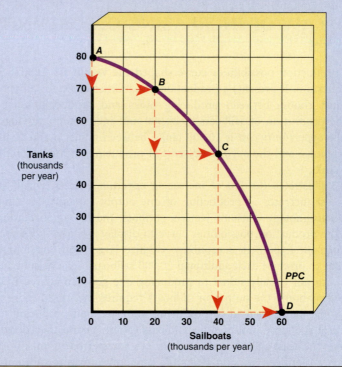

Production Possibilities Schedule for Tanks and Sailboats per Year				
Output	Production possibilities			
(thousands per year)	A	B	C	D
Tanks	80	70	50	0
Sailboats	0	20	40	60

2-6 SOURCES OF ECONOMIC GROWTH

Economic growth
The ability of an economy to produce greater levels of output, represented by an outward shift of its production possibilities curve.

The economy's production capacity is not permanently fixed. If either the resource base increases or technology advances, the economy experiences economic growth, and the production possibilities curve shifts outward. **Economic growth** is the ability of an economy to produce greater levels of output, represented by an outward shift of its production possibilities curve. Exhibit 4 illustrates the importance of an outward shift. (Note the

EXHIBIT 4 An Outward Shift of the Production Possibilities Curve for Computers and Pizzas

The economy begins with the capacity to produce combinations along the first production possibilities curve PPC_1. Growth in the resource base or technological advances can shift the production possibilities curve outward from PPC_1 to PPC_2. Points along PPC_2 represent new production possibilities that were previously impossible. This outward shift permits the economy to produce greater quantities of output. Instead of producing combination A, the economy can produce, for example, more computers at point B or more pizzas at point C. If the economy grows and produces at a point between B and C, more of both pizzas and computers can be produced, compared to point A.

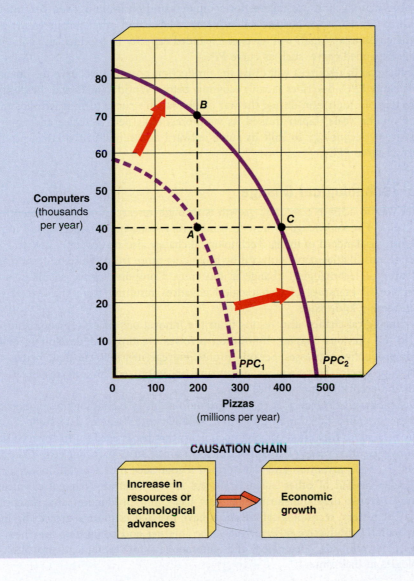

causation chain, which is often used in this text to focus on a model's cause-and-effect relationship.) At point *A* on PPC₁, a hypothetical full-employment economy produces 40,000 computers and 200 million pizzas per year. If the curve shifts outward to the new curve PPC₂, the economy can expand its full-employment output options. One option is to produce at point *B* and increase computer output to 70,000 per year. Another possibility is to increase pizza output to 400 million per year. Yet another choice is to produce more of both at some point between points *B* and *C* on PPC₂.

2-6a Changes in Resources

One way to accelerate economic growth is to obtain more resources. Any increase in resources, for example, more natural resources, a baby boom, or more factories will shift the production possibilities curve outward. In Exhibit 4, assume curve *PPC₁* represents Japan's production possibilities for computers and pizzas in a given year. Suddenly, Japan discovers within its borders new sources of labor and other resources. As a result of the new resources, Japan will have an expanded capacity to produce any combination along an expanded curve, such as curve *PPC₂*.

Reductions in resources will cause the production possibilities curve to shift inward. Assume curve *PPC₂* describes Japan's economy before World War II and the destruction of its factors of production during the war caused Japan's curve to shift leftward to curve *PPC₁*. Over the years, Japan trained its workforce, built new factories and equipment, and used new technology to shift its curve outward and surpass its original production capacity at curve *PPC₂*.

2-6b Technological Change

Another way to achieve economic growth is through research and development of new technologies. The knowledge of how to transform a stone into a wheel vastly improved the prehistoric standard of living. Technological change also makes it possible to shift the production possibilities curve outward by producing more from the same resources base. One source of technological change is *invention*. Computer chips, satellites, and the Internet are all examples of technological advances resulting from the use of science and engineering knowledge.

Technological change also results from the innovations of entrepreneurship, introduced in the previous chapter. Innovation involves creating and developing new products or productive processes. Seeking profits, entrepreneurs create new, better, or less expensive products. This requires organizing an improved mix of resources, which expands the production possibilities curve.

One entrepreneur, Henry Ford, changed auto industry technology by pioneering the use of the assembly line for making cars. Another entrepreneur, law student Chester Carlson, became so frustrated copying documents that he worked on his own to develop photocopying. After years of disappointment, a small firm named Xerox Corporation accepted Carlson's invention and transformed a good idea into a revolutionary product. These and a myriad of other business success stories illustrate that entrepreneurs are important because they transform their new ideas into production and practical use. Throughout history, technological advances have fostered economic growth by increasing our nation's productive power. Today, the Internet and computers are "new" technologies, but railroads, electricity, and automobiles, for example, were also "new" technologies in their time.

YOU'RE THE ECONOMIST

FedEx Wasn't an Overnight Success

Frederick W. Smith is a classic entrepreneurial success story. Young Fred went to Yale University, had a good new idea, secured venture capital, worked like crazy, and made a fortune, and the Smithsonian Institution rendered its ultimate accolade. It snapped up an early Federal Express jet for its collection, displaying it for a time in the National Air and Space Museum in Washington, D.C., not far from the Wright brothers' first airplane.

Smith's saga began with a college economics term paper that spelled out a nationwide overnight parcel delivery system that would be guaranteed to "absolutely, positively" beat the pants off the U.S. Postal Service. People, he said, would pay much more if their packages arrived at their destination the next morning. To accomplish his plan, planes would converge nightly on Memphis, Tennessee, carrying packages accepted at any location throughout the nation. Smith chose this city for its central U.S. location and because its airport has little bad weather to cause landing delays. In the morning hours, all items would be unloaded, sorted, and rerouted to other airports, where vans would battle rush-hour traffic to make deliveries before the noon deadline.

Smith's college term paper only got a C grade. Perhaps the professor thought the idea was too risky, and lots of others certainly agreed. In 1969, after college and a tour as a Marine pilot in Vietnam, the 24-year-old Smith began pitching his parcel delivery plan to mostly skeptical financiers. Nevertheless, with $4 million of his family's money, he persuaded a few venture capitalists to put up $80 million. At the time, this was the largest venture capital package ever assembled. In 1973, delivery service began with 33 jets connecting 25 cities, but on the first night, only 86 packages showed up.

It was years before Smith looked like a genius. The company posted a $27 million loss the first year, turned the corner in 1976, and then took off, helped by a 1981 decision to add letters to its basic package delivery service. Today, Smith's basic strategy hasn't changed, but the scale of the operation has exploded. FedEx is the world's largest express transportation company serving over 200 countries.

ANALYZE **THE ISSUE** Draw a production possibilities curve for an economy producing only pizzas and computers. Explain how Fred Smith and other successful entrepreneurs affect the curve.

What Does a War on Terrorism Really Mean?

With the disappearance of the former Soviet Union and the end of the Cold War, the United States became the world's only superpower and no longer engaged in an intense competition to build up its military. As a result, in the 1990s, Congress and the White House had the opportunity to reduce the military's share of the budget and spend more funds for nondefense goods. This situation was referred to as the "peace dividend." Now consider that the need to combat terrorism diverts resources back to military and security output. Does the peace dividend or a reversal to more military spending represent a possible shift of the production possibilities curve or a movement along it?

CHECKPOINT

2-7 PRESENT INVESTMENT AND THE FUTURE PRODUCTION POSSIBILITIES CURVE

When the decision for an economy involves choosing between capital goods and consumer goods, the output combination chosen for the present period can determine future production capacity. Exhibit 5 compares two countries producing different combinations of capital and consumer goods. Part (a) shows the production possibilities curve for the low-investment economy of Alpha. This economy was producing combination A in 2000, which is an output of C_a of consumer goods and an output of K_a of capital goods per year. This economy is currently producing relatively few capital goods and lots of consumer goods. Let's assume K_a is just enough capital output to replace the capital being worn out each year (depreciation). As a result, Alpha fails to accumulate the net gain of factories and equipment required to expand its production possibilities

---

EXHIBIT 5 Alpha's and Beta's Present and Future Production Possibilities Curves

In part (a), each year Alpha produces only enough capital (K_a) to replace existing capital that has worn out. Without more capital, and assuming other resources remain fixed as well, Alpha is unable to grow and shift its production possibilities curve outward. In part (b), each year Beta produces K_b capital, which is more than the amount required to replenish its depreciated capital. In 2018, this expanded capital provides Beta with the extra production capacity to shift its production possibilities curve to the right (outward). If Beta chooses point B on its curve, it has the production capacity to increase the amount of consumer goods from C_b to C_c without producing fewer capital goods. Because it now has more consumer goods, the country has increased its standard of living.

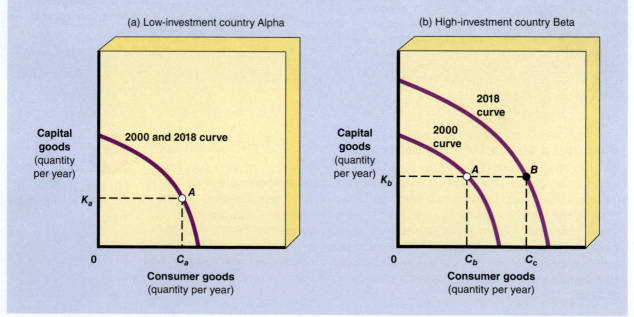

(a) Low-investment country Alpha

(b) High-investment country Beta

GLOBAL ECONOMICS

How Does Public Capital Affect a Nation's Curve?

Applicable Concept: Economic Growth

iStock.com/Robert Hackett

The discussion of low-investment country Alpha versus high-investment country Beta explained that sacrificing production of consumer goods for an increase in capital goods output can result in economic growth and a higher standard of living. Stated differently, there was a long-run benefit from the accumulation of capital that offset the short-run opportunity cost in terms of consumer goods foregone. Here the analysis was in terms of investment in private capital such as factories, machines, and inventories. However, public or government capital can also influence a nation's production possibilities over time.

For example, according to Josh Bivens at the Economic Policy Institute: "Public investment by federal, state, and local governments builds the nation's capital stock by devoting resources to the basic physical infrastructure (such as roads, bridges, rail lines, airports, and water distribution), innovative activity (basic research), green investments (clean power sources and weatherization), and education (both primary and advanced, as well as job training) that leads to higher productivity and/or higher living standards." Moreover, …"investments in public capital have significant

positive impacts on private-sector productivity, with estimated rates of return ranging from 15 percent to upwards of 45 percent," and "public investment has benefits that extend beyond simply increasing [overall production]: It also offers benefits that are more broadly shared by all… such as safer water and cleaner air."[1]

Finally, economic growth and development is a major goal of countries throughout the world, and there are numerous factors that cause some countries to experience greater economic growth compared to other countries. Note that this topic is discussed in more depth in the last chapter of the text.

ANALYZE THE ISSUE Construct a production possibilities curve for a hypothetical country. Put public capital goods per year on the vertical axis and consumer goods per year on the horizontal axis. Not shown directly in your graph, assume that this country produces just enough private capital per year to replace its depreciated capital. Assume further that this country is without public capital and is operating at point *A*, where consumer goods are at a maximum. Based on the above research and using a production possibilities curve, show and explain what happens to this country's private capital, production possibilities curve, and standard of living if it increases its output of public capital.

---

1. "Public Investment: The Next 'New Thing' for Powering Economic Growth," report by Josh Bivens, April 18, 2012, Economic Policy Institute, found at http://www.epi.org/publication/bp338-public-investments/. See also "The Short- and Long-Term Impact of Infrastructure Investments on Employment and Economic Activity in the U.S. Economy," report by Josh Bivens, July 1, 2014, Economic Policy Institute, found at http://www.epi.org/publication /impact-of-infrastructure-investments/. See also "The Macroeconomic and Budgetary Effects of Federal Investment," Congressional Budget Office, June 2016, found at https://www.cbo.gov/sites/default/files/114th-congress-2015-2016/reports/51628-Federal_Investment-OneCol.pdf.

---

curve outward in future years.[1] Why wouldn't Alpha simply move up along its production curve by shifting more resources to capital goods production? The problem is that sacrificing consumer goods for capital formation causes a lower standard of living, which can be unpopular.

---

[1]Recall from the Appendix to Chapter 1 that a third variable can affect the variables measured on the vertical and horizontal axes. In this case, the third variable is the quantity of capital worn out per year.

Investment
The accumulation of capital, such as factories, machines, and inventories, used to produce goods and services.

Comparing Alpha to Beta illustrates the importance of being able to do more than just replace worn out capital. Beta operated in 2000 at point A in part (b), which is an output of C_b of consumer goods and K_b of capital goods. Assuming K_b is more than enough to replenish worn-out capital, Beta is a high-investment economy, adding to its capital stock and creating extra production capacity. This process of accumulating capital (*capital formation*) is investment. **Investment** is the accumulation of capital, such as factories, machines, and inventories, used to produce goods and services. Newly built factories and machines in the present provide an economy with the capacity to expand its production options in the future. For example, the outward shift of its curve allows Beta to produce C_c consumer goods at point B in 2018. This means Beta will be able to improve its standard of living by producing $C_c - C_b$ extra consumer goods, while Alpha's standard of living remains unchanged because the production of consumer goods remains unchanged.

CONCLUSION   A nation can accelerate economic growth by increasing its production of capital goods in excess of the capital being worn out in the production process.

Key Concepts

What, How, and For Whom questions	Marginal analysis	Technology	Economic growth
Opportunity cost	Production possibilities curve	Law of increasing opportunity costs	Investment

Summary

- **Three fundamental economic questions** facing any economy are *What*, *How*, and *For Whom* to produce goods. The *What* question asks exactly which goods are produced and in what quantities. The *How* question requires society to decide the resource mix used to produce goods. The *For Whom* problem concerns the division of limited output among society's unlimited wants.

- **Opportunity cost** is the best alternative forgone for a chosen option. This means no decision can be made without cost.

- **Marginal analysis** examines the impact of changes from a current situation and is a technique used extensively in economics. The basic approach is to compare the additional benefits of a change with the additional costs of the change.

- A **production possibilities curve** illustrates an economy's capacity to produce goods, subject to the constraint of scarcity. The production possibilities curve is a graph of the maximum possible combinations of two outputs that can be produced in a given period of time, subject to three conditions: (1) All resources are fully employed. (2) The resource base is not allowed to vary during the time period. (3) **Technology**, which is the body of knowledge applied to the production of goods, remains constant.

- **Inefficient** production occurs at any point inside the production possibilities curve. All points along the curve are **efficient** points because each point represents a maximum output possibility.

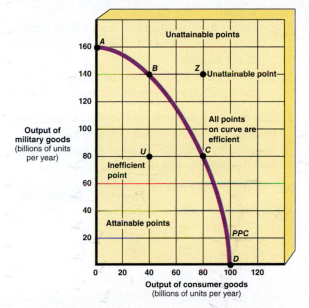

- The **law of increasing opportunity costs** states that the opportunity cost increases as the production of output expands. The explanation for this law is that the suitability of resources declines sharply as greater amounts are transferred from producing one output to producing another output.

- **Economic growth** is represented by the production possibilities curve shifting outward as the result of an increase in resources or an advance in technology. Economic growth is desired because it increases standards of living.

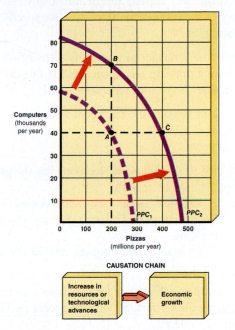

- **Investment** means that an economy is producing and accumulating capital. Investment consists of factories, machines, and inventories (capital) produced in the present that are used to shift the production possibilities curve outward in the future.

Summary of Conclusion Statements

- Scarcity limits an economy to points on or below its production possibilities curve.

- The production possibilities curve consists of all efficient output combinations at which an economy can produce more of one good only by producing less of the other good.

- Because resources are not equally well-suited to producing all products, it's common to

experience increasing opportunity costs and a bowed-out shaped production possibilities curve.

- A nation can accelerate economic growth by increasing its production of capital goods in excess of the capital being worn out in the production process.

Study Questions and Problems

Please see Appendix A for answers to the odd-numbered questions. Your instructor has access to the answers for even-numbered questions.

1. Explain why scarcity forces individuals and society to incur opportunity costs. Give specific examples.

2. Suppose a retailer promotes its store by advertising a drawing for a "free car." Is this car *free* because the winner pays *zero* for it?

3. Explain verbally the statement "There is no such thing as a free lunch" in relation to scarce resources.

4. Which of the following decisions has the greater opportunity cost? Why?
   a. A decision to use an undeveloped lot in Tokyo's financial district for an apartment building.
   b. A decision to use a square mile in the desert for a gas station.

5. Attending college is expensive, time consuming, and requires effort. So why do people decide to attend college?

6. The following is a set of hypothetical production possibilities for a nation.

Combination	Automobiles (thousands)	Beef (thousands of tons)
A	0	10
B	2	9
C	4	7
D	6	4
E	8	0

   a. Plot these production possibilities data. What is the opportunity cost of the first 2,000 automobiles produced? Between which points is the opportunity cost per thousand automobiles highest? Between which points is the opportunity cost per thousand tons of beef highest?
   b. Label a point *F* inside the curve. Why is this an inefficient point? Label a point *G* outside

the curve. Why is this point unattainable? Why are points *A* through *E* all efficient points?
   c. Does this production possibilities curve reflect the law of increasing opportunity costs? Explain.
   d. What assumptions could be changed to shift the production possibilities curve?

7. The following table shows the production possibilities for pies and flower boxes. Fill in the opportunity cost (pies forgone) of producing the first through the fifth flower box.

Combination	Pies	Flower boxes	Opportunity cost
A	30	0	____
B	26	1	____
C	21	2	____
D	15	3	____
E	8	4	____
F	0	5	____

8. Why does a production possibilities curve have a bowed-out shape?

9. Interpret the phrases "There is no such thing as a free lunch" and "A free lunch is possible" in terms of the production possibilities curve.

10. Suppose, unfortunately, your mathematics and economics professors have decided to give tests two days from now and you can spend a total of only twelve hours studying for both exams. After some thought, you conclude that dividing your study time equally between each subject will give you an expected grade of C in each course. For each additional three hours of study time for one of the subjects, your grade will increase one letter for that subject, and your grade will fall one letter for the other subject.

a. Construct a table for the production possibilities and corresponding number of hours of study in this case.
b. Plot these production possibilities data in a graph.
c. Does this production possibilities curve reflect the law of increasing opportunity costs? Explain.

11. Draw a production possibilities curve for a hypothetical economy producing capital goods and consumer goods. Suppose a major technological breakthrough occurs in the capital goods industry and the new technology is widely adopted only in this industry. Draw the new production possibilities curve. Now assume that a technological advance occurs in consumer goods production, but not in capital goods production. Draw the new production possibilities curve.

12. The present choice between investing in capital goods and producing consumer goods now affects the ability of an economy to produce in the future. Explain.

✔ CHECKPOINT ANSWERS

What Does a War on Terrorism Really Mean?
A "peace dividend" suggests resources are allocated away from military production and used for greater nonmilitary production. The war on terrorism arguably shifts resources in the opposite direction. If you said that this phrase represents a movement along the production possibilities curve, **YOU ARE CORRECT**.

Sample Quiz

Please see Appendix B for answers to Sample Quiz questions.

1. Which of the following *best* describes the three fundamental economic questions?
   a. What to produce, when to produce, and where to produce
   b. What time to produce, what place to produce, and how to produce
   c. What to produce, when to produce, and for whom to produce
   d. What to produce, how to produce, and for whom to produce

2. Suppose the alternative uses of an hour of your time in the evening, ranked from best to worst, are (1) study economics, (2) watch two half-hour sitcoms, (3) play video games, and (4) jog around town. You can choose only one activity. What is the opportunity cost of studying economics for one hour given this information?
   a. Jogging around town
   b. Watching two half-hour TV sitcoms
   c. Playing video games
   d. The sum of watching two half-hour TV sitcoms, playing pool, and doing your laundry

3. Which word or phrase *best* completes the following sentence? Marginal analysis means evaluating _____ changes from a current situation.
   a. positive or negative
   b. infinite
   c. no
   d. maximum

4. Which of the following is an example of an organization using marginal analysis?
   a. A hotel manager calculating the average cost per guest for the past year
   b. A farmer hoping for rain
   c. A government official considering the effect an increase in military goods

production will have on the production of consumer goods

d. A businessperson calculating economic profits

5. A production possibilities curve shows the various combinations of two outputs that
   a. consumers would like to consume.
   b. producers would like to produce.
   c. an economy can produce.
   d. an economy should produce.

6. A production possibilities curve is drawn based on which of the following assumptions?
   a. Resources are fixed and fully employed, and technology advances at the rate of growth of the economy overall.
   b. Resources such as nonrenewable resources will decline, but labor remains fully employed and technology is unchanged.
   c. Resources can vary; most resources experience times of unemployment; and technology advances, particularly during wartime.
   d. Resources such as labor and capital will grow and are fully employed, and technology is unchanged.
   e. None of the answers correct.

7. If an economy can produce various combinations of food and shelter along a production possibilities curve (PPC), then if we increase the production of shelter along the PPC, which of the following is true?
   a. We also increase the production of food.
   b. We must decrease the production of food. This forgone food production represents the opportunity cost of the increase in shelter.
   c. We cannot change the production of food.
   d. The concept of opportunity cost does not apply along PPC.

8. An economy can produce various combinations of food and shelter along a production possibilities curve (PPC). First, increase the production of shelter along the PPC; then continue to shift more and more production to shelter. Which of the following will most likely

happen to the opportunity cost of a unit of shelter?

a. Opportunity cost will increase because as more and more shelter is produced, labor and capital that is highly productive at producing food is being shifted to shelter production, and so more and more food is being given up to produce a unit of shelter.
b. Opportunity cost is the amount of labor (but not capital) that is used to produce the extra shelter.
c. Opportunity cost must stay constant if we are to stay on the production possibilities curve (PPC).
d. Opportunity cost includes all options given up to produce shelter.

9. An economy can produce various combinations of food and shelter along a production possibilities curve (PPC). Suppose a technological innovation resulted in a new, higher-yielding crop that generated more bushels of grain for a given set of land, labor, and capital resources. If this innovation did not affect the productivity of shelter production, which of the following would be *true*?
   a. The PPC will shift outward equally along both axes of the graph.
   b. The PPC will rotate inward along the food axis, but will not shift on the shelter axis.
   c. The PPC will rotate outward along the food axis, but will not shift on the shelter axis.
   d. The PPC will not change.

10. If a production possibilities curve (PPC) has capital on the vertical axis and consumer goods on the horizontal axis, which of the following is *true*?
    a. There is a trade-off between emphasizing the production of capital today to benefit people today versus emphasizing the production of consumer goods today that will generate benefits in the future.
    b. Greater emphasis on the production of capital today leads to future inward shifts in the

PPC, thus decreasing the wealth of people in the future.

c. Greater emphasis on the production of consumer goods today leads to greater outward shifts in the PPC, thus increasing the wealth of people in the future.

d. Greater emphasis on the production of capital today leads to greater outward shifts in the PPC, thus increasing the wealth of people in the future.

11. Which of the following reasons could explain why an economy would be operating inside its production possibilities curve (PPC)?
    a. Because shrinking population has reduced the number of productive workers in the economy
    b. Because technological innovations have increased the productivity of labor and capital
    c. Because damage to natural resources, such as damage caused by deforestation leading to erosion of topsoil, has shrunk the land resource
    d. Because of unemployment or underemployment of labor, perhaps due to discrimination against employing workers of a certain race or gender

12. Combinations of goods outside the production possibilities curve (PPC) have which of the following characteristics?
    a. They are attainable today only if we employ all unemployed or underemployed resources.
    b. They are not attainable given our existing stock of resources and technology.
    c. They imply that some resources, such as labor, are unemployed or underemployed.
    d. None of the answers is correct.

13. Suppose an economy can produce various combinations of fish and bread. If more people with strong fishing skills became employed in this economy, how would the production possibilities curve (PPC) change?
    a. The PPC would shift outward on the fish axis, but would not change on the bread axis.

b. The PPC would shift outward equally along both the fish and bread axes.
    c. The PPC would shift inward on the bread axis, but would not change on the fish axis.
    d. The PPC would shift inward equally along both the fish and bread axes.

14. Three different economies have made choices about the production of capital goods. Which of the following is most likely to produce the greatest growth in the production possibilities curve (PPC)?
    a. Capital goods produced at the exact rate needed to replace worn-out capital.
    b. Greater production of capital goods than what is needed to replace worn-out capital.
    c. Less production of capital goods than what is needed to replace worn-out capital.
    d. More production of consumption goods that replace worn-out capital.

15. In the study of economics, investment means
    a. the accumulation of capital that is used to produce goods and services.
    b. owning stocks and bonds.
    c. the principle that the opportunity cost increases as the production of one output expands.
    d. the effect of stock prices on the production possibilities curve.

16. Which of the following is *not* one of the three fundamental economic questions?
    a. What happens when you add to or subtract from a current situation?
    b. For whom to produce?
    c. How to produce?
    d. What to produce?

17. Opportunity cost
    a. represents the best alternative sacrificed for a chosen alternative.
    b. has no relationship to the various alternatives that must be given up when a choice is made in the context of scarcity.
    c. represents the worst alternative sacrificed for a chosen alternative.
    d. represents all alternatives not chosen.

18. Which words best complete the following sentence? A rational decision maker always chooses the option for which marginal benefit is _____ marginal cost.
    a. less than
    b. equal to
    c. unrelated to
    d. more than

19. The principle that the opportunity cost increases as the production of one output expands is the

    a. law of increasing opportunity costs.
    b. law of demand.
    c. law of supply.
    d. law of increasing returns to scale.

20. The ability of an economy to produce greater levels of output per time period is called
    a. positive economics.
    b. negative economics.
    c. economic growth.
    d. the law of specialization.

PART 1
Introduction to Economics

This road map feature helps you tie together material in the part as you travel the Economic Way of Thinking Highway. The following are review questions listed by chapter from the previous part. The key concept in each question is given for emphasis, and each question or set of questions concludes with an interactive game to reinforce the concepts. The correct answers to the multiple choice questions are given in Appendix C. If your instructor has included MindTap in your course, visit MindTap to play the interactive Causation Chain Game.

Chapter 1: Introducing the Economic Way of Thinking

1. Key Concept: Scarcity

Economists believe that scarcity forces everyone to

a. satisfy all wants.
b. abandon consumer sovereignty.
c. lie about their wants.
d. create unlimited resources.
e. make choices.

2. Key Concept: Economics

The subject of economics is primarily the study of

a. the government decision-making process.
b. how to operate a business successfully.
c. decision making because of the problem of scarcity.
d. how to make money in the stock market.

CAUSATION CHAIN GAME
The Relationship between Scarcity and Decision Making

3. Key Concept: Model

When building a model, an economist must

a. adjust for exceptional situations.
b. provide a complete description of reality.
c. make simplifying assumptions.
d. develop a set of behavioral equations.

4. Key Concept: Ceteris paribus

If the price of a textbook rises and students purchase fewer textbooks, an economic model can show a cause-and-effect relationship only if which of the following conditions holds?

a. Students' incomes fall.
b. Tuition decreases.
c. The number of students increases.
d. Everything else is constant.
e. The bookstore no longer accepts used book trade-ins.

5. Key Concept: Association versus causation

Someone notices that sunspot activity is high just prior to recessions and concludes that sunspots cause recessions. This person has

a. confused association and causation.
b. misunderstood the ceteris paribus assumption.
c. used normative economics to answer a positive question.
d. built an untestable model.

CAUSATION CHAIN GAME
The Steps in the Model-Building Process—Exhibit 2

Chapter 2: Production Possibilities, Opportunity Cost, and Economic Growth

6. Key Concept: Production possibilities curve

Which of the following is *not* true about a production possibilities curve? The curve

a. indicates the combinations of goods and services that can be produced with a given technology.
b. indicates the efficient production points.
c. indicates the nonefficient production points.
d. indicates the feasible (attainable) and nonfeasible production points.
e. indicates which production point will be chosen.

7. Key Concept: Production possibilities curve

Which of the following is *true* about the production possibilities curve when a technological progress occurs?

a. Shifts inward to the left
b. Becomes flatter at one end and steeper at the other end
c. Becomes steeper
d. Shifts outward to the right
e. Does not change

8. **Key Concept: Shifting the production possibilities curve**

An outward shift of an economy's production possibilities curve is caused by

a. entrepreneurship.
b. an increase in labor.
c. an advance in technology.
d. all of the above.

9. **Key Concept: Shifting the production possibilities curve**

Which would be *least* likely to cause the production possibilities curve to shift to the right?

a. An increase in the labor force
b. Improved methods of production
c. An increase in the education and training of the labor force
d. A decrease in unemployment

10. **Key Concept: Investment**

A nation can accelerate its economic growth by

a. reducing the number of immigrants allowed into the country.
b. adding to its stock of capital.
c. printing more money.
d. imposing tariffs and quotas on imported goods.

 CAUSATION CHAIN GAME
Economic Growth and Technology—Exhibit 4

PART 2

Microeconomics Fundamentals

In your study of the microeconomy, the chapters in Part 2 build on the basic concepts you learned in Part 1. Chapters 3 and 4 explain the market demand and supply model, which has a wide range of real-world applications. Chapter 5 takes a closer look at movements along the demand curve introduced in Chapter 3. Chapter 6 returns to the law of demand and explores in more detail exactly why consumers make their choices among goods and services. Part 2 concludes in Chapter 7 with an extension of the concept of supply that explains how various costs of production change as output varies.

Market Demand and Supply

CHAPTER PREVIEW

A cornerstone of the U.S. economy is the use of markets to answer the basic economic questions discussed in the previous chapter. Consider baseball cards, Blu-rays, physical fitness, gasoline, soft drinks, and sneakers. In a *market economy*, each is bought and sold by individuals coming together as buyers and sellers in markets. This chapter is extremely important because it introduces basic supply and demand analysis. This technique will prove to be valuable because it is applicable to a multitude of real-world choices of buyers and sellers facing the problem of scarcity. For example, the Global Economics feature asks you to consider the highly controversial issue of international trade in human organs.

Demand represents the choice-making behavior of consumers, whereas supply represents the choices of producers. The chapter begins by looking closely at demand and then at supply. Finally, it combines these forces to see how prices and quantities traded are determined in the marketplace. Market demand and supply analysis are the basic tools of microeconomic analysis.

IN THIS CHAPTER, YOU WILL LEARN TO SOLVE THESE ECONOMICS PUZZLES:

- What is the difference between a "change in quantity demanded" and a "change in demand"?

- Can Congress repeal the law of supply to control oil prices?

- Does the price system eliminate scarcity?

3-1 THE LAW OF DEMAND

Economics might be referred to as "graphs and laughs" because economists are so fond of using graphs to illustrate demand, supply, and many other economic concepts. Unfortunately, some students taking economics courses say they miss the laughs.

Exhibit 1 reveals an important "law" in economics called the law of demand. The **law of demand** states there is an inverse relationship between the price of a good and the quantity buyers are willing to purchase in a defined time period, ceteris paribus. The law of demand makes good sense. At a "sale," consumers buy more when the price of merchandise is cut.

In Exhibit 1, the *demand curve* is formed by the line connecting the possible price and quantity purchased responses of an individual consumer. The demand curve, therefore,

Law of demand
The principle that there is an inverse relationship between the price of a good and the quantity buyers are willing to purchase in a defined time period, ceteris paribus.

EXHIBIT 1 An Individual Buyer's Demand Curve for Blu-Rays

Bob's demand curve shows how many Blu-rays he is willing to purchase at different possible prices. As the price of Blu-rays declines, the quantity demanded increases, and Bob purchases more Blu-rays. The inverse relationship between price and quantity demanded conforms to the law of demand.

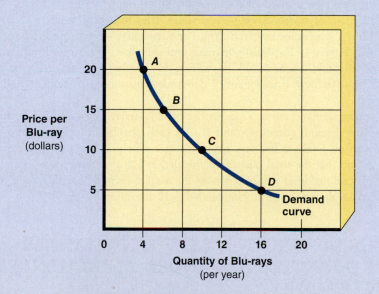

An Individual Buyer's Demand Schedule for Blu-rays

Point	Price per Blu-ray	Quantity demanded (per year)
A	$20	4
B	15	6
C	10	10
D	5	16

allows you to find the quantity demanded by a buyer at any possible selling price by moving along the curve. For example, Bob, a sophomore at Marketplace College, enjoys watching Blu-ray movies. Bob's demand curve shows that at a price of $15 per Blu-ray, his quantity demanded is six Blu-rays purchased annually (point *B*). At the lower price of $10, Bob's quantity demanded increases to ten Blu-rays per year (point *C*). Following this procedure, other price and quantity possibilities for Bob are read along the demand curve.

Note that until we know the actual price determined by both demand and supply, we do not know how many Blu-rays Bob will actually purchase annually. The demand curve is simply a summary of Bob's buying intentions. After we know the market price, a quick look at the demand curve tells us how many Blu-rays Bob will buy.

CONCLUSION

Demand curve is a curve or schedule showing the various quantities of a product consumers are willing to purchase at possible prices during a specified period of time, ceteris paribus.

Demand curve
A curve or schedule showing the various quantities of product consumers are willing to purchase at possible prices during a specified period of time, ceteris paribus.

3-1a Market Demand

To make the transition from an individual demand curve to a market demand curve, we total, or sum, the individual demand schedules. Suppose the owner of ZapMart, a small retail chain of stores serving a few states, tries to decide what to charge for Blu-rays and hires a consumer research firm. For simplicity, we assume Fred and Mary are the only two buyers in ZapMart's market, and they are sent a questionnaire that asks how many Blu-rays each would be willing to purchase at several possible prices. Exhibit 2 reports their price-quantity demanded responses in tabular and graphical form.

The market demand curve, D_{total}, in Exhibit 2 is derived by summing *horizontally* the two individual demand curves, D_1 and D_2, for each possible price. At a price of $20, for example, we sum Fred's 2 Blu-rays demanded per year and Mary's 1 Blu-ray demanded per year to find that the total quantity demanded at $20 is 3 Blu-rays per year. Repeating the same process for other prices generates the market demand curve, D_{total}. For example, at a price of $5, the total quantity demanded is 12 Blu-rays.

3-2 THE DISTINCTION BETWEEN CHANGES IN QUANTITY DEMANDED AND CHANGES IN DEMAND

Price is not the only variable that determines how much of a good or service consumers will buy. Recall from Exhibit A-4 of Appendix 1 that the price and quantity variables in our model are subject to the ceteris paribus assumption. If we relax this assumption and allow other variables held constant to change, a variety of factors can influence the position of the demand curve. Because these factors are not the price of the good itself, these variables are called *nonprice determinants*, or simply, *demand shifters*. The major nonprice determinants include (1) the number of buyers; (2) tastes and preferences; (3) income; (4) expectations of future changes in prices, income, and availability of goods; and (5) prices of related goods.

EXHIBIT 2 The Market Demand Curve for Blu-Rays

Individual demand curves differ for consumers Fred and Mary. Assuming they are the only buyers in the market, the market demand curve, D_{total}, is derived by summing horizontally the individual demand curves, D_1 and D_2.

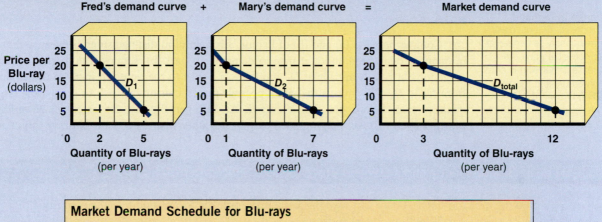

Market Demand Schedule for Blu-rays				
	Quantity demanded per year			
Price per Blu-ray	Fred	+	Mary	= Total demand
$25	1		0	1
20	2		1	3
15	3		3	6
10	4		5	9
5	5		7	12

Before discussing these nonprice determinants of demand, we must pause to explain an important and possibly confusing distinction in terminology. We have been referring to a change in quantity demanded, which results solely from a change in the price. A **change in quantity demanded** is a movement between points along a stationary demand curve, ceteris paribus. In Exhibit 3(a), at the price of $15, the quantity demanded is 20 million Blu-rays per year. This is shown as point *A* on the demand curve, *D*. At a lower price of, say, $10, the quantity demanded increases to 30 million Blu-rays per year, shown as point *B*. Verbally, we describe the impact of the price decrease as an increase in the quantity demanded of 10 million Blu-rays per year. We show this relationship on the demand curve as a movement down along the curve from point *A* to point *B*.

Change in quantity demanded
A movement between points along a stationary demand curve, ceteris paribus.

Under the law of demand, any decrease in price along the vertical axis will cause an increase in quantity demanded, measured along the horizontal axis, and appears as a movement along the demand curve.

CONCLUSION

A **change in demand** is an increase (rightward shift) or a decrease (leftward shift) in the quantity demanded at each possible price. If ceteris paribus no longer applies and if one of the five major nonprice factors changes, the location of the demand curve shifts.

CONCLUSION   Changes in nonprice determinants can produce only a shift in the demand curve and not a movement along the demand curve.

Change in demand
An increase or a decrease in the quantity demanded at each possible price. An increase in demand is a rightward shift in the entire demand curve. A decrease in demand is a leftward shift in the entire demand curve.

Comparing parts (a) and (b) of Exhibit 3 is helpful in distinguishing between a change in quantity demanded and a change in demand. In part (b), suppose the market demand curve for Blu-rays is initially at D_1 and there is a shift to the right (an increase in demand) from D_1 to D_2. This means that at all possible prices, consumers wish to purchase a larger quantity than before the shift occurred. At $15 per Blu-ray, for example, 30 million Blu-rays (point B) will be purchased each year, rather than 20 million Blu-rays (point A).

EXHIBIT 3 Movement along a Demand Curve versus a Shift in Demand

Part (a) shows the demand curve, D, for Blu-rays per year. If the price is $15 at point A, the quantity demanded by consumers is 20 million Blu-rays. If the price decreases to $10 at point B, the quantity demanded increases from 20 million to 30 million Blu-rays.

Part (b) illustrates an increase in demand. A change in some nonprice determinant can cause an increase in demand from D_1 to D_2. At a price of $15 on D_1 (point A), 20 million Blu-rays is the quantity demanded per year. At this price on D_2 (point B), the quantity demanded increases to 30 million.

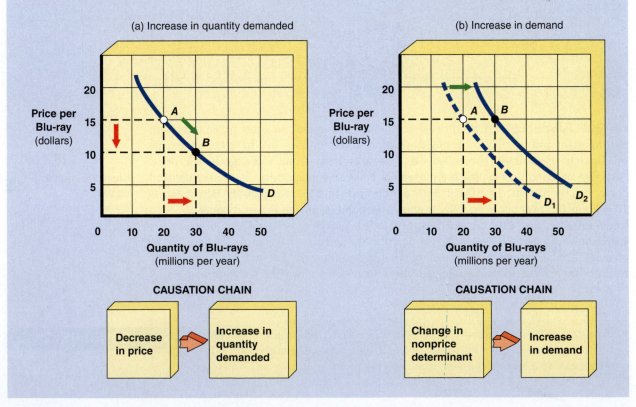

Now suppose a change in some nonprice factor causes demand curve D_1 to shift leftward (a decrease in demand). The interpretation in this case is that at *all* possible prices consumers will buy a smaller quantity than before the shift occurred.

Exhibit 4 summarizes the terminology for the effects of changes in price and non-price determinants on the demand curve.

3-3 NONPRICE DETERMINANTS OF DEMAND

Distinguishing between a change in quantity demanded and a change in demand requires some patience and practice. The following discussion of specific changes in nonprice factors, or demand shifters, will clarify how each nonprice variable affects demand.

EXHIBIT 4 Terminology for Changes in Price and Nonprice Determinants of Demand

Caution! It is important to distinguish between a change in quantity demanded, which is a movement along a demand curve (D_1) caused by a change in price, and a change in demand, which is a shift in the demand curve. An increase in demand (shift to D_2) or a decrease in demand (shift to D_3) is not caused by a change in price. Instead, a shift is caused by a change in one of the nonprice determinants.

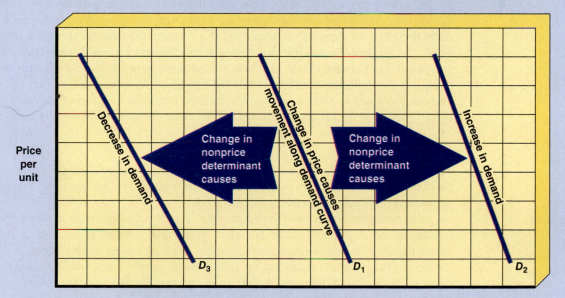

Change	Effect	Terminology
Price increases	Upward movement along the demand curve	Decrease in the quantity demanded
Price decreases	Downward movement along the demand curve	Increase in the quantity demanded
Nonprice determinant	Leftward or rightward shift in the demand curve	Decrease or increase in demand

3-3a Number of Buyers

Look back at Exhibit 2 and imagine the impact of adding more individual demand curves to the individual demand curves of Fred and Mary. At all possible prices, there is extra quantity demanded by the new customers, and the market demand curve for Blu-rays shifts rightward (an increase in demand). Population growth therefore tends to increase the number of buyers, which shifts the market demand curve for a good or service rightward. Conversely, a population decline shifts most market demand curves leftward (a decrease in demand).

The number of buyers can be specified to include both foreign and domestic buyers. Suppose the market demand curve D_1 in Exhibit 3(b) is for Blu-rays purchased in the United States by customers at home and abroad. Also assume that Japan restricts the import of Blu-rays into Japan. What would be the effect of Japan removing this trade restriction? The answer is that the demand curve shifts rightward from D_1 to D_2 when Japanese consumers add their individual demand curves to the U.S. market demand for Blu-rays.

3-3b Tastes and Preferences

A favorable or unfavorable change in consumer tastes or preferences means more or less of a product is demanded at each possible price. Fads, fashions, advertising, and new products can influence consumer preferences to buy a particular good or service. Beanie Babies, for example, became the rage in the 1990s, and the demand curve for these products shifted to the right. When people tire of a product, the demand curve will shift leftward. The physical fitness trend has increased the demand for health clubs and exercise equipment. On the other hand, have you noticed many stores selling hula hoops? Advertising can also influence consumers' taste for a product. As a result, consumers are more likely to buy more at every price, and the demand curve for the product will shift to the right. Concern for global climate change has increased the demand for hybrid cars.

3-3c Income

Most students are all too familiar with how changes in income affect demand. There are two possible categories of goods when it comes to changes in income and changes in demand: (1) Normal goods and (2) Inferior goods

A **normal good** is any good for which there is a direct relationship between changes in income and its demand curve. For many goods and services, an increase in income causes buyers to purchase more at any possible price. As buyers receive higher incomes, the demand curve shifts rightward for such *normal goods* as cars, steaks, vintage wine, cleaning services, and Blu-rays. A decline in income has the opposite effect, and the demand curve shifts leftward.

An **inferior good** is any good for which there is an inverse relationship between changes in income and its demand curve. A rise in income can result in reduced purchases of a good or service at any possible price. This might happen with such *inferior goods* as generic brands, Spam, discount clothes, and used cars. Instead of buying these inferior goods, consumers with higher incomes buy brand-name products, steaks, designer clothes, or new cars. Conversely, a fall in income causes the demand curve for inferior goods to shift rightward.

3-3d Expectations of Buyers

What is the effect on demand in the present when consumers anticipate future changes in prices, incomes, or availability? What happens when a war breaks out in the Middle East?

Normal good
Any good for which there is a direct relationship between changes in income and its demand curve.

Inferior good
Any good for which there is an inverse relationship between changes in income and its demand curve.

Expectations that there will be a shortage of gasoline induce consumers to say "fill 'er up" at every opportunity, and demand increases. Suppose students learn that the prices of the textbooks for several courses they plan to take next semester will double soon. Their likely response is to buy now, which causes an increase in the demand curve for these textbooks. Another example is a change in the weather, which can indirectly cause expectations to shift demand for some products. Suppose severe weather destroys a substantial portion of the peach crop. Consumers reason that the reduction in available supply will soon drive up prices, and they dash to stock up before it is too late. This change in expectations causes the demand curve for peaches to increase. For example, when a hurricane is expected to hit a major U.S. city, the sales of batteries and flashlights soar.

3-3e Prices of Related Goods

Possibly the most confusing nonprice factor is the influence of other prices on the demand for a particular good or service. The term *nonprice* seems to forbid any shift in demand resulting from a change in the price of *any* product. This confusion exists when one fails to distinguish between changes in quantity demanded and changes in demand. Remember that ceteris paribus holds all prices of other goods constant. Therefore, movement along a demand curve occurs solely in response to changes in the price of a product, that is, its "own" price. When we draw the demand curve for Coca-Cola, for example, we assume that the prices of Pepsi-Cola and other colas remain unchanged. What happens if we relax the ceteris paribus assumption and the price of Pepsi rises? Many Pepsi buyers switch to Coca-Cola, and the demand curve for Coca-Cola shifts rightward (an increase in demand). Coca-Cola and Pepsi-Cola are one type of related goods called substitute goods. A **substitute good** competes with another good for consumer purchases. As a result, there is a direct relationship between a price change for one good and the demand for its "competitor" good. Other examples of substitutes include margarine and butter, domestic cars and foreign cars, and Blu-rays and Internet movie downloads.

Blu-rays and Blu-ray players illustrate a second type of related goods called complementary goods. A **complementary good** is jointly consumed with another good. As a result, there is an inverse relationship between a price change for one good and the demand for its "go together" good. Although buying a Blu-ray and buying a Blu-ray player can be separate decisions, these two purchases are related. The more Blu-ray players consumers buy, the greater the demand for Blu-rays. What happens when the price of Blu-ray players falls sharply? The market demand curve for Blu-rays shifts rightward (an increase in demand) because new owners of players add their individual demand curves to those of people already owning players and buying Blu-rays. Conversely, a sharp rise in the price of desk jet printers would decrease the demand for ink cartridges.

Exhibit 5 summarizes the relationship between changes in the nonprice determinants of demand and the demand curve, accompanied by examples for each type of nonprice factor change.

Substitute good
A good that competes with another good for consumer purchases. As a result, there is a direct relationship between a price change for one good and the demand for its "competitor" good.

Complementary good
A good that is jointly consumed with another good. As a result, there is an inverse relationship between a price change for one good and the demand for its "go together" good.

Can Gasoline Become an Exception to the Law of Demand?
Suppose war in the Middle East threatened oil supplies, and gasoline prices began rising. Consumers feared future oil shortages, so they rushed to fill up their gas tanks. In this case, as the price of gas increased, consumers bought more, not less. Is this an exception to the law of demand?

CHECKPOINT

EXHIBIT 5 Summary of the Impact of Changes in Nonprice Determinants of Demand on the Demand Curve

Nonprice determinant of demand	Relationship to changes in demand curve	Shift in the demand curve	Examples
1. Number of buyers	Direct	Price / Quantity (D_1, D_2)	• Immigration from Mexico increases the demand for Mexican food products in grocery stores.
		Price / Quantity (D_2, D_1)	• A decline in the birthrate reduces the demand for baby clothes.
2. Tastes and preferences	Direct	Price / Quantity (D_1, D_2)	• For no apparent reason, consumers want Beanie Babies and demand increases.
		Price / Quantity (D_2, D_1)	• After a while, the fad dies and demand declines.
3. Income a. Normal goods	Direct	Price / Quantity (D_1, D_2)	• Consumers' incomes increase, and the demand for steaks increases.
		Price / Quantity (D_2, D_1)	• A decline in income decreases the demand for air travel.
b. Inferior goods	Inverse	Price / Quantity (D_2, D_1)	• Consumers' incomes increase, and the demand for hamburger decreases.
		Price / Quantity (D_1, D_2)	• A decline in income increases the demand for bus service.

(Continued)

Continued from previous page

Nonprice determinant of demand	Relationship to changes in demand curve	Shift in the demand curve	Examples
4. Expectations of buyers	Direct	Price / Quantity (D_1, D_2)	• Consumers expect that gasoline will be in short supply next month and that prices will rise sharply. Consequently, consumers fill the tanks in their cars this month, and there is an increase in demand for gasoline.
		Price / Quantity (D_2, D_1)	• Months later, consumers expect the price of gasoline to fall soon, and the demand for gasoline decreases.
5. Prices of related Goods a. Substitute goods	Direct	Price / Quantity (D_2, D_1)	• A reduction in the price of tea decreases the demand for coffee.
		Price / Quantity (D_1, D_2)	• An increase in the price of airfares causes higher demand for bus transportation.
b. Complementary goods	Inverse	Price / Quantity (D_1, D_2)	• A decline in the price of cellular service increases the demand for cell phones.
		Price / Quantity (D_2, D_1)	• A higher price for peanut butter decreases the demand for jelly.

3-4 THE LAW OF SUPPLY

In everyday conversations, the term *supply* refers to a specific quantity. A "limited supply" of golf clubs at a sporting goods store means there are only so many clubs for sale and that's all. This interpretation of supply is *not* the economist's definition. To economists, supply is the relationship between ranges of possible prices and quantities supplied, which is stated as the law of supply. The **law of supply** states there is a direct relationship between the price of a good and the quantity sellers are willing to offer for sale in a defined time period, ceteris paribus. Interpreting the individual *supply curve* for ZapMart shown in Exhibit 6 is basically the same as interpreting Bob's demand curve shown in Exhibit 1. Each point on the **supply curve** represents a quantity supplied (measured along the horizontal axis) at a particular price (measured along the vertical axis). For example, at a price of $10 per Blu-ray (point *C*), the quantity supplied by the seller,

Law of supply
The principle that there is a direct relationship between the price of a good and the quantity sellers are willing to offer for sale in a defined time period, ceteris paribus.

Supply curve
A curve or schedule showing the various quantities of a product sellers are willing to produce and offer for sale at possible prices during a specified period of time, ceteris paribus.

EXHIBIT 6 An Individual Seller's Supply Curve for Blu-Rays

The supply curve for an individual seller, such as ZapMart, shows the quantity of Blu-rays offered for sale at different possible prices. As the price of Blu-rays rises, a retail store has an incentive to increase the quantity of Blu-rays supplied per year. The direct relationship between price and quantity supplied conforms to the law of supply.

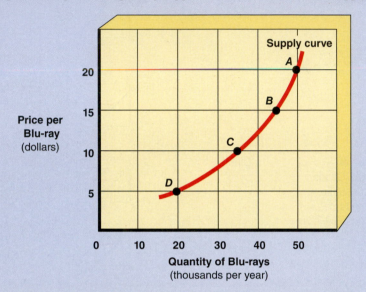

An Individual Seller's Supply Schedule for Blu-rays		
Point	Price per Blu-ray	Quantity supplied (thousands per year)
A	$20	50
B	15	45
C	10	35
D	5	20

ZapMart, is 35,000 Blu-rays per year. At the higher price of $15, the quantity supplied increases to 45,000 Blu-rays per year (point B).

CONCLUSION Supply curve is a curve or schedule showing the various quantities of a product sellers are willing to produce and offer for sale at possible prices during a specified period of time, ceteris paribus.

Why are sellers willing to sell more at a higher price? Suppose Farmer Brown is trying to decide whether to devote more of his land, labor, and barn space to the production of soybeans. Recall from Chapter 2 the production possibilities curve and the concept of increasing opportunity cost developed in Exhibit 3. If Farmer Brown devotes few of his resources to producing soybeans, the opportunity cost of, say, producing milk is small. But increasing soybean production means a higher opportunity cost, measured by the quantity of milk not produced. The logical question is: What would induce Farmer Brown to produce more soybeans for sale and overcome the higher opportunity cost of producing less milk? You guessed it! There must be the *incentive* of a higher price for soybeans.

> **CONCLUSION**
>
> Only at a higher price will it be profitable for sellers to incur the higher opportunity cost associated with producing and supplying a larger quantity.

CHECKPOINT

Can the Law of Supply Be Repealed for the Oil Market?
The United States experienced two oil shocks during the 1970s in the aftermath of Middle East tensions. Congress said no to high oil prices by passing a law prohibiting prices above a legal limit. Supporters of such price controls said this was a way to ensure adequate supply without allowing oil producers to earn excess profits. Did price controls increase, decrease, or have no effect on U.S. oil production during the 1970s?

3-4a Market Supply

To construct a market supply curve, we follow the same procedure used to derive a market demand curve. That is, we *horizontally* sum all the quantities supplied at various prices that might prevail in the market.

Let's assume that Entertain City and High Vibes are the only two firms selling Blu-rays in a given market. As you can see in Exhibit 7, the market supply curve, S_{total}, slopes upward to the right. At a price of $25, Entertain City will supply 25,000 Blu-rays per year, and High Vibes will supply 35,000 Blu-rays per year. Thus, summing the two individual supply curves, S_1 and S_2, *horizontally*, the total of 60,000 Blu-rays is plotted at this price on the market supply curve, S_{total}. Similar calculations at other prices along the price axis generate a market supply curve, telling us the total amount of Blu-rays these businesses offer for sale at different selling prices.

3-5 THE DISTINCTION BETWEEN CHANGES IN QUANTITY SUPPLIED AND CHANGES IN SUPPLY

As with demand, the price of a product is not the only factor that influences how much sellers offer for sale. Once we relax the ceteris paribus assumption, there are six principal *nonprice determinants* (also called *supply shifters*) that can shift the supply curve's

EXHIBIT 7 The Market Supply Curve for Blu-Rays

Entertain City and High Vibes are two businesses selling Blu-rays. If these are the only two firms in the Blu-ray market, the market supply curve, S_{total}, can be derived by summing horizontally the individual supply curves, S_1 and S_2.

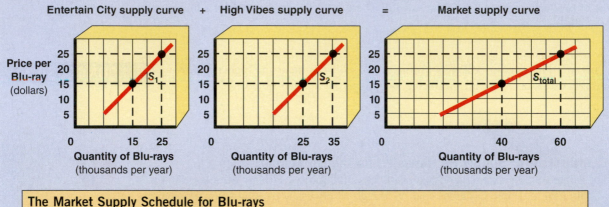

Entertain City supply curve + **High Vibes supply curve** = **Market supply curve**

Price per Blu-ray (dollars)

Quantity of Blu-rays (thousands per year)

The Market Supply Schedule for Blu-rays

	Quantity supplied (thousands per year)				
Price per Blu-ray	Entertain City	+	High Vibes	=	Total supply
$25	25		35		60
20	20		30		50
15	15		25		40
10	10		20		30
5	5		15		20

position: (1) The number of sellers, (2) Technology, (3) Resource prices, (4) Taxes and subsidies, (5) Expectations, and (6) Prices of other goods the firm can produce.

We will discuss these nonprice determinants in more detail momentarily, but first we must distinguish between a *change in quantity supplied* and a *change in supply*.

A **change in quantity supplied** is a movement between points along a stationary supply curve, ceteris paribus. In Exhibit 8(a), at the price of $10, the quantity supplied is 30 million Blu-rays per year (point *A*). At the higher price of $15, sellers offer a larger "quantity supplied" of 40 million Blu-rays per year (point *B*). Economists describe the effect of the rise in price as an increase in the quantity supplied of 10 million Blu-rays per year.

Change in quantity supplied
A movement between points along a stationary supply curve, ceteris paribus.

CONCLUSION
Under the law of supply, any increase in price along the vertical axis will cause an increase in the quantity supplied, measured along the horizontal axis, and appears as a movement along the supply curve.

EXHIBIT 8 Movement along a Supply Curve versus a Shift in Supply

Part (a) presents the market supply curve, S, for Blu-rays per year. If the price is $10 at point A, the quantity supplied by firms will be 30 million Blu-rays. If the price increases to $15 at point B, the quantity supplied will increase from 30 million to 40 million Blu-rays.

Part (b) illustrates an increase in supply. A change in some nonprice determinant can cause an increase in supply from S_1 to S_2. At a price of $15 on S_1 (point A), the quantity supplied per year is 30 million Blu-rays. At this same price on S_2 (point B), the quantity supplied increases to 40 million.

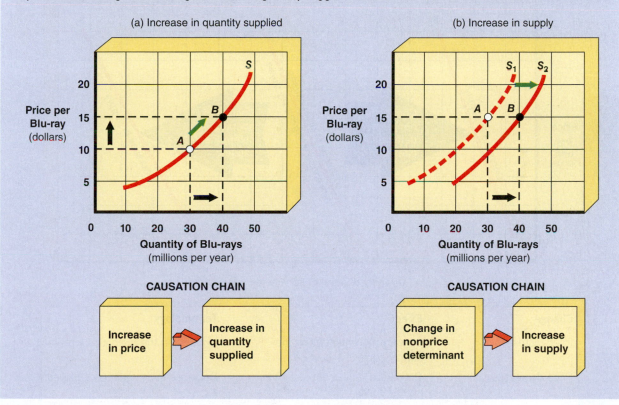

A **change in supply** is an increase (rightward shift) or a decrease (leftward shift) in the quantity supplied at each possible price. If ceteris paribus no longer applies and if one of the six nonprice factors changes, the impact is to alter the supply curve's location.

Changes in nonprice determinants can produce only a shift in the supply curve and not a movement along the supply curve.

CONCLUSION

Change in supply
An increase or a decrease in the quantity supplied at each possible price. An increase in supply is a rightward shift in the entire supply curve. A decrease in supply is a leftward shift in the entire supply curve.

In Exhibit 8(b), the rightward shift (an increase in supply) from S_1 to S_2 means that at all possible prices, sellers offer a greater quantity for sale. At $15 per Blu-ray, for instance, sellers provide 40 million for sale annually (point B), rather than 30 million (point A). On the other hand, if some nonprice factor changes in a way that causes a leftward shift (a decrease in supply) from supply curve S_1, a smaller quantity will be offered for sale at any price.

EXHIBIT 9 Terminology for Changes in Price and Nonprice Determinants of Supply

Caution! As with demand curves, you must distinguish between a change in quantity supplied, which is a movement along a supply curve (S_1) in response to a change in price, and a shift in the supply curve. An increase in supply (shift to S_2) or a decrease in supply occurs (shift to S_3) is caused by a change in some nonprice determinant and not by a change in the price.

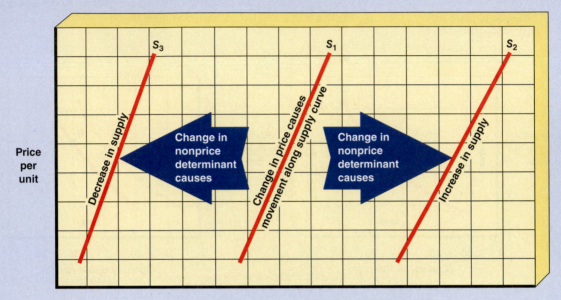

Quantity of good or service per unit of time

Change	Effect	Terminology
Price increases	Upward movement along the supply curve	Increase in the quantity supplied
Price decreases	Downward movement along the supply curve	Decrease in the quantity supplied
Nonprice determinant	Leftward or rightward shift in the supply curve	Decrease or increase in supply

Exhibit 9 summarizes the terminology for the effects of changes in price and non-price determinants on the supply curve.

3-6 NONPRICE DETERMINANTS OF SUPPLY

Now we turn to how each of the six basic nonprice factors affects supply.

3-6a Number of Sellers

What happens when a severe drought destroys wheat or a frost ruins the orange crop? The damaging effect of the weather may force orange growers out of business, and supply decreases. When the government eases restrictions on hunting alligators, the number of alligator hunters increases, and the supply curve for alligator meat and skins increases. Internationally, the United States may decide to lower trade barriers on textile imports, and this action increases supply by allowing new foreign firms to add their individual supply curves to the U.S. market supply curve for textiles. Conversely, higher U.S. trade barriers on textile imports shift the U.S. market supply curve for textiles leftward.

3-6b Technology

Never has society experienced such an explosion of new production techniques. Throughout the world, new and more efficient technology is making it possible to manufacture more products at any possible selling price. New, more powerful personal computers (PCs) reduce production costs and increase the supply of all sorts of goods and services. For example, computers are now milking cows. Computers admit the cows into the milking area and then activate lasers to guide milking cups into place. Dairy farmers no longer must wake up at 5:30 a.m., and cows get milked whenever they wish, day or night. As this technology spreads across the United States, it will be possible to offer more milk for sale at each possible price, and the entire supply curve for milk will shift to the right.

3-6c Resource Prices

Natural resources, labor, capital, and entrepreneurship are all required to produce products, and the prices of these resources affect supply. Suppose many firms are competing for computer programmers to design their software, and the salaries of these highly skilled workers increase. This increase in the price of labor adds to the cost of production. Along the original supply curve, extra costs must be added to each possible price. As a result, the supply of computer software shifts leftward (decreases) because sellers must charge more than before for any quantity supplied. Any reduction in production cost caused by a decline in the price of resources will have an opposite effect on the supply curve and it shifts rightward (increases). Along the original supply curve, cost declines, so the price can be reduced at each possible quantity supplied.

3-6d Taxes and Subsidies

Certain taxes, such as excise taxes imposed on sellers, have the same effect on supply as does an increase in the price of a resource. The impact of an excise tax (or "per unit" tax) that must be paid by sellers is similar to a rise in the cost of a microprocessor. The excise tax imposes an additional production cost on, for example, Blu-rays, and the supply curve shifts leftward. Conversely, a payment from the government for each Blu-ray produced (an unlikely subsidy) would have the same effect as lower prices for resources or a technological advance. That is, the supply curve for Blu-rays shifts rightward.

3-6e Expectations of Producers

Expectations affect both current demand and current supply. Suppose a war in the Middle East causes oil producers to believe that oil prices will rise dramatically.

Their initial response could be to hold back a portion of the oil in their storage tanks so that they can sell more and make greater profits later when oil prices rise. One approach used by the major oil companies might be to limit the amount of gasoline delivered to independent distributors. This response by the oil industry shifts the current supply curve to the left. Now suppose farmers anticipate that the price of wheat will soon fall sharply. The reaction is to sell their inventories stored in silos today before the price declines tomorrow. Such a response shifts the supply curve for wheat to the right.

3-6f Prices of Other Goods the Firm Could Produce

Businesses are always considering shifting resources from producing one good to producing another good. A rise in the price of one product relative to the prices of other products signals to suppliers that switching production to the product with the higher relative price yields higher profit. Suppose the price of corn rises because of government incentives to grow corn for ethanol while the price of wheat remains the same; then many farmers will divert more of their land to corn and less to wheat. The result is an increase in the supply of corn and a decrease in the supply of wheat. This happens because the opportunity cost of growing wheat, measured in forgone corn profits, increases.

Exhibit 10 summarizes the relationship between changes in the nonprice determinants of supply and the supply curve, accompanied by examples for each type of nonprice factor change.

EXHIBIT 10 Summary of the Impact of Changes in Nonprice Determinants of Supply on the Supply Curve

Nonprice determinant of supply	Relationship to changes in supply curve	Shift in the supply curve	Examples
1. Number of sellers	Direct		• The United States lowers trade restrictions on foreign textiles, and the supply of textiles in the United States increases.
			• A severe drought destroys the orange crop, and the supply of oranges decreases.
2. Technology	Direct		• New methods of producing automobiles reduce production costs, and the supply of automobiles increases.
			• Technology is destroyed in war, and production costs increase; the result is a decrease in the supply of good X.

(Continued)

Continued from previous page

Nonprice determinant of supply	Relationship to changes in supply curve	Shift in the supply curve	Examples
3. Resource prices	Inverse	Price / Quantity (S_1, S_2)	• A decline in the price of computer chips increases the supply of computers.
		Price / Quantity (S_2, S_1)	• An increase in the cost of farm equipment decreases the supply of soybeans.
4. Taxes and subsidies	Inverse	Price / Quantity (S_2, S_1)	• An increase in the per-pack tax on cigarettes reduces the supply of cigarettes.
	Direct	Price / Quantity (S_1, S_2)	• A government payment to dairy farmers based on the number of gallons produced increases the supply of milk.
5. Expectations	Inverse	Price / Quantity (S_2, S_1)	• Oil companies anticipate a substantial rise in future oil prices, and this expectation causes these companies to decrease their current supply of oil.
		Price / Quantity (S_1, S_2)	• Farmers expect the future price of wheat to decline, so they increase the present supply of wheat.
6. Prices of other goods and services	Inverse	Price / Quantity (S_2, S_1)	• A rise in the price of brand-name drugs causes drug companies to decrease the supply of generic drugs.
		Price / Quantity (S_1, S_2)	• A decline in the price of tomatoes causes farmers to increase the supply of cucumbers.

3-7 A MARKET SUPPLY AND DEMAND ANALYSIS

"Teach a parrot to say 'supply and demand' and you've got an economist." Drum roll, please! Buyer and seller actors are on center stage to perform a balancing act in a market. A **market** is any arrangement in which buyers and sellers interact to determine the price and quantity of goods and services exchanged. Let's consider the retail market for

Market
Any arrangement in which buyers and sellers interact to determine the price and quantity of goods and services exchanged.

YOU'RE THE ECONOMIST

PC Prices: How Low Can They Go?

Farknot Architect/Shutterstock.com

Radio was in existence for 38 years before 50 million people tuned in. Television took 13 years to reach that benchmark. Sixteen years after the first PC kit was introduced, 50 million people were using one. When available to the public, the Internet crossed that line in four years.[1] Before 1999, there were no blogs, and now there are millions. Today approximately 85 percent of U.S. households have a computer. Following are quotes from articles that illustrate changes in supply and demand for computers over time.

An Associated Press article reported in 1998:

Personal computers, which tumbled below the $1,000-price barrier just 18 months ago, now are breaking through the $400 price mark—putting them within reach of the average U.S. family. The plunge in PC prices reflects declining wholesale prices for computer parts, such as microprocessors, memory chips, and hard drives. "We've seen a massive transformation in the PC business," said Andrew Peck, an analyst with Cowen & Co., based in Boston.[2]

In 2001, an article in *The New York Times* described a computer price war:

We reached a situation where the market was saturated in 2000. People who needed computers had them. Vendors are living on sales of replacements, at least in the United States. But that doesn't give you the kind of growth these companies were used to. In the past, most price cuts came from falling prices for processors and other components. In addition, manufacturers have been narrowing profit margins for the last couple years. But when demand dried up last fall, the more aggressive manufacturers decided to try to gain market share by cutting prices to the bone. This is an all-out battle for market share.[3]

In 2016, analysts at *MarketWatch* observed the following decline in PC sales:

PCs are being left in the dust by the more preferred mobile devices such as smartphones and tablets. Worldwide growth of smartphone shipments skyrocketed by 1,000% between 2007 and 2015. PCs, meanwhile, have been on the decline since peaking at 362 million [in sales] in 2011, dropping by more than 20% over the past four years alone…[4]

Finally, Wikipedia reports that over time changes in supply and demand have continued to reduce PC prices. In 1982, for example, Dell offered a $3,000 PC. By 1998, the average selling price was below $1,000. Today, computers selling for less than $300 outperform computers from only a few years previously.

ANALYZE THE ISSUE Identify changes in quantity demanded, changes in demand, changes in quantity supplied, or changes in supply described in the article. For any change in demand or supply, also identify the nonprice determinant causing the change.

---

1. The Emerging Digital Economy (U.S. Department of Commerce, 1998), Chapter 1, P. 1.
2. David E. Kalish, "Pc Prices Fall Below $400, Luring Bargain-Hunters," Associated Press/Charlotte Observer, August 25, 1998, p. 3D.
3. Barnaby J. Feder, "Five Questions for Martin Reynolds: A Computer Price War Leaves Buyers Smiling," The New York Times, May 13, 2001.
4. Jon Swartz and Adam Ganucheau, "PCs Hang in, Tables … Don't," USA Today, "The Rise and Fall of the PC in One Chart," http://www.marketwatch.com/story/one-chart-shows-how-mobile-has-crushed-pcs-2016-04-20, April 24, 2016.

EXHIBIT 11 Demand, Supply, and Equilibrium for Sneakers (Pairs per Year)

(1) Price per pair	(2) Quantity demanded	(3) Quantity supplied	(4) Difference (3)–(2)	(5) Market condition	(6) Pressure on price
$105	25,000	75,000	+50,000	Surplus	Downward
90	30,000	70,000	+40,000	Surplus	Downward
75	40,000	60,000	+20,000	Surplus	Downward
60	50,000	50,000	0	Equilibrium	Stationary
45	60,000	35,000	−25,000	Shortage	Upward
30	80,000	20,000	−60,000	Shortage	Upward
15	100,000	5,000	−95,000	Shortage	Upward

sneakers. Exhibit 11 displays hypothetical market demand and supply data for this product. Notice in column 1 of the exhibit that price serves as a common variable for both supply and demand relationships. Columns 2 and 3 list the quantity demanded and the quantity supplied for pairs of sneakers per year.

The important question for market supply and demand analysis is this: Which selling price and quantity will prevail in the market? Let's start by asking what will happen if retail stores supply 75,000 pairs of sneakers and charge $105 a pair. At this relatively high price for sneakers, consumers are willing and able to purchase only 25,000 pairs. As a result, 50,000 pairs of sneakers remain as unsold inventory on the shelves of sellers (column 4), and the market condition is a surplus (column 5). A **surplus** is a market condition existing at any price where the quantity supplied is greater than the quantity demanded.

How will retailers react to a surplus? Competition forces sellers to bid down their selling price to attract more sales (column 6). If they cut the selling price to $90, there will still be a surplus of 40,000 pairs of sneakers, and pressure on sellers to cut their selling price will continue. If the price falls to $75, there will still be an unwanted surplus of 20,000 pairs of sneakers remaining as inventory, and pressure to charge a lower price will persist.

Now let's assume sellers slash the price of sneakers to $15 per pair. This price is very attractive to consumers, and the quantity demanded is 100,000 pairs of sneakers each year. However, sellers are willing and able to provide only 5,000 pairs at this price. The good news is that some consumers buy these 5,000 pairs of sneakers at $15. The bad news is that potential buyers are willing to purchase 95,000 more pairs at that price, but cannot because the shoes are not on the shelves for sale. This out-of-stock condition signals the existence of a shortage. A **shortage** is a market condition existing at any price where the quantity supplied is less than the quantity demanded.

In the case of a shortage, unsatisfied consumers compete to obtain the product by bidding to pay a higher price. Because sellers are seeking the higher profits that higher prices make possible, they gladly respond by setting a higher price of, say, $30 and increasing the quantity supplied to 20,000 pairs annually. At the price of $30, the shortage persists because the quantity demanded still exceeds the quantity supplied. Thus, a price of $30 will also be temporary because the unfulfilled quantity demanded provides an incentive for sellers to raise their selling price further and offer more sneakers for sale.

Surplus
A market condition existing at any price where the quantity supplied is greater than the quantity demanded.

Shortage
A market condition existing at any price at where the quantity supplied is less than the quantity demanded.

Suppose the price of sneakers rises to $45 a pair. At this price, the shortage falls to 25,000 pairs, and the market still gives sellers the message to move upward along their market supply curve and sell for a higher price.

3-7a Equilibrium Price and Quantity

Equilibrium
A market condition that occurs at any price and quantity at which the quantity demanded and the quantity supplied are equal.

Assuming sellers are free to sell their products at any price, trial and error will make all possible price-quantity combinations unstable except at equilibrium. **Equilibrium** occurs at any price and quantity where the quantity demanded and the quantity supplied are equal. Economists also refer to equilibrium as market clearing.

In Exhibit 11, $60 is the *equilibrium* price, and 50,000 pairs of sneakers is the *equilibrium* quantity per year. Equilibrium means that the forces of supply and demand are "in balance" or "at rest" and there is no reason for price or quantity to change, ceteris paribus. In short, all prices and quantities except a unique equilibrium price and quantity are temporary. Once the price of sneakers is $60, this price will not change unless a non-price factor changes demand or supply.

English economist Alfred Marshall (1842–1924) compared supply and demand to a pair of scissor blades. He wrote, "We might as reasonably dispute whether it is the upper or the under blade of a pair of scissors that cuts a piece of paper, as whether value is governed by utility [demand] or cost of production [supply]."[1] Joining market supply and market demand in Exhibit 12 allows us to clearly see the "two blades," that is, the demand curve, *D*, and the supply curve, *S*. We can measure the amount of any surplus or shortage by the horizontal distance between the demand and supply curves. At any price *above* the equilibrium—say, $90—there is an *excess quantity supplied* (surplus) of 40,000 pairs of sneakers. For any price *below* equilibrium—$30, for example—the horizontal distance between the curves tells us there is an *excess quantity demanded* (shortage) of 60,000 pairs. When the price per pair is $60, the market supply curve and the market demand curve intersect at point *E* and the quantity demanded equals the quantity supplied at 50,000 pairs per year. At this price, there is neither a shortage nor a surplus of sneakers.

CONCLUSION   Graphically, the intersection of the supply curve and the demand curve is the market equilibrium price-quantity point. When all other nonprice factors are held constant, this is the only stable coordinate on the graph.

3-7b Rationing Function of the Price System

Price system
A mechanism that uses the forces of supply and demand to create an equilibrium through rising and falling prices.

Our analysis leads to an important conclusion. The predictable or stable outcome in the sneakers example is that the price will eventually come to rest at $60 per pair. All other factors held constant, the price may be above or below $60, but the forces of surplus or shortage guarantee that any price other than the equilibrium price is temporary. This is the theory of how the price system operates, and it is the cornerstone of microeconomic analysis. The **price system** is a mechanism that uses the forces of supply and demand to create equilibrium through rising and falling prices. Stated simply, price plays a *rationing* role. The price system is important because it is a mechanism for distributing scarce goods and services. At the equilibrium price of $60, only those consumers willing to pay $60 per pair get sneakers, and there are no shoes for buyers unwilling to pay that price.

---

[1]Alfred Marshall, Principles of Economics, 8th ed. New York: Macmillan, 1982, p. 348.

EXHIBIT 12   The Supply and Demand for Sneakers

The supply and demand curves represent a market for sneakers. The intersection of the demand curve, *D*, and the supply curve, *S*, at point *E* indicates the equilibrium price of $60 and the equilibrium quantity of 50,000 pairs bought and sold per year. At any price above $60, a surplus prevails and pressure exists to push the price downward. At $90, for example, the excess quantity supplied of 40,000 pairs remains unsold. At any price below $60, a shortage provides pressure to push the price upward. At $30, for example, the excess quantity demanded of 60,000 pairs encourages consumers to bid up the price.

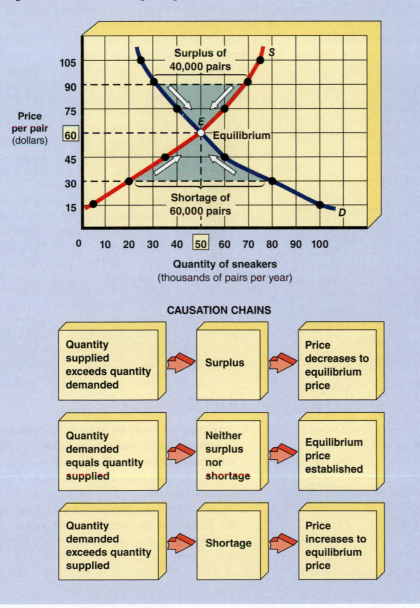

GLOBAL ECONOMICS

The Market Approach to Organ Shortages

Applicable Concept: Price System

There is a global market in human organs in spite of attempts to prevent these transactions. For example, China banned organ sales in 2006, and India did the same in 1994. Conversely, in Iran regulated kidney sales for profit are legal and currently there is no waiting list. The National Transplant Organ Act of 1984 made sale of organs illegal in the United States. Economist James R. Rinehart wrote the following on this subject:

> If you were in charge of a kidney transplant program with more potential recipients than donors, how would you allocate the organs under your control? Life and death decisions cannot be avoided. Some individuals are not going to get kidneys regardless of how the organs are distributed because there simply are not enough to go around. Persons who run such programs are influenced in a variety of ways. It would be difficult not to favor friends, relatives, influential people, and those who are championed by the press.
>
> The selection process frequently takes the form of having the patient wait at home until a suitable donor is found. What this means is that, at any given point in time, many potential recipients are just waiting for an organ to be made available. In essence, the organs are rationed to those who are able to survive the wait. In many situations, patients are simply screened out because they are not considered to be suitable candidates for a transplant. For instance, patients with heart disease and overt psychosis often are excluded. Others with end-stage liver disorders are denied new organs on the grounds that the habits that produced the disease may remain to jeopardize recovery…
>
> Under the present arrangements, owners receive no monetary compensation; therefore, suppliers are willing to supply fewer organs than potential recipients want. Compensating a supplier monetarily would encourage more people to offer their organs for sale. It also would be an excellent incentive for us to take better care of our organs. After all, who would want an enlarged liver or a weak heart…?[1]

The following illustrates the controversy: Apple CEO Steve Jobs had a temporary deliverance from death thanks to a liver transplant. This illustrates how the organ-donations system can be heavily weighted against poor potential recipients. Affluent patients like Steve Jobs can win the "transplant lottery" by listing simultaneously in different regions to increase their odds of finding a donor. In this case, a Palo Alto, Californian found his organ donor in Tennessee. The rules require that a prospective patient must be able to get to a center within seven or eight hours when an organ becomes available. This means a patient must be able to afford a private jet on standby and rent a place nearby the hospital. Such a system can be considered highly unfair. It should be noted that it is not known if Jobs was on more than one list, but this was allowed under the rules.

Based on altruism, the organ donor distribution system continues to result in shortages. In 2017, over 117,000 patients were on the waiting list for organs. When the price system is not allowed to allocate scarce items, alternative methods are often used to alleviate the shortage. For example, some European countries such as Spain, Belgium, and Austria have implemented an "opt out" organ donation system. In the opt out system, people are automatically considered as organ donors unless they officially declare that they do not wish to donate. Also, Facebook, encourages users to advertise their donor status on their pages.

ANALYZE THE ISSUE

1. Draw supply and demand curves for the U.S. organ market and compare the U.S. market to the market in a country where selling organs is legal.
2. What are some arguments against using the price system to allocate organs?
3. Should foreigners have the right to buy U.S. organs and U.S. citizens have the right to buy foreign organs?

---

1.   James R. Rinehart, "The Market Approach to Organ Shortages," *Journal of Health Care Marketing* 8, no. 1, March 1988, pp. 72–75.

Why would you prefer a world with all markets in equilibrium? If all markets were in equilibrium, there would be no shortages or surpluses for any good or service. In this world, consumers are not frustrated because they want to buy something and it is not on the shelf. Sellers are not upset because unsold merchandise is not piling up in their storerooms. Everyone is happy!

CHECKPOINT

Can the Price System Eliminate Scarcity?
You visit Cuba and observe that at "official" prices, there is a constant shortage of consumer goods in government stores. People explain that in Cuba, scarcity is caused by low prices combined with low production quotas set by the government. Many Cuban citizens say that the condition of scarcity would be eliminated if the government would allow markets to respond to supply and demand. Can the price system eliminate scarcity?

Key Concepts

Law of demand

Demand curve

Change in quantity demanded

Change in demand

Normal good

Inferior good

Substitute good

Complementary good

Law of supply

Supply curve

Change in quantity supplied

Change in supply

Market

Surplus

Shortage

Equilibrium

Price system

Summary

- The **law of demand** states there is an inverse relationship between the price and the quantity demanded, ceteris paribus. A market demand curve is the horizontal summation of individual demand curves.

- A **change in quantity demanded** is a movement along a stationary demand curve caused by a change in price.

- A **change in demand** occurs when any of the nonprice determinants of demand change, which causes the demand curve to shift. An *increase in demand* (rightward shift) or a *decrease in demand* (leftward shift) is caused by a change in one of the nonprice determinants.

Change in Quantity Demanded

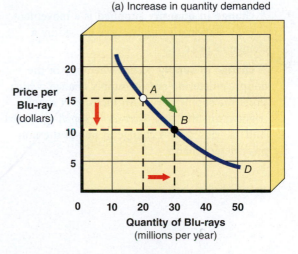

(a) Increase in quantity demanded

Change in Demand

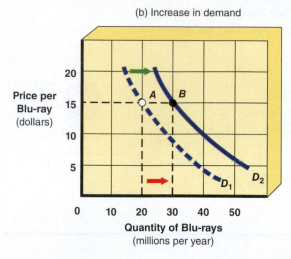

(b) Increase in demand

Change in Quantity Supplied

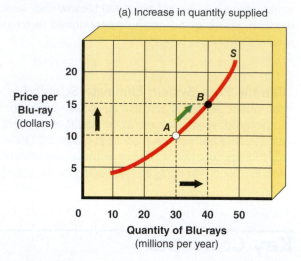

(a) Increase in quantity supplied

- **Nonprice determinants of demand** are as follows:
  a. Number of buyers
  b. Tastes and Preferences
  c. Income (normal and inferior goods)
  d. Expectations of future price and income changes
  e. Prices of related goods (substitutes and complements)

- The **law of supply** states there is a direct relationship between the price and the quantity supplied, ceteris paribus. The market supply curve is the horizontal summation of individual supply curves.

- A **change in quantity supplied** is a movement along a stationary supply curve caused by a change in price.

- A **change in supply** occurs when any of the nonprice determinants of supply change, which shifts the supply curve. An *increase in supply* (rightward shift) or a *decrease in supply* (leftward shift) is caused by a change in one of the nonprice determinants.

Change in Supply

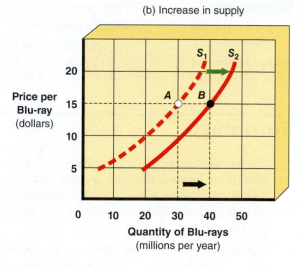

(b) Increase in supply

- **Nonprice determinants of supply** are as follows:
  a. Number of sellers
  b. Technology

c. Resource prices
d. Taxes and subsidies
e. Expectations of future price changes
f. Prices of other goods and services

- A **surplus** or **shortage** exists at any price where the quantity demanded and the quantity supplied are not equal. When the price of a good is higher than the equilibrium price, there is an excess quantity supplied, or *surplus*. When the price is less than the equilibrium price, there is an excess quantity demanded, or *shortage*.

- **Equilibrium** is the unique price and quantity established at the intersection of the supply and demand curves. Only at equilibrium does quantity demanded equal quantity supplied.

Equilibrium

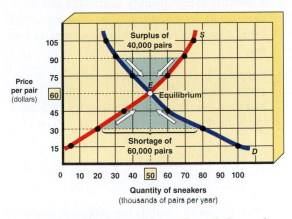

- The **price system** is the supply and demand mechanism that establishes equilibrium through the ability of prices to rise and fall.

Summary of Conclusion Statements

- **Demand curve** is a curve or schedule showing the various quantities of a product consumers are willing to purchase at possible prices during a specified period of time, ceteris paribus.

- Under the law of demand, any decrease in price along the vertical axis will cause an increase in quantity demanded, measured along the horizontal axis, and appears as a movement along the demand curve.

- Changes in nonprice determinants can produce only a shift in the demand curve and not a movement along the demand curve.

- **Supply curve** is a curve or schedule showing the various quantities of a product sellers are willing to produce and offer for sale at possible prices during a specified period of time, ceteris paribus.

- Only at a higher price will it be profitable for sellers to incur the higher opportunity cost associated with producing and supplying a larger quantity.

- Under the law of supply, any increase in price along the vertical axis will cause an increase in the quantity supplied, measured along the horizontal axis, and appears as a movement along the supply curve.

- Changes in nonprice determinants can produce only a shift in the supply curve and not a movement along the supply curve.

- Graphically, the intersection of the supply curve and the demand curve is the market equilibrium price-quantity point. When all other nonprice factors are held constant, this is the only stable coordinate on the graph.

Study Questions and Problems

Please see Appendix A for answers to the odd-numbered questions. Your instructor has access to the answers for even-numbered questions.

1. Some people will pay a higher price for brand-name goods. For example, some people buy Rolls Royce cars and Rolex watches to impress others. Does knowingly paying higher prices for certain items just to be a "snob" violates the law of demand?

2. Draw graphs to illustrate the difference between a decrease in the quantity demanded and a decrease in demand for Mickey Mantle baseball cards. Give a possible reason for change in each graph.

3. Suppose oil prices rise sharply for years as a result of war in the Persian Gulf region. What happens and why to the demand for each of the following?
   a. Cars
   b. Home insulation
   c. Coal
   d. Tires

4. Draw graphs to illustrate the difference between a decrease in quantity supplied and a decrease in supply for condominiums. Give a possible reason for change in each graph.

5. Use supply and demand analysis to explain why the quantity of word processing software exchanged increases from one year to the next.

6. Predict the direction of change for either supply or demand in the following situations:
   a. Several new companies enter the cell phone industry.
   b. Consumers suddenly decide SUVs are unfashionable.
   c. The U.S. surgeon general issues a report stating that tomatoes prevent colds.
   d. Frost threatens to damage the coffee crop, and consumers expect the price to rise sharply in the future.
   e. The price of tea falls. What is the effect on the coffee market?
   f. The price of sugar rises. What is the effect on the coffee market?
   g. Tobacco lobbyists convince Congress to remove the tax paid by sellers on each carton of cigarettes sold.
   h. A new type of robot is invented that will pick peaches.
   i. Nintendo anticipates that the future price of its games will fall much lower than the current price.

7. Explain the effect of the following situations:
   a. Population growth surges rapidly.
   b. The prices of resources used in the production of good X increase.
   c. The government is paying a $1-per-unit subsidy for each unit of a good produced.
   d. The incomes of consumers of normal good X increase.
   e. The incomes of consumers of inferior good Y decrease.
   f. Farmers are deciding what crop to plant and learn that the price of corn has fallen relative to the price of cotton.

8. Explain why the market price may not be the same as the equilibrium price.

9. If a new breakthrough in manufacturing technology reduces the cost of producing Blu-ray players by half, what will happen to the each of the following?
   a. Supply of Blue-ray players.
   b. Demand for Blu-ray players.
   c. Equilibrium price and quantity of Blu-ray players.
   d. Demand for Blu-rays.

10. The U.S. Postal Service is facing increased competition from firms providing overnight delivery of packages and letters. Additional competition has emerged because communications can be sent by emails, fax machine, and text messaging. What will be the effect of this competition on the market demand for mail delivered by the post office?

11. There is a shortage of college basketball and football tickets for some games, and a surplus occurs for other games. Why do shortages and surpluses exist for different games? Assume ticket prices are the same for all of a team's home games during a season.

12. Explain the statement "People respond to incentives and disincentives" in relation to the demand curve and supply curve for good X.

✓ CHECKPOINT ANSWERS

Can Gasoline Become an Exception to the Law of Demand?

As the price of gasoline began to rise, the expectation of still higher prices caused buyers to buy more now, and therefore, demand increased. As shown in Exhibit 13, suppose the price per gallon of gasoline was initially at P_1 and the quantity demanded was Q_1 on demand curve D_1 (point A). Then war in the Middle East caused the demand curve to shift rightward to D_2. Along the new demand curve, D_2, consumers increased their quantity demanded to Q_2 at the higher price of P_2 per gallon of gasoline (point B). The increased demand caused more to be purchased even though the price increased.

The expectation of rising gasoline prices in the future caused "an increase in demand," rather than "an increase in quantity demanded." If you said this is not an exception to the law of demand, **YOU ARE CORRECT**.

EXHIBIT 13 Increase in Demand

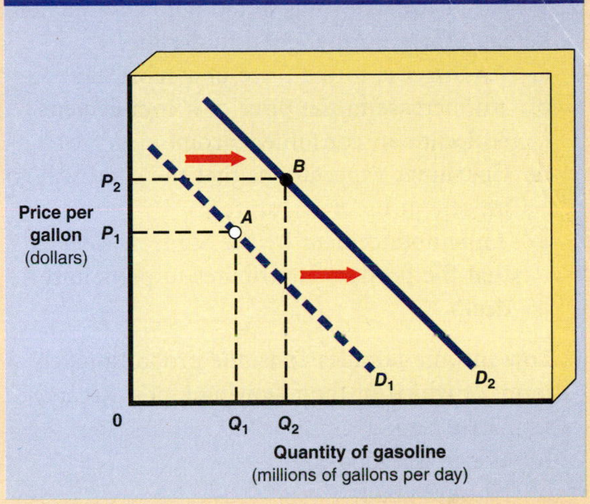

Can the Law of Supply Be Repealed for the Oil Market?

There is not a single quantity of oil—say, 3 million barrels—for sale in the world on a given day. The supply curve for oil is not vertical. As the law of supply states, higher oil prices will cause greater quantities of oil to be offered for sale. At lower prices, oil producers have less incentive to drill deeper for oil that is more expensive to discover.

The government cannot repeal the law of supply. Price controls discourage producers from oil exploration and production, which causes a reduction in the quantity supplied. If you said U.S. oil production decreased in the 1970s when the government put a lid on oil prices, **YOU ARE CORRECT**.

Can the Price System Eliminate Scarcity?

Recall from Chapter 1 that scarcity is the condition in which human wants are forever greater than the resources available to satisfy those wants. Using markets free from government interference will not solve the scarcity problem. Scarcity exists at any price for a good or service. This means scarcity occurs at any disequilibrium price at which a shortage or surplus exists, and scarcity remains at any equilibrium price at which no shortage or surplus exists.

Although the price system can eliminate shortages (or surpluses), if you said it cannot eliminate scarcity, **YOU ARE CORRECT**.

Sample Quiz

Please see Appendix B for answers to Sample Quiz questions.

1. Which of the following causes the demand for veggie burgers to increase?
   a. A decline in the price of veggie burgers

   b. An increase in the price of tofu burgers, perceived as a substitute by veggie burger consumers

c. An increase in the price of burger buns

d. A technological innovation that lowers the cost of producing veggie burgers

2. Which of the following would *not* cause market demand for a normal good to decline?

a. An increase in the price of a substitute

b. An increase in the price of a complement

c. A decline in consumer income

d. Consumer expectations that the good will go on sale in the near future

e. An announcement by the Surgeon General that the product contributes to premature death

3. Low-income families consume proportionately more of which of the following kinds of goods?

a. Luxury goods

b. Substitute goods

c. Normal goods

d. Inferior goods

4. Suppose each of the seven dwarfs buys four mugs of ginger ale per week from Snow White's café, when the price per mug is $2. If the seven dwarfs are the entire market demand for Snow White's ginger ale, which of the following is the correct value for market quantity demanded of ginger ale per week at a price of $2?

a. 4

b. 8

c. 28

d. 7

5. Which of the following increases the supply of corn?

a. The farm workers' union successfully negotiates a pay increase for corn harvest workers.

b. The Surgeon General announces that eating corn contributes to heart disease.

c. Congress and the President eliminate subsidies formerly paid to corn farmers.

d. Farmers who grow soybeans can also grow corn, and the price of soybeans drops by 75 percent.

6. With an upward-sloping supply curve, which of the following is *true*?

a. An increase in price results in a decrease in quantity supplied.

b. An increase in price results in an increase in supply.

c. A decrease in price results in a decrease in quantity supplied.

d. A decrease in price results in an increase in supply.

7. A rightward shift in the demand curve is called a(an)

a. decrease in output.

b. decrease in demand.

c. increase in demand.

d. increase in income.

8. A surplus occurs when

a. the quantity demanded exceeds the quantity supplied.

b. price is below the equilibrium price.

c. price is at the equilibrium.

d. price is above the equilibrium.

9. A shortage occurs when

a. the quantity supplied exceeds the quantity demanded.

b. price is below the equilibrium price.

c. price is at the equilibrium.

d. price is above the equilibrium.

10. Which of the following decreases supply in the market for pizza?

a. Pizza shop employees successfully organize a union and negotiate a pay increase.

b. The Surgeon General announces that eating pizza reduces the incidence of stomach cancer.

c. Cheese prices drop because price supports for dairy farmers are removed.

d. Some hot sandwich shops can also make and sell pizzas, and consumer demand for hot sandwiches declines sharply, reducing the profitability of producing hot sandwiches.

11. Which of the following results from an increase in the price of a one-week vacation at beach resorts on the coast of Mexico?

a. An increase in the supply of bicycle tires in Toledo, Ohio

b. An increase in the demand for vacations at resorts on Caribbean islands

c.   An increase in the supply of vacation opportunities at resorts on the coast of Mexico
d.   A decrease in the demand for vacations at resorts on Caribbean islands

12. There is news that the price of Tucker's Root Beer will increase significantly next week. If the demand for Tucker's Root Beer reacts *only* to this factor and shifts to the right, the position of this demand curve has reacted to a change in
a.   tastes.
b.   income levels.
c.   the prices of related goods.
d.   the number of buyers.
e.   expectations.

13. Which of the following causes a shortage to become larger?
a.   An increase in market price
b.   An increase in supply
c.   A decrease in demand
d.   A decrease in price

14. Which of the following is *true* in ski towns such as Crested Butte, Colorado, and Whistler, British Columbia during the peak winter ski season as compared to May and June?
a.   Demand for motel rooms is higher.
b.   Demand for motel rooms is lower.
c.   There is a surplus of motel rooms.
d.   The price of motel rooms will be lower.

15. In moving from a shortage toward the market equilibrium, which of the following is *true*?
a.   Price falls.
b.   Price rises.
c.   Quantity demanded increases.
d.   Quantity supplied decreases.

16. The law of demand is the principle that there is _____ relationship between the price of a good and the quantity buyers are willing to purchase in a defined time period, ceteris paribus.
a.   a direct
b.   no
c.   an inverse
d.   an independent

17. A curve that is derived by summing horizontally individual demand curves is called

a.   aggregate supply.
b.   market supply.
c.   aggregate demand.
d.   market demand.

18. A leftward shift in the demand curve is called a(an)
a.   decrease in demand.
b.   decrease in quantity demanded.
c.   increase in demand.
d.   increase in quantity demanded.

19. Under the law of demand, any increase in price will cause _____ in quantity demanded.
a.   a decrease
b.   an increase
c.   no change
d.   constant change

20. The law of supply is the principle that the relationship between the price of a good and the quantity sellers are willing to offer for sale in a defined time period, ceteris paribus, is
a.   inverse.
b.   direct.
c.   no relationship.
d.   independent.

EXHIBIT 14 Demand and Supply Data for Video Games

Price	Quantity demanded of video games	Quantity supplied of video games
$75	400	900
70	450	850
65	500	800
60	550	750
55	600	700
50	650	650
45	700	600
40	750	550

21. Exhibit 14 presents supply and demand data for the video game market. If the price of video games was currently $70, there would be an _____ of _____ video games in this market.
    a. excess demand; 450
    b. excess demand; 500
    c. excess supply; 400
    d. excess supply; 850
    e. excess demand; 400

22. In Exhibit 14, if the price of video games was currently $45, there would be an _____ of _____ video games in this market.
    a. excess demand; 700
    b. excess demand; 500
    c. excess supply; 100
    d. excess supply; 600
    e. excess demand; 100

23. In Exhibit 14, at any market price of video games above $50, a(n) _____ would result, causing price to _____.

    a. excess demand; rise
    b. excess supply; rise
    c. excess demand; fall
    d. excess supply; fall
    e. shortage; rise

24. In Exhibit 14, at any market price of video games below $50, a(n) _____ would result, causing price to _____.
    a. excess demand; rise
    b. excess supply; rise
    c. excess demand; fall
    d. excess supply; fall
    e. surplus; rise

25. In Exhibit 14, if there is a shortage of video games of 200 units, the current price of video games must be
    a. $60.
    b. $55.
    c. $50.
    d. $45.
    e. $40.

Consumer Surplus, Producer Surplus, and Market Efficiency

This chapter explained how the market forces of demand and supply establish the equilibrium price and output. Here it will be demonstrated that the equilibrium price and quantity determined in a competitive market are desirable because the result is *market efficiency*. To understand this concept, we use the area between the market price and the demand and supply curves to measure gains or losses from market transactions for consumers and producers.

3A-1 CONSUMER SURPLUS

Consider the market demand curve shown in Exhibit A-1(a). The height of this demand curve shows the maximum willingness of consumers to purchase ground beef at various prices per pound. At a price of $4.00 (point *X*), no one will purchase ground beef. But if the price drops to $3.50 at point *A*, consumers will purchase 1 million pounds of ground beef per year. Moving downward along the demand curve to point *B*, consumers will purchase an additional million pounds of ground beef per year at a lower price of $3.00 per pound. If the price continues to drop to $2.50 per pound at point *C* and lower, consumers are willing to purchase more pounds of ground beef consistent with the law of demand.

Assuming the market equilibrium price for ground beef is $2.00 per pound, we can use the demand curve to measure the net benefit, or *consumer surplus*, in this market. **Consumer surplus** is the value of the difference between the price consumers are willing to pay for a product on the demand curve and the price actually paid for it. At point *A*, consumers are willing to pay $3.50 per pound, but they actually pay the equilibrium price of $2.00. Thus, consumers earn a surplus of $1.50 ($3.50 − $2.00) per pound multiplied by 1 million pounds purchased, which is a $1.5 million consumer surplus. This value is represented by the gray shaded vertical rectangle formed at point *A* on the demand curve. At point *B*, consumers who purchase an additional million pounds of ground beef at $3.00 per pound receive a lower extra consumer surplus than at point *A*, represented by a rectangle of lower height. At point *C*, the marginal consumer surplus continues to fall until at equilibrium point *E*, where there is no consumer surplus.

The total value of consumer surplus can be interpreted from the explanation given above. As shown in Exhibit A-1(b), begin at point *X* and instead of selected prices, now imagine offering ground beef to consumers at each possible price downward along the demand curve until the equilibrium price of $2.00 is reached at point *E*. The result is that the entire green triangular area between the demand curve and the horizontal line at the equilibrium price represents total consumer surplus. Note that a rise in the

Consumer surplus
The value of the difference between the price consumers are willing to pay for a product on the demand curve and the price actually paid for it.

EXHIBIT A-1 Market Demand Curve and Consumer Surplus

As illustrated in part (a), consumers are willing at point *A* on the market demand curve to pay $3.50 per pound to purchase 1 million pounds of ground beef per year. Since the equilibrium price is $2.00, this means they receive a consumer surplus of $1.50 for each pound of ground beef and the vertical gray shaded rectangular area is the consumer surplus earned only at point *A*. Others who pay less at points *B*, *C*, and *E* receive less consumer surplus and the height of the corresponding rectangles falls at each of these prices. In part (b), moving downward along all possible prices on the demand curve yields the green shaded triangle, which is equal to total consumer surplus (net benefit).

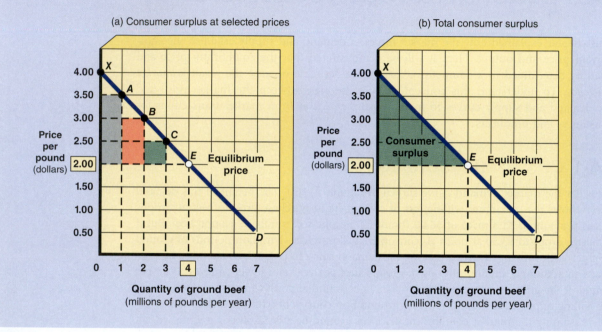

(a) Consumer surplus at selected prices

(b) Total consumer surplus

Quantity of ground beef
(millions of pounds per year)

Quantity of ground beef
(millions of pounds per year)

equilibrium price decreases total consumer surplus and a fall in the equilibrium price increases total consumer surplus.

CONCLUSION Total consumer surplus measured in dollars is represented by the total area under the market demand curve and above the equilibrium price.

3A-2 PRODUCER SURPLUS

Similar to the concept of consumer surplus, the height of the market supply curve in Exhibit A-2(a) shows the producers' minimum willingness to accept payment for ground beef offered for sale at various prices per pound. At point *X*, firms offer no ground beef for sale at a price of zero and they divert their resources to an alternative use. At a price of $0.50 per pound (point *A*), the supply curve tells us that 1 million pounds will be

EXHIBIT A-2 Market Supply Curve and Producer Surplus

In part (a), firms are willing at $0.50 (point *A*) to supply 1 million pounds of ground beef per year. Because $2.00 is the equilibrium price, the sellers earn a producer surplus of $1.50 per pound of ground beef sold. The first vertical shaded rectangle is the producer surplus earned only at point *A*. At points *B*, *C*, and *E*, sellers receive less producer surplus at each of these higher prices and the sizes of the rectangles fall. In part (b), moving upward along all possible selling prices on the supply curve yields the red-shaded triangle that is equal to total producer surplus (net benefit).

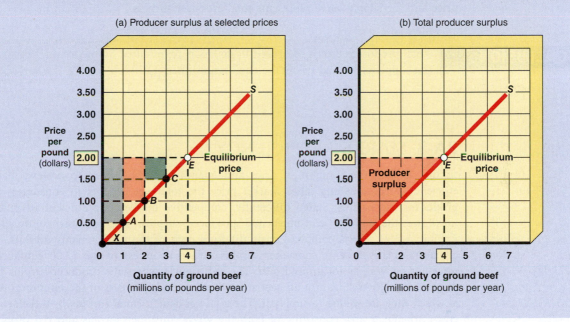

offered for sale. Moving upward along the supply curve to point *B*, firms will offer an additional million pounds of ground beef for sale at the higher price of $1.00 per pound. If the price rises to $1.50 at point *C* and higher, firms allocate more resources to ground beef production and another million pounds will be supplied along the supply curve.

Again, we will assume the equilibrium price is $2.00 per pound, and the supply curve can be used to measure the net benefit, or *producer surplus*. **Producer surplus** is the value of the difference between the actual selling price of a product and the price producers are willing to sell it for on the supply curve. Now assume the first million pounds of ground beef is sold at point *A* on the supply curve. In this case, producer surplus is the difference between the equilibrium selling price of $2.00 and the $0.50 price that is the minimum price that producers will accept to supply this quantity of ground beef. Thus, producer surplus is equal to $1.50 ($2.00−$0.50) per pound multiplied by 1 million pounds sold, which is a $1.5 million producer surplus. This value is represented by the vertical gray shaded rectangle formed at point *A* on the supply curve. The second million pounds of ground beef offered for sale at point *B* also generates a producer surplus because the selling price of $2.00 exceeds the $1.00

Producer surplus
The value of the difference between the actual selling price of a product and the price producers are willing to sell it for on the supply curve.

price at which firms are willing to supply this additional quantity of ground beef. Note that producer surplus is lower at point *B* compared to point *A*, and marginal producer surplus continues to fall at point *C* until it reaches zero at the equilibrium point *E*.

The total value of producer surplus is represented in Exhibit A-2(b). Start at point *X*, where none of the product will be supplied at the price of zero. Now consider the quantities of ground beef producers are willing to offer for sale at each possible price upward along the supply curve until the equilibrium price of $2.00 is reached at point *E*. The result is that the entire red triangular area between the horizontal line at the equilibrium price and the supply curve represents total producer surplus.

CONCLUSION   Total producer surplus measured in dollars is represented by the total area above the supply curve and below the equilibrium price.

3A-3 MARKET EFFICIENCY

In this section, the equilibrium price and quantity will be shown to achieve market efficiency because at any other market price the total net benefits to consumers and producers will be less. Stated differently, competitive markets are efficient when they maximize the sum of consumer and producer surplus. The analysis continues in Exhibit A-3(a), which combines parts (b) from each of the two previous exhibits. The green triangle represents consumer surplus earned in excess of the $2.00 equilibrium price consumers pay for ground beef. The red triangle represents producer surplus producers receive by selling ground beef at $2.00 per pound in excess of the minimum price at which they are willing to supply it. The total net benefit (total surplus) is therefore the entire triangular area consisting of both the green consumer surplus and red producer surplus triangles.

Now consider in Exhibit A-3(b) the consequences to market efficiency of producers devoting fewer resources to ground beef production and only 2 million pounds being bought and sold per year compared with 4 million pounds at the equilibrium price of $2.00. The result is a deadweight loss. **Deadweight loss** is the net loss of consumer and producer surplus from underproduction or overproduction of a product. In Exhibit A-3 (b), the deadweight loss is equal to the gray triangle *ABE*, which represents the total surplus of green and red triangles in part (a) that is not obtained because the market is operating below equilibrium point *E*.

Exhibit A-3(c) illustrates that a deadweight loss of consumer and producer surplus can also result from overproduction. Now suppose more resources are devoted to production and 6 million pounds of ground beef are bought and sold at the equilibrium price. However, from the producers' side of the market, the equilibrium selling price is only $2.00 and is below any possible selling price on the supply curve between points *E* and *C*. Therefore, firms have a net loss for each pound sold beyond 4 million pounds, represented by the area under the supply curve and bounded below by the horizontal equilibrium price line. Similarly, consumers pay the equilibrium price of $2.00, but this price exceeds any price consumers are willing to pay between points *E* and *D* on the demand curve. This means consumers experience a total net benefit

Deadweight loss
The net loss of consumer and producer surplus from underproduction or over-production of a product.

EXHIBIT **A-3** Comparison of Market Efficiency and Deadweight Loss

In part (a), the green triangle represents consumer surplus and the red triangle represents producer surplus. The total net benefit, or total surplus, is the entire triangle consisting of the consumer and producer surplus triangles.

In part (b), too few resources are used to produce 2 million pounds of ground beef compared to 4 million pounds at equilibrium point *E*. The market is inefficient because the deadweight loss gray triangle *ABE* is no longer earned by either consumers or producers. As shown in part (c), overproduction at the equilibrium price of $2.00 can also be inefficient. If 6 million pounds of ground beef are offered for sale, too many resources are devoted to this product and a deadweight loss of area *EDC* occurs.

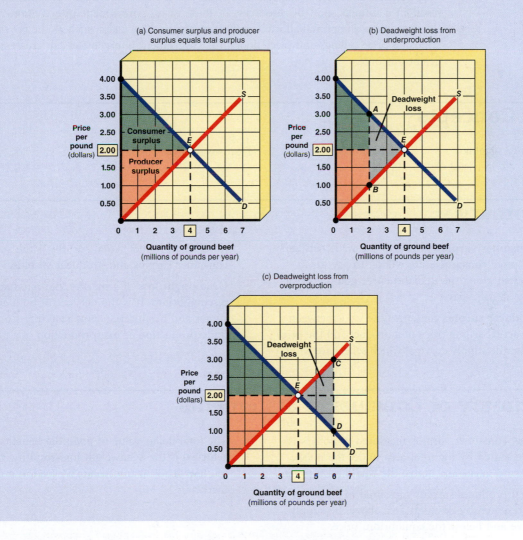

loss for each pound purchased, represented by the portion of the gray area above the demand curve but below the horizontal equilibrium price line. The total net loss of consumer and producer surplus (deadweight loss) is equal to the gray-shaded area *EDC*.

CONCLUSION   The total dollar value of potential benefits not achieved is the deadweight loss resulting from too few or too many resources used in a given market.

Looking ahead, the conclusion drawn from this appendix is that market equilibrium is efficient, but this conclusion is not always the case. In the next chapter, the topic of *market failure* will be discussed, in which market equilibrium under certain conditions can result in too few or too many resources being used to produce goods and services. For example, the absence of a competitive market, the existence of pollution, or vaccinations to prevent a disease can establish equilibrium conditions which are inefficient and result in a misallocation of resources. In these cases, government intervention may be able to achieve an optimal allocation of resources. In other cases, such as the government imposing price ceilings and price floors, the government intervention can create an inefficient outcome.

Key Concepts

Consumer surplus   Producer surplus   Deadweight loss

Summary

- **Consumer surplus** measures the value between the price consumers are willing to pay for a product along the demand curve and the price they actually pay.

- **Producer surplus** measures the value between the actual selling price of a product and the price along the supply curve at which sellers are willing

to sell the product. Total surplus is the sum of consumer surplus and producer surplus.

- **Deadweight loss** of a market that operates in disequilibrium. It is the net loss of both consumer and producer surplus resulting from underproduction or overproduction of a product.

Summary of Conclusion Statements

- Total consumer surplus measured in dollars is represented by the total area under the market demand curve and above the equilibrium price.

- Total producer surplus measured in dollars is represented by the total area above the supply curve and below the equilibrium price.

- The total dollar value of potential benefits not achieved is the deadweight loss resulting from too few or too many resources used in a given market.

Study Questions and Problems

Please see Appendix A for answers to the odd-numbered questions. Your instructor has access to the answers for even-numbered questions.

1. Consider the market for used textbooks. Use Exhibit A-4 to calculate the total consumer surplus.

EXHIBIT **A-4** Used Textbook Market

Potential buyer	Willingness to pay	Market price
Brad	$60	$30
Juan	45	30
Sue	35	30
Jamie	25	30
Frank	10	30

2. Consider the market for used textbooks. Use Exhibit A-5 to calculate the total producer surplus.

EXHIBIT **A-5** Used Textbook Market

Potential seller	Willingness to sell	Market price
Forest	$60	$30
Betty	45	30
Alan	35	30
Paul	25	30
Alice	10	30

3. Using Exhibits A-4 and A-5 above, calculate the total surplus. Then calculate the effect on consumer surplus, producer surplus, and total surplus of a fall in the equilibrium price of textbooks from $30 to $15 each. Explain the meaning of your calculations.

4. Using Exhibit A-6, and assuming the market is in equilibrium at Q_E, identify areas *ACD*, *DCE*, and *ACE*. Now explain the result of underproduction at Q in terms of areas *BCG*, *GCF*, and *BCF*.

EXHIBIT **A-6** Used Textbook Market

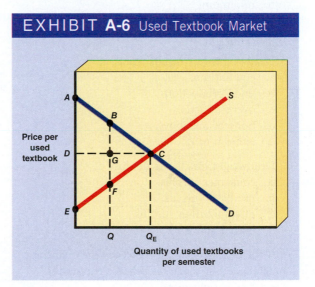

Price per used textbook

Quantity of used textbooks per semester

Sample Quiz

Please see Appendix B for answers to Sample Quiz questions.

1. Consumer surplus measures the value between the price consumers are willing to pay and the
   a. producer surplus price.
   b. deadweight gain price.
   c. actual price paid.
   d. preference price.

2. If Sam is willing to pay $50 for one good *X*, $30 for a second, $20 for a third, $8 for a fourth, and

the market price is $10. What is Sam's consumer surplus?
a. $10
b. $40
c. $70
d. $100

3. Suppose Tucker Inc. is willing to sell one gizmo for $10, a second gizmo for $15, a third for $20, and the market price is $25. What is Tucker Inc.'s producer surplus?
a. $10
b. $15
c. $30
d. $50

4. In an efficient market, deadweight loss is
a. maximum.
b. minimum.
c. constant.
d. zero.

5. Deadweight loss results from
a. equilibrium.
b. underproduction.
c. overproduction.
d. none of the above.
e. either b or c.

6. Deadweight loss is the net loss of
a. consumer surplus.
b. producer surplus.
c. disequilibrium surplus.
d. both a and b.

7. If the quantity supplied exceeds the quantity demanded in a market, what is the result?
a. Deadweight loss
b. Inefficiency
c. Overproduction
d. All of the above answers are correct

8. Suppose a consumer is willing to pay $20 for one good X, $10 for a second, and $5 for a third, and the market price is $4. What is the consumer surplus?
a. $16
b. $6
c. $1
d. $23

9. Producer surplus measures the value between the actual selling price and the
a. price sellers are willing to sell the product.
b. deadweight loss price.
c. lowest price sellers are willing to sell the product.
d. profit-maximization price.

10. Suppose seller X is willing to sell one good X for $5, a second good X for $10, a third for $16, a fourth for $25, and the market price is $20. What is seller X's producer surplus?
a. $15
b. $20
c. $22
d. $29

11. Deadweight loss is the result of
a. disequilibrium.
b. underproduction.
c. overproduction.
d. all of the above.

12. Deadweight loss is computed as the net of
a. consumer surplus minus producer surplus.
b. disequilibrium surplus plus consumer surplus.
c. producer surplus minus disequilibrium surplus.
d. consumer surplus plus producer surplus.

13. Deadweight loss is *not* the result of
a. an efficient market.
b. an inefficient market.
c. zero consumer surplus.
d. zero producer surplus.

14. At the equilibrium price, deadweight loss is
a. minimized.
b. zero.
c. maximized.
d. equal to the equilibrium price multiplied by the quantity exchanged.

15. If the quantity demanded exceeds the quantity supplied in a market, what is the result?
a. Deadweight loss
b. Inefficiency
c. Underproduction
d. All of the above answers are correct

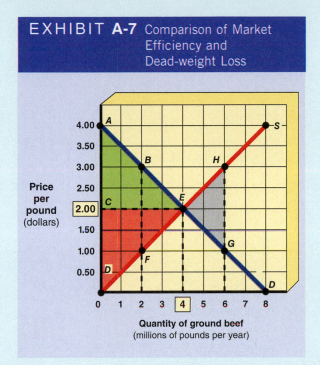

EXHIBIT A-7 Comparison of Market Efficiency and Dead-weight Loss

16. As shown in Exhibit A-7, if the market is in equilibrium, _____ represents consumer surplus.
    a. *ABEC*
    b. *AED*
    c. *EGH*
    d. *BEF*

17. As shown in Exhibit A-7, if the market is in equilibrium, _____ represents producer surplus.

a. *ADFB*
b. *CEFD*
c. *EGH*
d. *BEF*

18. As shown in Exhibit A-7, if the quantity supplied is 2 million pounds of ground beef per year, what is the result?
    a. Deadweight loss
    b. Inefficiency
    c. Underproduction
    d. All of the above
    e. None of the above

19. As shown in Exhibit A-7, if the quantity supplied is 6 million pounds of ground beef per year, what is the result?
    a. Deadweight loss
    b. Inefficiency
    c. Overproduction
    d. All of the above
    e. None of the above

20. As shown in Exhibit A-7, if the quantity supplied is 2 million pounds of ground beef per year, the result is a deadweight loss represented by area
    a. *ABEC.*
    b. *CEFD.*
    c. *EGH.*
    d. *BEF.*

CHAPTER 4

Markets in Action

CHAPTER PREVIEW

When you understand how buyers and sellers respond to changes in equilibrium prices, you begin to understand the economic way of thinking. This chapter starts by showing that changes in supply and demand influence the equilibrium price and quantity of goods and services exchanged around you every day. For example, you will study the impact of changes in supply and demand curves on the markets for Caribbean cruises, new homes, and AIDS vaccinations. Then you will see why the laws of supply and demand cannot be repealed. Using market supply and demand analysis, you will learn that government policies to control markets have predictable consequences. For example, you will understand what happens when the government limits the maximum rent landlords can charge and who benefits and who loses from the federal minimum-wage law.

In this chapter, you will also study situations in which the market mechanism fails. Have you visited a city and lamented the smog that blankets the beautiful surroundings? Or have you ever wanted to swim or fish in a stream, but could not because of industrial waste? These are obvious cases in which market-system magic failed and the government must consider cures to reach socially desirable results.

IN THIS CHAPTER, YOU WILL LEARN TO SOLVE THESE ECONOMICS PUZZLES:

- How can a spotted owl affect the price of homes?

- How do demand and supply affect the price of high-definition televisions?

- Why might government warehouses overflow with cheese and milk?

- What do ticket scalping and rent controls have in common?

- Can vouchers fix our schools?

4-1 CHANGES IN MARKET EQUILIBRIUM

Using market supply and demand analysis is like putting on glasses if you are near-sighted. Suddenly, the fuzzy world around you comes into clear focus. Many people believe that prices are set by sellers adding a certain percentage to their costs. If costs rise, sellers simply raise their prices by that percentage. In free markets, there is more to the story. In the following examples, you will open your eyes and see that economic theory has something important to say about so many things in the real world.

4-1a Changes in Demand

The Caribbean cruise market shown in Exhibit 1(a) assumes market supply, S, is constant and market demand increases from D_1 to D_2. Why has the demand curve shifted rightward in the figure? We will assume the popularity of cruises to these vacation islands has suddenly risen sharply due to extensive advertising that influenced tastes and preferences. Given supply curve S and demand curve D_1, the initial equilibrium price is $600 per cruise, and the initial equilibrium quantity is 8,000 cruises per year, shown as point E_1. After the impact of advertising, the new equilibrium point, E_2, becomes 12,000 cruises per year at a price of $900 each. Thus, the increase in demand causes both the equilibrium price and the equilibrium quantity to increase.

It is important to understand the force that caused the equilibrium to shift from E_1 to E_2. When demand initially increased from D_1 to D_2, there was a temporary shortage of 8,000 cruises (16,000 – 8,000) at $600 per cruise. Firms in the cruise business responded to the excess demand by hiring more workers, offering more cruises to the Caribbean, and raising the price. The cruise lines therefore move upward along the supply curve (increasing quantity supplied, but not changing supply). During some period of trial and error, Caribbean cruise sellers increase their price and quantity supplied until a shortage no longer exists at point E_2. Therefore, the increase in demand causes both the equilibrium price and the equilibrium quantity to increase.

What will happen to the demand for gas-guzzling automobiles (for example, SUVs) if the price of gasoline triples? Because gasoline and automobiles are complements, a rise in the price of gasoline decreases the demand for gas guzzlers from D_1 to D_2 in Exhibit 1(b). At the initial equilibrium price of $30,000 per gas guzzler ($E_1$), the quantity supplied now exceeds the quantity demanded by 20,000 automobiles per month (30,000 – 10,000). This unwanted inventory forces automakers to reduce the price and quantity supplied. As a result of this movement downward on the supply curve, market equilibrium changes from E_1 to E_2. The equilibrium price falls from $30,000 to $20,000, and the equilibrium quantity falls from 30,000 to 20,000 gas guzzlers per month.

4-1b Changes in Supply

Now reverse the analysis by assuming demand remains constant and allow some non-price determinant to shift the supply curve. In Exhibit 2(a), begin at point E_1 in a market for babysitting services at an equilibrium price of $9 per hour and 4,000 babysitters hired per month. Then assume there is a population shift and the number of people available to babysit rises. This increase in the number of sellers shifts the market supply curve rightward from S_1 to S_2 and creates a temporary surplus of 4,000 babysitters (8,000 – 4,000) at

EXHIBIT 1 The Effects of Shifts in Demand on Market Equilibrium

In part (a), demand for Caribbean cruises increases because of extensive advertising and the demand curve shifts rightward from D_1 to D_2. This shift in demand causes a temporary shortage of 8,000 cruises per year at the initial equilibrium of E_1. This disequilibrium condition encourages firms in the cruise business to move upward along the supply curve to a new equilibrium at E_2.

Part (b) illustrates a decrease in the demand for gas-guzzling automobiles (SUVs) caused by a sharp rise in the price of gasoline (a complement). This leftward shift in demand from D_1 to D_2 results in a temporary surplus of 20,000 gas guzzlers per month at the initial equilibrium of E_1. This disequilibrium condition forces sellers of these cars to move downward along the supply curve to a new equilibrium at E_2.

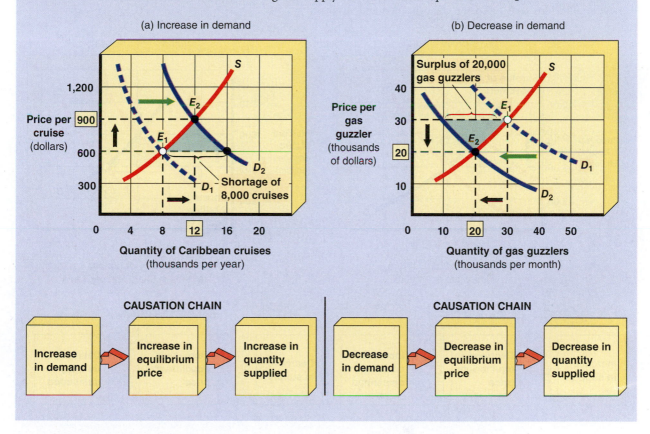

point E_1 who offer their services but are not hired. The unemployed babysitters respond by reducing the price and the number of babysitters available for hire, which is a movement downward along S_2. As the price falls, buyers move down along their demand curve and hire more babysitters per month. When the price falls to $6 per hour, the market is in equilibrium again at point E_2, instead of E_1, and consumers hire 6,000 babysitters per month.

Exhibit 2(b) illustrates the market for lumber. Suppose this market is at equilibrium at point E_1, where the going price is $400 per thousand board feet, and 8 billion board feet are bought and sold per year. Now suppose a new Endangered Species Act is passed, and the federal government sets aside huge forest resources to protect the

EXHIBIT 2 The Effects of Shifts in Supply on Market Equilibrium

In part (a), begin at equilibrium E_1 in the market for babysitters, and assume an increase in the number of babysitters shifts the supply curve rightward from S_1 to S_2. This shift in supply causes a temporary surplus of 4,000 unemployed babysitters per month. This disequilibrium condition causes a movement downward along the demand curve to a new equilibrium at E_2. At E_2, the equilibrium price declines, and the equilibrium quantity rises.

In part (b), steps to protect the environment cause the supply curve for lumber to shift leftward from S_1 to S_2. This shift in supply results in a temporary shortage of 4 billion board feet per year. Customer bidding for the available lumber raises the price. As a result, the market moves upward along the demand curve to a new equilibrium at E_2, and the quantity demanded falls.

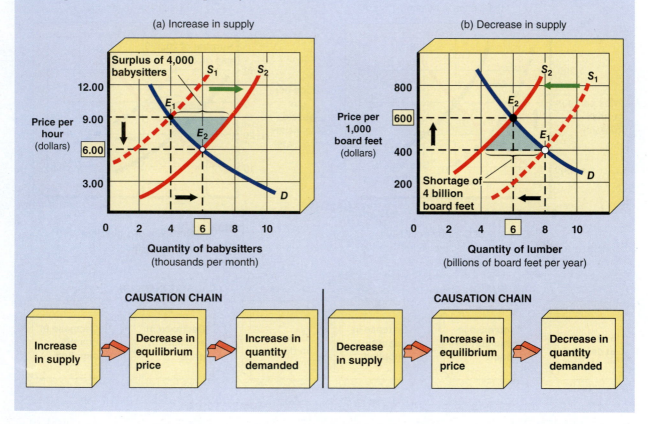

spotted owl and other wildlife. This means the market supply curve shifts leftward from S_1 to S_2, and a temporary shortage of 4 billion board feet of lumber exists (8 billion–4 billion) at point E_1. Suppliers respond by hiking their price from $400 to $600 per thousand board feet, and a new equilibrium is established at E_2, where the quantity is 6 billion board feet per year. This higher cost of lumber, in turn, raises the price of a new home.

Exhibit 3 gives a concise summary of the impact of changes in demand or supply on market equilibrium.

EXHIBIT 3 The Effects of Shifts in Supply on Market Equilibrium

Change	Effect on equilibrium price	Effect on equilibrium quantity
Demand increases	Increases	Increases
Demand decreases	Decreases	Decreases
Supply increases	Decreases	Increases
Supply decreases	Increases	Decreases

Why the Lower Price for Big-Screen High-Definition Televisions?
Suppose more consumers were willing and able to purchase more big-screen high-definition televisions because of their increased popularity, and at the same time, producers manufactured more of these sets. Within one year, the price of big-screen hi-def televisions would fall dramatically. During this period, which would increase more—demand, supply, or neither?

CHECKPOINT

4-1c Trend of Equilibrium Prices over Time

Basic demand and supply analysis allows us to explain a trend in prices over a number of years. Exhibit 4 shows the effect of changes in nonprice determinants that increase both the demand and supply curves for good *X* between 2010, 2015, and 2020. A line connects the equilibrium prices for each year in order to summarize the trend of equilibrium price and quantity changes over this time period. In this case, the observed prices trace an upward-sloping trend line.

4-2 CAN THE LAWS OF SUPPLY AND DEMAND BE REPEALED?

The government intervenes in some markets with the objective of preventing prices from rising to the equilibrium price. In other markets, the government's goal is to intervene and maintain a price higher than the equilibrium price. Market supply and demand analysis is a valuable tool for understanding what happens when the government fixes prices. There are two types of price controls: *price ceilings* and *price floors*.

4-2a Price Ceilings

Case 1: Rent Controls

What happens if the government prevents the price system from setting a market price "too high" by mandating a price ceiling? A **price ceiling** is a legally established maximum price a seller can charge. Rent controls are an example of the imposition of a price

Price ceiling
A legally established maximum price a seller can charge.

EXHIBIT 4 Trend of Equilibrium Prices over Time

Nonprice determinants of demand and supply for good X have caused both the demand and supply curves to shift rightward between 2010 and 2020. As a result, the equilibrium price and quantity in this example rise along the upward-sloping trend line connecting each observed equilibrium price.

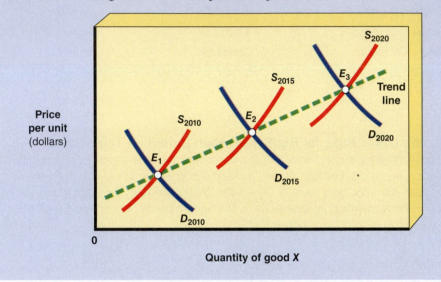

ceiling in the market for rental units. New York City, Washington, D.C., Los Angeles, San Francisco, and other communities in the United States have some form of rent control. Since World War I, rent controls have been widely used in Europe. The rationale for rent controls is to provide an "essential service" that would otherwise be unaffordable by many people at the equilibrium rental price. Let's see why most economists believe that rent controls are counterproductive.

Exhibit 5 is a supply and demand diagram for the quantity of rental units demanded and supplied per month in a hypothetical city. We begin the analysis by assuming no rent controls exist and equilibrium is at point E, with a monthly rent of $1,200 per month and 6 million units occupied. Next, assume the city council imposes a rent control (ceiling price) that by law forbids any landlord from renting a unit for more than $800 per month. What does market supply and demand theory predict will happen? At the low rent ceiling of $800, the quantity demanded of rental units will be 8 million, but the quantity supplied will be only 4 million. Consequently, the price ceiling creates a persistent market shortage of 4 million rental units because suppliers cannot raise the rental price without being subjected to legal penalties.

Note that a rent ceiling at or above $1,200 per month would have no effect. If the ceiling is set at the equilibrium rent of $1,200, the quantity of rental units demanded and the quantity of rental units supplied are equal regardless of the rent control. If the rent ceiling is set above the equilibrium rent, the quantity of rental units supplied exceeds the quantity of rental units demanded, and this surplus will cause the market to adjust to the equilibrium rent of $1,200.

EXHIBIT 5 Rent Control Results in a Shortage of Rental Units

If no rent controls exist, the equilibrium rent for a hypothetical apartment is $1,200 per month at point *E*. However, if the government imposes a rent ceiling of $800 per month, a shortage of 4 million rental units occurs. Because rent cannot rise by law, one outcome is that consumers must search for available units instead of paying a higher rent. Other outcomes include a black market, bribes, discrimination, and other illegal methods of dealing with a shortage of 4 million rental units per month.

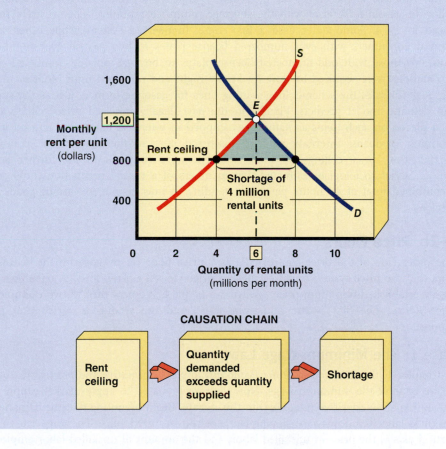

CAUSATION CHAIN

Rent ceiling → Quantity demanded exceeds quantity supplied → Shortage

What is the impact of rent controls on consumers? First, as a substitute for paying higher prices, consumers must spend more time on waiting lists and searching for housing. This means consumers incur an *opportunity cost* added to the $800 rent set by the government. Second, an illegal market, or *black market*, can arise because of the excess quantity demanded. Because the price of rental units is artificially low, the profit motive encourages tenants to risk breaking the law by subletting their unit to the highest bidder over $800 per month.

From the seller's perspective, rent control encourages two undesirable effects. First, faced with a mandated low rent, landlords may cut maintenance expenses, and housing deterioration will reduce the stock of rental units in the long run. Second, landlords may use discriminatory practices to replace the price system. Once owners realize there is an excess quantity demanded for rentals at the controlled price, they may resort to preferences based on pet ownership or family size to determine how to allocate scarce rental space.

Case 2: Gasoline Price Ceiling

The government placed ceilings on most nonfarm prices during World War II and, to a lesser extent, during the Korean War. In 1971, President Nixon "froze" virtually all wages, prices, and rents until 1973 in an attempt to control inflation. As a result of an oil embargo in late 1973, the government imposed a price ceiling of 55 cents per gallon of gasoline. To deal with the shortage, nonprice rationing schemes were introduced in 1974. Some states used a first-come, first-served system, while other states allowed consumers with even-numbered license plates to buy gas on even-numbered days and those with odd-numbered license plates to buy gas on odd-numbered days. Gas stations were required to close on Friday night and not open until Monday morning. Regardless of the scheme, long waiting lines for gasoline formed, just as the supply and demand model predicts. Finally, in the past, legally imposed price ceilings have been placed on such items as natural gas shipped in interstate commerce and on interest rates for loans. Internationally, as discussed later in the chapter on economies in transition, price ceilings on food and rent were common in the former Soviet Union. Soviet sociologists estimated that members of a typical urban household spent a combined total of 40 hours per week standing in lines to obtain various goods and services.

4-2b Price Floors

Price floor
A legally established minimum price a seller can be paid.

The other side of the price-control coin is a price floor set by government because it fears that the price system might establish a price viewed as "too low." A **price floor** is a legally established minimum price a seller can be paid. We now turn to two examples of price floors. The first is the minimum wage, and the second is agricultural price supports.

Case 1: The Minimum-Wage Law

In Chapter 1, the second *You're the Economist* applied *normative* and *positive* reasoning to the issue of the minimum wage. Now you are prepared to apply market supply and demand analysis (positive reasoning) to this debate. Begin by noting that the demand for unskilled labor is a downward-sloping curve as shown in Exhibit 6. The wage rate on the vertical axis is the price of unskilled labor, and the amount of unskilled labor employers are willing to hire varies inversely with the wage rate. At a higher wage rate, businesses will hire fewer workers. At a lower wage rate, they will employ a larger quantity of workers.

On the supply side, the wage rate determines the number of unskilled workers willing and able to work per year. At higher wages, workers will give up leisure or schooling to work, and at lower wages, fewer workers will be available for hire. The upward-sloping curve in Exhibit 6 is the supply of labor.

Assuming the freedom to bargain, the price system will establish an equilibrium wage rate of W_e and an equilibrium quantity of labor employed of Q_e. But suppose the government enacts a minimum wage, W_m, which is a price floor above the equilibrium wage, W_e. The intent of the legislation is to "wave a carrot" in front of people

EXHIBIT 6 A Minimum Wage Results in a Surplus of Labor

When the federal or state government sets a wage-rate floor above the equilibrium wage, a surplus of unskilled labor develops. The supply curve is the number of workers offering their labor services per year at possible wage rates. The demand curve is the number of workers employers are willing and able to hire at various wage rates. Equilibrium wage, W_e, will result if the price system is allowed to operate without government interference. At the minimum wage of W_m, there is a surplus of unemployed workers, $Q_s - Q_d$.

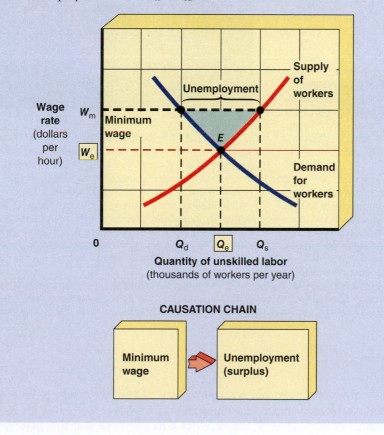

CAUSATION CHAIN

who will not work at W_e and to make lower-paid workers better off with a higher wage rate. But consider the undesirable consequences. One result of an artificially high minimum wage is that the number of workers willing to offer their labor increases upward along the supply curve to Q_s, but there are fewer jobs because the number of workers firms are willing to hire decreases to Q_d on the demand curve. The predicted outcome is a labor surplus of unskilled workers, $Q_s - Q_d$, who are unemployed. Moreover, employers are encouraged to substitute machines and skilled labor for the unskilled labor previously employed at equilibrium wage W_e. The minimum wage is therefore considered counterproductive because employers lay off the lowest-skilled workers, who ironically are the type of workers minimum wage legislation intends to help.

YOU'RE THE ECONOMIST

Applicable Concept: Price Supports

Rigging the Market for Milk

For many years the milk industry faced an important question: What does the federal government plan to do about its dairy price support program, which has helped boost farmers' income since 1949? Under the price support program, the federal government agrees to buy storable milk products, such as cheese, butter, and dry milk. If the farmers cannot sell all their products to consumers at a price exceeding the price support level, the federal government will purchase any unsold grade A milk production. Although state-run dairy commissions set their own minimum prices for milk, these legal minimums were similar to the federally set prices. To reduce the interstate price competition for milk, each state set its minimum milk price within 3 percent of the prices set by bordering states. The result has been that government essentially bought up surplus production at supported prices—prices above what would otherwise exist in the market.

These federal price supports on dairy products, as well as other agricultural products, have been controversial. Critics argue that price support programs force consumers to face considerably higher prices for milk and milk-based foods. They also argue that these programs waste taxpayer money. For example, each year the federal government pays billions of dollars to dairy farmers for milk products that sometimes are destroyed or held in storage at a huge cost. Moreover, the problem is compounded because the federal government encourages dairy farmers to use ultramodern farming techniques to increase the production per cow. Another concern

smereka/Shutterstock.com

is that instead of helping small family farmers, these price supports are a corporate welfare program, and the biggest government price support checks go to the largest farmers. This enables these corporate farms to buy smaller, less-efficient farmers, pushing up land values that prevent young people from entering farming and contributing to the decline in the number of dairy farmers. Finally, opponents of the dairy price support program argue that the market for milk is inherently a competitive industry and that consumers and taxpayers would be better served without government price supports for milk.

Perhaps as a result of the critics, Congress did take action with the passage of the Agricultural Act of 2014, which repealed price supports on dairy products. This legislation,

Also, loss of minimum wage jobs represents a loss of entry-level jobs to those who seek to enter the workforce.

Supporters of the minimum wage are quick to point out that those employed (Q_d) are better off. Moreover, when their additional income is spent, it generates more sales, more production, and some job creation that can offset at least some of the initial unemployment over a period of time. Even though the minimum wage causes a reduction in employment, some economists argue that a more equal or fairer income distribution is worth the loss of some jobs. Moreover, the shape of the labor demand curve may be much more vertical than shown in Exhibit 6. If this is the case, the unemployment effect of a rise in the minimum wage would be small. In addition, they claim opponents ignore the possibility that unskilled workers lack bargaining power versus employers.

Finally, a minimum wage set at or below the equilibrium wage rate is ineffective. If the minimum wage is set at the equilibrium wage rate of W_e, the quantity of labor demanded and the quantity of labor supplied are equal regardless of the minimum

TOOS
USA

"I always wondered how the government set milk prices."

© Andrew Toos. Reproduction rights obtainable from www.CartoonStock.com

charged farmers). The Dairy Product Donation Program (DPDP) requires the Secretary of Agriculture to purchase dairy products for donation to low-income groups when the dairy margin falls below $4.00.

The Agricultural Act of 2014 is due to expire December 31, 2018. We will have to see what the future holds as government balances the interests of farmers, consumers, and taxpayers.

ANALYZE THE ISSUE

1. Draw a supply and demand graph to illustrate the problem of a price support on milk described in the case study.
2. Who benefits and who is hurt by dairy price supports?
3. What do you think the impact is on dairy farmers, consumers, and taxpayers as a result of the Margin Protection Program for Dairy (MPP-Dairy)? Is this an improvement over the price support program?
4. What do you think the impact is on dairy farmers, consumers, and taxpayers as a result of the Dairy Product Donation Program (DPDP)? Is this an improvement over the price support program?

however, has not stopped government from trying to assist farmers. Two new government programs were established with this act: the Margin Protection Program for Dairy (MPP-Dairy) and the Dairy Product Donation Program (DPDP).

The Margin Protection Program for Dairy (MPP-Dairy) offers dairy producers catastrophic insurance coverage at virtually no cost to them, and some additional insurance at their expense, should the difference between current market prices and the costs of production fall below a certain amount (called the "margin"—currently between $4, which is the basic catastrophic amount, and up $8, where a premium is

wage. If the minimum wage is set below the equilibrium wage, the forces of supply of and demand for labor establish the equilibrium wage regardless of the minimum wage rate.

Case 2: Agricultural Price Supports

A farm price support is a well-known example of a price floor, which results in government purchases of surplus food and in higher food prices. Agricultural price support programs began in the 1930s as a means of raising the income of farmers, who were suffering from low market prices during the Great Depression. Under these programs, the government guarantees a minimum price above the equilibrium price and agrees to purchase any quantity the farmer is unable to sell at the legal price.

A few of the crops that have received price supports are corn, peanuts, soybeans, wheat, cotton, rice, tobacco, and dairy products. As predicted by market supply and demand analysis, a price support above the equilibrium price causes surpluses. Government warehouses therefore often overflow with such perishable products as butter, cheese, and dry milk purchased with taxpayers' money. The previous "You're the Economist" section on the dairy industry examines one of the best-known examples of U.S. government interference with agricultural market prices.

CONCLUSION	A price ceiling or price floor prevents market adjustment in which competition among buyers and sellers bids the price upward or downward to the equilibrium price.

CHECKPOINT

Is There Price Fixing at the Ticket Window?
At sold-out concerts, sports contests, and other events, some ticket holders try to resell their tickets for more than they paid—a practice known as scalping. For scalping to occur, must the original ticket price be legally set by a price floor, at the equilibrium price, or by a price ceiling?

4-3 MARKET FAILURE

In this chapter and the previous chapter, you gained an understanding of how markets operate. Through the price system, society coordinates economic activity, but markets are not always "Prince Charmings" that achieve *market efficiency* without a misallocation of resources. It is now time to step back with a critical eye and consider markets that become "ugly frogs" by allocating resources inefficiently. **Market failure** occurs when market equilibrium results in too few or too many resources being used in the production of a good or service. In this section, you will study four important cases of market failure: lack of competition, externalities, public goods, and income inequality. Market failure is discussed in more detail in the chapter on environmental economics, except for the macroeconomics version of the text.

Market failure
A situation in which market equilibrium results in too few or too many resources being used in the production of a good or service. This inefficiency may justify government intervention.

4-3a Lack of Competition

There must be competition among both producers and consumers for markets to function properly. But what happens if the producers fail to compete? In *The Wealth of Nations*, Adam Smith stated, "People of the same trade seldom meet together, even for merriment and diversion, but the conversation ends in a conspiracy against the public, or in some diversion to raise prices."[1] This famous quotation clearly underscores the fact that in the real world businesses seek ways to replace consumer sovereignty with "big business sovereignty." What happens when a few firms rig the market and they become the market's boss? By restricting supply through artificial limits on the output of a good,

---

[1]Adam Smith, *An Inquiry into the Nature and Causes of the Wealth of Nations*, 1776; reprint, New York: Random House, The Modern Library, 1937, p. 128.

firms can enjoy higher prices and profits. As a result, firms may waste resources and retard technology and innovation.

Exhibit 7 illustrates how IBM, Apple, Gateway, Dell, and other suppliers of personal computers (PCs) could benefit from rigging the market. Without collusive action, the competitive price for PCs is $1,500, the quantity of 200,000 per month is sold, and efficient equilibrium prevails at point E_1. It is in the best interest of sellers, however, to take steps that would make PCs artificially scarce and raise the price. Graphically, the sellers wish to shift the competitive supply curve, S_1, leftward to the restricted supply curve, S_2. This could happen for a number of reasons, including an agreement among sellers to restrict supply (collusion) and government action. For example, the sellers could lobby the government to pass a law allowing an association of PC suppliers to set production quotas. The proponents might argue this action raises prices, revenues, and, in turn, profits. Higher profits enable the industry to invest in new capital and become more competitive in world markets.

EXHIBIT 7 Rigging the PC Market

At efficient equilibrium point E_1, sellers compete. As a result, the price charged per PC is $1,500, and the quantity of PCs exchanged is 200,000. Suppose suppliers use collusion, government intervention, or other means to restrict the supply of this product. The decrease in supply from S_1 to S_2 establishes inefficient market equilibrium E_2. At E_2, firms charge the higher price of $2,500, and the equilibrium quantity of PCs falls to 150,000. Thus, the outcome of restricted supply is that the market fails because firms use too few resources to produce fewer than the optimal number of PCs, while charging an artificially high price.

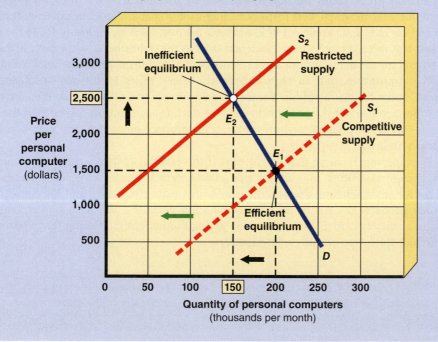

Opponents of artificially restricted supply argue that, although the producers benefit, the lack of competition means the economy loses. The result of restricting supply is that the efficient equilibrium point, E_1, changes to the inefficient equilibrium point, E_2. At point E_2, the higher price of $2,500 is charged, and the lower equilibrium quantity means that firms devote too few resources to producing PCs and charge an artificially high price. Note that under U.S. antitrust laws, the Justice Department is responsible for prosecuting firms that collude to restrict supply to force higher prices.

4-3b Externalities

Externality
A cost or benefit imposed on people other than the consumers and producers of a good or service.

Even when markets are competitive, some markets may still fail because they suffer from the presence of side effects economists call externalities. An **externality** is a cost or benefit imposed on people other than the consumers and producers of a good or service. Externalities are also called *spillover effects* or *neighborhood effects*. People other than consumers and producers who are affected by these side effects of market exchanges are called *third parties*. Externalities may be either negative or positive; that is, they may be detrimental or beneficial. Suppose you are trying to study and your roommate is listening to Steel Porcupines at full blast. The action of your roommate is imposing an unwanted *external cost* or *negative externality* on you and other third parties who are trying to study or sleep. Externalities can also result in an *external benefit* or *positive externality* to nonparticipating parties. When a community proudly displays its neat lawns, gorgeous flowers, and freshly painted homes, visitors are third parties who did none of the work, but enjoy the benefit of the pleasant scenery.

A Graphical Analysis of Pollution

Exhibit 8 provides a graphical analysis of two markets that fail to include externalities in their market prices unless the government takes corrective action. Exhibit 8(a) shows a market for steel in which steel firms burn high-sulfur coal and pollute the environment. Demand curve D and supply curve S_1 establish the inefficient equilibrium, E_1, in the steel market. Not included in S_1 are the *external costs* to the public because the steel firms are not paying for the damage from smoke emissions. If steel firms discharge smoke and ash into the atmosphere, foul air reduces property values, raises health care costs, and, in general, erodes the quality of life. Because supply curve S_1 does not include these external costs, they are also not included in the price of steel, P_1. In short, the absence of the cost of pollution in the price of steel means the firms produce more steel and pollution than is socially desirable.

S_2 is the supply curve that would exist if the external costs of respiratory illnesses, dirty homes, and other undesirable side effects were included. Once S_2 includes the charges for environmental damage, the equilibrium price rises to P_2, and the equilibrium quantity becomes Q_2. At the efficient equilibrium point, E_2, the steel market achieves allocative efficiency. At E_2, steel firms are paying the full cost and using fewer resources to produce the lower quantity of steel at Q_2.

CONCLUSION   When the supply curve fails to include external costs, the equilibrium price is artificially low, and the equilibrium quantity is artificially high. External costs cause the market to overallocate resources.

EXHIBIT 8 Externalities in the Steel and AIDS Vaccination Markets

In part (a), resources are overallocated at inefficient market equilibrium E_1 because steel firms do not include the cost per ton of pollution in the cost per ton of steel. Supply curve S_2 includes the external costs of pollution. If firms are required to purchase equipment to remove the pollution or to pay a tax on pollution, the economy achieves the efficient equilibrium of E_2.

Part (b) demonstrates that external benefits cause an underallocation of resources. The efficient output at equilibrium point E_2 is obtained if people are required to purchase AIDS shots or if the government pays a subsidy equal to the external benefit per shot.

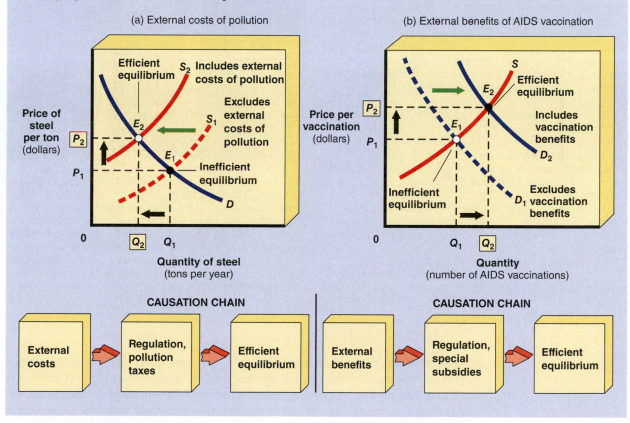

Regulation and pollution taxes are two ways society can correct the market failure of pollution:

1. **Regulation.** Legislation can set standards that force firms to clean up their emissions as a condition of remaining in business. This means firms must buy, install, and maintain pollution-control equipment. When the extra cost of the pollution equipment is added to the production cost per ton of steel, the initial supply curve, S_1, in Exhibit 8(a), shifts leftward to supply curve S_2. This means regulation has forced the market equilibrium to change from E_1 to E_2. At point E_2, the firms use fewer resources to produce Q_2 compared to Q_1 output of steel per year, and S_2 reflects all costs of production, including the external costs; therefore, the firms operate efficiently.

YOU'RE THE ECONOMIST

Applicable Concept: Public Goods versus Private Goods

Can Vouchers Fix Our Schools?

In their book *Free to Choose*, published in 1980, economists Milton Friedman and his wife Rose Friedman proposed a voucher plan for schools.[1] The objective of their proposal was to retain government financing, but give parents greater freedom to choose the schools their children attend. The Friedmans pointed out that under the current system parents face a strong incentive not to remove their children from the public schools. The reason is because if parents decide to withdraw their children from a public school and send them to a private school, they must pay private tuition in addition to the taxes that finance children enrolled in the public schools.

To remove the financial penalty that limits the freedom of parents to choose schools, the government could give parents a voucher, which is a piece of paper redeemable for a sum of money payable to any approved school. For example, if the government spends $8,000 per year to educate a student, then the voucher could be for this amount. The voucher plan embodies the same principle as the GI Bill that provides educational benefits to military veterans. The veteran receives a voucher good only for educational expenses and is free to choose the school where it is used, provided the school satisfies certain standards.

The Friedmans argue that parents could, and should, be permitted to use the vouchers not only at private schools, but also at other public schools—and not only at schools in their own

Marjorie Kamys Cotera/Bob Daemmrich Photography/Alamy Stock Photo

district, city, or state, but at any school that is willing to accept their child. That option would give every parent a greater opportunity to choose and at the same time would require public schools to charge tuition. The tuition would be competitive because public schools must compete for students both with other public schools and with private schools. It is important to note that this plan relieves no one of the burden of taxation to pay for schooling. It simply gives parents a wider choice as to which competing schools their children can attend, given the

2. **Pollution Taxes.** Another approach would be for the government to levy a tax per ton of steel equal to the external cost imposed on society when the firm emits pollution into the air. This action inhibits production by imposing an additional production cost per ton of steel from the pollution taxes and shifts the supply curve leftward from S_1 to S_2 as shown in Exhibit 8(a). Again, the objective is to change the equilibrium from E_1 to E_2 and eliminate the overuse of resources devoted to steel production and its pollution. The tax revenue could be used to compensate those damaged by the pollution.

A Graphical Analysis of AIDS Vaccinations

As explained earlier, the supply curve may not include the *external costs* of a product. Now you will see that the demand curve may not include the *external benefits* of a product. Suppose a vaccination is discovered that prevents AIDS. Exhibit 8(b) illustrates the market for immunization against AIDS. Demand curve D_1 reflects the price consumers would pay for shots to receive the benefit of a reduced probability of infection by AIDS. Supply curve S shows the quantities of shots suppliers offer for sale at different prices.

amount of funding per student that the community has obligated itself to provide. The plan also does not affect the present standards imposed on private schools to ensure that students attending them satisfy the compulsory attendance laws.

In 1990, Milwaukee began an experiment with school vouchers. The program gave selected children from low-income families taxpayer-funded vouchers to allow them to attend private schools. There has been a continuing heated debate among parents, politicians, and educators over the results. In 1998, Wisconsin's highest court ruled in a 4–2 decision that without violating the constitutional separation of church and state, Milwaukee could use public money for vouchers for students who attend religious schools.

A 2002 article in *USA Today* reported:

> Opponents of vouchers have repeatedly argued that they would damage the public schools, draining them of resources and better students. A recent study of the Milwaukee voucher program by Caroline Hoxby, a Harvard economist, suggests just the opposite. She wrote that "schools that faced the most potential competition from vouchers had the best productivity response." No doubt, the nation's experience with vouchers is limited, yet the evidence cited in a recent Brookings Institution report shows that they do seem to benefit African-American youngsters.[2]

The controversy continues: For example, in a 2002 landmark case, the U.S. Supreme Court ruled that government vouchers for private or parochial schools are constitutional. In 2003, however, a Denver judge struck down Colorado's new school voucher law, ruling that it violated the state's constitution by stripping local school boards of their control over education. In 2006, the Florida Supreme Court ruled that Florida's voucher program for students in the lowest-rated public schools was unconstitutional. Then in 2010, Florida legislated a tax-credit voucher plan for low-income students. In 2013 the Indiana Supreme Court upheld the state's voucher program, which is the nation's broadest school voucher program. And in the 2014–2015 school year, North Carolina awarded vouchers to students whose families meet certain income requirements. In 2017, a renewed debate was sparked by President Trump's appointment of Betsy DeVos, a long-time supporter of school vouchers, as Secretary of Education.

ANALYZE THE ISSUE

1. In recent years, school choice has been a hotly debated issue. Explain whether education is a public good. If education is not a public good, why should the government provide it?

2. The Friedmans present a one-sided view of the benefits of a voucher system. Other economists disagree about the potential effectiveness of vouchers. Do you support a voucher system for education? Explain your reasoning.

1. Milton Friedman and Rose Friedman, *Free to Choose: A Personal Statement*, New York: Harcourt Brace Jovanovich, 1980, pp. 160–161.
2. Robert J. Bresler, "Vouchers and The Constitution," *USA Today*, May 2002, p. 15.

At equilibrium point E_1, the market fails to achieve an efficient allocation of resources. The reason is that when buyers are vaccinated, other people who do not purchase AIDS shots (called *free riders*) also benefit because this disease is less likely to spread. Once demand curve D_2 includes external benefits to nonconsumers of AIDS vaccinations (increase in the number of buyers), the efficient equilibrium of E_2 is established. At Q_2, sellers devote greater resources to AIDS vaccinations, and the underallocation of resources is eliminated.

How can society prevent the market failure of AIDS vaccinations? Two approaches follow:

1. **Regulation.** The government can boost consumption and shift the demand curve rightward by requiring all citizens to purchase AIDS shots each year. This approach to capturing external benefits in market demand explains why all school-age children must have polio and other shots before entering school.

2. **Special Subsidies.** Another possible solution would be for the government to increase consumer income by paying consumers for each AIDS vaccination. This would mean the government pays each citizen a dollar payment equal to the amount

of external benefits per shot purchased. Because the subsidy amount is payable at any price along the demand curve, the demand curve shifts rightward until the efficient equilibrium price and quantity are reached.

CONCLUSION   When the demand curve fails to include external benefits the equilibrium price is artificially low, and the equilibrium quantity is artificially low. External benefits cause the market to underallocate resources.

4-3c Public Goods

Private goods are produced through the price system. In contrast, national defense is an example of a public good provided by the government because of its special characteristics. A **public good** is a good or service that, once produced, has two properties: (1) Users collectively consume benefits, (2) There is no way to bar people who do not pay (free riders) from consuming the good or service.

To see why the marketplace fails, imagine that Patriot Missiles Inc. offers to sell missile defense systems to people who want private protection against attacks from incoming missiles. First, once the system is operational, everyone in the defense area benefits from increased safety. Second, the *nonexclusive* nature of a public good means it is impossible or very costly for any owner of a Patriot missile defense system to prevent nonowners, the free riders, from reaping the benefits of its protection.

Given the two properties of a public good, why would any private individual purchase a Patriot missile defense system? Why not take a free ride and wait until someone else buys a missile system? Thus, each person wants a Patriot system, but does not want to bear the cost of the system when everyone shares in the benefits. As a result, the market fails to provide Patriot missile defense systems, and everyone hopes no missile attacks occur before someone finally decides to purchase one. Government can solve this public goods problem by producing Patriot missiles and taxing the public to pay. Unlike a private citizen, the government can use force to collect payments and prevent the free-rider problem. Other examples of public goods include global agreements to reduce emissions, the judicial system, the national emergency warning system, air traffic control, prisons, dams, city roads, and traffic lights.

Public good
A good or service with two properties: (1) users collectively consume benefits, and (2) there is no way to bar people who do not pay (free riders) from consuming the good or service.

CONCLUSION   If public goods are available only in the marketplace, people wait for someone else to pay, and the result is an underproduction or zero production of public goods.

4-3d Income Inequality

In the cases of insufficient competition, externalities, and public goods, the marketplace allocates too few or too many resources to producing output. The market may also result in a very unequal distribution of income, thereby raising a very controversial issue. Under the impersonal price system, movie stars earn huge incomes for acting in movies, while homeless people roam the streets penniless. The controversy is therefore over how equal the distribution of income should be and how much government intervention is required to achieve this goal. Some people wish to remove most inequality of income. Others argue for the government to provide a "safety net" minimum income level for all citizens. Still others see high income as an incentive and a "fair" reward for productive resources.

To create a more equal distribution of income, the government uses various programs to transfer money from people with high incomes to those with low incomes. Unemployment compensation and food stamps are examples of such programs. The federal minimum wage is another example of a government attempt to raise the earnings of low-income workers.

Should There Be a War on Drugs?

The U.S. government fights the use of drugs, such as marijuana and cocaine, in a variety of ways, including spraying crops with poisonous chemicals; imposing jail sentences for dealers and users; and confiscating drug-transporting cars, boats, and planes. Which market failure motivates the government to interfere with the market for drugs: lack of competition, externalities, public goods, or income inequality?

CHECKPOINT

Key Concepts

Price ceiling   Market failure   Public good

Price floor   Externalities

Summary

- **Price ceilings** and **price floors** are maximum and minimum prices enacted by law, rather than allowing the forces of supply and demand to determine prices. A *price ceiling* is a maximum price mandated by government, and a *price floor*, or *support price*, is a minimum legal price. If a price ceiling is set below the equilibrium price, a shortage will persist. If a price floor is set above the equilibrium price, a surplus will persist.

Price Ceiling

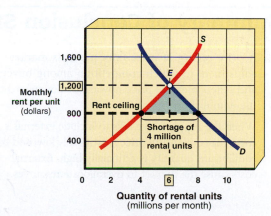

Price Floor

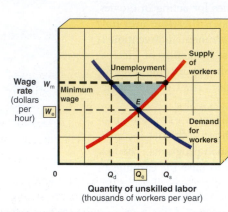

Quantity of unskilled labor
(thousands of workers per year)

- **Market failure** occurs when the market mechanism does not achieve an efficient allocation of resources. Sources of market failure include lack of competition, externalities, public goods, and income inequality. Although controversial, government intervention is a possible way to correct market failure.

- An **externality** is a cost or benefit of a good imposed on people who are not buyers or sellers of that good. Pollution is an example of an *external cost,* which means too many resources are used to produce the product responsible for the pollution. Two basic approaches to solve this market failure are regulation and pollution taxes. Vaccinations provide *external benefits*, which means sellers devote too few resources to producing this product. Two basic solutions to this type of market failure are laws to require consumption of shots and special subsidies.

Externalities

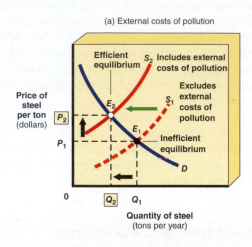

(a) External costs of pollution

Quantity of steel
(tons per year)

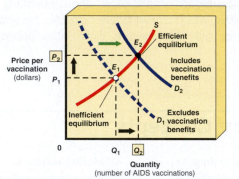

(b) External benefits of AIDS vaccination

Quantity
(number of AIDS vaccinations)

- **Public goods** are goods that are consumed by all people in a society regardless of whether they pay or not. National defense, air traffic control, and other public goods can benefit many individuals simultaneously and are provided by the government.

Summary of Conclusion Statements

- A price ceiling or price floor prevents market adjustment in which competition among buyers and sellers bids the price upward or downward to the equilibrium price.

- When the supply curve fails to include external costs, the equilibrium price is artificially low, and the equilibrium quantity is artificially high. External costs cause the market to overallocate resources.

- When the demand curve fails to include external benefits, the equilibrium price and the equilibrium quantity are artificially low. External benefits cause the market to underallocate resources.

- If public goods are available only in the marketplace, people wait for someone else to pay, and the result is an underproduction or zero production of public goods.

Study Questions and Problems

Please see Appendix A for answers to the odd-numbered questions. Your instructor has access to the answers for even-numbered questions.

1. Market researchers have studied the market for milk, and their estimates for the supply of and the demand for milk per month are as follows:

Price per gallon	Quantity demanded (millions of gallons)	Quantity supplied (millions of gallons)
$10.00	100	500
8.00	200	400
6.00	300	300
4.00	400	200
2.00	500	100

   a. Using the data, graph the demand for and the supply of milk. Identify the equilibrium point as *E*, and use dotted lines to connect *E* to the equilibrium price on the price axis and the equilibrium quantity on the quantity axis.

   b. Suppose the government enacts a milk price support of $8 per gallon. Indicate this action on your graph, and explain the effect on the milk market. Why would the government establish such a price support?

   c. Now assume the government decides to set a price ceiling of $4 per gallon. Show and explain how this legal price affects your graph of the milk market. What objective could the government be trying to achieve by establishing such a price ceiling?

2. Use a graph to show the impact on the price of Japanese cars sold in the United States if the United States imposes import quotas and other trade restrictions that decrease the supply of Japanese cars. Now draw another graph to show how the change in the price of Japanese cars affects the price of American-made cars in the United States. Explain the market outcome in each graph and the link between the two graphs.

3. Using market supply and demand analysis, explain why labor union leaders are strong advocates of raising the minimum wage above the equilibrium wage.

4. What are the advantages and disadvantages of the price system?

5. Suppose a market is in equilibrium and both demand and supply curves increase. What happens to the equilibrium price if demand increases more than supply?

6. Consider this statement: *"Government involvement in markets is inherently inefficient."* Do you agree or disagree? Explain.

7. Suppose coal-burning firms are emitting excessive pollution into the air. Suggest two ways the government can deal with this market failure.

8. Explain the impact of external costs and external benefits on resource allocation.

9. Why are public goods not produced in sufficient quantities by private markets?

10. Which of the following are public goods?
    a. Air bags
    b. Pencils
    c. Cycle helmets
    d. City streetlights
    e. Contact lenses

✔ CHECKPOINT ANSWERS

Why the Lower Price for Big-Screen High-Definition Televisions?

As shown in Exhibit 9, an increase in demand leads to higher TV prices, while an increase in supply leads to lower prices. Because the overall direction of the market price of TVs was down, the increase in supply must have been larger than the increase in demand. If you said supply increased by more than demand, **YOU ARE CORRECT**.

Is There Price Fixing at the Ticket Window?

Scalpers are evidence of a shortage whereby buyers are unable to find tickets at the official price. As shown in Exhibit 10, scalpers (often illegally) profit from the shortage by selling tickets above the official price. Shortages result when prices are restricted below equilibrium, as is the case when there is a price ceiling. If you said scalping occurs when there is a price ceiling because scalpers charge more than the official maximum price, **YOU ARE CORRECT**.

Should There Be a War on Drugs?

Drug use often affects not only the person using the drugs, but also other members of society as well. For example, higher crime rates are largely attributable to increased drug usage, and AIDS is often spread when users inject drugs using nonsterile needles. When one person's actions affect others not involved in the decision to buy or sell, the market fails to operate efficiently. If you said the market failure motivating government intervention in the drug market is externalities because drug users impose costs on nonusers, **YOU ARE CORRECT**.

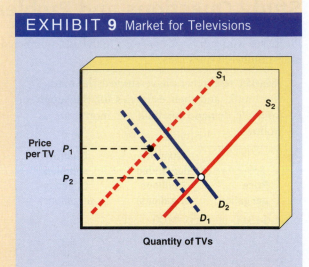

EXHIBIT 9 Market for Televisions

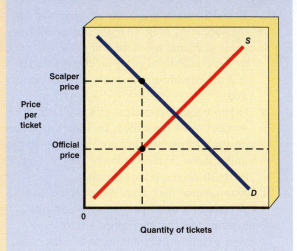

EXHIBIT 10 Market for Tickets

Sample Quiz

Please see Appendix B for answers to Sample Quiz questions.

1. A decrease in demand with the supply held constant leads to a(an)
   a. increased equilibrium price and an increased equilibrium quantity.
   b. decreased equilibrium price and a decreased equilibrium quantity.
   c. decreased equilibrium price and an increased equilibrium quantity.
   d. increased equilibrium price and a decreased equilibrium quantity.

2. An increased equilibrium price and a decreased equilibrium quantity results from a(an)
   a. decrease in demand.
   b. increase in supply.
   c. decrease in supply.
   d. increase in demand.

3. Assume no price ceiling exists in a market. Then a price ceiling is established below the market equilibrium. What would result?
   a. Shortage
   b. Equilibrium
   c. Surplus
   d. Exchange price

4. Which of the following is *not* an example of market failure?
   a. Lack of competition
   b. Externalities
   c. Efficient equilibrium
   d. Extreme income inequality

5. A cost imposed on people other than the consumers of a good or service is a
   a. price floor.
   b. negative externality.
   c. positive externality.
   d. price ceiling.

6. Suppose X and Y are substitutes. If the price of Y increases, how will this change the market equilibrium for X?
   a. Both equilibrium price and quantity decline.
   b. Both equilibrium price and quantity rise.
   c. Equilibrium price declines, and equilibrium quantity rises.

   d. Equilibrium price rises, and equilibrium quantity falls.

7. If the cost of producing a good rises for sellers, how will this affect the market equilibrium for that good?
   a. Price will rise, and quantity will fall.
   b. Price will fall, and quantity will rise.
   c. Both price and quantity will rise.
   d. Both price and quantity will fall.

8. If goods A and B are complements, and the price of good B rises, how will this affect the market equilibrium for good A?
   a. Price will rise, and quantity will fall.
   b. Price will fall, and quantity will rise.
   c. Both price and quantity will rise.
   d. Both price and quantity will fall.

9. Suppose Big-Cat and Fat-Cat are rival cat food brands and the price of Fat-Cat is reduced. Following this price drop, is there a shortage or a surplus of Big-Cat at the old price of Big-Cat?
   a. Shortage
   b. Surplus
   c. Neither because equilibrium exists
   d. Neither because a price drop cannot cause a shortage or a surplus

10. Suppose the average equilibrium monthly rental price of apartments and rooms in a college town has been steady at $600, but then the college expands enrollment from 10,000 to 12,000. Suddenly, there is a shortage of rental housing at the prevailing price of $600. Which of the following is *most* likely true?
    a. The shortage occurred because demand increased, and a new market equilibrium will feature higher rental prices and more rental units available on the market.
    b. The shortage occurred because supply increased, and a new market equilibrium will feature lower rental prices and fewer rental units available on the market.
    c. The shortage occurred because demand decreased, and a new market equilibrium will

feature lower rental prices and fewer rental units available on the market.

d. The shortage occurred because demand increased, and a new market equilibrium will feature higher rental prices and fewer rental units available on the market.

11. If a price ceiling is set at $10, and the equilibrium market price is $8, which price will consumers actually pay?
    a. $10
    b. $8
    c. $18
    d. $2

12. Suppose the state of California imposes a minimum wage of $15 per hour. In the entry-level labor market in California fast-food restaurants, the quantity of labor demanded at $15 per hour is 800,000 and the quantity of labor supplied is 1.2 million. Which of the following is true?
    a. There is a shortage of 800,000 workers in the labor market.
    b. There is a surplus of 400,000 workers in the labor market.
    c. There is a shortage of 400,000 workers in the labor market.
    d. There is a surplus of 1.2 million workers in the labor market.

13. Suppose the federal government imposes a price floor (support price) in the milk market at a price of $6 per gallon. If market quantity demanded at $6 is 1 billion gallons, and market quantity supplied is 1.5 billion gallons, which of the following is true?
    a. There is a shortage of 500 million gallons of milk, and the federal government will buy 1 billion gallons to maintain the $6 price.
    b. There is a surplus of 500 million gallons of milk, and the federal government will buy these 500 million gallons to maintain the $6 price.
    c. There is a shortage of 500 million gallons of milk, and the federal government will buy an additional 500 million gallons to maintain the $6 price.

d. There is a surplus of 1 billion gallons of milk, and the federal government will buy 1.5 billion gallons to maintain the $6 price.

14. Suppose the city of Arcata, California, imposes rent control so that rents cannot exceed $1,000 per month on one-bedroom rental units. Suppose $1,000 had also been the equilibrium rental price in Arcata before a huge new apartment complex was built in the nearby town of McKinleyville, where rents are $800 per month. Which of the following is *most* likely true?
    a. There will be a shortage of rental housing in Arcata at the rent control price of $1,000.
    b. There will be a lasting surplus of rental housing in Arcata after the new apartment complex is built in McKinleyville.
    c. The equilibrium rental price in Arcata will fall below $1,000; thus, rent control will not affect the rental market in Arcata.
    d. The equilibrium price of $1,000 per month in Arcata will not change.

15. Suppose the federal government provides wheat farmers with a price floor above the market equilibrium price of wheat, creating a surplus. Which of the following causes a reduction in the surplus of wheat?
    a. Elimination of the price floor
    b. An increase in the price of wheat
    c. A decrease in the demand for wheat
    d. An increase in the supply of wheat

16. If society allows firms to freely pollute the environment, which of the following is *true*?
    a. Market equilibrium output will be too high relative to the efficient output level.
    b. Market equilibrium output will be too low relative to the efficient output level.
    c. Market equilibrium output will be equivalent to the efficient output level.
    d. The efficient output level can be achieved by giving firms a subsidy for the pollution they generate.

17. If there are external benefits for good X, which of the following is true?
    a. The socially efficient amount of good X can be achieved if society taxes consumers of good X.

b. The socially efficient amount of good X can be achieved if society subsidizes consumers of good X.

c. The socially efficient amount of good X will be equivalent to the free market equilibrium quantity.

d. The socially efficient amount of good X does not exist.

18. Suppose the federal government imposes a new pollution tax of $0.01 per kilowatt-hour of electricity on coal-fired power producers. Which of the following describes how this tax will affect the market for electricity served by these power plants?

a. Demand for electricity will decrease.

b. Demand for electricity will increase.

c. The supply of electricity will decrease.

d. The supply of electricity will increase.

19. Why don't competitive markets do a good job providing public goods?

a. Because people do not receive benefits from public goods

b. Because firms cannot produce enough goods to satisfy market demand

c. Because public goods generate negative externalities and pollution taxes reduce the incentive for firms to supply public goods

d. Because it is difficult to exclude people from gaining benefits from public goods without paying for them; so market demand does not reflect the benefits to society from the public good

20. Which of the following is *not* an example of market failure?

a. Lack of competition

b. Externalities

c. Efficient equilibrium

d. Extreme income inequality

Applying Supply and Demand Analysis to Health Care

One out of every six dollars spent in the United States is spent for health care services. This is a greater percentage than in any other industrialized country.[1] And in 2010, historic health care legislation (the Affordable Care Act, commonly called Obamacare) was enacted to dramatically reform the U.S. system. The topic of health care arouses deep emotions and generates intense media coverage. How can we understand many of the important health care issues? One approach is to listen to the normative statements made by politicians and other concerned citizens. Another approach is to use supply and demand theory to analyze the issue. Here again the objective is to bring textbook theory to life and use it to provide you with a deeper understanding of third-party health service markets.

4A-1 THE IMPACT OF HEALTH INSURANCE

There is a downward-sloping demand curve for health care services just as there is for other goods and services. Following the same law of demand that applies to cars, clothing, entertainment, and other goods and services, movements along the demand curve for health care occur because consumers respond to changes in the price of health care. As shown in Exhibit A-1, we assume that health care, including doctor visits, medicine, hospital bills, and other medical services, can be measured in units of health care. Without health insurance, consumers buy Q_1 units of health care services per year at a price of P_1 per unit. Assuming supply curve S represents the quantity supplied, the market is in equilibrium at point A. At this point, the total cost of health care can be computed by the price of health care (P_1) times the quantity demanded (Q_1) or represented geometrically by the rectangle $0P_1AQ_1$.

Analysis of the demand curve for health care is complicated by the way health care is financed. About 80 percent of all health care is paid for by *third parties*, including private insurance companies and government programs, such as Medicare and Medicaid. The price of health care services paid by patients, therefore, depends on the *copayment rate*, which is the percentage of the cost of services consumers pay out of pocket. To understand the impact, it is more realistic to assume consumers are insured and extend the analysis represented in Exhibit A-1. Because patients pay only 20 percent of the bill, the quantity of health care demanded in the figure increases to Q_2 at a lower

---

[1]Source Bureau of Economic Analysis, *Health Care Satellite Account*, http://www.bea.gov/industry/index.htm.

EXHIBIT **A-1** The Impact of Insurance on the Health care Market

Without health insurance, the market is in equilibrium at point A, with a price of P_1 and a quantity demanded of Q_1. Total spending is $0P_1AQ_1$. With copayment health insurance, consumers pay the lower price of P_2, and the quantity demanded increases to Q_2. Total health care costs rise to $0P_3CQ_2$, with $0P_2BQ_2$ paid by consumers and P_2P_3CB paid by insurers. As a result, the quantity supplied increases from point A to point C, where it equals the quantity demanded of Q_2.

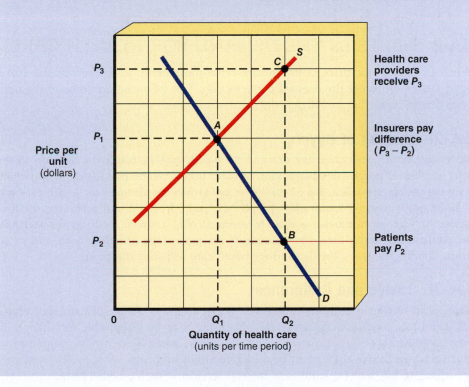

Health care providers receive P_3

Insurers pay difference $(P_3 - P_2)$

Patients pay P_2

Price per unit (dollars)

Quantity of health care (units per time period)

price of P_2. At point B on the demand curve, insured consumers pay an amount equal to rectangle $0P_2BQ_2$, and insurers pay an amount represented by rectangle P_2P_3CB. Health care providers respond by increasing the quantity supplied from point A to point C on the supply curve S, where the quantity supplied equals the quantity demanded of Q_2. The reason that there is no shortage in the health care market is that the combined payments from the insured consumers and insurers equal the total payment required for the movement upward along the supply curve. Stated in terms of rectangles, the total health care payment of $0P_3CQ_2$ equals $0P_2BQ_2$ paid by consumers plus P_2P_3CB paid by insurers.

CONCLUSION

Compared to a health care market without insurance, the quantity demanded, the quantity supplied, and the total cost of health care are increased by copayment health care insurance.

Finally, note that Exhibit A-1 represents an overall or general model of the health care market. Individual health care markets are subject to *market failure*. For example, there would be a lack of competition if hospitals, doctors, or drug companies conspired to fix prices. Externalities provide another source of market failure, as illustrated previously for vaccinations in Exhibit 8(b). We are also concerned that health care should be distributed in a fair way. This concern explains why the government Medicare and Medicaid programs help the elderly and poor afford health care. In fact, as a result of market failure, some nations have chosen to have their governments provide health care to all that is paid for through taxes.

4A-2 SHIFTS IN THE DEMAND FOR HEALTH CARE

While changes in the price of health care cause movements along the demand curve, other factors can cause the demand curve to shift. The following are some of the non-price determinants that can change the demand for health care.

4A-2a Number of Buyers

As the population increases, the demand for health care increases. In addition to the total number of people, the distribution of older people in the population is important. As more people move into the 65-and-older age group, the demand for health care services becomes greater because older people have more frequent and prolonged spells of illness. An increase in substance abuse involving alcohol, tobacco, or drugs also increases the demand for health care. For example, if the percentage of babies born into drug-prone families increases, the demand for health care will shift rightward.

4A-2b Tastes and Preferences

Changes in consumer attitudes toward health care can also change demand. For example, television, movies, magazines, and advertising may be responsible for changes in people's preferences for cosmetic surgery. Moreover, medical science has improved so much that we believe there must be a cure for most ailments. As a result, consumers are willing to buy larger quantities of medical services at each possible price.

Doctors also influence consumer preferences by prescribing treatment. It is often argued that some doctors guard against malpractice suits or boost their incomes by ordering more tests or office visits than are really needed. Some estimates suggest that fraud and abuse account for as much as 10 percent of total health care spending. These studies reveal that as many as one-third of some procedures are inappropriate.

4A-2c Income

Health care is a normal good. Rising inflation-adjusted incomes of consumers in the United States cause the demand curve for health care services to shift to the right. On the other hand, if real median family income remains unchanged, there is no influence on the demand curve.

4A-2d Prices of Substitutes

The prices of medical goods and services that are substitutes can change and, in turn, influence the demand for other medical services. For example, treatment of a back problem by a chiropractor is an alternative for many of the treatments provided by orthopedic doctors. If the price of orthopedic therapy rises, then some people will switch to treatment by a chiropractor. As a result, the demand curve for chiropractic therapy shifts rightward.

4A-3 SHIFTS IN THE SUPPLY OF HEALTH CARE

Changes in the following nonprice factors change the supply of health care.

4A-3a Number of Sellers

Sellers of health care include hospitals, nursing homes, physicians in private practice, drug companies, chiropractors, psychologists, and a host of other suppliers. To ensure the quality and safety of health care, virtually every facet of the industry is regulated and licensed by the government or controlled by the American Medical Association (AMA). Primarily through medical school accreditation and licensing requirements, the AMA limits the number of people practicing medicine. The federal Food and Drug Administration (FDA) requires testing that delays the introduction of new drugs. Tighter restrictions on the number of sellers shift the health care supply curve leftward and reduced restrictions shift the supply curve rightward.

4A-3b Resource Prices

An increase in the costs of resources underlying the supply of health care shifts the supply curve leftward. By far the single most important factor behind increasing health care spending has been technological change. New diagnostic, surgical, and therapeutic equipment is used extensively in the health care industry, and the result is higher costs. Wages, salaries, and other costs, such as the costs of malpractice suits, also influence the supply curve. If hospitals, for example, are paying higher prices for inputs used to produce health care, the supply curve shifts to the left because the same quantities may be supplied only at higher prices.

CHAPTER 5

Price Elasticity of Demand and Supply

CHAPTER PREVIEW

Elasticity concerns how *sensitive* changes in quantity are to changes in price. Suppose you are the manager of the Steel Porcupines rock group. You are considering raising your ticket price, and you wonder how the fans will react. You have studied economics and know the law of demand. When the price of a ticket rises, the quantity demanded goes down, ceteris paribus. So you really need to know to what extent will ticket sales fall. If the lawn seating ticket price for a Steel Porcupines concert is $25, you will sell 20,000 tickets. At $30 per ticket, only 10,000 tickets will be sold. Thus, a $5 increase per ticket cuts the number of tickets sold in half.

Which ticket price should you choose? Is it better to charge a higher ticket price and sell fewer tickets or to charge a lower ticket price and sell more tickets? The answer depends on changes in *total revenue*, or sales, as we move along points on Steel Porcupines' demand curve. At $30 per ticket, sales will be $300,000. If you charge $25, the group will take in $500,000 for a concert. Okay, you say, what happens at $20 per ticket?

This chapter teaches you to calculate the percentage change in the quantity demanded when the price changes by a given percentage. Then you will see how this relates to total revenue. This knowledge of the sensitivity of the quantity demanded as price changes is vital for pricing and targeting markets for goods and services. Next, you will see how changes in consumer income and the prices of related goods affect percentage changes in the quantity demanded. The chapter concludes by relating the concept of price elasticity to supply and the impact of taxation.

IN THIS CHAPTER, YOU WILL LEARN TO SOLVE THESE ECONOMICS PUZZLES:

- Can total revenue from a Steel Porcupines concert remain unchanged regardless of changes in the ticket price?

- How sensitive is the quantity of cigarettes demanded to changes in the price of cigarettes?

- What would happen to the sales of Mercedes, BMWs, and Jaguars in the United States if Congress prohibited sales of Japanese luxury cars in this country?

- Can Honda compete with itself?

5-1 PRICE ELASTICITY OF DEMAND

In Chapter 3, when you studied the demand curve, the focus was on the law of demand. This law states there is an inverse relationship between the price and the quantity demanded of a good or service. In this chapter, the emphasis is on measuring the *relative size* of changes in the price and the quantity demanded. Now we ask: By *what percentage* does the quantity demanded rise when the price falls by, say, 10 percent?

5-1a The Price Elasticity of Demand Midpoints Formula[1]

Price elasticity of demand

The ratio of the percentage change in the quantity demanded of a product to a percentage change in its price.

Economists use a price elasticity of demand formula to measure the degree of consumer responsiveness, or sensitivity, to a change in price. **Price elasticity of demand** is the ratio of the percentage change in the quantity demanded of a product to a percentage change in its price. Price elasticity of demand explains how strongly consumers react to a change in price. Think of quantity demanded as a rubber band. Price elasticity of demand measures how "stretchy" the rubber band is when the price changes. Suppose a university's enrollment drops by 20 percent because tuition rises by 10 percent. Therefore, the price elasticity of demand is 2 (-20 percent/+10 percent). The number 2 means that the quantity demanded (enrollment) changes 2 percent for each 1 percent change in price (tuition). Note there should be a minus sign in front of the 2 because, under the law of demand, price and quantity move in *opposite* directions. However, economists drop the minus sign because we know from the law of demand that quantity demanded and price are inversely related.

The number 2 is an *elasticity coefficient*, which economists use to measure the degree of elasticity. The elasticity formula is

$$E_d = \frac{\text{percentage change in quantity demanded}}{\text{percentage change in price}}$$

where E_d is the elasticity of demand coefficient. Here you must take care. *There is a problem using this formula.* Let's return to the rock group example from the chapter preview. Suppose Steel Porcupines raises its ticket price from $25 to $30 and the number of seats sold falls from 20,000 to 10,000. We can compute the elasticity coefficient as

$$E_d = \frac{\%\Delta Q}{\%\Delta P} = \frac{\dfrac{10{,}000 - 20{,}000}{20{,}000}}{\dfrac{30 - 25}{25}} = \frac{50\%}{20\%} = 2.5$$

Now consider the elasticity coefficient computed between these same points on Steel Porcupines' demand curve when the price is lowered. Starting at $30 per ticket and lowering the ticket price to $25 causes the number of seats sold to rise from 10,000 to 20,000. In this case, the rock group computes a much different elasticity coefficient, as

$$E_d = \frac{\%\Delta Q}{\%\Delta P} = \frac{\dfrac{20{,}000 - 10{,}000}{10{,}000}}{\dfrac{25 - 30}{30}} = \frac{100\%}{17\%} = 5.9$$

[1]The midpoints formula is also commonly called the *arc elasticity formula*.

There is a reason for the different elasticity coefficients between the same two points on a demand curve (2.5 if price is raised, 5.9 if price is cut). The natural approach is to select the initial point as the base and then compute a percentage change. But price elasticity of demand involves changes between two possible initial base points (P_1, Q_1 or P_2, Q_2). Economists solve this problem of different base points by using the *midpoints* as the base points of changes in prices and quantities demanded. The *midpoints formula* for price elasticity of demand is

$$E_d = \frac{\text{change in quantity}}{\text{sum of quantities}/2} \div \frac{\text{change in price}}{\text{sum of prices}/2}$$

which can be expressed as

$$E_d = \frac{\%\Delta Q}{\%\Delta P} = \frac{\dfrac{Q_2 - Q_1}{Q_1 + Q_2}}{\dfrac{P_2 - P_1}{P_1 + P_2}}$$

where Q_1 represents the first quantity demanded, Q_2 represents the second quantity demanded, and P_1 and P_2 are the first and second prices. Expressed this way, we divide the change in quantity demanded by the *average* quantity demanded. Then this value is divided by the change in the price divided by the *average* price.

It does not matter if Q_1 or P_1 is the first or second number in each term because we are finding averages. Also note that you can drop the 2 as a divisor of both the $(Q_1 + Q_2)$ and $(P_1 + P_2)$ terms because the 2s in the numerator and the denominator cancel out. Now we can use the midpoints formula to calculate the price elasticity of demand to be equal to 3.7 regardless of whether Steel Porcupines raises the ticket price from \$25 to \$30 or lowers it from \$30 to \$25.

$$E_d = \frac{\dfrac{Q_2 - Q_1}{Q_1 + Q_2}}{\dfrac{P_2 - P_1}{P_1 + P_2}} = \frac{\dfrac{10{,}000 - 20{,}000}{20{,}000 + 10{,}000}}{\dfrac{30 - 25}{25 + 30}} = \frac{33\%}{9\%} = 3.7$$

and

$$E_d = \frac{\dfrac{Q_2 - Q_1}{Q_1 + Q_2}}{\dfrac{P_2 - P_1}{P_1 + P_2}} = \frac{\dfrac{20{,}000 - 10{,}000}{10{,}000 + 20{,}000}}{\dfrac{25 - 30}{30 + 25}} = \frac{33\%}{9\%} = 3.7$$

The value of 3.7 tells us that for every 1 percent change in the price of the Steel Porcupines tickets, the quantity demanded will change in the opposite direction by 3.7 percent.

5-1b The Total Revenue Test of Price Elasticity of Demand

As reflected in the midpoints formula, the *responsiveness* of the quantity demanded to a change in price determines the value of the elasticity coefficient. There are three possibilities: (1) the numerator is greater than the denominator, (2) the numerator is less than the denominator, and (3) the numerator equals the denominator. Exhibit 1 presents three cases that the Steel Porcupines rock band may confront.

EXHIBIT 1 The Impact of a Decrease in Price on Total Revenue

These three different demand curve graphs show the relationship between a decrease in concert ticket price and a change in total revenue.

In part (a), the demand curve is elastic between points A and B. The percentage change in quantity demanded is greater than the percentage change in price, $E_d > 1$. As the ticket price falls from $30 to $20, total revenue increases from $300,000 to $600,000.

Part (b) shows a case in which the demand curve is inelastic between points C and D. The percentage change in quantity demanded is less than the percentage change in price, $E_d < 1$. As the ticket price decreases over the same range, total revenue falls from $600,000 to $500,000.

Part (c) shows a unitary elastic demand curve. The percentage change in quantity demanded equals the percentage change in price between points E and F, $E_d = 1$. As the concert ticket price decreases, total revenue remains unchanged at $600,000.

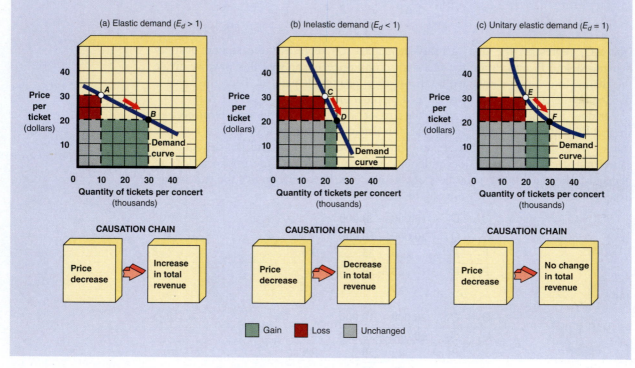

5-1c Elastic Demand ($E_d > 1$)

Suppose Steel Porcupines' demand curve is as depicted in Exhibit 1(a). Using the above midpoints formula, which drops the 2 as a divisor, if the group lowers its ticket price from $30 to $20, the quantity demanded increases from 10,000 to 30,000. Using the midpoints formula, we obtain a value for the price elasticity of demand of 2.5 and this means, for example, that a 20 percent reduction in ticket price brings a 50 percent increase in quantity demanded. Whenever $E_d > 1$, like $E_d = 2.5$, we say that demand is elastic. **Elastic demand** is a condition in which the percentage change in quantity demanded is greater than the percentage change in price. Demand is elastic when the elasticity coefficient is greater than 1. Because the percentage change in quantity

Elastic demand
A condition in which the percentage change in quantity demanded is greater than the percentage change in price.

demanded is greater than the percentage change in price, the drop in price causes total revenue to rise. **Total revenue (TR)** is the total number of dollars a firm earns from the sale of a good or service, which is equal to its price multiplied by the quantity demanded. Perhaps the simplest way to tell whether demand is elastic, unitary elastic, or inelastic is to observe the response of total revenue as the price of a product changes. For example, in Exhibit 1(a), the total revenue at $30 is $300,000. The total revenue at $20 is $600,000. Compare the shaded rectangles under the demand curve, representing total revenue at each price. The gray area is an amount of total revenue unaffected by the price change. Note that the green shaded area gained at $20 per ticket ($400,000) is greater than the red shaded area lost at $30 per ticket ($100,000). This net gain of $300,000 causes the total revenue to increase by this amount when Steel Porcupines lowers the ticket price from $30 to $20.

Total revenue (TR)
The total number of dollars a firm earns from the sale of a good or service, which is equal to its price multiplied by the quantity demanded.

5-1d Inelastic Demand ($E_d < 1$)

The demand curve in Exhibit 1(b) is inelastic. The quantity demanded is less responsive to a change in price. Here a fall in Steel Porcupines' ticket price from $30 to $20 causes the quantity demanded to increase by just 5,000 tickets (20,000 to 25,000 tickets). Using the midpoints formula, $E_d = 0.55$. This means for every one percent change in the price there is only a 0.55 percent change in the quantity demanded. For example, a 20 percent fall in the ticket price causes an 11 percent rise in the quantity demanded. Therefore, demand is inelastic. **Inelastic demand** is a condition in which the percentage change in quantity demanded is less than the percentage change in price. Demand is inelastic when the elasticity coefficient is less than 1. When demand is inelastic, the drop in price causes total revenue to fall from $600,000 to $500,000. Note the net change in the shaded rectangles.

Inelastic demand
A condition in which the percentage change in quantity demanded is less than the percentage change in price.

5-1e Unitary Elastic Demand ($E_d = 1$)

An interesting case exists when a demand curve is neither elastic nor inelastic. Exhibit 1 (c) shows a demand curve for which any percentage change in price along the curve causes an exact proportional change in quantity demanded. When this situation occurs, the total amount of money spent on a good or service does not vary with changes in price. If Steel Porcupines drops the ticket price from $30 to $20, the quantity demanded rises from 20,000 to 30,000; therefore, using the midpoints formula, $E_d = 1$ and this means that for every 1 percent change in the price there is a 1 percent change in the quantity demanded. For example, a 20 percent decrease in price brings about a 20 percent increase in quantity demanded. If this is the case, demand is unitary elastic ($E_d = 1$), and the total revenue remains unchanged at $600,000. **Unitary elastic demand** is defined as a condition in which the percentage change in quantity demanded is equal to the percentage change in price. Because the percentage change in price equals the percentage change in quantity, total revenue does not change regardless of changes in price.

Unitary elastic demand
A condition in which the percentage change in quantity demanded is equal to the percentage change in price.

5-1f Perfectly Elastic Demand ($E_d = \infty$)

Two extreme cases are shown in Exhibit 2. These represent the limits between which the three demand curves explained earlier fall. Suppose for the sake of argument that a demand curve is perfectly horizontal, as shown in Exhibit 2(a). At a price of $20, buyers

EXHIBIT 2 Perfectly Elastic and Perfectly Inelastic Demand

Here two extreme demand curves for Steel Porcupines' concert tickets are presented. Part (a) shows a demand curve that is a horizontal line. Such a demand curve is perfectly elastic. At $20 per ticket, Steel Porcupines can sell as many concert tickets as it wishes. At any price above $20, the quantity demanded falls from an infinite number to zero.

Part (b) shows a demand curve that is a vertical line. This demand curve is perfectly inelastic. No matter what the ticket price is, the quantity demanded remains unchanged at 20,000 tickets.

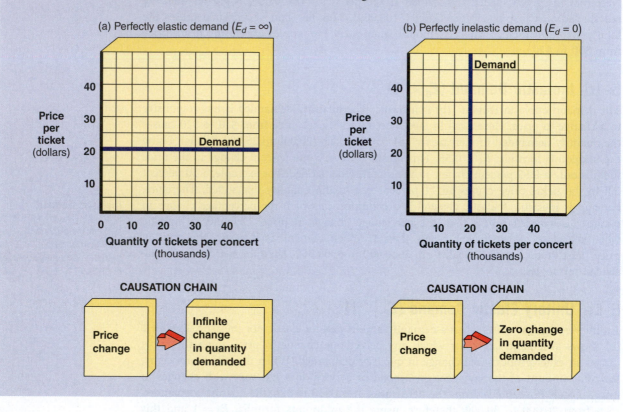

Perfectly elastic demand

A condition in which a small percentage change in price brings about an infinite percentage change in quantity demanded.

Perfectly inelastic demand

A condition in which the quantity demanded does not change as the price changes.

are willing to buy as many tickets as the Steel Porcupines band is willing to offer for sale. At higher prices, buyers buy nothing. For example, at $20.01 per ticket or higher, buyers will buy zero tickets. If so, $E_d = \infty$, and demand is perfectly elastic. **Perfectly elastic demand** is a condition in which a small percentage change in price brings about an infinite percentage change in quantity demanded.

5-1g Perfectly Inelastic Demand ($E_d = 0$)

Exhibit 2(b) shows the other extreme case, which is a perfectly vertical demand curve. No matter how high or low Steel Porcupines' ticket price is, the quantity demanded remains the same, at 20,000 tickets. Such a demand curve is perfectly inelastic, and $E_d = 0$. **Perfectly inelastic demand** is a condition in which the quantity demanded does not change as the price changes.

Exhibit 3 summarizes the ranges for price elasticity of demand.

EXHIBIT 3 Price Elasticity of Demand Terminology

Elasticity coefficient	Definition	Demand	Graph
$E_d > 1$	Percentage change in quantity demanded is greater than the percentage change in price	Elastic	
$E_d < 1$	Percentage change in quantity demanded is less than the percentage change in price	Inelastic	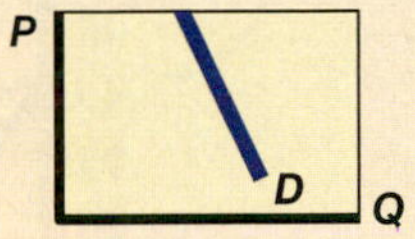
$E_d = 1$	Percentage change in quantity demanded is equal to the percentage change in price	Unitary elastic	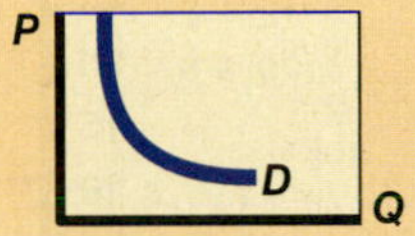
$E_d = \infty$	Percentage change in quantity demanded is infinite in relation to the percentage change in price	Perfectly elastic	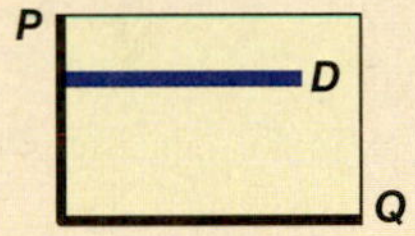
$E_d = 0$	Quantity demanded does not change as the price changes	Perfectly inelastic	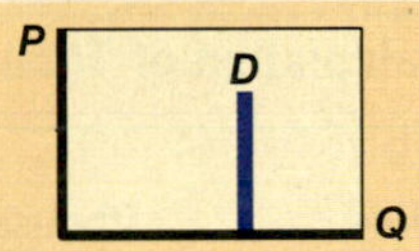

5-2 PRICE ELASTICITY OF DEMAND VARIATIONS ALONG A DEMAND CURVE

The price elasticity of demand for a downward-sloping straight-line demand curve varies as we move along the curve. Look at Exhibit 4, which shows a linear demand curve in part (a) and the corresponding total revenue curve in part (b). Begin at $40 on the demand curve and move down to $35, to $30, to $25, and so on. The table in Exhibit 4 lists variations in the total revenue and the elasticity coefficient (E_d) at different ticket prices. As we move down the upper segment of the demand curve, price elasticity of demand falls, and total revenue rises. For example, measured over the price range of $35 to $30, the price elasticity of demand is 4.33, so this segment of demand is elastic ($E_d > 1$). Between these two prices, total revenue increases from $175,000 to $300,000. At $20, price elasticity is unitary elastic ($E_d = 1$), and total revenue is maximized at $400,000. As we move down the lower segment of the demand curve, price elasticity of demand falls below a value of 1.0, and total revenue falls. Over the price range of $15 to $10, for example, the price elasticity of demand is 0.45, and, therefore, this segment of

EXHIBIT 4   The Variation in Elasticity and Total Revenue along a Hypothetical Demand Curve

Part (a) shows a straight-line demand curve and its three elasticity ranges. In the $40–$20 price range, demand is elastic. As price decreases in this range, total revenue increases. At $20, demand is unitary elastic, and total revenue is at its maximum. In the $20–$5 price range, demand is inelastic. As price decreases in this range, total revenue decreases. The total revenue (TR) curve is plotted in part (b) to trace its relationship to price elasticity.

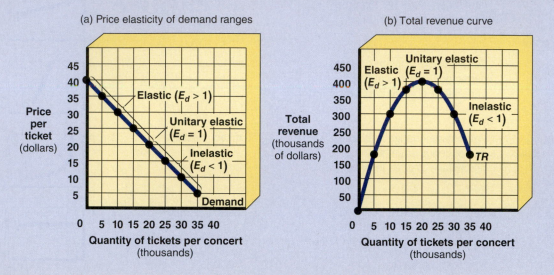

(a) Price elasticity of demand ranges

(b) Total revenue curve

Calculation of Total Revenue and Elasticity along a Hypothetical Demand Curve

Price	Quantity (thousands of tickets)	Total revenue (thousands of dollars)	Elasticity coefficient (E_d)	Price elasticity of demand
$40	0	$0		
			15.00	Elastic
35	5	175		
			4.33	Elastic
30	10	300		
			2.20	Elastic
25	15	375		
			1.29	Elastic
20	20	400	1.00	Unitary elastic
			0.78	Inelastic
15	25	375		
			0.45	Inelastic
10	30	300		
			0.23	Inelastic
5	35	175		

demand is inelastic $(E_d < 1)$. Between these two prices, total revenue decreases from $375,000 to $300,000.

CONCLUSION

The price elasticity coefficient of demand applies only to a specific range of prices.

It is no coincidence that the demand curve in Exhibit 4(a) has elastic, unitary elastic, and inelastic segments. In fact, *any downward-sloping straight-line demand curve has ranges of all three of these types of price elasticity of demand.* As we move downward from the top of the demand curve, first there is an elastic range; next a unitary elastic range, and finally an inelastic range. Why? Recall that price elasticity of demand is a ratio of percentage changes. At the upper end of the demand curve, quantities demanded are lower, and prices are higher. A change of 1 unit in quantity demanded is a large percentage change. On the other hand, a $1 price change is a relatively small percentage change. At the lower end of the curve, the situation reverses. A 1-unit change in quantity demanded is a small percentage change. A $1 price change is a relatively larger percentage change. Now pause and refer back to parts (a) and (b) of Exhibit 1. If we examine changes in price along the entire length of these demand curves, we will find elastic, unitary elastic, and inelastic segments.

Exhibit 5 summarizes the relationships between elasticity, price change, and total revenue.

CHECKPOINT

Will Fliers Flock to Low Summer Fares?
The marketing staff at American Airlines is concerned over low sales revenues and announces special cuts in its fares this summer. The New York to Los Angeles fare, for example, is reduced from $500 to $420. Does the American Airlines staff think demand is elastic, unitary elastic, or inelastic?

EXHIBIT 5 Relationships among Elasticity, Price Change, and Total Revenue

Price elasticity of demand	Elasticity coefficient	Price	Total revenue
Elastic	$E_d > 1$	↓	↑
Elastic	$E_d > 1$	↑	↓
Unitary elastic	$E_d = 1$	↑↓	No change
Inelastic	$E_d < 1$	↓	↓
Inelastic	$E_d < 1$	↑	↑

5-3 DETERMINANTS OF PRICE ELASTICITY OF DEMAND

Economists have estimated price elasticity of demand for various goods and services. Exhibit 6 presents some of these estimates, and as you can see, the elasticity coefficients vary a great deal. For example, the demand for automobiles and for chinaware is elastic. On the other hand, the demand for jewelry and watches and for theater and opera tickets is inelastic. The demand for tires is approximately unitary elastic. Why do the price elasticities of demand for these products vary so much? The following factors cause these differences.

5-3a Availability of Substitutes

By far, the most important influence on price elasticity of demand is the availability of substitutes. Demand becomes more elastic for a good or service when the number of close substitutes increases. If the price of cars rises, consumers can switch to buses, trains, bicycles, and walking. The more public transportation is available, the more responsive quantity demanded is to a change in the price of cars. When consumers have limited alternatives, the demand for a good or service is more price inelastic.

EXHIBIT 6 Estimated Price Elasticities of Demand

Item	Elasticity coefficient	
	Short run	Long run
Automobiles	1.87	2.24
Chinaware	1.54	2.55
Movies	0.87	3.67
Tires	0.86	1.19
Commuter rail fares	0.62	1.59
Jewelry and watches	0.41	0.67
Medical care	0.31	0.92
Housing	0.30	1.88
Gasoline	0.34	0.84
Theater and opera tickets	0.18	0.31
Foreign travel	0.14	1.77
Air travel	0.10	2.40

SOURCES: Martijn Brons, PeterNijkamp, Eric Pels, and Piet Rietveld, "A Meta-Analysis of the Price Elasticity of Gasoline Demand. A SUR Approach," *Energy Economics*, Volume 30, Issue 5, September 2008, pp. 2105–2122; Robert Archibald and Robert Gillingham, "An Analysis of the Short-Run Consumer Demand for Gasoline Using Household Survey Data," *Review of Economics and Statistics* 62 (November 1980), pp. 622–628; Hendrik S. Houthakker and Lester D. Taylor, *Consumer Demand in the United States: Analyses and Projections* (Cambridge, MA: Harvard University Press, 1970, pp. 56–149; Richard Voith, "The Long-Run Elasticity of Demand for Commuter Rail Transportation," *Journal of Urban Economics* 30 (November 1991), pp. 360–372.

If the price of tobacco rises, people addicted to it have few substitutes because not smoking is unappealing to most users.

CONCLUSION

The price elasticity coefficient of demand is directly related to the availability of suitable substitutes for a product.

Price elasticity also depends on the market used to measure demand. For example, studies show the price elasticity of Toyota Camrys is greater than that of automobiles in general. Camrys compete with other cars sold by Toyota, GM, Ford, Chrysler, Honda, and other automakers and with buses and trains—all of which are substitutes for Camrys. But using the broad class of cars eliminates these specific types of cars as competitors. Instead, substitutes for automobiles include buses and trains, which are also substitutes for Camrys. In short, there are more close substitutes for Camrys than there are for all cars.

CHECKPOINT

Can Trade Sanctions Affect Elasticity of Demand for Cars?
Assume Congress prohibits the sale of Japanese luxury cars, such as Lexus, Acura, and Infiniti, in the United States. How would this affect the price elasticity of demand for Mercedes, BMWs, and Jaguars in the United States?

5-3b Share of Budget Spent on the Product

When the price of salt changes, consumers pay little attention. Why should they notice? The price of salt or toothpicks can double, and this purchase will remain a small percentage of one's budget. If, however, college tuition, the price of dinners at restaurants, or housing prices double, people will look for alternatives. These goods and services account for a large part of people's budgets.

CONCLUSION

The price elasticity coefficient of demand is directly related to the percentage of one's budget spent for a good or service.

5-3c Adjustment to a Price Change Over Time

Exhibit 6 separates the elasticity coefficients into short-run and long-run categories. As time passes, buyers can respond fully to a change in the price of a product by finding more substitutes. Consider the demand for gasoline. In the short run, people find it hard to cut back the amount they buy when the price rises sharply. They are accustomed to driving back and forth to work alone in their cars. The typical short-run response is to cut luxury travel and reduce speed on trips. If high prices persist over time, car buyers will find ways to cut back. They can buy cars with better fuel economy (more miles per gallon), form car pools, and ride buses or commuter trains. This explains why the

YOU'RE THE ECONOMIST

Applicable Concept: Price Elasticity of Demand

Cigarette Smoking Price Elasticity of Demand

Tobacco use is one of the chief preventable causes of death in the world. Since 1964, health warnings have been mandated in the United States on tobacco advertising, including billboards and printed advertising. In 1971, television advertising was prohibited. Most states have banned smoking in state buildings, and the federal government has restricted smoking in federal offices and military facilities.

One way to curb smoking is to raise cigarette taxes. This can be especially effective in preventing teenagers from picking up the habit. The passage of the Children's Health Insurance Program Reauthorization Act of 2009 more than doubled the cigarette tax per pack from $0.39 to $1.01 per pack.[1] Critics argue that this price increase would be a massive tax on low-income Americans that would generate huge revenues to finance additional government programs and spending. In fact, proponents in part raised the cigarette tax to fund the increased costs of expanding the State Children Health Insurance Program (SCHIP). In addition, proponents argued that it is not about taxes. Instead, the legislation is an attack on the death march of Americans who die early from tobacco-related diseases.

Estimates of the price elasticity of demand for cigarettes in the United States and other high-income countries fall in the inelastic range of 0.62. This means that if prices rise by 10 percent, cigarette consumption will fall by about 6 percent.[2] Moreover, estimates of the price elasticity of demand range significantly across states from 2.00 (Kentucky) to 0.09 (Mississippi).[3] The price elasticity of demand for cigarettes also appears to vary by education. Less-educated adults are more responsive to price changes than better-educated adults. This finding supports the theory that less-educated people are more present-oriented, or "myopic," than people with more education. Thus, less-educated individuals tend to

© yurchello108/Shutterstock.com

be more influenced by current changes in the price of a pack of cigarettes.[4] Another study in 2000 confirmed that education has strong negative effects on the quantity of cigarettes smoked, especially for high-income individuals. The presence of young children reduces smoking, with the effect most pronounced for women.[5]

A study published in *Health Economics* estimated the relationship between cigarette smoking and price for 34,145 respondents aged 15–29. The price elasticity of smoking was inelastic and varied inversely with age: 0.83 for ages 15–17, 0.52 for ages 18–20, 0.37 for ages 21–23, 0.20 for ages 24–26, and 0.09 for ages 27–29. Thus, younger people were more likely to reduce the number of cigarettes smoked in response to increased prices.[6] Although elasticity measures for cigarettes have been very stable of the last numerous decades, this could be changing with the introduction of substitutes like smokeless tobacco and e-cigarettes.[7]

ANALYZE THE ISSUE According to the previous discussion, what factors influence the price elasticity of demand for cigarettes? What other factors not mentioned in the article might influence the price elasticity of demand for cigarettes?

1. Michael C. Fiore, "Tobacco Control in the Obama Era—Substantial Progress, Remaining Challenges," *New England Journal of Medicine*, 2016; 375:1410-1412, October 13, 2016, DOI: 10.1056/NEJMP 1607850.

2. Jon P. Nelson, "Cigarette Demand, Structural Change, and Advertising Bans: International Evidence, 1970–1995," *Contribution to Economic Analysis and Policy* 2, no. 1, (2003), article 10.

3. Craig A. Gallet, "Health Information and Cigarette Consumption: Supply and Spatial Consideration," *Empirica* 33, no. 1, (March 2006), pp. 35–47.

4. Frank Chaloupka et al., "Tax, Price and Cigarette Smoking," *Tobacco Control* 11, no. 1, (March 2002): pp. 62–73.

5. Joni Hersch, "Gender, Income Levels, and the Demand for Cigarettes," *Journal of Risk and Uncertainty* 21, no. 2–3 (November 2000): pp. 263–282.

6. Jeffrey E. Harris and Sandra W. Chan, "The Continuum of Addiction: Cigarette Smoking in Relation to Price among Americans Aged 15–29," *Health Economics* 8, no. 1, (February 1999), pp. 81–86.

7. "Big Tobacco Takes Its Last Drag as Economic Change Looms," *Forbes*, September 6, 2013. Found at https://www.forbes.com/sites/thestreet/2013/09/06/big-tobacco-takes-its-last-drag-as-economic-change-looms/#68452384819f.

short-run elasticity coefficient of gasoline in the exhibit is more inelastic at 0.34 than the long-run elasticity coefficient of 0.84.

> In general, the price elasticity coefficient of demand is higher the longer a price change persists.

CONCLUSION

5-4 OTHER ELASTICITY MEASURES

The elasticity concept has other applications beyond calculating the price elasticity of demand. Broadly defined, it is a technique for measuring the response of one variable to changes in some other variable.

5-4a Income Elasticity of Demand

Recall from Chapter 3 that an increase in income can increase demand (shift the demand curve rightward) for a normal good or service and decrease demand (shift the demand curve leftward) for an inferior good or service. To measure exactly how consumption responds to changes in income, economists calculate the income elasticity of demand. **Income elasticity of demand** is the ratio of the percentage change in the quantity demanded of a good or service to a given percentage change in income. We use a midpoints formula similar to the one we used for calculating price elasticity of demand:

Income elasticity of demand
The ratio of the percentage change in the quantity demanded of a good or service to a given percentage change in income.

$$E_I = \frac{\text{percentage change in quantity demanded}}{\text{percentage change in income}}$$

$$E_I = \frac{\%\Delta Q}{\%\Delta I} = \frac{\dfrac{Q_2 - Q_1}{Q_1 + Q_2}}{\dfrac{I_2 - I_1}{I_1 + I_2}}$$

Where E_I is the income elasticity of demand coefficient, Q_1 and Q_2 represent quantities demanded before and after the income change, and I_1 and I_2 represent income before and after the income change.

For a *normal* good or service, the income elasticity of demand is *positive*, $E_I > 0$. Recall that for this type of good, demand and income move in the same direction. Thus, the variables in the numerator and denominator change in the same direction. For an *inferior* good or service, the reverse is true, and the income elasticity of demand is *negative*, $E_I < 0$.

Why is the income elasticity coefficient important? Returning to our rock group example, the Steel Porcupines band needs to know the impact of a recession on ticket sales. During a downturn when consumers' incomes fall, if a rock concert is a *normal good*, the quantity of ticket sales falls. Conversely, if a rock concert is an *inferior good*, the quantity of ticket sales rises. To illustrate, suppose consumers' incomes increase from \$1,000 to \$1,250 per month. As a result, the quantity of tickets demanded increases from 10,000 to 15,000. Based on these data, is a rock concert a normal or an inferior good? We compute as follows:

$$E_I = \frac{\dfrac{Q_2 - Q_1}{Q_1 + Q_2}}{\dfrac{I_2 - I_1}{I_1 + I_2}} = \frac{\dfrac{15,000 - 10,000}{10,000 + 15,000}}{\dfrac{1,250 - 1,000}{1,250 + 1,000}} = \frac{0.20}{0.11} = 1.8$$

The computed income elasticity of demand coefficient of 1.8 (technically equal to 1.81818181…) summarizes the relationship between changes in rock concert ticket purchases and changes in income. E_I is a positive number; therefore, a rock concert is a normal good because people buy more when their incomes rise. Also, ticket purchases are very responsive to changes in income. When income rises by 11 percent, ticket sales increase by more (20 percent = 11 × 1.81818181…).

Exhibit 7 lists estimated income elasticity of demand for selected products.

5-4b Cross-Elasticity of Demand

In Chapter 3, we learned that a change in the price of one good, say, Y, can cause the consumption of another good, say, X, to change (see prices of related goods in Exhibit 5 in Chapter 3). In Exhibit 1(b) in Chapter 4, for example, a sharp rise in the price of gasoline (a complement) causes the number of gas guzzlers purchased to decline. This responsiveness of the quantity demanded to changes in the price of some other good is

EXHIBIT 7 Estimated Income Elasticities of Demand

Item	Elasticity coefficient	
	Short run	Long run
Potatoes	N.A.	0.81
Furniture	2.60	0.53
Dental services	0.38	1.00
Automobiles	5.50	1.07
Physician services	0.28	1.15
Clothing	0.95	1.17
Shoes	0.90	1.50
Gasoline and oil	0.55	1.36
Jewelry and watches	1.00	1.60
Toilet articles	0.25	3.74

SOURCES: Hendrik S. Houthakker and Lester D. Taylor, *Consumer Demand in the United States: Analyses and Projections* (Cambridge, MA: Harvard University Press, 1970); Dale M. Helen, "The Structure of Food Demand: Interrelatedness and Duality," *American Journal of Agricultural Economics* 64, no. 2 (May 1982): 213–221.

estimated by the cross-elasticity of demand. **Cross-elasticity of demand** is the ratio of the percentage change in the quantity demanded of a good or service to a given percentage change in the price of another good or service. Again, we use the midpoints formula as follows to compute the cross-elasticity coefficient of demand:

Cross-elasticity of demand
The ratio of the percentage change in the quantity demanded of a good or service to a given percentage change in the price of another good or service.

$$E_c = \frac{\text{percentage change in quantity demanded of one good}}{\text{percentage change in price of another good}}$$

$$E_c = \frac{\%\Delta Q_x}{\%\Delta P_Y} = \frac{\dfrac{Q_{x_2} - Q_{x_1}}{Q_{x_1} + Q_{x_2}}}{\dfrac{P_{Y_2} - P_{Y_1}}{P_{Y_1} + P_{Y_2}}}$$

where E_c is the cross-elasticity coefficient, Q_1 and Q_2 represent quantities before and after the price of another good or service changes, and P_1 and P_2 represent the price of another good or service before and after the price change.

The cross-elasticity coefficient reveals whether a good or service is a *substitute* or a *complement*. For example, suppose Coke increases its price 10 percent, which causes consumers to buy 5 percent more Pepsi. The cross-elasticity of demand for Pepsi is a *positive* 0.50 (+5 percent/+10 percent). Since $E_c > 0$, Coke and Pepsi are *substitutes* because the numerator and denominator variables change in the same direction. The larger the positive coefficient, the greater the substitutability between the two goods.

Now suppose there is a 50 percent increase in the price of motor oil and the quantity demanded of gasoline decreases by 10 percent. The cross-elasticity of demand for gasoline is a *negative* 0.20 (-10 percent/+50 percent). The variables in the numerator and denominator change in opposite directions. Since $E_c < 0$, these two goods are *complements*. The larger the negative coefficient, the greater the complementary relationship between the two goods.

5-4c Price Elasticity of Supply

The price elasticity of supply closely follows the price elasticity of demand concept. **Price elasticity of supply** is the ratio of the percentage change in the quantity supplied of a product to the percentage change in its price. This elasticity coefficient is calculated using the following formula:

Price elasticity of supply
The ratio of the percentage change in the quantity supplied of a product to the percentage change in its price.

$$E_s = \frac{\text{percentage change in quantity supplied}}{\text{percentage change in price}}$$

where E_s is the price elasticity of supply coefficient. Since price and quantity supplied change in the same direction, the elasticity coefficient is a positive value. Economists use terminology corresponding to that for the elasticity of demand. Supply is *elastic* when $E_s > 1$, *unit elastic* when $E_s = 1$, *inelastic* when $E_s < 1$, *perfectly elastic* when $E_s = \infty$, and *perfectly inelastic* when $E_s = 0$. Exhibit 8 shows three of these cases.

In Chapter 8, we will explain why the time period of analysis is a primary determinant of the shape of the supply curve. More specifically, it will be shown that price elasticity of supply is greater in the long run than in the short run. Thus, the long-run supply curve will be flatter.

Exhibit 9 gives a summary of the three elasticity concepts presented in this section.

EXHIBIT 8 Price Elasticity of Supply

This figure shows three supply curves. As shown in part (a), a small change in price changes the quantity supplied by an infinite amount: $E_s = \infty$. Part (b) shows the quantity supplied is unaffected by a change in price, $E_s = 0$, and supply is perfectly inelastic. In part (c), the percentage change in quantity supplied is equal to the percentage change in price: $E_s = 1$.

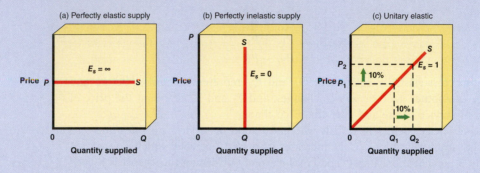

EXHIBIT 9 Summary of Other Elasticity Concepts

Type	Definition	Elasticity coefficient possibilities	Terminology
Income elasticity of demand	$\dfrac{\text{Percentage change in quantity demanded}}{\text{Percentage change in income}}$	$E_I > 0$	Normal good
		$E_I < 0$	Inferior good
		$E_I > 1$	Income elastic
		$E_I < 1$	Income inelastic
		$E_I = 1$	Income unitary elastic
Cross-elasticity of demand	$\dfrac{\text{Percentage change in quantity demanded of one good}}{\text{Percentage change in price of another good}}$	$E_c < 0$	Complements
		$E_c > 0$	Substitutes
Price elasticity of supply	$\dfrac{\text{Percentage change in quantity supplied}}{\text{Percentage change in price}}$	$E_s > 1$	Elastic
		$E_s = 1$	Unitary elastic
		$E_s < 1$	Inelastic
		$E_s = \infty$	Perfectly elastic
		$E_s = 0$	Perfectly inelastic

5-5 PRICE ELASTICITY AND THE IMPACT OF TAXATION

Who pays a tax levied on sellers of goods such as gasoline, cigarettes, and alcoholic beverages? One way to answer this question is to say that if the government places an excise ("per unit") tax on, say, gasoline, the gasoline companies pay the tax. They collect the tax when they sell gas and write the checks to the government for the tax. But this is not the whole story. Instead of looking simply at who writes the checks, economists use the elasticity concept to analyze who "really" pays a tax. **Tax incidence** is the share of a tax ultimately paid by consumers and sellers. In this section, we show that even though taxes are collected from sellers, buyers do not escape a share of the tax burden. The tax incidence depends on the price elasticities of demand and supply. Let's look at two examples.

Tax incidence
The share of a tax ultimately paid by consumers and sellers.

Suppose the federal government decides to raise the gasoline tax $0.50 per gallon. Exhibit 10 shows the impact of the tax on different demand curves. At E_1 in part (a), the equilibrium price before the tax is $3.00 per gallon and the equilibrium quantity is 30 million gallons per day. The effect of the tax is to shift the supply curve upward equal to the amount of the tax; or otherwise stated, it shifts the supply curve leftward from S_1 to S_2. From the sellers' viewpoint, the cost of each gallon of gasoline increases $0.50 per gallon at any possible selling price. The effect is exactly the same as if the price of crude oil or any resource used to produce gasoline increased.

Sellers would like consumers to pay the entire amount of the tax. This would occur if consumers would pay $3.50 per gallon for the same 30 million gallons per day they purchased before the tax. But the leftward shift in supply establishes a new equilibrium at E_2. The new equilibrium price is $3.25 per gallon, and the equilibrium quantity falls to 25 million gallons per day. At E_2, the entire shaded area represents the tax revenue. The government collects $12.5 million per day, which equals the $0.50 per gallon tax times the 25 million gallons sold each day. The vertical line between points E_2 and T represents the $0.50 tax per gallon. Since consumers now pay $3.25 instead of $3.00 per gallon, they pay one-half of the tax. The sellers pay the remaining half of the tax. Now the sellers send $0.50 to Uncle Sam and keep $2.75 compared to the $3.00 per gallon they kept before the tax.

> **CONCLUSION**
>
> If the demand curve slopes downward and the supply curve slopes upward, sellers cannot raise the price by the full amount of the tax.

Part (b) of Exhibit 10 is a special case in which the market price increases by the full amount of the tax per gallon. Here the demand for gasoline is perfectly inelastic. In this case, buyers do not decrease the quantity demanded in response to the decrease in supply caused by the tax. The quantity demanded is 30 million gallons per day before and after the tax. The price, however, increases from E_1 to E_2 by exactly the amount of tax per unit from $3.00 to $3.50 per gallon, and therefore consumers pay the entire burden of the tax. After paying the tax, sellers receive a net price of $3.00 per gallon. The total tax revenue collected by the government is the shaded area. Each day $15 million is collected, which equals the $0.50 per gallon tax multiplied by 30 million gallons sold each day.

> **CONCLUSION**
>
> In the case where demand is perfectly inelastic, sellers can raise the price by the full amount of a tax.

EXHIBIT 10   The Tax Incidence of a Tax on Gasoline

In parts (a) and (b), S_1 is the supply curve before the imposition of a tax of $0.50 per gallon on gasoline. The demand curve is not affected by this tax collected from the sellers. The initial equilibrium is E_1. Before the tax, the price is $3.00 per gallon, and 30 million gallons are bought and sold.

In part (a), the equilibrium price rises to $3.25 per gallon at E_2 as a result of the tax. After the tax is paid, sellers receive only $2.75 per gallon (point T) instead of the $3.00 they received before the tax. Thus, buyers pay $0.25 of the tax per gallon, and sellers bear the remaining $0.25. The shaded area is the total tax collected.

As shown in part (b), a tax collected from sellers can be fully shifted to buyers in the unlikely case that demand is perfectly inelastic. Since the quantity of gasoline purchased is unresponsive to a change in price, sellers receive $3.00 per gallon before and after they pay the tax.

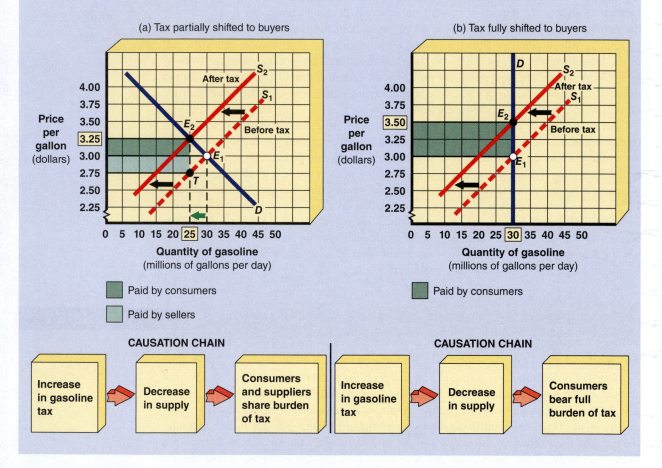

Can Honda Compete with Itself?

When Honda introduced the Acura to compete with European luxury cars, there was a danger that the new line would take sales away from Honda's Accord. To make Acura more competitive with other luxury cars, suppose Honda cuts the price of Acura while keeping the price of Accord unchanged. If Honda's fear comes true, will it find a negative cross-elasticity of demand, or a positive cross-elasticity of demand?

CHECKPOINT

Key Concepts

Price elasticity of
  demand

Elastic demand

Total revenue (TR)

Inelastic demand

Unitary elastic demand

Perfectly elastic demand

Perfectly inelastic
  demand

Income elasticity of
  demand

Cross-elasticity of
  demand

Price elasticity of supply

Tax incidence

Summary

- **Price elasticity of demand** is a measure of the responsiveness of the quantity demanded to a change in price. Specifically, price elasticity of demand is the ratio of the percentage change in quantity demanded to the percentage change in price.

$$E_d = \frac{\%\Delta Q}{\%\Delta P} = \frac{\dfrac{Q_2 - Q_1}{Q_1 + Q_2}}{\dfrac{P_2 - P_1}{P_1 + P_2}}$$

- **Elastic demand** occurs where there is a change of more than 1 percent in quantity demanded in response to a 1 percent change in price. Demand is elastic when the elasticity coefficient is greater than 1 and *total revenue* (price times quantity) varies inversely with the direction of the price change.

- **Inelastic demand** occurs where there is a change of less than 1 percent in quantity demanded in response to a 1 percent change in price. Demand is inelastic when the elasticity coefficient is less than 1 and total revenue varies directly with the direction of the price change.

- **Unitary elastic demand** occurs where there is a 1 percent change in quantity demanded in response to a 1 percent change in price. Demand is unitary elastic when the elasticity coefficient equals 1 and total revenue remains constant as the price changes.

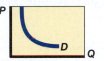

- **Perfectly elastic demand** occurs when the quantity demanded declines to zero for even the slightest rise or fall in price. This is an extreme case in which the demand curve is horizontal and the elasticity coefficient equals infinity.

- **Perfectly inelastic demand** occurs when the quantity demanded does not change in response to price changes. This is an extreme case in which the demand curve is vertical and the elasticity coefficient equals zero.

- **Determinants of price elasticity of demand** include

    the availability of substitutes,

    the percentage of one's budget spent on the product, and

    the length of time allowed for adjustment.

    Each of these factors is directly related to the elasticity coefficient.

- **Income elasticity of demand** is the percentage change in quantity demanded divided by the percentage change in income. For a *normal* good or service, income elasticity of demand is positive. For an *inferior* good or service, income elasticity of demand is negative.

- **Cross-elasticity of demand** is the percentage change in the quantity demanded of one product caused by a change in the price of another product. When the cross-elasticity of demand is positive, the two products are substitutes. When the cross-elasticity of demand is negative, the two products are complements.

- **Price elasticity of supply** is a measure of the responsiveness of the quantity supplied to a change in price. Price elasticity of supply is the ratio of the percentage change in quantity supplied to the percentage change in price.

- **Tax incidence** is the share of a tax ultimately paid by buyers and sellers. Facing a downward-sloping demand curve and an upward-sloping supply curve, sellers cannot raise the price by the full amount of the tax. If the demand curve is vertical, sellers will raise the price by the full amount of the tax.

Tax Incidence of Gasoline Tax

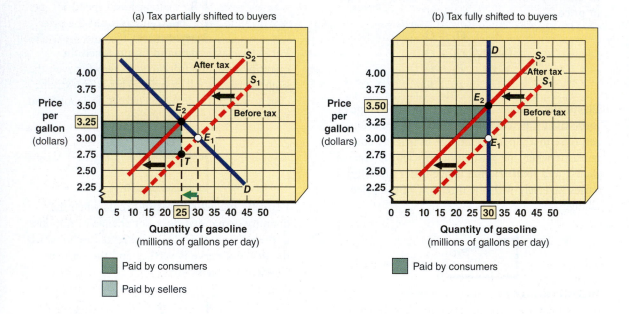

Summary of Conclusion Statements

- The price elasticity coefficient of demand applies only to a specific range of prices.

- The price elasticity coefficient of demand is directly related to the availability of suitable substitutes for a product.

- The price elasticity coefficient of demand is directly related to the percentage of one's budget spent for a good or service.

- In general, the price elasticity coefficient of demand is higher the longer a price change persists.

- If the demand curve slopes downward and the supply curve slopes upward, sellers cannot raise the price by the full amount of the tax.

- In the case where demand is perfectly inelastic, sellers can raise the price by the full amount of a tax.

Study Questions and Problems

Please see Appendix A for answers to the odd-numbered questions. Your instructor has access to the answers for even-numbered questions.

1. If the price of a good or service increases and the total revenue received by the seller declines, is the demand for this good over this segment of the demand curve elastic or inelastic? Explain.

2. Suppose the price elasticity of demand for farm products is inelastic. If the federal government wants to follow a policy of increasing income for farmers, what type of programs will the government enact?

3. Suppose the price elasticity of demand for used cars is estimated to be 3. What does this mean? What will be the effect on the quantity demanded for used cars if the price rises by 10 percent?

4. Consider the following demand schedule:

Price	Quantity demanded	Elasticity coefficient
$25	20	
20	40	_____
15	60	_____
10	80	_____
5	100	_____

What is the price elasticity of demand between
a. $P = \$25$ and $P = \$20$?
b. $P = \$20$ and $P = \$15$?
c. $P = \$15$ and $P = \$10$?
d. $P = \$10$ and $P = \$5$?

5. Suppose a university raises its tuition from $3,000 to $3,500. As a result, student enrollment falls from 5,000 to 4,500. Calculate the price elasticity of demand. Is demand elastic, unitary elastic, or inelastic?

6. Will each of the following changes in price cause total revenue to increase, decrease, or remain unchanged?
a. Price falls, and demand is elastic.
b. Price rises, and demand is elastic.

c. Price falls, and demand is unitary elastic.
d. Price rises, and demand is unitary elastic.
e. Price falls, and demand is inelastic.
f. Price rises, and demand is inelastic.

7. Suppose a movie theater raises the price of popcorn 10 percent, but customers do not buy any less popcorn. What does this tell you about the price elasticity of demand? What will happen to total revenue as a result of the price increase?

8. Charles loves Mello Yello and will spend $10 per week on the product no matter what the price. What is his price elasticity of demand for Mello Yello?

9. Which of the following pairs of goods has the higher price elasticity of demand?
a. Oranges or Sunkist oranges.
b. Cars or salt.
c. Foreign travel in the short run or foreign travel in the long run.

10. The Energizer Bunny that "keeps going and going" has been a very successful ad campaign for batteries. Explain the relationship between this slogan and the firm's price elasticity of demand and total revenue.

11. Suppose the income elasticity of demand for furniture is 3.0 and the income elasticity of demand for physician services is 0.3. Compare the impact on furniture and physician services of a recession that reduces consumers' incomes by 10 percent.

12. How might you determine whether Nike and Reebok are in competition with each other?

13. Assume the cross-elasticity of demand for car tires with respect to the price of cars is −2. What does this tell you about the relationship between car tires and cars when the price of cars rises by 10 percent?

14. Consider the following supply schedule:

Price	Quantity supplied	Elasticity coefficient
$10	50	
8	40	_____
6	30	_____
4	20	_____
2	10	_____
0	0	_____

What is the price elasticity of supply between
   a. $P = \$10$ and $P = \$8$?
   b. $P = \$8$ and $P = \$6$?
   c. $P = \$6$ and $P = \$4$?
   d. $P = \$4$ and $P = \$2$?
   e. $P = \$2$ and $P = \$0$?

15. Why would consumers prefer that the government tax products with elastic, rather than inelastic demand?

16. Opponents of increasing the tax on gasoline argue that the big oil companies just pass the tax along to the consumers. Do you agree or disagree? Explain your answer.

✔ CHECKPOINT ANSWERS

Will Fliers Flock to Low Summer Fares?

American Airlines must believe the quantity of airline tickets demanded during the summer is quite responsive to a price cut. For total revenue to rise with a price cut, the quantity demanded must increase by a larger percentage than the percentage decrease in the price. For this to occur, the price elasticity of demand must exceed 1. If you said American Airlines believes demand is elastic, **YOU ARE CORRECT**.

Can Trade Sanctions Affect Elasticity of Demand for Cars?

Because substitutes (Japanese luxury cars) are no longer available to U.S. consumers, the quantity demanded of Mercedes, BMWs, and Jaguars in the United States would be less responsive to changes in the prices for these cars. If you said the price elasticity of demand for Mercedes, BMWs, and Jaguars would become less elastic, **YOU ARE CORRECT**.

Can Honda Compete with Itself?

Determining the effect of cutting the Acura's price on sales of Accords calls for cross-elasticity. Once the price of Acura is cut, Honda would calculate the change in the quantity of Accords demanded. If Acura's decrease in price causes people to buy fewer Accords, Honda is indeed competing with itself. If you said a positive cross-elasticity of demand indicates the two goods are substitutes and they would compete with each other, **YOU ARE CORRECT**.

Sample Quiz

Please see Appendix B for answers to Sample Quiz questions.

1. A perfectly elastic demand curve has an elasticity coefficient of
   a. 0.
   b. 1.
   c. less than 1.
   d. infinity.

2. If the percentage change in the quantity demanded of a good is less than the percentage change in price, price elasticity of demand is
   a. elastic.
   b. inelastic.
   c. perfectly inelastic.
   d. unitary elastic.

3. As shown in Exhibit 11, the price elasticity of demand for good X between points E and B is
   a. $3/7 = 0.43$.
   b. $7/3 = 2.33$.

EXHIBIT **11** Supply and Demand Curves for Good *X*

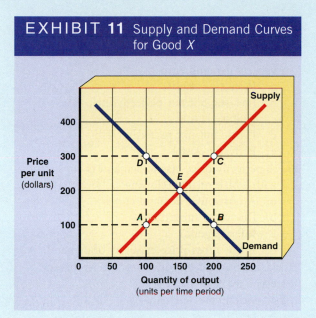

c. unitary elastic.
d. perfectly elastic.

8. The president of Tucker Motors says, "Lowering the price won't sell a single additional Tucker car." The president believes that the price elasticity of demand is
   a. perfectly elastic.
   b. perfectly inelastic.
   c. unitary elastic.
   d. elastic.

9. If a straight-line demand curve slopes down, price elasticity will
   a. remain the same at all points on the demand curve.
   b. change between points along the demand curve.
   c. always be greater than 1.
   d. always equal 1.

10. Along a segment of the demand curve where the price elasticity of demand is less than 1, a decrease in price
    a. is impossible.
    b. will increase total revenue.
    c. will decrease total revenue.
    d. decreases quantity demanded.

11. If Tucker University increases tuition to increase its revenue, it will
    a. not be successful if the demand curve slopes downward.
    b. be successful if demand is elastic.
    c. be successful if demand is inelastic.
    d. be successful if supply is elastic.

12. A demand curve that has constant price elasticity of demand coefficient equal to 1 at *all* points is a (an)
    a. rectangular hyperbola.
    b. downward-sloping straight line.
    c. upward-sloping straight line.
    d. None of the above answers are correct.

13. In Exhibit 12, if the area 0*ABC* equals the area 0*DEF*, the demand curve is
    a. elastic.
    b. inelastic.
    c. unitary elastic.
    d. nonelastic.

14. In Exhibit 12, the change in total revenue resulting from a change in price from *A* to *D* indicates that the demand curve is
    a. elastic.
    b. inelastic.
    c. unitary elastic.
    d. quasi-elastic.

c. 1/2 = 0.50.
d. 1.

4. Which of the following is *true* about the price elasticity of demand on the top part of a linear demand curve?
   a. Demand is inelastic.
   b. Demand is unitary elastic.
   c. Demand is elastic.
   d. It is impossible to tell.

5. Price elasticity of demand tends to be larger in the long run than in the short run. Which of the following is a reason that this statement is true?
   a. Over time, people's incomes rise.
   b. If price rises, over time, producers will be able to offer more substitutes.
   c. Over time, the good will become a smaller and smaller share of people's budgets.
   d. People see fewer and fewer substitutes for the good in the long run.

6. If a decrease in the price of movie tickets increases the total revenue of movie theaters, this is evidence that demand is
   a. price elastic.
   b. price inelastic.
   c. unit elastic with respect to price.
   d. perfectly inelastic.

7. Suppose the president of a college argues that a 25 percent tuition increase will raise revenues for the college. It can be concluded that the president thinks that demand to attend this college is
   a. elastic.
   b. inelastic, but not perfectly inelastic.

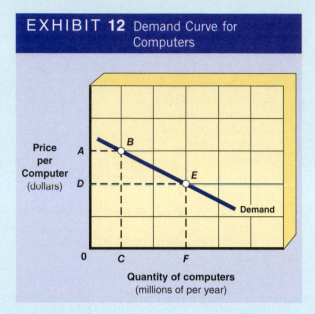

EXHIBIT 12 Demand Curve for Computers

Price per Computer (dollars)

Quantity of computers (millions of per year)

15. If the price elasticity of demand is elastic, then
  a. $E_d < 1$.
  b. consumers are not very responsive to a price increase.
  c. an increase in the price will increase total revenue.
  d. there are a large number of substitute products available.

16. If the quantity of bread demanded rises 2 percent when the price of bread declines 10 percent, then the price elasticity of demand is
  a. 0.2.
  b. 1.
  c. 2.
  d. 10.
  e. cannot be determined.

17. Suppose Sally buys exactly five bars of English toffee each week, regardless of whether the toffee bars are regularly priced at $1 or on sale for $0.50. Based on this information, what is Sally's price elasticity of demand for English toffee in this price range?
  a. 0
  b. 1
  c. Infinity
  d. Cannot be determined.

18. Suppose Bill budgets exactly $50 each month for fresh shrimp regardless of whether shrimp is priced at $10 per pound, or is on sale for $4 per pound. Based on this information, Bill's price elasticity of demand is
  a. 0.
  b. 1.

  c. infinite.
  d. cannot be determined.

19. What is the price elasticity of demand for a vertical demand curve?
  a. Perfectly inelastic
  b. Inelastic but not perfectly inelastic
  c. Unitary elastic
  d. Elastic but not perfectly elastic
  e. Perfectly elastic

20. A perfectly price-elastic demand is consistent with which of the following?
  a. A horizontal demand curve
  b. Few close substitutes
  c. Inferior goods
  d. A low cross-price elasticity of demand

21. If bus travel is an inferior good, its income elasticity of demand is
  a. strictly greater than 1.
  b. positive.
  c. equal to zero.
  d. negative.

22. If a good is inferior in an economic sense,
  a. it is demand price elastic.
  b. it is demand price inelastic.
  c. the income elasticity of demand is negative.
  d. it is a low-quality good.

23. If automobiles and gasoline are complements, then their cross-elasticity coefficient is
  a. strictly greater than 1.
  b. positive.
  c. equal to zero.
  d. negative.

24. Suppose that when price is $10, quantity supplied is 20 units, and when the price is $6, the quantity supplied is 12 units. What is the price elasticity of supply?
  a. 0.5
  b. 0.8
  c. 1.0
  d. 1.5

25. Using supply and demand analysis, which of the following is *true*, the more elastic the demand curve?
  a. The larger the portion of a sales tax that is passed on to the consumer.
  b. The smaller the portion of a sales tax that is passed on to the consumer.
  c. It does not make any difference how flat the demand curve is; the tax is always split evenly between buyer and seller.
  d. The full tax is always passed on to the consumer no matter how flat the demand curve is.

CHAPTER 6

Consumer Choice Theory

CHAPTER PREVIEW

This chapter expands our understanding of demand by investigating more deeply *why* people buy goods and services. In Chapter 3, the law of demand rested on a foundation of common sense and everyday observation. When the price of a Big Mac falls, people *do* buy more, and a price rise causes people to buy less. But there is more to the story.

The focus of this chapter is the logic of consumer behavior. Why does a consumer buy one bundle of goods rather than another? Suppose someone asked why you bought a milkshake and french fries, rather than a Coke and a hot dog. You would probably answer that given the money you had to spend; the Coke and hot dog would have given you less satisfaction. In this chapter, you will transform this simple explanation into consumer choice theory and then connect this theory to the law of demand. The chapter ends with another way to explain the demand curve, which involves effects related to income and the prices of other goods.

IN THIS CHAPTER, YOU WILL LEARN TO SOLVE THESE ECONOMICS PUZZLES:

- Under what conditions might you be willing to pay $10,000 for a gallon of water and 1 cent for a one-carat diamond?

- When ordering Big Macs, milkshakes, pizza, and other goods, how can you obtain the highest possible satisfaction?

- Do white rats obey the law of demand?

6-1 FROM UTILITY TO THE LAW OF DEMAND

The basis of the law of demand is self-interested behavior. Consumers spend their limited budget to satisfy some want, such as listening to a compact disc or driving a new car. The motivation to consume goods and services is to gain utility. **Utility** is the satisfaction, or pleasure, that people receive from consuming a good or service. Utility is want-satisfying power "in the eye of the beholder." Just as wants differ among people, utility received from consumption varies from person to person. Fred's utility from consuming a BMW will probably differ from Maria's utility. In spite of the subjective nature of utility, this section develops in steps the derivation of a demand curve based on the utility concept.

6-1a Total Utility and Marginal Utility

Actual measurement of utility is impossible because only you know the satisfaction from consuming, say, four Big Macs in one day. But suppose we could gauge your total utility of consuming four Big Macs in a day. **Total utility** is the amount of satisfaction received from all the units of a good or service consumed. That is, the utility of the first unit consumed added to that of the second unit, and so on. What units can be used to measure total utility? Economists use a mythical unit called a *util*, which allows us to quantify our thinking about consumer behavior.

No one has invented a "utility meter," but assume we could connect such a meter to your brain. Like taking your temperature, we could read the marginal utility each time you eat a Big Mac. **Marginal utility** is the change in total utility from one additional unit of a good or service. Instead of the total pleasure from eating X number of Big Macs, the question is how much *extra* satisfaction the first, second, or third Big Mac gives you. For example, Exhibit 1(a) shows your marginal utility data for eating four Big Macs in a day. You munch down the first Big Mac. Ah, the util meter hits an 8. You grab another Big Mac and eat it a little more slowly. The util meter hits 4 this time. You're starting to feel full, but you eat a third Big Mac. This one gets a 2. Even though you are pretty full, there is room for one more. You eat the fourth Big Mac very slowly, and it gives you less satisfaction than any of the previous burgers. Your utility meter reads 1. This trend conforms to the law of diminishing marginal utility. The **law of diminishing marginal utility** is the principle that the extra satisfaction provided by a good or service declines as people consume more in a given period. Economists have found that this is a universal principle of human consumption behavior.

Exhibit 1(a) is a marginal utility (MU) graph. Consistent with the law of diminishing marginal utility, the MU curve slopes downward as you consume more Big Macs. This reflects a steady decline in the utility of each additional Big Mac consumed. If you continue to eat Big Macs, a quantity of Big Macs is eventually reached at which the marginal utility is zero. Here you say to yourself, "If I eat another bite, I'll be sick." Then if you did eat another bite after all, marginal utility would be negative. A rational person never consumes goods when the marginal utility is negative (disutility) unless he or she is paid enough to do so. In our example, we assume you are rational and will not eat a Big Mac that gives you a negative marginal utility and a stomach ache. Also keep in mind that the MU curve for a good is different for different circumstances and individuals. Your MU curve would be much higher if you had not eaten in days. On the other hand, a vegetarian would receive no positive marginal utility from consuming a Big Mac.

Exhibit 1(b) shows how the shape of the total utility (TU) curve varies with marginal utility as you consume more Big Macs each day. The total utility of Big Macs increases steadily because each hamburger provides *additional* satisfaction to the sum of all the Big Macs already consumed. However, the TU curve becomes flatter as the marginal utility diminishes. This is because, as you consume more, the positive pleasure per Big Mac declines, and, in turn, each Big Mac adds less to total utility.

Utility
The satisfaction, or pleasure, that people receive from consuming a good or service.

Total utility
The amount of satisfaction received from all the units of a good or service consumed.

Marginal utility
The change in total utility from one additional unit of a good or service

Law of diminishing marginal utility
The principle that the extra satisfaction provided by a good or service declines as people consume more in a given period.

EXHIBIT 1 Diminishing Marginal Utility and Total Utility Curves for Consuming Big Macs

Part (a) shows that as more Big Macs are consumed per day, the utility from each additional Big Mac declines. The utils are only imaginary because utility cannot be measured. When the marginal utility of each Big Mac consumed is summed, we obtain the total utility curve shown in part (b).

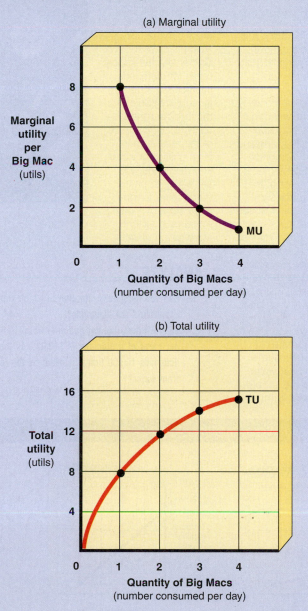

YOU'RE THE ECONOMIST

Applicable Concepts: Total Utility and Marginal Utility

Why Is Water Less Expensive than Diamonds?

Adam Smith posed a paradox in *The Wealth of Nations*. Water is essential to life and therefore should be of great value. On the other hand, diamonds are not essential to life, so people should value them less than water. Yet, even though water provides individuals with more total utility, it is cheaper than diamonds. Smith's puzzle came to be known as the diamond–water paradox. Now you can use marginal utility analysis to explain something that baffled the father of economics.

Early economists failed to find the key to the diamond–water puzzle because they did not distinguish between marginal and total utility. Marginal utility theory was not developed until the late nineteenth century. Water is life-giving and does indeed yield much higher total utility than diamonds; however, marginal utility, and not total utility, determines the price one is willing to pay. Water is plentiful in most of the world, so its marginal utility is low and therefore one's willingness to pay for water is low. This follows the law of diminishing marginal utility.

Jewelry-quality diamonds, on the other hand, are scarce. Because we have relatively few diamonds, the quantity of diamonds consumed is not large. As a result, the marginal utility of diamonds and the price buyers are willing to pay for them are quite high. Thus, scarcity raises marginal utility and the price one is willing to pay regardless of the size of total utility.

Exhibit 2 presents a graphical analysis that you can use to unravel the alleged paradox. Part (a) shows the marginal utility per carat you receive from each diamond consumed, and part (b) represents marginal utility per gallon of water consumed. The vertical line, *S*, in each graph is the supply of water or diamonds available per year. Since water is much

more plentiful than diamonds, the supply curve for water intersects the marginal utility curve at MU_w, which is close to zero. Conversely, the supply curve for diamonds intersects the marginal utility curve at a much higher marginal utility, MU_d. Because of the relative marginal utilities of water and diamonds, you are willing to pay much more for one more carat of a diamond than for one more gallon of water.

Denis Vrublevski/Shutterstock.com

ANALYZE THE ISSUE

1. Can you imagine a situation in which water would be more expensive than diamonds?

2. Suppose the price per gallon of water is 1 cent and the price per carat of a diamond is $10,000. Is the total utility of diamonds 10,000 times as great as the total utility received from water?

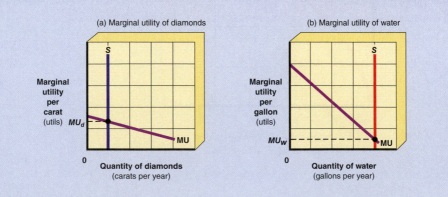

EXHIBIT 2 The Diamond–Water Paradox

(a) Marginal utility of diamonds

Marginal utility per carat (utils) MU_d

S

MU

0   **Quantity of diamonds** (carats per year)

(b) Marginal utility of water

Marginal utility per gallon (utils) MU_w

S

MU

0   **Quantity of water** (gallons per year)

6-1b **Consumer Equilibrium**

We will now make our example of consumer choice more realistic. Let's examine how Bob Moore, a sophomore at Seaview College, might behave, given a limited budget and the choice between two goods. Suppose Bob goes to McDonald's for lunch with $8 in his pocket to spend for Big Macs and milkshakes. The price of a Big Mac is $2, and the price of a milkshake is also $2. How can Bob enjoy the maximum total utility with his limited money?

Recall from Chapter 2 the concept of *marginal analysis*. This is the method Bob uses to decide how many Big Macs and milkshakes to order. Exhibit 3 shows Bob's marginal utility for each Big Mac and milkshake consumed. The *marginal utility per dollar* (MU/P) is the ratio of the marginal utility of each good to its price. In making purchases, the key consideration is how additional satisfaction relates to price. Using marginal decision-making before ordering his lunch, Bob compares the marginal utility of one Big Mac to the marginal utility of one milkshake. Being a rational consumer, Bob sees that spending his first $2 on a Big Mac gives more "bang for the buck." The first Big Mac gives him 4 utils per dollar, but the same $2 spent on a milkshake gives him 3 utils per dollar. Next, Bob ponders how to spend his next $2. The best buy now is a milkshake because it gives 3 utils per dollar compared to 2 utils per dollar for a second Big Mac.

Spending Bob's last $4 is a toss-up. Both the second Big Mac and the second milkshake give the same 2 utils per dollar. So Bob can spend $2 for a second Big Mac and his last $2 for a second milkshake. Or he can spend $2 for a second milkshake and his last $2 for a second Big Mac. The order does not matter. Now that Bob has spent all his income, the marginal utility per dollar of the last Big Mac is equal to the marginal utility per dollar of the last milkshake.

> If the marginal utility per last dollar spent on each good is equal and the entire budget is spent, total utility is maximized.

CONCLUSION

To convince yourself that two Big Macs and two milkshakes do indeed maximize total utility, consider any other combination Bob could buy with $8. All others yield

---

EXHIBIT 3   Marginal Utility for Big Macs and Milkshakes (Utils per Day)

Quantity	Big Macs MU	Big Macs MU/P	Milkshakes MU	Milkshakes MU/P
1	8	4	6	3
2	4	2	4	2
3	2	1	1	1/2
4	1	1/2	0	0

NOTE: The price per Big Mac and per milkshake is $2.

lower total utility. Suppose Bob were to buy three Big Macs and one milkshake. The third Big Mac adds 2 utils, but giving up the second milkshake subtracts 4 utils. As a result, total utility falls by 2 utils. Or can Bob maximize utility if he were to eat only one Big Mac and drink three milkshakes? The extra utility of the third milkshake is 1 util, but this is less than the 4 utils he would lose by saying no to the second Big Mac. In this case, total utility would fall by 3 utils.

Consumer equilibrium
A condition in which total utility cannot increase by spending more of a given budget on one good and spending less on another good.

This example demonstrates the utility-maximizing concept of consumer equilibrium. **Consumer equilibrium** is a condition in which total utility cannot increase by spending more of a given budget on one good and spending less on another good. Suppose Bob knows not only the exact marginal utility of consuming Big Macs and milkshakes, but also the marginal utility of french fries, pizza, and other goods. To obtain the highest possible satisfaction, Bob allocates his budget so that the last dollar spent on good *A*, the last on good *B*, and so on, yield equal MU/P ratios. Consumer equilibrium can be restated algebraically as follows:

$$\frac{\text{MU of good } A}{\text{Price of good } A} = \frac{\text{MU of good } B}{\text{Price of good } B} = \frac{\text{MU of good } Z}{\text{Price of good } Z}$$

The letters *A*, *B*, … *Z* indicate all the various goods and services purchased by the consumer with a given budget.

6-1c From Consumer Equilibrium to the Law of Demand

Understanding the law of diminishing marginal utility and consumer equilibrium provides you with a new set of tools to explore the law of demand. Let's begin with a straightforward link between the law of diminishing marginal utility and the demand curve. Declining marginal utility from consuming more Big Macs and milkshakes means each extra quantity consumed is less important or valuable to the consumer. Therefore, as the quantity consumed increases and the marginal utility falls, Bob is willing to pay less per Big Mac and milkshake. Thus, Bob's individual demand curve conforms to the law of demand and is downward sloping.

A more complete explanation of the law of demand combines diminishing marginal utility and consumer equilibrium. Suppose Bob reaches consumer equilibrium as follows:

$$\frac{\text{MU of Big Mac}}{\text{Price of Big Mac}} = \frac{\text{MU of milkshake}}{\text{Price of milkshake}}$$

$$\frac{4 \text{ utils}}{\$2} = \frac{4 \text{ utils}}{2}$$

Now suppose the price of a Big Mac falls to $1 and upsets the above equality. This changes the formula to the following:

$$\frac{\text{MU of Big Mac}}{\text{Price of Big Mac}} > \frac{\text{MU of milkshake}}{\text{Price of milkshake}}$$

$$\frac{4 \text{ utils}}{1} > \frac{4 \text{ utils}}{2}$$

Now Bob gains more utility per dollar by buying a Big Mac rather than a milkshake. To restore maximum total utility, he spends more on Big Macs. The marginal utility of a Big Mac must fall as he buys more. At the same time, the marginal utility of a milkshake must rise as Bob buys fewer milkshakes. A fall in the price of Big Macs therefore causes Bob to buy more Big Macs. Voila! The law of demand.

When Dining Out, Do You Eat Smart?

Welcome to Jose's Hacienda! Beside each dish, the menu lists the total utility from each item. If you have $15 to spend, which combination of menu items will you order to achieve consumer equilibrium (to maximize your total utility given prices and your limited budget)? Hint: Fill in the tables first.

CHECKPOINT

Jose's Hacienda Menu

Tacos—$3 each	Total Utility	Marginal Utility (MU)	(Marginal Utility)/ Price (MU/P)
1 taco	99 utils		
2 tacos	162 utils		
3 tacos	174 utils		

Flan*—$2 each	Total Utility	Marginal Utility (MU)	(Marginal Utility)/ Price (MU/P)
1 flan	40 utils		
2 flans	48 utils		
3 flans	50 utils		

Coke—$1 each	Total Utility	Marginal Utility (MU)	(Marginal Utility)/ Price (MU/P)
1 Coke	25 utils		
2 Cokes	29 utils		
3 Cokes	32 utils		

*Mexican dessert.

6-2 INCOME AND SUBSTITUTION EFFECTS AND THE LAW OF DEMAND

Since utility is not measurable, it is desirable to have an alternative explanation of demand. Economists offer the following two complementary explanations for the law of demand, which do not rely on utility.

6-2a Income Effect

One reason people buy more of a good when the price falls is the effect of a price change on real income. The *nominal*, or *money*, amount of your paycheck is simply the number of dollars you earn. On the other hand, price changes alter your *real* income. A rise in prices decreases purchasing power, and a fall in prices increases purchasing power, ceteris paribus.

Suppose your weekly nominal income is $100, and you decide to stock up on Pepsi-Cola (a normal good). If the price per quart is $1, you can afford to buy 100 quarts this week. If the price is instead $0.50 per quart and the prices of other goods remain constant, you are richer because of the rise in purchasing power. As a result, you can afford to buy 200 quarts of Pepsi-Cola without giving up any other goods, or purchase less than 200 quarts and more of other goods. As predicted by the law of demand, the lower price for Pepsi-Cola causes real income to rise and, in turn, causes the quantity demanded to rise. This relationship between changes in real income and your ability to buy goods and services is the income effect. The **income effect** is the change in quantity demanded of a good or service caused by a change in real income (purchasing power).

Income effect
The change in quantity demanded of a good or service caused by a change in real income (purchasing power).

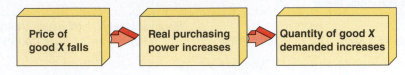

6-2b Substitution Effect

There is another reason the change in a good's price causes a change in the quantity demanded. This reason has to do with changing *relative prices*, that is, the price of one good compared to that of another. If the price of Pepsi falls and the price of Coke remains unchanged, Pepsi becomes a better buy. As a result, many consumers will switch from Coke and other beverages and buy more Pepsi. Just as the law of demand predicts, this is an increase in quantity demanded. With the price of Pepsi lower than before, the substitution effect causes people to substitute Pepsi for the now relatively more expensive Coke. The **substitution effect** is the change in quantity demanded of a good or service caused by a change in its price relative to substitutes.

Substitution effect
The change in quantity demanded of a good or service caused by a change in its price relative to substitutes.

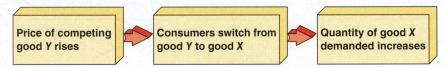

Although we discussed the income and the substitution effects separately, they are complementary explanations for the downward-sloping demand curve.

CONCLUSION When the price of a normal good falls, the income effect and the substitution effect combine to cause the quantity demanded to increase.

Some students express relief that this conclusion has no reference to the untidy word *utility*.

CHECKPOINT

Does the Substitution Effect Apply to Buying a Car?

Jenny Tanaka wants to buy a new car, and the annual gasoline expense is a major consideration. Her present car gets 25 miles per gallon (mpg), and she is looking at a new car that gets 40 mpg. Jenny now drives about 12,000 miles per year and pays $3.25 per gallon of gasoline. She therefore calculates an annual gasoline consumption of 480 gallons for her 25 mpg car (12,000 miles/25 mpg) compared to 300 gallons consumed per year for the 40 mpg car (12,000 miles/40 mpg). Since driving the higher-mileage car would use 180 gallons less per year, Jenny estimates the new car will save her $585 in gasoline expense per year (180 gallons × $3.25 per gallon). Suppose Jenny buys the 40 mpg car. Do you predict Jenny will have an annual gasoline savings equal to $585, less than $585, or more than $585?

YOU'RE THE ECONOMIST

Applicable Concept: Substitution Effect

Testing the Law of Demand with White Rats

Economists often envy the controlled laboratory experiments of biologists and other scientists. In the real world, the economist is unable to observe consumer behavior without the prices of other goods, expectations, and other factors changing. So it is no wonder that the idea of studying the behavior of white rats to test the law of demand was intriguing. The question was whether the consumer choice of a white rat supports the downward-sloping demand curve.

Standard laboratory rats were placed in experimental cages with two levers. If a rat pressed one lever, nonalcoholic Collins mix was the reward. Pressing the second lever rewarded the rat with root beer. It seems rats are fond of these two beverages. Each rat was given a limited "income" of lever presses per day. After, say, 300 presses, a light above the lever went out, signaling the daily budget was gone. The next day the light was turned on, and the rat was given a new income of lever presses. The "price" of each good corresponded to the number of lever pushes required to obtain 1 milliliter of liquid. For example, if the number of pushes per milliliter for Collins mix released increased by 10 percent, this equaled a 10 percent increase in the price of Collins mix.

The crucial test was to measure the substitution effect resulting from a change in price. As explained in the text, a change in price sets in motion both an income effect and a substitution effect. In the experiment, the price of Collins mix was lowered by decreasing the number of pushes required per milliliter. At the same time, the price of root beer was raised by increasing the number of pushes required per milliliter. To eliminate the income effect, the number of lever presses was raised to compensate for loss of purchasing power. For example, if a rat purchased 4 milliliters of Collins mix per day and 11 milliliters of root beer before the price change, it would be given enough extra pushes after the price change to still purchase these quantities.

In one experiment, a male albino rat was given 300 pushes per day for two weeks, and both liquids were priced at 20 pushes per milliliter. The rat soon settled into a consistent consumption pattern of 4 milliliters of Collins mix and 11 milliliters of root beer per day. Then the experimenters made changes in prices and income. The price (pushes per milliliter) of Collins mix was cut in half, and the price of root beer was doubled. At the same time, the total income of pushes was increased just enough to allow the rat to afford its initial consumption pattern. Stated differently, the income effect was eliminated in order to focus on the substitution effect. After two weeks of decisions under the new conditions, the rat changed its consumption pattern to 17 milliliters of Collins mix and 8 milliliters of root beer per day.

ANALYZE **THE ISSUE**   Based on the behavior of the rat described earlier, what do you conclude about the substitution effect and the slope of the demand curve?

SOURCE: John H. Kagel, Raymond C. Battalio, Howard Rachlin, and Leonard Green, "Demand Curves for Animal Consumers," *Quarterly Journal of Economics* 96 (February 1981), pp. 1–16.

Key Concepts

Utility	Marginal utility	Consumer equilibrium	Substitution effect
Total utility	Law of diminishing marginal utility	Income effect	

Summary

- **Utility** is the satisfaction or pleasure derived from consumption of a good or service. Actual measurement of utility is impossible, but economists assume it can be measured by a fictitious unit called the *util*.

- **Total utility** is the total level of satisfaction derived from all units of a good or service consumed. **Marginal utility** is the change in total utility from a 1-unit change in the quantity of a good or service consumed.

Relationship between Marginal and Total Utility

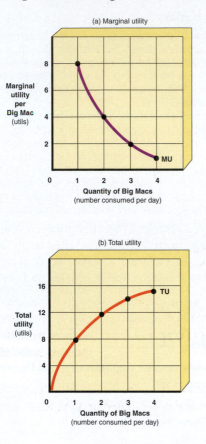

(a) Marginal utility

Marginal utility per Big Mac (utils)

Quantity of Big Macs (number consumed per day)

(b) Total utility

Total utility (utils)

Quantity of Big Macs (number consumed per day)

• The **law of diminishing marginal utility** states that the marginal utility of a good or service eventually declines as consumption increases.

• **Consumer equilibrium** is the condition of reaching the maximum level of satisfaction, given a budget, when the marginal utility per dollar spent on each good purchased is equal. Consumer equilibrium and the law of diminishing marginal utility can be used to derive a downward-sloping demand curve. When the price of a good falls, consumer equilibrium no longer holds because the marginal utility per dollar for the good rises. To restore equilibrium, the consumer must increase consumption. As the quantity demanded increases, the marginal utility falls until equilibrium is again achieved. Thus, the price falls, and the quantity demanded rises, as predicted by the law of demand.

$$\frac{\text{MU of good } A}{\text{Price of good } A} = \frac{\text{MU of good } B}{\text{Price of good } B} = \frac{\text{MU of good } Z}{\text{Price of good } Z}$$

• The **income effect** and **substitution effect** are complementary explanations for the law of demand. When the price changes, these effects work in combination to change the quantity demanded in the opposite direction. As the price falls, real purchasing power increases, causing an increase in the consumer's willingness and ability to purchase a good or service. This is the *income effect*. Also, as the price falls, the consumer substitutes the cheaper good for other goods that are now relatively more expensive. This is the *substitution effect*.

Summary of Conclusion Statements

• If the marginal utility per last dollar spent on each good is equal and the entire budget is spent, total utility is maximized.

• When the price of a normal good falls, the income effect and the substitution effect combine to cause the quantity demanded to increase.

Study Questions and Problems

Please see Appendix A for answers to the odd-numbered questions. Your instructor has access to the answers for even-numbered questions.

1. Does a dollar given to a rich person raise the rich person's total utility more than a dollar given to a poor person raises the poor person's total utility?

2. Do you agree with the following statement? "If you like tacos, you should consume as many as you can."

3. This week you have gone to two parties. Assume the total utility you gained from these parties is 100 utils. Then you go to a third party, and your total utility rises to 110 utils. What is the marginal utility of the third party attended per week? Given the law of diminishing marginal utility, what will happen to total utility and marginal utility when you go to a fourth party this week?

4. Suppose your marginal utility for meals at the campus cafeteria this week has fallen to zero. Explain what has happened to your total utility curve derived from consuming these meals. Now explain what will happen to total utility if you eat more meals at the cafeteria this week.

5. Suppose you consume 3 pounds of beef and 5 pounds of pork per month. The price of beef is $1.50 per pound, and pork is $2.00 per pound. Assuming you have studied economics and achieved consumer equilibrium, what is the ratio of the marginal utility of beef to the marginal utility of pork?

6. Suppose the marginal utility of a Coke is 15 utils and its price is $1. The marginal utility of a pizza is 20 utils, and its price is $2. If you buy 1 unit of each good, will you achieve consumer equilibrium? If not, how can greater total utility be obtained?

7. Explain the relationship between the law of diminishing marginal utility and the law of demand.

8. Consider the following table, which lists James's marginal utility schedule for steak and hamburger meals:

Steak meals per month	Marginal utility of steak meals	Price per steak meal	Hamburger meals per month	Marginal utility of hamburger meals	Price per hamburger meal
1	20	$10	1	15	$5
2	15	10	2	8	5
3	12	10	3	6	5
4	10	10	4	4	5
5	8	10	5	2	5

Given a budget of $45, how many steak and hamburger meals will James buy per month to maximize his total utility? What is the total utility realized?

9. Using the marginal utility schedule in question 8, begin in consumer equilibrium and assume the price per hamburger meal falls from $5 to $2, all other factors held constant. What is the total utility realized?

10. Suppose the price of a BMW falls. Explain the law of demand based on the income and substitution effects.

 CHECKPOINT ANSWERS

When Dining Out, Do You Eat Smart?

Start with 1 taco (99 marginal utils/$3, or 33 marginal utils/$1). Then order a Coke (25 marginal utils/$1). Next, order another taco (63 marginal utils/$3, or 21 marginal utils/$1). Now treat yourself to a flan (40 marginal utils/$2, or 20 marginal utils/$1). Finish it all with a second flan (4 marginal utils/$1), another Coke (4 marginal utils/$1), and a third taco (4 marginal utils/$1). You have now spent your entire $15 budget and the MU/P are equal for all goods. If you said, following the principle of consumer equilibrium, you would order 2 Cokes, 2 flans, and 3 tacos, although not a very nutritious choice, **YOU ARE CORRECT**.

Checkpoint: Does the Substitution Effect Apply to Buying a Car?

Buying a higher mpg car will reduce the cost per mile of driving relative to substitutes, such as riding a bus, a train, or an airplane. As the cost of driving falls, the substitution effect predicts Jenny will drive more in the 40 mpg car than the 12,000 miles she now drives per year in the 25 mpg car. The extra cost of gasoline for driving over 12,000 miles per year in the 40 mpg car must be subtracted from the $585 savings that was based on the assumption that Jenny's miles driven per year would remain unchanged when she bought the 40 mpg car. If you said Jenny will save less than $585, **YOU ARE CORRECT**.

Jose's Hacienda menu			
Tacos—$3 each	**Total Utility**	**Marginal Utility (MU)**	**(Marginal Utility)/Price (MU/P)**
1 taco	99 utils	99	99/3 = 33
2 tacos	162 utils	63	63/3 = 21
3 tacos	174 utils	12	12/3 = 4
Flan*—$2 each	**Total Utility**	**Marginal Utility (MU)**	**(Marginal Utility)/Price (MU/P)**
1 flan	40 utils	40	40/2 = 20
2 flans	48 utils	8	8/2 = 4
3 flans	50 utils	2	2/2 = 1
Coke—$1 each	**Total Utility**	**Marginal Utility (MU)**	**(Marginal Utility)/Price (MU/P)**
1 Coke	25 utils	25	25/1 = 25
2 Cokes	29 utils	4	4/1 = 4
3 Cokes	32 utils	3	3/1 = 3

*Mexican desert

Sample Quiz

Please see Appendix B for answers to Sample Quiz questions.

1. The term *utility* refers to the
   a. usefulness of a good in relation to its scarcity.
   b. necessity of a good.
   c. price of a good.
   d. number of goods a consumer has.
   e. pleasure, or satisfaction, a consumer receives upon consuming a good.

2. When total utility is at a maximum, marginal utility is
   a. zero.
   b. positive.
   c. negative.
   d. one.

3. The marginal utilities associated with the first 4 units of consumption of good Y are 10, 12, 9, and 7. What is the total utility associated with the third unit?
   a. 3
   b. 9

   c. 25
   d. 31
   e. The amount cannot be determined from the marginal utilities.

4. Generally speaking, as more of a particular good is purchased, a consumer's marginal utility _____ and total utility _____.
   a. increases; decreases
   b. decreases; increases
   c. increases; increases
   d. decreases; decreases
   e. Generalizations cannot be made.

5. Marginal utility is defined as the
   a. extra satisfaction the consumer receives from an extra $1 of income.
   b. total level of satisfaction a consumer receives upon the consumption of a certain number of goods.

c. number of hours a consumer would be willing to work to receive a certain product.

d. extra satisfaction a person derives from consuming an additional unit of a good.

6. The statement "As more of a good is consumed, the utility a person derives from each additional unit diminishes" is known as the
   a. water and diamond paradox.
   b. law of diminishing marginal utility.
   c. law of total utility.
   d. marginal-utility-to-price ratio equalization rule.

7. The law of diminishing marginal utility indicates that the marginal utility curve is
   a. downward sloping.
   b. upward sloping.
   c. U-shaped.
   d. flat.

EXHIBIT 4 Marginal Utility for Data for Clothes and Amusement

Quantity	Clothes	Amusement
1	15	20
2	13	18
3	10	13
4	8	12
5	6	10

8. Refer to Exhibit 4. Clothes and amusements are priced at $10 each. The marginal utility per dollar for the first unit of amusement is
   a. 0.5.
   b. 1.5.
   c. 2.0.
   d. 5.0.

9. Refer to Exhibit 4. Your budget is $50. The price of amusement goods is $10. If the price of clothes falls to $4, which of the following statements is true?
   a. The marginal-utility-to-price ratio for clothes will decrease.
   b. The marginal-utility-to-price ratio for clothes will increase.
   c. The quantity demanded of clothes will decrease.
   d. Both b and c are true.

10. Refer to Exhibit 4. Clothes and amusements are priced at $10 each. If you had a budget of $50,

which of the following combinations of goods would you buy?
   a. 4 units of clothes and 1 unit of amusement
   b. 3 units of clothes and 2 units of amusement
   c. 2 units of clothes and 3 units of amusement
   d. 1 unit of clothes and 4 units of amusement

11. Total utility is maximized in the consumption of two goods by equating the
   a. prices of both goods for the last dollar spent on each good.
   b. marginal utilities of both goods for the last dollar spent on each good.
   c. ratios of marginal utility to the price of both goods for the last dollar spent on each good.
   d. marginal utility of one good to the price of the other good.

12. The MU/P equalization principle means consumers will exhaust their expenditure budget so that, in the end, the MU/P ratio is
   a. zero for each good.
   b. higher for goods the consumer wants the most.
   c. maximized for the goods the consumer wants the most.
   d. the same for each good.

13. When the price of a good falls, consumers may increase the quantity consumed because they have greater total purchasing power. Which of the following does this statement describe?
   a. Substitution effect
   b. Income effect
   c. Consumer equilibrium effect
   d. Price effect

14. When the price of a good falls, consumers buy more of the good because it is cheaper relative to competing goods. Which of the following does this statement describe?
   a. Consumer equilibrium effect
   b. Price effect
   c. Income effect
   d. Substitution effect

15. When the price of a normal good falls,
   a. both the income and substitution effects combine to cause the quantity demanded to increase.
   b. the substitution effect will cause people to buy more because the good is relatively less expensive.
   c. the income effect will cause people to buy more because of the increased purchasing power associated with the lower price.
   d. All of the above answers are correct.

16. If utility is *not* maximized,
    a. some change in consumption will increase satisfaction.
    b. no change in consumption will increase utility.
    c. only a change in income will increase utility.
    d. only a change in price will increase utility.

17. A utility-maximizing consumer would never purchase a good if the
    a. MU/P were positive.
    b. marginal utility were positive.
    c. marginal utility were negative.
    d. None of the above answers are correct.

18. Diminishing marginal utility means that as you consume more of a good, other things constant, the
    a. total satisfaction you obtain from consuming this good falls.
    b. total amount produced begins to fall.
    c. marginal product begins to fall.
    d. additional satisfaction you obtain from each additional unit of the good falls.

19. Assume that an individual consumes only hot dogs and colas and that the last hot dog consumed yields 15 utils and the last cola yields 10 utils. If the price of a hot dog is $1.00 and the price of a cola is $0.50, we can conclude that the
    a. consumer should consume more hot dogs and less cola.
    b. price of hot dogs is too high.
    c. consumer should consume fewer hot dogs and more cola.
    d. consumer is in equilibrium.

20. Assume the price of Coca-Cola increases. As a result, your real income decreases and you decrease the quantity of Coca-Cola purchased each month. This is an example of the
    a. income effect.
    b. consumer price effect.
    c. revenue effect.
    d. substitution effect.

21. When the price of a good rises, one effect of this change in price is that some consumers switch to more affordable substitutes, which helps us understand the law of demand. What is this effect called?
    a. Marginal utility effect
    b. Substitution effect
    c. Price effect
    d. Income effect

22. According to the utility model of consumer demand, the demand curve is downward sloping because of the law of
    a. diminishing marginal utility.
    b. diminishing consumer equilibrium.
    c. consumer equilibrium.
    d. diminishing utility maximization.

23. As shown in Exhibit 5, assume that the price of both goods is $1 per unit and you consume 3 units of good X and 3 units of good Y. To maximize total utility without a budget, you should consume
    a. neither X nor Y.
    b. more of X and less of Y.
    c. less of X and more of Y.
    d. more of both X and Y.
    e. less of both X and Y.

EXHIBIT 5 Marginal Utility Data for Goods X and Y

Units of good X	Marginal utility of good X	Units of good Y	Marginal utility of good Y
1	20	1	14
2	16	2	12
3	12	3	10
4	8	4	8
5	4	5	6

24. As shown in Exhibit 5, assume that the price of both goods is $1 per unit and your budget is $5. Also assume that you consume 4 units of good X and 1 unit of good Y. To maximize utility, you should consume
    a. neither X nor Y.
    b. more of X and less of Y.
    c. less of X and more of Y.
    d. more of both X and Y.
    e. less of both X and Y.

25. As shown in Exhibit 5, assume that the price of good X is $2 per unit and the price of good Y is $1 per unit and your budget is $11. If you consume 3 units of good X and 4 units of good Y and maximize utility, you should consume
    a. neither X nor Y.
    b. more of X.
    c. more of Y.
    d. more of both X and Y.
    e. less of both X and Y.

Indifference Curve Analysis

This appendix explains another version of consumer choice theory based on indifference curves and budget lines.

6A-1 CONSTRUCTING AN INDIFFERENCE CURVE

Let's begin with an experiment to find out a consumer's consumption preferences for quantities of two goods. The consumer samples a number of pairs of servings with various ounces of lobster tail and steak (surf and turf). Each time the same question is asked, "Would you prefer serving *A* or serving *B*?" After numerous trials, suppose the consumer states indifference between eating choices *A−D* shown in Exhibit A-1. This means the consumer is just as satisfied having either 7 ounces of steak and 4 ounces of lobster (*A*), or 3 ounces of steak and 8 ounces of lobster (*D*), or either of the other two combinations of *B* or *C*. Interpretation of the curve connecting these points is that each of these choices yields the same total utility because no choice is preferred to any other choice. Since, as explained in the chapter, there is no such thing as a utility meter, this approach is actually a method for determining equal levels of satisfaction or total utility for different bundles of goods without an exact measure of utils. The curve derived from this experimental data is called an indifference curve. An **indifference curve** is a curve showing the different combinations of two products that yield the same satisfaction or total utility to a consumer. Note that not only points *A*, *B*, *C*, and *D*, but also all other points on the smooth curve connecting them are equally satisfactory combinations to the consumer.

Indifference curve
A curve showing the different combinations of two products that yield the same satisfaction or total utility to a consumer.

6A-1a Why Indifference Curves Are Downward Sloping and Convex

If total utility is the same at all points along the indifference curve, then consuming more of one good must mean consuming less of the other good. Given this condition, movement along the indifference curve generates a curve with a negative slope. Suppose a consumer moves in marginal increments between any two combination points in Exhibit A-1. For instance, say the consumer decides to move from point *A* to point *B* and consume an extra ounce of lobster. To do so, the consumer increases total utility (+MU) by consuming an extra quantity of lobster. However, since by definition total utility is constant everywhere along the curve, the consumer must give up a quantity of steak (2 ounces) in order to reduce total utility (−MU) by precisely enough to offset the gain in total utility from the extra lobster.

The inverse relationship between goods along the downward-sloping indifference curve means that the absolute value of the slope of an indifference curve equals what is

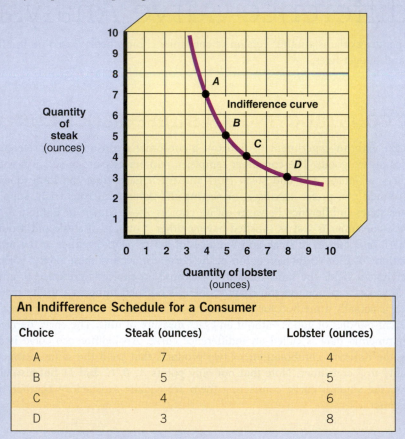

EXHIBIT A-1 A Consumer's Indifference Curve

Points *A*, *B*, *C*, *D*, and each point along the curve represent a combination of steak and lobster that yields equal total utility for a given consumer. Stated differently, the consumer is indifferent between consuming servings having quantities represented by all points composing the indifference curve.

An Indifference Schedule for a Consumer

Choice	Steak (ounces)	Lobster (ounces)
A	7	4
B	5	5
C	4	6
D	3	8

Marginal rate of substitution (MRS)

The rate at which a consumer is willing to substitute one good for another without a change in total utility. The MRS equals the slope of the indifference curve at any point on the curve.

called the marginal rate of substitution. The **marginal rate of substitution (MRS)** is the rate at which a consumer is willing to substitute one good for another with no change in total utility. Begin at *A* and move to *B* along the curve. The slope and MRS of the curve is −2/1, or simply 2, when the minus sign is removed to give the absolute value. This is the consumer's subjective willingness to substitute *A* for *B*. At point *A*, the consumer has a substantial amount of steak and relatively little lobster. Therefore, the consumer is willing to forgo or "substitute" 2 ounces of steak to get 1 more ounce of lobster. In other words, the marginal utility of losing each ounce of steak between *A* and *B* is low compared to the marginal utility of gaining each ounce of lobster. In fact, the MRS is really the ratio of the marginal utility of good X (placed on the X axis—in this case, X is lobster) in relation to the marginal utility of good Y (placed on the Y axis—in this case, Y is steak). This can be written: MUx/MUy. So, moving from point *A* to *B*, the

MU of lobster is twice that for steak because the consumer was willing to give up 2 ounces of steak to get an additional ounce of lobster.

Now suppose the consumer moves from *B* to *C*, and the slope changes to 1/1 (MRS = 1). Between these two points, the consumer is willing to substitute 1 ounce of steak for an equal quantity of lobster. This means that between *B* and *C* the marginal utility lost per ounce of steak equals the marginal utility gained from an ounce of lobster, while total utility remains constant. The ratio of MUx in relation to MUy (MUx/MUy) equals one.

Finally, assume the consumer moves from *C* to *D*. Here the ratio of MUx/MUy which equals the slope, equals ½ (MRS = ½) because the consumer at point *C* has a substantial amount of lobster and relatively little steak. Consequently, the marginal utility lost from giving up 1 ounce of steak equals twice the marginal utility gained from an additional ounce of lobster.

As we see in this example, as the quantity of lobster increases along the horizontal axis, the marginal utility of additional ounces of lobster decreases. Correspondingly, as the quantity of steak decreases along the vertical axis, its marginal utility increases. So moving down the curve means the consumer is willing to give up smaller and smaller quantities of steak on the vertical axis to obtain each additional ounce of lobster on the horizontal axis.

> The slope of the indifference curve is negative and equal to the marginal rate of substitution (MRS), which declines as one moves downward along the curve. The result is a curve with a diminishing slope that is convex (bowed inward) to the origin.

CONCLUSION

6A-1b **The Indifference Map**

As explained earlier, any point selected along an indifference curve gives the same level of satisfaction or total utility. Actually, there are other indifference curves that can be drawn for a consumer. As shown in Exhibit A-2, indifference curves I_1 to I_6 also exist to form an indifference map. An **indifference map** is a selection of indifference curves with each curve representing a different level of satisfaction or total utility. In fact, if all possible curves were drawn, they would completely fill the space between the axes because there would be so many. And it is important to note that each curve reflects a different level of total utility. Also, each curve moving from the origin in the northeasterly direction from I_1 to I_6 and beyond yields higher total utility. This is reasonable because at each higher indifference curve, the consumer is able to select more of both goods and therefore is better off. To verify this concept, select a combination on one indifference curve in Exhibit A-2 and then select a combination of more of both goods on a higher indifference curve.

Indifference map
A selection of indifference curves with each curve representing a different level of satisfaction or total utility.

> Each consumer has a set of indifference curves that form a map. Because consumers want to achieve the highest possible total utility, they always prefer curves farther from the origin where they can select more quantities of two goods.

CONCLUSION

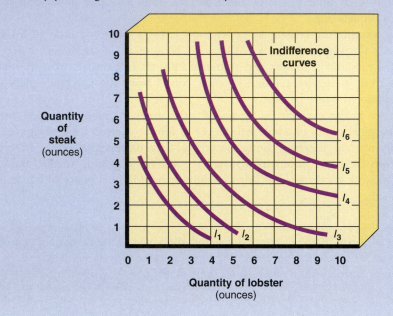

EXHIBIT A-2 A Consumer's Indifference Map

An indifference map is a selected set of indifference curves. Along curves farther from the origin, it is possible to select more of both goods compared to indifference curves closer to the origin. Therefore, curves farther from the origin are preferred because they yield higher levels of total utility.

6A-2 THE BUDGET LINE

Having considered the consumer's preferences for steak and lobster in the indifference map, the next step is to see what the consumer can afford. The consumer's ability to purchase steak and lobster is limited, or constrained, by the amount of money (income) that the consumer has to spend and the prices of the two goods. Suppose the consumer likes to go to a fine restaurant and budgets $10 per week to dine on surf and turf. The price of steak is $1 per ounce, and the price of lobster is $2 an ounce. If the consumer spends the entire budget on steak, 10 ounces of steak can be purchased. At the other extreme, the whole budget could be spent for lobster, and 5 ounces would be purchased. As shown in Exhibit A-3, and given the consumption possibilities of buying fractions of ounces of steak and lobster, a range of choices can be purchased along the budget line ranging from 10 ounces on the steak axis to 5 ounces on the lobster axis. A **budget line** is a line that shows the different combinations of two goods a consumer can purchase with a given amount of money and at given prices. The table in Exhibit A-3 computes selected whole-unit combinations of steak and lobsters that each equal a $10 total expenditure.

Budget line
A line that shows the different combinations of two goods a consumer can purchase with a given amount of money and at given prices.

CONCLUSION The budget line represents various combinations of goods that a consumer can purchase at given prices with a given budget.

EXHIBIT A-3 A Consumer's Budget Line

A budget line shows all the possible combinations of goods that can be purchased with a given budget and given prices for these goods.

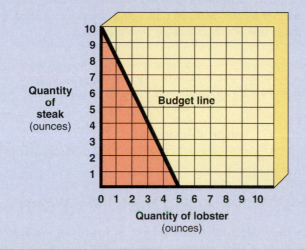

Quantity of steak (ounces) — vertical axis

Budget line

Quantity of lobster (ounces) — horizontal axis

Selected Whole-Unit Combinations of Steak and Lobster Affordable with a $10 Budget

(1) Choice	(2) Ounces of steak (price = $1/ounce)	(3) Ounces of lobster (price = $2/ounce)	(4) Total expenditure
A	10	0	$10 ($10 + $0)
B	8	1	$10 ($8 + $2)
C	4	3	$10 ($4 + $6)
D	2	4	$10 ($2 + $8)
E	0	5	$10 ($0 + $10)

Computing the slope of the budget line requires some shorthand mathematical notation. Let B represent the amount of money the consumer has to spend on steak and lobster. Also, let P_l and P_s represent the prices of lobster and steak, respectively, and L and S represent the ounces of lobster and steak, respectively. Given this notation, the budget line may be expressed as

$$P_l L + P_s S = B$$

In order to express the equation in slope-intercept form, divide both sides by P_s and get

$$\frac{P_l}{P_s} L + S = \frac{B}{P_s}$$

Solving for S yields

$$S = \frac{B}{P_s} - \frac{P_1}{P_s} L$$

Note that S is a linear function of L with a vertical intercept of B/P_s and a slope of P_1/P_s. Since the price of lobster is \$2 an ounce and the price of steak is \$1 per ounce, the slope of the budget line is -2 or 2 as an absolute value.

CONCLUSION	The slope of the budget line equals the ratio of the price of good X on the horizontal axis divided by the price of good Y on the vertical axis. Expressed as a formula: **slope of budget line $= P_x/P_y$**

6A-3 A CONSUMER EQUILIBRIUM GRAPH

Exhibit A-4 shows the budget line from Exhibit A-3 superimposed on an indifference map. This allows us to easily compare consumer preferences and affordability. The utility-maximizing combination is the equilibrium point X where the budget line is just tangent to the highest attainable indifference curve I_2, and the quantity of steak purchased is 4 ounces and the quantity of lobster is 3 ounces.

As explained in Exhibit A-4 of the appendix to Chapter 1, the slope of a straight line tangent to a curve is equal to the slope of the curve at that point. This mathematical relationship translates into the economic interpretation of the tangency condition in this appendix. At the point of tangency, the MRS (MUx/MUy) equals the slope of the budget line (Px/Py)—where "X" is lobster and "Y" is steak. At point X, the slope of budget line $= P_x/P_y = 2$ (from Exhibit A-3), and, therefore, it follows that $MU_x/MU_y = MRS = 2$ at point X on curve I_2 in Exhibit A-4. So, at the point of tangency $MU_x/MU_y = P_x/P_y$. If we divide both sides of this equation by Px and multiply both sides by MUy we finally get: $MU_x/P_x = MU_y/P_y$ and this is the consumer equilibrium condition explained in the chapter! It tells us that the marginal utility per last dollar spent on each good is equal, and therefore total utility is maximized.

At any other combination, the MRS will not be equal to the price ratio (and MUx/Px will *not* equal MUy/Py), and the consumer will reallocate the budget until equilibrium is achieved at point X.

CONCLUSION	Consumer equilibrium occurs where the budget line is tangent to the highest attainable indifference curve. At this unique point, MRS = slope (price ratio of P_x/P_y).

6A-4 DERIVATION OF THE DEMAND CURVE

This appendix concludes with Exhibit A-5, which shows how the demand curve for lobster can be derived from a map of two indifference curves. The table in this exhibit

EXHIBIT A-4 Consumer Equilibrium

Consumer equilibrium is at point X, where the budget line is tangent to the highest attainable indifference curve, I_2. Only at this point does the marginal rate of substitution (MRS) along I_2 equal the slope of the budget line, which equals the price ratio P_1/P_s. Although point Y is on a higher curve, I_3, and would yield a greater total utility than X, point Y is beyond the budget line and therefore is unattainable by the consumer. Point Z is on a lower indifference curve, but it will not be chosen. The consumer can move upward along the budget line by shifting dollars from purchases of lobster to purchases of steak and reach point X on the higher indifference curve I_2.

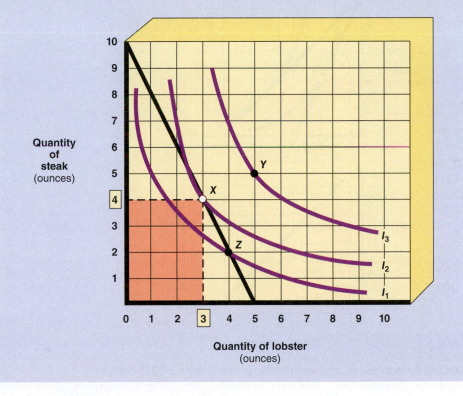

reproduces the table from Exhibit A-3 and adds column (4) with the price of lobster equal to $1 per ounce, rather than $2 per ounce. Now compare columns (3) and (4) in the table. Holding the price of steak constant at $1 per ounce and the budget equal to $10, the consumer can afford to purchase more lobster at each choice except A where the entire budget is spent on steak. The top graph is drawn from Exhibit A-4 where at point X the price of lobster is $2 per ounce and the quantity demanded of lobster is 3 ounces. The bottom graph of Exhibit A-5 shows one point on the demand curve for lobster at X'. To find another point on the demand curve, we decrease the price of lobster to $1 per ounce and trace the new budget line points from column (4) of the table onto the top graph. The budget line swings outward along the horizontal axis, but the original vertical intercept remains unchanged. The reason the vertical axis remains at

EXHIBIT A-5 Deriving the Demand Curve

In the top part of this exhibit, the initial budget line intersects the highest attainable indifference curve I_2 at point X with the price of steak equal to $1 per ounce and the price of lobster equal to $2 per ounce. Holding the budget and the price of steak constant at $10 and $1, respectively, the price of lobster drops to $1 per ounce. As a result, the budget line shifts to intersect the higher indifference curve I_3 at point Y.

The bottom part of the exhibit corresponds points X and Y to points X' and Y', respectively, on the demand curve for lobster. At $2 per ounce for lobster, the consumer buys 3 ounces. At $1 per ounce for lobster, the consumer buys 7 ounces. Connecting these two points results in a downward-sloping demand curve.

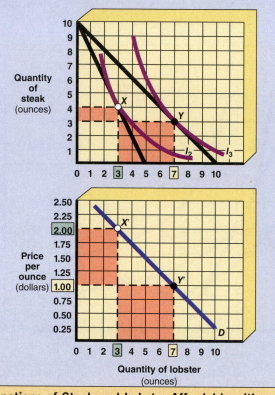

Selected Whole-Unit Combinations of Steak and Lobster Affordable with a $10 Budget

(1) Choice	(2) Ounces of steak (price $1/ounce)	(3) Ounces of lobster (price $2/ounce)	(4) Ounces of lobster (price $1/ounce)	(5) Total expenditure
A	10	0	0	$10 ($10 + $0)
B	8	1	2	$10 ($8 + $2)
C	4	3	6	$10 ($4 + $6)
D	2	4	8	$10 ($2 + $8)
E	0	5	10	$10 ($0 + $10)

10 ounces of steak is because the price of steak is still at $1 per ounce, and if the consumer spends the entire $10 on steak, then the price of lobster is irrelevant to the vertical intercept. However, at a lower price for lobster, the consumer can afford more lobster moving downward along the new budget line with the same $10 budget because lobster is cheaper.

Given the new budget line shown in the top graph in Exhibit A-5, the consumer finds that higher indifference curve I_3 is now attainable. As a result, consumer equilibrium moves from point X to point Y, where 7 ounces of lobster are purchased. This gives the corresponding second point Y' shown in the lower graph. Connecting these two points allows us to draw the consumer's demand curve for lobster. Voila! Consistent with the law of demand, the demand curve is indeed downward sloping.

Key Concepts

Indifference curve   Marginal rate of   Indifference map   Budget line
                         substitution (MRS)

Summary

- An **indifference curve** shows the different quantity combinations of two goods that give the same satisfaction or total utility to a consumer.

Indifference Curve

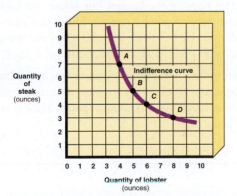

- The **marginal rate of substitution (MRS)** is the rate at which a consumer is willing to substitute one good for another with no change in total utility.

- An **indifference map** is a selection of a consumer's indifference curves.

Indifference Map

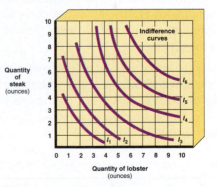

- The **budget line** gives the different combinations of two goods that a consumer can purchase with a given amount of money and relative prices for the goods. The slope of the budget line equals the price of the good on the horizontal axis divided by the price on the vertical axis.

Budget Line

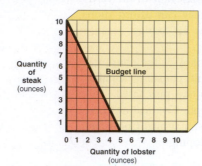

Deriving the Demand Curve

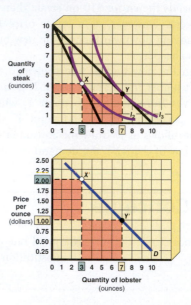

- To **Derive the Demand Curve,** find where the budget line is tangent to the highest possible indifference curve, as shown originally at point X. Next, let the price of one good fall, so the consumer's equilibrium changes to point Y on a higher indifference curve. Connecting the two corresponding price-quantity points X' and Y' generates a downward-sloping demand curve.

Summary of Conclusion Statements

- The slope of the indifference curve is negative and equal to the marginal rate of substitution (MRS), which declines as one moves downward along the curve. The result is a curve with a diminishing slope that is convex (bowed inward) to the origin.

- Each consumer has a set of indifference curves that form a map. Since consumers wish to achieve the highest possible total utility, they always prefer curves farther from the origin where they can select more quantities of two goods.

- The budget line represents various combinations of goods that a consumer can purchase at given prices with a given budget.

- The slope of the budget line equals the ratio of the price of good X on the horizontal axis divided by the price of good Y on the vertical axis. Expressed as a formula: slope $= P_x/P_y$.

- Consumer equilibrium occurs where the budget line is tangent to the highest attainable indifference curve. At this unique point, MRS = slope (price ratio of P_x/P_y).

Study Questions and Problems

Please see Appendix A for answers to the odd-numbered questions. Your instructor has access to the answers for even-numbered questions.

1. Suppose a consumer's marginal rate of substitution is three slices of pizza for one Coke. If the price of a Coke is $1 and the price of three slices of pizza is $2, would the consumer change his or her consumption combination?

2. Let M represent the quantity of medical services, such as the number of doctor visits, and let O

represent the quantity of other goods purchased by a consumer in a given year. Let the budget (B) be in thousands of dollars and the price of medical services and other goods be in terms of dollars per unit, with $B = 60$, $P_m = 6$, and $P_o = 10$.

a. Graph the budget line and determine the slope.

b. Show the result if the price of medical services (P_o) decreases to $5.

c. Add two indifference curves to the graph that are tangent to the budget line and explain the result.

3. Assume that the data in the following table are an indifference curve for a consumer:

Choice	Units of *Y*	Units of *X*
A	10	2
B	6	4
C	4	6
D	2	12

a. Graph this indifference curve and label "Quantity of *Y*" on the vertical axis and "Quantity of *X*" on the horizontal axis. Label the points *A*−*D*.

b. Assume the consumer's budget is $12 and the prices of *X* and *Y* are $1.00 and $1.50, respectively. Draw the budget line in the above graph.

c. What combination of *X* and *Y* will the consumer purchase?

d. What is the value of the MRS and the slope of the budget line (P_x/P_y) at consumer equilibrium?

e. Beginning with the graph drawn in Part (a), explain and draw graphs to derive a demand curve for *X*.

Sample Quiz

Please see Appendix B for answers to Sample Quiz questions.

1. The slope of an indifference curve is _____, and a movement along the curve causes the loss in marginal utility (MU) of one good to _____ the marginal utility (MU) gained from another good.
   a. zero; maximize
   b. positive; exceed
   c. concave; reduce
   d. negative; equal

2. The _____ is the absolute value of the slope of the indifference curve.
   a. marginal rate of substitution
   b. average rate of transitivity
   c. relative rate of utility
   d. marginal rate of transposition

3. Consumers always _____ indifference curves that are farther from the origin.
   a. reject
   b. cross
   c. prefer
   d. maximize

4. Given the prices of two goods, all quantity combinations inside the budget line are
   a. indifferent.
   b. efficient.
   c. unattainable.
   d. attainable.

5. Consumer equilibrium occurs where the budget line is _____ to the _____ possible indifference curve.
   a. tangent; highest
   b. equal; lowest
   c. marginal; maximum
   d. differential; highest

6. An indifference curve consists of quantity combinations of two goods that yield
   a. equal marginal utilities.
   b. negative marginal utilities.
   c. the same price ratios.
   d. the same total satisfaction.

7. The slope of an indifference curve is equal to the ratio of the _____ of the good on the horizontal axis to the _____ of the good on the vertical axis.
   a. marginal utility (MU); marginal utility (MU)
   b. total utility (TU); total utility (TU)

c. marginal product (MP); marginal product (MP)
d. price (P); total utility (TU)

8. The equation for a budget line for goods X and Y, with P_x being the price of X, P_y being the price of Y, and B being the budget, can be written as
    a. $P_xX + P_yY = B$.
    b. $P_xX + P_yY = 1/B$.
    c. $P_xX = B + P_yY$.
    d. $P_xX/P_yY = 1 - B$.

9. Given the budget line and indifference curves shown in Exhibit A-6, consumer equilibrium occurs at point
    a. A.
    b. B.
    c. C.
    d. D.
    e. E.

10. Given the budget line and indifference curves shown in Exhibit A-6, assume the consumer is initially at point C. To maximize total utility, the consumer should
    a. purchase more of good X and less of good Y.
    b. remain at point C.
    c. move to point B and then to point A.
    d. purchase more of good Y and less of good X.

a. marginal utility of one good.
b. total utility of one good.
c. marginal substitution value (MSV).
d. marginal transitivity of one good.

12. The marginal rate of substitution _____ as one moves downward along the indifference curve.
    a. increases
    b. remains constant
    c. decreases
    d. increases and then decreases

13. Assume P_x is the price of good X on the horizontal axis and P_y is the price of good Y on the vertical axis. The slope of the budget line equals
    a. P_y/P_xY.
    b. P_yQ_y/P_xQ_x.
    c. $(1 - P_y/P_x)$.
    d. P_x/P_y.

14. As shown in Exhibit A-7, the marginal rate of substitution (MRS) at point B is equal to
    a. 0.33.
    b. 2.0.
    c. 0.5.
    d. 3.0.

EXHIBIT A-7 Consumer Equilibrium

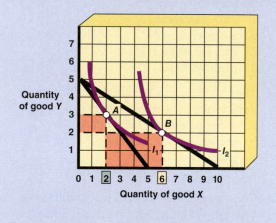

11. An indifference curve has a negative slope because movement along the curve requires the consumer to give up the

EXHIBIT A-6 Consumer Equilibrium

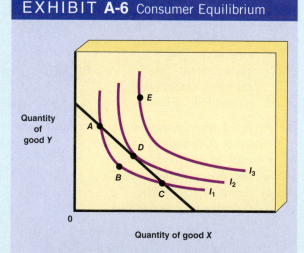

15. As shown in Exhibit A-7, movement from consumer equilibrium at point A to point B is caused by a(an)
    a. increase in the price of good X.
    b. decrease in the price of good X.
    c. increase in the price of good Y.
    d. decrease in the price of good Y.

CHAPTER 7

Production Costs

CHAPTER PREVIEW

Suppose you dream of owning your own company. That's right! You want to be an entrepreneur. You crave the excitement of starting your own firm and making it successful. Instead of working for someone else, you want to be your own boss. You are under no illusions; it is going to take hard work and sacrifice.

You are an electrical engineer who is an expert at designing electronic components for cell phones and similar applications. So you quit your job and invest your nest egg in starting Computech (a mythical company). You lease factory space, hire employees,

and purchase raw materials, and soon your company's products begin rolling off the assembly line. And then you find that production cost considerations influence each decision you make in this new business venture.

The purpose of this chapter is to study production and its relationship to various types of costs. Whether your company is new and small or an international giant, understanding costs is essential for success. In this chapter and the next two chapters, you will follow Computech and learn the basic principles of production and the way various types of costs vary with output.

IN THIS CHAPTER, YOU WILL LEARN TO SOLVE THESE ECONOMICS PUZZLES:

- Why would an accountant say a firm is making a profit and an economist say it is losing money?

- What is the difference between the short run and the long run?

- How can a company make a profit with a free website?

7-1 COSTS AND PROFIT

A basic assumption in economics is that the motivation for business decisions is profit maximization. Economists realize that managers of firms sometimes pursue other goals, such as contributing to the United Way or building an empire for the purpose of ego satisfaction. Nevertheless, the profit maximization goal has proved to be the best theory to explain why managers of firms choose a particular level of output or price. To understand profit as a driving force for business firms, we must distinguish between the way economists measure costs and the way accountants measure costs.

7-1a Explicit and Implicit Costs

Economists define the total opportunity cost of a business as the sum of *explicit costs* and *implicit costs*. **Explicit costs** are payments to nonowners of a firm for their resources. In our Computech example, explicit costs include the wages paid to labor, the rental charges for a plant, the cost of electricity, the cost of materials, and the cost of medical insurance. These resources are owned outside the firm and must be purchased with actual payments to these "outsiders."

Implicit costs are the opportunity costs of using resources owned by a firm. These are opportunity costs of resources because the firm makes no actual payments to outsiders. When you started Computech, you gave up the opportunity to earn a salary as an electrical engineer for someone else's firm. When you invested your nest egg in your own enterprise, you gave up the opportunity to earn interest. You also used a building you own to warehouse Computech products. Although you made no payment to anyone, you gave up the opportunity to earn rental payments.

Explicit costs
Payments to nonowners of a firm for their resources.

Implicit costs
The opportunity costs of using resources owned by a firm.

7-1b Economic and Accounting Profit

In everyday use, the word *profit* is defined as follows:

$$\textbf{Profit} = \textbf{total revenue} - \textbf{total cost}$$

Economists call this concept *accounting profit*. This popular formula is expressed in economics as

$$\textbf{Accounting profit} = \textbf{total revenue} - \textbf{total explicit cost}$$

Because economic decisions include implicit as well as explicit costs, economists use the concept of economic profit instead of accounting profit. **Economic profit** is total revenue minus explicit and implicit costs. Economic profit can be positive, zero, or negative (an economic loss). Expressed as an equation:

$$\textbf{Economic profit} = \textbf{total revenue} - \textbf{total opportunity costs}$$

or

$$\textbf{Economic profit} = \textbf{total revenue} - (\textbf{explicit costs} + \textbf{implicit costs})$$

Economic profit
Total revenue minus explicit and implicit costs.

Exhibit 1 illustrates the importance of the difference between accounting profit and economic profit. Computech must know how well it is doing, so you hire an accounting firm to prepare a financial report. The exhibit shows that Computech earned total revenue of $500,000 in its first year of operation. Explicit costs for wages, materials, interest,

EXHIBIT 1 Computech's Accounting Profit versus Economic Profit

Item	Accounting profit	Economic profit
Total revenue	$500,000	$500,000
Less explicit costs:		
Wages and salaries	400,000	400,000
Materials	50,000	50,000
Interest paid	10,000	10,000
Other payments	10,000	10,000
Less implicit costs:		
Forgone salary	0	50,000
Forgone rent	0	10,000
Forgone interest	0	5,000
Equals profit	$30,000	−$35,000

and other payments totaled $470,000. Based on standard accounting procedures, this left an accounting profit of $30,000.

If the analysis ends with accounting profit, Computech is profitable. But accounting practice overstates profit. Because implicit costs are subjective and therefore difficult to measure, accounting profit ignores implicit costs. A few examples will illustrate the importance of implicit costs. Your $50,000-a-year salary as an electrical engineer was forgone in order to spend all your time as owner of Computech. Also forgone were $10,000 in rental income and $5,000 in interest that you would have otherwise earned by keeping your savings in the bank. Subtracting both explicit and implicit costs from total revenue, Computech had an economic loss of $35,000. The firm is failing to cover all the opportunity costs of using its resources in the electronics industry. Thus, the firm's resources would earn a higher return if used for other alternatives.

How would you interpret a zero economic profit? It's not as bad as it sounds. Economists call this condition normal profit. **Normal profit** is the minimum profit necessary to keep a firm in operation. Zero economic profit signifies there is just enough total revenue to pay the owners for all explicit and implicit costs. Stated differently, there is no benefit from reallocating resources to another use. For example, assume an owner earns zero economic profit, including an implicit (forfeited) cost of $50,000 per year that could have been earned working for someone else. This means the owner earned as much as would have been earned in the next best employment opportunity.

Normal profit
The minimum profit necessary to keep a firm in operation. A firm that earns normal profits earns total revenue equal to its total opportunity cost.

Since business decision making is based on economic profit, rather than accounting profit, the word *profit* in this text always means economic profit.

CONCLUSION

CHECKPOINT

> **Should the Professor Go or Stay?**
> Professor Martin is considering leaving the university and opening a consulting business. For her services as a consultant, she would be paid $110,000 a year. To open this business, Professor Martin must convert a house from which she collects rent of $20,000 per year into an office and hire an assistant at a salary of $25,000 per year. The university pays Professor Martin $75,000 a year. Based only on economic decision making, do you predict the professor will leave the university to start a new business?

7-2 SHORT-RUN PRODUCTION COSTS

Having presented the basic definitions of total cost, the next step is to study cost theory. In this section, we explore the relationship between output and cost in the short run. In the next section, the time horizon shifts to the long run.

7-2a Short Run versus Long Run

Suppose I asked you, "What is the difference between the short run and the long run?" Your answer might be that the short run is less than a year and the long run is over a year. Good guess, but wrong! Economists do not partition production decisions based on any specific number of days, months, or years. Instead, the distinction depends on the ability to vary the quantity of inputs or resources used in production. There are two types of inputs—*fixed inputs* and *variable inputs*. A **fixed input** is any resource for which the quantity cannot change during the period of time under consideration. For example, the physical size of a firm's plant and the production capacity of heavy machines cannot easily change within a short period of time. They must remain as fixed amounts while managers decide to vary output. In addition to fixed inputs, the firm uses *variable inputs* in the production process. A **variable input** is any resource for which the quantity can change during the period of time under consideration. For example, managers can hire fewer or more workers during a given year. They can also change the amount of raw materials and electricity used in production.

Now we can link the concepts of fixed and variable inputs to the *short run* and the *long run*. The **short run** is a period of time so short that there is at least one fixed input. For example, the short run is a period of time during which a firm can increase output by hiring more workers (variable input), while the size of the firm's plant (fixed input) remains unchanged. The firm's plant is the most difficult input to change quickly. The **long run** is a period of time so long that all inputs are variable. In the long run, the firm can build new factories or purchase new machinery. New firms can enter the industry, and existing firms may leave the industry.

7-2b The Production Function

Having defined inputs, we can now describe how these inputs are transferred into outputs using a concept called a production function. A **production function** is the relationship between the maximum amounts of output a firm can produce and various quantities of inputs. An assumption of the production function model we are about to develop is that the level of technology is fixed. Technological advances would mean more output is possible from a given quantity of inputs.

Fixed input
Any resource for which the quantity cannot change during the period of time under consideration.

Variable input
Any resource for which the quantity can change during the period of time under consideration.

Short run
A period of time so short that there is at least one fixed input.

Long run
A period of time so long that all inputs are variable.

Production function
The relationship between the maximum amounts of output a firm can produce and various quantities of inputs.

Exhibit 2(a) presents a short-run production function for Eaglecrest Vineyard. The variable input is the number of workers employed per day, and each worker is presumed to have equal job skills. The acreage, amount of fertilizer, and all other inputs are assumed to be fixed; therefore, our production model is operating in the short run. Employing zero workers produces no bushels of grapes. A single worker can produce 10 bushels per day, but a lot of time is wasted when one worker picks, loads containers, and transports the grapes to the winery. Adding a second worker raises output to 22 bushels per day because the workers divide the tasks and specialize, allowing the vineyard to more than double the output produced by just one worker. Adding four more workers raises total production to 50 bushels per day.

7-2c Marginal Product

The relationship between changes in total output and changes in labor is called the marginal product of labor. **Marginal product** is the change in total output produced by adding one unit of a variable input, with all other inputs used being held constant. When Eaglecrest increases labor from zero to one worker, output rises from 0 to 10 bushels produced per day. This increase is the result of the addition of one more worker; therefore, the marginal product of the first worker is 10 bushels per day. Adding the second worker increases total output by 12 bushels per day; therefore, the marginal ("extra") product of the second worker is 12 bushels per day. Similar marginal product calculations generate the marginal product curve shown in Exhibit 2(b). Note that marginal product is plotted at the midpoints shown in the table because the change in total output occurs between each additional unit of labor used.

Marginal product
The change in total output produced by adding one unit of a variable input, with all other inputs used being held constant.

7-2d The Law of Diminishing Returns

A long-established economic law called the law of diminishing returns determines the shape of the marginal product curve. The **law of diminishing returns** states that beyond some point the marginal product decreases as additional units of a variable factor are added to a fixed factor. Because the law of diminishing returns assumes at least one fixed input, this principle is a short-run, rather than a long-run, concept.

This law applies to production of both agricultural and nonagricultural products. Returning to Exhibit 2, we can identify and explain the law of diminishing returns in our Eaglecrest example. Initially, the total output curve rises quite rapidly as this firm hires the first two workers. The marginal product curve reflects the change in the total output curve because marginal product is the slope of the total output curve. As shown in Exhibit 2(b), the range from zero to two workers hired is called *increasing marginal returns*. In this range of output, the last worker hired adds more to total output than the previous worker.

Diminishing returns begin after the second worker is hired and the marginal product reaches its peak. Beyond two workers, diminishing returns occur because the marginal product declines. The short-run assumption guarantees this condition. Eventually, marginal product falls because the amount of land per worker falls as more workers are added to fixed quantities of land and other inputs used to produce wine. Similar reasoning applies to the Computech example introduced in the chapter preview. Assume Computech operates with a fixed plant size and a fixed number of machines and all other inputs except the number of workers are fixed. Those in the first group of workers hired divide the most important tasks among themselves, specialize, and achieve

Law of diminishing returns
The principle that beyond some point the marginal product decreases as additional units of a variable factor are added to a fixed factor.

EXHIBIT 2 A Production Function and the Law of Diminishing Returns

Part (a) shows how the total output of bushels of grapes per day increases and the number of workers increases while all other inputs remain constant. This figure is a short-run production function, which relates outputs to a one-variable input while all other inputs are fixed.

Part (b) illustrates the law of diminishing returns. The first worker adds 10 bushels of grapes per day, and marginal product is 10 bushels per day. Adding a second worker adds another 12 bushels of grapes per day to total output. This is the range of increasing marginal returns. After two workers, diminishing marginal returns set in, and marginal product declines continuously.

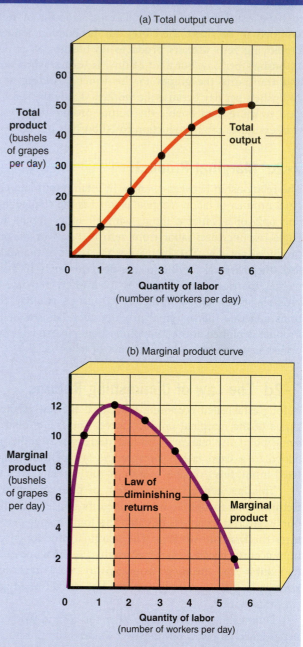

(a) Total output curve

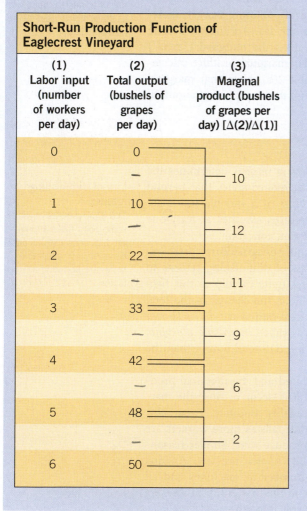

Short-Run Production Function of Eaglecrest Vineyard

(1) Labor input (number of workers per day)	(2) Total output (bushels of grapes per day)	(3) Marginal product (bushels of grapes per day) [Δ(2)/Δ(1)]
0	0	
		10
1	10	
		12
2	22	
		11
3	33	
		9
4	42	
		6
5	48	
		2
6	50	

(b) Marginal product curve

increasing returns. Then diminishing returns begin and continue as Computech employs each additional worker. The reason is that as more workers are added, they must share fixed inputs, such as machinery. Some workers are underemployed because they are standing around waiting for a machine to become available. Also, as more workers are hired, there are fewer important tasks to perform. As a result, marginal product declines. In the extreme case, marginal product would be negative. At some number of workers, they must work with such limited floor space, machines, and other fixed inputs that they start stepping on each other's toes. No profit-seeking firm would ever hire workers with zero or negative marginal product. Chapter 11 explains the labor market in more detail and shows how Computech decides exactly how many workers to hire.

7-3 SHORT-RUN COST FORMULAS

To make production decisions in either the short run or the long run, a business must determine the costs associated with producing various levels of output. Using Computech, you will study the relationship between two "families" of short-run costs and output: (1) the total cost curves, and (2) the average cost curves.

7-3a Total Cost Curves

Total Fixed Cost

As production expands in the short run, costs are divided into two basic categories— *total fixed cost* and *total variable cost*. **Total fixed cost (TFC)** consists of costs that do not vary as output varies and that must be paid even if output is zero. These are payments that the firm must make in the short run, regardless of the level of output. Even if a firm, such as Computech, produces nothing, it must still pay rent, interest on loans, property taxes, and fire insurance. Fixed costs are therefore beyond management's control in the short run. Fixed costs are sometimes referred to as "overhead costs." The total fixed cost for Computech is $100, as shown in column (2) of Exhibit 3.

Total fixed cost (TFC) Costs that do not vary as output varies and that must be paid even if output is zero. These are payments that the firm must make in the short run, regardless of the level of output.

Total Variable Cost

As the firm expands from zero output, total variable cost is added to total fixed cost. **Total variable cost (TVC)** consists of costs that are zero when output is zero and vary as output varies. These costs relate to the costs of variable inputs. Examples include wages for hourly workers, electricity, fuel, and raw materials. As a firm uses more input to produce output, its variable costs will increase. Management can influence variable costs in the short run by changing the level of output. Exhibit 3 lists the total variable cost for Computech in column (3).

Total variable cost (TVC) Costs that are zero when output is zero and vary as output varies.

Total Cost

Given total fixed cost and total variable cost, the firm can calculate total cost. **Total cost (TC)** is the sum of total fixed cost and total variable cost at each level of output. As a formula:

Total cost (TC) The sum of total fixed cost and total variable cost at each level of output.

$$TC = TFC + TVC$$

Total cost for Computech is shown in column (4) of Exhibit 3. Exhibit 4(a) uses the data in Exhibit 3 to construct graphically the relationships between total cost, total fixed cost, and total variable cost. Note that the TVC curve varies with the level of output and the

EXHIBIT 3 Short-Run Cost Schedule for Computech

(1) Total product (Q)	(2) Total fixed cost (TFC)	(3) Total variable cost (TVC)	(4) Total cost (TC)	(5) Marginal cost (MC)	(6) Average fixed cost (AFC)	(7) Average variable cost (AVC)	(8) Average total cost (ATC)
0	$100	$ 0	$100		–	–	–
				$50			
1	100	50	150		$100	$50	$150
				34			
2	100	84	184		50	42	92
				24			
3	100	108	208		33	36	69
				19			
4	100	127	227		25	32	57
				23			
5	100	150	250		20	30	50
				30			
6	100	180	280		17	30	47
				38			
7	100	218	318		14	31	45
				48			
8	100	266	366		13	33	46
				59			
9	100	325	425		11	36	47
				75			
10	100	400	500		10	40	50
				95			
11	100	495	595		9	45	54
				117			
12	100	612	712		8	51	59

TFC curve does not. The TC curve is simply the TVC curve plus the vertical distance between the TC and TVC curves, which represents TFC.

7-3b Average Cost Curves

In addition to total cost, firms are interested in the *per-unit cost* or *average cost*. Average cost, like product price, is stated on a per-unit basis. The last three columns in Exhibit 3

EXHIBIT 4 Short-Run Cost Curves

The curves in this exhibit are derived by plotting data from Exhibit 3. Part (a) shows that the total cost (TC) at each level of output is the sum of total variable cost (TVC) and total fixed cost (TFC). Because the TFC curve does not vary with output, the shape of the TC curve is determined by the shape of the TVC curve. The vertical distance between the TC and the TVC curves is TFC.

In part (b), the marginal cost (MC) curve decreases at first, then reaches a minimum, and then increases as output increases. The MC curve intersects both the average variable cost (AVC) curve and the average total cost (ATC) curve at the minimum point on each of these cost curves. The average fixed cost (AFC) curve declines continuously as output expands. AFC is also the difference between the ATC and the AVC curves at any quantity of output.

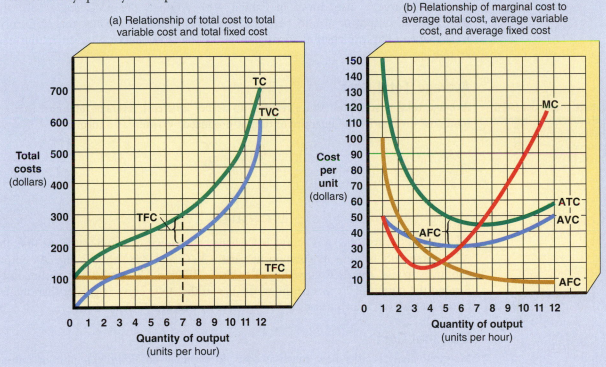

(a) Relationship of total cost to total variable cost and total fixed cost

(b) Relationship of marginal cost to average total cost, average variable cost, and average fixed cost

are *average fixed cost* (AFC), *average variable cost* (AVC), and *average total cost* (ATC). These average, or per-unit, curves are also shown in Exhibit 4(b). These three concepts are defined as follows:

Average Fixed Cost

As output increases, average fixed cost falls continuously. **Average fixed cost (AFC)** is total fixed cost divided by the quantity of output produced. Written as a formula:

$$AFC = \frac{TFC}{Q}$$

Average fixed cost (AFC)
Total fixed cost divided by the quantity of output produced.

As shown in Exhibit 4(b), the AFC curve approaches the horizontal axis, or zero, as output expands. This is because larger output numbers (a larger denominator) divide into TFC (a fixed numerator) and cause AFC to become smaller and smaller.

Average Variable Cost

Average variable cost (AVC)
Total variable cost divided by the quantity of output produced.

The average variable cost in our example forms a U-shaped curve. **Average variable cost (AVC)** is total variable cost divided by the quantity of output produced. Written as a formula:

$$\text{AVC} = \frac{\text{TVC}}{\text{Q}}$$

The AVC curve is also drawn in Exhibit 4(b). At first, the AVC curve falls, and then after an output of 6 units per hour, the AVC curve rises. Thus, the AVC curve is U-shaped. The explanation for the shape of the AVC curve is given in the next section.

Average Total Cost

Average total cost (ATC)
Total cost divided by the quantity of output produced.

Average total cost is sometimes referred to as *per-unit cost*. **Average total cost (ATC)** is total cost divided by the quantity of output produced. Written as a formula:

$$\text{ATC} = \frac{\text{TC}}{\text{Q}}$$

or

$$\text{ATC} = \text{AFC} + \text{AVC}$$

Like the AVC curve, the ATC curve is U-shaped, as shown in Exhibit 4(b). At first, the ATC curve falls because its component parts—AVC and AFC—are falling. As output continues to rise, the AVC curve begins to rise, while the AFC curve falls continuously. Beyond the output of 7 units per hour, the rise in the AVC curve is greater than the fall in the AFC curve, which causes the ATC curve to rise in a U-shaped pattern.

Marginal Cost

Marginal cost (MC)
The change in total cost when one additional unit of output is produced.

Marginal analysis asks how much it costs to produce an *additional* unit of output. Column (5) in Exhibit 3 is marginal cost. **Marginal cost (MC)** is the change in total cost when one additional unit of output is produced. Stated differently, marginal cost is the ratio of the change in total cost to a 1-unit change in output. Written as a formula:

$$\text{MC} = \frac{\text{change in TC}}{\text{change in Q}}$$

Changing output by one unit at a time simplifies the marginal cost calculations in our Computech example. The marginal cost data are listed between output levels to show that marginal cost is the change in total cost as the output level changes. Exhibit 4(b) shows this marginal cost schedule graphically. In the short run, a firm's marginal cost initially falls as output expands, eventually reaches a minimum, and then rises, forming a J-shaped curve. Note that marginal cost is plotted at the midpoints because the change in cost actually occurs between each additional unit of output.

Exhibit 5 summarizes a firm's short-run cost relationships.

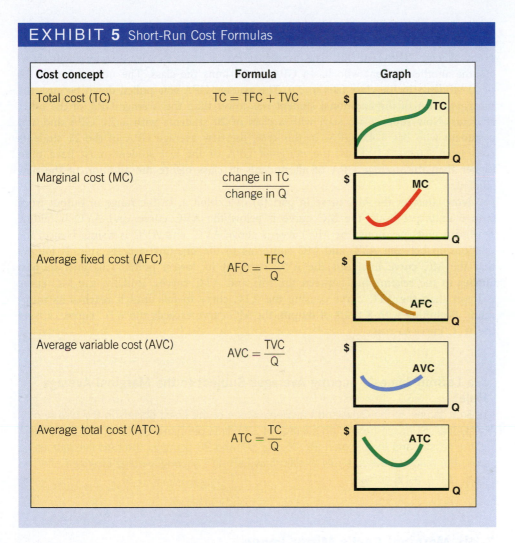

EXHIBIT 5 Short-Run Cost Formulas

Cost concept	Formula	Graph
Total cost (TC)	$TC = TFC + TVC$	
Marginal cost (MC)	$\dfrac{\text{change in TC}}{\text{change in Q}}$	
Average fixed cost (AFC)	$AFC = \dfrac{TFC}{Q}$	
Average variable cost (AVC)	$AVC = \dfrac{TVC}{Q}$	
Average total cost (ATC)	$ATC = \dfrac{TC}{Q}$	

7-4 MARGINAL COST RELATIONSHIPS

Part (b) of Exhibit 4 presents two important relationships that require explanation. First, we will explain the rule that links the marginal cost curve to the average cost curves. Second, we will return to the marginal product curve in Exhibit 2(b) and explain its connection to the marginal cost curve.

7-4a The Marginal-Average Rule

Observe that the MC curve in Exhibit 4(b) intersects both the AVC curve and the ATC curve at their minimum points. This is not accidental. It is a result of a relationship called the marginal-average rule. The **marginal-average rule** states that when marginal cost is below average cost, average cost falls. When marginal cost is above average cost, average cost rises. When marginal cost equals average cost, average cost is at its minimum point. The marginal-average rule applies to grades, weights, and any average figure.

Marginal-average rule
The rule that states when marginal cost is below average cost, average cost falls. When marginal cost is above average cost, average cost rises. When marginal cost equals average cost, average cost is at its minimum point.

Perhaps the best way to understand this rule is to apply it to a noneconomic example. Suppose there are 20 students in your class and each student has a grade point average (GPA) of 4.0. The average GPA of the class is, therefore, 4.0. Now assume another student who has a GPA of 2.0 joins the class. The new average GPA of 21 students in the class falls to 3.9. The average GPA was pulled down because the *marginal* GPA of the additional student was lower than the *average* GPA of the other students. Now suppose we start with a class of 20 students with a 2.0 GPA and add a student who has a 4.0 GPA. In this case, the new average GPA of the 21 students rises from 2.0 to 2.1. Thus, the *marginal* GPA of the last student must have been higher than the *average* GPA of all students in class before the addition of the new student.

Now consider the MC curve in part (b) of Exhibit 4. In the range of output from 0 to 6 units per hour, the MC curve is below the AVC curve, and AVC is falling. Beyond 6 units per hour, the MC curve is above AVC, and AVC is rising. Hence, the relationship between AVC and MC conforms to the marginal-average rule. It follows that the MC curve intersects the AVC curve at its lowest point. This analysis also applies to the relationship between the MC and ATC curves. Initially, the MC curve is lower than the ATC curve causing the ATC curve to fall until it reaches its minimum. Beginning with 8 units of output, the MC curve exceeds the ATC curve, causing the ATC curve to rise.

CHECKPOINT

Are LeBron James's Scoring Averages Subject to the Marginal-Average Rule?

LeBron James, of the Cleveland Cavaliers, is one of the finest players in the history of basketball. Suppose he had an average of 33 points per game over the first 10 games of the season and then scored 20, 25, 40, 50, and 20 points in the next five games. Does the marginal-average rule explain how LeBron's scoring average changed after each of the last 5 games?

7-4b Marginal Cost's Mirror Image

Since the MC curve determines the U-shape of the AVC and ATC curves, we must explain the J-shape of the MC curve. Exhibit 6 illustrates that the shape of the MC curve is the mirror reflection of the shape of the marginal product (MP) curve. Comparing parts (a) and (b) of Exhibit 6 gives the following:

CONCLUSION

The marginal cost declines as the marginal product of a variable input rises. Beginning at the point of diminishing returns, the marginal cost rises as the marginal product of a variable input declines.

As explained earlier in this chapter, the law of diminishing returns is the declining portion of the MP curve, and this range of production corresponds to the rising portion of the MC curve. To understand why this relationship exists, we return to the case of Eaglecrest Vineyard presented earlier in Exhibit 2. Now we again assume that labor is

EXHIBIT 6 The Inverse Relationship between Marginal Product and Marginal Cost

Part (a) represents the marginal product (MP) of labor curve. At first each additional worker hired adds more to output than does the previously hired worker and the MP curve rises until a maximum is reached at 2 workers hired. At 3 workers the law of diminishing returns sets in and each additional worker hired adds less output than previously hired workers.

Part (b) shows the marginal cost (MC) curve is a J-shaped curve that is inversely related to the MP curve. Assuming the wage rate remains constant, as the MP curve rises, the MC curve falls. When the MP curve reaches a maximum at two workers, the MC curve is at a minimum. As diminishing returns set in and the MP curve falls, the MC curve rises.

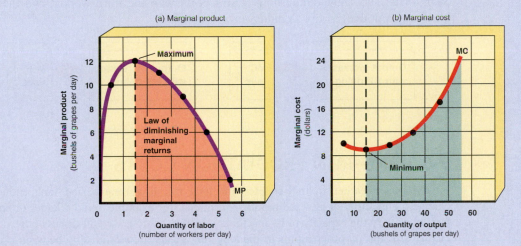

(1) Labor input (number of workers per day)	(2) Total output (bushels of grapes per day)	(3) Marginal product (bushels of grapes per day) [Δ(2)/Δ(1)]	(4) Total cost per day [$100 × (1)]	(5) Marginal cost [Δ(4)/(3)]
0	0		$0	
		10		$10.00
1	10		100	
		12		8.33
2	22		200	
		11		9.09
3	33		300	
		9		11.11
4	42		400	
		6		16.67
5	48		500	
		2		50.00
6	50		600	

the only variable input and add the new important assumption that the wage rate is constant at $100 per day. When Eaglecrest moves from zero labor to hire one worker, its total output rises from 0 to 10 bushels of grapes per day. As explained earlier, the marginal product is also 10 bushels, and the marginal cost is $100/10 = $10 ($\Delta TC / \Delta Q = \Delta TC/MP$). When Eaglecrest hires the second worker, total output rises by 12 bushels per day. Hiring this worker increases the firm's total cost by $100, while the marginal product rises to 12 bushels. The marginal cost of the second worker therefore falls to a minimum at $100/12 = $8.33. At this point, it is noteworthy that the minimum point on the MC curve corresponds to the maximum point on the MP curve. The third worker hired yields only 11 additional bushels of grapes per day, so marginal cost rises to $9.09 ($100/11). Thus, diminishing returns begin with the third worker, and the marginal cost continues to rise as more workers are hired.

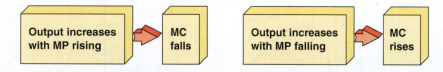

7-5 LONG-RUN PRODUCTION COSTS

As mentioned earlier in this chapter, the long run is a time period long enough to change the quantity of all fixed inputs. A firm can, for example, build a larger or smaller factory or vary the capacity of its machinery. In this section, we will discuss how varying factory size and *all* other inputs in the long run affects the relationship between production and costs.

7-5a Long-Run Average Cost Curves

Suppose Computech is making its production plans for the future. Taking a long-run view of production means the firm is not locked into a small, medium-sized, or large factory. However, once a factory of any particular size is built, the firm operates in the short run because the plant becomes a fixed input.

CONCLUSION A firm operates in the short run when there is insufficient time to alter some fixed input. The firm plans in the long run when all inputs are variable.

Exhibit 7 illustrates a situation in which there are only three possible factory sizes Computech might select. Short-run cost curves representing these three possible plant sizes are labeled $SRATC_s$, $SRATC_m$, and $SRATC_l$. SR is the abbreviation for short run, and ATC stands for average total cost. The subscripts s, m, and l represent small, medium, and large plant sizes, respectively. In the previous sections, there was no need to use SR for short run because we were discussing only short-run cost curves and not long-run cost curves.

Suppose Computech estimates that it will be producing an output level of 6 units per hour for the foreseeable future. Which plant size should the company choose? It will build the

EXHIBIT 7 The Relationship between Three Factory Sizes and the Long-Run Average Cost Curve

Each of the three short-run ATC curves in the exhibit corresponds to a different plant size. Assuming these are the only three plant-size choices, a firm can choose any one of these plant sizes in the long run. For example, a young firm may operate a small plant represented by the U-shaped short-run average total cost curve $SRATC_s$. As a firm matures and demand for its product expands, it can decide to build a larger factory, corresponding to either $SRATC_m$ or $SRATC_l$. The long-run average cost curve, LRAC, is the green shaded scalloped curve joining the short-run curves below their intersections.

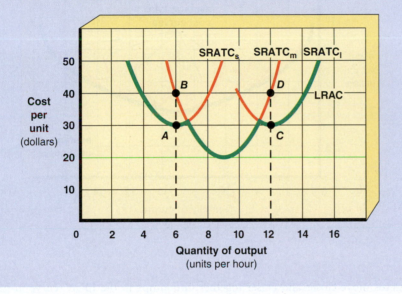

plant size represented by $SRATC_s$ because this affords a lower cost of $30 per unit (point A) than the factory size represented by $SRATC_m$, which has a cost of $40 per unit (point B).

What if production is expected to be 12 units per hour? In this case, the firm will choose the plant size represented by $SRATC_l$. At this plant size, the cost is $30 per unit (point C), which is lower than $40 per unit (point D).

The plant size selected by a firm in the long run depends on the expected level of production.

CONCLUSION

Using the three short-run average cost curves shown in Exhibit 7, we can construct the firm's long-run average cost curve. The **Long-run average cost curve (LRAC)** curve traces the lowest cost per unit at which a firm can produce any level of output after the firm can build any desired plant size. The LRAC curve is often called the firm's planning curve. In Exhibit 7, the green curve represents the LRAC curve.

Exhibit 8 shows there are actually an infinite number of possible plant sizes from which managers can choose in the long run. As the intersection points of the short-run

Long-run average cost curve (LRAC)
The curve that traces the lowest cost per unit at which a firm can produce any level of output when the firm can build any desired plant size.

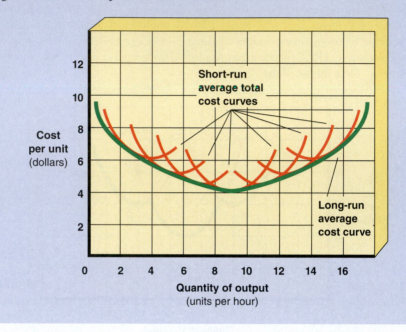

ATC curves move closer and closer together, the lumps in the LRAC curve in Exhibit 7 disappear. With a great variety of plant sizes, the corresponding short-run ATC curves trace a smooth LRAC curve in Exhibit 8. Over the range of output when the LRAC curve falls, the tangency points are to the left of the minimum points on the short-run ATC curves. As output expands and the LRAC curve rises, the tangency points are to the right of the minimum points on the short-run ATC curves.

7-5b Different Scales of Production

Exhibit 8 depicts long-run average cost as a U-shaped curve. In this section, we will discuss the reasons why the LRAC curve first falls and then rises when output expands in the long run. In addition, we will learn that the LRAC curve can have a variety of shapes. Note that the law of diminishing returns is not an explanation here because in the long run there are no fixed inputs.

For simplicity, Exhibit 9 excludes possible short-run ATC curves that touch points along the LRAC curve. Typically, a young firm starts small and builds larger plants as it matures. As the scale of operation expands, the LRAC curve can follow three different patterns. Over the lowest range of output from zero to Q_1, the firm experiences economies of scale. **Economies of scale** exist when the long-run average cost curve declines as the firm increases output.

Economies of scale
A situation in which the long-run average cost curve declines as the firm increases output.

EXHIBIT 9 A Long-Run Average Cost Curve with Constant Returns to Scale

The long-run average cost curve LRAC illustrates a firm that experiences economies of scale until output level Q_1 is reached. Between output levels Q_1 and Q_2, the LRAC curve is flat, and there are constant returns to scale. Beyond output level Q_2, the firm experiences diseconomies of scale, and the LRAC curve rises.

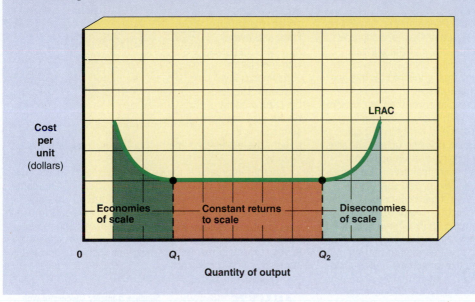

There are several reasons for economies of scale. First, a larger firm can increase its *division of labor* and *use of specialization*. Adam Smith noted in *The Wealth of Nations*, published in 1776, that the output of a pin factory is greater when one worker draws the wire, a second straightens it, a third cuts it, a fourth grinds the point, and a fifth makes the head of the pin. As a firm initially expands, having more workers allows managers to break a job into small tasks. Then each worker—including managers—can specialize by mastering narrowly defined tasks rather than trying to be a jack-of-all-trades.[1] The classic example is Henry Ford's assembly line, which greatly reduced the cost of producing automobiles. Today, McDonald's trains its workers at "Hamburger University; then some workers prepare food, some specialize in taking orders, and a few workers specialize in the drive-through window operation.

Second, economies of scale result from greater *efficiency of capital*. Suppose machine A costs $1,000 and produces 1,000 units per day. Machine B costs $4,000, but it is technologically more efficient and has a capacity of 8,000 units per day. The low-output firm will find it too costly to purchase machine B, so it uses machine A, and its average cost is $1. The large-scale firm can afford to purchase machine B and produce more efficiently at a per-unit cost of only $0.50.

The LRAC curve may not have a flat, or horizontal portion as shown in Exhibit 8. But, between some levels of output, such as Q_1 and Q_2 in Exhibit 9, the LRAC curve no

---

[1]Adam Smith, *An Inquiry into the Nature and Causes of the Wealth of Nations* (1776; reprint, New York: Random House, 1937), pp. 4–6.

YOU'RE THE ECONOMIST

YOU'RE THE ECONOMIST

Applicable Concept: Economies and Diseconomies of Scale

Why Is That Website You're Using Free?

Pick the best price that you want to pay for a product. Is zero reserved only for those who believe in Santa Claus? Recall the famous saying by economist Milton Friedman that "there's no such thing as a free lunch." Well, today more and more Web companies are using digital technology and the principles of *freeconomics* to make profits by giving something away free of charge. And the key to understanding this radical business model is the concept of economies of scale.

How is it possible for companies to cover their production costs with a price of zero? Don't Web businesses have huge fixed costs to buy computer servers and design web pages? This is true, but once the servers are powered up and the sites are online, the marginal cost of logging in each additional customer is very small. Then as the companies scale expands over time, the cost of servers, bandwidth, and software are spread out over millions of users, and the long-run cost curve declines to almost zero, which is economies of scale.

In the Web land of free payments called *freemiums*, the basic idea is to shift from the view of a market price matching buyers and sellers of a product to a free system with many participants and only a few who exchange cash. After customers get used to the free services, the companies hope that people will pay for more advanced services. Examples of freemiums are Adobe Reader, search engines, blogging platforms, and Skype-to-Skype phone calls. The revenue from the premiums for more powerful services covers the cost of both the premium and free activities. This is the cross-subsidy approach. A legendary example of this marketing strategy is King Gillette, who in the early 1900s was having no success selling men on the idea of shaving with disposable thin blades rather than with a straight razor. The solution was

to bundle free razors with gum, coffee, marshmallows, and even new bank deposits with the slogan "Shave and Save" attached. The freebie razor without blades was useless so customers bought the blades and the rest of this success story is history.

Another approach is to use free services to deliver advertising, just like traditional broadcast TV or radio. One company that has very successfully applied the advertising approach to freemiums is Google. There is no cost to use its search engine, but the results pages feature "Sponsored Links," which are advertisements paid for by websites related to your search terms. Google used this model to achieve impressive financial results.

ANALYZE THE ISSUE Suppose a hugely successful Web company has used freeconomics, expanded its scale of operations, and spread its long-run costs over larger and larger audiences. However, after years of profits, its continued growth has now caused the company's profits to fall. Using production costs theory, explain why this situation might be occurring.

---

longer declines or rises. In this range of output, the firm increases its plant size, but the LRAC curve remains flat. Economists call this situation constant returns to scale. **Constant returns to scale** exists when the LRAC curve does not change as the firm increases output. Economists believe this is the shape of the LRAC curve in many real-world industries. The scale of operation is important for competitive reasons. Consider a young firm producing less than output Q_1 and competing against a more established firm producing in the constant-returns-to-scale range of output. The LRAC curve shows that the older firm has an average cost advantage.

As a firm becomes large and expands output beyond some level, such as Q_2 in Exhibit 9, it encounters diseconomies of scale. **Diseconomies of scale** exists when the long-run average cost curve rises as the firm increases output. A very large-scale firm becomes harder to manage. As the firm grows, the chain of command lengthens, and communication becomes more complex. People communicate through forms instead of

Constant returns to scale
A situation in which the long-run average cost curve does not change as the firm increases output.

Diseconomies of scale
A situation in which the long-run average cost curve rises as the firm increases output.

direct conversation. The firm becomes too bureaucratic, and operations bog down in red tape. Layer upon layer of managers are paid big salaries to shuffle papers that have little or nothing to do with beating the competition by producing output at a lower cost. Consequently, it is no surprise that a firm can become too big, and these management problems can cause the average cost of production to rise.

Steven Jobs, founder of Apple Computer Company, stated:

When you are growing [too big], you start adding middle management like crazy... People in the middle have no understanding of the business, and because of that, they screw up communications. To them, it's just a job. The corporation ends up with mediocre people that form a layer of concrete.[2]

Ideally, firms want to operate at a scale that minimizes their LRAC. Operating in the diseconomies of scale region can motivate firms to downsize, to reduce their costs in order to remain price competitive. On the other hand, if economies of scale can be experienced, firms are motivated to expand output, moving down their LRAC curve.

Key Concepts

Explicit costs
Implicit costs
Economic profit
Normal profit
Fixed input
Variable input
Short run
Long run

Production function
Marginal product
Law of diminishing returns
Total fixed cost (TFC)
Total variable cost (TVC)
Total cost (TC)

Average fixed cost (AFC)
Average variable cost (AVC)
Average total cost (ATC)
Marginal cost (MC)
Marginal-average rule

Long-run average cost curve (LRAC)
Economies of scale
Constant returns to scale
Diseconomies of scale

Summary

- **Economic profit** is equal to total revenue minus both *explicit* and *implicit* costs. **Explicit costs** are payments to nonowners of a firm for their resources. **Implicit costs** are the opportunity costs of forgone returns to resources owned by a firm. Economic profit is total revenue minus explicit and implicit costs. Economic profit can be positive, zero, or negative (an economic loss). Economic profit is important for decision-making purposes because it includes implicit costs and accounting profit does not. Accounting profit equals total revenue minus explicit costs.

- **Normal profit** is the minimum profit necessary to keep a firm in operation. A normal profit is a zero economic profit, and it signifies there is just enough total revenue to pay the owners for all explicit and implicit costs.

- A **fixed input** is any resource for which the quantity cannot change during the period of time under consideration. A **variable input** is any resource for which the quantity can change during the period of time under consideration.

[2]Deborah Wise and Catherine Harris, "Apple's New Crusade," *Business Week*, November 26, 1984, p. 156.

- The **short run** is a time period during which a firm has at least one fixed input, such as its factory size. The **long run** for a firm is defined as a period during which all inputs are variable.

- A **production function** is the relationship between output and inputs. Holding all other factors of production constant, the production function shows the total output as the amount of one input, such as labor, varies.

- **Marginal product** is the change in total output caused by a one-unit change in a variable input, such as the number of workers hired. The **law of diminishing returns** states that after some level of output in the short run, each additional unit of the variable input yields smaller and smaller marginal product. This range of declining marginal product is the region of diminishing returns.

- **Total fixed cost (TFC)** consists of costs that do not vary with the level of output, such as rent for office space. Total fixed cost is the cost of inputs that do not change as a firm changes output in the short run. **Total variable cost (TVC)** consists of costs that vary with the level of output, such as wages. Total variable cost is the cost of variable inputs used in production. **Total cost (TC)** is the sum of total fixed cost (TFC) and total variable cost (TVC).

Total Cost Curves

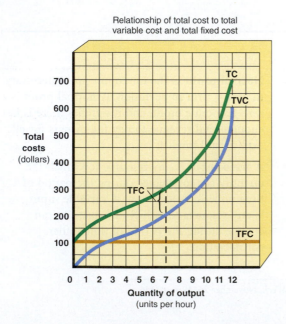

Relationship of total cost to total variable cost and total fixed cost

- **Marginal cost (MC)** is the change in total cost associated with one additional unit of output. **Average fixed cost (AFC)** is the total fixed cost divided by total output. **Average variable cost (AVC)** is the total variable cost divided by total output. **Average total cost (ATC)** is the total cost divided by output, or the sum of average fixed cost and average variable cost.

Average and Marginal Cost Curves

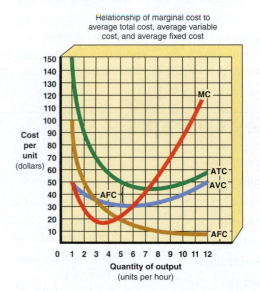

Relationship of marginal cost to average total cost, average variable cost, and average fixed cost

- The **marginal-average rule** explains the relationship between marginal cost and average cost. When marginal cost is less than average cost, average cost falls. When marginal cost is greater than average cost, average cost rises. Following this rule, the marginal cost curve intersects the average variable cost curve and the average total cost curve at their minimum points.

- **Marginal cost (MC)** and **marginal product (MP)** are mirror images of each other. Assuming a constant wage rate, marginal cost equals the wage rate divided by the marginal product. Increasing returns cause marginal cost to fall, and diminishing returns cause marginal cost to rise. This explains the J-shaped marginal cost curve.

Marginal Product Curve

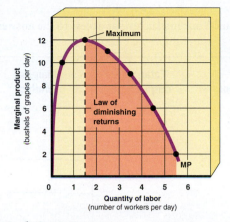

Marginal Cost Curve

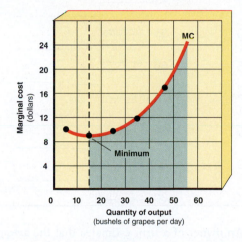

- The **long-run average cost curve (LRAC)** is a curve drawn tangent to all possible short-run average total cost curves. When the LRAC curve decreases as output increases, a firm experiences **economies of scale**. If the LRAC curve remains unchanged as output increases, a firm experiences **constant returns to scale**. If the LRAC curve increases as output increases, a firm experiences **diseconomies of scale**.

Long-Run Average Cost Curve

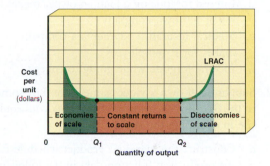

Summary of Conclusion Statements

- Because business decision making is based on economic profit, rather than accounting profit, the word *profit* in this text always means economic profit.

- The marginal cost declines as the marginal product of a variable input rises. Beginning at the point of diminishing returns, the marginal cost rises as the marginal product of a variable input declines.

- A firm operates in the short run when there is insufficient time to alter some fixed input. The firm plans in the long run when all inputs are variable.

- The plant size selected by a firm in the long run depends on the expected level of production.

Study Questions and Problems

Please see Appendix A for answers to the odd-numbered questions. Your instructor has access to the answers for even-numbered questions.

1. Indicate whether each of the following is an explicit cost or an implicit cost.
   a. A manager's salary
   b. Payments to Dell for computers
   c. A salary forgone by the owner of a firm by operating his or her own company
   d. Interest forgone on a loan an owner makes to his or her own company
   e. Medical insurance payments a company makes for its employees
   f. Income forgone while going to college

2. Suppose you own a video game store. List some of the fixed inputs and variable inputs you would use in operating the store.

3. a. Construct the marginal product schedule for the production function data in the following table.
   b. Graph the total output and marginal product curves, and identify increasing and diminishing marginal returns.

4. Consider this statement: "Total output starts falling when diminishing returns occur." Do you agree or disagree? Explain.

5. What effect might a decrease in the demand for high definition televisions have on the short-run average total cost curve for this product?

6. a. Construct the cost schedule using the data below for a firm operating in the short run.
   b. Graph the average variable cost, average total cost, and marginal cost curves.

7. Explain why the average total cost curve and the average variable cost curve move closer together as output expands.

8. Ace Manufacturing produces 1,000 hammers per day. The total fixed cost for the plant is $5,000 per day, and the total variable cost is $15,000 per day. Calculate the average fixed cost, average variable cost, average total cost, and total cost at the current output level.

Labor	Total output	Marginal product
0	0	
1	8	
2	18	
3	30	
4	43	
5	55	
6	65	
7	73	
8	79	
9	82	
10	80	

9. An owner of a firm estimates that the average total cost is $6.71 and the marginal cost is $6.71 at the current level of output. Explain the relationship between these marginal cost and average total cost figures.

10. What short-run effect might a decline in the demand for electronic components for automatic teller machines have on Computech's average total cost curve?

11. For mathematically minded students, what is the algebraic relationship between the equation for output and the equation for marginal product in Exhibit 2? Explain the circumstances under which the long-run supply curve for an industry is a horizontal line. Next, explain the circumstances under which the long-run supply curve for an industry is an upward-sloping line.

Total output (Q)	Total fixed cost (TFC)	Total variable cost (TVC)	Total cost (TC)	Marginal cost (MC)	Average fixed cost (AFC)	Average variable cost (AVC)	Average total cost (ATC)
0	$50	$____	$50		$____	$____	$____
				$____			
1	____	____	$70		____	____	____
				____			
2	____	____	$85		____	____	____
				____			
3	____	____	$95		____	____	____
				____			
4	____	____	$100		____	____	____
				____			
5	____	____	$110		____	____	____
				____			
6	____	____	$130		____	____	____
				____			
7	____	____	$165		____	____	____
				____			
8	____	____	$215		____	____	____
				____			
9	____	____	$275		____	____	____

✓ CHECKPOINT ANSWERS

Should the Professor Go or Stay?

In the consulting business, the accounting profit is $85,000. An accountant would calculate profit as the annual revenue of $110,000 less the explicit cost of $25,000 per year for the assistant's salary. However, the accountant would neglect implicit costs. Professor Martin's business venture would have implicit costs of $20,000 in forgone rent and $75,000 in forgone earnings. Her economic profit is −$10,000, calculated as the accounting profit of $85,000 less the total implicit costs of $95,000. If you said the professor will pass up the potential accounting profit and stay with the university to avoid an economic loss, **YOU ARE CORRECT**.

Are LeBron James's Scoring Averages Subject to the Marginal-Average Rule?

Since James's marginal points in games 11 and 12 were below his average points per game, his average points per game fell from 33 to 31. Games 13 and 14 lifted his average from 31 to 33 points per game because his marginal points in both of these games exceeded his average points per game. Finally, the 20 points in game 15 again reduced his average back to 32 points per game. Thus, when James's marginal points scored in a game were below his season's average points per game, his average fell. When James's marginal points scored in a game were above his season's average points per game, his average rose.

Game	Marginal points	Average points
10		33 over 10 games
11	20	$32 = (33 \times 10 + 20)/11$ games
12	25	$31 = (32 \times 11 + 25)/12$ games
13	40	$32 = (31 \times 12 + 40)/13$ games
14	50	$33 = (32 \times 13 + 50)/14$ games
15	20	$32 = (33 \times 14 + 20)/15$ games

If you said even LeBron James cannot beat the marginal-average rule, **YOU ARE CORRECT**.

Sample Quiz

Please see Appendix B for answers to Sample Quiz questions.

1. A firm has $200 million in total revenue and explicit costs of $190 million. Suppose its owners have invested $100 million in the company at an opportunity cost of 10 percent interest per year. What is the firm's economic profit?
   a. $400 million
   b. $100 million
   c. $80 million
   d. zero

2. The units of variable input in a production process are 1, 2, 3, 4, and 5, and the corresponding total outputs are 30, 34, 37, 39, and 40, respectively. What is the marginal product of the fourth unit?
   a. 2
   b. 1
   c. 37
   d. 39

3. The situation in which the marginal product of labor is greater than zero and declining as more labor is hired is called the law of
   a. negative response.
   b. inverse return to labor.
   c. diminishing returns.
   d. demand.

4. Which of the following is true if the total variable cost curve is rising?
   a. Average fixed cost is increasing.
   b. Marginal cost is decreasing.
   c. Marginal cost is increasing.
   d. Average fixed cost is constant.

5. If the minimum points of all possible short-run average total cost curves become successively lower as quantity of output increases,
   a. the firm should try to produce less output.
   b. total fixed costs are constant along the LRAC curve.
   c. there are economies of scale.
   d. the firm is probably having significant management problems.

6. A young chef is considering opening his own sushi bar. To do so, he would have to quit his current job, which pays $20,000 a year, and take

over a store building that he owns and currently rents to his brother for $6,000 a year. His expenses at the sushi bar would be $50,000 for food and $2,000 for gas and electricity. What are his explicit costs?

a. $26,000
b. $66,000
c. $78,000
d. $52,000

7. An economist left her $100,000-a-year teaching position to work full-time in her own consulting business. In the first year, she had total revenue of $200,000 and business expenses of $150,000. She made an

a. implicit profit.
b. economic loss.
c. economic profit.
d. accounting loss but not an economic loss.

8. Which of the following *best* describes total fixed cost?

a. The change in total cost when one additional unit of output is produced
b. Total cost divided by the quantity of output produced
c. Total variable cost divided by the quantity of output produced
d. Total fixed cost divided by the quantity of output produced
e. Costs that do not vary as output varies

9. A farm can produce 10,000 bushels of wheat per year with five workers and 13,000 bushels with six workers. What is the marginal product of the sixth worker for this farm?

a. 10,000 bushels
b. 3,000 bushels
c. 500 bushels
d. 23,000 bushels

10. The law of diminishing returns applies to which of the following segments of the marginal product of labor curve?

a. The entire curve
b. The downward-sloping segment only
c. The upward-sloping segment only
d. The point where labor input is zero

11. Which of the following is *true* at the point where diminishing returns set in?

a. Both marginal product and marginal cost are at a maximum.
b. Both marginal product and marginal cost are at a minimum.
c. Marginal product is at a maximum, and marginal cost is at a minimum.
d. Marginal product is at a minimum, and marginal cost is at a maximum.

12. In the long run, total fixed cost

a. falls.
b. rises.
c. is constant.
d. does not exist.

13. Which of the following is considered a fixed cost of operating an automobile?

a. Gasoline
b. Tires
c. Oil changes
d. Maintenance
e. Registration fees

14. Which of the following is an example of a fixed cost for a fishing company?

a. The cost of hiring a fishing crew
b. The fuel costs of running the boat
c. The monthly loan payment on the boat
d. The supply of nets, hooks, and fishing lines

15. The decreasing portion of a firm's long-run average cost curve is attributable to

a. increasing marginal cost.
b. economies of scale.
c. diseconomies of scale.
d. constant returns to scale.

16. Diseconomies of scale exist over the range of output for which the long-run average cost curve is

a. constant.
b. falling.
c. rising.
d. none of the above.

17. Assume both the marginal cost and the average variable cost curves are U-shaped. At the minimum point on the AVC curve, marginal cost must be

a. greater than the average variable cost.
b. less than the average variable cost.
c. equal to the average variable cost.
d. at its minimum.

EXHIBIT 10 Costs Schedules for Producing Pizza

Pizzas	Fixed cost	Variable cost	Total cost	Marginal cost
0	$	$	$	$
1		5		
2		13		
3				10
4	100		140	
5				20
6		85		
7			215	

18. By filling in the blanks in Exhibit 10 the total cost of producing zero pizzas is shown to be equal to
    a. zero.
    b. $100.
    c. $5.
    d. $105.
    e. $95.

19. By filling in the blanks in Exhibit 10 the fixed cost of producing six pizzas is shown to be equal to
    a. $100.
    b. $150.
    c. $200.
    d. $185.
    e. $85.

20. By filling in the blanks in Exhibit 10 the average variable cost of producing four pizzas is shown to be equal to
    a. $10.
    b. $15.
    c. $20.
    d. $40.
    e. $85.

21. By filling in the blanks in Exhibit 10 the average total cost of producing 5 pizzas is shown to be equal to
    a. $12.
    b. $15.
    c. $32.
    d. $85.
    e. $160.

22. By filling in the blanks in Exhibit 10 the marginal cost of the fourth pizza is shown to be equal to
    a. $10.
    b. $15.
    c. $17.
    d. $23.
    e. $40.

EXHIBIT 11 Long-Run Average Cost Curves

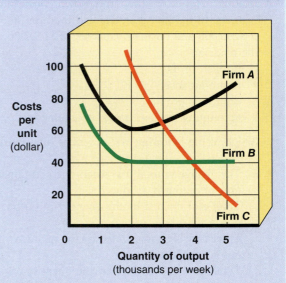

23. In Exhibit 11 which firm's long-run average cost curve experiences constant returns to scale?
    a. Firm A
    b. Firm B
    c. Firm C
    d. Firms A and C

24. Which firm in Exhibit 11 displays a long-run average cost curve with diseconomies of scale beginning at 2,000 units of output per week?
    a. Firm A
    b. Firm B
    c. Firm C
    d. Firms A and C

25. Which firm in Exhibit 11 displays a long-run average cost curve with economies of scale throughout the range of output shown?
    a. Firm A
    b. Firm B
    c. Firm C
    d. Firms A and B

ROAD MAP

PART 2
Microeconomics Fundamentals

This road map feature helps you tie together material in the part as you travel the Economic Way of Thinking Highway. The following are review questions listed by chapter from the previous part. The key concept in each question is given for emphasis, and each question or set of questions concludes with an interactive game to reinforce the concepts. The correct answers to the multiple choice questions are given in Appendix C. If your instructor has included MindTap in your course, visit MindTap to play the interactive Causation Chain Game.

Chapter 3: Market Demand and Supply

1. Key Concept: Movement along versus shift in demand

Which of the following would shift the demand curve for autos to the right?

a. A fall in the price of autos
b. A fall in the price of auto insurance
c. A fall in consumers' incomes
d. A fall in the price of steel

CAUSATION CHAIN GAME
Movement along a Demand Curve versus a Shift in Demand—Exhibit 3

2. Key Concept: Movement along versus shift in supply

Assuming that both soybeans and tobacco can be grown on the same land, a decrease in the price of tobacco, other things being equal, causes a(an)

a. rightward shift of the supply curve for tobacco.
b. upward movement along the supply curve for soybeans.
c. rightward shift in the supply curve for soybeans.
d. leftward shift in the supply curve for soybeans.

CAUSATION CHAIN GAME
Movement along a Supply Curve versus a Shift in Supply—Exhibit 8

3. Key Concept: Surplus

Assume Q_s represents the quantity supplied at a given price and Q_d represents the quantity demanded at the same given price. Which of the following market conditions produce a downward movement of the price?

a. $Q_s = 1,000$, $Q_d = 750$
b. $Q_s = 750$, $Q_d = 750$

c. $Q_s = 750$, $Q_d = 1,000$
d. $Q_s = 1,000$, $Q_d = 1,000$

4. Key Concept: Shortage

Which of the following situations results from a ticket price to a concert set below the equilibrium price?

a. A long line of people wanting to purchase tickets to the concert
b. No line of people wanting to buy tickets to the concert
c. Tickets available at the box office, but no line of people wanting to buy them
d. None of the above

CAUSATION CHAIN GAME
Supply and Demand for Sneakers—Exhibit 12

Chapter 4: Markets in Action

5. Key Concept: Change in demand

A decrease in consumer income decreases the demand for compact discs. As a result of the change to a new equilibrium, there is a(an)

a. leftward shift of the supply curve.
b. rightward shift of the supply curve.
c. upward movement along the supply curve.
d. downward movement along the supply curve.

CAUSATION CHAIN GAME
The Effects of Shifts in Demand on Market Equilibrium—Exhibit 1

6. Key Concept: Change in supply

Consider the market for grapes. An increase in the wage paid to grape pickers will cause the

a. demand curve for grapes to shift to the right, resulting in a higher equilibrium price for grapes and a reduction in the quantity consumed.
b. demand curve for grapes to shift to the left, resulting in a lower equilibrium price for grapes and an increase in the quantity consumed.
c. supply curve for grapes to shift to the left, resulting in a lower equilibrium price for grapes and a decrease in the quantity consumed.
d. supply curve for grapes to shift to the left, resulting in a higher equilibrium price for grapes and a decrease in the quantity consumed.

CAUSATION CHAIN GAME
The Effects of Shifts in Supply on Market Equilibrium—Exhibit 2

7. Key Concept: Rent control

Rent controls create distortions in the housing market by

a. increasing rents received by landlords.
b. raising property values.
c. encouraging landlords to overspend for maintenance.
d. discouraging new housing construction.
e. increasing the supply of housing in the long run.

CAUSATION CHAIN GAME
Rent Control—Exhibit 5

8. Key Concept: Minimum wage
Which of the following is a good example of a price floor?

a. Rent controls on apartments in major cities
b. General admission tickets to concerts
c. The minimum wage law
d. Food stamp regulations
e. Rock concert tickets

CAUSATION CHAIN GAME
Minimum Wage—Exhibit 6

Chapter 5: Price Elasticity of Demand and Supply

9. Key Concept: Price elasticity of demand
Suppose Good Food's supermarket raises the price of its steak and finds that its total revenue from steak sales does *not* change. This is evidence that price elasticity of demand for steak is

a. perfectly elastic.
b. perfectly inelastic.
c. unitary elastic.
d. inelastic.
e. elastic.

10. Key Concept: Tax incidence
Assuming the demand curve is more elastic (flatter) than the supply curve, which of the following is *true*?

a. The full tax is always passed on to the consumer no matter how flat (elastic) the demand curve is.
b. The full tax is always passed on to the seller no matter how flat (elastic) the demand curve is.
c. The smaller the portion of a sales tax that is passed on to the consumer.
d. It does not make any difference how flat (elastic) the demand curve is; the tax is always split evenly between buyer and seller.

CAUSATION CHAIN GAME
The Incidence of a Tax on Gasoline—Exhibit 10

Chapter 6: Consumer Choice Theory

11. Key Concept: Income effect
The income effect refers to a change in

a.   income because of changes in the CPI.
b.   the quantity demanded of a good because of a change in the buyer's real income.
c.   the quantity demanded of a good because of a change in the buyer's money income.
d.   None of the above.

CAUSATION CHAIN GAME
Income Effect

12. Key Concept: Substitution effect
Which of the following is the *best* example of the substitution effect?

a.   Joe buys fewer apples and more oranges as the result of an increase in the price of apples.
b.   Joe buys more apples when his income increases.
c.   Joe buys an apple slicer when the price of apples decreases.
d.   Joe buys less sugar as the result of an increase in the price of apples.

CAUSATION CHAIN GAME
Substitution Effect

Chapter 7: Production Costs

13. Key Concept: Marginal product and marginal cost
Which of the following is *true* at the point where diminishing returns set in?

a.   Both marginal product and marginal cost are at a maximum.
b.   Both marginal product and marginal cost are at a minimum.
c.   Marginal product is at a maximum, and marginal cost is at a minimum.
d.   Marginal product is at a minimum, and marginal cost is at a maximum.

CAUSATION CHAIN GAME
Marginal Product Effects on Marginal Cost

PART 3
Market Structures

This part focuses on different types of markets, each defined by a set of characteristics that determine corresponding demand and supply conditions. Chapter 8 describes a highly competitive market consisting of an extremely large number of competing firms, and Chapter 9 explains the theory for a market with only a single seller. Between these extremes, Chapter 10 discusses two markets that have some characteristics of both competition and monopoly. This part concludes by developing labor market theory in Chapter 11.

CHAPTER 8

Perfect Competition

CHAPTER PREVIEW

Ostrich farmers in Iowa, Texas, Oklahoma, and other states in the Midwest "stuck their necks out." Many invested millions of dollars converting a portion of their farms into breeding grounds for ostriches. The reason was that mating pairs of ostriches were selling for $75,000 during the late 1990s. Ostrich breeders claimed that ostrich meat would become the low-cholesterol, low-fat health treat, and ostrich prices rose. The high prices for ostriches fueled profit expectations, and many cattle ranchers deserted their cattle and went into the ostrich business.

Adam Smith concluded that competitive forces are like an "invisible hand" that leads people who simply pursue their own interests and, in the process, serve the interests of society. In a competitive market, when the profit potential in the ostrich business looked good, firms entered this market and started raising ostriches. Over time, more and more ostrich farmers flocked to this market, and the population of these big, flightless birds exploded. As a result, the price of a breeding pair plummeted to only a few thousand dollars, profits tumbled, and the number of ostrich farms declined. A decade later, demand increased unexpectedly because mad cow disease plagued Europe, and people bought alternatives

to beef. Suppliers could not meet the demand for ostrich burgers, and profits rose again, causing farmers to increase supply by investing in more ostriches. In more recent times, two groups of people have purchased enough ostrich meat to keep the demand for ostriches high. The first group is composed of health conscious consumers who are attracted to the low-fat main course; high-end restaurant managers make up the other group, and they view ostrich as an exotic meal option they can offer their customers.

This chapter combines the demand, cost of production, and marginal analysis concepts from previous chapters to explain how competitive markets determine prices, output, and profits. Here firms are small, like an ostrich ranch or an alligator farm, rather than huge, like Wal-Mart or Microsoft. In the short run, when there are profits, additional firms enter the market and start producing output. In contrast, when there are losses, some firms leave the market, halting their production. The entry and exit of firms drives economic profit to zero, which is a long-run equilibrium. Without economic profits or losses, firms no longer have an incentive to enter or leave the competitive market, and the number of firms remains stable. Other types of markets in which large and powerful firms operate are discussed in the next two chapters.

IN THIS CHAPTER, YOU WILL LEARN TO SOLVE THESE ECONOMICS PUZZLES:

- Why is the demand curve horizontal for a firm in a perfectly competitive market?

- Why would a firm stay in business while losing money?

- In the long run, can alligator farms earn an economic profit?

8-1 PERFECT COMPETITION

Firms sell goods and services under different market conditions, which economists call market structures. A **market structure** describes the key traits of a market, including the number of firms, the similarity of the products they sell, and the ease of entry into and exit from the market. Examination of the business sector of our economy reveals firms operating in different market structures. In this chapter and the two chapters that follow, we will study four market structures. The first is perfect competition, to which this entire chapter is devoted. **Perfect, or pure, competition** is a market structure characterized by three specific points: (1) a large number of small firms, (2) a homogeneous product, and (3) easy entry into or exit from the market. Let's discuss each of these characteristics.

8-1a Characteristics of Perfect Competition

Large Number of Small Firms

How many sellers comprise a large number? And how small is a small firm? Certainly, one, two, or three firms in a market would not be a large number. In fact, the exact number cannot be stated. This condition is fulfilled when each firm in a market has no significant share of total output and, therefore, no ability to affect the product's price. Each firm acts independently, rather than coordinating decisions collectively. For example, there are thousands of independent egg farmers in the United States. If any single egg farmer decides to alter the number of eggs she produces, the change in egg output will be so small that it will have no measurable impact on the market supply; therefore, the famer's decision will not influence the market price.

> The large-number-of-sellers condition is met when each firm is so small relative to the total market that no single firm can influence the market price.

CONCLUSION

Homogeneous Product

In a perfectly competitive market, all firms produce a standardized or **homogeneous product**. This means the good or service of each firm is identical. Farmer Brown's wheat is identical to Farmer Jones's wheat. Buyers may believe the transportation services of one independent trucker are about the same as another's services. This assumption rules out rivalry among firms in advertising and quality differences.

> If a product is homogeneous, buyers are indifferent as to which seller's product they buy.

CONCLUSION

Very Easy Entry and Exit

Very easy entry into a market means that a new firm faces no barrier to entry. A **barriers to entry** is any obstacle that makes it difficult for a new firm to enter a market. Barriers

Market structures
A classification system for the key traits of a market, including the number of firms, the similarity of the products they sell, and the ease of entry into and exit from the market.

Perfect competition
A market structure characterized by (1) a large number of small firms, (2) a homogeneous product, and (3) very easy entry into or exit from the market. Perfect competition is also referred to as *pure competition*.

Homogeneous product
A good or service that is identical regardless of which firm produces it.

Barriers to entry
Any obstacle that makes it difficult for a new firm to enter a market.

can be financial, technical, or government-imposed, such as licenses, permits, and patents. Such barriers do not exist for ostrich farming. Anyone who wants to try his or her hand at raising ostriches needs only a plot of land and feed.

CONCLUSION   Perfect competition requires that resources be completely mobile to freely enter or exit a market.

No real-world market exactly fits the three assumptions of perfect competition. The perfectly competitive market structure is a theoretical or ideal model, but some actual markets do approximate the model fairly closely. Examples include farm products' markets, the stock market, and the foreign exchange market.

8-1b The Perfectly Competitive Firm as a Price Taker

For model-building purposes, suppose a firm operates in a market that conforms to all three of the requirements for perfect competition. This means that the perfectly competitive firm is a price taker. A **price taker** is a seller that has no control over the price of the product it sells. From the individual firm's perspective, the price of its products is determined by market supply and demand conditions over which the firm has no influence. Look again at the characteristics of a perfectly competitive firm: A small firm that is one among many firms, sells a homogeneous product, and is exposed to competition from new firms entering the market. These conditions make it impossible for the perfectly competitive firm to have the market power to affect the market price. Instead, the firm must adjust to, or "take," the market price.

Exhibit 1 is a graphical presentation of the relationship between the market supply and demand for electronic components and the demand curve facing a firm in a perfectly competitive market. Here we will assume that the electronic components industry is perfectly competitive, keeping in mind that the real-world market does not exactly fit the model. Exhibit 1(a) shows market supply and demand curves for the quantity of output per hour. The theoretical framework for this model was explained in Chapter 4. The equilibrium price is $70 per unit, and the equilibrium quantity is 60,000 units per hour.

Because the perfectly competitive firm "takes" the equilibrium price, the individual firm's demand curve in Exhibit 1(b) is *perfectly elastic* (horizontal) at the $70 market equilibrium price. (Note the difference between the firm's units per hour and the industry's thousands of units per hour.) Recall from Chapter 5 that when a firm facing a perfectly elastic demand curve tries to raise its price one penny higher than $70, no buyer will purchase its product [Exhibit 2(a) in Chapter 5]. The reason is that many other firms are selling the same product at $70 per unit. Hence, the perfectly competitive firm will not set the price above the prevailing market price and risk selling zero output. Nor will the firm set the price below the market price because a lower price would reduce the firm's revenue, and the firm can sell all it wants to at the going price.

Price taker
A seller that has no control over the price of the product it sells.

8-2 SHORT-RUN PROFIT MAXIMIZATION FOR A PERFECTLY COMPETITIVE FIRM

Since the perfectly competitive firm has no control over price, what does the firm control? The firm makes only one decision—what quantity of output to produce that

EXHIBIT 1 The Market Price and Demand for the Perfectly Competitive Firm

In part (a), the market equilibrium price is $70 per unit. The perfectly competitive firm in part (b) is a price taker because it is so small relative to the market. At $70, the individual firm faces a horizontal demand curve, *D*. This means that the firm's demand curve is perfectly elastic. If the firm raises its price even one penny, it will sell zero output.

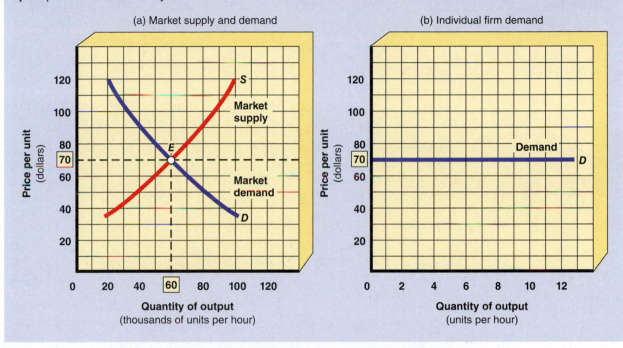

maximizes profit. This section develops two profit maximization methods that determine the output level for a competitive firm. We begin by examining the total revenue-total cost approach for finding the profit-maximizing level of output. Next, marginal analysis is used to show another method for determining the profit-maximizing level of output. The framework for the analysis is the short run with some fixed input, such as factory size.

8-2a The Total Revenue-Total Cost Method

Exhibit 2 provides hypothetical data on output, total revenue, total cost, and profit for our typical electronic components producer—Computech. Using Computech as our example allows us to extend the data and analysis presented in previous chapters. The cost figures are taken from Exhibit 3 in Chapter 7. Total fixed cost at zero output is $100. Total revenue is reported in column (3) of Exhibit 2 and is computed as the product price times the quantity. In this case, we assume the market equilibrium price is $70 per unit, as determined in Exhibit 1. Because Computech is a price taker, the total revenue from selling 1 unit is $70, from selling 2 units is $140, and so on. Subtracting total cost in column (6) from total revenue in column (3) gives the total profit or loss [column (9)] that the firm earns at each level of output. From 0 to 2 units, the

EXHIBIT 2 Short-Run Profit Maximization Schedule for Computech as a Perfectly Competitive Firm

(1) Output (units per hour) (Q)	(2) Price per unit (P)	(3) Total revenue (TR)	(4) Marginal revenue (MR)	(5) Marginal cost (MC)	(6) Total cost (TC)	(7) Average variable cost (AVC)	(8) Average total cost (ATC)	(9) Profit (+) or loss (−) [(3) − (6)]
0	$70	$0			$100	–	–	−$100
			$70	$50				
1	70	70			150	$50	$150	−80
			70	34				
2	70	140			184	42	92	−44
			70	24				
3	70	210			208	36	69	2
			70	19				
4	70	280			227	32	57	53
			70	23				
5	70	350			250	30	50	100
			70	30				
6	70	420			280	30	47	140
			70	38				
7	70	490			318	31	45	172
			70	48				
8	70	560			366	33	46	194
			70	59				
9	70	630	70	70	425	36	47	205
			70	75				
10	70	700			500	40	50	200
			70	95				
11	70	770			595	45	54	175
			70	117				
12	70	840			712	51	59	128

firm incurs losses, and then a *break-even point* (zero economic profit) occurs at about 3 units per hour. Recall from the previous chapter that at zero economic profit, the firm earns only a normal profit, which is the minimum profit necessary to keep a firm in operation. If the firm produces 9 units per hour, it earns the maximum profit of $205 per hour. As output expands between 9 and 12 units of output, the firm's profit diminishes. Exhibit 3 illustrates graphically that the maximum profit occurs where the vertical distance between the total revenue and the total cost curves is at a maximum.

EXHIBIT 3 Short-Run Profit Maximization Using the Total Revenue-Total Cost Method for a Perfectly Competitive Firm

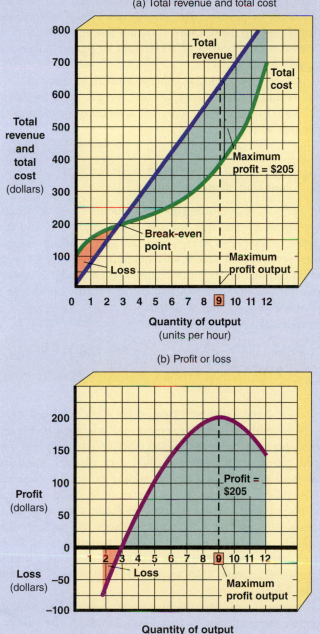

This exhibit shows the profit-maximizing level of output chosen by a perfectly competitive firm, Computech. Part (a) shows the relationships between total revenue, total cost, and output, given a market price of $70 per unit. The maximum profit is earned by producing 9 units per hour. At this level of output, the vertical distance between the total revenue and the total cost curves is the greatest. At an output level below 3 units per hour, the firm incurs losses.

Profit maximization is also shown in part (b). The maximum profit of $205 per hour corresponds to the profit-maximizing output of 9 units per hour, represented in part (a).

8-2b The Marginal Revenue Equals Marginal Cost Method

A second approach uses *marginal analysis* to determine the profit-maximizing level of output by comparing marginal revenue (marginal benefit) and marginal cost. Recall from the previous chapter that a synonym for marginal is "extra" and that marginal cost is the change in total cost as the output level increases by one unit. Also recall that these marginal cost data are listed between the quantity of output line entries because the change in total cost occurs between each additional whole unit of output rather than exactly at each listed output level.

Now we introduce marginal revenue (MR), a concept similar to marginal cost. **Marginal revenue** is the "extra" revenue or the change in total revenue from the sale of one additional unit of output. Stated another way, marginal revenue is the ratio of the change in total revenue to a change in output.

Marginal revenue (MR)
The change in total revenue from the sale of one additional unit of output.

Mathematically,

$$MR = \frac{\textbf{change in total revenue}}{\textbf{one-unit change in output}}$$

As shown in Exhibit 1(b), the perfectly competitive firm faces a perfectly elastic demand curve. Because the competitive firm is a price taker, the sale of each additional unit adds to total revenue an amount equal to the price (average revenue, TR/Q). In our example, Computech adds $70 to its total revenue each time it sells one unit. Therefore, $70 is the marginal revenue for each additional unit of output in column (4) of Exhibit 2. As with MC, MR is also listed between the quantity of output line entries because the change in total revenue occurs between each additional unit of output.

| CONCLUSION | In perfect competition, the firm's marginal revenue equals the price, which the firm views as a horizontal demand curve. |

Columns (3) and (6) in Exhibit 2 show that both total revenue and total cost rise as the level of output increases. Now compare marginal revenue and marginal cost in columns (4) and (5). As explained, marginal revenue remains equal to the price, but marginal cost follows the J-shaped pattern introduced in Exhibit 4 of Chapter 7. At first, marginal revenue exceeds marginal cost, and the firm is adding more to its revenues than to its costs as output increases. Economic profit therefore increases as output expands from zero until the output level reaches 9 units per hour. Over this output range, Computech moves from a $100 loss to a $205 profit per hour. Beyond an output level of 9 units per hour, marginal cost exceeds marginal revenue, and profit falls. This is because each additional unit of output per hour raises total cost by more than it raises total revenue. In this case, profit falls from $205 to only $128 per hour as output increases from 9 to 12 units per hour.

Our example leads to this question: How does the firm use its marginal revenue and marginal cost curves to determine the profit-maximizing level of output? The answer is that the firm follows a guideline called the MR = MC rule: *The firm maximizes profit by producing the output where marginal revenue equals marginal cost.* Exhibit 4 relates the marginal revenue curve equals marginal cost curve condition to profit maximization. In Exhibit 4(a), the perfectly elastic demand curve is drawn at the industry-determined price of $70. The average total cost (ATC) and average variable cost (AVC) curves are

EXHIBIT 4 Short-Run Profit Maximization Using the Marginal Revenue Equals Marginal Cost Method for a Perfectly Competitive Firm

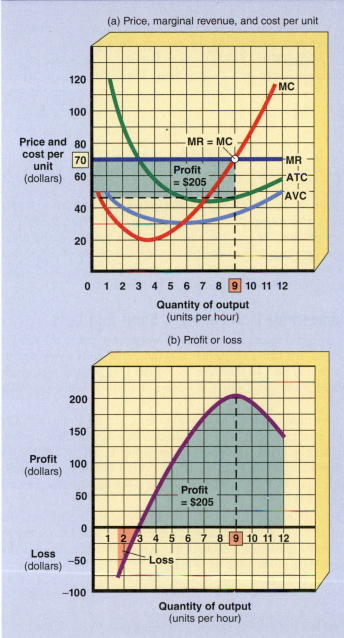

(a) Price, marginal revenue, and cost per unit

(b) Profit or loss

In addition to comparing total revenue and total cost, a firm can find the profit-maximizing level of output by comparing marginal revenue (MR) and marginal cost (MC). As shown in part (a), profit is at a maximum where marginal revenue equals marginal cost at $70 per unit. The intersection of the marginal revenue and marginal cost curves establishes the profit-maximizing output at 9 units per hour.

A profit curve is depicted separately in part (b) to show that the maximum profit occurs when the firm produces at the level of output corresponding to the MR = MC point. Below 3 units per hour output, the firm incurs losses.

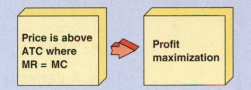

traced from Exhibit 2. Using marginal analysis, we can relate the MR = MC rule to the same profit data given in Exhibit 2. Between 8 and 9 units of output, the MR curve is above the MC curve ($70 > $59), and the profit curve rises to its peak at $205. Beyond 9 units of output, the MC curve is above the MR curve, and the profit curve falls. For example, between 9 and 10 units of output, marginal cost is $75, and marginal revenue is $70. Therefore, if the firm produces at 9 units of output rather than, say, at 8 or 10 units of output, the MR curve equals the MC curve, and profit is maximized.

You can also calculate profit directly from Exhibit 4(a). At the profit-maximizing level of output of 9 units, the vertical distance between the demand curve and the ATC curve is the *average profit per unit*. Multiplying the average profit per unit times the quantity of output gives the profit [($70 − $47.22) × 9 = $205.02].[1] The shaded rectangle also represents the maximum profit of $205 per hour. Note that we have arrived at the same profit maximization amount ($205) derived earlier by comparing the total revenue and the total cost curves.

8-3 SHORT-RUN LOSS MINIMIZATION FOR A PERFECTLY COMPETITIVE FIRM

Because the perfectly competitive firm must take the price determined by market supply and demand forces, market conditions can change the prevailing price. When the market price drops, the firm can do nothing but adjust its output to make the best of the situation. Here only the marginal approach is used to predict output decisions of firms. Our model, therefore, assumes that business managers make their output decisions by comparing the *marginal* effect on profit of a *marginal* change in output.

8-3a A Perfectly Competitive Firm Facing a Short-Run Loss

Suppose a decrease in the market demand for electronic components causes the market price to fall to $35. As a result, the firm's horizontal demand curve shifts downward to the new position shown in Exhibit 5(a). In this case, there is no level of output at which the firm earns a profit because any price along the demand curve is below the ATC curve.

Since Computech cannot make a profit, what output level should it choose? The logic of the MR = MC rule given in the profit maximization case applies here as well. At a price of $35, MR = MC at 6 units per hour. Comparing parts (a) and (b) of Exhibit 5 shows that the firm's loss will be minimized at this level of output. The minimum loss of $70 per hour is equal to the shaded area, which is the *average loss per unit* times the quantity of output [($35 − $46.66) × 6 = −$70].

Note that although the price is not high enough to pay the average total cost, the price is high enough to pay the average variable cost. Each unit sold also contributes to paying a portion of the average fixed cost, which is the vertical distance between the ATC and the AVC curves. This analysis leads us to extend the MR = MC rule so that it applies to losses as well as to profits.

CONCLUSION The firm maximizes profit or minimizes loss by producing the output where marginal revenue equals marginal cost.

---

[1]In Exhibit 3 in Chapter 7, the average total cost figure at 9 units of output was rounded to $47. It also should be noted that there is often no level of output for which marginal revenue exactly equals marginal cost when dealing with whole units of output.

EXHIBIT 5 Short-Run Loss Minimization Using the Marginal Revenue Equals Marginal Cost Method for a Perfectly Competitive Firm

If the market price is less than the average total cost, the firm will produce a level of output that keeps its loss to a minimum. In part (a), the given price is $35 per unit, and marginal revenue (MR) equals marginal cost (MC) at an output of 6 units per hour.

Part (b) shows that the firm's loss will be greater at any output other than where the marginal revenue and the marginal cost curves intersect. Because the price is above the average variable cost, each unit of output sold pays for the average variable cost and a portion of the average fixed cost.

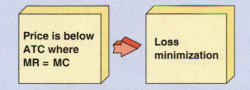

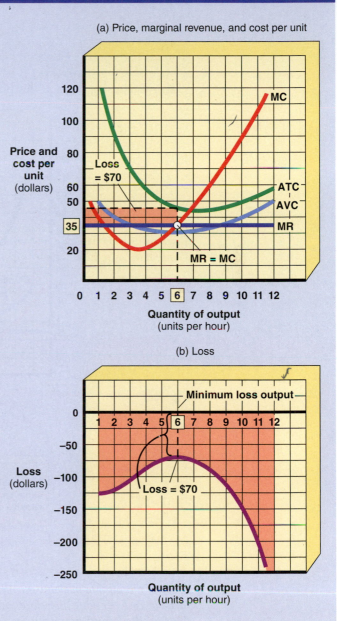

(a) Price, marginal revenue, and cost per unit

(b) Loss

8-3b A Perfectly Competitive Firm Shutting Down

What happens if the market price drops below the AVC curve, as shown in Exhibit 6? For example, if the price is $25 per unit, should Computech produce some level of output? The answer is no. The best course of action is for the firm to shut down. *If the price*

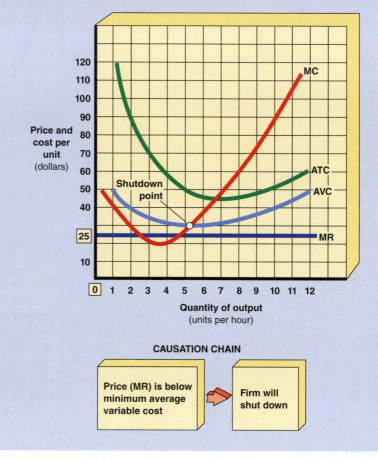

EXHIBIT 6 The Short-Run Shutdown Point for a Perfectly Competitive Firm

The shutdown point of $30 per unit is the minimum point on the average variable cost (AVC) curve. If the price falls below this price, the firm shuts down. The reason is that operating losses are now greater than total fixed cost. In this exhibit, the price of $25 per unit (MR) is below the AVC curve at any level of output, and the firm would shut down at this price.

CAUSATION CHAIN

| Price (MR) is below minimum average variable cost | → | Firm will shut down |

is below the minimum point on the AVC curve, each unit produced would not cover the variable cost per unit; therefore, operating would increase losses. The firm is better off shutting down and producing zero output. While shut down, the firm might keep its factory, pay fixed costs, and hope for higher prices soon. If the firm does not believe market conditions will improve, it will avoid fixed costs by going out of business.

CONCLUSION

The firm will shut down when the price drops below the minimum average variable cost (AVC).

CHECKPOINT

Should Motels Offer Rooms at the Beach for Only $70 a Night?
Myrtle Beach, South Carolina, with its famous Grand Strand and Calabash seafood, is lined with virtually identical motels. Summertime rates run about $250 a night. During the winter, one can find rooms for as little as $70 a night. Assume the average fixed cost of a room per night, including insurance, taxes, and depreciation, is $30. The average guest-related cost (average variable cost) for a room each night, including cleaning service and linens, is $65. The average total cost, which is the sum of the average fixed cost ($30) and the average variable cost ($65), is $95. Would these motels be better off renting rooms for $70 in the off-season or shutting down until summer?

8-4 SHORT-RUN SUPPLY CURVES UNDER PERFECT COMPETITION

The preceding examples provide a framework for a more complete explanation of the supply curve than was given earlier in Chapter 3. We now develop the short-run supply curve for an individual firm and then derive it for an industry.

8-4a The Perfectly Competitive Firm's Short-Run Supply Curve

Exhibit 7 reproduces the cost curves from our Computech example. Also represented in the exhibit are three possible demand curves the firm might face—MR_1, MR_2, and MR_3. As the marginal revenue curve moves upward along the marginal cost curve, the $MR = MC$ point changes.

Suppose demand for electronic components begins at a market price close to $30. Point A therefore corresponds to a price equal to MR_1, which equals MC at the lowest point on the AVC curve. At any lower price, the firm cuts its loss by shutting down. At a price of about $30, however, the firm produces 5.5 units per hour. Point A is, therefore, the lowest point on the individual firm's short-run supply curve.

If the price rises to $45, represented in the exhibit by MR_2, the firm breaks even and earns a normal profit at point B with an output of 7 units per hour. As the marginal revenue curve rises, the firm's supply curve is traced by moving upward along its MC curve. At a price of $90, point C is reached. Now MR_3 intersects the MC curve at an output of 10 units per hour, and the firm earns an economic profit. If the price rises higher than $90, the firm will continue to increase the quantity supplied and increase its maximum profit.

We can now define a perfectly competitive firm's short-run supply curve. The **perfectly competitive firm's short-run supply curve** is its marginal cost curve above the minimum point on its average variable cost curve.

8-4b The Perfectly Competitive Industry's Short-Run Supply Curve

Understanding that the firm's short-run supply curve is the segment of its MC curve above its AVC curve sets the stage for derivation of the perfectly competitive industry's short-run supply curve. The **perfectly competitive industry's short-run supply curve** is the

Perfectly competitive firm's short-run supply curve
A firm's marginal cost curve above the minimum point on its average variable cost curve.

Perfectly competitive industry's short-run supply curve
The supply curve derived from horizontal summation of the marginal cost curves of all firms in the industry above the minimum point of each firm's average variable cost curve.

EXHIBIT 7 The Perfectly Competitive Firm's Short-Run Supply Curve

This exhibit shows how the short-run supply curve for Computech is derived. When the price is $30, the firm will produce 5.5 units per hour at point A. If the price rises to $45, the firm will move upward along its marginal cost (MC) curve to point B and produce 7 units per hour. At $90, the firm continues to set price equal to marginal cost, and it produces 10 units per hour. Thus, the firm's short-run supply curve is the MC curve above its AVC curve.

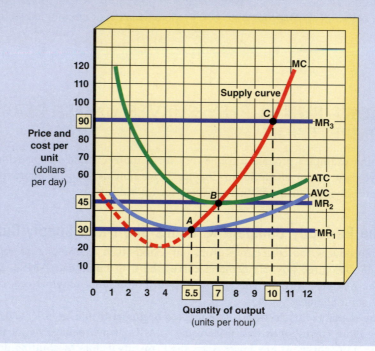

horizontal summation of the marginal cost curves of all firms in the industry above the minimum point of each firm's average variable cost curve.

In Exhibit 7 in Chapter 3, we drew a market supply curve. Now we will reconstruct this market, or industry, supply curve using more precision. Although in perfect competition there are many firms, we suppose for simplicity that the industry has only two firms, Computech and Western Computer Co. Exhibit 8 illustrates the MC curves for these two firms. Each firm's MC curve is drawn for prices above the minimum point on the AVC curve. At a price of $45, the quantity supplied by Computech is 7 units, and the quantity supplied by Western Computer Co. is 11 units. Now horizontally add these two quantities and obtain one point on the industry supply curve corresponding to a price of $45 and 18 units. Following this procedure for all prices, we generate the short-run industry supply curve.

Note that the industry supply curve derived above is based on the assumption that input prices remain unchanged as output expands. In the next section, we will learn how changes in input prices affect the derivation of the industry supply curve.

EXHIBIT 8 Deriving the Industry Short-Run Supply Curve

Assuming input prices remain constant as output expands, the short-run supply curve for an industry is derived by horizontally summing the quantities supplied at each price by all firms in the industry. In this exhibit, we assume there are only two firms in an industry. At $45, Computech supplies 7 units of output, and Western Computer Co. supplies 11 units. The quantity supplied by the industry is therefore 18 units. Other points forming the industry short-run supply curve are obtained similarly.

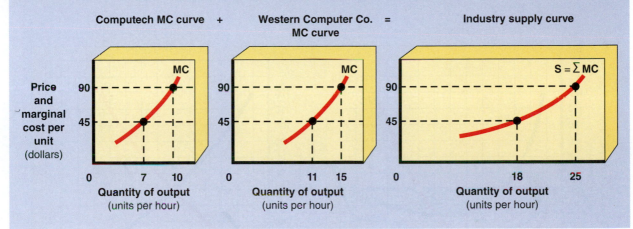

8-4c **Short-Run Equilibrium for a Perfectly Competitive Firm**

Exhibit 9 illustrates a condition of short-run equilibrium under perfect competition. Exhibit 9(a) represents the equilibrium price and cost situation for one of the many firms in an industry. As shown in the exhibit, the firm earns an economic profit in the short run by producing 9 units. Exhibit 9(b) depicts short-run equilibrium for the industry. As explained earlier, the industry supply curve is the aggregate of each firm's MC curve above the minimum point on the AVC curve. Including industry demand establishes the equilibrium price of $60 that all firms in the industry must take. The industry's equilibrium quantity supplied is 60,000 units. This state of short-run equilibrium will remain until some factor changes and causes a new equilibrium condition in the industry.

8-5 **LONG-RUN SUPPLY CURVES UNDER PERFECT COMPETITION**

Recall from Chapter 7 that *all* inputs are variable in the long run. Existing firms in an industry can react to profit opportunities by building larger or smaller plants, buying or selling land and equipment, or varying other inputs that are fixed in the short run. Profits also attract new firms to an industry, while losses cause some existing firms to leave the industry. As you will now see, the free entry and exit characteristic of perfect competition is a crucial determinant of the shape of the long-run supply curve.

8-5a **Long-Run Equilibrium for a Perfectly Competitive Firm**

As discussed in Chapter 7, in the long run a firm can change its plant size or any input used to produce a product. This means that an established firm can decide to *leave* an

EXHIBIT 9 Short-Run Perfectly Competitive Equilibrium

Short-run equilibrium occurs at point *E*. The intersection of the industry supply and demand curves shown in part (b) determines the price of $60 facing the firm shown in part (a). Given this equilibrium price, the firm represented in part (a) establishes its profit-maximizing output at 9 units per hour and earns an economic profit shown by the shaded area. Note in part (b) that the short-run industry supply curve is the horizontal summation of the marginal cost (MC) curves of all individual firms above their minimum average variable cost points.

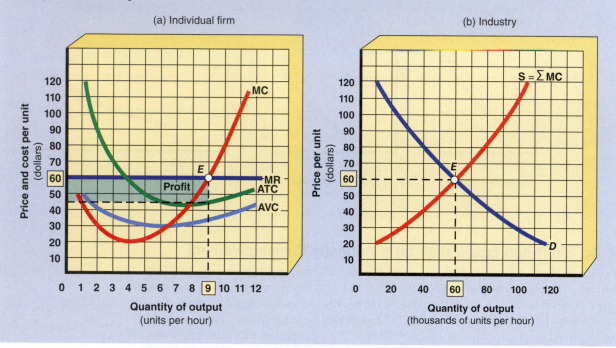

(a) Individual firm   (b) Industry

industry if it earns below normal profits (negative economic profits) and that new firms may enter an industry in which earnings of established firms exceed normal profits (positive economic profits). This process of entry and exit of firms is the key to long-run equilibrium. If there are economic profits, new firms enter the industry and shift the short-run industry supply curve to the right. This increase in short-run supply causes the price to fall until economic profits reach zero in the long run. On the other hand, if there are economic losses in an industry, existing firms leave, causing the short-run supply curve to shift to the left, and the price rises. This adjustment continues until economic losses are eliminated and economic profits equal zero in the long run.

Exhibit 10 shows a typical firm in long-run equilibrium. Supply and demand for the market as a whole set the equilibrium price. Thus, in the long run, the firm faces an equilibrium price of $60. Following the MR = MC rule, the firm produces an equilibrium output of 6 units per hour. At this output level, the firm earns a normal profit (zero economic profit) because marginal revenue (price) equals the minimum point on both the short-run average total cost (SRATC) curve and the long-run average cost (LRAC) curve. Given the U-shaped LRAC curve, the firm is producing with the optimal factory size.

EXHIBIT **10** Long-Run Perfectly Competitive Equilibrium

Long-run equilibrium occurs at point *E*. In the long run, the firm earns a normal profit. The firm operates where the price equals the minimum point on its long-run average cost (LRAC) curve. At this point, the short-run marginal cost (SRMC) curve intersects both the short-run average total cost (SRATC) curve and the long-run average cost (LRAC) curve at their minimum points.

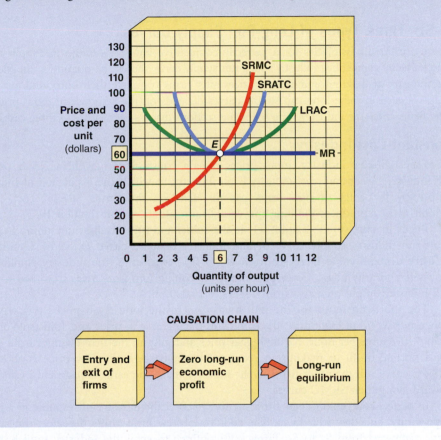

With SRMC representing short-run marginal cost, the conditions for long-run perfectly competitive equilibrium can also be expressed as an equality:

$$P = MR = SRMC = SRATC = LRAC$$

As long as none of the variables in the above formula changes, there is no reason for a perfectly competitive firm to change its output level, factory size, or any aspect of its operation. Everything is just right! Because the typical firm is in a state of equilibrium, the industry is also at rest. Under long-run equilibrium conditions, there are neither positive economic profits to attract new firms to enter the industry nor negative economic profits to force existing firms to leave. In long-run equilibrium, maximum efficiency is achieved. The adjustment process of firms moving into or out of the industry is complete, and the firms charge the lowest possible price to consumers. Next, we will discuss how the firm and industry adjust when market demand changes.

CHECKPOINT

8-5b Three Types of Long-Run Supply Curves

There are three possibilities for a perfectly competitive industry's long-run supply curve. The **perfectly competitive industry's long-run supply curve** shows the quantities supplied by the industry at different equilibrium prices after firms complete their entry and exit. The shape of each of these long-run supply curves depends on the response of input prices as new firms enter the industry. The following sections discuss each of these three cases.

Constant-Cost Industry

In a constant-cost industry, input prices remain constant as new firms enter or exit the industry. A **constant-cost industry** is an industry in which the expansion of industry output by the entry of new firms has no effect on the firm's SRATC cost curve. Exhibit 11(a) reproduces the long-run equilibrium situation from Exhibit 10.

Begin in part (b) of Exhibit 11 at the initial industry equilibrium point E_1 with short-run industry supply curve S_1 and industry demand curve D_1. Now assume the industry demand curve increases from D_1 to D_2. As a result, the industry equilibrium moves temporarily to E_2. Correspondingly, the equilibrium price rises from $60 to $80, and industry output increases from 50,000 to 70,000 units.

The short-run result for the individual firm in the industry happens this way. As shown in part (a) of Exhibit 11, the firm takes the increase in price and adjusts its output from 6 to 7 units per hour. At the higher price and output, the firm changes from earning a normal profit to making an economic profit because the new price is above its SRATC curve. All the other firms in the industry make the same adjustment by moving upward along their SRMC curves.

In perfect competition, new firms are free to enter the industry in response to a profit opportunity, and they will do so. The addition of new firms shifts the short-run supply curve rightward from S_1 to S_2. Firms will continue to enter the industry until profit is eliminated. This occurs at equilibrium point E_3, where short-run industry demand curve D_2 intersects short-run supply curve S_2. Thus, the entry of new firms has restored the initial equilibrium price of $60. The firm responds by moving downward along its SRMC curve until it once again produces 6 units and earns a normal profit.

As shown in the exhibit, the path of these changes in industry short-run equilibrium points traces a horizontal line, which is the industry's long-run supply curve.

CONCLUSION

Now we reconsider Exhibit 11 and ask what happens when the demand curve shifts leftward from D_2 to D_1. Beginning in part (b) at point E_3, the decrease in demand causes the price to fall temporarily below $60. As a result, firms incur short-run losses, and

---

Perfectly competitive industry's long-run supply curve
The curve that shows the quantities supplied by the industry at different equilibrium prices after firms complete their entry and exit.

Constant-cost industry
An industry in which the expansion of industry output by the entry of new firms has no effect on the individual firm's average total cost curve.

EXHIBIT 11 Long-Run Supply in a Constant-Cost Industry

Part (b) shows an industry in equilibrium at point E_1, producing 50,000 units per hour and selling them for $60 per unit. In part (a), the firm is in equilibrium, producing 6 units per hour and earning a normal profit. Then industry demand increases from D_1 to D_2, and the equilibrium price rises to $80. Industry output rises temporarily to 70,000 units per hour, and the individual firm increases output to 7 units per hour. Firms are now earning an economic profit, which attracts new firms into the industry. In the long run, the entry of these firms causes the short-run supply curve to shift rightward from S_1 to S_2, the price is reestablished at $60, and a new industry equilibrium point, E_1, is established. At E_3, industry output rises to 90,000 units per hour, the SRATC curve remains constant, and the firm's output returns to 6 units per hour. Now the typical firm earns a normal profit, and new firms stop entering the industry. Connecting point E_1 to point E_3 generates the long-run supply curve.

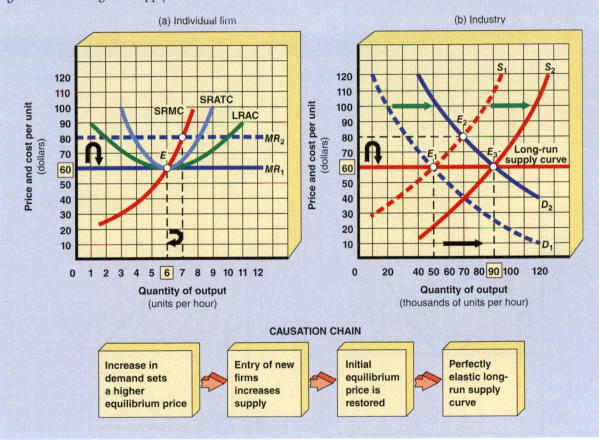

some firms leave the industry. The exodus of firms shifts the short-run supply curve leftward from S_2 to S_1, establishing a new equilibrium at point E_1. This decrease in supply restores the equilibrium price to the initial price of $60 per unit. Once equilibrium is reestablished at E_1, there are a smaller number of firms, each earning a normal profit.

Decreasing-Cost Industry

Input prices fall as new firms enter a decreasing-cost industry, and output expands. A **decreasing-cost industry** is an industry in which the expansion of industry output by

Decreasing-cost industry
An industry in which the expansion of industry output by the entry of new firms decreases the individual firm's average total cost curve (cost curve shifts downward).

the entry of new firms decreases each individual firm's cost curve (cost curve shifts downward). For example, as production of electronic components expands, the price of computer chips may decline. The reason is that greater sales volume allows the suppliers to achieve economies of scale and lower their input prices to firms in the electronic components industry. Exhibit 12 illustrates the adjustment process of an increase in demand based on the assumption that our example is a decreasing-cost industry.

CONCLUSION   The long-run supply curve in a perfectly competitive decreasing-cost industry is downward sloping.

EXHIBIT 12 Long-Run Supply in a Decreasing-Cost Industry

The long-run supply curve for a decreasing-cost industry is downward sloping. The increase in industry demand shown in part (b) causes the price to rise to $80 in the short run. Temporarily, the individual firm illustrated in part (a) earns an economic profit. Higher profits attract new firms, and supply increases. As the industry expands, input prices fall causing the SRATC curve for the firm to shift downward from $SRATC_1$ to $SRATC_2$, and the firm reestablishes long-run equilibrium at the lower price of $50.

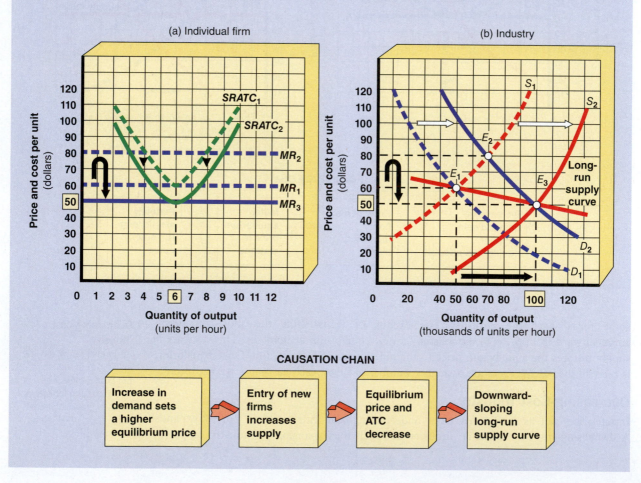

Increasing-Cost Industry

In an increasing-cost industry, input prices rise as new firms enter the industry, and output expands. As this type of industry uses more labor and machines, the demand for greater quantities of these inputs drives up input prices. An **increasing-cost industry** is an industry in which the expansion of industry output by the entry of new firms increases the individual firm's cost curve (cost curve shifts upward). Suppose the electronic component business uses a significant proportion of all electrical engineers in the country. In this case, electrical engineering salaries will rise as firms hire more electrical engineers to expand industry output. In practice, most industries are increasing-cost industries, and, therefore, the long-run supply curve is upward sloping.

Exhibit 13 shows what happens in an increasing-cost industry when an increase in demand causes output to expand. In part (b), the industry is initially in equilibrium at

Increasing-cost industry
An industry in which the expansion of industry output by the entry of new firms increases the individual firm's average total cost curve (cost curve shifts upward).

EXHIBIT 13 Long-Run Supply in an Increasing-Cost Industry

This pair of graphs derives the long-run supply curve based on the assumption that input prices rise as industry output expands. Part (b) shows that an increase in demand from D_1 to D_2 causes the price to increase in the short run from $60 to $80. The individual firm represented in part (a) earns an economic profit, and new firms enter the industry, causing an increase in industry supply from S_1 to S_2. As output expands, input prices rise and push up the firm's SRATC curve from $SRATC_1$, to $SRATC_2$. As a result, a new long-run equilibrium price is established at $70, which is above the initial equilibrium price. The long-run supply curve for an increasing-cost industry is upward sloping.

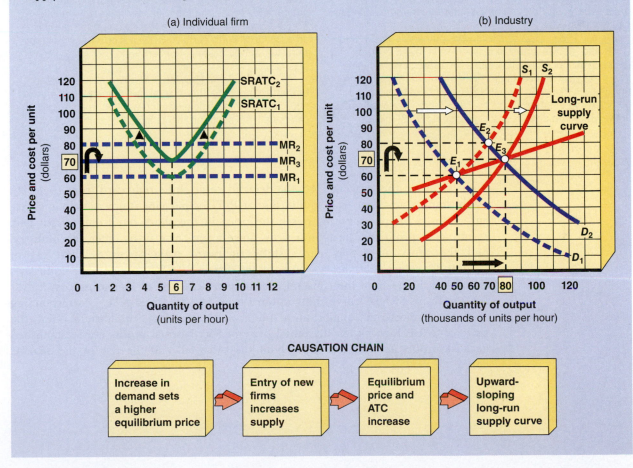

(a) Individual firm

(b) Industry

CAUSATION CHAIN

| Increase in demand sets a higher equilibrium price | ⇨ | Entry of new firms increases supply | ⇨ | Equilibrium price and ATC increase | ⇨ | Upward-sloping long-run supply curve |

YOU'RE THE ECONOMIST

Applicable Concepts: Short-Run and Long-Run Competitive Equilibrium

Recession Takes a Bite Out of Gator Profits

In the late 1980s, many farmers who were tired of milking cows, roping steers, and slopping hogs decided to try their hand at a new animal. Anyone feeding this animal, however, could require a gun for protection.

Prior to the late 1970s, alligators were on the endangered species list. Under this protection, their numbers grew so large that wandering alligators became pests in Florida neighborhoods and police were exhausted from chasing them around. Consequently, the ban on hunting was removed, and shrewd entrepreneurs began seeking big profits by turning gators into farm animals. In fact, gator farming became one of Florida's fastest-growing businesses.

The gators spawned several hot industries. The lizard "look" came back into vogue and the fashionable sported gator-skin purses, shoes, and belts. Chic didn't come cheap. In New York, gator cowboy boots sold for $1,800, and attaché cases retailed for $4,000. And you could order gator meat at trendy restaurants all along the East Coast. "Why not gator?" asked Red Lobster spokesman Dick Monroe. "Today's two-income households are looking for more variety. And they think it's neat to eat an animal that can eat them."[1]

Before 1983, alligator farms were primarily tourist attractions, and the two active farms in Florida raised enough gators to produce only 184 hides. In 1984, however, there was a substantial increase in the demand for alligator skin, and the price of alligator hides doubled. The high price attracted more farmers, and by 1986 there were fourteen active gator farms in the state, producing 3,921 hides.[2]

David Huntley Creative/Shutterstock.com

Revenues soared as well. As the *Washington Post* tells the story, "During the late 1980s gator ranching was booming, and the industry was being compared to a living gold mine. People rushed into the industry. Some farmers became temporarily rich."[3] Frank Godwin, owner of Gatorland in Orlando, is one example. He netted an estimated $270,000 annually.[4]

In 1995, however, a *USA Today* interview with a gator hunter provided evidence that the profits had disappeared and that this industry was at its long-run equilibrium: "Armed with a pistol barrel attached to the end of an 8-foot wooden pole, alligator hunter Bill Chaplin fires his 'bank stick' and dispatches a six-foot gator with a single round of .44 magnum ammunition. What's in it for him? Financially, very little. At $3.50 a pound for the meat and $45 a foot for the hide, an alligator is worth perhaps $100 a foot. After paying for skinning and processing, neither hunter nor landowner gets rich."[5]

A 2000 article in *The Dallas Morning News* provided further evidence that the market had reached its long-run equilibrium. In the article, Mark Glass, who began raising gators in 1995 south of Atlanta stated, "I can honestly say

point E_1. As in the previous case, the demand curve shifts rightward from D_1 to D_2, establishing a new short-run equilibrium at E_2. This movement upward along short-run industry supply curve S_1 raises the price in the short run from $60 to $80, resulting in profit for the typical firm. Once again, new firms enter the industry, and the short-run supply curve shifts rightward from S_1 to S_2. Part (a) of Exhibit 13 shows that the response of the firm's SRATC curve to the industry's expansion differs from the constant-cost industry case. In an increasing-cost industry, the firm's SRATC curve shifts upward from SRATC$_1$ to SRATC$_2$, corresponding to the new short-run equilibrium at point E_3. At this final equilibrium point, the price of $70 is higher than the initial price of $60. Normal profits are reestablished because profits are squeezed from both the price fall and the rise in the SRATC curve.

I haven't made any money yet, but I hope that's about to change."[6] And a 2003 article from *Knight Ridder/Tribune Business News* gave a pessimistic report for Florida: "Revenue from alligator harvesting has flattened in recent years, despite Florida's efforts to promote the alligator as part of a viable 'aquaculture' industry. It's a tough business."[7]

And beginning in 2009, alligator skin bags, belts, shoes, watch straps, and purses were victims of the recession. As a result, many alligator farms were overrun with an unprecedented surplus of unsold alligators and falling prices. The price of an alligator hide dropped from $43.75 a foot in 2008 to $15.00 a foot in 2009. The low price caused some farms to cut back on production. For instance, Wayne Sagrera, co-owner of Vermilion Gator Farm near Lafayette, Louisiana, stated, "We can't invest in eggs if the demand is not there. They're just not selling."[8] This low price also caused thirteen active farms in Florida to drop to ten within a three-year span.

Alligator farmers can easily start or stop producing alligators in response to price changes. We see this when the number of active alligator farms varies over time. In 1991, which was a time when hide prices were relatively high, thirty-one farms were active out of the fifty-eight that were licensed; that is, about one in two licensed farms was active. When the prices and the profitability of producing hides dropped, some licensed farms stopped raising alligators. By 2015, there were only seventeen active farms out of the sixty-nine that were licensed.[9] Put another way, roughly one in four licensed farms were active in 2015. Should the prices of hides increase, some licensed farms will start raising alligators again.

ANALYZE THE ISSUE

1. Draw short-run firm and industry competitive equilibriums for a perfectly competitive gator-farming industry before the number of alligator farms in Florida doubled. For simplicity, assume the gator farm is earning zero economic profit. Then show the short-run effect of an increase in demand for alligators.

2. Assuming gator farming is perfectly competitive, explain the long-run competitive equilibrium condition for the typical gator farmer and the industry as a whole.

1. Ron Moreau and Penelope Wang, "Gators: Snapping Up Profits," *Newsweek*, December 8, 1986, p. 68.
2. Alligator Management Team of Florida Fish and Wildlife Conservation Commission, "Table 2. Estimated producer value of alligator harvests on Florida farms during 1977-2015," http://www.myfwc.com/media/31019/alligator-farm-value.pdf.
3. William Booth, "Bag a Gator and Save the Species," *The Washington Post*, August 25, 1993, p. A1.
4. Ron Moreau and Penelope Wang, "Gators: Snapping Up Profits," *Newsweek*, December 8, 1986, p. 68.
5. J. Taylor Buckley, "S. Carolina Lets Hunters Go for Gators Again," *USA Today*, September 21, 1995, News Section, p. A1.J.
6. "More Bite for the Buck," *The Dallas Morning News*, December 6, 2000, p. 2A.
7. Jerry W. Jackson, "Alligators Are Growing Part of Florida's Agricultural Landscape," *Knight Ridder/Tribune Business News*, January 26, 2003.
8. Rick Jervis, "Recession Eats into Gator Industry," *USA Today*, October 22, 2009, News Section, p. 2A.
9. Alligator Management Team of Florida Fish and Wildlife Conservation Commission, "Table 2. Estimated producer value of alligator harvests on Florida farms during 1977-2015," http://www.myfwc.com/media/31019/alligator-farm-value.pdf.

The long-run industry supply curve is drawn by connecting the two long-run equilibrium points of E_1 and E_3. Equilibrium point E_2 is not a long-run equilibrium point because it is not established after the entry of new firms has restored normal profits.

The long-run supply curve in a perfectly competitive increasing-cost industry is upward sloping.

CONCLUSION

Finally, given the three models presented, you may ask which is the best choice. The answer is that all three versions are possible for any given industry. Only direct observation of the industry can tell which type of industry it is.

Key Concepts

Market structure

Perfect competition

Homogeneous product

Barrier to entry

Price taker

Marginal revenue (MR)

Perfectly competitive firm's short-run supply curve

Perfectly competitive industry's short-run supply curve

Perfectly competitive industry's long-run supply curve

Constant-cost industry

Decreasing-cost industry

Increasing-cost industry

Summary

- **Market structure** consists of three market characteristics: (1) the number of sellers, (2) the nature of the product, and (3) the ease of entry into or exit from the market.

- **Perfect competition** is a market structure in which an individual firm cannot affect the price of the product it produces. Each firm in the industry is very small relative to the market as a whole, all the firms sell a homogeneous product, and firms are free to enter and exit the industry.

- A **homogeneous product** is a good or service that is identical regardless of which firm produces it.

- A **price-taker** firm in perfect competition faces a perfectly elastic demand curve. It can sell all it wishes at the market-determined price, but it will sell nothing above the given market price. This is because so many competitive firms are willing to sell the same product at the going market price.

- The **total revenue-total cost method** is one way a firm determines the level of output that maximizes profit. Profit reaches a maximum when the vertical difference between the total revenue and the total cost curves is at a maximum.

Total Revenue-Total Cost Method

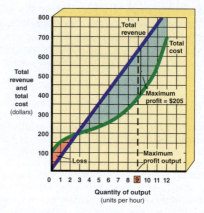

- The **marginal revenue equals marginal cost method** is a second approach to finding where a firm maximizes profits. **Marginal revenue (MR)** is the change in total revenue from a one-unit change in output. Marginal revenue for a perfectly competitive firm equals the market price. The MR = MC rule states that the firm maximizes profit or minimizes loss by producing the output where marginal revenue equals marginal cost. If the price (average revenue) is below the minimum point on the average variable cost curve, the MR = MC rule does not apply, and the firm shuts down to minimize its losses.

Marginal Revenue Equals Marginal Cost Method

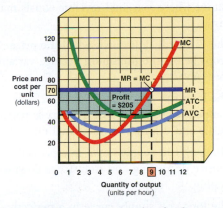

- The **perfectly competitive firm's short-run supply curve** is a curve showing the relationship between the price of a product and the quantity supplied in the short run. The individual firm always produces along its marginal cost curve above its intersection with the average variable cost curve. The **perfectly competitive industry's short-run supply curve** is the horizontal summation of the short-run supply curves of all firms in the industry.

Short-Run Supply Curve

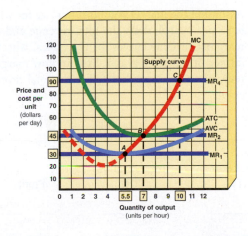

- **Long-run perfectly competitive equilibrium** occurs when a firm earns a normal profit by producing where price equals the minimum long-run average cost, the minimum short-run average total cost, and the short-run marginal cost.

Long-Run Perfectly Competitive Equilibrium

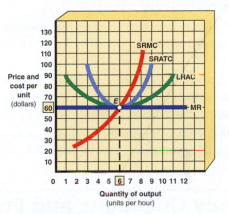

- In a **constant-cost industry**, total output can be expanded without an increase in the individual firm's average total cost. Because input prices remain constant, the long-run supply curve in a constant-cost industry is perfectly elastic.

- In a **decreasing-cost industry**, lower input prices result in a downward-sloping industry long-run supply curve. As industry output expands, an individual firm's average total cost curve declines (shifts downward), and the long-run equilibrium market price falls.

- In an **increasing-cost industry**, input prices rise as industry output increases. As a result, an individual firm's average total cost curve rises (shifts upward), and the industry long-run supply curve for an increasing-cost industry is upward sloping.

Summary of Conclusion Statements

- The large-number-of-sellers condition is met when each firm is so small relative to the total market that no single firm can influence the market price.

- If a product is homogeneous, buyers are indifferent as to which seller's product they buy.

- Perfect competition requires that resources be completely mobile to freely enter or exit a market.

- In perfect competition, the firm's marginal revenue equals the price, which the firm views as a horizontal demand curve.

- In perfect competition, the firm maximizes profit or minimizes loss by producing the output where marginal revenue equals marginal cost.

- The firm will shut down when the price drops below the minimum average variable cost (AVC).

- The long-run supply curve in a perfectly competitive constant-cost industry is perfectly elastic and drawn as a horizontal line.

- The long-run supply curve in a perfectly competitive decreasing-cost industry is downward sloping.

- The long-run supply curve in a perfectly competitive increasing-cost industry is upward sloping.

Study Questions and Problems

Please see Appendix A for answers to the odd-numbered questions. Your instructor has access to the answers for even-numbered questions.

1. Explain why a perfectly competitive firm would or would not advertise.

2. Does a Kansas wheat farmer operate in a perfectly competitive market structure? Explain.

3. Suppose the market equilibrium price of wheat is $2 per bushel in a perfectly competitive industry. Draw the industry supply and demand curves and the demand curve for a single wheat farmer. Explain why the wheat farmer is a price taker.

4. Assuming the market equilibrium price for wheat is $5 per bushel, draw the total revenue and the marginal revenue curves for the typical wheat farmer in the same graph. Explain how marginal revenue and price are related to the total revenue curve.

Output (Q)	Total fixed cost (TFC)	Total variable cost (TVC)	Total cost (TC)	Total revenue (TR)	Profit
1	$100	$120	$_____	$_____	$_____
2	100	200	_____	_____	_____
3	100	290	_____	_____	_____
4	100	430	_____	_____	_____
5	100	590	_____	_____	_____

5. Consider the following cost data for a perfectly competitive firm in the short run:

   If the market price is $150, how many units of output will the firm produce in order to maximize profit in the short run? Specify the amount of economic profit or loss. At what level of output does the firm break even?

6. Consider this statement: "A firm should increase output when it makes a profit." Do you agree or disagree? Explain.

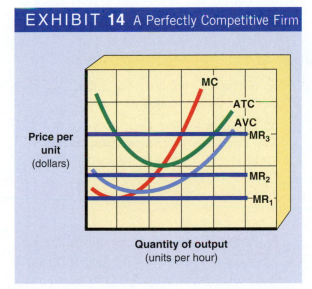

EXHIBIT 14 A Perfectly Competitive Firm

Price per unit (dollars)

MC

ATC

AVC

MR₃

MR₂

MR₁

Quantity of output (units per hour)

7. Consider this statement: "When marginal revenue equals marginal cost, total cost equals total revenue, and the firm makes zero profit." Do you agree or disagree? Explain.

8. Consider Exhibit 14, which shows the graph of a perfectly competitive firm in the short run.
   a. If the firm's demand curve is MR₃, does the firm earn an economic profit or loss?
   b. Which demand curve(s) indicate(s) the firm incurs a loss?
   c. Which demand curve(s) indicate(s) the firm would shut down?
   d. Identify the firm's short-run supply curve.

9. Consider this statement: "The perfectly competitive firm will sell all the quantity of output consumers will buy at the prevailing market price." Do you agree or disagree? Explain your answer.

10. Suppose a perfectly competitive firm's demand curve is below its average total cost curve. Explain the conditions under which a firm continues to produce in the short run.

11. Suppose the industry equilibrium price of residential housing construction is $100 per square foot and the minimum average variable cost for a residential construction contractor is $110 per square foot. What would you advise the owner of this firm to do? Explain.

12. Suppose independent truckers operate in a perfectly competitive constant-cost industry. If these firms are earning positive economic profits, what happens in the long run to the following: the price of trucking services, the industry quantity of output, and the profits of trucking firms?

 CHECKPOINT ANSWERS

Should Motels Offer Rooms at the Beach for Only $70 a Night?

As long as price exceeds average variable cost, the motel is better off operating than shutting down. Since $70 is more than enough to cover the guest-related (average variable) cost of $65 per room, the firm will operate. The $5 remaining after average variable costs are covered can be put toward the $30 average fixed costs. Were the motel to shut down, it would make no contribution to these overhead costs. If you said the Myrtle Beach motels should operate during the winter because they can get a price that exceeds their average variable cost, **YOU ARE CORRECT**.

Are You in Business for the Long Run?

In the long run, surviving firms will operate at the minimum of the long-run average cost curve. The average cost of 50 storage units is $4,000 ($200,000/50), the average cost of 100 storage units is $3,000 ($300,000/100), and the average cost of 200 storage units is $3,500 ($700,000/200). Of the three storage-unit quantities given, the one with the lowest average cost is closest to the minimum point on the LRAC curve. If you chose 100 storage units, **YOU ARE CORRECT**.

Sample Quiz

Please see Appendix B for answers to Sample Quiz questions.

1. As shown in Exhibit 15, suppose the firm's price is *OB*. The firm's total economic profit at this price is equal to the area of
   a. *CJID*.
   b. *BFHD*.
   c. *AEXD*.
   d. *CGHD*.
   e. zero.

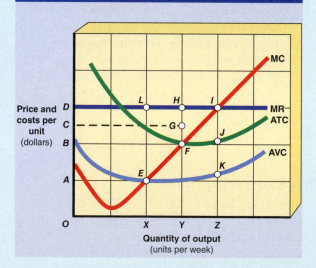

EXHIBIT 15 Marginal Revenues and Cost per Unit Curves

2. The firm shown in Exhibit 15 will
   a. produce where marginal cost equals marginal revenue.
   b. be a price taker.

   c. not produce below a price of *OA*.
   d. All of the above answers are correct.

3. As shown in Exhibit 15, if the price is *OD*, a perfectly competitive firm maximizes profit at which point on its marginal cost curve?
   a. *E*
   b. *F*
   c. *I*
   d. Between *E* and *I*

4. As shown in Exhibit 15, if the price is *OB*, the firm's total cost of producing at its most profitable level of output is
   a. *YF*.
   b. *XL*.
   c. *OYFB*.
   d. *OXEA*.

5. As shown in Exhibit 15, if the price is *OD*, the firm's total revenue at its most profitable level of output is
   a. *OZID*.
   b. *OYHD*.
   c. *OXLD*.
   d. *OYFB*.

6. As shown in Exhibit 15, suppose the firm's price is OD. At this price the firm
   a. will maximize profits by producing OX units.
   b. will maximize profits by producing OY units.
   c. will shut down.
   d. is earning a zero economic profit.
   e. is earning positive economic profits.

7. As shown in Exhibit 15, if the price is *OB*, the firm's total revenue of producing at its most profitable level of output is
   a. *YF*.
   b. *XL*.
   c. *OYFB*.
   d. *OXEA*.

8. When there is a permanent increase in market demand in a constant-cost industry, a firm's Short-run Average Total Cost Curve will
   a. become vertical
   b. shift up
   c. shift down
   d. remain the same

9. Perfect competition is defined as market structure in which
   a. there are many small sellers.
   b. the product is homogeneous.
   c. it is very easy for firms to enter or exit the market.
   d. All of the above answers are correct.

10. Under perfect competition, which of the following are the same (equal) at all levels of output?
    a. Price and marginal cost
    b. Price and marginal revenue
    c. Marginal cost and marginal revenue
    d. All of the above answers are correct

11. A portrait photographer produces output in packages of 100 photos each. If the output sold increases from 600 to 700 photos, total revenue increases from $1,200 to $1,400. What is the marginal revenue per photo?
    a. $200
    b. $100
    c. $20
    d. $2
    e. $1

12. In the short run, a perfectly competitive firm is producing at a price below average total cost. What is its economic profit?
    a. Positive
    b. Zero
    c. Negative
    d. Normal

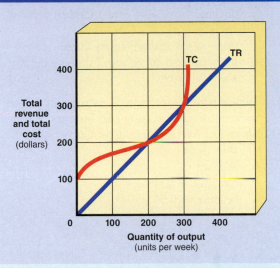

EXHIBIT 16 Total Revenue and Total Cost Graph

13. In Exhibit 16, if output is 200 units per week, economic profit for the firm is
    a. zero.
    b. at its minimum.
    c. at its maximum.
    d. None of the above answers are correct.

14. In Exhibit 16, economic profit for the firm is at a maximum when output per week equals
    a. 0 units.
    b. 100 units.
    c. 200 units.
    d. 250 units.

15. The point of maximum profit for a business firm is where
    a. *P* = AC.
    b. TR = TC.
    c. MR = AR.
    d. MR = MC.

16. When there is a permanent increase in market demand in a decreasing-cost industry, a firm's Short-run Average Total Cost Curve will
    a. become vertical
    b. shift down
    c. remain the same
    d. shift up

17. A perfectly competitive firm's short-run supply curve is the
    a. average total cost curve.
    b. demand curve above the marginal revenue curve.
    c. same as the market supply curve.
    d. marginal cost curve above the average variable cost curve.

18. When there is a permanent increase in market demand in an increasing-cost industry, a firm's Short-run Average Total Cost Curve will
    a. shift down
    b. shift up
    c. remain the same
    d. become vertical

19. In long-run equilibrium, the perfectly competitive firm sets its price equal to which of the following?
    a. Short-run average total cost
    b. Short-run marginal cost
    c. Long-run average cost
    d. All of the above answers are correct

20. If there is a permanent increase in demand for the product of a perfectly competitive industry, the process of transition to a new long-run equilibrium will include
    a. the entry of new firms.
    b. temporarily higher profits.
    c. both a and b.
    d. neither a nor b.

CHAPTER 9

Monopoly

CHAPTER PREVIEW

Playing the popular board game of Monopoly teaches some of the characteristics of monopoly theory presented in this chapter. In the game version, players win by gaining as much economic power as possible. They strive to own railroads, utilities, Boardwalk, Park Place, and other valuable real estate. Then each player tries to bankrupt opponents by purchasing hotels that charge high prices. A player who rolls the dice and lands on another player's property has no choice—either pay the price or lose the game.

In the last chapter, we studied perfect competition, which may be viewed as the paragon of economic virtue. Why? Under perfect competition, there are many sellers, each lacking any power to influence price. Perfect competition and monopoly are polar extremes. The word *monopoly* is derived from two Greek words meaning "single seller." A monopoly has the market power to set its price and not worry about competitors. Perhaps your college or university has only one bookstore where you can buy textbooks. If so, students are likely to pay higher prices for textbooks than they would if many sellers competed in the campus textbook market.

This chapter explains why firms do not or cannot enter a particular market and compete with a monopolist. Then we explore some of the interesting actual monopolies around the world. We study how a monopolist determines what price to charge and how much to produce. The chapter ends with a discussion of the pros and cons of monopoly. Most of the analytical tools required here have been introduced in previous chapters.

IN THIS CHAPTER, YOU WILL LEARN TO SOLVE THESE ECONOMICS PUZZLES:

- Why doesn't the monopolist gouge consumers by charging the highest possible price?

- How can price discrimination be fair?

- Are medallion cabs in New York City monopolists?

9-1 THE MONOPOLY MARKET STRUCTURE

The model at the opposite extreme from perfect competition is monopoly. Under monopoly, the consumer has a simple choice—either buy the monopolist's product or do without it. **Monopoly** is a market structure characterized by (1) a single seller, (2) a unique product, and (3) impossible entry into the market.

Monopoly
A market structure characterized by (1) a single seller, (2) a unique product, and (3) impossible entry into the market.

Unlike perfect competition, there are no close substitutes for the monopolist's product. Monopoly, like perfect competition, corresponds only approximately to real-world industries, but it serves as a useful benchmark model. Following are brief descriptions of each monopoly characteristic.

9-1a Characteristics of Monopoly

Single Seller

In perfect competition, many firms make up the industry. In contrast, a monopoly means that a single firm is the industry. One firm provides the total supply of a product in a given market. Local monopolies are more common real-world approximations of the model than national or world market monopolies. For example, a campus bookstore, a cable television company, and an electric power company may be local monopolies. The only gas station, drugstore, or grocery store in Nowhere County, Utah, and a hotdog stand at a football game are also examples of monopolies. Nationally, the U.S. Postal Service monopolizes first-class mail.

Unique Product

A unique product means there are *no close substitutes* for the monopolist's product. Thus, the monopolist faces little or no competition. In reality, however, there are few, if any, products that have no close substitutes. Students can buy used textbooks from sources other than the campus bookstore, and textbooks can be purchased over the Internet. Satellite television competes with cable television. Natural gas, oil furnaces, and solar energy are substitutes for electric heat. Similarly, the fax machine and email are substitutes for mail service.

Impossible Entry

In perfect competition, there are no constraints to prevent new firms from entering an industry. In the case of monopoly, extremely high barriers make it very difficult or impossible for new firms to enter an industry. Following are the three major barriers that prevent new firms from entering a market and competing with a monopolist.

- **Ownership of a Vital Resource** Sole control of the entire supply of a strategic input is one way a monopolist can prevent a newcomer from entering an industry. A famous historical example is Alcoa's monopoly of the U.S. aluminum market from the late nineteenth century until the end of World War II. The source of Alcoa's monopoly was its control of bauxite ore, which is necessary to produce aluminum. Today, it is very difficult for a new professional sports league to compete with the National Football League (NFL) and the National Basketball Association (NBA). Why? NFL and NBA teams have contracts with the best players and leases for the best stadiums and arenas.

- **Legal Barriers** The oldest and most effective barriers protecting a firm from potential competitors are the result of government franchises and licenses. The government permits a single firm to provide a certain product and excludes competing firms by law. For example, water and sewer service, natural gas, and cable television operate under monopoly franchises established by state and local governments. In many states, the state government runs monopoly liquor stores and lotteries. The U.S. Postal Service has a government franchise to deliver first-class mail. Government-granted licenses restrict entry into some industries and occupations. For example, the Federal Communications Commission (FCC) must license radio and television stations. In most states, physicians, lawyers, dentists, nurses, teachers, real estate agents, hair stylists, taxicabs, liquor stores, funeral homes, and other professions and businesses are required to have a license. Patents and copyrights are another form of government barriers to entry. The government grants patents to inventors, thereby legally prohibiting other firms from selling the patented product for 20 years. Copyrights give creators of literature, art, music, and movies exclusive rights to sell or license their works. The purpose behind granting patents and copyrights is to encourage innovation and new products by guaranteeing exclusive rights to profit from new ideas for a limited period.

- **Economies of Scale** Why might competition among firms be unsustainable so that one firm becomes a monopolist? Recall the concept of *economies of scale* from Chapter 7 on production costs. As a result of large-scale production, the long-run average cost (LRAC) of production falls, allowing a firm to lower its per-unit cost as it expands output, which in turn enables this firm to charge lower prices than its smaller competitors. The smaller firms can't compete with these lower prices and are driven out of the market. Thus, if a large firm continues to grow and obtain enough of a cost advantage over its rivals, it can become a monopoly and remain dominant in an industry. In addition, even if the monopolist does not own an essential resource, and if it is not protected by legal barriers, its sheer size may be enough to scare away potential competition. Would-be competitors may find it virtually impossible to raise enough money to set up operations on a large-enough scale to effectively compete in this industry.

Economists call the situation in which one seller emerges in an industry because of economies of scale a natural monopoly. A **natural monopoly** is an industry in which the long-run average cost of production declines over the full range of output demanded in the market. As a result, a single firm, rather than two or more firms, can supply the entire market demand at the lowest possible cost. Public utilities, such as natural gas, water, and cable television, are examples of natural monopolies. The government grants these industries an exclusive franchise in a geographic area so consumers can benefit from the cost savings that occur when one firm in an industry with significant economies of scale sells a large enough output to satisfy the entire market demand. The government then regulates these monopolies through a board of commissioners to prevent exploitation.

Exhibit 1 depicts the LRAC curve for a natural monopoly. A single firm can produce 100 units at an average cost of $15 and a total cost of $1,500. If two firms each produce 50 units, the total cost rises to $2,500. With five firms producing 20 units each, the total cost rises to $3,500. In the chapter on antitrust and regulation, regulation of a natural monopoly will be explored in greater detail.

Natural monopoly
An industry in which the long-run average cost of production declines throughout the entire market. As a result, a single firm can supply the entire market demand at a lower cost than two or more smaller firms.

EXHIBIT 1 Minimizing Costs in a Natural Monopoly

In a natural monopoly, a single firm, rather than multiple firms, provides the lowest cost option for producing the industry's output. The single firm's cost advantage occurs because the LRAC curve for any firm decreases over the full range of output demanded in the market. For example, one firm can produce 100 units at an average cost of $15 and a total cost of $1,500. Two firms in the industry can produce 100 units of output (50 units each) for a total cost of $2,500, and five firms can produce the same output for a total cost of $3,500.

CONCLUSION Because of economies of scale, a single firm in an industry can produce enough output to satisfy market demand and produce this output at a lower per-unit cost than would be possible if the market were served by more than one firm.

9-1b Network Good

Network good
A good that increases in value to each user as the total number of users increases. As a result, a firm can achieve economies of scale. Examples include Facebook and Match.com.

Economies of scale and monopoly power can exist because consumers choose a product that everyone else is using. A **network good** is a good that increases in value to each user as the total number of users increases. Examples include Internet products such as Facebook and Match.com. People post on Facebook to belong to the same network where everyone can see their posts. Similarly, Match.com is the largest dating service with the largest selections of potential dates.

CONCLUSION As the number of people connected to a network goods system increases, the greater the benefits each person receives from being in the network.

By selling network goods, a firm can increase sales rapidly and thus achieve economies of scale, as illustrated in Exhibit 1. One large firm emerges because smaller firms

GLOBAL ECONOMICS

Monopolies around the World

Applicable Concept: Monopoly

Interesting examples of monopolies can be found in other countries. Let's begin with a historical example. In the sixteenth through eighteenth centuries, monarchs granted monopoly rights to a variety of businesses. For example, in 1600, Queen Elizabeth I chartered the British East India Company and gave it a monopoly over England's trade with India. This company was even given the right to coin money and to make peace or war with non-Christian powers. As a result of its monopoly, the company made substantial profits from the trade in Indian cotton goods, silks, and spices. In the late 1700s, the growing power of the company and huge personal fortunes of its officers provoked more and more government control. Finally, in 1858, the company was abolished, ending its trade monopoly, great power, and patronage.

"Diamonds are forever," has been the De Beers slogan, but will De Beers be the diamond monopoly forever? De Beers, a South African corporation, was close to being a world monopoly. It owns the world's largest diamond mine, which was discovered in 1866 on a farm in South Africa owned by Johannes De Beer. Through its Central Selling Organization (CSO) headquartered in London, De Beers controlled 80 percent of all the diamonds sold in the world. De Beers controlled the price of jewelry-quality diamonds by requiring suppliers in Russia, Australia, Congo, Botswana, Namibia, and other countries to sell their rough diamonds through De Beers's CSO. Why did suppliers of rough diamonds allow De Beers to set the price and quantity of diamonds sold throughout the world? The answer was that the CSO could put any uncooperative seller out of business. All the CSO had to do was to reach into its huge stockpile of diamonds and flood the market with the type of diamonds being sold by an independent seller. As a result, the price of diamonds would plummet in the competitor's market, and the independent seller would cease to sell diamonds.

In recent years, De Beers lost some of its control of the market. Mines in Australia became more independent, diamonds were found in Canada, and Russian mines began selling to independents. To deal with the new conditions, De Beers changed its policy in 2001 by closing the CSO

and promoting its own brand of diamonds rather than trying to control the world diamond supply. De Beers proclaimed its strategy to be "the diamond supplier of choice." Will this monopoly continue? It is an interesting question.

Michael Kraus/Shutterstock.com

Genuine caviar, the salty black delicacy, is naturally scarce because it comes from the eggs of sturgeon harvested by fisheries from the Caspian Sea near the mouth of the Volga River. After the Bolshevik revolution in Russia in 1917, a caviar monopoly was established under the control of the Soviet Ministry of Fisheries and the Paris-based Petrosian Company. The Petrosian brothers limited exports of caviar and pushed prices up as high as $1,000 a pound for some varieties. As a result of this worldwide monopoly, both the Soviet government and the Petrosian Company earned handsome profits. It is interesting to note that the vast majority of the tons of caviar harvested each year was consumed at government banquets or sold at bargain prices to top Communist Party officials. With the fall of the Soviet Union, it was impossible for the Ministry of Fisheries to control all exports of caviar. Various former Soviet republics claimed jurisdiction and negotiated independent export contracts. As a result, caviar export prices dropped sharply.

ANALYZE THE ISSUE

1. Explain why the price of Indian cotton goods should have dropped after 1858.
2. Explain why the caviar monopoly was willing to sell caviar to Soviet government officials at bargain prices.

are left with high costs, which prevent them from matching the price set by a large volume producer.

9-2 PRICE AND OUTPUT DECISIONS FOR A MONOPOLIST

The major difference between perfect competition and monopoly is the shape of the demand curve a single firm faces, not the shapes of the cost curves. As explained in the previous chapter, a perfectly competitive firm is a *price taker*. In contrast, the next sections explain that a monopolist is a price maker. A **price maker** is a firm that faces a downward-sloping demand curve. This means a monopolist has the ability to select the product's price. In short, a monopolist can set the price with its corresponding level of output, rather than being a helpless pawn at the mercy of the going industry price. To understand the monopolist, we again apply the marginal approach to our hypothetical electronics company—Computech.

Price maker
A firm that faces a downward-sloping demand curve and therefore it can choose among price and output combinations along the demand curve.

9-2a Marginal Revenue, Total Revenue, and Price Elasticity of Demand

Suppose engineers at Computech discover an inexpensive, miraculous electronic device called SAV-U-GAS that anyone can easily attach to a car's engine. Once installed, the device raises gasoline mileage to over 100 miles per gallon. The government grants Computech a patent, and the company becomes a monopolist selling this gas-saving gizmo. Because of this barrier to entry, Computech is the only seller in the industry. Although other firms try to compete with this invention, they create poor substitutes. As a result, everyone in the market buys from the monopoly. This means the downward-sloping market demand curve is also the demand curve the monopolist faces.

Exhibit 2(a) illustrates the demand and the marginal revenue (MR) curves for a monopolist such as Computech. As the monopolist lowers its price to increase the quantity demanded in its market, changes in both price and quantity affect the firm's total revenue (price times quantity), as shown graphically in Exhibit 2(b). If Computech charges $150, consumers purchase 0 units, and, therefore, total revenue is zero. To sell 1 unit, Computech must lower the price to $138, and total revenue rises from zero to $138. Because the marginal revenue is the increase in total revenue that results from a 1-unit change in output, the MR curve at the first unit of output is $138 ($138 − 0). Thus, the price and the marginal revenue from selling 1 unit are equal at $138. To sell 2 units, the monopolist must lower the price to $125, and total revenue rises to $250. The marginal revenue from selling the second unit is $112 ($250 − $138), which is $13 less than the price received.

As shown in Exhibit 2(a), the marginal revenue curve always lies below the demand curve, which is a result of the monopolist charging all of its customers the same price. For example, to increase sales from one to two units, the monopolist must reduce the price from $138 to $125 for *both* units. Although it is true that the monopolist generates an extra $125 in revenue from selling the second item, it also earns $13 less from selling its first unit of output, now that it has reduced the price for *both* items to make the additional sale. Therefore, the marginal revenue of selling the second unit is $112 ($125 − $13), which, of course, is less than $125, the price given by the demand curve

EXHIBIT 2 Demand, Marginal Revenue, and Total Revenue for a Monopolist

Part (a) shows the relationship between the demand and the marginal revenue curves. The MR curve is below the demand curve. Between 0 and 6 units of output, MR > 0; at 6 units of output, MR = 0; beyond 6 units of output, MR < 0.

The relationship between demand and total revenue is shown in part (b). When the price is $150, total revenue is zero. When the price is set at zero, total revenue is also zero. Between these two extreme prices, the price of $75 maximizes total revenue. This price corresponds to 6 units of output, which is where the MR curve intersects the quantity axis, halfway between the origin and the intercept of the demand curve.

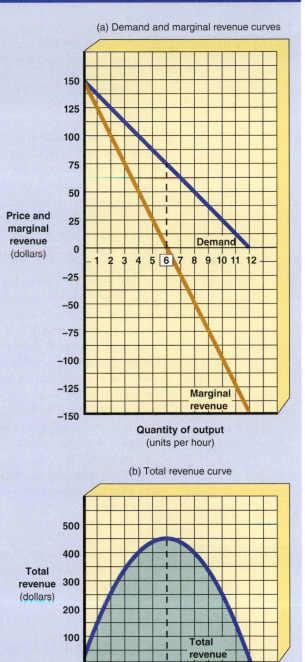

(a) Demand and marginal revenue curves

Price and marginal revenue (dollars)

Quantity of output (units per hour)

(b) Total revenue curve

Total revenue (dollars)

Quantity of output (units per hour)

Demand, Marginal Revenue, and Total Revenue for Computech as a Monopolist

Output per hour	Price	Total revenue	Marginal revenue
0	$150	$0	
			$138
1	138	138	
			112
2	125	250	
			89
3	113	339	
			61
4	100	400	
			40
5	88	440	
			10
6	75	450	0
			−9
7	63	441	
			−41
8	50	400	
			−58
9	38	342	
			−92
10	25	250	
			−107
11	13	143	
			−143
12	0	0	

at this quantity. Expanding production and sales continues to generate marginal revenues that are less than the successively lower prices found on the demand curve.

CONCLUSION

The demand and marginal revenue curves of the monopolist are downward sloping, in contrast to the horizontal demand and corresponding marginal revenue curves facing the perfectly competitive firm [compare Exhibit 2(a) with Exhibit 1(b) of the previous chapter].

Refer to the table in Exhibit 2. Starting from zero output, as the price falls, total revenue rises until it reaches a maximum at 6 units, and then it falls, tracing the "revenue hill" drawn in part (b). The explanation was presented earlier in the discussion of price elasticity of demand in Chapter 5. Recall that a straight-line demand curve has an elastic ($E_d > 1$) segment along the upper half, a unit elastic ($E_d = 1$) segment at the midpoint, and an inelastic ($E_d < 1$) segment along the lower half (see Exhibit 4 in Chapter 5). Recall from Chapter 5 that when $E_d > 1$, total revenue rises as the price drops, and total revenue reaches a maximum where $E_d = 1$. When $E_d < 1$, total revenue falls as the price falls.

As shown in Exhibit 2(b), total revenue for a monopolist is related to marginal revenue. When the MR curve is above the quantity axis (elastic demand), total revenue is increasing. At the intersection of the MR curve and the quantity axis (unit elastic demand), total revenue is at its maximum. When the MR curve is below the quantity axis, total revenue is decreasing (inelastic demand). The monopolist will never operate on the inelastic range of its demand curve that corresponds to a negative marginal revenue. The reason is that, in this inelastic range, the monopolist can increase total revenue by cutting output and raising price. In our example, Computech would not charge a price lower than $75 or produce an output greater than 6 units per hour. Now we turn to the question of what quantity will the monopolist produce and what price will it charge to maximize profit.

In Exhibit 2(a), observe that the MR curve cuts the quantity axis at 6 units, which is *half* of 12 units, the quantity where the demand curve intersects the *x*-axis. Following this easy rule helps you locate the point along the quantity axis where marginal revenue equals zero.

CONCLUSION

The marginal revenue curve for a straight-line demand curve intersects the quantity axis halfway between the origin and the quantity axis intercept of the demand curve.

9-2b Short-Run Profit Maximization for a Monopolist Using the Total Revenue–Total Cost Method

Exhibit 3 reproduces the demand, total revenue, and marginal revenue data from Exhibit 2 and adds cost data from the previous two chapters. These data illustrate a situation in which Computech can earn monopoly economic profit in the short run. Subtracting total cost in column 6 from total revenue in column 3 gives the total profit

EXHIBIT 3 Short-Run Profit Maximization Schedule for Computech as a Monopolist

(1) Output per hour (Q)	(2) Price per unit (P)	(3) Total revenue (TR)	(4) Marginal revenue (MR)	(5) Marginal cost (MC)	(6) Total cost (TC)	(7) Average total cost (ATC)	(8) Profit (+) or loss (−)
0	$150	$0			$100	–	−$100
			$138	$50			
1	138	138			150	$150	−12
			112	34			
2	125	250			184	92	66
			89	24			
3	113	339			208	69	131
			61	19			
4	100	400			227	57	173
			40	23			
5	88	440	25	25	250	50	190
			10	30			
6	75	450			280	47	170
			−9	38			
7	63	441			318	45	123
			−41	48			
8	50	400			366	46	34
			−58	59			
9	38	342			425	47	−83
			−92	75			
10	25	250			500	50	−250
			−107	95			
11	13	143			595	54	−452
			−143	117			
12	0	0			712	59	−712

or loss in column 8 that the firm earns at each level of output. From 0 to 1 unit, the monopolist incurs losses, and then a break-even point occurs before 2 units per hour. If the monopolist produces 5 units per hour, it earns the maximum profit of $190 per hour. As output expands between 5 and 8 units of output, the monopolist's profit diminishes. After 8 units of output, there is a second break-even point, and losses increase as output expands. Exhibit 4 graphically illustrates the values of total cost, total revenue, and profit over a range of quantities the monopolist could produce. Total

EXHIBIT 4 Short-Run Profit Maximization for a Monopolist Using the Total Revenue–
Total Cost Method

The profit-maximizing level of output for Computech as a monopolist is shown in this exhibit.
Part (a) shows that maximum profit is earned by
producing 5 units per hour and charging a price of
$88 per unit where the vertical distance between
the total revenue and total cost curves is the
greatest. In part (b), the maximum profit of $190
per hour corresponds to the profit-maximizing
output of 5 units per hour illustrated in part (a).
At output levels below 2 or above 8, the
monopolist incurs losses.

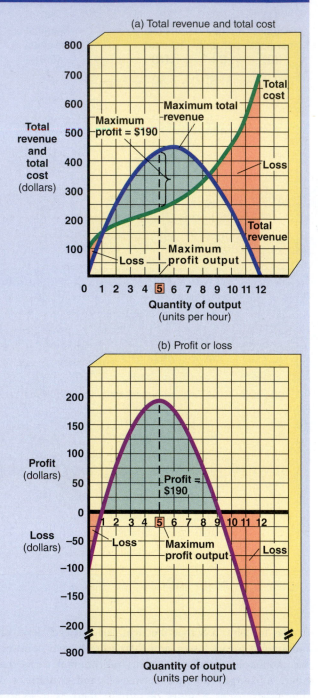

revenue is depicted by the hill-shaped curve and is maximized at the top of the hill, which occurs at a quantity of 6 units. Profit is maximized where the vertical distance between the total revenue and total cost curves is greatest, which occurs at 5 units of output. Note that the total revenue-maximizing output level of 6 units is greater than the profit-maximizing output at 5 units.

9-2c Short-Run Profit Maximization for a Monopolist Using the Marginal Revenue Equals Marginal Cost Method

Exhibit 5 reproduces the demand and cost curves from the table in Exhibit 3. Like the perfectly competitive firm, a monopolist maximizes profit by producing the quantity of output where MR = MC and charging the corresponding price on its demand curve. In this case, 5 units is the quantity at which MR = MC. As represented by point *A* on the demand curve, the price at 5 units is $88. Point *B* represents an average total cost (ATC) of $50 at 5 units. Because the price of $88 is above the ATC curve at the MR = MC output, the monopolist earns a profit of $38 per unit. At the hourly output of 5 units, total profit is $190 per hour, as shown by the shaded area ($38 per unit × 5 units).

Observe that a monopolist charges neither the highest possible price nor the total revenue-maximizing price. In Exhibit 5(a), $88 is not the highest possible price. Because Computech is a *price maker*, it could have set a price above $88 and sold less output than 5 units. However, the monopolist does not maximize profit by charging the highest possible price. Any price above $88 does not correspond to the intersection of the MR and MC curves. Now note that 5 units is below the output level where MR intersects the quantity axis and total revenue reaches its peak. Because MR = 0 and $(E_d = 1)$ when total revenue is maximum at 6 units of output, MC = 0 must also hold to maximize revenue and profit at the same time. A monopolist producing with zero marginal cost is an unlikely case. Hence, the price charged to maximize profit is higher on the demand curve than the price that maximizes total revenue. Remember: The objective is to maximize profits, not total revenue!

The monopolist always maximizes profit by producing at a price on the elastic segment of its demand curve.

CONCLUSION

9-2d A Monopolist Facing a Short-Run Loss

Having a monopoly does not guarantee profits. A monopolist has no protection against changes in demand or cost conditions. Exhibit 6 shows a situation in which the demand curve is lower at any point than the ATC curve, and total cost therefore exceeds total revenue at any price charged. Because the point where MR = MC at a price of $50 (point *A*) on the demand curve is above the AVC curve, but below the ATC curve, the best Computech can do is to minimize its loss. This means the monopolist, like the perfectly competitive firm, produces in the short run at a quantity of 5 units per hour where MR = MC. At a price of $50 (point *A*), the ATC is $70 (point *B*), and Computech incurs a loss of $100 per hour, represented by the shaded area ($20 × 5 units).

What if MR = MC at a price on the demand curve that is below the AVC for a monopolist? As under perfect competition, the monopolist will shut down. To operate would only add further to its losses.

EXHIBIT 5 Short-Run Profit Maximization for a Monopolist Using the Marginal Revenue Equals Marginal Cost Method

Part (a) illustrates a monopolist electronics firm, Computech, maximizing profit by producing 5 units of output where the marginal revenue (MR) and the marginal cost (MC) curves intersect. The profit-maximizing price the monopolist charges at 5 units of output is $88, which is point *A* on the demand curve. Because $88 is above the average total cost (ATC) of $50 at point *B*, the monopolist earns a short-run profit of $190 per hour, represented by the shaded area ($38 profit per unit × 5 units).

At a price of $88 and output of 5 units per hour in part (a), the shaded area in part (b) shows that the profit curve is maximized at $190 per hour. At output levels below 2 or above 8, the monopolist incurs losses.

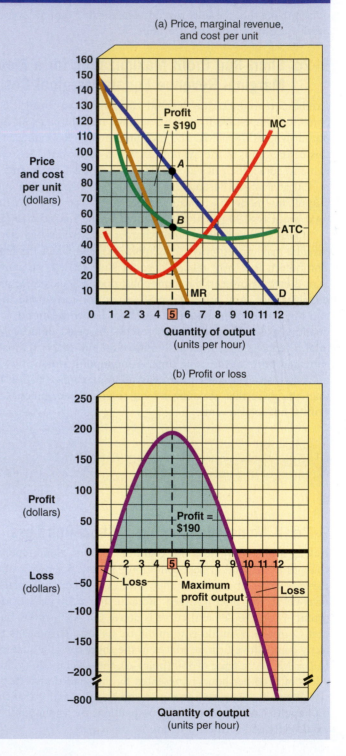

(a) Price, marginal revenue, and cost per unit

(b) Profit or loss

EXHIBIT 6 Short-Run Loss Minimization for a Monopolist Using the Marginal Revenue Equals Marginal Cost Method

In part (a), all points along the demand curve lie below the ATC curve. If the market price charged corresponds to the output where the marginal revenue (MR) and marginal cost (MC) curves intersect, the firm will keep its loss to a minimum. At an output of 5 units per hour, the marginal revenue equals the marginal cost, the loss-minimizing price is $50 per unit (point *A*), and the ATC equals $70 per unit (point *B*). The short-run loss represented by the shaded area is $100 ($20 loss per unit × 5 units).

Part (b) shows that the firm's short-run loss will be greater at any output other than where the marginal revenue and the marginal cost curves intersect at an output of 5 units per hour. Because the price of $50 is above the average variable cost, each unit of output sold pays for the average variable cost and a portion of the average fixed cost.

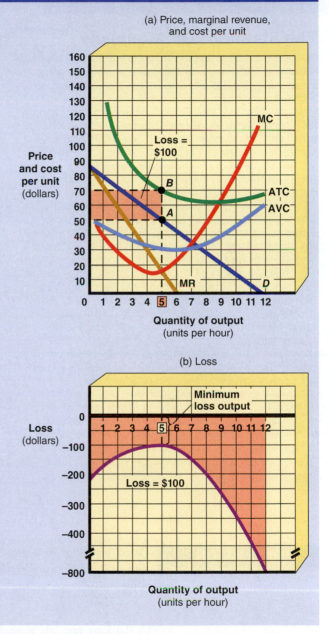

9-2e **Monopoly in the Long Run**

In perfect competition, economic profits are impossible in the long run. The entry of new firms into the industry drives the product's price down until profits reach zero. Extremely high barriers to entry, however, protect a monopolist from potential competitors.

YOU'RE THE ECONOMIST

The Standard Oil Monopoly

Oil was discovered in western Pennsylvania by Colonel Edwin L. Drake in 1859, and after the Civil War, oil wells sprang up across the landscape. Because oil was plentiful, there was cutthroat competition, and the result was low prices and profits. At this time, John D. Rockefeller, who had grown up selling eggs, was a young produce wholesaler in Cleveland during his early twenties. He was doing well in produce, but realized that greater profits could be made in refining oil, where there was less competition than in drilling for oil. So in 1869, Rockefeller borrowed all the money he could and began with two small oil refineries.

To boost his market power, Rockefeller's Standard Oil of Ohio negotiated secret agreements with the railroads. In addition to getting the railroads to provide him with information on his competitors' shipments, Rockefeller negotiated contracts with the railroads to pay rebates to Standard Oil, not only on Standard Oil's oil shipments, but also on its competitors' shipments. Soon Standard Oil was able to buy 21 of its 26 refining competitors in the Cleveland area. As its profits grew, Standard Oil expanded its refining empire by acquiring its own oil fields, railroads, pipelines, and ships. The objective was to control oil from the oil well to the consumer. Over time, Rockefeller came to own a major part of the petroleum industry. Competitors found railroads and pipelines closed to their oil shipments. Rivals that could not be forced out of business were merged with Standard Oil.

In 1870, Standard Oil controlled only 10 percent of the oil industry in the United States. By 1880, Standard Oil controlled over 90 percent of the industry, and its oil was being shipped throughout the world. The more Standard Oil monopolized the petroleum industry, the higher its profits

Carl Mydans/Getty Images

rose, and the greater its power to eliminate competition became. As competitors dropped out of the industry, Rockefeller became a price maker. He raised prices, and Standard Oil's profits soared. Finally, in 1911, Standard Oil was broken up under the Sherman Antitrust Act of 1890 into competing companies, including companies that eventually became ExxonMobil and Chevron.

ANALYZE THE ISSUE   If Standard Oil was a natural monopoly, what would happen to the average cost of producing gasoline after the company was split up? Explain using a LRAC curve.

CONCLUSION   If the positions of a monopolist's demand and cost curves give it a profit and nothing disturbs these curves, the monopolist will earn profit in the long run.

In the long run, the monopolist has great flexibility. The monopolist can alter its plant size to lower cost just as a perfectly competitive firm does. But firms such as Computech will not remain in business in the long run when losses persist—regardless of their monopoly status. Facing long-run losses, the monopolist will transfer its resources to a more profitable industry.

In reality, no monopolist can depend on barriers to protect it fully from competition in the long run. One threat is that entrepreneurs will find innovative ways to compete with a monopoly. For example, Computech must fear that firms will use their ingenuity and new electronic discoveries to develop a better and cheaper gasoline-saving device. To dampen the enthusiasm of potential rivals, one alternative for the monopolist is to sacrifice short-run profits to earn greater profits in the long run. Returning to part (a) of Exhibit 5, the monopolist might wish to charge a price below $88 and produce an output greater than 5 units per hour. At a lower selling price, potential entrants may be discouraged from entering the market, which would allow Computech to earn profits for a longer period of time.

9-3 PRICE DISCRIMINATION

Our discussion so far has assumed the monopolist charges each customer the same price. What if Computech decides to sell identical SAV-U-GAS units for, say, $50 to truckers and $100 to everyone else? Under certain conditions, a monopolist may practice price discrimination to maximize profit. **Price discrimination** occurs when a seller charges different prices for the same product that are not justified by cost differences.

Price discrimination
The practice of a seller charging different prices for the same product that are not justified by cost differences.

9-3a Conditions for Price Discrimination

Not all firms can engage in price discrimination. The following three conditions must exist before a seller can price discriminate:

1. The seller must be a price maker and, therefore, face a downward-sloping demand curve. This means that monopoly is not the only market structure in which price discrimination may occur.
2. The seller must be able to segment the market by distinguishing between consumers willing to pay different prices. Momentarily, this separation of buyers will be shown to be based on different price elasticities of demand.
3. It must be impossible or too costly for customers to engage in arbitrage. **Arbitrage** is the practice of earning a profit by buying a good at a low price and reselling the good at a higher price. For example, suppose your campus bookstore tried to boost profits by selling textbooks at a 50 percent discount to seniors. It would not take seniors long to cut the bookstore's profits by buying textbooks at the low price, selling these texts under the list price to all students who are not seniors, and pocketing the difference. In so doing, even without knowing the word *arbitrage*, the seniors would destroy the bookstore's price discrimination scheme.

Arbitrage
The practice of earning a profit by buying a good at a low price and reselling the good at a higher price.

Although not monopolies, college and university tuition policies meet the conditions for price discrimination. For example, colleges and universities have some control over the tuition they charge, and lower tuition increases the quantity of students applying for entrance. Applicants' high school grades and SAT scores allow the admissions office to classify "consumers" with different price elasticities of demand. Students with lower grades and SAT scores have fewer substitutes, and their demand curve is less elastic than that of students with higher grades and SAT scores. If the tuition rises at University X, few students with lower grades will be lost because they have few offers of admission from other universities. On the other hand, the loss of students with higher grades and SAT scores is greater because they have more admissions opportunities. Further, the nature of the product prevents arbitrage. A student cannot buy University X admission at one price and sell it to another student for a higher price.

EXHIBIT 7 Price Discrimination

To maximize profit, University X separates students applying for admission into two distinct markets. The demand curve for admission of average students in part (a) is less elastic than the demand curve for admission of superior students in part (b). Profit maximization occurs when MR = MC in each market. Therefore, University X sets a tuition of T_1 for average students and gives scholarships to superior students, which lowers their tuition to T_2. Using price discrimination, University X earns a greater profit than it would by charging a single tuition to all students.

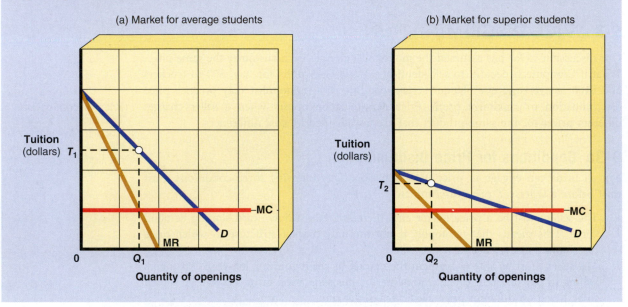

Exhibit 7 illustrates how University X price discriminates. For simplicity, assume the marginal cost of providing education to students is constant and therefore is represented by a horizontal MC curve. To maximize profit, University X follows the MR = MC rule in each market. Given the different price elasticities of demand, the price at which MR = MC differs for average and superior students. As a result, University X sets a higher tuition, T_1, in the average-student market, where demand is less responsive to the higher price. In the superior-student market, where demand is more responsive, these students receive scholarships, and their tuition is lower at T_2.

9-3b Is Price Discrimination Unfair?

Examples of price discrimination abound. Movie theaters offer lower prices for children than for adults. Electric utilities, which are monopolies, charge industrial users of electricity lower rates than residential users. Hotels and restaurants often give discounts to senior citizens, and airlines offer lower fares to vacationers who buy weeks early.

The typical reaction to price discrimination is that it is unfair. From the viewpoint of buyers who pay the higher prices, it is. But, look at the other side of price discrimination. The seller is pleased because price discrimination increases profits. And many buyers benefit from price discrimination, which gives them the opportunity to pay lower prices. In Exhibit 7, price discrimination makes it possible for superior students who could not afford to pay a higher tuition to attend University X. Price discrimination also allows retired persons to enjoy hotels and restaurants they could not otherwise afford and enables more children to attend movies.

CHECKPOINT

Why Don't Adults Pay More for Popcorn at the Movies?
At the movies, adults pay a higher ticket price than children, and each group gets a different-colored ticket. However, when adults and children go to the concession stand, both groups pay the same amount for popcorn and other snacks. Which of the following statements best explains why price discrimination stops at the ticket window?

1. The demand curve for popcorn is perfectly elastic.
2. The theater has no way to divide the buyers of popcorn based on different price elasticities of demand.
3. The theater cannot prevent resale.

9-4 COMPARING MONOPOLY AND PERFECT COMPETITION

Now that the basics of the two extremes of perfect competition and monopoly have been presented, we can compare and evaluate these market structures. This is an important assessment because the contrast between the disadvantages of monopoly and the advantages of perfect competition is the basis for many government policies, such as antitrust laws. To keep the analysis simple, we assume the monopolist charges a single price, rather than engaging in price discrimination.

9-4a The Monopolist as a Resource Misallocator

Recall the discussion of market efficiency in Chapter 4. This condition exists when a firm charging the equilibrium price uses neither too many nor too few resources to produce a product, so there is no *market failure*. Now you can state this definition of market efficiency in terms of price and marginal cost, as follows: *A perfectly competitive firm that produces the quantity of output at which P = MC achieves an efficient allocation of resources.* This means production reaches the level of output when the price of the last unit produced matches the marginal cost of producing it.

Exhibit 8(a) shows that a perfectly competitive firm produces the quantity of output at which $P = MC$. To evaluate this condition, recall that people continue to make purchases until the value of a product is equal to its price; therefore, the price of a product is equal to the value of the last item purchased. As a result, since the price, P_c, which measures the marginal benefit of the last unit consumed, equals the marginal cost of the resources used to produce it, just the right amount is produced. In contrast, the monopolist shown in Exhibit 8(b) charges a price, P_m, greater than marginal cost, $P > $ MC.

EXHIBIT 8 Comparing a Perfectly Competitive Firm and a Monopolist

The perfectly competitive firm in part (a) sets $P = MC$ and produces Q_c output. Therefore, at the last unit of output, the marginal benefit, measured by the price, is equal to the marginal cost of resources used to produce it. This condition means perfect competition achieves efficiency.

Part (b) shows that the monopolist produces output Q_m where $P > MC$. By so doing, consumers are shortchanged because the marginal benefit of the last unit produced exceeds the marginal cost of producing it. Under monopoly, inefficiency occurs because the monopolist underallocates resources to the production of its product. As a result, Q_m is less than Q_c.

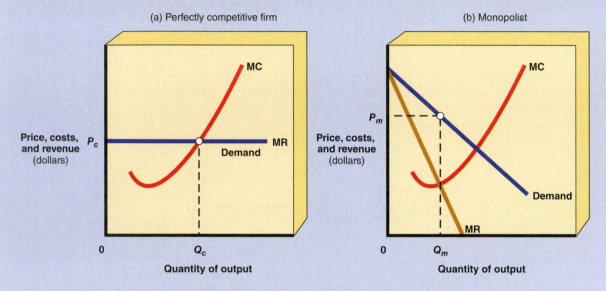

Therefore, consumers are short-changed because the marginal benefit of the last unit consumed exceeds the marginal cost of producing it. Consumers want the monopolist to use more resources to produce additional units, but the monopolist restricts output to maximize its profits.

CONCLUSION   A monopolist is characterized by inefficiency because resources are underallocated to the production of its product.

9-4b Perfect Competition Means More Output for Less

Exhibit 9 presents a comparison of perfect competition and monopoly in the same graph. Suppose the industry begins as perfectly competitive. The market demand curve, D (equal to MR), and the market supply curve, S, establish a perfectly competitive price, P_c, and output, Q_c. Recall from Exhibit 8 in the previous chapter that the competitive industry's supply curve, S, is the horizontal sum of the marginal cost (MC) curves of all the firms in the industry.

EXHIBIT 9 The Impact of Monopolizing an Industry

Assume an industry is perfectly competitive, with market demand curve D and market supply curve S. The market supply curve is the horizontal summation of all the individual firms' marginal cost curves above their minimum average variable costs. The intersection of market supply and market demand establishes the equilibrium price of P_c and the equilibrium quantity of Q_c. Now assume the industry suddenly changes to a monopoly. The monopolist produces the MR = MC output of Q_m, which is less than Q_c. By restricting output to Q_m, the monopolist is able to charge the higher price of P_m.

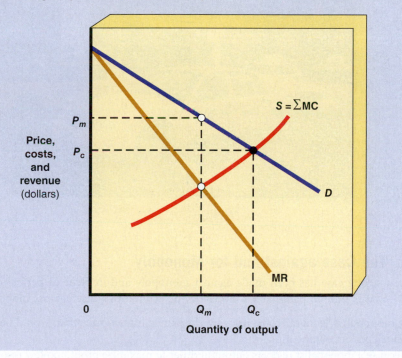

Now let's suppose the market structure changes when one firm buys out all the competing firms and the industry becomes a monopoly. Assume further that the demand and cost curves are unaffected by this dramatic change. In a monopoly, the industry demand curve *is* the monopolist's demand curve. Because the single firm is a price maker, the MR curve lies below the demand curve. The industry supply curve now becomes the MC curve for the monopolist. To maximize profit, the monopolist sets MR = MC by restricting the output to Q_m and raising the price to P_m.

CONCLUSION

Monopoly harms consumers on two fronts. The monopolist charges a higher price and produces a lower output than would result under a perfectly competitive market structure.

YOU'RE THE ECONOMIST

Applicable Concept: Perfect Competition Versus Monopoly

New York Taxicabs: Where Have All the Fare Flags Gone?

Yellow taxicabs in New York City, which are today one of the most famous icons of the city, engender a love and hate relationship. The upside is that you can stick your arm in the air to hail a cab that will take you to your destination. The downside is the traffic jams speckled with yellow cabs that service the city. Flash back to the 1920s, when New York taxicabs were competitive. There was no limit on the number of taxis, and hack licenses were only $10. In addition to a low barrier to entry, taxis engaged in price competition. Cabbies could choose among three different flags to attach to their cars. A red flag cab charged a surcharge for extra passengers. A white flag signaled no surcharge for extra passengers. A green flag meant the cabbie was offering a discount fare. Price wars often erupted, and the vast majority of cabbies flew green flags

© Vacclav/Shutterstock.com

9-4c The Case against and for Monopoly

So far, a strong case has been made against monopoly and in favor of perfect competition. Now it is time to pause and summarize the economist's case against monopoly:

- A monopolist "gouges" consumers by charging a higher price than would be charged under perfect competition.
- Because a monopolist restricts output in order to maximize profit, too few resources are used to produce the product. Stated differently, the monopolist misallocates resources by charging a price greater than marginal cost. In perfectly competitive industries, price is set equal to marginal cost, and the result is an optimal allocation of resources.
- Long-run economic profit for a monopolist exceeds the zero economic profit earned in the long run by a perfectly competitive firm.
- To the extent that the monopolist is a rich John D. Rockefeller, for example, and consumers of oil are poor, monopoly alters the distribution of income in favor of the monopolist.

Not all economists agree that monopoly is bad. Joseph Schumpeter and John Kenneth Galbraith, for example, argued that the rate of technological change is likely to be greater under monopoly than under perfect competition. In their view, monopoly profits afford giant monopolies the financial strength to invest in the well-equipped laboratories and skilled labor necessary to create technological change.

The counterargument is that monopolists are slow to innovate. Freedom from direct competition means the monopolist is not motivated and, therefore, tends to stick to the and charged bargain fares. One strategy was to fly the red flag (high rate) during rush hour and the green flag to offer discounts at off-peak times. Taxi companies also offered a variety of cabs—old, new, big, and small.[1]

As years passed, the system changed because of the concern that competition was causing an overabundance of taxis that congested city streets. The solution was to create a monopoly by law in 1937 designed to limit the number of cabs by requiring all cabs accepting street hails to be painted yellow and possess a medallion on the hood of the taxi. The Taxi and Limousine Commission (TLC) set rates and imposed regulations. For years, there were no price wars, and the barrier to entry was high because there was a very limited supply of medallions. With so few medallions available, taxicab companies bid up the price until these aluminum badges sold for $1.1 million in 2013. Although it is illegal for cabs without medallions to cruise and pick up passengers who hail them, there is a loophole in this regulation that has caused taxicabs to have to compete for passengers. Nonmedallion cabs are authorized to respond to customers who have ordered the cab in advance by phone or other means. There's no limit on the number of nonmedallion cabs or what the drivers may charge.[2]

Companies like Uber and Lyft have taken advantage of this loophole, and they provide their customers with a cheaper ride option. The average cost of a yellow taxi cab ride is $34.62, whereas the average Uber ride costs only $24.75. In the face of this competition, taxi cabs provided 37 percent fewer rides in 2016 than they did in 2014. As a result, taxi cab medallions, and the barrier to entry that they represent, are now worth half of what they were worth only a few years ago.[3]

ANALYZE THE ISSUE Use a graph to compare the price and output of medallion yellow cabs in New York City today with the taxi market before the 1920s.

1. John Tierney, "You'll Wonder Where the Yellow Went," *The New York Times,* July 12, 1998, Section 6, p. 18.
2. Jennifer Surane, "Uber's Manhattan Invasion is Killing the Loan Market for Taxis," *Bloomberg,* July 15, 2015.
3. Shelly Hagan, "Uber Takes Majority of Ground Transport Market for U.S. Business Travelers," *Bloomberg,* January 26, 2017.

"same old ways of doing things." As Nobel laureate Sir John Hicks put it, "The best of all monopoly profit is a quiet life." In short, monopoly offers the opportunity to relax a bit and not worry about the "rat race" of technological change.

What does the research on this issue suggest? Not surprisingly, many attempts have been made to verify or refute the effect of market structure on technological change. Unfortunately, the results to date have been inconclusive. For all we know, the best market structure for promoting innovation may be different for each industry.

Key Concepts

Monopoly	Network good	Price discrimination
Natural monopoly	Price maker	Arbitrage

Summary

- **Monopoly** is a single seller that faces the entire industry demand curve because it is the only seller. The monopolist sells a unique product, and extremely high barriers to entry protect it from competition.

- **Barriers to entry** that prevent new firms from entering an industry are:
  - Ownership of an essential resource
  - Legal barriers
  - Economies of scale

Government franchises, licenses, patents, and copyrights are the most obvious legal barriers to entry.

- A **natural monopoly** arises because of the existence of economies of scale in which the long-run average cost (LRAC) curve falls over the full range of output demanded in the market. Economies of scale allow a single firm, rather than several firms, to produce enough output to satisfy the entire market demand at the lowest possible cost. Whichever firm expands first gains a cost advantage and monopoly status, as smaller firms leave the industry because of their high costs.

Natural Monopoly

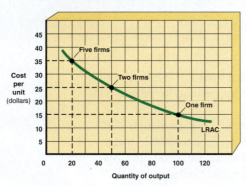

- A **network good** is a good that increases in value to each user as the total number of users increases. Examples are Facebook and Match.com.

- A **price-maker** firm faces a downward-sloping demand curve. It therefore searches its demand curve to find the price-output combination that maximizes its profit (or minimizes its loss).

- The **marginal revenue** and demand curves are downward sloping for a monopolist. The marginal revenue curve for a monopolist lies below the demand curve, and the total revenue curve reaches its maximum where marginal revenue equals zero.

- **Price elasticity of demand** corresponds to sections of the marginal revenue curve. When MR is positive, price elasticity of demand is elastic, $E_d > 1$. When MR is equal to zero, price elasticity of demand is unit elastic, $E_d = 1$. When MR is negative, price elasticity of demand is inelastic, $E_d < 1$.

- The **short-run profit-maximizing monopolist**, like the perfectly competitive firm, locates the profit-maximizing price by producing the output where the MR and MC curves intersect. If this price is greater than average total cost (ATC), the firm earns an economic profit. If the price is less than ATC but greater than average variable cost (AVC), the firm loses money but remains in operation. Finally, if the price is less than the AVC, the monopolist shuts down to minimize losses.

Short-Run Profit Maximizing Monopolist

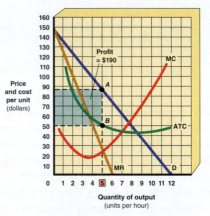

Short-Run Loss-Minimizing Monopolist

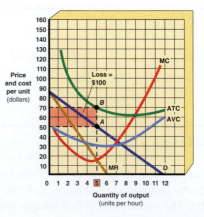

- The **long-run profit-maximizing monopolist** earns a profit because of barriers to entry. If demand is low and/or costs are high, thus creating the prospect of long-run losses, the monopolist will leave the industry.

- **Price discrimination** allows the monopolist to increase profits by charging buyers different prices rather than a single price. Three conditions are necessary for price discrimination:

  - The seller possesses some price-setting ability.

  - Buyers in different markets must have different price elasticities of demand.

  - Buyers must be prevented from reselling the product at a price higher than the purchase price.

- **Monopoly disadvantages** include the following:

  - A monopolist charges a higher price and produces less output than a perfectly competitive firm.

  - Resource allocation is inefficient because the monopolist produces less than if competition existed.

  - Monopoly produces higher long-run profits than if competition existed.

  - Monopoly transfers income from consumers to producers to a greater degree than under perfect competition.

Monopoly Disadvantages

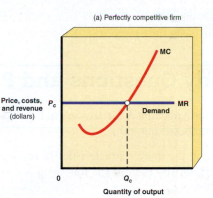

(a) Perfectly competitive firm

Price Discrimination

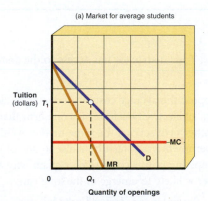

(a) Market for average students

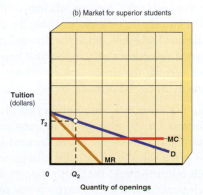

(b) Market for superior students

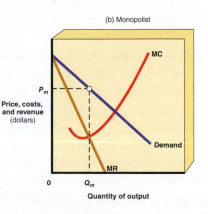

(b) Monopolist

Summary of Conclusion Statements

- Because of economies of scale, a single firm in an industry will produce output at a lower per-unit cost than two or more firms.

- As the number of people connected to a network goods system increases, the greater the benefit each person receives from the network good.

- The demand and marginal revenue curves of the monopolist are downward sloping in contrast to the horizontal demand and corresponding marginal revenue curves facing the perfectly competitive firm.

- The marginal revenue curve for a straight-line demand curve intersects the quantity axis halfway between the origin and the quantity axis intercept of the demand curve.

- The monopolist always maximizes profit by producing at a price on the elastic segment of its demand curve.

- If the positions of a monopolist's demand and cost curves give it a profit and nothing disturbs these curves, the monopolist will earn profit in the long run.

- A monopolist is characterized by inefficiency because resources are under-allocated to the production of its product.

- Monopoly harms consumers on two fronts. The monopolist charges a higher price and produces a lower output than would result under a perfectly competitive market structure.

Study Questions and Problems

Please see Appendix A for answers to the odd-numbered questions. Your instructor has access to the answers for even-numbered questions.

1. Using the three characteristics of monopoly, explain why each of the following is a monopolist:
   a. Local water service
   b. A newly invented cancer drug with patent protection
   c. U.S. postal service

2. Why is the demand curve facing a monopolist downward sloping while the demand curve facing a perfectly competitive firm is horizontal?

3. Suppose an investigator finds that the prices charged for drugs at a hospital are higher than the prices charged for the same products at drugstores in the area served by the hospital. What might explain this situation?

4. Explain why you agree or disagree with the following statements:
   a. "All monopolies are created by the government."
   b. "The monopolist charges the highest possible price."
   c. "The monopolist never takes a loss."

5. Suppose the average cost of producing a kilowatt-hour of electricity is lower for one firm than for another firm serving the same market. Without the government granting a franchise to one of these competing power companies, explain why a single seller is likely to emerge in the long run.

6. Use the following demand schedule for a monopolist to calculate total revenue and marginal revenue. For each price, indicate whether demand is elastic, unit elastic, or inelastic. Using the data from the demand schedule, graph the demand curve, the marginal revenue curve, and the total revenue curve. Identify the elastic, unit elastic, and inelastic segments along the demand curve.

7. Make the unrealistic assumption that production is costless for the monopolist in question 6. Given the data from the above demand schedule, what price will the monopolist charge and how much output should the firm produce? How much profit will the firm earn? When marginal cost is above zero, what will be the effect on the price and output of the monopolist?

Price (P)	Quantity demanded (Q)	Total revenue (TR)	Marginal revenue (MR)	Price elasticity of demand (E_d)
$5.00	0	$_____	$_____	_____
4.50	1	_____	_____	_____
4.00	2	_____	_____	_____
3.50	3	_____	_____	_____
3.00	4	_____	_____	_____
2.50	5	_____	_____	_____
2.00	6	_____	_____	_____
1.50	7	_____	_____	_____
1.00	8	_____	_____	_____
0.50	9	_____	_____	_____
0	10	_____	_____	_____

8. Explain why a monopolist would never produce in the inelastic range of the demand curve.

9. In each of the following cases, state whether the monopolist would increase or decrease output:
   a. Marginal revenue exceeds marginal cost at the output produced.
   b. Marginal cost exceeds marginal revenue at the output produced.

10. Suppose the demand and cost curves for a monopolist are as shown in Exhibit 10. Explain what price the monopolist should charge and how much output it should produce.

11. Which of the following constitute price discrimination and which does not?
    a. A department store has a 25 percent off sale.
    b. A publisher sells economics textbooks at a lower price in North Carolina than in New York, even though it can deliver its textbooks to any state at the same costs.
    c. The Japanese sell cars at higher prices in the United States than in Japan, even though the cost to the companies of selling these cars is the same across different countries.

12. Suppose the candy bar industry approximates a perfectly competitive industry. Suppose also that a single firm buys all the assets of the candy bar

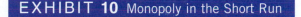

EXHIBIT 10 Monopoly in the Short Run

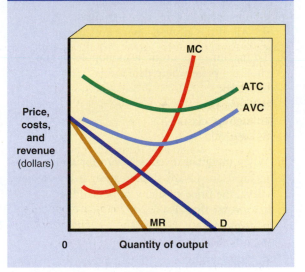

firms and establishes a monopoly. Contrast these two market structures with respect to price, output, and allocation of resources. Draw a graph of the market demand and market supply for candy bars before and after the takeover.

13. Name three places you frequent that use price discrimination and explain the discrimination used.

✔ CHECKPOINT ANSWERS

Why Don't Adults Pay More for Popcorn at the Movies?

First, there are no other popcorn sellers in the lobby, so the theater is a price maker for popcorn and the demand curve slopes downward. Second, the theater could easily set up different lines for adults and children and charge different prices for popcorn. Third, is there a practical way to prevent resale? Does the theater want to try to stop children who resell popcorn to their parents, friends, and other adults? If you said theaters do not practice price discrimination at the concession counter because resale cannot be prevented, **YOU ARE CORRECT**.

Sample Quiz

Please see Appendix B for answers to Sample Quiz questions.

1. The monopolist faces
   a. a perfectly inelastic demand curve.
   b. a perfectly elastic demand curve.
   c. the entire market demand curve.
   d. All of the answers above are correct.

2. To maximize its profit, a monopoly should choose a price where demand is
   a. elastic.
   b. inelastic.
   c. unitary elastic.
   d. vertical.

3. When marginal revenue is zero for a monopolist facing a downward-sloping straight-line demand curve, the price elasticity of demand is
   a. greater than 1.
   b. equal to 1.
   c. less than 2.
   d. equal to 0.

4. Both a perfectly competitive firm and a monopolist
   a. always earn an economic profit.
   b. maximize profit by setting marginal cost equal to marginal revenue.
   c. maximize profit by setting marginal cost equal to average total cost.
   d. are price takers.

5. Suppose a monopolist's demand curve lies below its average variable cost curve. The firm will
   a. stay in operation in the short run.
   b. earn an economic profit.
   c. earn an economic profit in the long run.
   d. shut down.

6. Which of the following statements best describes the price, output, and profit conditions of monopoly?
   a. Price will equal marginal cost at the profit-maximizing level of output, and profits will be positive in the long run.
   b. Price will always equal average variable cost in the short run, and either profits or losses may result in the long run.
   c. In the long run, positive economic profit will be earned.
   d. All of the answers above are correct.

7. Which of the following is true for the monopolist?
   a. Marginal revenue is less than the price charged.
   b. Economic profit is possible in the long run.
   c. Profit maximizing or loss minimizing occurs when marginal revenue equals marginal cost.
   d. All of the answers above are correct.

8. Although a monopoly can charge any price it wishes, it chooses
   a. the highest price.
   b. the price equal to marginal cost.
   c. the price that maximizes profit.
   d. competitive prices.
   e. a fair price.

9. As shown in Exhibit 11, the profit-maximizing price for the monopolist is
   a. OP_1.
   b. OP_2.
   c. OP_3.
   d. OP_4.
   e. OP_5.

10. As shown in Exhibit 11, if the monopolist produces the profit-maximizing output, total revenue is the rectangular area
    a. $OQ_1 AP_1$.
    b. $OQ_2 BP_2$.
    c. $OQ_3 CP_3$.
    d. $OQ_2 DP_4$.

11. As shown in Exhibit 11, the monopolist's total cost is which of the following areas?
    a. $P_1 AEP_5$
    b. $P_2 BDP_4$
    c. $P_3 CDP_5$

d. $P_4 DEP_5$
e. None of the answers above are correct

12. The profit-maximizing output for the monopolist in Exhibit 11 is
    a. zero.
    b. OQ_1.
    c. OQ_2.
    d. OQ_3.

13. Consider the monopolist's profit maximizing output in exhibit 11. At this level of output, consumers will want the monopolist to
    a. charge a higher price.
    b. use more resources to produce less output.
    c. use fewer resources to produce less output.
    d. use more resources to produce additional output.

14. As shown in Exhibit 11, the monopolist's profit-maximizing price-quantity point is
    a. *A*.
    b. *B*.
    c. *C*.
    d. *D*.
    e. *E*.

15. Suppose a monopolist charges a price corresponding to the intersection of marginal cost and marginal revenue. If the price is between its average variable cost and average total cost curves, the firm will
    a. earn an economic profit.
    b. stay in operation in the short run, but shut down in the long run if demand remains the same.
    c. shut down.
    d. None of the above answers is correct.

16. The act of buying a commodity in one market at a lower price and selling it in another market at a higher price is known as
    a. buying long.
    b. selling short.
    c. a tariff.
    d. arbitrage.

17. One necessary condition for effective price discrimination is
    a. identical tastes among buyers.
    b. a difference in the price elasticity of demand among buyers.

EXHIBIT 11 Profit Maximizing for a Monopolist

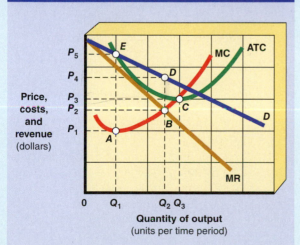

c. a single, homogeneous market.

d. two or more markets with easy resale of products between them.

18. An example of price discrimination is the price charged for
    a. an economics textbook at a campus bookstore.
    b. gasoline.
    c. theater tickets that offer lower prices for children.
    d. a postage stamp.

19. Suppose a monopolist and a perfectly competitive firm have the same cost curves. The monopolistic firm would
    a. charge a lower price than the perfectly competitive firm.
    b. charge a higher price than the perfectly competitive firm.

c. charge the same price as the perfectly competitive firm.

d. refuse to operate in the short run unless an economic profit could be made.

20. Suppose there are two markets for football games: (1) rich alumni as fully committed to their alma mater as the lower-income students and (2) students. Based on this information, which market will have the lower elasticity, and thus the higher price, if the university can price-discriminate?
    a. The student market
    b. The alumni market
    c. Both markets have the same price elasticity
    d. Impossible to infer based on the given scenario

CHAPTER 10

Monopolistic Competition and Oligopoly

CHAPTER PREVIEW

Suppose your favorite restaurant is Ivan's Oyster Bar. Ivan's does not fit either of the two extreme models studied in the previous two chapters. Instead, Ivan's characteristics are a blend of monopoly and perfect competition. For starters, like a monopolist, Ivan's demand curve is downward sloping. This means Ivan's is a *price maker* because it can charge a higher price for seafood and lose some customers, but many loyal customers will keep coming. The reason is that Ivan's successfully distinguishes its product from the competition by advertising, as well as by offering first-rate service, a great salad bar, and other unique attributes. In short, like a monopolist, Ivan's has a degree of *market power*, which allows it to restrict output and to set its prices to maximize profit. But like a perfectly competitive firm and unlike a monopolist, Ivan's is not the only place to buy a seafood dinner in town. It must share the market with many other restaurants within an hour's drive.

The small Ivan's Oyster Bars and the gigantic Microsofts of the world represent most of the firms with which you deal. These firms compete in two different market structures: *monopolistic competition* or *oligopoly*. Ivan's operates in the former, and Microsoft belongs to the latter. The theories of perfect competition and monopoly from the previous two chapters will help you understand the impact of monopolistic competition and oligopoly market structures on the price and output decisions of real-world firms.

IN THIS CHAPTER, YOU WILL LEARN TO SOLVE THESE ECONOMICS PUZZLES:

- Why will Ivan's Oyster Bar make zero economic profit in the long run?

- Why do OPEC and other cartels tend to break down?

- Are Cheerios, Rice Krispies, and other brands sold by firms in the breakfast cereal industry produced under monopolistic competition or oligopoly?

- How does the NCAA Final Four basketball tournament involve imperfect competition?

10-1 THE MONOPOLISTIC COMPETITION MARKET STRUCTURE

Monopolistic competition
A market structure characterized by (1) many small sellers, (2) a differentiated product, and (3) easy market entry and exit.

Economists define **monopolistic competition** as a market structure characterized by (1) many small sellers, (2) a differentiated product, and (3) easy market entry and exit.

Most real-world businesses operate within a monopolistically competitive market environment. The following briefly explains the characteristics of this market structure.

10-1a Characteristics of Monopolistic Competition

Many Small Sellers

Under monopolistic competition, as under perfect competition, the exact number of firms cannot be stated. But in monopolistic competition, the number of sellers is smaller than in perfect competition. In this market structure, consumers have many different varieties of products from which to choose. A single seller does not have enough market share to have very much control over market prices, but it does have some influence over its own price. Ivan's Oyster Bar, described in the chapter preview, is an example of a monopolistic competitor. Ivan assumes that his restaurant can set prices slightly higher or improve service *independently* without fear that competitors will react with a large change in their prices or in their level of service. Thus, if any single seafood restaurant raises its price, the going market price for seafood dinners increases by a very small amount.

CONCLUSION The many-sellers condition is met when each firm is so small relative to the total market that its pricing decisions have a negligible effect on the market price.

Differentiated Product

Product differentiation
The process of creating real or apparent differences between goods and services.

The key feature of monopolistic competition is product differentiation. **Product differentiation** is the process of creating real or apparent differences between goods and services. A differentiated product has close, but not perfect, substitutes. Although the products of each firm are highly similar, the consumer views them as somewhat different or distinct. There may be 25 seafood restaurants in a given city, but they are not all the same. They differ in location, atmosphere, quality of food, quality of service, and so on.

Product differentiation can be real or imagined. It does not matter which is correct so long as consumers believe such differences exist. For example, many customers think Ivan's has the best seafood in town even though other restaurants actually offer a similar product. What is important is that consumers are willing to pay a slightly higher price for Ivan's seafood. To maintain these high prices, Ivan goes to great lengths to make potential customers believe his food is unique. For example, he buys ads that show him personally catching the seafood he serves. These ads leave people with the impression that Ivan has the freshest seafood in town.

A firm can charge higher prices if it makes its products seem unique.	**CONCLUSION**

The example of Ivan's restaurant makes it clear that under monopolistic competition rivalry centers on nonprice competition in addition to price competition. With **nonprice competition**, a firm competes by using advertising, packaging, product design, better quality, better service, more convenient hours of operation, and a better location, rather than by using lower prices. Nonprice competition is an important characteristic of monopolistic competition that distinguishes it from perfect competition and monopoly. Under perfect competition, there is no nonprice competition because firms sell identical products. Likewise, the monopolist has little incentive to engage in nonprice competition because it sells a unique product.

Nonprice competition
The situation in which a firm competes using advertising, packaging, product development, better quality, and better service, rather than lower prices.

Easy Entry and Exit

Unlike a monopoly, firms in a monopolistically competitive market face low barriers to entry. But entry into a monopolistically competitive market is not quite as easy as entry into a perfectly competitive market. People who want to enter the seafood restaurant business can get loans, lease space, and start serving seafood without too much trouble. However, if they want to survive, they have to do something new and exciting; otherwise, people will stick with Ivan's, the restaurant with the established reputation for the best seafood in town.

Monopolistic competition is by far the most common market structure in the United States. Examples include retail firms, such as grocery stores, hair salons, gas stations, diet centers, clothing stores, and restaurants.

10-1b The Monopolistically Competitive Firm as a Price Maker

Given the characteristics of monopolistic competition, you might think the monopolistic competitor is a *price taker*, but it is not. The primary reason is that its product is differentiated. This gives the monopolistically competitive firm, like the monopolist, some control over its price. When the price is raised, brand loyalty ensures some customers will remain steadfast. Similar to a monopolist, the demand curve and the corresponding marginal revenue curve for a monopolistically competitive firm are downward sloping. But the existence of close substitutes causes the demand curve for the monopolistically competitive firm to be much more elastic than the demand curve for a monopolist. When Ivan's raises its prices 10 percent, the quantity of seafood dinners demanded declines, say, 30 percent. Instead, if Ivan's had a monopoly, no close substitutes would exist, and consumers would be less sensitive to price changes. As a monopolist, the same 10 percent price hike might lose Ivan's only, say, 15 percent of its quantity of seafood dinners demanded.

The demand curve for a monopolistically competitive firm is less elastic (steeper) than for a perfectly competitive firm and more elastic (flatter) than for a monopolist.	**CONCLUSION**

10-1c Advertising Pros and Cons

Before presenting the complete graphical models for monopolistic competition, let's pause to examine the topic of advertising. As explained at the beginning of this chapter, a distinguishing feature of a monopolistically competitive firm is that it engages in non-price competition, which may entail using expensive ads to differentiate its product. Instead of lowering the price, the firm's goal is to convince customers that its product is really different from its rivals' products. Monopolistically competitive firms are frequently running ads that feature lower prices, a higher quality of service, or new products to win customers. Ads proclaim that products make you smarter, better looking, or nicer to be around. Graphically, the firm hopes advertising will make the demand curve less elastic and shift it rightward by changing consumers' tastes in favor of its product. Profit rises when advertising increases the firm's revenue by more than it increases the combined cost of the advertising and the cost of producing the greater quantity demanded.

Exhibit 1 illustrates the effect of advertising on the long-run average cost (LRAC) curve for Yummy Frozen Yogurt. Yummy competes with It Can't Be

EXHIBIT 1 The Effect of Advertising on Average Cost

When Yummy Frozen Yogurt increases its advertising costs to sell more yogurt, the firm's average cost curve shifts upward from $LRAC_1$ to $LRAC_2$. If advertising increases the quantity demanded from 6,000 to 12,000 dishes per month, average total cost falls from $2.00 (point A) to $1.50 (point B). However, if the extra cost of advertising fails to increase the quantity demanded, average total cost rises from $2.00 (point A) to $3.00 (point C).

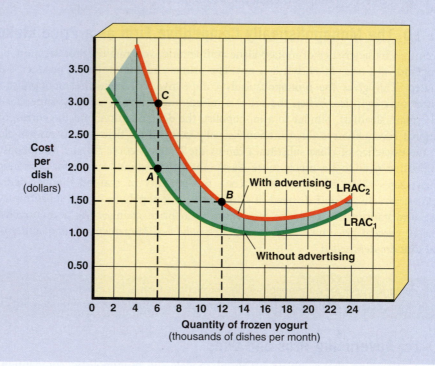

Yogurt and five other stores in the northeastern part of town. Without advertising, the $LRAC_1$ curve represents Yummy's average cost. At the given price charged, the quantity demanded is 6,000 frozen yogurt dishes per month, and the average cost is $2.00 per dish (point *A*).

To increase profits in the short run, Yummy decides to advertise. Yummy knows, however, that in the long run new entrants and rising costs will shrink all yogurt stores' economic profits to zero. Then Yummy must come up with some new product to boost sales. But for now, suppose Yummy's advertising campaign is successful and demand increases. Then two short-run effects occur. One is an upward shift in the average cost curve at any level of output from $LRAC_1$ to $LRAC_2$. The vertical distance between these two curves measures the additional average fixed cost of advertising. Another effect is that the quantity demanded increases to 12,000 frozen yogurt dishes per month. Now the average cost is $1.50 at point *B* on $LRAC_2$.

So far, our story illustrates a social benefit of advertising. Look again at Exhibit 1. The increased volume of sales caused by advertising leads to *economies of scale*, explained in Chapter 7. Without advertising, Yummy operated with a lower output and a higher average cost. With advertising, the firm sells more, and the reduction in average total cost from *A* to *B* outweighs the boost in cost per unit from advertising.

On the other hand, suppose Yummy's advertising campaign is not successful and demand remains unchanged. In this case, the quantity demanded remains at the original 6,000 frozen yogurt dishes per month, but the average total cost rises to $3.00 (point *C*). Critics of advertising argue this is the typical case and there is no reduction in unit cost, such as a firm would achieve by moving from *A* to *B*. Rather than believing that advertising enables economies of scale, they argue that advertising just adds extra cost without providing a benefit. In their view, Yummy, It Can't Be Yogurt, and other firms spend large outlays on advertising just to keep their present market share. And in the process, the cost, and therefore the price, of yogurt is increased. Moreover, the additional cost of advertising does not improve the yogurt at all. The only purpose is to persuade or mislead consumers into buying something they do not need. From society's viewpoint, the resources used in advertising could be used for schools, hospitals, bridges, or other more useful purposes.

Proponents of advertising counter the argument that advertising is valueless. They argue that ads provide information. Advertising informs consumers of sales, the availability of products, and the advantages of products. Even if the product costs a little more, this information saves consumers money and time. Ads also increase price competition among sellers. When Yummy offers discount coupons, other yogurt stores see these ads and respond with lower prices. Finally, they argue that consumers are rational and cannot be fooled by advertising. If a product is undesirable, customers will not buy it.

Does monopolistic competition lead to lower prices, greater output, and better-informed consumers? Or does this market structure simply raise prices and annoy customers with useless and often misleading information? This fascinating and ongoing debate is perhaps best analyzed on a case-by-case basis. In a latter section, you will learn that advertising to differentiate a product is also a key characteristic of an oligopoly market environment as well.

YOU'RE THE ECONOMIST

Applicable Concept: Product Differentiation

Social Networking Sites: The New Advertising Game

A key characteristic of the market structures discussed in this chapter is that they use advertising to promote product differentiation, which is a form of nonprice competition. The television commercial is considered the most effective method of mass-market advertising. This explains why TV networks charge such high prices for commercial airtime during prominent events, such as the Super Bowl. However, the days when television commercials dominate the advertising world could be fading away. Don't want to be bothered by those advertisements? It's easy: Just press the fast-forward button on the remote of a digital video recorder (DVR). Advertisers are therefore competing to get the attention of consumers by tapping into the popularity of such social networking sites as Facebook, Twitter, Google Plus, and YouTube. These sites connect individuals who interact through personal profiles, games, video clips, and more. There are also niche sites focused on very specific activities for a hyper-targeted audience. For example, Dogster.com is a site for dog lovers and Zappos.com is a popular site for women's and men's shoes. ProductWiki is a resource for shoppers. It gives access to product reviews and lets you compare prices. Other new forms of advertisement include ads on apps, such as Pandora (music), used on iPhones, iPads, and smartphones.

The challenge for web economy entrepreneurs is to earn profits by differentiating their product and creating innovative ways to include advertising. The search engine is a highly successful business model. If someone googles for golf clubs, sponsored links for golf clubs appear on the screen. Social networks provide the prospect of tailoring ads to people's

Ingvar Björk/Alamy Stock Photo

specific interests. Now suppose a golf club company pays Facebook, the crown jewel of social networking, for a page where you and your friends can register and play a game of video golf. What does the company get out of it? A database of tens of thousands of names, all potential customers. Another form of advertising is called "retargeting" ads. Suppose you browse a swimsuit on Nordstrom.com and then an ad for this swimsuit shows up on your Facebook page. Do users enjoy personalized ads or are they alienated by such intrusive tracking?

Some ideas are not winners. Facebook implemented a new approach that informed friends whenever a member purchased something from online retailers. Consumers protested this was an invasion of privacy, and the program was abandoned. And in 2012, GM decided to cancel its advertising because it thought Facebook ads had little effect on car purchases.

ANALYZE THE ISSUE Advertising is tasteless, offensive, and a nuisance that wastes resources. Give three arguments against this idea.

10-2 PRICE AND OUTPUT DECISIONS FOR A MONOPOLISTICALLY COMPETITIVE FIRM

Now we are prepared to develop the short-run and long-run graphical models for monopolistic competition. In the short run, you will see that monopolistic competition resembles monopoly. In the long run, however, entry by new firms leads to a more competitive market outcome. This section presents a graphical analysis that shows why a monopolistically competitive firm is part perfectly competitive and part monopolistic.

10-2a Monopolistic Competition in the Short Run

Exhibit 2 shows the short-run equilibrium position for Ivan's Oyster Bar—a typical firm under monopolistic competition. As explained earlier, the demand curve slopes downward because customers believe, rightly or wrongly, that Ivan's product is a little better than its competitors' products. Customers like Ivan's family atmosphere, location, and quality of service. These nonprice factors differentiate Ivan's product and allow the restaurant to raise the price of sautéed alligator, shrimp, and oysters at least slightly without losing many sales. Remember: Successful differentiation not only increases demand but also makes the demand curve less elastic (steeper).

Like the monopolist, the monopolistically competitive firm maximizes short-run profit by following the MR = MC rule. In this case, the marginal cost (MC) and marginal revenue (MR) curves intersect at an output of 600 seafood meals per week. The price per meal of $18 is the point on the demand curve corresponding to this level of output. Because the price exceeds the average total cost (ATC) of $15 per meal, Ivan's

EXHIBIT 2 A Monopolistically Competitive Firm in the Short Run

Ivan's Oyster Bar is a monopolistically competitive firm that maximizes short-run profit by producing the output where marginal revenue equals marginal cost. At an output of 600 seafood dinners per week, the price of $18 per dinner is dictated by the firm's demand curve. Given the firm's costs, output, and prices, Ivan's will earn a short-run profit of $1,800 per week.

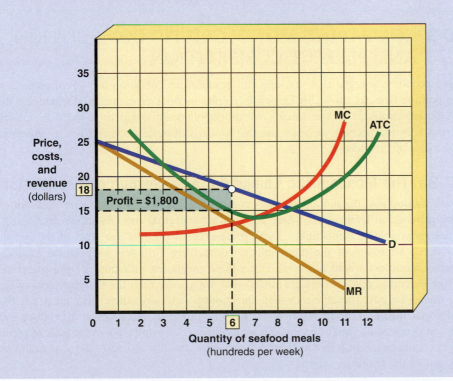

earns a short-run economic profit of $1,800 ($3 × 600) per week. As under monopoly, if the price equals the ATC, the firm earns no economic profit. If the price is below the ATC, the firm suffers a short-run loss, and if the price is below the average variable cost (AVC), the firm shuts down.

10-2b Monopolistic Competition in the Long Run

The monopolistically competitive firm, unlike a monopolist, will not earn an economic profit in the long run. Rather, like a perfect competitor, the monopolistically competitive firm earns only a normal profit (that is, zero economic profit) in the long run. Recall from the chapter on production costs that *normal profit* is the minimum profit necessary to keep a firm in operation. The reason is that short-run profits and easy entry attract new firms into the industry. When Ivan's Oyster Bar earns a short-run profit, as shown in Exhibit 2, two things happen. First, Ivan's demand curve shifts downward as some of each seafood restaurant's market share is taken away by new firms seeking profit. Second, Ivan's, and other seafood restaurants as well, tries to recapture market share by advertising, improving its decor, and utilizing other forms of nonprice competition. As a result, long-run average costs increase, and the firm's LRAC curve shifts upward.

The combination of the leftward shift in the firm's demand curve and the upward shift in its LRAC curve continues until a long-run equilibrium is reached where the monopolistic competitive firm earns zero or normal economic profit. The result is the long-run equilibrium condition shown in Exhibit 3. At a price of $17 per meal, the demand curve is tangent to the LRAC curve at the MR = MC output of 500 meals per week. Once long-run equilibrium is achieved in a monopolistically competitive industry, there is no incentive for new firms to enter or for established firms to leave.

10-3 COMPARING MONOPOLISTIC COMPETITION AND PERFECT COMPETITION

Some economists argue that the long-run equilibrium condition for a monopolistically competitive firm, as shown in Exhibit 3, results in poor economic performance. Other economists contend that the benefits of a monopolistically competitive industry outweigh the costs. In this section, we again use the standard of perfect competition to understand both sides of this debate.

10-3a The Monopolistic Competitor as a Resource Misallocator

Like a monopolist, the monopolistically competitive firm fails the efficiency test. An efficient production level occurs where price equals marginal cost. As shown in Exhibit 3, under monopolistic competition, Ivan's price exceeds the marginal cost of the last unit produced. Therefore, if the monopolistic competitive firm was to produce additional meals, consumers would place values on these meals (as measured by the prices read off the demand curve at these quantities) that are greater than the marginal cost of serving them. To pass the efficiency test, the monopolist competitive firm must sell these additional meals. Although Ivan could devote additional resources and produce more seafood dinners, he won't because this would lower his profits. So, monopolistic competition results in too little production and, therefore, too few resources devoted to the production of the goods or service.

EXHIBIT 3 A Monopolistically Competitive Firm in the Long Run

In the long run, the entry of new seafood restaurants decreases the demand for Ivan's seafood. In addition, Ivan's shifts its average cost curve upward by increasing advertising and other expenses in order to compete against new entrants. In the long run, the firm earns zero economic profit at a price of $17 per seafood meal and produces an MR = MC output of 500 meals per week.

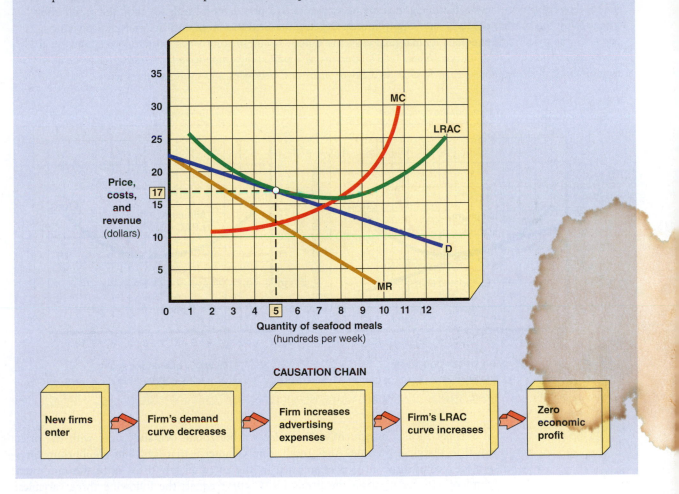

CAUSATION CHAIN

New firms enter ⇨ Firm's demand curve decreases ⇨ Firm increases advertising expenses ⇨ Firm's LRAC curve increases ⇨ Zero economic profit

10-3b Monopolistic Competition Means Less Output for More

Exhibit 4(a) reproduces the long-run condition from Exhibit 3. Exhibit 4(b) assumes that the seafood restaurant market is perfectly competitive. Recall from Chapter 8 that the characteristics of perfect competition include the condition that customers perceive seafood meals as *homogeneous* and, as a result, no firms engage in advertising or in other forms of nonprice competition. Because we now assume for the sake of argument that Ivan's product is identical to all other seafood restaurants, Ivan's becomes a *price taker*. In this case, the industry's long-run supply and demand curves set an equilibrium price

EXHIBIT 4 A Comparison of Monopolistic Competition and Perfect Competition in the Long Run

In part (a), Ivan's Oyster Bar is a monopolistically competitive firm that sets its price at $17 per seafood meal and produces 500 meals per week. As a monopolistic competitor, Ivan's earns zero economic profit in the long run and does not produce at the lowest point on its LRAC curve.

Under conditions of perfect competition in part (b), Ivan's becomes a price taker, rather than a price maker. Here the firm faces a flat demand curve at a price of $16 per seafood meal, which is the equilibrium price set by the market demand and supply curves. Because the firm produces until its marginal revenue, given by the price of $16, equals its marginal cost, the output is 800 meals a week, which corresponds to the lowest point on the LRAC curve. When Ivan's operates as a perfectly competitive firm, rather than as a monopolistically competitive firm, it charges a lower price and produces 300 more meals a week.

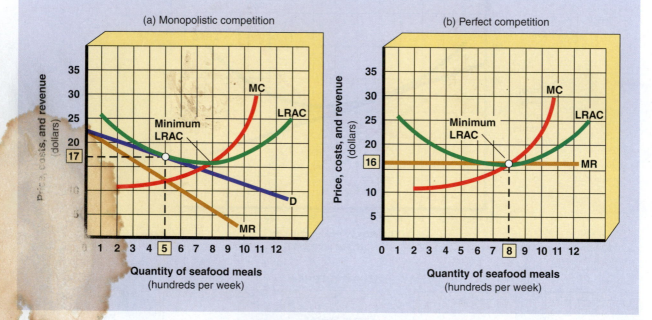

of $16 per meal. Consequently, Ivan's faces a horizontal demand curve with the price equal to marginal revenue. Also, recall from Chapter 8 that long-run equilibrium for a perfectly competitive firm is established by the entry of new firms until the minimum point of $16 per meal on the firm's LRAC curve equals the following three variables: price, MR, and MC. Stated as a formula:

$$P = MR = MC = LRAC$$

A comparison of parts (a) and (b) of Exhibit 4 reveals two important points. First, the firms in both monopolistically competitive and perfectly competitive industries earn zero economic profit in the long run. Second, the long-run equilibrium output of the monopolistically competitive firm is to the left of the minimum point on the LRAC curve and the price exceeds MC. Like a monopolist, monopolistically competitive firms, therefore, charge higher prices and produce less output than if they were perfectly competitive firms.

In our example, suppose the price is $16, and the firm produces until the price is equal to the marginal cost, as it would in a perfectly competitive market. In this case,

Ivan's would charge $1 less per meal and produce 300 more seafood meals per week The extra 300 meals not produced are *excess capacity*, which represents underutilized resources. The criticism of monopolistic competition, then, is that there are too many firms producing too little output at inflated prices, wasting society's resources in the process. For example, on many nights, there are not enough customers for all the restaurants in town. Servers, cooks, tables, and other resources are therefore underutilized. If, instead, monopolistically competitive firms acted like perfectly competitive firms, each restaurant would produce a greater output at a lower price and with a lower average cost. But, of course, all the food would be identical. Boring!

Opinions vary concerning whether the benefits of monopolistic competition exceed the costs. Having many different kinds of seafood restaurants offers consumers more choice and variety. Having Ivan's Oyster Bar and many similar competitors gives consumers extra quality and service options. If you do not like Ivan's sautéed alligator, you may be able to find another restaurant that serves this dish, but more to your liking. Is the greater variety of options available worth the higher prices? What do you think?

10-4 OLIGOPOLY—COMPETITION AMONG THE FEW

Now we turn to oligopoly, an imperfectly competitive market structure in which a few large firms dominate the market. Many manufacturing industries, such as steel, aluminum, automobiles, aircraft, drugs, and tobacco, are best described as oligopolistic. This is the "big business" market structure in which firms aggressively compete by bombarding us with advertising on television and filling our mailboxes with junk mail.

Economists define an **oligopoly** as a market structure characterized by (1) few large sellers, (2) either a homogeneous or a differentiated product, and (3) difficult market entry. Like monopolistic competition, oligopoly is found in many real-world industries. Let's examine each characteristic.

Oligopoly
A market structure characterized by (1) few large sellers, (2) either a homogeneous or a differentiated product, and (3) difficult market entry.

10-4a Characteristics of Oligopoly

Few Sellers

Oligopoly is competition "among the few." Here we refer to the "Big Three" or "Big Four" to mean that three or four firms dominate an industry. But what does "a few" firms really mean? Does this mean at least two, but less than ten? As with other market structures, the answer is there is no specific number of firms that must dominate an industry before it is an oligopoly. Basically, an oligopoly is a consequence of mutual interdependence. **Mutual interdependence** is a condition in which an action by one firm may cause a reaction from other firms. Stated another way, a market structure with a few powerful firms requires oligopolists to consider the likely reaction of other firms if it changes its prices or alters its output in some way. The large number of firms under perfect competition or monopolistic competition and the absence of other firms in a market served by a monopoly enable firms operating in these types of market structures to ignore the actions and reactions of other firms.

Mutual interdependence
A condition in which an action by one firm may cause a reaction from other firms.

When General Motors (GM) considers a price hike or a style change, it must predict how Ford, Chrysler, and Toyota will change their prices and styling in response. Therefore, the decisions under oligopoly are more complex than under perfect competition, monopoly, and monopolistic competition.

CONCLUSION   The few-sellers condition is met when these few firms are so large relative to the total market that they can affect the market price.

Homogeneous or Differentiated Product

Under oligopoly, firms can produce either a homogeneous (identical) or a differentiated product. The steel produced by USX is identical to the steel from Republic Steel. The oil sold by Saudi Arabia is identical to the oil from Iran. Similarly, zinc, copper, and aluminum are standardized or homogeneous products. But cars produced by the major automakers are differentiated products. Tires, detergents, and breakfast cereals are also differentiated products sold by oligopolies.

CONCLUSION   Buyers in an oligopoly may or may not be indifferent as to which seller's product they buy.

Difficult Entry

Similar to a monopoly, an oligopoly is protected from the threat of new entrants by formidable barriers to entry. These barriers include exclusive financial requirements, control over an essential resource, patent rights, and other legal barriers. But the most significant barrier to entry in an oligopoly is *economies of scale*. For example, larger automakers achieve lower average total costs than those incurred by smaller automakers. Consequently, the U.S. auto industry has moved over time from more than 60 firms to only two major U.S.-owned firms.

10-5 PRICE AND OUTPUT DECISIONS FOR AN OLIGOPOLIST

Mutual interdependence among firms in an oligopoly makes this market structure more difficult to analyze than perfect competition, monopoly, or monopolistic competition. The price-output decision of an oligopolist is not simply a matter of charging the price where MR = MC. Making price and output decisions in an oligopoly is like playing a game of chess. One player's move depends on the anticipated reactions of the opposing player. One player thinks, "If I move my rook here, my opponent might move her knight there." Likewise, a firm in an oligopoly can have many different possible reactions to the price, nonprice, and output changes of another firm. Consequently, there are different oligopoly models because no single model can cover all cases. The following is a discussion of five well-known oligopoly models: (1) nonprice competition, (2) the kinked demand curve, (3) price leadership, (4) the cartel, and (5) game theory.

10-5a Nonprice Competition

Major oligopolists often compete using advertising and product differentiation. Instead of "slugging it out" with price cuts, oligopolists may try to capture business away from their rivals through better advertising campaigns and improved products. This model of behavior explains why advertising expenditures often are large in the cigarette, soft drink, athletic shoe, and automobile industries. It also explains why the research and development (R&D) function is so important to oligopolists. For example, much engineering effort is aimed largely at developing new products and improving existing products all in an attempt at product differentiation.

Why might oligopolists compete through nonprice competition, rather than price competition? The answer is that each oligopolist perceives that its rival will easily and quickly match any price reduction. In contrast, it is much more difficult to combat a clever and/or important product improvement.

10-5b The Kinked Demand Curve

Unlike other market structures, different assumptions define different models for any given oligopolistic industry. Over time, the "rules of the game" change, and a new model becomes the best predictor of the behavior of oligopolists. We begin with the kinked demand curve. The strange shape of this curve explains why a firm in an oligopolistic market selling cars changes prices far less often than firms change prices in a perfectly competitive market selling wheat.

The **kinked demand curve** is a demand curve facing an oligopolist that assumes rivals will match a price decrease, but ignore a price increase. Without collusion, the kinked demand curve exists because management tacitly believes that the competition will not be "undersold." On the other hand, a price hike by one firm allows competitors to capture its share of the market. Oligopolistic firms must make pricing decisions, so they are *price makers*, rather than price takers. But as we will soon see in the kinked demand model, the high degree of interdependence among oligopolists restricts their pricing discretion.

In Exhibit 5, a kinked demand curve is drawn for Tucker Motor Company, which we assume competes with GM, Ford, Toyota, and Chrysler in the automobile market. (I suggest you check out the 1988 movie titled *Tucker: The Man and His Dreams*.) The current price per Tucker car is $25,000, and the quantity demanded at this price is 3 million cars per year. Tucker's management assumes that if it raises its price even slightly above $25,000, the other automakers *will not follow* with higher prices. This price gap between the Tucker cars and other cars would drive many of Tucker's customers over to its rivals. The segment of the demand curve above $25,000 is therefore relatively flat. Stated differently, above the "kink" in the demand curve, demand is relatively elastic. If Tucker raises the price to, say, $27,250 at point *X*, this price hike cuts Tucker's quantity demanded to 1.5 million cars per year (reducing revenues significantly). Because raising its price is ill-advised, management can consider a price reduction strategy. Suppose Tucker cuts the price of its cars from $25,000 to $22,250 at point *Y*. The model shows that Tucker gains few customers and the quantity demanded rises only slightly from 3 million to 3.2 million cars per year (and again, revenues fall significantly). The reason for such a small sales boost is that other automakers also cut their prices to protect their market share. However, the lower price does attract some new buyers who could not afford a car at the higher price. The segment of the demand curve below the kink is therefore relatively steep. Here demand is less elastic, meaning the quantity demanded is not very responsive to a price drop.

Given the kinked demand curve facing the oligopolist, management fears the worst and is afraid to raise or lower the price of its product. Under this model of oligopoly, the

Kinked demand curve
A demand curve facing an oligopolist that assumes rivals will match a price decrease, but ignore a price increase.

EXHIBIT 5 The Kinked Demand Curve

An oligopolist's demand curve may be kinked. A price hike from $25,000 to $27,250 per auto causes a sizable reduction in the quantity demanded from 3 million to 1.5 million autos (point X). Demand above the kink is elastic, because rivals ignore the firm when it raises the price. Below the kink, the demand curve is less elastic. A price reduction from $25,000 to $22,250 per auto causes rivals to drop their prices as well. Consequently, the firm attracts very few new customers, and the quantity demanded increases from 3 million to only 3.2 million autos per year (point Y). Under the kinked demand curve theory, prices tend to be rigid.

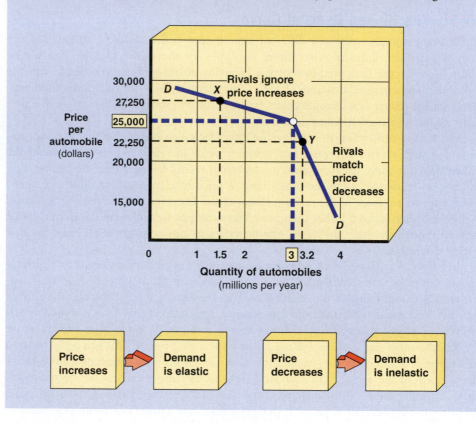

price established at the kink changes very infrequently. However, oligopolists will change their prices after large cost increases or decreases force a new kinked demand curve with the kink at a higher or lower price.

Economists continue to debate the importance of the kinked demand model. Critics challenge the theory on theoretical and empirical grounds. On a theoretical level, there is no explanation for how the original price at the kink was determined. On empirical grounds, studies of certain oligopolistic industries fail to find price stickiness. On the other hand, widespread use of price lists in catalogs that remain fixed for a long time is consistent with kinked demand theory. In any case, the kinked demand theory does not provide a complete explanation of price and output decisions.

GLOBAL ECONOMICS

Major Cartels in Global Markets

Applicable Concept: Cartel

Cartels flourished in Germany and other European countries in the first half of the twentieth century. Many had international memberships. After World War II, European countries passed laws against such restrictive trade practices. The following are some of the most important cartels today:

- **Organization of the Petroleum Exporting Countries (OPEC).** OPEC was created by Iran, Iraq, Kuwait, Saudi Arabia, and Venezuela in Baghdad in 1960. Today, the Vienna-based OPEC's membership consists of 12 countries that control about 70 percent of the world's oil reserves. Cartels are anticonsumer. OPEC's objective is to set oil production quotas for its members and, in turn, influence global prices of oil and gasoline.

- **International Telecommunication Union (ITU).** Perhaps the world's least-known and most effective cartel of about 193 member nations is based in Geneva, Switzerland. The ITU was founded in 1865 and became an agency of the United Nations in 1947.

It is responsible for international regulations and standards governing global telecommunications including satellite communications, Internet access, and radio and TV broadcasting.

- **International Air Transport Association (IATA).** Originally founded in 1919, most of the world's international airlines belong to the IATA. This cartel, headquartered in Montreal, sets international airline ticket prices and safety and security standards for passenger and cargo shipping. It controls access to airports and challenges rules and regulations considered to be unreasonable. The IATA also is concerned with minimizing the impact of air transport on the environment.

ANALYZE THE ISSUE Given today's oil and gasoline prices, how successful do you suppose OPEC has recently been in restricting the supply of oil? Explain.

10-5c Price Leadership

Without formal agreement, firms can play a game of follow-the-leader that economists call price leadership. **Price leadership** is a pricing strategy in which a dominant firm sets the price for an industry and the other firms follow. Following this tactic, firms in an industry simply match the price of perhaps, but not necessarily, the biggest firm.

Price leadership is not uncommon. In addition to GM, USX Corporation (steel), Alcoa (aluminum), DuPont (nylon), R.J. Reynolds (cigarettes), and Goodyear Tire and Rubber (tires) are examples of price leaders in U.S. industries.

Price leadership
A pricing strategy in which a dominant firm sets the price for an industry and the other firms follow.

10-5d The Cartel

The price leadership model assumes that firms do not collude (or "get-together") to avoid price competition. Instead, firms avoid price wars by informally playing by the established pricing rules. Another way to avoid price wars is for oligopolists to agree to a peace treaty. Instead of allowing mutual interdependence to lead to rivalry, firms openly or secretly conspire to form a monopoly by establishing a cartel. A **cartel** is a group of firms that formally agree to reduce competition by coordinating the price and output of a product. The goal of a cartel is to reap monopoly profits by replacing competition with cooperation. Cartels are illegal in the United States, but not in other nations. The best-known cartel is the Organization of the Petroleum Exporting Countries

Cartel
A group of firms that formally agree to reduce competition by coordinating the price and output of a product.

(OPEC). The members of OPEC divide "black gold" output among themselves according to quotas openly agreed upon at meetings of the OPEC oil ministries. Saudi Arabia is the largest producer and has the largest quota. The Global Economics feature provides a brief summary of some of today's major global cartels.

Using Exhibit 6, we can demonstrate how a cartel works and why keeping members from cheating is a problem. Our analysis begins before oil-producing firms have formed a cartel. Assume each firm has the same cost curve shown in the exhibit. Price wars have

---

EXHIBIT 6 Why a Cartel Member Has an Incentive to Cheat

A representative oil producer operating in a perfectly competitive industry would be in long-run equilibrium at a price of $75 per barrel, producing 6 million barrels per day and making zero economic profit. A cartel can agree to raise the price of oil from $75 to $120 per barrel by restricting the firm to 4 million barrels per day. As a result of this quota, the cartel price is above $90 on the LRAC curve, and the firm earns a daily profit of $120 million. However, if the firm cheats on the cartel agreement, it will want to produce 8 million barrels per day. At this quantity, marginal revenue (which is also the price of $120) equals marginal cost, and the firm can earn a total profit of $240 million instead of the $120 million it would earn if it did not cheat. If all firms cheat, the original long-run equilibrium will be reestablished.

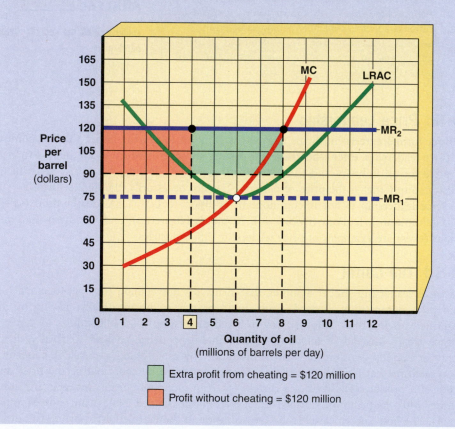

driven each firm to charge $75 a barrel, which is equal to the minimum point on its LRAC curve. Because oil is a standardized product, as under perfect competition, each firm fears raising its price because it will lose all its customers. Thus, the typical firm is in long-run competitive equilibrium at a price of $75 per barrel ($MR_1$), producing 6 million barrels per day. In this condition, economic profits are zero, and the firms decide to organize a meeting of all oil producers to establish a cartel.

Now assume the cartel is formed and each firm agrees to reduce its output to 4 million barrels per day and charge $120 per barrel. If no firms cheat, each firm faces a higher horizontal demand curve, represented by MR_2. At the cartel price, each firm earns an economic profit of $120 million ($30 × 4 million), rather than a normal profit. But what if one firm decides to cheat on the cartel agreement by stepping up its output while other firms stick to their quotas? The profit-maximizing output corresponding to the point at which $MR_2 = MC$ is 8 million barrels per day. If a cheating firm expands its output to this level, it can double its profit by earning an extra $120 million. Of course, if all firms cheat, the cartel breaks up, in which case the price and output of each firm return to the initial levels, and economic profit again falls to zero.

10-5e **Game Theory**

Game theory is a model of the strategic moves and countermoves of rivals. To illustrate, let's use a noncollusive example of Delta Air Lines competing with American Airlines. Each airline independently sets its fare, and Exhibit 7 is a *payoff matrix* that shows profit

Game theory
A model of the strategic moves and countermoves of rivals.

EXHIBIT 7 A Two-Firm Payoff Matrix

Game theory is a method of analyzing the oligopoly puzzle. Two fare options of charging either a high fare or a low fare are given for Delta Air Lines and American Airlines. The profit or loss that each earns in cells A–D depends on the pricing decisions of these two rivals. Their collective interest is best served in cell A where each charges the high fare and each makes the maximum profit of $8 billion. But once either airline independently seeks the higher profit of $10 billion by using a low-fare strategy in cell B or C, the other airline counters with a low fare, and both end up charging the low fare in cell D. As a result, mutual profits are $5 billion, rather than $8 billion in cell A. Cell D is the equilibrium outcome because both airlines fear changing the price and causing the other to counter.

		Delta Air Lines' options	
		High fare	**Low fare**
American Airlines' options	**High fare**	**A** Delta Air Lines' profit = $8 billion American Airlines' profit = $8 billion	**B** Delta Air Lines' profit = $10 billion American Airlines' loss = −$2 billion
	Low fare	**C** Delta Air Lines' loss = −$2 billion American Airlines' profit = $10 billion	**D** Delta Air Lines' profit = $5 billion American Airlines' profit = $5 billion

outcomes for the two airlines resulting from charging either a high fare or a low fare. If both charge the high fare in cell A, they split the market, and each makes a profit of $8 billion. If both decide to charge the low fare in cell D, they also split the market, and the profit for each falls to $5 billion. If one charges the high fare and the other charges the low fare in cell B or cell C, then the low-fare airline attracts most of the customers and earns the maximum possible profit of $10 billion, while the high-fare airline loses $2 billion.

Both rivals in our example are clearly *mutually interdependent* because an action by one firm may cause a reaction from the other firm. Suppose both airlines initially select the most mutually profitable solution and both charge high fares in cell A. This outcome creates an incentive for either airline to charge a lower fare in cell B or cell C and earn the highest possible profit by pulling customers away from its rival. Consequently, assume the next day one airline cuts its fare to gain higher profits. In order to avoid losing customers, this action causes the other airline to counter with an equally low fare. Price competition has therefore forced both airlines to charge the low fare in cell D and earn less than maximum joint profits. Once cell D is reached, neither airline has an incentive to increase the fare since doing so would create a loss of $2 billion. Note that when both firms charge the low fare in equilibrium at cell D, consumers benefit from not paying the higher fares found in the other cells.

CONCLUSION   The payoff matrix demonstrates why a competitive oligopoly tends to result in both rivals using a low-price strategy that does not maximize mutual profits.

How can these oligopolists avoid the low-fare outcome in cell D and instead stabilize the more jointly profitable high-fare payoffs in cell A? One possible strategy is called *tit-for-tat*. Under this approach, a player will do whatever the other player did the last time. If one airline defects from cell A by cutting its fare to gain a profit advantage, the other competitor will also cut its fare. After repeated trials, these price-cutting responses serve as a signal that says, "You are not going to get the best of me, so move your fare up!" Once the defector responds by moving back to the high fare, the other airline cooperates and also moves to the high fare. The result is that both players return to cell A without a formal agreement.

Another informal approach is for rivals to coordinate their pricing decisions based on price leadership, as discussed earlier in this chapter. For example, one airline may be much more established or dominant, and the other airline follows whatever price the leader sets. Another approach would be to informally rotate the leadership. Thus, without a formal agreement, the leader sets the profit-maximizing high price in cell A and the other competitor follows. However, this system does not eliminate the threat that the price follower will cheat.

Finally, if cartels were legal in the United States, the airlines could collude and make a formal agreement that each will charge the high fare. However, as explained in the previous section, there is always the incentive for one firm to cheat by moving from cell A to either cell B or cell C, and therefore cartels tend to break down. A remedy might be for the rivals to agree on a penalty for any party that reneges by lowering its fare.

CONCLUSION   As long as the benefits exceed the costs, cheating can threaten formal or informal agreements among oligopolists to maximize joint profits.

10-5f An Evaluation of Oligopoly

Oligopoly is much more difficult to evaluate than other market structures. None of the models just presented gives a definite answer to the question of efficiency under oligopoly. Depending on the assumptions made, an oligopolist can behave much like a perfectly competitive firm or more like a monopoly. Nevertheless, let's assume some likely changes that occur if a perfectly competitive industry is suddenly turned into an oligopoly selling a differentiated product.

First, the price charged for the product will be higher than under perfect competition. The smaller the number of firms in an oligopoly and the more difficult it is to enter the industry, the higher the oligopoly price will be in comparison to the perfectly competitive price.

Second, an oligopoly is likely to spend money on advertising, product differentiation, and other forms of nonprice competition. These expenditures can shift the demand curve to the right. As a result, both price and output may be higher under oligopoly than under perfect competition. Moreover, as with a monopoly, the oligopoly may promote technological advances that enhance the quality of life for many people.

Third, in the long run, a perfectly competitive firm earns zero economic profit. The oligopolist, however, can earn an economic profit in the long run because it is more difficult for competitors to enter the industry.

Which Model Fits the Cereal Aisle?

As you walk along the cereal aisle, notice the many different cereals on the shelf. For example, you will probably see General Mills' Wheaties, Total, and Cheerios; Kellogg's Corn Flakes, Cracklin' Oat Bran, Frosted Flakes, and Rice Krispies; Quaker Oats' Cap'n Crunch and 100% Natural; and Post's Golden Crisp, to name only a few. There are many different brands of the same product, cereal, on the shelves. Each brand is slightly different from the others. Is the breakfast cereal industry's market structure monopolistic competition or oligopoly?

CHECKPOINT

10-6 REVIEW OF THE FOUR MARKET STRUCTURES

Now that we have completed the discussion of perfect competition, monopoly, monopolistic competition, and oligopoly, you are prepared to compare these four market structures. Exhibit 8 summarizes the characteristics and gives examples of each market structure.

EXHIBIT 8 Comparison of Market Structures

Market structure	Number of sellers	Type of product	Entry condition	Control of Price	Examples
Perfect competition	Large	Homogeneous	Very easy	Price taker	Agriculture
Monopoly	One	Unique	Impossible	Price maker	Public utilities
Monopolistic competition	Many	Differentiated	Easy	Price maker	Retail trade
Oligopoly	Few	Homogeneous or differentiated	Difficult	Price maker	Auto, steel, oil, pharmaceuticals

YOU'RE THE ECONOMIST

Applicable Concept: Oligopoly

How Oligopolists Compete at the Final Four

Suppose March Madness included your basketball team making it all the way to the Final Four and you were going to be there. Before leaving, you checked the official website and noticed a Coke ad giving a prize to the person who submitted the best video commercial for a new Coke product. But this was only the beginning of the Great Cola Wars. Shortly after leaving the plane at the airport, you encountered a group of students who were giving away huge inflatable plastic hands with index fingers sticking up in the air signaling that your team is number one. The plastic hands were imprinted with the Pepsi-Cola logo and your choice of a Final Four team. And the group was also giving away free ice-cold cans of Pepsi. As you walked along the streets to your hotel, giant inflatable "cans" of Pepsi appeared all over the downtown area on the sidewalks and on top of gas stations. And not to be outdone, the entire side of a prominent three-story building was painted Coca-Cola red and white with the 64 NCAA basketball finalists and all the winners listed bracket by bracket. Following the first-round games, painters were on scaffolding three stories up filling in the Coke sign's brackets for the final two teams, in school colors no less. Inside the arena, the colas continued their battle by scrolling cola ads with other ads under the press rows along either side of the basketball court. This was indeed competition between showboating industry giants worthy of the Final Four competition among the basketball teams.

Many fascinating markets function during the Final Four basketball tournament, including competitive markets that

Chris Steppig/NCAA Photos/Getty Images

determine prices for parking lots, restaurants, and tickets. (Recall the Checkpoint in Chapter 4 on ticket scalping.) Then there were the hotels surrounding the arena, which joined a centralized booking service. Each hotel had raised its normal price by 75 percent for the weekend.

ANALYZE THE ISSUE In this feature, two forms of oligopoly were discussed. Identify each of these forms and explain why it is being used by the oligopolists.

Key Concepts

Monopolistic competition	Oligopoly	Price leadership
Product differentiation	Mutual interdependence	Cartel
Nonprice competition	Kinked demand curve	Game theory

Summary

- **Monopolistic competition** is a market structure characterized by (1) many small sellers, (2) a differentiated product, and (3) easy market entry and exit. Given these characteristics, firms in monopolistic competition have a negligible effect on the market price.

- **Product differentiation** is a key characteristic of monopolistic competition. It is the process of creating real or apparent differences between products.

- **Nonprice competition** includes advertising, packaging, product development, better quality, and better service. Under monopolistic competition and oligopoly, firms may compete using nonprice competition, rather than price competition.

- **Short-run equilibrium for a monopolistic competitor** can yield economic losses, zero economic profits, or economic profits. In the long run, monopolistic competitors make zero economic profits.

Short-Run Equilibrium for a Monopolistic Competitor

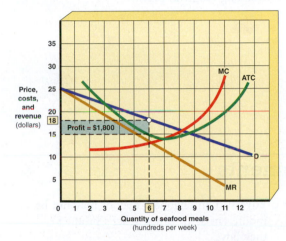

- **Comparing monopolistic competition with perfect competition**, we find that in the long run the monopolistically competitive firm does not achieve allocative efficiency, charges a higher price, restricts output, and does not produce where average costs are at a minimum.

Comparison of Monopolistic and Perfect Competition

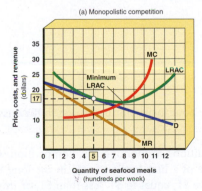

(a) Monopolistic competition

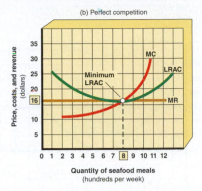

(b) Perfect competition

- **Oligopoly** is a market structure characterized by (1) few sellers, (2) either a homogeneous or a differentiated product, and (3) difficult market entry. Oligopolies are **mutually interdependent** because an action by one firm may cause a reaction from other firms.

- The **nonprice competition model** is a theory that might explain oligopolistic behavior. Under this theory, firms use advertising and product differentiation, rather than price reductions, to compete.

- The **kinked demand curve** model explains why prices may be rigid in an oligopoly. The kink occurs because an oligopolist assumes that rivals will match a price decrease, but ignore a price increase.

Kinked Demand Curve

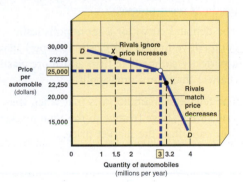

- **Price leadership** is another theory of pricing behavior under oligopoly. When a dominant firm in an industry raises or lowers its price, other firms follow suit.

- A **cartel** is a formal agreement among firms to set prices and output quotas. The goal is to maximize joint profits, but firms have an incentive to cheat, which is a constant threat to a cartel.

Cartel

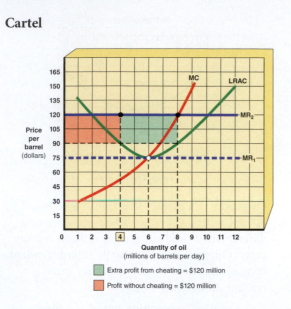

Extra profit from cheating = $120 million

Profit without cheating = $120 million

- **Game theory** reveals that (1) oligopolies are mutually interdependent in their pricing policies, (2) without collusion, oligopoly prices and mutual profits are lower, and (3) oligopolists have a temptation to cheat on any collusive agreement.

- **Comparing oligopoly with perfect competition**, we find that the oligopolist allocates resources inefficiently, charges a higher price, and restricts output so that price may exceed average cost enabling long-run profits.

Summary of Conclusion Statements

- The many-sellers condition is met when each firm is so small relative to the total market that its pricing decisions have a negligible effect on the market price.

- A firm can charge higher prices if it makes its products seem unique.

- The demand curve for a monopolistically competitive firm is less elastic (steeper) than for a perfectly competitive firm and more elastic (flatter) than for a monopolist.

- The few-sellers condition is met when these few firms are so large relative to the total market that they can affect the market price.

- Buyers in an oligopoly may or may not be indifferent as to which seller's product they buy.

- The payoff matrix demonstrates why a competitive oligopoly tends to result in both rivals using a low-price strategy that does not maximize mutual profits.

- As long as the benefits exceed the costs, cheating can threaten formal or informal agreements among oligopolists to maximize joint profits.

Study Questions and Problems

Please see Appendix A for answers to the odd-numbered questions. Your instructor has access to the answers for even-numbered questions.

1. Compare the monopolistically competitive firm's demand curve to those of a perfect competitor and a monopolist.

2. Suppose the minimum point on the LRAC curve of a soft-drink firm's cola is $1 per liter. Under conditions of monopolistic competition, will the price of a liter bottle of cola in the long run be above $1, equal to $1, less than $1, or impossible to determine?

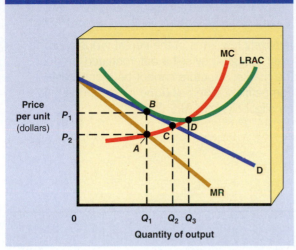

EXHIBIT 9 Firm in Long-Run Equilibrium

7. List four goods or services that you have purchased that were produced by an oligopolist. Why are these industries oligopolistic, rather than monopolistically competitive?

8. Why is mutual interdependence important under oligopoly, but not so important under perfect competition, monopoly, or monopolistic competition?

9. Suppose the jeans industry is an oligopoly in which each firm sells its own distinctive brand of jeans. Each firm believes its rivals will not follow its price increases, but will follow its price cuts. Explain the demand curve facing each firm. Does this demand curve mean that firms in the jeans industry do or do not compete against one another?

10. What might be a general distinction between oligopolists that advertise and those that do not?

11. Suppose Canon raised the price of its printers, but Hewlett-Packard (the largest seller) refused to follow. Two years later Canon cut its price, and Hewlett-Packard retaliated with an even deeper price cut, which Canon was forced to match. For the next five years, Hewlett-Packard raised its prices five times, and each time Canon followed suit within 24 hours. Does the pricing behavior of these printer industry firms follow the cartel model or the price leadership model? Why?

12. Evaluate the following statement: "A cartel will put an end to price war, which is a barbaric form of competition that benefits no one."

13. Assume the payoff matrix in Exhibit 7 applies to spending for advertising rather than airline fares. Substitute "*Don't Advertise*" for "*High fare*" and "*Advertise*" for "*Low fare*." Assume the same profit and loss figures in each cell, but substitute "*Marlboro*" for "*Delta Airlines,*" and "*Camel*" for "*American Airlines.*" Explain the dynamics of the model and why cigarette companies might be pleased with a government ban on all cigarette advertising.

3. Exhibit 9 represents a monopolistically competitive firm in long-run equilibrium.
   a. Which price represents the long-run equilibrium price?
   b. Which quantity represents the long-run equilibrium output?
   c. At which quantity is the LRAC curve at its minimum?
   d. Is the long-run equilibrium price greater than, less than, or equal to the marginal cost of producing the equilibrium output?

4. Consider this statement: "Because price equals long-run average cost and profits are zero, a monopolistically competitive firm is efficient." Do you agree or disagree? Explain.

5. Assuming identical long-run cost curves, draw two graphs, and indicate the price and output that result in the long run under monopolistic competition and perfect competition. Evaluate the differences between these two market structures.

6. Draw a graph that shows how advertising affects a firm's ATC curve. Explain how advertising can lead to lower prices in a monopolistically competitive industry.

✓ CHECKPOINT ANSWERS

Which Model Fits the Cereal Aisle?

The fact that there is a differentiated product does not necessarily mean that many firms are competing along the cereal aisle. The different cereals listed in this example are produced by only four companies: General Mills, Kellogg's, Quaker Oats, and Post. In fact, there are relatively few firms in the cereal industry, so even though they sell a differentiated product, the market structure cannot be monopolistic competition. If you said the cereal industry is an oligopoly, **YOU ARE CORRECT**.

Sample Quiz

Please see Appendix B for answers to Sample Quiz questions.

1. Clothing stores in cities are an illustration of
   a. perfect competition.
   b. monopoly.
   c. monopolistic competition.
   d. oligopoly.

2. Firms in a monopolistically competitive industry produce
   a. homogeneous goods and services.
   b. differentiated products.
   c. competitive goods only.
   d. consumption goods only.

3. Monopolistic competitive firms in the long run earn
   a. positive economic profits.
   b. zero pure economic profits.
   c. negative economic profits.
   d. None of the above answers are correct.

4. The theory of monopolistic competition predicts that in long-run equilibrium, a monopolistically competitive firm will
   a. produce at the level in which price equals long-run average cost.
   b. operate at minimum long-run average cost.
   c. overutilize its insufficient capacity.
   d. None of the above answers are correct.

5. Which of the following statements *best* describes the price, output, and profit conditions of monopolistic competition?

   a. Price will equal marginal cost at the profit-maximizing level of output; profits will be positive in the long run.
   b. Price will always equal average variable cost in the short run, and either profits or losses may result in the long run.
   c. Marginal revenue will equal marginal cost in the short run profit-maximizing level of output; in the long run economic profit will be zero.
   d. Marginal revenue will equal average total cost in the short run; long-run economic profits will be zero.

6. Entry of new firms will occur in a monopolistic competitive industry until
   a. marginal cost equals zero.
   b. marginal revenue equals zero.
   c. marginal revenue equals marginal cost.
   d. economic profit equals zero.
   e. economic profit is negative.

7. As presented in Exhibit 10, what is the short-run profit-maximizing output for the monopolistic competitive firm?
   a. 0 units per day
   b. 200 units per day
   c. 400 units per day
   d. 600 units per day

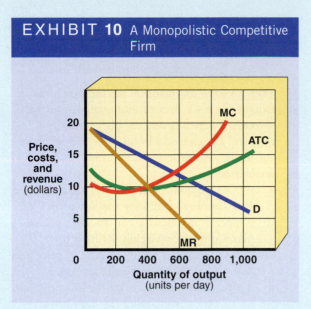

EXHIBIT 10 A Monopolistic Competitive Firm

Price, costs, and revenue (dollars)

Quantity of output (units per day)

8. As presented in Exhibit 10, what is the short-run profit per unit of output for the monopolistic competitive firm?
   a. Zero
   b. $5
   c. $10
   d. $15

9. In which of the following market structures can firms be price makers?
   a. monopoly, monopolistic competition, and oligopoly.
   b. perfect competition, monopolistic competition, and oligopoly.
   c. monopoly, perfect competition, and oligopoly.
   d. monopoly, monopolistic competition, and perfect competition.

10. An oligopoly is a market structure in which
   a. one firm has 100 percent of a market.
   b. there are many small firms.
   c. there are many firms with no control over price.
   d. there are few firms selling either a homogeneous or differentiated product.

11. Mutual interdependence among firms in an oligopoly means that
   a. firms never practice price leadership.
   b. firms never form a cartel.

   c. it is difficult to know how firms will react to decisions of rivals.
   d. no formal agreement is possible among firms.

12. A common characteristic of oligopolies is
   a. interdependence in pricing decisions.
   b. independent pricing decisions.
   c. low industry concentration.
   d. few or no plant-level economies of scale.

13. Which of the following *best* describes a cartel?
   a. A group of monopolistically competitive firms that jointly reduces output and raise price in imitation of a monopolist. When entry is very costly, these high prices can persist.
   b. A group of monopolistically competitive firms that agree to increase the variety of goods that they sell.
   c. A monopolist that reduces output and raises price. When entry is very costly, these high prices can persist.
   d. A group of cooperating oligopolists that jointly reduce output and raise price in imitation of a monopolist. When entry is very costly, these high prices can persist.

14. Which of the following is *true* about an oligopoly equilibrium compared with equilibrium under similar circumstances but with perfect competition?
   a. Output is larger and price is lower than under perfect competition.
   b. Output is larger but price is higher than under perfect competition.
   c. Output is smaller and price is higher than under perfect competition.
   d. Output is smaller and price is lower than under perfect competition.

15. Which of the following market structures describes an industry in which a group of firms formally agrees to control prices and output of a product?
   a. Perfect competition
   b. Monopoly
   c. Oligopoly
   d. Cartel
   e. Monopolistic competition

16. Assume costs are identical for the two firms in Exhibit 11. If both firms were allowed to form a

EXHIBIT 11 Two-Firm Payoff Matrix

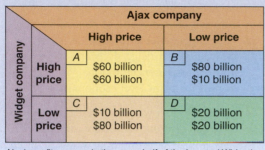

Ajax's profits appear in the upper half of the box and Widget's profits appear in the lower half of the box.

cartel and agree on their prices, equilibrium would be established by

a. Widget Company charging the low price and Ajax Company charging the high price.
b. Widget Company charging the high price and Ajax Company charging the low price.
c. Widget Company charging the low price and Ajax Company charging the low price.
d. Widget Company charging the high price and Ajax Company charging the high price.

17. Suppose costs are identical for the two firms in Exhibit 11. If both firms assume the other will compete and charge a lower price, equilibrium will be established by

a. Widget Company charging the low price and Ajax Company charging the low price.
b. Widget Company charging the high price and Ajax Company charging the low price.

c. Widget Company charging the low price and Ajax Company charging the high price.
d. Widget Company charging the high price and Ajax Company charging the high price.

18. Suppose costs are identical for the two firms in Exhibit 11. Each firm assumes without formal agreement that if it sets the high price, its rival will *not* charge a lower price. Under these "tit-for-tat" conditions, equilibrium will be established by

a. Widget Company charging the high price and Ajax Company charging the low price.
b. Widget Company charging the high price and Ajax Company charging the high price.
c. Widget Company charging the low price and Ajax Company charging the low price.
d. Widget Company charging the low price and Ajax Company charging the high price.

19. As a result of a kinked demand curve, the price

a. fluctuates.
b. falls below the kink.
c. settles at the kink.
d. rises above the kink.

20. The "kinked" oligopoly demand curve is a result of the assumption by an oligopolist that

a. price increases will be matched, but price reductions will not.
b. price increases will not be matched, but price reductions will.
c. both price increases and price reductions will be matched.
d. neither price increases nor price reductions will be matched.

CHAPTER **11**

Labor Markets

CHAPTER PREVIEW

In 2016, singer Lady Gaga earned the impressive figure of $59 million, but Taylor Swift did even better. She earned $80 million. Whereas one headline reports a sports team signed its star player to a contract paying $10 million annually, another cites a recent survey showing chief executive officers (CEOs) of America's biggest corporations are paid millions of dollars in compensation. The Chief Justice of the Supreme Court is paid $258,100 per year. The worker with a bachelor's degree or more earns an average of over $66,000. The average high school graduate earns just over $36,000, whereas many others, including college students, toil for the minimum wage.

How are earnings determined? What accounts for the wide differences in earnings? This chapter provides answers by explaining different types of labor markets that determine workers' compensation and the quantity of workers firms hire. Understanding hiring decisions is indeed a key to understanding why some become rich and famous by playing baseball—a kid's game—while other workers might be exploited by firms with labor market power.

The chapter begins with the development of a competitive labor market in which no single buyer or seller can influence the price (wage rate) of labor. The chapter concludes with a discussion of the ways in which employees and firms can each increase their bargaining power in negotiations. When they have more negotiating power, unions or employers can alter wage and employment outcomes. For example, the chapter explains how unions affect wages and examines trends in union membership in the United States.

IN THIS CHAPTER, YOU WILL LEARN TO SOLVE THESE ECONOMICS PUZZLES:

- What determines the wage rate an employer pays?

- How do labor unions influence wages and employment?

- Does the NCAA exploit college athletes?

11-1 THE LABOR MARKET UNDER PERFECT COMPETITION

In Chapters 8, 9, and 10, you studied the price and quantity determinations of goods and services produced by firms operating under different market structures—perfect competition, monopoly, oligopoly, and monopolistic competition. As you have learned, market structure affects the price and the quantity of a good or service sold by firms to consumers. Similarly, as this chapter will demonstrate, the price (wage rate) paid to labor and the quantity of labor hired by firms are influenced by whether or not the labor market is competitive.

Recall from Chapter 8 that we assumed the hypothetical firm called Computech produces and sells electronic components in a perfectly competitive market. In the same chapter, we also assumed Computech hires workers in a perfectly competitive labor market. In a perfectly competitive labor market, there are many sellers and buyers of labor services. Consequently, wages and salaries are determined by the intersection of the demand for labor and the supply of labor.

11-1a The Demand for Labor

How many workers should Computech hire? To answer this question, Computech must know how much workers contribute to its output. Column (1) of Exhibit 1 lists possible numbers of workers Computech might hire per day, and as discussed earlier in Chapter 7 on production costs, column (2) shows the total output per day. One worker would produce 5 units per day, 2 workers together would produce 9 units per day, and so on. Note that columns (1) and (2) constitute a *production function,* as represented earlier in Exhibit 2(a) in Chapter 7. Column (3) lists the additional output from hiring each worker. The first worker hired would add 5 units of output per day, the second would produce an additional 4 units (found as the difference in the total product: 9 – 5 units produced), and so on. Recall from Chapter 7 that the additional output from hiring another unit of labor is defined as the *marginal product of labor* [see Exhibit 2(b) in Chapter 7]. Consistent with the *law of diminishing returns,* the marginal product of labor falls as the firm hires more workers.[1]

Marginal revenue product (MRP)
The increase in a firm's total revenue resulting from hiring an additional unit of labor or other variable resource.

The next step in Computech's hiring decision is to convert the marginal product of labor into dollars by calculating the **marginal revenue product (MRP)**, which is the increase in a firm's total revenue resulting from hiring an additional unit of labor. Although only labor is considered in this chapter, keep in mind that Computech also faces a similar decision in determining how many machines to purchase to aid its production process. The company will calculate its MRP when it increases its purchases of machines as well.

Stated simply, MRP is the dollar value of worker productivity. It is the extra revenue a firm earns from selling the output of an extra worker. Returning to Exhibit 1 in Chapter 8 on perfect competition, suppose the market equilibrium price per unit is $70. Because Computech operates in a perfectly competitive market, the firm can sell any quantity of its product at the $70 market-determined price. Given a $70 market price, the first unit of labor contributes a MRP of $350 per day to revenue ($70 per unit times the 5 units of output). Column (5) of Exhibit 1 lists the MRP of each additional worker hired.

---

[1]Recall from Chapter 7 that at low rates of output, the marginal product may increase with the addition of more labor due to specialization and division of labor. Then, as output expands in the short run, the law of diminishing returns will cause marginal product to decrease.

EXHIBIT 1 Computech's Demand for Labor

Points	(1) Labor Input (workers per day)	(2) Total Output (units per day)	(3) Marginal Product (units per day)	(4) Product Price	(5) Marginal Revenue Product [(3) × (4)]
	0	0		$70	
			5		$350
A	1	5		70	
			4		280
B	2	9		70	
			3		210
C	3	12		70	
			2		140
D	4	14		70	
			1		70
E	5	15		70	

CONCLUSION

A perfectly competitive firm's marginal revenue product is equal to the marginal product of its labor times the price of its product. Expressed as a formula: $MRP = P \times MP$.

Now assuming all other inputs are fixed, Computech can derive its demand curve for labor, which conforms to the law of demand explained in Chapter 3. The **demand curve for labor** is a curve showing the different quantities of labor employers are willing to hire at different wage rates. It is equal to the MRP of labor. The MRP numbers from Exhibit 1 are duplicated in Exhibit 2. As shown in Exhibit 2, the price of labor in terms of daily wages is measured on the vertical axis. The quantity of workers Computech will hire per day at each wage rate is measured on the horizontal axis. The demand curve for labor is downward sloping: As the wage rate falls, Computech will hire more workers per day. If the wage rate is above $350 (point *A*), Computech will hire no workers because the cost of a worker is more than the dollar value of any worker's contribution to total revenue (MRP). But what happens if Computech pays each worker $280 per day? At point *B*, Computech finds it profitable to hire 2 workers because the MRP of the first worker is greater than the wage rate (extra cost) and the second worker's MRP equals the wage rate. If the wage rate is $140 per day at point *D*, Computech will find it profitable to hire 4 workers. In this case, Computech will not hire the fifth worker. Why? The fifth worker contributes an MRP of $70 to total revenue (point *E*), but this amount is below the wage rate paid of $140. Consequently, Computech cannot maximize profits by hiring the fifth worker because it would be adding more to costs than to revenue.

Demand curve for labor
A curve showing the different quantities of labor employers are willing to hire at different wage rates in a given time period, ceteris paribus. It is equal to the marginal revenue product of labor.

EXHIBIT 2 Computech's Demand Curve for Labor

Computech's downward-sloping demand curve for labor is derived from the marginal revenue product (MRP) of labor, which declines as additional workers are hired. The MRP is the change in total revenue that results from hiring one more worker (see Exhibit 1). At point *B*, Computech pays $280 per day and finds it profitable to pay this wage to two workers because each worker's MRP equals or exceeds the wage rate. If Computech pays a lower wage rate of $140 per day at point *D*, it is not profitable for the firm to hire the fifth worker because this worker's MRP of $70 is below the wage rate of $140 per day. At a wage rate of $70, the fifth worker would be hired.

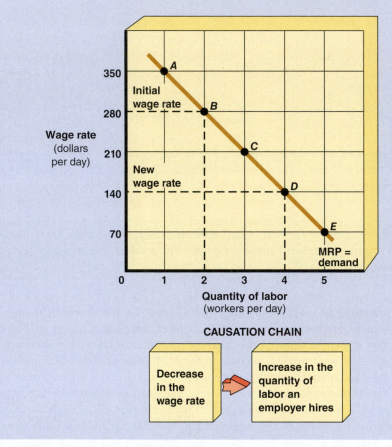

CAUSATION CHAIN

Specifically, Computech would lose $70 per day by hiring the fifth worker. At a wage rate of $70, however, the fifth worker would be hired.

| CONCLUSION | A firm hires additional workers up to the point where the MRP equals the wage rate. |

Each firm in the market has a demand for labor based on its MRP data. Summing these individual demand curves for labor provides the market demand curve for labor in the electronic components industry. Another important point must be made. The demand for labor is called derived demand. The **derived demand** for labor and other factors of production depends on the consumer demand for the final goods and services the factors produce. If consumers are not willing to purchase products requiring electronic components, such as bank teller machines, there is no MRP, and firms will hire no workers to make electronic components for them. On the other hand, if customer demand for bank teller machines soars, the price of these machines rises, and the MRP of firms in the electronic components industry also rises. The result is a rightward shift in the market demand curve for labor.

Derived demand
The demand for labor and other factors of production that depends on the consumer demand for the final goods and services the factors produce.

11-1b **The Supply of Labor**

The supply curve of labor is also consistent with the law of supply discussed in Chapter 3. The **supply curve of labor** shows the different quantities of labor workers are willing to offer employers at different wage rates. Summing the individual supply curves of labor for firms producing electronic units for automated teller machines provides the market supply curve of labor. As shown in Exhibit 3, as the wage rate rises, more workers are willing to supply their labor. Each point indicates the wage rate that must be paid to attract the corresponding number of workers. At point *A*, 20,000 workers offer their services to the industry for $140 per day. At the higher wage rate of $280 per day (point *B*), the quantity of labor supplied is 40,000 workers. More people are willing to work at higher wage rates because as the wage rate increases, workers are willing to give up their time that they would otherwise use for other activities. Higher wages also attract workers from other industries that require similar skills, but have lower wage rates.

Supply curve of labor
A curve showing the different quantities of labor workers are willing to offer employers at different wage rates in a given time period, ceteris paribus.

Ignoring differences in wage scales, why might the supply of less-skilled workers (e.g., carpenters) be greater than that of more-skilled workers (e.g., physicians)? The explanation for this difference is the human capital required to perform various occupations. **Human capital** is the accumulation of education, training, and experience, as well as the condition of a person's health that enables a worker to enter an occupation and be productive. Less human capital is required to be a carpenter than a physician. Because so many more people are qualified to be carpenters than physicians, the supply of carpenters is larger than the supply of physicians.

Human capital
The accumulation of education, training, experience, and the level of good health that enables a worker to enter an occupation and be productive.

11-1c **The Equilibrium Wage Rate**

Wage rates are determined in perfectly competitive markets by the interaction of labor supply and demand. The equilibrium wage rate for the entire electronic components market, shown in Exhibit 4(a), is $210 per day. This wage rate clears the market because the quantity of 30,000 workers demanded equals the quantity of 30,000 workers who are willing to supply their labor services at that wage rate. In a competitive labor market, no single worker can set his or her wage above the equilibrium wage. Such a worker fears not being hired because there are so many workers who will work for $210 per day. Similarly, so many firms are hiring labor that a single firm cannot influence the wage by paying workers more or less than the prevailing wage. Hence, a wage rate above $210 per day would create a surplus of workers seeking employment (unemployment) in the electronic components market, and a wage rate below $210 per day would cause a shortage.

EXHIBIT 3 The Market Supply Curve of Labor

The upward-sloping supply curve of labor for the electronic components industry indicates that a direct relationship exists between the wage rate and the quantity of labor supplied. At point A, 20,000 workers are willing to work for $140 per day in this market. If the wage rate rises to $280 per day, 40,000 workers will supply their services to the electronic components labor market.

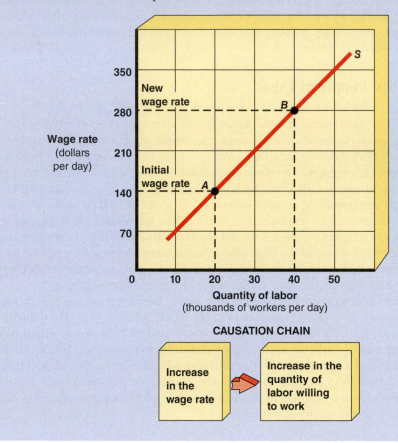

CAUSATION CHAIN

Increase in the wage rate → Increase in the quantity of labor willing to work

Why does a cardiologist make a much higher hourly wage than a server in a restaurant? As demonstrated in Exhibit 4(a), wage differentials are determined by the demand and supply curves in labor markets for these two occupations. In this case, compared to the market for servers, the demand for cardiologists is much greater and the supply is much lower; therefore, the equilibrium wage rate for cardiologists greatly exceeds the equilibrium wage rate for servers. In the next chapter, this labor market model is used to explain differences in wages resulting from racial discrimination.

Although the supply curve of labor is upward sloping for the electronic components market, this is not the case for an individual firm, such as Computech, shown in Exhibit 4 (b). Because a competitive labor market assumes that each firm is too small to influence the wage rate, Computech is a "wage taker" and therefore pays the market-determined wage rate of $210 per day regardless of the quantity of labor it employs. For this reason,

EXHIBIT 4 A Competitive Labor Market Determines the Firm's Equilibrium Wage

In part (a), the intersection of the supply of labor and the demand for labor curves determines the equilibrium wage rate of $210 per day in the electronic components industry. Part (b) illustrates that a single firm, such as Computech, is a "wage taker." The firm can hire all the workers it wants at this equilibrium wage, so its supply curve, S, is a horizontal line. Computech chooses to hire three workers, where the firm's demand curve for labor intersects its supply curve of labor.

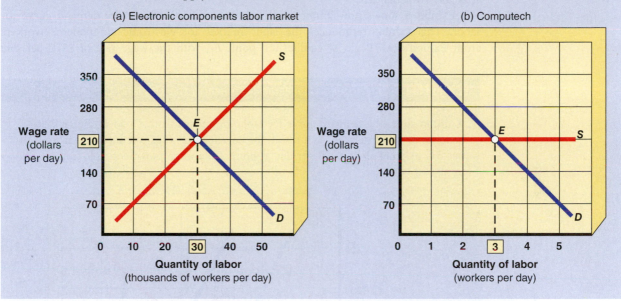

(a) Electronic components labor market   (b) Computech

the labor supply to Computech is represented by a horizontal line at the equilibrium wage rate. Given this wage rate of $210 per day, Computech then hires labor up to the equilibrium point, *E*, where the wage rate equals the third worker's marginal revenue product.

11-2 LABOR UNIONS: EMPLOYEE POWER

The perfectly competitive model does not apply to workers who belong to unions. Unions arose because workers recognized that acting together gave them more bargaining power than acting individually and being at the mercy of their employers. Some of the biggest unions are the Teamsters, United Auto Workers, National Education Association, and American Federation of Government Employees. Two primary objectives of unions are to improve working conditions and raise the wages of union members above the level that would exist in a competitive labor market. To raise wages, unions use three basic strategies: (1) increase the demand for labor, (2) decrease the supply of labor, and (3) exert power to force employers to pay a wage rate above the equilibrium wage rate.

11-2a Unions Increase the Demand for Labor

Now suppose the workers form a union. One way to increase wages is to use a method called *featherbedding*. This means the union forces firms to hire more workers than the firm would otherwise employ or to impose work rules that reduce output per worker.

For example, contract provisions may prohibit any workers but carpenters from doing even the simplest carpentry work. Another approach is to boost domestic demand for labor by decreasing competition from other nations. For example, the union might lobby Congress to protect the U.S. electronic parts industry against competition from China. Another approach might be to advertise and try to convince the public to "Look for the Union Label." Effective advertising would boost the demand for electronic products with union-made components and, in turn, the demand for union labor because it is *derived demand*.

Exhibit 5 shows how union power can be used to increase the demand curve for labor. This exhibit reproduces the labor market for electronic components workers from Exhibit 4(a). Begin at equilibrium point E_1, with the wage rate of $210 per day

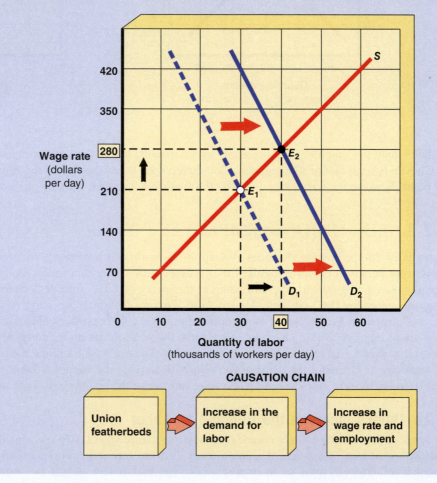

EXHIBIT 5 A Union Causes an Increase in the Demand Curve for Labor

A union shifts the demand curve for labor rightward from D_1 to D_2 by featherbedding or other devices. As a result, the equilibrium wage rate increases from $210 per day at point E_1 to $280 per day at point E_2, and employment rises from 30,000 to 40,000 workers.

CAUSATION CHAIN

Union featherbeds → Increase in the demand for labor → Increase in wage rate and employment

paid to each of 30,000 workers. Then the union successfully increases the demand curve for labor from D_1 to D_2. At the new equilibrium point, E_2, firms hire an additional 10,000 workers and pay each worker an extra $70 per day.

11-2b Unions Decrease the Supply of Labor

Exhibit 6 shows another way unions can use their power to increase the wage rate of their members by restricting the supply of labor. Now suppose the labor market is in equilibrium at point E_1, with 40,000 workers making electronic units and earning $210 per day. Then the union uses its power to shift the supply curve of labor leftward from

EXHIBIT 6 A Union Causes a Decrease in the Supply Curve of Labor

A union shifts the supply curve of labor leftward from S_1 to S_2 by restricting union membership or by using other techniques. As a result, the equilibrium wage rate rises from $210 per day at point E_1 to $280 per day at point E_2, and the number of workers hired falls from 40,000 to 30,000.

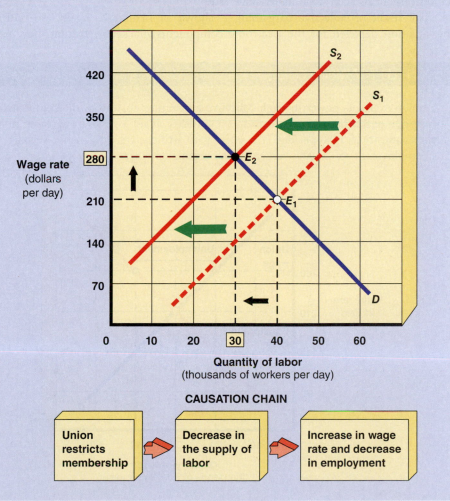

CAUSATION CHAIN

| Union restricts membership | Decrease in the supply of labor | Increase in wage rate and decrease in employment |

S_1 to S_2 by, say, requiring a longer apprenticeship, charging higher membership fees, or using some other device designed to reduce union membership. For example, the union might lobby for legislation to reduce immigration or to shorten working hours. As a result of these union actions, the equilibrium wage rate rises to $280 per day at point E_2, and employment is artificially reduced to 30,000 workers. It should be noted that self-serving practices of unions to limit the labor supply and raise wages can be disguised as standards of professionalism, such as those required by the American Medical Association and the American Bar Association, teacher certification requirements, Ph.D. requirements for university faculty, and so on.

11-2c Labor Unions Use Collective Bargaining to Boost Wages

Collective bargaining
The process of negotiating labor contracts between the union and management concerning wages and working conditions.

A third way to raise the wage rate above the equilibrium level is to use collective bargaining. **Collective bargaining** is the process of negotiating labor contracts between the union and management concerning wages and working conditions. By law, after a union has been certified as the representative of a majority of the workers, employers must deal with the union. If employers deny union demands, the union can strike and reduce profits until the firms agree to a higher wage rate.

The result of collective bargaining is shown in Exhibit 7. Again, we return to the situation depicted for the electronic components market in Exhibit 4(a). At the

---

EXHIBIT 7 Union Collective Bargaining Causes a Wage Rate Increase

A union exerts its power through collective bargaining. Instead of the competitive wage rate of $210 at point E, firms in the industry avoid a strike by agreeing in a labor contract to $280 per day. The effect is to artificially create a labor surplus (unemployment) of 20,000 workers at the negotiated wage.

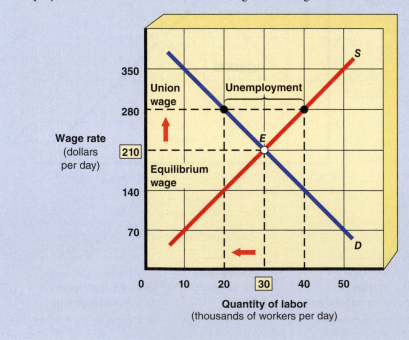

EXHIBIT 8 Factors Causing Changes in Labor Demand and Labor Supply

Changes in labor demand	Changes in labor supply
1. Unions	1. Unions
2. Prices of substitute inputs	2. Demographic trends
3. Technology	3. Expectations of future income
4. Demand for final products	4. Changes in immigration laws
5. Marginal product of labor	5. Education and training

equilibrium wage rate of $210 per day (point *E*), there is no surplus or shortage of workers. Then the industry is unionized, and a collective bargaining agreement takes effect in which firms agree to pay the union wage rate of $280 per day. At the higher wage rate, employment falls from 30,000 to 20,000 workers. However, 40,000 workers want to work for $280 per day, so there is a surplus of 20,000 unemployed workers in the industry. How might firms react to a situation in which they hire fewer workers and pay higher wages? Employers might respond by substituting capital for labor or by transferring operations overseas, where labor costs are lower than in the United States.

Finally, several factors can cause either the demand curve for labor or the supply curve of labor to shift. Exhibit 8 provides a list of these factors.

11-2d Union Membership

How important are unions as measured by the percentage of the labor force that belongs to a union? Let's start during the Great Depression, when millions of people were out of work and union membership was relatively low (see Exhibit 9). To boost employment and earnings, President Franklin D. Roosevelt's National Industrial Recovery Act (NIRA) of 1933 established the right of employees to bargain collectively with their employers, but the act was declared unconstitutional by the Supreme Court in 1935. However, the 1935 National Labor Relations Act (NLRA), known as the Wagner Act, incorporated the labor provisions of the NIRA. The Wagner Act guaranteed workers the right to form unions and to engage in collective bargaining. The combined impact of this legislation and the production demands of World War II created a surge in union membership between 1935 and 1945.

Since World War II, union power has declined. Union membership has fallen from about 35 percent of the labor force in 1945 to 11 percent today. Since 1985, union membership of public-sector workers has changed little and is currently at 34 percent. On the other hand, union membership for private-sector workers has declined significantly from 14 percent to 7 percent over the same period of time.

Exhibit 10 shows the unionization rates in several states. While the U.S. unionization rate is just under 11 percent, this rate varies considerably across the states, ranging from a high of 23.6 percent in New York and a low of 1.6 percent in South Carolina. Generally, Rust Belt states, such as Illinois and Michigan, have high unionization rates,

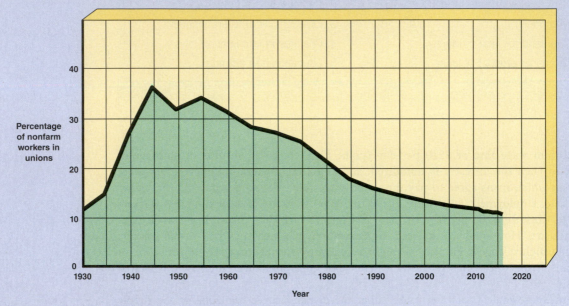

EXHIBIT 9 U.S. Union Membership, 1930–2016

As a percentage of nonfarm workers, union membership in the United States grew rapidly during the decade 1935–1945. Since its peak in 1945, union membership as a percentage of the labor force has fallen to about the level not seen since the early 1930s.

SOURCE: *Statistical Abstract of the United States, 2016*, http://www.census.gov/compendia/statab/, Table 648; and Percentage of Employed, Members of Unions, *Current Population Survey*, Bureau of Labor and Statistics, https://www.bls.gov, accessed May 2017.

whereas southern states like Louisiana, and non-coastal western states like New Mexico, have low unionization rates.

CHECKPOINT

Where Should Toyota Build the Factory?

At Toyota, the top management wants to build a new factory in the United States, but they are worried that unions could make wage demands that would prevent the factory from being profitable. As a result, management wants to build the factory in the state with the lowest unionization rate. Which of the seven states listed in Exhibit 10 should be home to the new factory?

11-3 EMPLOYER POWER

Monopsony
A labor market in which a single firm hires labor.

So far, labor markets have been explained with employees possessing varying degrees of power to influence wage rates and employment while employers were competitive with no market power. However, significant power can exist on the employer side of the labor market. The extreme case occurs in a monopsony. **Monopsony** is a labor market in which

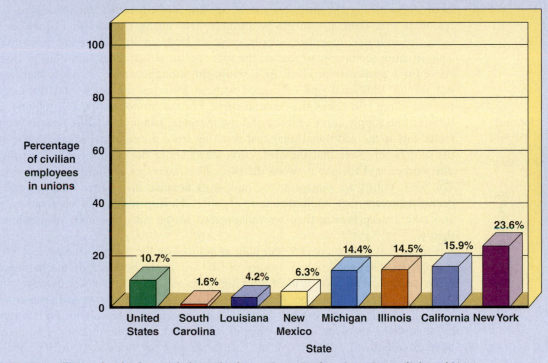

EXHIBIT 10 Union Membership for Selected States, 2016

Union membership as a percentage of the civilian labor force is above average in New York, California, and the mid-western industrial states. In contrast, the percentage of the workforce that is unionized is below average in the southern states and in the western states that do not border the Pacific Ocean.

SOURCE: Union Affiliation of employed wage and salary workers by state, *Current Population Survey*, Bureau of Labor and Statistics, https//www.bls.gov, accessed May 2017.

a single firm hires labor. For example, a single textile mill, mining company, or housing contractor might be the only buyer of labor in a particular market. The classical phrase for this situation is the "company town," where for miles around a small town everyone's livelihood depends on a single employer. The reason for the monopsony is the absence of other firms in the area competing for relatively immobile labor because workers must acquire new skills to find work outside the company town market. Even if a firm doesn't dominate a local labor market, it may have monopsony power over certain types of labor. A hospital, for example, may be the only large employer of nurses in a local market; therefore, it has monopsony power.

11-3a **Marginal Factor Cost**

This chapter began by assuming Computech operated in a competitive labor market in which no single employer in the electronic components market had any direct influence on the market wage rate. Recall from Exhibit 4 that Computech is a wage taker. More precisely, Computech hires the quantity of labor at the prevailing labor market equilibrium wage rate, which is determined by the point where the firm's downward-sloping MRP curve (demand curve for labor) intersects the horizontal supply curve of labor. The equilibrium wage rate is established by a competitive labor market beyond Computech's power to control.

Now we visit the isolated small town of Plainsville and find General Griffin's, which is a monopsonist producing turkeys. As shown in Exhibit 11, the supply of labor curve facing the monopsonist is upward sloping rather than horizontal. The reason is that General Griffin's is the only firm hiring workers in Plainsville, so it faces the industry, or entire, supply curve of labor in the Plainsville labor market. This situation compares to that of the monopolist, which faces the industry demand curve for a particular product. As a result, the monopolist in a product market cannot sell an additional unit of a good without lowering the price, and the marginal revenue curve falls below the demand curve. For the monopsonist, a distinction exists between the supply curve of labor and the marginal factor cost (MFC) curve. **Marginal factor cost** is the additional total cost resulting from a one-unit increase in the quantity of a factor. Note that the MFC curve starts above the supply curve when there is one worker, and the gap between the two curves increases as more workers are hired. The MFC points are plotted at the midpoints because the change in total wage cost occurs between each additional unit of labor. Having made this observation, relax and take a deep breath; then we will proceed to the nuts and bolts of monopsonist theory.

If General Griffin's pays $3 per hour at point *A* on the upward-sloping supply curve of labor in Plainsville, only 1 worker will be willing to be hired. If the monopsonist wants to hire more labor, it must offer higher wages. If the firm raises its wage offer to $6 per hour for each worker (point *B*), the quantity of labor supplied increases to 2 workers per hour. In the exhibit, the total wage cost per hour in column (3) is computed by multiplying the wage rate per hour in column (1) times the number of workers per hour in column (2). At point *A*, the total wage cost per hour is $3, which equals the wage rate. At point *B*, the total wage cost per hour rises to $12. The MFC is determined by the change in the firm's total wage cost caused by each additional hire. For example, hiring the second worker increases this labor cost from $3 to $12. The $9 difference between these costs is the MFC and is shown in column 4. Notice that among 1 and 2 workers, the $9 MFC is greater than the wage rate of $6 per hour. The explanation is that all workers are assumed to perform the same job. Consequently, the first worker will demand to be paid the same wage rate as the second worker hired at the higher wage rate. Stated differently, General Griffin's must pay a higher wage not only to each additional worker but also to all previously hired workers. If General Griffin's attempts to pay different wage rates for the same job, worker morale will deteriorate causing labor unrest. Comparing points *A* through *D* confirms that MFC is greater than the wage rate for a monopsonist, much like the monopolist's price, which is greater than the marginal revenue.

Marginal factor cost
The additional total cost resulting from a one-unit increase in the quantity of a factor.

CONCLUSION   Because the monopsonist can hire additional workers only by raising the wage rate for all workers, the marginal factor cost exceeds the wage rate.

EXHIBIT 11 A Monopsonist Determines Its Wage Rate

The monopsonist, General Griffin's, faces the industry upward-sloping supply curve of labor in the small town of Plainsville. As the wage rate rises, all workers must be paid the same higher wage. As a result, the change in total wage cost [marginal factor cost in column (4)] exceeds the wage paid to the last worker [column (1)]. The MFC curve therefore lies above the supply curve of labor.

The demand curve for labor is the marginal revenue product (MRP), or the worth to the monopsonist of each worker it hires. The intersection of the MFC and MRP curves at point *E* determines that General Griffin's hires 2 workers per hour. Because this firm has a monopsony in the Plainsville labor market, it can pay $6 per hour at point *B* on the supply curve of labor, which is enough to attract 2 workers. However, the worker is exploited because the MRP at point *E* for the second worker is $12 per hour and the wage rate is only $6. In a competitive labor market, the equilibrium would be at point *C*, and General Griffin's would pay a higher wage and employ more workers.

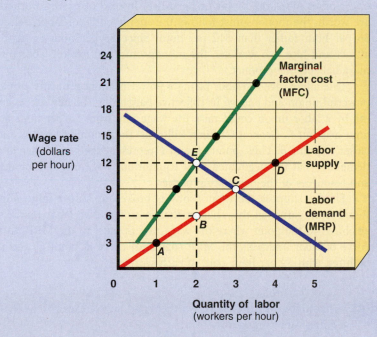

Points	(1) Wage Rate (per hour)	(2) Labor Input (workers per hour)	(3) Total Wage Cost (per hour) [(1) × (2)]	(4) Marginal Factor Cost (MFC) [Δ(3)/Δ(2)]
	$ 0	0	$ 0	
				$ 3
A	3	1	3	
				9
B	6	2	12	
				15
C	9	3	27	
				21
D	12	4	48	

11-3b Monopsonistic Equilibrium

How many workers will General Griffin's hire? To answer this question requires the demand curve for labor that traces labor's marginal revenue product (MRP), explained earlier in this chapter. Recall that MRP reflects the value or contribution of each additional worker because MRP is the increase in total revenue produced by hiring each additional worker. Also, as explained in Chapter 8, the profit-maximizing producer selects the level of output where marginal revenue equals marginal cost. Similarly, *the monopsonist in the labor market hires the quantity of labor at which the marginal revenue product of labor equals its marginal factor cost.*

In Exhibit 11, General Griffin's will follow the MRP = MFC rule by hiring 2 workers, determined by the intersection of the MRP and MFC curves at point *E*. But pay special attention to this point: The monopsonist is a "wage maker." It has labor market power and does not have to pay $12 per hour, which equals the contribution of the second worker measured by his or her MRP. Instead of paying workers what their services are worth, the monopsonist follows the supply curve of labor, selects point *B*, and pays $6 per hour rather than $12 per hour. Since $6 per hour is all the firm must pay to attract and hire two workers, the monopsonist can exploit labor by paying less than its marginal revenue product.

One alternative for labor facing a powerful monopsonistic employer is to organize a powerful union and engage in collective bargaining. Totally successful collective bargaining by a labor union could raise the wage rate from $6 per hour at point *B* to $12 per hour at point *E*. General Griffin's will resist the union's demands and offer a lower wage closer to point *B*. Thus, points *B* and *E* represent the boundaries of a potential settlement. What the negotiated final equilibrium wage rate will be depends on the tactics and resources of the negotiating parties.

Finally, suppose the monopsony is broken up into a large number of small firms. Recall from earlier in this chapter that in competitive labor markets additional workers are hired to the point where the wage rate is equal to the MRP. In this case, the supply curve of labor intersects the MRP (demand) curve at point *C*, and more workers would be hired with $9 per hour paid to each worker.

CONCLUSION

A monopsonist hires fewer workers and pays a lower wage than a firm in a competitive labor market.

CHECKPOINT

Can the Minimum Wage Create Jobs?

In Chapter 4, Exhibit 6 explained that the effect of the minimum wage in a competitive labor market is to decrease the number of unskilled workers employed. Assume the minimum wage is $9, and consider the effect on the monopsonist represented in Exhibit 11. This means by law the monopsonist cannot hire a worker for a lower wage. In the case of monopsony, contrary to the case of perfect competition, can the minimum wage increase the number of persons working? Explain your answer using Exhibit 11.

YOU'RE THE **ECONOMIST**   Applicable Concept: Monopsony

Should College Athletes Be Paid?

It was perfect football weather on a beautiful autumn Saturday at Nebraska State's stadium. There was a hush in the crowd of 80,000 as the clock showed 5 seconds left in the game and the scoreboard read Home 26 Visitor 30. The Screaming Eagles were playing the Fighting Irish, and the season was on the line. With time running out, the Eagles All-American quarterback Joe Wyoming launched a desperation pass from his 45-yard line. The pass hit the extended fingers of a wide receiver who leaped over three defenders at the Irish 25-yard line and then ran into the end zone all alone. The home crowd roared with joy after staring defeat in the face.

Aspen Photo/Shutterstock.com

So the season had been in the hands of Joe Wyoming, who received a full scholarship that cost the university more than $120,000 over four years. Because Joe led the Eagles to victory over Notre Dame, the team played in the Sugar Bowl, which paid Nebraska State $18 million for the appearance. In addition, the next year's ticket sales, alumni contributions, and trademark licensing boosted revenues $30 million, while applications for admission to the university increased sharply.

Economist Robert Brown argued that college athletes are clearly underpaid because players cannot be paid salaries under National Collegiate Athletic Association (NCAA) rules. His study estimated that a star college football player, who was drafted into the National Football League (NFL), generates a marginal revenue product of over $1,000,000 per year for the university.[1] Yet that athlete is paid only a $40,000 scholarship per year.

In Chapter 10, a cartel was explained as a group of firms that use a collusive agreement to act as a monopoly. NCAA regulations serve as a collusive agreement among colleges and universities to act as a monopsony and hire the services of college-bound athletes. Just like an output or sellers' cartel, such as the Organization of Petroleum Exporting Countries (OPEC), the NCAA must enforce the rules against cheaters.

Because this agreement holds players' wages far below their marginal revenue product, the gap creates an incentive for schools to offer "illegal" inducements of cars, money,

clothes, and trips to attract good players. Such cheating benefits the college athletes whose wages are raised closer to their marginal revenue products. A school that is not caught benefits by recruiting better players, achieving athletic success, and receiving greater sports revenue. Schools that follow the rules must depend on the NCAA to punish cheaters by taking away TV appearances, tournament play, bowl invitations, and scholarships.

In January of 2015, the NCAA's "power five" conferences passed legislation that allows universities to provide stipends to cover the cost of attendance. The exact monetary value will vary by school and other conferences are implementing payments to athletes in addition to scholarships.

ANALYZE **THE ISSUE** Do you favor paying college athletes salaries determined by a competitive labor market rather than by an NCAA agreement? Explain.

---

1. Robert Brown, "Research Note: Estimates of College Football Player Rents," *Journal of Sports Economics*, 2011, 12 (2), pp. 200–212.

CHECKPOINT

If You Don't like It, Mickey, Take Your Bat and Go Home
Mickey Mantle described his salary negotiations with the Yankees in his autobiography *The Mick*. After winning baseball's Triple Crown in 1956, his salary increased from about $85,000 to $100,000. The next season, he raised his batting average even higher, and the Yankee team owner offered him a pay cut. What is the most likely explanation for the owner's behavior—an increase in the supply of star baseball players, owner's monopsony power, or the owner's desire that Mantle find another team?

Key Concepts

Marginal revenue product (MRP)

Demand curve for labor

Derived demand

Supply curve of labor

Human capital

Collective bargaining

Monopsony

Marginal factor cost (MFC)

Summary

- **Marginal revenue product (MRP)** is determined by a worker's contribution to a firm's total revenue. Algebraically, the marginal revenue product equals the price of the product times the worker's marginal product: $MRP = P \times MP$.

- The **demand curve for labor** shows the quantities of labor a firm is willing to hire at different prices of labor. The marginal revenue product (MRP) of labor curve is the firm's demand curve for labor. Summing individual firm's demand for labor curves gives the market demand curve for labor.

- **Derived demand** is the demand for labor and other factors of production that depends on the consumer demand for the goods and services the factors produce. Changes in consumer demand for a product cause changes in the demand for labor and for other resources used to make the product.

- The **supply curve of labor** shows the quantities of workers willing to work at different prices of labor. The market supply curve of labor is derived by adding the individual supply curves of labor.

Demand Curve for Labor

[A graph titled "Demand Curve for Labor" with Wage rate (dollars per day) on the vertical axis ranging from 70 to 350, and Quantity of labor (workers per day) on the horizontal axis from 0 to 5. A downward-sloping line labeled "MRP = demand" passes through points A (1, 350), B (2, 280), C (3, 210), D (4, 140), and E (5, 70). Horizontal dashed lines mark "Initial wage rate" at 280 and "New wage rate" at 140.]

Supply Curve of Labor

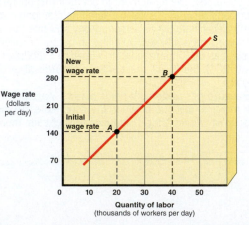

- **Human capital** is the accumulated investment people make in education, training, experience, and a level of good health that makes them more productive. One explanation for earnings differences is differences in human capital.

- **Collective bargaining** is the process through which a union and management negotiate a labor contract.

- **Monopsony** is a labor market in which a single firm hires labor. Because the monopsonist faces the market supply curve of labor and each worker is paid the same wage, changes in total wage cost exceed the wage rate necessary to hire each additional worker. As a result, the **marginal factor cost (MFC)** of labor curve, which measures changes in total wage cost per worker, lies above the supply curve of labor. The monopsonist's wage rate and quantity of labor are determined

where the MFC equals MRP. Since at this point the worker's MRP is greater than the wage paid, the monopsonist exploits workers.

Monopsony

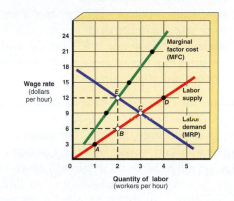

Summary of Conclusion Statements

- A perfectly competitive firm's marginal revenue product is equal to the marginal product of its labor times the price of its product. Expressed as a formula: MRP = P × MP

- A firm hires additional workers up to the point where the MRP equals the wage rate.

- Because the monopsonist can hire additional workers only by raising the wage rate for all workers, the marginal factor cost exceeds the wage rate.

- A monopsonist hires fewer workers and pays a lower wage than a firm in a competitive labor market.

Study Questions and Problems

Please see Appendix A for answers to the odd-numbered questions. Your instructor has access to the answers for even-numbered questions.

1. Consider this statement: "Workers demand jobs, and employers supply jobs." Do you agree or disagree? Explain.

2. The Zippy Paper Company has no control over either the price of paper or the wage it pays its workers. The following table shows the relationship between the number of workers Zippy hires and total output:

Labor Input (workers per day)	Total Output (boxes of paper per day)
0	0
1	15
2	27
3	36
4	43
5	48
6	51

Assuming the selling price is $10 per box, answer the following questions:

a. What is the marginal revenue product (MRP) of each worker?

b. How many workers will Zippy hire if the wage rate is $100 per day?

c. How many workers will Zippy hire if the wage rate is $75 per day?

d. Assume the wage rate is $75 per day and the price of a box of paper is $20. How many workers will Zippy hire?

3. Assume the Grand Slam Baseball Store sells $100 worth of baseball cards each day, with 1 employee operating the store. The owner decides to hire a second worker, and the 2 workers together sell $150 worth of baseball cards. What is the second worker's marginal product (MP)? If the price per card sold is $5, what is the second worker's marginal revenue product (MRP)?

4. What is the relationship between the marginal revenue product (MRP) and the demand curve for labor?

5. The market supply curve of labor is upward sloping, but the supply curve of labor for a single firm is horizontal. Explain why.

6. Assume the labor market for loggers is perfectly competitive. How would each of the following events influence the wage rate loggers are paid?

a. Consumers boycott products made with wood.

b. Loggers form a union that requires longer apprenticeships, charges high fees, and uses other devices designed to reduce union membership.

7. How does a human capital investment in education increase your lifetime earnings?

8. Suppose states pass laws requiring public school teachers to have a master's degree in order to retain their teaching certificates. What effect would this legislation have on the labor market for teachers?

9. Use the data in question 2, and assume the equilibrium wage rate is $90 per day, determined in a perfectly competitive labor market. Now explain the impact of a union-negotiated collective bargaining agreement that changes the wage rate to $100 per day.

10. Some economists argue that the American Medical Association and the American Bar Association create an effect on labor markets similar to that of a labor union. Do you agree?

11. Assume the Jaguars were in the process of hiring players. Using the following hypothetical table of data, construct a graph to determine the number of quarterbacks the Jaguars hired and the salary paid to each quarterback. Assuming the labor market was competitive, what would be the number of quarterbacks hired and the salary each was paid?

(1) Salary (thousands of dollars)	(2) Number of quarterbacks	(3) Total cost of quarterbacks (thousands of dollars)	(4) Marginal factor cost (MFC) (thousands of dollars)	(5) Marginal revenue product (MRP) (thousands of dollars)
$ 0	0	$ 0	–	–
100	1	100	$100	$700
200	2	400	300	600
300	3	900	500	500
400	4	1,600	700	400
500	5	2,500	900	300

✓ **CHECKPOINT ANSWERS**

Where Should Toyota Build the Factory?

Among the seven states listed in Exhibit 10, South Carolina has the lowest unionization rate at only 1.6 percent. If you said that Toyota should build its new plant in South Carolina to maximize its profits, **YOU ARE CORRECT**.

Can the Minimum Wage Create Jobs?

The minimum wage of $9 corresponds to point C in Exhibit 11. At this point, the labor supply and labor demand (MRP) curves intersect. Thus, the effect of the minimum wage is to force the monopsonist to operate at the equilibrium that would be established in a competitive labor market. If you said that under monopsony the minimum wage could raise the wage rate and create additional employment, **YOU ARE CORRECT**.

If You Don't like It, Mickey, Take Your Bat and Go Home

Baseball players had no free-agent rights in the 1950s. If Mantle did not like the salary offer, his only choice was to go back to his home in Oklahoma. Faced with that alternative, he accepted the salary cut. If you said the team owner achieved monopsony power by prohibiting players from going to another team, **YOU ARE CORRECT**.

Sample Quiz

Please see Appendix B for answers to Sample Quiz questions.

1. Alan Jones owns a company that sells life insurance. When he employs 10 salespersons, his firm sells $200,000 worth of contracts per week, and when he employs 11 salespersons, total revenue is $210,000. The marginal revenue product of the 11th salesperson is
   a. $410,000.
   b. $10,000.
   c. $20,000.
   d. $210,000.

2. The demand for labor is
   a. derived demand.
   b. featherbedding demand.
   c. marginal utility demand.
   d. All of the answers above are correct.

3. In which of the following years did the U.S. have the highest percentage of its labor force unionized?
   a. 2016
   b. 1970
   c. 1945
   d. 1930

4. Which of the following statements is *true*?
   a. Derived demand for labor depends on the demand for the product labor produces.
   b. Unions can either increase demand or decrease the supply of labor.
   c. Investment in human capital is expected to increase the demand for those workers.
   d. All the answers above are correct.

5. In a perfectly competitive labor market, the optimal hiring rule is to employ labor up to the point where
   a. wage = MFC.
   b. wage = MP.
   c. wage = MR.
   d. wage = MRP.

6. In Exhibit 12, when the marginal revenue product is $20, firms should
   a. continue hiring.
   b. stop hiring.
   c. start firing.
   d. pay a wage above $15 to its workers.

EXHIBIT 12 A Perfectly Competitive Labor Market

Quantity of labor (thousands)	Marginal revenue product	Total labor cost
5	$25	$ 5
10	20	10
15	15	15
20	10	20
25	5	25

7. In Exhibit 12, how many thousands of workers are the firms willing to hire?
   a. 20
   b. 10
   c. 25
   d. 15

8. What happens to the MP of labor when the market price of the good produced increases?
   a. Increases proportional to price
   b. Decreases proportional to price
   c. Stays the same
   d. Falls because quantity demanded falls

9. A union can influence the demand for labor by
   a. requiring union fees.
   b. raising union fees.
   c. using effective advertising that convinces customers to buy the "union label."
   d. doing all of the above.

10. A union can influence the equilibrium wage rate by
   a. collective bargaining.
   b. featherbedding.
   c. lobbying for legislation to reduce immigration.
   d. doing all of the above.

11. Which of the following states has the largest union membership measured as the percentage of civilian employees in unions?
   a. Michigan
   b. Illinois
   c. New Mexico
   d. New York

12. Suppose a firm can hire 100 workers at $8.00 per hour but must pay $8.05 per hour to hire 101 workers. Marginal factor cost (MFC) for the 101st worker is approximately equal to
   a. $8.00.
   b. $8.05.
   c. $13.05.
   d. $13.00.

EXHIBIT 13 A Labor Market

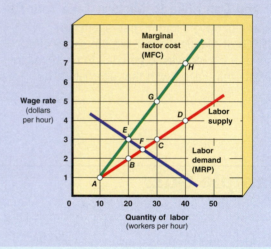

13. If the labor market shown in Exhibit 13 is competitive, the wage rate and number of workers employed will be determined at point
   a. A.
   b. B.
   c. C.
   d. D.
   e. F.

14. If the labor market shown in Exhibit 13 is a monopsony, the wage rate and number of workers employed will be determined at point
   a. A.
   b. B.
   c. C.
   d. D.
   e. F.

15. Which of the following is *true* for a monopsonist?
    a. wage > TWC
    b. wage > MFC
    c. wage = MFC
    d. wage = MRP
    e. wage < MFC

16. A technological advance that increases the productivity of teachers can be expected to have what effects on the equilibrium labor market for teachers?
    a. Wages will rise, and quantity of labor will fall.
    b. Wages will rise, and quantity of labor will rise.
    c. Wages will fall, and quantity of labor will fall.
    d. Wages will fall, and quantity of labor will rise.
    e. Wages and quantity of labor will remain the same.

17. In Exhibit 14, the marginal factor cost of the tenth employee is
    a. $23.
    b. $19.
    c. $25.
    d. $21.

18. A technological advance that increases labor productivity will
    a. lower wages.
    b. decrease the demand for labor as fewer workers are needed.

EXHIBIT 14 Labor and Wage Rate Data

Labor	Wage
6	$12
7	13
8	14
9	15
10	16

c. decrease the supply of labor as fewer workers are needed.
d. increase the demand for labor as MP rises.
e. decrease the demand for labor as MP falls.

19. A monopsonist's marginal factor cost (MFC) curve lies above its supply curve because the firm must
    a. lower the factor price to hire more.
    b. increase the price of its product to sell more.
    c. increase the factor price to hire more.
    d. lower the product price to sell more.

20. In Exhibit 14, the marginal factor cost of the eighth employee is
    a. $14.
    b. $13.
    c. $21.
    d. $23.
    e. $112.

PART 3
Market Structures

This road map feature helps you tie together material in the part as you travel the Economic Way of Thinking Highway. The following are review questions listed by chapter from the previous part. The key concept in each question is given for emphasis, and each question or set of questions concludes with an interactive game to reinforce the concepts. The correct answers to the multiple choice questions are given in Appendix C. If your instructor has included MindTap in your course, visit MindTap to play the interactive Causation Chain Game.

Chapter 8: Perfect Competition

1. Key Concept: Short-Run Shutdown Point

Suppose product price is fixed at $24, MR = MC at Q = 200, AFC = $6, AVC = $25. What do you advise this firm to do?

a. Increase output.
b. Decrease output.
c. Shut down operations.
d. Stay at the current output; the firm is earning a profit of $1,400.
e. Stay at the current output; the firm is losing $1,400.

CAUSATION CHAIN GAME
The Short-Run Shutdown Point—Exhibit 6

2. Key Concept: Long-Run Equilibrium

Consider a firm operating with the following: price = 10, MR = 10, MC = 10, ATC = 10. This firm is

a. making an economic profit of 10.
b. an example of monopolistic competition.
c. going to go out of business in the long run.
d. a monopolist for a product with a relatively inelastic demand.
e. perfectly competitive in long-run equilibrium.

CAUSATION CHAIN GAME
Long-Run Perfectly Competitive Equilibrium—Exhibit 10

3. Key Concept: Constant-Cost Industry

Assume the short-run average total cost for a perfectly competitive industry remains constant as the output of the industry expands. In the long run, the industry supply curve will

a. have a positive slope.
b. have a negative slope.
c. be perfectly horizontal.
d. be perfectly vertical.

CAUSATION CHAIN GAME
Long-Run Supply in a Constant-Cost Industry—Exhibit 11

4. Key Concept: Decreasing-Cost Industry

Assume the short-run average total cost for a perfectly competitive industry decreases as the output of the industry expands. In the long run, the industry supply curve will

a. have a positive slope.
b. have a negative slope.
c. be perfectly horizontal.
d. be perfectly vertical.

CAUSATION CHAIN GAME
Long-Run Supply in Decreasing-Cost Industry—Exhibit 12

5. Key Concept: Increasing-Cost Industry

Suppose that, in the long run, the price of feature films rises as the movie production industry expands. We can conclude that movie production is a(an)

a. increasing-cost industry.
b. constant-cost industry.
c. decreasing-cost industry.
d. marginal-cost industry.

CAUSATION CHAIN GAME
Long-Run Supply in an Increasing-Cost Industry—Exhibit 13

Chapter 9: Monopoly

6. Key Concept: Profit Maximization

Assume a monopolist's marginal cost and marginal revenue curves intersect and the demand curve passes above its average total cost curve. The firm will

a. make an economic profit.
b. stay in operation in the short run, but shut down in the long run.
c. shut down in the short run.
d. lower the price.

7. Key Concept: Price discrimination

Suppose there are two markets for college football games, and each market contains the same number of potential consumers. The first market consists of rich alumni, and the second market is made up of low-income students. Based on this information, which group will be charged a higher price for football tickets?

a. students.
b. Alumni.
c. Students and alumni will be charged equal prices.
d. Cannot be determined.

CAUSATION CHAIN GAME
Profit Maximization and Loss Minimization—Exhibits 4 and 5

Chapter 10: Monopolistic Competition and Oligopoly

8. Key Concept: Long-Run Monopolistic Competition

In the long run, the economic profits of Hoot's Chicken 'n' Ribs, a monopolistic competitor, are

a. not eliminated, because competition is not perfect.
b. not eliminated, because the demand curve slopes downward.
c. eliminated due to firms entering the industry.
d. eliminated due to firms leaving the industry.
e. not eliminated, because firms cannot enter the industry.

CAUSATION CHAIN GAME
A Monopolistically Competitive Firm in the Long Run—Exhibit 3

Chapter 11: Labor Markets

9. Key Concept: Market Supply Curve of Labor

Which of the following statements concerning the supply of labor is true?

a. The supply curve of labor shifts when the prevailing wage rate changes.
b. The labor supply curve is downward sloping.
c. The wage rate has no effect on the quantity of labor supplied.
d. None of the answers above are correct.

CAUSATION CHAIN GAME
The Market Supply Curve of Labor—Exhibit 3

10. Key Concept: Increase in Demand for Labor

Featherbedding allows unions to increase wages by

a. limiting the supply of labor.
b. increasing firms' demand for labor.
c. forcing firms to accept higher-than-equilibrium wages.
d. reducing labor share of payroll taxes.

CAUSATION CHAIN GAME
A Union Causes an Increase in the Demand Curve for Labor—Exhibit 5

11. Key Concept: Decrease in Supply of Labor

Which of the following statements is true?

a. Derived demand for labor depends on the demand for the product labor produces.
b. Unions can either increase demand or decrease the supply of labor.
c. Investment in human capital is expected to increase the demand for those workers.
d. All of the answers above are correct.

CAUSATION CHAIN GAME
A Union Causes a Decrease in the Supply Curve of Labor—Exhibit 6

PART 4

Microeconomics Policy Issues

These three chapters apply micro principles learned in previous chapters to explore policy issues concerning some important economic topics. The first chapter in this part extends the theory of labor markets into an examination of actual data on income distribution and poverty. The second chapter mixes politics and economic theory to discuss such interesting topics as the Microsoft case and the deregulation of energy. The third chapter takes a closer look at ways to deal with externalities, such as pollution permits, which are actually traded on the Chicago Board of Trade.

CHAPTER 12

Income Distribution, Poverty, and Discrimination

CHAPTER PREVIEW

The previous chapter examined how variations in wages are determined in competitive and monopsonistic labor markets. These labor supply and demand models do not give the complete picture of labor markets. In this chapter, we turn our attention to the distribution of income, poverty, and discrimination, which are important topics related to labor market wage decisions. The chapter begins by exploring the controversial issue of how the national income "pie" is cut into various size "slices" or shares for different groups of families. You will examine government data that indicate the trend over the years in the share of income for the richest fifth of the population and the poorest fifth. Here the hotly contested issue of whether the "rich got richer" at the expense of the poor is addressed. In addition, the inequality of income in the United States is compared to that of other countries.

Poverty is an unhappy consequence of an unequal income distribution. Eighteenth-century English poet and essayist Samuel Johnson stated, "A decent provision for the poor is the true test of civilization." One purpose of this chapter is to define poverty and who are the poor. Another objective is to discuss government programs that aid the poor and provide criticisms of these programs. A special feature concerns the important issue of Social Security, past, present, and future.

The chapter concludes with the subject of discrimination, which is one possible explanation for unequal income distribution and poverty. Here you will apply the supply and demand model to explain why women earn less on average than men and African Americans earn less than whites.

IN THIS CHAPTER, YOU WILL LEARN TO SOLVE THESE ECONOMICS PUZZLES:

- Could the rich become richer and other income groups also become better off?

- How can a negative income tax solve the welfare controversy?

- Is pay for females fair?

12-1 THE DISTRIBUTION OF INCOME

One function of labor markets is to determine the *distribution of income*—that is, how wages and salaries are divided among members of society. Recall from Chapter 2 that the *For Whom* question is one of the three basic questions that any economic system must answer. Here we study the *For Whom* question in more detail.

12-1a Trends in Income Distribution

One way to analyze the distribution of income in the United States is illustrated in Exhibit 1. In column 1 of this exhibit, families are divided into six groups according to the percentage of the total annual money income they received. The remaining columns of the table give the percentages of the total money income for each of the six groups in selected years since 1929. These data reveal changes in the distribution of income among families over time. For example, families with income in the top 5 percent in 1929 earned about 9 percentage points more of the total income pie than they did in 2016. However, there is concern that since 1970 the percentage of income received by families in the lowest 20 percent group has fallen, while the income percentages received by the families in the highest fifth and the highest 5 percent have risen.

As shown in Exhibit 1, there is an unequal distribution of income among families. Why didn't each fifth of the families receive 20 percent of the total income? There are many reasons. For example, Exhibit 2 reveals that families headed by a college graduate fare better than those headed by an individual with less education. Recall from the previous chapter that human capital refers to education and skills that increase a worker's productivity. Workers with a greater investment in human capital are likely to be worth more to an employer. Data in this exhibit also indicate that families headed by a male generally earn more than those headed by a female.

12-1b Equality versus Efficiency

Because the data presented in Exhibits 1 and 2 show that an unequal distribution of income exists in the United States, the normative question to be debated concerns the pros and cons of a more equal income distribution. Those who favor greater equality

EXHIBIT 1 The Division of Total Annual Money Income among Families, 1929–2016

Percentage of families	1929	1947	1970	1980	1990	2016
Highest 5%	30%	18%	16%	15%	17%	21%
Highest fifth	54	43	41	41	44	49
Second-highest fifth	19	23	24	24	24	23
Middle fifth	14	17	18	18	17	15
Second-lowest fifth	9	12	12	12	11	9
Lowest fifth	4	5	5	5	5	4

SOURCE: U.S. Bureau of the Census, Historical Income Tables, https://census.gov/data/tables/time-series/demo/income-poverty/historical-income-families.html, Table F-2.

EXHIBIT 2   Median Money Income of Families, 2016

Characteristic	Median income*
All families	$70,697
Families headed by a male	49,772
Families headed by a female	34,126
Families with head aged 25–34 years	56,775
Families with head aged 65 years and over	57,360
Families headed by person with less than 9th-grade education	35,542
Families headed by a high school graduate	52,906
Families headed by a person with at least a bachelor's degree	111,270

*Fifty percent of families earn less than the median income and 50 percent earn more.

SOURCE: U.S. Bureau of the Census, Historical Income Tables, https://census.gov/data/tables/time-series/demo/income-poverty/historical-income-families.html, Tables F-7, F-11, and F-18.

fear the link between the rich and political power. The wealthy may well use their money to influence national policies that benefit the rich. It is also argued that income inequality results in unequal opportunities for various groups. For example, children of the poor have difficulty obtaining a college education. Consequently, their underutilized productive capacity is a waste of human capital. The poor are also unable to afford health care, and this is a national concern.

Advocates of income inequality pose this question. Suppose you had your choice of living in egalitarian society *A,* where every person earns $40,000 a year, or society *B,* where 20 percent earn $100,000 and 80 percent earn $30,000. You may likely choose society *B* because the incentive to earn more and live better is worth the risk of earning less and living worse. After all, why is the average income higher in society *B*? The answer is that income inequality gives people an incentive to be productive. In contrast, people in society *A* lack such motivation because everyone earns the same income. Although no one argues that every worker should earn the same amount, the point is that some people believe income inequality is not necessary for workers to be motivated. They believe motivation can come from nonmonetary incentives, such as pride in one's work or in one's nation. Moreover, they point to concerns surrounding notions of fairness, human dignity, and economic security.

A frequently debated topic concerning income inequality is whether the "rich are getting richer." As we observed earlier, the data in Exhibit 1 reveal that the percentages of total income received by the highest 5 percent and the highest fifth have increased in recent decades, while the percentages received by each of the fifths below the highest decreased slightly.

CONCLUSION   Measured by distribution of family money income, the richest families as a group have become a little richer and the rest of the family groups a little poorer in recent decades.

It is important to note that simply observing changes in income distribution over time does not tell the whole story. Exhibit 3 traces real median family income, adjusted for rising prices, for the period 1980–2016. This measure indicates the trend of the median level of income received by all groups. The overall trend for real median income since the 1980s has been upward. This means the size of the income "pie" grew, and, therefore, all of the slices grew larger. However, consistent with the distribution data in Exhibit 1, the relative share of the pie for those with the biggest slices grew slightly larger. In 2000, real median income reached a new high before falling following the recession of 2001 and the Great Recession of 2007–2009. The trend has reversed and is rising again in recent years.

12-1c **The Lorenz Curve**

The distribution of income data presented in Exhibit 1 can be represented by the Lorenz curve. The **Lorenz curve** is a graph of the actual cumulative distribution of income compared to a perfectly equal cumulative distribution of income. This curve is a primary

Lorenz curve
A graph of the actual cumulative distribution of income compared to a perfectly equal cumulative distribution of income.

EXHIBIT 3 Real Median Family Income, 1980–2016

Real median income measures the income adjusted for inflation received by all families in the United States. Fifty percent of families earn less and 50 percent earn more than the median income. The trend of this measure was generally upward until 2000. In 2000, real median income reached a new high before falling during the recession of 2001 and the Great Recession of 2007–2009. The long-term upward trend has returned in recent years. In 2016, median family income increased over the previous year to $70,697.

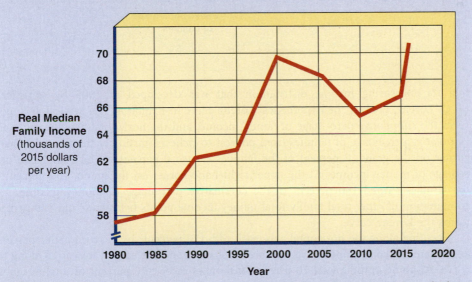

SOURCE: U.S. Bureau of the Census, Historical Income Tables, http://www.census.gov/hhes/www/income/income.html, Table F-7.

EXHIBIT 4 A Hypothetical Lorenz Curve

The Lorenz curve shows the cumulative percentage of money income earned from 0 to 100 percent by the cumulative percentage of families, also from 0 to 100 percent. If the income distribution follows the 45-degree perfect equality line, 20 percent of the families earn 20 percent of total money income, 40 percent receive 40 percent of total money income, and so on. The shaded area between the perfect equality line and the Lorenz curve measures the degree of inequality in the distribution of income. The more the Lorenz curve is bowed outward, the more unequal the distribution of income is.

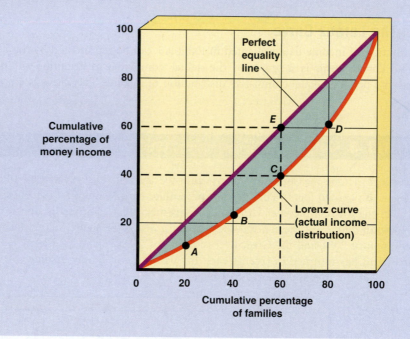

tool for measuring income distribution that was developed in 1905 by statistician M. O. Lorenz. Look at the hypothetical Lorenz curve in Exhibit 4. The vertical axis measures the *cumulative* percentage of family income, and the horizontal axis measures the *cumulative* percentage of families from poorest to richest. Starting at the lower left-hand corner on the graph, 0 percent of the families earned 0 percent of the cumulative percentage of money income. At the upper right-hand corner on the graph, 100 percent of the families earned 100 percent of the cumulative percentage of money income. The combination of other total family-total money income points between 0 and 100 percent forms the Lorenz curve.

Reading along the horizontal axis, each fifth (20 percent) of the cumulative percentage of families corresponds to its cumulative share of income earned measured along the curve. At point *A*, the lowest 20 percent of families receive 10 percent of total or cumulative income. To read this, go from the 20 percent point on the horizontal axis up to point *A* on the Lorenz curve. Then draw a horizontal line to the vertical axis, and read that it intersects this axis at 10 percent. Point *B* is interpreted as the lowest 40 percent of families earning 10 percent plus 15 percent, which equals a cumulative share of 25 percent. Similarly, point *C* is the cumulative share earned by the lowest 60 percent of families, which equals 40 percent. Finally, point *D* is a bit tricky to interpret. At this point, the lowest 80 percent of families receive about 62 percent of total income. And here is the twist. You must interpret that the richest 20 percent of families earn 38 percent of income (100 percent – 62 percent).

We now turn to the 45-degree line above the Lorenz curve that cuts the box in half. This line represents perfect equality: 20 percent of the families receive 20 percent of total income, 40 percent of the families receive 40 percent of total income, and so on. The distance of the Lorenz curve from the perfect equality line is therefore a measure of unequal income distribution. The gap between points *C* and *E*, for example, indicates that 60 percent of families earn 20 percent less of total income than required for perfect equality. Similar measurements generate the shaded area between the Lorenz curve and the perfect equality line. Thus, the shaded area is a measure of the degree of income inequality for our hypothetical data. A larger shaded area would mean greater income inequality, and the shape of the Lorenz curve would become more bowed outward. A smaller shaded area would represent a more equal income distribution, and the Lorenz curve would be a flatter curve.

It is important to note that there are limitations associated with using money income statistics. Such data are not adjusted for government-provided food stamps, medical care, housing, or other goods and services. Money income also reflects income before taxes and does not measure unreported income. At the same time, the Lorenz curve makes no mention of wealth distribution. Wealth, or the accumulated value of assets, is much more unequally distributed in the population than is income. Still, used carefully, the Lorenz curve is a convenient tool for visualizing the degree of income inequality.

12-1d Income Distribution Trend in the United States

In Exhibit 1, we looked at income distributions for selected years between 1929 and 2016. What can we conclude from these data using the Lorenz curve? Has the overall income distribution become more or less equal? The table in Exhibit 5 restates the income share data for 1929 and 2016 from Exhibit 1, and the cumulative percentage shares of families of quintiles are calculated from the percentage shares.

Exhibit 5 suggests that overall money income distribution has changed little over the period. In the exhibit, there is only a small shaded area between the 1929 and 2016 Lorenz curves. However, the share of income received by the highest fifth of families fell from 54 percent in 1929 to 49 percent in 2016. Note that comparing other years can lead to different conclusions. For example, as shown in Exhibit 1, the distribution of income is less equal than it was in 1970.

CONCLUSION

The Lorenz curve has shifted only slightly inward, and therefore closer to the perfect equality line between 1929 and 2016.

12-1e Global Comparisons of Income Distribution

How does the distribution of income in the United States compare with that of other countries? Exhibit 6 presents separate Lorenz curves for the United States, Norway, and

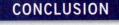

GLOBAL ECONOMICS

EXHIBIT 5 Lorenz Curves for Family Income Distribution in the United States, 1929 and 2016

Since 1929, the Lorenz curve has shifted somewhat inward toward the perfect equality line. Thus, there has been a reduction in the inequality of distribution of family money income since 1929.

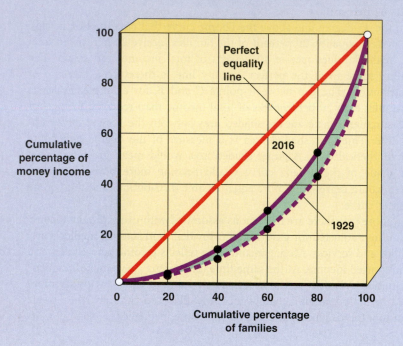

Percentage of families	1929		2016	
	Percentage share	Cumulative share	Percentage share	Cumulative share
Lowest fifth	4%	4%	4%	4%
Second-lowest fifth	9	13	9	13
Middle fifth	14	27	15	28
Second-highest fifth	19	46	23	51
Highest fifth	54	100	49	100

Brazil. This exhibit indicates that the degree of income inequality in the United States exceeds that of Norway. On the other hand, income distribution is more equal in the United States than in Brazil. In general, the distribution of income in developed nations, such as the United States, Germany, Italy, and Sweden, is more equal than in developing nations, such as Brazil, Mexico, and Zimbabwe.

EXHIBIT 6 Lorenz Curves for Selected Countries

Comparing Lorenz curves for the United States, Norway, and Brazil reveals that income is distributed more equally in Norway than in the United States and Brazil. As illustrated by the Lorenz curve for Brazil, income inequality is usually greater in less-developed countries.

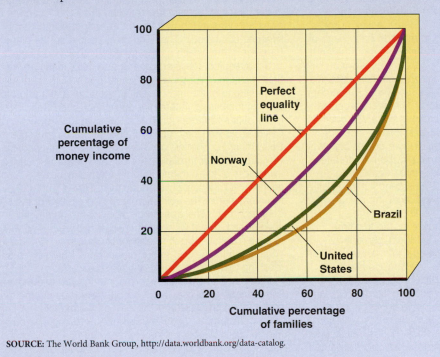

SOURCE: The World Bank Group, http://data.worldbank.org/data-catalog.

12-2 POVERTY

Having discussed the broader question of how the degree of income distribution inequality is measured, we now turn the spotlight on the fiercely debated issue of poverty. We are all disturbed by homelessness and hungry children. How can poverty exist in a nation of abundance such as the United States? Can economists offer useful ideas to reform and improve our current welfare system? Most of the nation agrees that the welfare system must undergo reforms to reduce poverty, cut welfare dependency, and save taxpayers money. The first step to understanding the problem is to ask this question: Who is poor?

12-2a Defining Poverty

What is poverty? Is it eating Spam when others are eating steak? Or is poverty a family having one car when others have two or more? Indeed, the term *poverty* is difficult to define. A person whose income is comparatively low in the United States may be viewed as being well off in a less-developed country. Or what we in the United States regard as poverty today might have seemed to be a life of luxury 200 years ago.

YOU'RE THE ECONOMIST

Pulling Back the Curtain on Income and Wealth Distribution

The reward for working hard and innovating is necessary for a well-functioning economy. But, when does income and wealth inequality become a problem? Here's a look at the amount of income one would have to make to be in each of the income quintiles in 2015, and to be in the top 5 percent, top 1 percent and top 0.1 percent:[1]

Income inequality has been on the rise in recent decades. "In 1928, the top 1 percent of families received 23.9 percent of all pretax income, while the bottom 90 percent received 50.7 percent. By 1944 the top 1 percent's share was down to 11.3 percent, while the bottom 90 percent were receiving 67.5 percent, levels that would remain more or less constant for the next three decades. But starting in the mid- to late 1970s, the uppermost tier's income share began rising dramatically, while that of the bottom 90 percent started to fall. By 2012, the top 1 percent group was receiving nearly 22.5 percent of all pretax income, while the bottom 90 percent's share is below 50 percent for the first time ever. For the United States overall, the top 1 percent captured 85.1 percent of total income growth between 2009 and 2013. In 2013 the top 1 percent of families nationally made 25.3 times as much as the bottom 99 percent."[2] CEO compensation was around 30 times greater than the average pay of their employees in 1978. Now it is around 300 times greater.

Wealth (the value of assets, like stock, bonds, real estate and other things of value) is even more unequally distributed than income and is also becoming increasingly concentrated in the hands of the very few. All told, the top 0.1 percent now owns about as much wealth as the bottom 90 percent of America combined.[3] The 80 richest people on the planet have the same wealth as the poorest 3.5 billion people.[4]

As a result of these staggering numbers, many are voicing their concerns over growing income and wealth inequality. Perhaps one of the most vocal economists in the effort to combat increasing income inequality is Robert Reich, Chancellor's Professor of Public Policy at the University of California at Berkeley, Senior Fellow at the Blum Center for Developing Economies, and former Secretary of Labor under President Clinton. Professor Reich has sought to increase awareness of the dangers income inequality poses to our economy for the last several decades. He said in a 2014 testimony before the Joint Economic Committee of the U.S. Congress that, "The question is not whether inequality is good or bad. It is at what point inequality becomes so wide as to pose a serious threat to economic growth, to our ideal of equal opportunity, and to our democracy. I believe we are reaching that tipping point, or have already reached it."[5]

According to Robert Reich income inequality threatens our economy because when people have less income to spend, spending falls and the economy contracts. "We cannot have a growing economy without a growing and buoyant middle class. We cannot have a growing middle class if almost all of the economic gains go to the top 1 percent."

Lowest 20%	Second Lowest 20%	Middle 20%	Second highest 20%	Highest 20%	Highest 5%	Highest 1%	Highest 0.1%
<$30,000	$30,000–$55,000	$55,000–$86,000	$86,000–$134,000	>$134,000	>$240,000	>$429,000	>$1,900,000

There are two views of poverty. One defines poverty in *absolute* terms, and the other defines poverty in *relative* terms. Absolute poverty can be defined as a dollar figure that represents some level of income per year required to purchase some minimum amount of goods and services essential to meeting a person's or a family's basic needs. In contrast, relative poverty might be defined as a level of income that places a person or family in the lowest, say, 20 percent of all persons or families receiving incomes. An unequal distribution of income guarantees that some persons or families will occupy in relative terms the bottom rung of the income ladder. The U.S. government first established an official definition of the poverty line in 1964. The **poverty line** is the level of

Poverty line
The level of income below which a person or a family is considered to be poor.

Equal opportunity can be threatened because it becomes more difficult for people to move up the economic ladder. Moreover, he argues, democracy itself may be at stake "as income and wealth flow upward, political power follows. Money flowing to political campaigns, lobbyists, think tanks, 'expert' witnesses and media campaigns buys disproportionate influence."[6]

What has caused the growing gap between the rich and poor and the shrinking middle class in the last 30 years? Professor Reich points to technological advances and globalization that have put downward pressure on wages, keeping them low—even as the productivity of workers has grown. "Instead of responding to these gale-force winds with policies designed to upgrade the skills of Americans, modernize our infrastructure, strengthen our safety net and adapt the workforce—and pay for much of this with higher taxes on the wealthy—we did the reverse. We began disinvesting in education, job training and infrastructure. We began shredding our safety net. We made it harder for many Americans to join unions. (The decline in unionization directly correlates with the decline of the portion of income going to the middle class.) And we reduced taxes on the wealthy…We also deregulated."[7]

What to do? According to Secretary Reich, we should:

- Raise the minimum wage.
- Unionize low-wage workers.
- Invest in education.
- Invest in infrastructure.
- Pay for these investments with higher taxes on the wealthy.
- Make the payroll tax progressive.
- Raise the estate tax and eliminate the "stepped-up basis" for determining capital gains at death.
- Constrain Wall Street.
- Give all Americans a share in future economic gains.
- Get big money out of politics.

What is a "fair" distribution of income and wealth is a normative issue that equally reasonable people can disagree over. If you believe this is a problem, then it will likely take some time to turn this ship around, even if there is agreement on what needs to be done and there's the political will to take the necessary steps to do so.

ANALYZE THE ISSUE

1. What would happen to the Lorenz curve if it also included wealth distribution?

2. Do you think income and wealth are fairly or unfairly distributed? Should we be concerned with this issue? If you think we should be concerned with growing income and wealth inequality, what remedies would you recommend?

---

1. U.S. Census Bureau, Historical Income Tables, https://census.gov/data/tables/time-series/demo/income-poverty/historical-income-families.html and Economic Policy Institute, http://www.epi.org/publication/income-inequality-in-the-us/, and Business Insider, http://www.businessinsider.com/top-one-percent-every-us-state-2016-11/#-1

2. Estelle Sommeiller, Mark Price and Ellis Wazeter, "Income inequality in the U.S. by State, Metropolitan area, and county, Economic Policy Institute, June 16, 2016, http://www.epi.org/publication/income-inequality-in-the-us/ and drew desilver, U.S. income inequality, on rise for decades, is now highest since 1928." Pew research center, http://www.pewresearch.org/fact-tank/2013/12/05/u-s-income-inequality-on-rise-for-decades-is-now-highest-since-1928/.

3. The economist, November 6, 2014, http://www.economist.com/news/finance-and-economics/21631129-it-001-who-are-really-getting-ahead-america-forget-1.

4. Faith Karim, "Wealthiest 1% will soon own more than rest of us combined, Oxfam Says." CNN, January 19, 2015, http://www.cnn.com/2015/01/19/world/wealth-inequality/index.html.

5. https://www.jec.senate.gov/public/_cache/files/3455c373-7557-4581-8cd8-34b43b759f53/reich-testimony.pdf.

6. http://robertreich.org/post/85532751265.

7. ibid.

income below which a person or a family is considered poor. The poverty line is defined in absolute terms: It is based on the cost of a minimal diet multiplied by three because it is assumed low-income families should spend about one-third of their income on food. In 1964, the poverty income level for a family of four was $3,000 ($750 for food × 4). Since 1969, the poverty line figure has been adjusted upward each year for inflation. In 1992, for example, the official poverty income level was $13,400 or below for a family of four. In 2017, a family of four needed an income of $24,600 to clear the poverty threshold.

Exhibit 7(a) shows the percentage of all persons in the U.S. population below the poverty level, beginning with 1959. The poverty rate for all persons was on a downward

EXHIBIT 7 Persons below the Poverty Level as a Percentage of the U.S. Population, 1959–2015

In part (a), the official poverty rate for all persons declined sharply between 1959 and the 1970s. After the Great Recession of 2007, the poverty rate rose. Comparison of parts (b) and (c) reveals that the poverty rate for African Americans fell sharply between 1959 and 1970, but since then it remained almost three times the poverty rate of whites until 1995. In 2015, the ratio was twice as great.

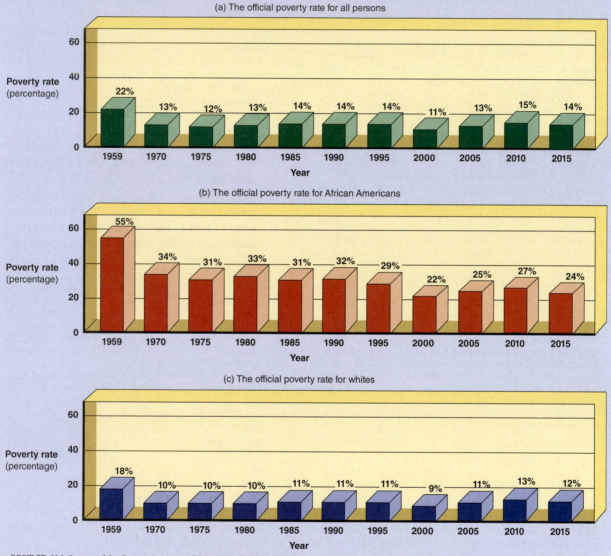

(a) The official poverty rate for all persons

(b) The official poverty rate for African Americans

(c) The official poverty rate for whites

SOURCE: U.S. Bureau of the Census, *Income and Poverty in the United States, 2015*, http://www.census.gov/index.html, Table 3.

trend until the early 1980s. After 1980, the percentage remained between 13 and 14 percent until the rate dropped to 11 percent in 2000. This was the lowest level in more than a quarter-century. Following the Great Recession of 2007–2009, the poverty rate rose to 15 percent in 2010. The exhibit also gives an idea of poverty levels by race for selected years. As shown by comparing parts (b) and (c), the percentage of African Americans below the poverty line remained almost three times the percentage of whites between 1970 and 1990. In 2015, the ratio was twice as great.

The poverty rate shown in Exhibit 7 has two major problems. First, this percentage gives no indication of how poor the people included are. A person with an income $1 below the poverty line counts, and so does a person whose income is $5,000 below the threshold. Second, the poverty rate is computed by comparing a family's census cash income from all sources to the poverty line. Cash income includes cash payments from Social Security, unemployment compensation, and Temporary Assistance for Needy Families (TANF). Cash income for the poor does not include noncash transfers, called in-kind transfers. **In-kind transfers** are government payments in the form of goods and services, rather than cash, including such government programs as food stamps, Medicaid, and housing. These antipoverty programs will be discussed in more detail in the next section.

In-kind transfers
Government payments in the form of goods and services, rather than cash, including such government programs as food stamps, Medicaid, and housing.

12-2b **Who Are the Poor?**

Exhibit 8 lists selected characteristics of families below the poverty level in 2016. Geographically, poor families are most likely to live in the South. An important characteristic

EXHIBIT 8 Characteristics of U.S. Persons and Families below the 2016 Poverty Level

Characteristic	Percentage below the poverty line
Region	
South	15%
West	13
Midwest	12
Northeast	12
Type of Family	
Headed by married couple	5
Headed by male, no wife	16
Headed by female, no husband	28
Education of Household Head	
No high school diploma	26
High school diploma, no college	13
Bachelor's degree or more	5

SOURCE: U.S. Bureau of the Census, Income, Poverty, and Health Insurance in the United States: 2016, http://www.census.gov/hhes/www/poverty.html, Tables 3, 5 and POV29.

of families living below the poverty line in the United States is family structure. The poverty rate was 28 percent for families headed by a female with no husband present and 16 percent for families headed by a male with no female present, compared to only 5 percent for married couples. Finally, poverty is greatly influenced by the lack of educational achievement of the head of household. As shown in the exhibit, 26 percent of families with household heads who have not received a high school diploma are below the poverty line compared to only 5 percent of families whose heads have at least a bachelor's degree.

12-3 ANTIPOVERTY PROGRAMS

The government has a number of programs specifically designed to aid the poor. The groups eligible for such assistance include disabled persons, elderly persons, and poor families with dependent children. People become eligible for public assistance if their income is below certain levels as measured by a *means test*. A **means test** is a requirement that a family's income not exceed a certain level to be eligible for public assistance. People who pass the means test may be *entitled* to government assistance. Thus, government welfare programs are often called *entitlement programs*.

Means test
A requirement that a family's income not exceed a certain level to be eligible for public assistance.

Federal programs to assist the poor in the United States are classified into two broad types of programs: *cash* assistance and *in-kind transfers*. As explained previously, the current definition of the poverty threshold excludes in-kind transfers because these programs did not exist when the poverty rate measure was adopted decades ago.

12-3a Cash Transfer Programs

The following are major government programs that alleviate poverty by providing eligible persons with cash payments needed to purchase food, shelter, clothing, and other basic needs.

Social Security (OASDHI)

The technical name for our gigantic social insurance program is Old Age, Survivors, Disability, and Health Insurance (OASDHI). Under the Social Security Act passed in 1935, each worker must pay a payroll tax matched in equal amount by his or her employer. Look at your paycheck, and you will find this deduction under FICA, which stands for Federal Insurance Contribution Act. Most of this money is used on a "pay-as-you-go" basis to pay current benefit recipients, and the remainder goes into the Social Security Trust Fund. Now, workers may retire at the age of 66, but the retirement age is scheduled to increase to 67 soon. Workers may also retire at age 62, with reduced benefits. If a wage earner dies, Social Security provides payments to survivors, including spouse and children. In addition, payments are made to disabled workers.

Earned-Income Tax Credit (EITC)

This is a refundable federal tax credit based on earned income below a maximum amount provided to low-income wage earners with the purpose of offsetting Social Security payroll taxes paid by the workers. In short, EITC is designed to avoid taxing the working poor further into poverty. Under this program, the tax credit reduces federal income taxes or provides a cash payment if the credit exceeds the tax liability.

Unemployment Compensation

Unemployment compensation is a government insurance program that pays income for a short time period to unemployed workers. This unemployment insurance is financed by a payroll tax on employers, which varies by state and according to the size of the firm's payroll. This means nothing is deducted from employees' paychecks for unemployment compensation. Although the federal government largely collects the taxes and funds this program, it is administered by the states. Any insured worker who becomes unemployed, and did not just quit his or her job, can become eligible for benefit payments after a short waiting period of usually one week.

Temporary Assistance for Needy Families (TANF)

TANF gives states broad discretion to determine eligibility and benefit levels. However, families may not receive benefits for longer than 60 months. Unwed teenage parents must stay in school and live at home, and people convicted of drug-related felonies are banned from receiving TANF or food stamp benefits. In addition, nonworking adults must participate in community service within two months of receiving benefits, and must find work within two years. Parents with children under age one are exempt from the work requirements (under age six if child care is not available).

Social Security: Past, Present, and Future

President Franklin D. Roosevelt signed the Social Security Act in 1935 as a bedrock of the New Deal program to help Americans besieged by the Great Depression. On December 1, 1936, the first official Social Security card was drawn arbitrarily from a stack of applications. The recipient was John D. Sweeney, Jr., who was the son of a wealthy factory owner and had grown up in a 15-room home staffed with servants. Unfortunately, Mr. Sweeney died at the age of 61 without ever receiving any benefits from the Social Security program.

Prior to 2010, the Social Security Trust Fund collected more revenue than it paid out in benefits. The balance was invested exclusively in interest-bearing U.S. Treasury securities. After 2010, revenue fell below benefits. Now the system is dipping into the trust fund to make up the difference. In 2034, it is estimated that the trust fund will be depleted. The problem, and it is a good problem to have, is that life expectancy is rising and there is a larger number of baby boomers born between 1945 and 1964 who are retiring. Excluding increasing the retirement age, the solution to financing a secure retirement program for future generations is to reduce benefits and/or increase revenues.

One idea to restore the trust fund is to allow people to obtain a higher return on their investment by channeling all or some of the money into their own private stock market account because stocks generally outperform U.S. Treasury securities by a significant margin. Unanswered questions of such partial privatization system include:

How much money could workers divert from Social Security into their private investment account?

What are the transition costs for new government debt required to pay benefits to current retirees not financed by payroll taxes because of money diverted to private accounts? and

How should workers be protected if their investments lose money?

Another reform idea is to increase tax revenue by lifting the cap on income subject to Social Security taxes. Currently, employers and employees each pay a fixed percentage payroll tax on worker earnings up to a maximum amount of each employee's salary.

However, no tax is paid on the income above that maximum amount, which is currently $118,500. The effect would be to raise revenue by expanding the tax base to include highest-paid employees.

12-3b In-Kind Transfers

The following are important government in-kind transfer programs that raise the standard of living for the poor.

Medicare

This federal health care program is available to Social Security beneficiaries and persons with certain disabilities. Coverage is provided for hospital care and post-hospital nursing services. It also makes available supplementary low-cost insurance programs that help pay for doctor services and prescription drug expenses. Medicare is financed by payroll taxes on employers and employees.

Medicaid

This is one of the largest in-kind transfer program. Medicaid provides medical services to eligible poor under age 65 who pass a means test. TANF families qualify for Medicaid in all states. It is financed by general tax revenues.

Supplemental Nutrition Assistance Program (SNAP)

SNAP (formerly food stamps) began in 1964 as a federally financed program administered by state governments. The government issues coupons to the poor, who use them like money at the grocery store. The grocer cashes the stamps at a local bank, which redeems them at face value from the government. The cash value of stamps issued varies with the eligible recipient's income and family size. The SNAP program has become a major part of the welfare system in the United States.

Housing Assistance

Federal and state governments have a number of different programs to provide affordable housing for poor people. The federal agency overseeing most of these programs is the Department of Housing and Urban Development (HUD). These programs include housing projects owned and operated by the government and subsidies to assist people who rent private housing. In both cases, recipients pay less than the market value for apartments and therefore receive an in-kind transfer.

12-3c Welfare Criticisms

The majority of objections to welfare can be classified into the following major criticisms:

- **Work Disincentives** Critics have argued that because welfare provides income that is easier to obtain than by working, the poor are often induced to reduce their work effort. In fact, the more a recipient earns from a job, the fewer the benefits he or she receives. Moreover, the taxes to finance welfare payments have some disincentive effects on the work effort of taxpayers. Taxes reduce take-home pay and thus reduce the reward for work.
- **Inefficiencies** Critics have charged that the huge welfare bureaucracy in Washington, D.C., and throughout the nation results in more money in the pockets of bureaucrats

than in the pockets of the poor. This major criticism was expressed by economics professor Thomas Sowell as follows:

> *The amount necessary to lift every man, woman, and child in America above the poverty line has been calculated, and it is one-third of what is in fact spent on poverty programs. Clearly, much of the transfer ends up in the pockets of highly paid administrators, consultants, and staff as well as higher income recipients of benefits from programs advertised as antipoverty efforts.*[1]

- **Inequities** Today, many critics argue that poor persons with equal needs receive different benefits. For example, a needy family in California might receive welfare benefits twice as great as those received by a needy family of the same size in South Carolina. The reason is that benefits under TANF and Medicaid are essentially controlled by the states.

12-4 REFORM PROPOSALS

Although there have been numerous proposals for reforming welfare, the various ideas can be classified into two broad approaches. First, the negative income tax offers a major transformation of the entire patchwork of federal, state, and local welfare programs. Second, workfare, which is the cornerstone of TANF, is a departure from the previous welfare system because it is based on work rather than entitlement. However, workfare is not without considerable debate and controversy.

12-4a Negative Income Tax

The idea of negative income tax was first advanced by the prominent economist Milton Friedman in the early 1960s to reduce work disincentives and welfare bureaucracy while providing for the poor. The **negative income tax (NIT)** is a plan under which families below a certain break-even level of income would receive cash payments that decrease as their incomes increase. A NIT system would combine all cash and in-kind transfer welfare programs into a single program administered by a single agency. This would mean an end to such programs as unemployment compensation, Medicaid, SNAP, and housing assistance.

Exhibit 9 illustrates how a negative income tax might work. A low-income family of four receives a cash payment until it reaches a *break-even income* at, say, $20,000 per year, where the family neither receives a payment nor pays income taxes. Above $20,000, the family pays income taxes. For example, a family with an income of $30,000 pays $5,000 in taxes, while a family with an income of $10,000 is paid a NIT subsidy of $5,000. A family with zero income receives a NIT payment of $10,000. Thus, the government pays families an amount that varies inversely (negatively) with income.

Negative income tax (NIT)
A plan under which families below a certain breakeven level of income would receive cash payments that decrease as their incomes increase.

CONCLUSION

The negative income tax is the reverse of a positive income tax system, in which people pay the government an amount that varies directly with their income.

The basic idea behind the NIT system is simple: Families with incomes above the break-even income finance payments to families with incomes below the break-even

---
[1]Thomas Sowell, *Markets and Minorities* (New York: Basic Books, 1981), p. 122.

EXHIBIT 9 A Negative Income Tax Plan

In this example, a family with no earned income receives a $10,000 payment from the government. From $0 to $20,000, payments are reduced by a phase-out rate of $0.50 for each $1.00 of additional income. When income exceeds $20,000, payments fall to zero, and the family pays income taxes. Thus, a family with an income of $30,000 pays $5,000 in taxes.

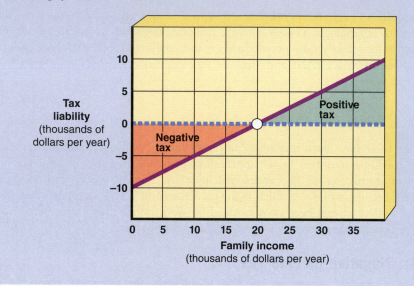

income. Begin at zero income in the exhibit, and assume the income guarantee is set at the poverty income threshold of $10,000. Beyond the guaranteed minimum income of $10,000, government payments are reduced by, say, $0.50 for each $1.00 earned. This rate, called the *phase-out rate*, determines the cash transfers to low-income families until the break-even income is reached.

The NIT system offers several potential advantages. First, bureaucratic costs would be cut because a NIT program could be administered by a single agency. Second, poor people would not suffer the stigma of repeatedly standing in line at the welfare office or using food stamps in the grocery store, which could reduce some truly needy from seeking out assistance. The needy would simply file annual, or perhaps quarterly, income returns with the IRS. Third, many economists argue that individuals are rational and know best how to spend their money. Thus, a cash subsidy is preferable to an in-kind transfer. In sum, many economists argue that the NIT system is preferable to the numerous current poverty-relief programs because it reduces taxpayers' expense, it increases poverty relief to those who are truly poor, and it creates a greater incentive to work.

After years of discussion and study, the NIT has not gained wide political support. The NIT system is perceived as a political liability because voters perceive it as a "giveaway" of taxpayers' money. These critics believe in-kind welfare is preferable to cash assistance. When a recipient is given food stamps or a housing subsidy, he or she acquires food and housing, rather than, say, buying drugs and gambling. NIT proponents point out, however, it is known that some food stamps are sold illegally for cash, which is used to buy drugs, alcohol, or whatever. Finally, some critics argue that a generous guaranteed minimum income paid in cash might create a disincentive to work rather than an incentive to work.

CHECKPOINT

Does a Negative Income Tax Discourage Work?
Under a negative income system, people who work receive reduced payments from the government. Even worse, beyond the break-even income, workers must pay taxes. This means there is no basis in a NIT system to argue that the poor will have an incentive to work. Explain why you agree or disagree. (Hint: Construct a table using Exhibit 9, and consider after-tax income.)

12-4b Workfare

The 1996 welfare reform bill titled the *Personal Responsibility and Work Reconciliation Opportunity Act* created TANF, and gave the states block grants to run welfare programs. To overcome the disincentive to work characteristic of earlier welfare programs based on entitlement, the current approach is to increase the work performed by welfare recipients and encourage their participation in job-training programs. To keep their benefits, welfare recipients must perform some work activities within two years of receiving welfare or risk losing benefits. This idea is called *workfare*. Workfare programs require able-bodied adults to work for the local government or any available private-sector employer in order to be eligible for welfare benefits. The paramount question thus becomes how to create jobs for welfare recipients who often lack basic literacy skills. A large public job plan would be costly and politically unpopular, especially among public employees who fear losing their jobs. Another option is for the government to pay employers to hire welfare recipients with the intent of providing on-the-job training. A variation on this idea is for the government to hire personnel firms that would earn a fee for each person placed in a job.

There are potential problems with providing subsidies for companies that hire welfare recipients. One problem is that subsidies can stigmatize welfare recipients and reduce their long-term employment prospects. Another potential problem is that subsidies could be a windfall payment to employers for hiring people who would have been hired without the subsidies. Finally, there is a displacement problem because a subsidized welfare-recipient worker can take the job of an unsubsidized worker who has never received welfare benefits.

12-5 DISCRIMINATION

Poverty and discrimination in the workplace are related. Nonwhites and females earn less income when employer prejudice prevents them from receiving job opportunities. Discrimination also occurs when nonwhites and females earn less, but do basically the same work as whites and males. Exhibit 10 uses labor market theory to explain how discrimination can cause the equilibrium wage to be lower for nonwhites than for whites.

Exhibit 10(a) assumes that employers do not discriminate. This means employers hire workers regardless of race—that is, on the basis of their contribution to revenue (their marginal revenue products, MRPs). Hence, the intersection of the market demand curve, *D*, and the market supply curve, *S*, determines the equilibrium wage rate of $245

YOU'RE THE ECONOMIST

Applicable Concept: Welfare Reform

Pulling on the Strings of the Welfare Safety Net

It may be surprising that welfare reform can be argued to be a success. The number of recipients on welfare receiving cash assistance (TANF) has fallen from 12.3 million in 1996 to 4.1 million in 2016.[1] In contrast, other entitlement programs, such as SNAP (formerly food stamps), have increased sharply from 17.2 million participants in 2000 to 44.2 million in 2016.[2] The following is a sampling of articles describing the evolution of welfare after the Personal Responsibility and Work Opportunity Reconciliation Act of 1996.

As reported in *The Washington Post*, Los Angeles County provides a striking contrast of welfare before and after reform in 1996. Prior to 1996, Los Angeles County had a traditional welfare program that provided education and job training without work requirements. After the welfare reform act of 1996, independent researchers found that 43 percent of poor families who were required to participate in the city's new welfare reform program with work requirements got jobs, while only 32 percent of families randomly selected to remain in the traditional welfare program did. This represented an increase of one-third over the old welfare program. The typical welfare family subject to the new reform initiatives earned $1,286 in the first six months of the program, while "control group" families earned $879, a difference of 46 percent.[3]

A 2002 article in the *Los Angeles Times* concerned the new approach of the federal government providing block grants to states and mandating that the needy find jobs rather than just handing them welfare checks:

Before 1996, when the nation's welfare laws were radically altered, welfare families might have gotten a monthly welfare check for the rest of their lives. Martha Soria's job would have been mostly to shuffle their paperwork. But with welfare reform came time limits on such benefits and strict new work requirements. And while Soria still shuffles a lot of paperwork, her job as well as the jobs of welfare caseworkers across the state and nation have changed. They have had to master hundreds of new rules and regulations under welfare reform and take on new responsibilities as guidance counselor, job finder, cheerleader, and taskmaster.[4]

The following article argues that the states must do more to avoid racial bias:

Under the 1996 law, states have the option to enforce time limits of their choosing. Because of this flexibility, states are left open to discriminate freely. Across the board, race was the determining factor affecting time limit lengths and their application. Observation of the enforcement of time limits shows that states with a higher proportion of African Americans or Latinos possess shorter time limits than the five-year guideline of the law. Over 20 states have opted to not allow exemptions to these time limits. Over 50 percent of African American families under welfare are subject to time limits shorter than the federal cutoff, as opposed to 30 percent of whites under welfare[5]

Reforms continue: A new federal rule in 2008 made it easier for welfare recipients to attend college by counting a year's worth of study, including homework time, as work. And in 2013, a bill was introduced in Congress, but not passed that would require states to randomly drug test people who receive TANF payments. At the state level in 2014, a U.S. Circuit Court of Appeals upheld a lower court ruling that Florida's testing requirement violated the Constitution's ban on unreasonable search. In 2015, at least 12 states have passed legislation requiring drug testing for welfare recipients.

Critics of welfare reform point out that about one-third of the states have enacted even more stringent limits beyond the federal government's 5-year life-time limit on any cash assistance (TANF) an individual may receive, as well as other measures, that makes living in poverty unnecessarily harsh in these states. However, as reported in a *New York Times* article in May, 2016:

Ronald T. Haskins, who helped write the 1996 federal law as an aide to House Republicans, said that for some poor people, the erosion of cash benefits had been offset by increases in other programs, including the earned-income tax credit, nutrition assistance, and Medicaid. But, Mr. Haskins said, "It is reasonable and appropriate to worry about mothers and children in families with no earnings and no cash welfare."

ANALYZE THE ISSUE The current approach to welfare reform is to cut the growth of welfare by shifting control from the federal government to the states. The idea is that because state and local officials are closer to the people, welfare programs will improve. Analyze the results presented above based on work disincentives, inefficiencies, and inequities.

1. U.S. Census Bureau, *Statistical Abstract of the United States*, 2016, http://www.census.gov/compendia/statab/, Table 563, and Robert Pear, "Political Rifts over Bill Clinton's Welfare Law Resurface as Aid Shrinks." *New York Times*, May 20, 2016.
2. Ibid., Table 570, and United States Department of Agriculture: https://www.fns.usda.gov/pd/supplemental-nutrition-assistance-program-snap
3. Judith Havemann, "Welfare Reform Success Cited in L.A.," *The Washington Post*, August 20, 1998, p. A1.
4. Carla Rivera, "Welfare Reform's Enforcers," *Los Angeles Times*, May 28, 2002, p. A1.
5. Gordon Hurd, "Safety Net Sinking," *Colorline Magazine*, Summer 2002, p. 17.

EXHIBIT 10 Labor Markets without and with Racial Discrimination

In part (a), there is no labor market discrimination against African Americans. In this case, the equilibrium wage for all labor is $245 per day. Under discrimination in part (b), the labor demand and labor supply curves for white and African-American workers differ. As a result, the equilibrium wage rate for white workers, $280, is higher than that for African Americans, $210.

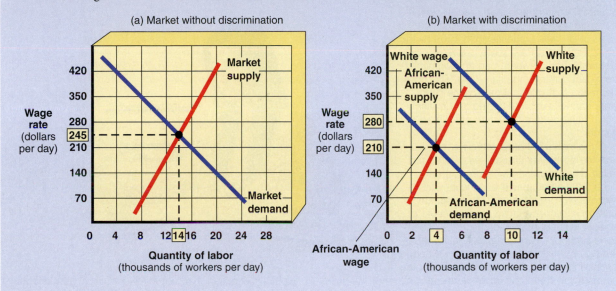

per day paid by nondiscriminating employers. The total number of African American and white workers hired is 14,000 workers.

Now assume for the sake of argument that employers do practice job discrimination against African-American workers. The result, shown in Exhibit 10(b), is two different labor markets—one for whites and one for African Americans. Because discrimination exists, the demand curve for labor for African Americans is to the left of the demand curve for labor for whites, reflecting unjustified restricted employment practices. The supply curve of labor for African Americans is also to the left of the supply curve of labor for white workers because there are fewer African Americans seeking employment than whites.

Given the differences in the labor market demand and supply curves, the equilibrium wage rate for white workers of $280 is higher than the $210 paid to African Americans. Comparison of these wage rates with the labor market equilibrium wage rate of $245 reveals that the effect of discrimination is to change the relative wages of white and African-American workers. Whites earn a higher wage rate than they would earn in a labor market that did not favor hiring them. Conversely, the African-American wage rate is lower as a result of discrimination.

12-5a **Comparable Worth**

A controversial public policy aimed at eliminating labor market pay inequities is a concept called comparable worth. **Comparable worth** is the principle that employees who work for the same employer must be paid the same wages when their jobs, even if different, require similar levels of education, training, experience, and responsibility. Comparable worth is a nonmarket wage-setting remedy to the situation where jobs dominated by women pay less

Comparable worth
The principle that employees who work for the same employer must be paid the same wage when their jobs, even if different, require similar levels of education, training, experience, and responsibility. A nonmarket wage-setting process is used to evaluate and compensate jobs according to point scores assigned.

YOU'RE THE ECONOMIST

Applicable Concept: Comparable Worth

Is Pay for Females Fair?

Women working full-time earn on average about 20 percent less than men. Discrimination in wages and employment on the basis of sex was made illegal in 1963 by the Equal Pay Act (EPA), which outlawed pay discrimination between men and women doing substantially the same job. This does not mean that unequal pay for the same work cannot exist, but if it does, the differential must be due to factors other than gender.

Proponents of comparable worth argue that the equal-pay-for-equal-work idea has failed. They maintain that women crowd into such female-dominated occupations as secretarial work, nursing, school teaching, and social work because of discrimination against women in male-dominated occupations such as engineering. The increased supply of female labor in female-crowded professions lowers the prevailing wage. If the courts follow the comparable worth principle, they will not consider whether employers intentionally pay less for "women's jobs," but only whether the employers are in compliance with a quantitative rating scheme. The best-known case occurred in the 1980s, when the American Federation of State, County, and Municipal Employees won the first federal court case against the state of Washington. The state was found guilty of wage discrimination against

Rostislav_Sedlacek/Shutterstock.com

women because it had not followed a comparable worth point system. According to the point system, male-dominated jobs often paid more than female-dominated jobs even though the female jobs had greater "worth" and therefore "underpaid" female job classes should be raised rather than lowering the "overpaid" male job classes. The court ordered Washington to upgrade nearly 15,000 female employees and award back pay estimated at $377 million.

than jobs dominated by men. Because women's work is alleged to be undervalued, the solution is equal pay for jobs evaluated as having "comparable worth" according to point scores assigned to different jobs. In essence, comparable worth replaces labor-market-determined wages with bureaucratic judgments about the valuation of different jobs. For example, compensation paid to an elevator inspector and a nurse can be computed based on quantitative scores in a job-rating scheme. If the jobs' point totals are equal, the average elevator inspector and nurse must be paid equally by law.

CHECKPOINT

Should the Law Protect Women?

Do you want women mining coal and building skyscrapers? Suppose laws are enacted that "protect" women by keeping them out of jobs deemed "too strenuous" or "too dangerous." Would the likely effect of such laws be to decrease wages in male-dominated occupations, increase wages in female-intensive occupations, or decrease wages in female-intensive occupations?

The decision was appealed to higher courts, and the union ultimately lost the case.

Critics of comparable worth argue that it is nearly impossible to measure all of the factors that determine compensation for jobs, and the fact that female occupations earn less than male occupations is not necessarily evidence of discrimination. For example, women often seek occupations more compatible with childrearing. Over the years, it appeared that comparable worth had faded into a golden oldie until the Fair Pay Act of 2007 was introduced by Senator Tom Harkin (D-Iowa) and included then-Senator Barack Obama (D-Illinois) as one of the cosponsors. The premise is that the government has the duty to decide a job's worth. Under its provisions, employers must send the Equal Employment Opportunity Commission (EEOC) annual reports of how pay is determined in any jobs dominated by one gender. The goal is for the EEOC to decide pay for workers in dissimilar but "equivalent" jobs based on criteria established by the EEOC. Such calculations would serve as a basis for workers to sue their employers based on not being paid the same for "equivalent" work. Although this bill was not enacted, the Lilly Ledbetter Fair Pay Act of 2009 was passed to reset the statute of limitation for pay discrimination.

Finally, the National Equal Pay Task Force was created in 2010 to crack down on violations of equal pay laws. In addition to the Labor Department, members include the Equal Employment Opportunity Commission, the Department of Justice, and the Office of Personnel Management. In 2012, the Paycheck Fairness Act failed in the Senate that would require employers to prove that pay differences between men and women are based on qualifications, education, and other "bona fides." And in 2013, a National Partnership For Women And Families study reported that a gender-based wage gap exists in every state and in the country's 50 largest metropolitan areas. In 2015 an article in *International New York Times* examined female discrimination in Hollywood. The conclusion was that women in film are routinely denied jobs, credits, prizes, and equal pay.[1] Comparable worth pay efforts hit the headlines again with the passage of the California Equal Pay Act that went into effect on January 1, 2016. It "bars California employers from paying workers of one sex more than the workers of the opposite sex for 'substantially similar' work unless the employer can show that any pay gap is justified by a factor other than sex, such as a system that determines pay based on quantity or quality of production or that resulted from differences in education, training, or experience."[2] Perhaps, the principles of this Fair Pay Act will be extended to compensation differences across race and ethnicity as well. We shall see.

ANALYZE THE ISSUE Suppose the EEOC uses a job-scoring system and determines that the wage rate for a secretary is $50 per hour, while the competitive labor market wage rate is $10 per hour. What would be the effect of such a comparable worth law?

1. Manohla Dargis "Lights, Camera, Women Taking Action: They Are Fighting for Better Directing Roles in Hollywood," *International New York Times*, January 24, 2015, p. 18.
2. Dan Eaton "Two changes to the California equal pay law coming in 2017 that all employees need to know," *The San Diego Union-Tribune*, December 12, 2016. Found at http://www.sandiegouniontribune.com/pomerado-news/business/sd-fi-eaton-20161212-story.html.

Key Concepts

Lorenz curve

Poverty line

In-kind transfers

Means test

Unemployment compensation

Negative income tax (NIT)

Comparable worth

Summary

- The **Lorenz curve** is a measure of inequality of income. Since 1947, the share of money income for each fifth of families ranked according to their income has been quite stable. Also, the degree of income inequality among families in the United States has changed little since 1929. In recent decades, the richest families have become richer; however, the median income of all groups has increased.

Lorenz Curve

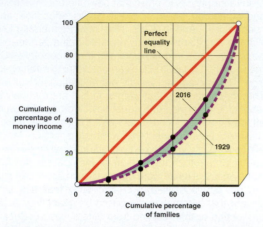

- The **poverty line** is a level of cash income below which a family is classified as poor. The poverty income threshold is three times the cost of a minimal diet for a family. Today, about 14 percent of the U.S. population is officially classified as poor.

- **In-kind transfers** are payments to the poor in the form of goods and services, rather than cash. Calculation of the poverty line counts only cash income. In-kind transfers, such as food stamps, Medicaid, and housing, do not count as income for families classified as officially poor. Government cash transfers counted in calculating the poverty line include payments from Social Security, unemployment compensation, and Temporary Assistance for Needy Families.

- A **means test** is a requirement that a family's income not exceed a certain level to be eligible for public assistance.

- **Welfare criticisms** include three major arguments:

  - Welfare reduces the incentive for the poor to work, and for taxpayers to work when increased taxes used to finance welfare reduces their take-home pay.

  - Welfare is inefficient because much of the money covers administrative costs, rather than providing benefits for the poor.

  - Because many antipoverty programs are controlled by the state, welfare benefits vary widely.

- The **negative income tax** is a plan to guarantee a certain amount of income for all families. As a low-income family earns income, government payments (negative income tax) are phased out. After reaching a break-even income, families become taxpayers instead of being on the welfare rolls.

Negative Income Tax

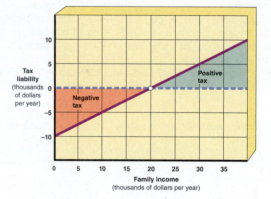

- **Comparable worth** is the theory that workers in jobs determined to be of equal value by means of point totals should be paid equally. Instead of allowing labor markets to set wages, independent consultants award points to different jobs on the basis of such criteria as knowledge, experience, and working conditions.

Summary of Conclusion Statements

- Measured by distribution of family money income, the richest families as a group have become a little richer and the rest of the family groups a little poorer in recent decades.

- The Lorenz curve has shifted only slightly inward, and therefore closer to the perfect equality line between 1929 and 2016.

- The negative income tax is the reverse of a positive income tax system, in which people pay the government an amount that varies directly with their income.

Study Questions and Problems

Please see Appendix A for answers to the odd-numbered questions. Your instructor has access to the answers for even-numbered questions.

1. The following table contains data on the distribution of income in the countries of Alpha and Beta:
   a. Compute the cumulative distribution of income for each country.
   b. Construct the Lorenz curve for each country.
   c. For which country is the distribution of income more equal?

	Alpha			Beta	
Percentage of families	Percentage share	Cumulative share		Percentage share	Cumulative share
Lowest fifth	17.7%	—		9.0%	—
Second-lowest fifth	19.9	—		14.2	—
Middle fifth	20.4	—		17.5	—
Second-highest fifth	20.7	—		21.9	—
Highest fifth	21.3	—		37.4	—

2. Suppose each family in the United States earned an equal money income. What would be the effect?

3. Explain the difference between poverty defined absolutely and poverty defined relatively. Which definition is the basis of the poverty line?

4. Calculate the official poverty threshold annual income for a family of four. Assume the minimally acceptable diet is estimated to be $5 per person per day and the minimum wage is $5 per hour. Will a head of a family of four earn the poverty threshold you have calculated?

5. What are in-kind transfers? Give examples. How are in-kind transfers considered in determining whether a family is below the poverty income threshold?

6. Would free health care reduce poverty, as measured by the government? Would free public housing, day care, and job training for the poor reduce the poverty rate? Explain.

7. What percentage of families in the United States is classified as poor? Which demographic groups have higher poverty rates?

8. List the major government cash assistance and in-kind transfer programs to assist the poor. Which of the programs are not exclusively for the poor?

9. What are three major criticisms of welfare?

10. Assume the government implements a negative income tax plan with a guaranteed minimum income of $5,000 and a phase-out rate for payments of 50 percent. Provide the missing data in the following table:

A Negative Income Tax Plan		
Family income	Negative tax	Total after-tax income
$ 0	_____	_____
2,000	_____	_____
4,000	_____	_____
6,000	_____	_____
8,000	_____	_____
10,000	_____	_____

11. Critics of welfare argue that the role of government should be to break down legal barriers to employment rather than use programs that directly provide cash or goods and services. For example, advocates of this approach would remove laws mandating minimum wages, comparable worth, union power, professional licensing, and other restrictive practices. Do you agree or disagree? Why?

✓ CHECKPOINT ANSWERS

Does a Negative Income Tax Discourage Work?

The following table is interpreted from Exhibit 9. Even though payments from the government decrease (with a 50 percent phase-out rate in this case), total after-tax income increases from the combination of the income earned and the negative tax. After the break-even income of $20,000, total after-tax income continues to rise. If you said the NIT system assumes the poor are rational people who are motivated to earn more total after-tax income by working, **YOU ARE CORRECT**.

Family income	Negative tax	Positive tax	Total after-tax income
$ 0	$10,000	$ 0	$10,000
5,000	7,000	0	12,000
10,000	5,000	0	15,000
15,000	2,500	0	17,500
20,000	0	0	20,000
25,000	0	−2,500	22,500
30,000	0	−5,000	25,000
35,000	0	−7,500	27,500

Should the Law Protect Women?

A law that limits women's access to certain occupations results in their crowding into the remaining occupations. The obstacles facing women in male-dominated occupations artificially restrict competition with men. If you said the increased labor supply in female-intensive occupations decreases their wages, while the decreased labor supply in male-intensive occupations increases wages for males, **YOU ARE CORRECT**.

Sample Quiz

Please see Appendix B for answers to Sample Quiz questions.

1. "Dividing the economic pie more equally may reduce the size of the economic pie." This argument is characterized as
   a. untrue.
   b. a form of discrimination.
   c. a conflict between equity and efficiency.
   d. a conflict between full employment and economic growth.

2. The highest fifth of all families receive approximately what percent of the distribution of annual money income among families?
   a. 5 percent
   b. 10 percent
   c. 25 percent
   d. 50 percent

EXHIBIT 11 Lorenz Curve

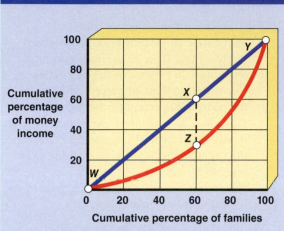

3. Which of the following graphs shows the cumulative shares of income received by a family?
   a. Distribution curve
   b. Lorenz curve
   c. Ricardian curve
   d. Quintile curve

4. As shown in Exhibit 11, the perfect equality line is drawn between points
   a. *W* and *Z*.
   b. *Z* and *Y*.
   c. *W* and *Y* along the straight line.
   d. *W* and *Y* along the curve.

5. As shown in Exhibit 11, 60 percent of families earned a cumulative share of about what percent of income?
   a. 5 percent
   b. 15 percent
   c. 30 percent
   d. 50 percent

6. When the Lorenz curve lies above the diagonal,
   a. the poorest 20 percent of the population receive more than 20 percent of income.
   b. the richest 20 percent of the population receive more than 20 percent of income.
   c. everyone receives the same income.
   d. the curve is wrong because it is impossible for the graph to look like this.

7. The poverty line
   a. separates those on welfare from those not on welfare.
   b. equals three times an economy food budget.
   c. equals the median income level.
   d. includes all of the above answers.

8. Which of the following government programs provides recipients with unrestricted cash payments?
   a. Temporary Assistance to Needy Families (TANF)
   b. Medicaid
   c. The food stamp program
   d. Housing assistance programs

9. Medicaid and food stamps are
   a. available only to families.
   b. counterproductive.
   c. forms of in-kind assistance.
   d. forms of cash assistance.

10. As shown in Exhibit 12, a family of four pays income taxes at
    a. an income of $5,000.
    b. any income between zero and $40,000.
    c. all levels of income.
    d. any income above $40,000.

11. As shown in Exhibit 12, a family of four with no earned income receives _____ from the government.
    a. Zero payment
    b. The break-even income of $40,000

EXHIBIT 12 Negative Income Tax

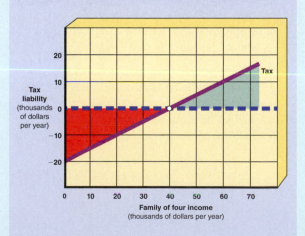

c. A $20,000 payment

d. A $20,000 tax deferment

12. Under the negative income tax scheme in Exhibit 12, families earning between $10,000 and $40,000 would
    a. receive the maximum negative income tax payment of $20,000.
    b. receive payments under the negative income tax.
    c. pay no income taxes, but receive no payments.
    d. do none of the answers above.

13. Which of the following might increase the supply curve of labor?
    a. Eliminating discrimination against blacks
    b. Eliminating discrimination against females
    c. Easing licensing requirements
    d. Doing all of the answers above

14. Consider a law that limits women's access to certain "dangerous" occupations such as coal mining and military combat service. Such a law would likely reduce women's wages because
    a. women would be overqualified for "non-dangerous" jobs.
    b. labor supply in female-intensive occupations would increase.
    c. women would be less likely to obtain college degrees.
    d. comparable worth would no longer exist between men's and women's occupations.

15. Comparable worth is the principle that
    a. goods and services priced the same have about the same worth.
    b. the wage rate equals the value of productivity.
    c. men and women should be paid comparably.
    d. employees who perform comparable jobs should be paid the same wage.

16. Which of the following graphs shows the percentage of the families on one axis and the percentage of income on the other?
    a. Budget-distribution curve
    b. Income-consumption curve

c. Lorenz curve

d. Marx curve

17. If the Lorenz curve lies on the diagonal,
    a. the poorest 20 percent of the population receives more than 20 percent of income.
    b. the richest 20 percent of the population receives more than 20 percent of income.
    c. the poorest 20 percent of the population and the richest 20 percent of the population each receive 20 percent of income.
    d. the country's income has been rising over time.
    e. the curve is wrong because it is impossible for the graph to look like this.

18. The official U.S. poverty line for a family is calculated by taking 3 times the annual cost of
    a. public housing.
    b. basic medical care.
    c. utilities and transportation.
    d. a minimal diet.

19. Which of the following program(s) is (are) an example of in-kind assistance to fight poverty in the United States?
    a. b and e
    b. Medicaid
    c. Unemployment benefits
    d. Temporary Assistance to Needy Families (TANF)
    e. SNAP (food stamps)

20. The incentive to work is an ingredient of the negative income tax because
    a. if families work, they will be eliminated from the program.
    b. if families don't work, they will be eliminated from the program.
    c. the more income earned in the workplace, the higher the family's after-tax income.
    d. the more income earned in the workplace, the higher the payment from the government.

CHAPTER 13

Antitrust and Regulation

CHAPTER PREVIEW

People of the same trade seldom meet together, even for merriment and diversion, but the conversation ends in a conspiracy against the public, or in some contrivance to raise prices.[1]

—Adam Smith

When Microsoft dominated the personal computer software industry, the U.S. government charged the firm and Bill Gates, its founder, with anticompetitive business practices. The media compared the case to John D. Rockefeller's Standard Oil monopoly and the robber barons of the 1890s. In the past, antitrust laws have been successfully used against the nation's largest corporations. This threat of the high legal costs of defending against an antitrust suit serves as a powerful deterrent, discouraging monopolies from engaging in unfair actions intended to eliminate rivals. Here you will explore and form opinions on the Microsoft case, the Standard Oil case, and other major antitrust cases.

When antitrust policy is successful, consumers benefit from lower prices and more output. As you study antitrust policy in this chapter, you will learn that antitrust is somewhat of an art form that blends economic theory and politics—perhaps more politics than economic theory. Interestingly, certain industries and organizations are exempt from antitrust legislation: labor unions, professional baseball teams, public utilities, public transit companies, schools, hospitals, and suppliers of military equipment.

The second half of this chapter turns to government regulation, which affects virtually every business and consumer. Our food is regulated, our environment is regulated, airline safety is regulated, and most industries must deal with some form of regulation. What are the reasons for regulation, and what are its consequences? The explanation begins with a brief survey of regulation in the United States. In the last section, we discuss the rationale for three different types of regulation justified on the basis of market failure.

IN THIS CHAPTER, YOU WILL LEARN TO SOLVE THESE ECONOMICS PUZZLES:

* Can universities and colleges improve education by engaging in price fixing?

* Why doesn't the water company or electric company compete?

* Why is market failure an economic rationale for regulation?

---

[1]Adam Smith, *An Inquiry into the Nature and Causes of the Wealth of Nations* (1776, reprint, New York: Random House, The Modern Library, 1937), p. 128.

13-1 ANTITRUST

Before the Civil War, industries were populated by small firms, and few economic problems were caused by monopoly. After the Civil War, during the rapid industrialization of the 1870s and 1880s, the railroads and telegraph linked diverse regions of the country and enabled firms to expand into national markets. To gain more control of expanding industries, many competing companies merged or formed a trust. A **trust** is a combination or cartel consisting of firms that place their assets in the custody of a board of trustees. The trust allows firms that have not actually merged to form a cartel, or a cohesive group of firms that controls an industry in order to charge monopoly prices and earn higher profits. The long list of trusts formed during this period included the iron trust, sugar trust, copper trust, steel trust, coal trust, oil trust, tobacco trust, and even the paper-bag trust. The organizers of many of these trusts became widely known as *robber barons* because they exploited and bullied anyone in their way as they sought ever higher profits.

During the last decades of the nineteenth century, many trusts used various tactics to avoid competition. Recall from Chapter 9 on monopoly that Standard Oil acquired oil fields, railroads, pipelines, and ships and then denied access to rivals. Thus, competing firms had to merge with Standard Oil or go out of business. With the competition eliminated, John D. Rockefeller, the best-known so-called robber baron, raised Standard Oil's prices and limited production, and consumers suffered along with Standard Oil's competitors.

Another anticompetitive strategy used by the industrial giants was predatory pricing. **Predatory pricing** is the practice of one or more firms temporarily reducing prices in order to eliminate competition and then raising prices. Often trusts would sell a product below cost until their weaker competitors were unable to withstand mounting losses and were forced from the industry. Perhaps even more alarming, some trusts resorted to political corruption. For example, the railroad and petroleum trusts employed corrupt legislators and judges to gain a competitive edge.

By the end of the nineteenth century, the threat of continuing economic and political abuses created a public opinion quite hostile to big business. Newspapers regularly printed news of the trusts' questionable business practices. The numerous and politically influential farmers blamed the trusts for the high railroad charges that were making farming unprofitable. Consumers and labor unions also raised their voices against monopoly power. The influence of the trusts was discussed constantly in the halls of Congress. In 1888, both major political parties added antimonopoly planks to their campaign platforms. Hatred and distrust of the centralization of economic and political power originated in the Jeffersonian tradition of the United States. Against this background of populist (pro-people) fear of big business and its political power, Congress passed laws aimed at preventing firms from engaging in anticompetitive activities.

The following is a brief description of the major antitrust legislation that constitutes basic antitrust law.

13-1a The Sherman Act

The first antitrust law was the Sherman Act. The **Sherman Act of 1890** is the federal antitrust law that prohibits monopolization and conspiracies to restrain trade. Today, this act remains the cornerstone of antitrust policy in the United States. It has two main provisions:

Section 1: Every contract, combination in the form of trust or otherwise, or conspiracy in restraint of trade or commerce among the several States, or with foreign nations, is hereby declared to be illegal….

Trust
A combination or cartel consisting of firms that place their assets in the custody of a board of trustees.

Predatory pricing
The practice of one or more firms temporarily reducing prices in order to eliminate competition and then raising prices.

Sherman Act of 1890
The federal antitrust law enacted in 1890 that prohibits monopolization and conspiracies to restrain trade.

Section 2: Every person who shall monopolize, or attempt to monopolize, or combine or conspire with any other person or persons, to monopolize any part of the trade or commerce among the several States, or with foreign nations, shall be deemed guilty of a misdemeanor, and, on conviction thereof, shall be punished by a fine not exceeding five thousand dollars, or by imprisonment not exceeding one year, or by both said punishments, in the discretion of the court.[2]

In response to the public outcry, Congress intended to craft this law with sweeping language against the trusts. But what does the Sherman Act really say? It is unclear exactly which business practices constitute a "restraint of trade" and therefore a violation of the law. As a result of the extremely vague language, there were numerous court battles, and the act was ineffective for years. For example, the federal government did not win its first notable cases until 1911; these cases were against Standard Oil and American Tobacco.

The serious consequences of violating the Sherman Act are reflected in the more recent case of Archer Daniels Midland (ADM) Company. In 1995, this agribusiness giant pleaded guilty to price fixing involving lysine and citric acid. It paid a $100 million fine. In 1998, a federal jury convicted three past and present executives of conspiring with competitors to fix the prices of these products. They were sentenced to serve two years in prison and to pay fines of $350,000 each.

13-1b **The Clayton Act**

As explained above, the Sherman Act initially proved to be little more than a legislative mandate for the courts to spell out the meaning of antitrust laws. To define anticompetitive acts more precisely, Congress passed the Clayton Act. The **Clayton Act of 1914** is an amendment that strengthened the Sherman Act by making it illegal for firms to engage in certain anticompetitive business practices. Under this act, the following business practices are illegal when they "substantially lessen competition or tend to create a monopoly":

Clayton Act of 1914
A 1914 amendment that strengthens the Sherman Act by making it illegal for firms to engage in certain anticompetitive business practices.

1. **Price Discrimination.** A firm charges different customers different prices for the same product when these price differences are not related to cost differences. (Recall the discussion of this topic in the chapter on monopoly.)
2. **Exclusive Dealing.** A manufacturer requires a retailer to sign an agreement stipulating the condition that the retailer will not carry any rival products of the manufacturer.
3. **Tying Contracts.** The seller of one product requires the buyer to purchase some other product(s). For example, movie distributors cannot force theaters to purchase projection rights to a blockbuster movie only on the condition that they pay for a bundle of films with much less box office potential.
4. **Stock Acquisition of Competing Companies.** One firm buys the stock of a competing firm.
5. **Interlocking Directorates.** The directors of one company serve on the board of directors of another company in the same industry. Interlocking directorates are illegal, whether or not the effect may be to "substantially lessen competition."

---

[2]In 1974, the act was amended so that violations would be treated as felonies.

Although more specific than the Sherman Act, the Clayton Act is also vague and leaves a key question unanswered: Exactly when does a situation or action "substantially lessen competition"? To this day, the task of interpreting this ambiguous phrase remains with the courts and the interpretation changes over time.

13-1c The Federal Trade Commission Act

Since the federal government faced a growing antitrust responsibility in the early 1900s, an agency was needed to investigate alleged anticompetitive practices and reach judgments. The Federal Trade Commission Act was enacted for this purpose. The **Federal Trade Commission Act of 1914** established the Federal Trade Commission (FTC) to investigate unfair competitive practices of firms. This act contains perhaps the most general language of any antitrust act. It declares illegal "unfair methods of competition in commerce." The act established a five-member commission appointed by the president to determine the exact meaning of "unfair methods." Today, the FTC is concerned primarily with

Federal Trade Commission Act of 1914

The federal act that in 1914 established the Federal Trade Commission (FTC) to investigate unfair competitive practices of firms.

- enforcing consumer protection legislation
- prohibiting deceptive advertising
- preventing collusion

When a complaint is filed with the FTC, the commission investigates. If there is a violation, the FTC can negotiate a settlement, issue a cease-and-desist order, or initiate a lawsuit.

13-1d The Robinson–Patman Act

The Clayton Act has been amended twice. Although price discrimination became illegal under the Clayton Act, that section was not widely enforced at first. This situation changed with the passage of the Robinson–Patman Act. The **Robinson–Patman Act of 1936** is an amendment to the Clayton Act that strengthens the Clayton Act's provisions against price discrimination. The Robinson–Patman Act is complex and controversial. Its basic purpose is to prevent large sellers from offering different prices to different buyers where the effect is to harm even a single small firm. In fact, the Robinson–Patman Act is often called the "Chain Store Act" because it was an outgrowth of the competition between small independent sellers and chain stores that developed after World War I.

Robinson–Patman Act of 1936

A 1936 amendment to the Clayton Act that strengthens the Clayton Act's provision against price discrimination.

The Robinson–Patman Act encourages lawsuits by small independent firms because it broadens the list of illegal price discrimination practices. This act, for example, makes it illegal for a firm to offer quantity discounts, free advertising, or promotional allowances to one buyer if the firm does not offer the same concessions to all buyers. Be careful to note that the prohibition on price discrimination in the Robinson–Patman Act is limited to situations where the effect is to "substantially lessen competition or tend to create a monopoly." The first You're the Economist offers the opportunity to debate issues concerning this act.

13-1e The Celler–Kefauver Act

Prior to 1950, the U.S. Supreme Court interpreted the Sherman Act as prohibiting mergers between competing firms by stock acquisition, but not prohibiting mergers by the sale of physical assets (plant, equipment, and so on). The Celler–Kefauver Act was the second amendment to the Clayton Act, and it was enacted to address this problem. The **Celler–Kefauver Act of 1950** is an amendment to the Clayton Act that prohibits one firm from merging with a competitor by purchasing its physical assets if the effect is to substantially lessen competition. Consequently, this act is sometimes called the Antimerger Act because it closed the loophole in the Clayton Act and thereby prohibited anticompetitive mergers, which were the target of the original Clayton Act.

The five major antitrust laws are summarized in Exhibit 1.

Celler–Kefauver Act of 1950

A 1950 amendment to the Clayton Act that prohibits one firm from merging with a competitor by purchasing its physical assets if the effect is to substantially lessen competition.

13-2 KEY ANTITRUST CASES

Antitrust policy can be compared to the rules of baseball or other sports. The House and Senate of the U.S. Congress set the "rules of the game" for antitrust cases, just as the American and National Leagues set the rules of baseball. For example, the rules of baseball say that a player hitting a homer must run from first base to home plate, rather than from third base to home plate. Similarly, the Sherman Act forbids monopolization through predatory pricing by businesses. This brings us to the role of the umpire. After a game, a Little League player asked the first-base umpire, "What do you call when the runner and the ball reach first base at exactly the same time?" The umpire replied, "There's no such thing as a tie. It's always the way I call it." That's how it is with court decisions on antitrust laws, and just like many of the umpire's calls, all the courts' decisions are not "crowd pleasers." With this point in mind, let's look at some important "calls" of courts on antitrust cases.

EXHIBIT 1 Summary of Major Antitrust Laws

Law (date enacted)	Key provisions
Sherman Act (1890)	• Prohibits interstate price fixing and other conspiracies and combinations that restrain trade and attempt to monopolize.
Clayton Act (1914)	• Bolsters and clarifies the Sherman Act by prohibiting specific business practices, including exclusive dealing, tying contracts, stock acquisition of competitors, and interlocking directorates.
Federal Trade Commission Act (1914)	• Established an agency (the FTC) to help enforce antitrust laws by investigating unfair and deceptive business practices.
Robinson–Patman Act (1936)	• Amends the Clayton Act by broadening the list of illegal price discrimination practices to include quantity discounts, free advertising, and promotional allowances offered to large buyers and not to small buyers. The Robinson–Patman Act is often called the Chain Store Act.
Celler–Kefauver Act (1950)	• Amends the Clayton Act by closing the loophole that permitted firms to merge by buying assets of rivals, rather than by acquisition of stocks, as outlawed in the original Clayton Act. The Celler–Kefauver Act is often called the Antimerger Act.

YOU'RE THE ECONOMIST

Applicable Concept: Robinson–Patman Act

Is Utah Pie's Slice of the Pie Too Small?

The following is a classic and controversial case: In the 1950s, the market for frozen dessert pies was small, but growing. The Salt Lake City market was supplied by distant plants in California that were owned by Carnation, Continental Baking, and Pet Milk. Until 1957, these three firms accounted for almost all the frozen fruit pies sold in the Salt Lake City market.

The Utah Pie Company had been baking dessert pies in Salt Lake City and selling them fresh for 30 years. This family-owned-and-operated business entered the frozen pie market in 1957. It was immediately successful and grabbed a huge share of the Salt Lake City market. During the relevant years, the market shares of the various competitors were as follows:

Utah Pie's strategy for penetrating the market was to set its prices below those of its competitors. Due to its immediate success, it built a new plant in 1958. Its local plants gave Utah Pie a locational advantage over its competitors. For most of the time in question, Utah Pie's prices were the lowest in the Salt Lake City market. The incumbent firms, of course, responded to Utah Pie's entry and lower prices by reducing their own prices. As a result, all the larger firms sold frozen pies in Salt Lake City at prices lower than those charged for pies of like grade and quality in other geographic markets considerably closer to their California plants. When the California firms lowered their pie prices in Utah,

customers found these out-of-state pies more attractive and Utah Pie Company's market share dropped from 67 percent in 1958 to 46 percent or less in each of the next three years.

Utah Pie sued these three firms, claiming price discrimination. Ultimately, the case was reviewed by the Supreme Court in 1967, which took a dim view of such pricing behavior: "Sellers may not sell like goods to different purchasers at different prices if the result may be to injure competition in either the sellers' or the buyers' market unless such discriminations are justified as permitted by the Act." Consequently, the Supreme Court found the defendants guilty of price discrimination. Inasmuch as no competitors had been forced from the market, it appears that price discrimination does not have to have an obviously predatory impact to be ruled illegal. All the Court saw in this case was a pattern of falling prices. It feared that such a pattern could result in a lessening of competition if one or more competitors dropped out of the market.

	1958	1959	1960	1961
Utah Pie	67%	34%	46%	45%
Pet	16	36	28	29
Carnation	10	9	12	9
Continental	1	3	2	8
All others	6	18	12	9

ANALYZE THE ISSUE Utah Pie sued its three outside competitors under the Robinson–Patman Act. Some have criticized this case because it is an example of the type of bizarre result that can be produced by antitrust policy. Do you agree? Explain.

SOURCE: David L. Kaserman and John W. Mayo, *Government and Business: The Economics of Antitrust and Regulation* (Fort Worth: Dryden Press, 1995), p. 282.

13-2a The Standard Oil Case (1911)

President Theodore Roosevelt's administration took action to break up Standard Oil under the Sherman Act. After ten years of litigation, the Supreme Court ruled in 1911 that Standard Oil had achieved its monopoly position in the oil refining industry through illegal business practices. John D. Rockefeller's trust had used railroad rebates, discounts, espionage, control of supplies to rivals, and predatory pricing to gain a monopoly. The remedy was for the Standard Oil Trust to be broken into competing companies: Standard Oil of New York became Mobil, Standard Oil of California became Chevron, Standard Oil of Indiana became Amoco, and Standard Oil of New Jersey became Exxon.

The Standard Oil Trust case established a standard for antitrust rulings. The Supreme Court ruled that

(1) Standard Oil was a monopoly with a 90 percent share of the refined-oil market

(2) Standard Oil achieved its monopoly through illegal business behavior intended to exclude rivals

The Court stated that point (2) was critical to its decision and not point (1). This doctrine became known as the **rule of reason**. The **rule of reason** is the antitrust doctrine that the existence of monopoly alone is not illegal unless the monopoly engages in illegal business practices. Stated differently, monopoly *per se* is not illegal. Thus, "big is not necessarily bad." Standard Oil and other dominant firms would be broken up not merely because of their dominance, but also because of their abusive behavior.

Between 1911 and 1920, the courts applied the rule of reason in breaking up the American Tobacco Trust and other trusts. In 1920, the Supreme Court also applied the rule of reason when it decided that U.S. Steel was not guilty under the Sherman Act. Although U.S. Steel controlled almost 75 percent of the domestic iron and steel industry, the Supreme Court ruled that it is not *size* that violates the law. Since there was no evidence of unfair pricing practices, U.S. Steel was a "good citizen" not in violation of the Sherman Act.

Rule of reason
The antitrust doctrine that the existence of monopoly alone is not illegal unless the monopoly engages in illegal business practices.

13-2b The Alcoa Case (1945)

Thirty-four years after the Standard Oil case, the courts did a "flip flop" on the rule of reason. In 1940, the Aluminum Company of America (Alcoa) was the only producer of aluminum in the United States. Alcoa's monopoly was primarily the result of its patents and its ownership of a unique resource, bauxite. Moreover, Alcoa kept its prices low to avoid competition and prosecution, behaving as a "good citizen" despite its size. A federal appeals court ruled that Alcoa had violated the Sherman Act and declared:

> Having proved that Alcoa had a monopoly of the domestic ingot market the government had gone far enough.... Congress did not condone "good trusts" and condemn "bad" ones; it forbade all.[3]

With the *Alcoa* decision, the courts turned from "big is not necessarily bad" to "big is bad." The rule of reason was transformed into the per se rule. The **per se rule** is the antitrust doctrine that the existence of monopoly alone is illegal, regardless of whether or not the monopoly engages in illegal business practices. Instead of judgments based on the performance of a monopoly, antitrust policy in the United States was switched by the court's interpretation to judgments based solely on the market structure. Interestingly, the court's solution was not to break up Alcoa. Instead, the federal government subsidized Alcoa's competitors. War plants were sold at bargain prices to Reynolds Aluminum and Kaiser Aluminum, and later more rivals entered the aluminum industry.

Per se rule
The antitrust doctrine that the existence of monopoly alone is illegal, regardless of whether or not the monopoly engages in illegal business practices.

[3]*U.S. v. Aluminum Co. of America*, 148 F.2d 416 (2d Cir. 1945).

Apple Does It Again! Now It Brings to Life Applications of Artificial Intelligence!

Imagine Apple develops a new chip that is implanted in its latest i-Phones, i-Pads, i-Watches, and digital eyeglasses that enables applications of artificial intelligence tasks, such as facial recognition, self-driving cars, and speaker systems. This new technology opens the door for a vast array of new applications that enhance the quality of life for millions. No other company can produce these products. Apple possesses 100 percent market share, but is not otherwise undertaking illegal business practices. A suit is brought against Apple as a monopoly and the courts rule that Apple is not in violation of any antitrust laws. Did the courts apply the rule of reason antitrust doctrine, or did they use the per-se rule in their decision?

13-2c The IBM Case (1982)

In 1969, the U.S. Department of Justice brought antitrust action against IBM because of its dominance in the mainframe computer market. The government argued that IBM had a 72 percent share of the electronic digital computing industry. IBM argued that the relevant market was broader and included programmable calculators and other information-processing products. After 13 years of litigation, IBM had spent over $100 million on its defense and had constructed an entire building to store case documents. Finally, in 1982, the government dropped the case. One reason was that Digital Equipment, Apple Computer, and Japanese companies were competing with IBM. Another reason illustrates the mix of politics and antitrust policy. In 1982, Ronald Reagan was president, and he believed in a much less restrictive interpretation of antitrust laws. In any event, the IBM case represented a shift in the general sentiment among those enforcing the antitrust laws from the per se rule back to the rule of reason.

13-2d The AT&T Case (1982)

In 1978, the U.S. Department of Justice brought an antitrust suit against AT&T and the Bell System. The issue was complicated. At this time, AT&T was a *natural monopoly* regulated by the government. (Regulation of a natural monopoly will be explained later in this chapter; see Exhibit 4.) The government allowed AT&T to have a monopoly in long-distance and local telephone service and in the production of telephones. The Federal Communications Commission (FCC) regulated long-distance rates, and state utility commissioners regulated local rates. What was the objective of giving one company the exclusive right to provide telephone services in the United States? In order to provide everyone with low-cost local services, the regulatory commissions set AT&T's local charges low and its long-distance rates high to cover the lower local rates.

In the 1970s, advances in technology changed the nature of the long-distance telephone industry. Telephone service was no longer a natural monopoly because fiber optics and satellites made cable connections obsolete. Competitors developed, and the government alleged that these rivals were being charged unfairly high fees for access to AT&T's local telephone lines.

On the same day the IBM case ended in 1982, AT&T and the Department of Justice announced this case was settled. AT&T ("Ma Bell") divested itself of 22 local companies ("Baby Bells"), but retained its long-distance telephone service, its research facilities (Bell

Laboratories); and its manufacturing facilities (Western Electric Company). As a result, local companies became regulated monopolies in their areas, and local phone rates rose sharply. In nationwide long-distance telephone service, AT&T's competition with MCI and Sprint lowered the price of long-distance telephone service. Moreover, individual customers became responsible for buying their own phones, rather than using only AT&T phones. The result was a highly competitive market, offering a wide range of phone prices and a wide variety of phones.

13-2e The MIT Case (1992)

For years, the presidents of many of the nation's top universities—Cornell, Harvard, Yale, Columbia, Brown, Princeton, The University of Pennsylvania, Dartmouth, and MIT—attended annual meetings to discuss tuition, faculty salaries, and financial aid packages. After such meetings, these schools often adjusted tuition charges, salary increases, and even fees for room and board. For example, one year Dartmouth planned to raise faculty salaries by 8.5 percent. The other schools wanted to hold the line at 6.5 percent, so Dartmouth was persuaded to cave in. At other meetings, the group's goal was to make sure each student who applied to more than one of the schools would be offered the same financial aid. At another meeting, Harvard and Yale accused Princeton of offering excessively generous scholarships to top students.

The U.S. Justice Department investigated and charged the eight Ivy League universities and MIT with an illegal conspiracy to fix prices. The Ivy League schools settled the case with a consent decree. This agreement required these schools to cease colluding on tuition, salaries, and financial aid in the future, and in return, none of the schools admitted guilt for a price conspiracy. MIT refused to sign the consent order, and in 1992, a federal district judge ruled that MIT had violated antitrust laws and concluded that students and parents have the right to compare prices when choosing a university. In 1993, an appeals court ordered a new trial and the Justice Department dropped charges with the agreement that MIT would cease comparing financial packages.

Does Price Fixing Improve Your Education?

Price-fixing agreements are among the monopolistic restraint-of-trade practices prohibited by Section 1 of the Sherman Act. The Supreme Court has concluded that a formal agreement is not necessary to prove conspiracy. Instead, conspiracy may be inferred from the acts of the accused even if the consequences might be considered socially desirable. The presidents of the universities charged with price fixing in the MIT case defended their business practices with the argument that they openly met to fix prices in order to improve education. With tuition and the amount of financial aid fixed, students and parents will choose their university on the basis of academic quality alone. Consider the discussion of pricing strategies for an oligopoly discussed in Chapter 10. Can you give the presidents a better argument for their defense?

CHECKPOINT

13-2f The Microsoft Case (2001)

Microsoft Corporation dominated the personal computer (PC) software industry with about a 90 percent share of the PC operating system software and Internet browser markets. And Microsoft had tied its Windows operating systems at zero price (predatory pricing) to its Internet Explorer browser in order to eliminate competition and establish a monopoly in the browser market. The remedies discussed included both conduct and structural remedies. A conduct remedy was a judicial instruction against engaging in specific behavior. For example, Microsoft could be required to include major rival browsers with its browser. Bill Gates likened this proposal to "requiring Coca-Cola to include three cans of Pepsi in every six-pack it sells." Moreover, Microsoft claimed that by integrating Internet Explorer with Windows, it was creating one product and not tying two products. In short, no one using the Windows operating system needed a separate browser.

A structural remedy is a "surgical fix" aimed at permanently altering a company so substantially that further violations are not possible. For example, Microsoft could be split into three companies. One company would have operating systems, such as Windows. A second company could have applications, such as Word, Excel, and PowerPoint. The third company would get Internet Explorer and related Internet business. A major concern with this remedy was that a three-headed monopoly monster might destroy innovation and a seamless transition between Windows and other software applications. Another fear was that prices might rise and software would become much more complicated.

In 2001, a federal appeals court ruled that Microsoft did violate antitrust law to protect a monopoly for its Windows operating system. However, the court ruled the government had failed to prove Microsoft illegally attempted to monopolize the Internet browser market. In response, Microsoft announced that it would allow PC manufacturers to continue adding icons of other technology companies to Microsoft's operating system. In 2002, a federal judge approved most of the provisions of the antitrust settlement reached the previous year with Microsoft.

The major antitrust cases are summarized in Exhibit 2.

EXHIBIT 2 Summary of Major Antitrust Cases

Case (date)	Key provision
Standard Oil (1911)	• This case established the rule of reason, allowing monopoly unless it engages in illegal practices.
Alcoa (1945)	• This case overturned the rule of reason and established the per se rule, under which all monopolies are illegal.
IBM (1982)	• The government dropped its case after 13 years and shifted antitrust policy back to the rule of reason.
AT&T (1982)	• Technology made this government-regulated natural monopoly obsolete, and AT&T was found guilty of anticompetitive pricing.
MIT (1992)	• Eight Ivy League schools agreed to stop colluding to fix prices, and MIT was found guilty of price fixing while attending open meetings. MIT and the Justice Department reached an agreement after an appeals court ordered new trial.
Microsoft (2001)	• Microsoft and the government reached settlement after an appeals court held that the firm illegally protected its Windows monopoly.

13-3 MERGERS AND GLOBAL ANTITRUST POLICY

The decades of the 1980s and 1990s were characterized by a wave of mergers. Mergers are a concern to antitrust regulators because firms can avoid charges of price fixing by merging into one firm. The antitrust policy toward mergers depends on the type of merger and its likely effect on the relevant market.

13-3a Types of Mergers

A **horizontal merger** is a merger of firms that compete in the same market. The mergers of Coca-Cola and PepsiCo, Ford Motor Company and General Motors, and Anheuser Bush and Coors would be hypothetical examples of horizontal mergers. Horizontal mergers raise a red flag because they decrease competition in a market. For example, in 1986, the government blocked the proposed merger between Coca-Cola and Seven Up. Likewise, the merger between T-Mobile and Sprint was blocked by the Obama administration in 2016, but company leaders are expected to try again under the Trump administration.

Horizontal merger
A merger of firms that compete in the same market.

A **vertical merger** is a merger of a firm with its suppliers. This type of merger occurs between companies at different stages of a production process. Hypothetical examples of vertical mergers would be General Motors merging with a major tire company and Ford Motor Company merging with a large number of car dealerships. Although the government often challenges vertical mergers, global competition has reduced antitrust scrutiny of vertical mergers. This is especially true if this type of merger lowers costs by eliminating unnecessary supplier charges and U.S. firms become more competitive in world markets.

Vertical merger
A merger of a firm with its suppliers.

A **conglomerate merger** is a merger between firms in unrelated markets. Suppose an insurance company buys a computer software company or a cigarette company merges with a hotel chain. Actual examples are Philip Morris merging with Miller Brewing Company and General Motors merging with Electronic Data Systems Corporation. No antitrust action was taken to prevent these mergers because the products of the two firms were considered to be unrelated. Conglomerate mergers are generally allowed because they do not significantly decrease competition.

Conglomerate merger
A merger between firms in unrelated markets.

13-3b Antitrust Policies in Other Countries

Early antitrust laws were aimed at the domestic economy with little concern for global competitiveness. Because of the internationalization of competition in recent decades, some economists call for a relaxation of antitrust laws to allow firms to merge and compete more effectively in the world economy. Other economists disagree and argue that strong antitrust laws are necessary because small firms create most jobs and innovations.

One reason firms in other countries are so competitive with U.S. firms is that other countries' antitrust laws are weak in comparison to U.S. antitrust laws. For example, no other country breaks up companies for antitrust violations. There are two basic explanations. First, most other countries have smaller populations than the United States. Because other countries have fewer potential customers, they view the global market as the target and design weak antitrust laws accordingly. Stated differently, other countries must sell their products globally in order to achieve economies of scale and be competitive.

Second, other countries have weak antitrust laws based on their culture and history. In the United States, there is a strong belief in Adam Smith's individualistic competition among small firms. This "big is bad" ideology is the foundation of U.S. antitrust laws, but this belief is not prevalent in other countries. In other countries, "big is better," and in countries such as Japan and Germany, government and business work together to compete globally. In contrast, there is a general mistrust of big government working directly with big businesses in the United States.

13-4 REGULATION

The same distrust of big business that is the basis of antitrust laws also led to the evolution of regulation and federal regulatory agencies in the United States. The regulatory process in the United States has gone through several phases. In the first phase, from 1887 to the Great Depression, the railroads were the primary target. During the 1930s, the Great Depression created a favorable environment in which regulation spread to the communications, financial, and other industries. After 1970, regulation increased steadily in the areas of health, safety, and the environment until the 1980s, when a deregulation movement began. That deregulation movement continued until the Obama administration where regulation of the financial and healthcare industries, as well as environment regulation, re-emerged. We will have to see what the future holds for the role of regulation in our economy. In any event, most economists are generally less interested in political or philosophical arguments over whether there ought to be more or less regulation per se. Instead, they are generally more pragmatic and focus on scientific evidence to suggest when it might be appropriate to regulate as well as how and to what extent should more or less regulation be undertaken where it does exist.

13-4a Historical Origins of Regulation

The Early Years

The railroads came under regulation in the late nineteenth century as a result of their unfair pricing practices. At that time in history, railroads faced little competition from other carriers, so there was little to prevent railroads from overcharging. Railroads also practiced price discrimination against isolated rural customers by charging them higher rates for short hauls than they charged city customers for long hauls. In 1887, the Interstate Commerce Commission (ICC) was established to regulate rail prices and to cut the costs of rail transportation by reducing duplicate trains, depots, and tracks. The Food and Drug Administration (FDA) was established in 1906 to oversee the safety of food and drugs.

The Great Depression Era

During the 1930s, regulation was extended to other industries. All surface transportation, including trucks, barges, and oil pipelines, came to be regulated by the Interstate Commerce Commission (ICC). The Civil Aeronautics Board (CAB) was created in 1938 to regulate air travel, and the Federal Communications Commission (FCC) was established in 1934 to regulate telephones, telegraphs, and broadcasting industries. In 1934, as a result of the stock market crash of 1929, the Securities and Exchange Commission (SEC) was created to combat fraud and malpractice in the securities industry.

The Health, Safety, and Environment Era

The Occupational Safety and Health Administration (OSHA) was created in 1970 to reduce the incidence of injury and death in the workplace. This agency cites and fines employers who violate safety and health rules. In the same year, the Environmental Protection Agency (EPA) was established to set and enforce pollution standards. In 1972, the Consumer Product Safety Commission (CPSC) was established to protect the public against injury from unsafe products. The CPSC has the power to ban the sale of hazardous products.

13-4b The Deregulation Trend

Deregulation
The elimination or phasing out of government restrictions on economic activity.

In the 1970s, the higher production costs resulting from regulation generated widespread dissatisfaction with government regulation. The result was a movement toward deregulation in the late 1970s and 1980s. **Deregulation** is the elimination or phasing out of government restrictions on economic activity. Initially, the major thrust of deregulation was in the transportation and telecommunications industries. The *Airline Deregulation Act of 1978* removed regulated airfares and restrictions against competition in air travel markets. The *Staggers Rail Act of 1980* deregulated the railroads, the *Motor Carrier Act of 1980* deregulated trucking, the *Depository Institutions Deregulation and Monetary Control Act of 1980 deregulated banking,* and the *Bus Regulatory Reform Act of 1982* deregulated bus transportation. The Civil Aeronautics Board (CAB), established in 1938 to regulate airline fares and air routes, was abolished in 1984. The You're the Economist at the end of the chapter examines the effects on the airline industry.

In telecommunications, the most important case was the deregulation and dismantling of AT&T. As explained previously, technological innovations made competition in telecommunications possible, and as a result of an antitrust lawsuit, AT&T was broken up and forced to compete with MCI, Sprint, and other companies for long-distance service. In 1996, Congress passed a telecommunications bill that made additional changes in U.S. telecommunications. This bill deregulated cable television rates, while allowing local and long-distance telephone companies and cable companies to compete. This bill also required television manufacturers to equip new sets with a computer chip to block shows parents do not wish their children to watch.

For nearly 100 years, electricity was a regulated industry in the United States. Privately held utility companies obtained the right to operate a monopoly in exchange for government regulations that set rates and capped profits. In 1992, Congress started the deregulation movement for power companies when it approved the *Energy Policy Act*, which opened competition at the wholesale level. By 2001, 24 states and the District of Columbia had approved deregulation plans, but the California power shortage created a deregulation backlash (see You're the Economist on California electricity deregulation later in the chapter).

The principal functions of the federal regulatory agencies discussed are summarized in Exhibit 3.

13-5 THREE CASES FOR GOVERNMENT REGULATION

Government regulation involves political, social, and economic factors, and the general justification for regulation is to protect the public. In this section, we examine three basic situations in which regulation is often imposed:

- Natural monopoly
- Externalities
- Imperfect information

In each of these cases, the argument in favor of regulation is *market failure*. Recall from Chapter 4 that market failure is a situation in which the market operating on its own fails to lead to an efficient allocation of resources.

13-5a Natural Monopoly

The objective of antitrust policy is to create a level playing field for competing firms. Depending on the case, antitrust policy can result in breaking up a monopoly, preventing the formation of a monopoly, and/or punishing anticompetitive business practices of a monopoly. But what happens when it is inefficient for more than one company to operate in a particular market? Stated another way, creation of a level playing field for competitors

EXHIBIT 3 Federal Regulatory Agencies

Agency	Year created	Function
Interstate Commerce Commission (ICC)	1887*	Regulated interstate ground transportation, including the railroad, trucking, bus, and water carrier industries.
Food and Drug Administration (FDA)	1906	Protects the health of the nation against impure and unsafe foods, drugs, and cosmetics. Develops policy regarding labeling of all drugs.
Securities and Exchange Commission (SEC)	1934	Provides for complete financial disclosure and protects investors in stock and other securities against fraud.
Federal Communications Commission (FCC)	1934	Regulates television, radio, telephone, and telegraph services; satellite transmissions; and cable TV.
Civil Aeronautics Board (CAB)	1938[†]	Regulated airline fares and routes.
Occupational Safety and Health Administration (OSHA)	1970	Enforces rules in cases involving safety and health violations in the workplace.
Environmental Protection Agency (EPA)	1970	Regulates pollution in the areas of air, water, waste, noise, radiation, and toxic substances.
Consumer Product Safety Commission (CPSC)	1972	Protects the public against unreasonable risks of injury from consumer products.

*Abolished in 1995.
[†]Abolished in 1984.

may not be in the best interest of economic efficiency or society. This situation exists in a *natural monopoly*. As explained earlier in Exhibit 1 in Chapter 9 on monopoly, a natural monopoly is an industry in which long-run average cost is minimized when only one firm serves the market. Recall that the services of such public utilities as gas, electric, cable TV, and water companies are natural monopolies subject to government regulation. To avoid abuse of this type of monopoly, the prices or rates these public utilities can charge are determined by a federal, state, or local regulatory commission or board.

Exhibit 4 illustrates the demand curve, long-run marginal cost curve (LRMC), and long-run average cost curve (LRAC) for a natural monopoly in the cable TV market—say, a company called Vision Cable. Because of *economies of scale*, the LRAC curve is negatively sloped. Following the *marginal-average rule* explained in Chapter 7, the LRMC curve is below the falling LRAC curve. Given this condition, the firm's demand curve intersects the LRAC curve at a quantity of 80,000 subscribers and a cost of $90 per month equal to the price (point *B*). Suppose this output is divided equally between Vision Cable and another cable company, so that each firm has 40,000 subscribers and operates at point D on the LRAC curve, leaving the firms with an average cost of $120 per subscription. As discussed in Exhibit 1 of Chapter 9, the result of competition between cable TV companies is that the cost per subscriber is much higher—and even higher if output is divided among more than two cable companies.

To take advantage of the lower cost, the policy prescription is to create a cable TV market served by only one producer—Vision Cable. The policy problem now is how to keep this unregulated natural monopoly from enjoying a substantial monopoly profit.

EXHIBIT 4 A Regulated Monopoly

If an unregulated monopolist serves the cable TV market, it will set MR = LRMC, charge a price of $150 per month, and provide service to only 40,000 customers (point *A*). To improve the efficiency of the market by taking advantage of the lower costs of a natural monopoly, government regulators could set the price at $60, which equals long-run marginal cost (point *C*). This policy is efficient, but losses require public subsidies. The typical solution is to set a "fair-return" price of $90, which allows the monopolist to earn zero economic profit and serve 80,000 customers at point *B*. This condition does not fully correct the underallocation of resources caused by an unregulated natural monopoly.

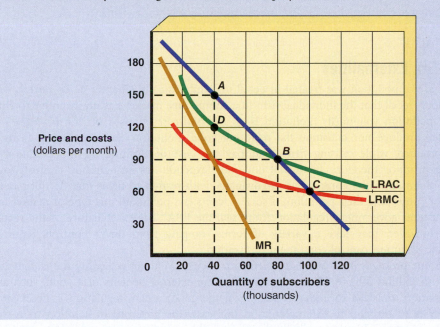

Instead of providing services for 80,000 customers, Vision Cable will service only 40,000 customers by following the MR = MC rule to maximize profits. The price that corresponds to this output is $150 per month at point *A*. Because the profit-maximizing price exceeds the LRAC curve, monopoly pricing creates too high a price and too small an output. Stated differently, the result is an inefficient cable TV market in which there is an under allocation of resources to produce cable TV service.

For the cable television market to be efficient, regulators must set a price ceiling at $60 per month, which is equal to long-run marginal cost at point *C* on the demand curve. This pricing strategy follows the competitive principle of marginal cost pricing. **Marginal cost pricing** is a system of pricing in which the price charged equals the marginal cost of the last unit produced. The problem, however, is that at a price of $60, Vision Cable suffers a loss because although the price covers long-run marginal cost, the price is not high enough to cover long-run average cost. This means the firm can survive in the long run only if the government subsidizes the loss.

What to do? Is there an option that does not require taxpayers' money? Yes! In practice, regulatory commissions have relaxed the objective of efficiency (marginal cost

Marginal cost pricing
A system of pricing in which the price charged equals the marginal cost of the last unit produced.

pricing) and have focused on establishing a "fair-return" price to be charged by the monopolist. In Exhibit 4, the commission would establish the fair-return price at $90 per month at point *B*, where the demand curve intersects the LRAC curve. Because the price ceiling equals long-run average cost, Vision Cable earns zero economic profit and serves 80,000 customers in the long run. However, remember from the chapter on production costs, that in economics, cost includes a normal profit, which is just enough to keep the firm in the cable industry.

CONCLUSION Government regulators can achieve efficiency for a natural monopoly by setting a price ceiling equal to the intersection of the demand and the marginal cost curves, but this policy results in losses. An alternative is to set a price ceiling, called the fair-return price that yields a normal profit, but is somewhat inefficient.

13-5b **Externalities**

The case of pollution was treated in detail in Exhibit 8(a) in Chapter 4. To refresh your memory, recall that the individual firm in a competitive market has no incentive to eliminate pollution voluntarily. Pollution is an *external cost* imposed on *third parties* who neither produce nor consume the polluting good. Pollution causes polluting firms to overproduce, while causing firms that pay the cost of cleaning up the pollution to under produce; therefore, firms that undertake expenditures on pollution control would place themselves at a competitive disadvantage with respect to firms that do not pay the cost of controlling their pollution. If society wants less pollution, this type of market failure justifies government regulation from, say, the EPA. The exact nature of the regulation, however, may take a variety of forms, ranging from direct controls requiring specific pollution-control equipment to taxation.

Some products have *external benefits* for society. Without repeating the explanation given in Exhibit 8(b) in Chapter 4, note that the external benefits of a good, such as a vaccination, can lead to underproduction of the good. Again, regulation is necessary if society is to respond to externalities. In this case, the government solution to correct for the underproduction can take various forms, including requiring consumption or providing special subsidies.

CHECKPOINT

Why Doesn't the Water Company Compete?
The local water company is considered to be a natural monopoly, and the government prohibits other firms from competing with it. If a natural monopoly can produce water at a lower price than other firms, then why would the government protect the water company from competitors?

13-6 IMPERFECT INFORMATION

In some cases, consumers lack important information about a product, and they cannot make rational decisions. Without complete and reliable information, consumers may be unaware of the dangers of unsafe drugs, hazardous chemicals, and defective products. The source of imperfect information about products may be company errors. Much

YOU'RE THE ECONOMIST

Applicable Concept: Price Ceiling Regulation

Who Turned out the Lights in California?

In order to keep electricity cheap for its state, the California legislature in 1996 set a retail ceiling price of 10 cents per kilowatt-hour. Moreover, no new power-generating plants were built during the 1990s. The plan was to require utilities to sell their power plants and import electricity as needed from the "spot market" through high-speed transmission lines from other states. In the deregulated wholesale electricity market, a spot market is one in which the price of electricity is determined by supply and demand conditions each hour.

The stage was set for the forces of supply and demand to "turn out the lights." First, demand soared during a heat wave in the summer of 2000 as consumers turned on their air conditioners. Second, there was a leftward shift in supply. High natural gas prices increased the cost of producing electricity in all states. Also, low snowpacks and a drought in the Pacific Northwest reduced the capacity of hydroelectric dams in this region.

Facing shortages from both increased demand and decreased supply, California utilities had no choice but to buy electricity on the spot market as prices soared tenfold over their normal levels. Since customer rates were capped, the price paid by consumers did not cover what the utilities were paying for electricity. The utilities quickly found themselves facing bankruptcy, and this threat caused additional spot rate increases. Duke Power Company of North Carolina, for example, stated that 8 percent of its spot price was a premium to cover the risk of selling to California utilities that might not pay their bills. A subsequent investigation by the Federal Energy Regulatory Commission (FERC) reported evidence that power companies such as Enron developed strategies to drive up prices.

Faced with this crisis, Gray Davis, who was governor of California at the time, called for more price caps. He convinced the FERC to cap wholesale prices in the West during

Tony Craddock/Shutterstock.com

hours of highest demand, combined with a daily regime of rolling blackouts and calls for conservation. In April 2001, Davis abandoned the 1996 price ceiling, thus sharply increasing the retail electricity price. Prices have oscillated ever since but remain high to this day.

ANALYZE THE ISSUE Draw a graph illustrating California's electricity crisis. Put the label "Price of electricity (cents per kilowatt-hour)" on the vertical axis and "Quantity of electricity (megawatts per hour)" on the horizontal axis. As explained in Chapter 4, draw the changes in demand and supply for electricity in California described above. (Hint: Begin the graph in equilibrium below the price ceiling.)

---

worse, companies may be able to boost sales by withholding valuable information about a problem with their products.

Let's consider a hypothetical case in which an unsafe Tucker Motors (TM) truck is sold. Suppose the safety defect is a gas tank that is located too close to the side of the truck. As a result, another vehicle can crash into the side of the TM truck and hit the gas tank. Such an accident can cause a deadly explosion. Assume further that TM is aware of this safety problem, but the cost of recalling and fixing the trucks exceeds the estimated cost of lawsuits caused by the defective gas tanks. The market incentive is therefore for TM to withhold knowledge of this defect from uninformed consumers.

Exhibit 5 illustrates this case. With consumers unaware of the defect, the interaction of the supply and demand curves for TM trucks yields an equilibrium at E_1, with 100,000 trucks being sold per year at a price of $30,000 per truck. Next, suppose the Consumer Product Safety Commission (CPSC) exposes the problem, and the media

EXHIBIT 5 The Impact of Imperfect Information on the Market for TM Trucks

An initial equilibrium is established at point E_1, with 100,000 TM trucks purchased each year for $30,000 per truck. This equilibrium is reached without consumers having knowledge of a safety defect. Once consumers are informed of the safety defect, the demand curve shifts leftward from D_1 to D_2. At the new equilibrium point E_2, 75,000 TM trucks are purchased each year for $20,000 per truck. Thus, imperfect information has resulted in a waste of the resources used to produce 25,000 TM trucks.

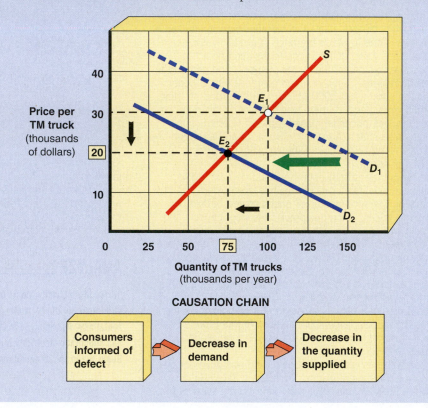

CAUSATION CHAIN

| Consumers informed of defect | → | Decrease in demand | → | Decrease in the quantity supplied |

report stories about crash victims who have been severely burned or even killed by flames from the exploding gas tanks in TM trucks. Once the consuming public is aware of the defect, consumers' preferences for TM trucks change, and the demand curve decreases from D_1 to D_2. The result is a new equilibrium at E_2, with 75,000 TM trucks being sold per year at a price of $20,000 per truck. In other words, this case is an application of market supply and demand analysis as presented in Chapter 4.

CONCLUSION   Deficient information on unsafe products can cause consumers to overconsume a product.

In the TM truck example, resources were used to produce 25,000 trucks that consumers would not purchase when given complete information. These resources were

Does Airline Deregulation Mean Friendlier Skies?

A much publicized case of deregulation is the airline industry. Under regulation by the Civil Aeronautics Board (CAB), airfare competition and the incentive to control costs were reduced or eliminated. The CAB set both fares and routes for carriers. Unable to compete with price, the carriers could compete only with costly nonprice competition, such as advertising. Once the CAB authorized a carrier to provide service between two cities, the frequency of service remained unregulated. When carriers purchased fleets of planes and provided too many flights for their protected routes, profits were squeezed because the percentage of seats filled with passengers (load factor) fell, and the average cost rose. Carriers would then attempt to boost profits by lobbying the CAB for higher fares. In addition to eliminating price competition between established carriers, the CAB restricted entrants into the industry. From 1938 until 1977, the CAB never awarded a major route to any new airline.

Successful deregulation of an industry would be expected to provide the following three results:

- The average price of the service falls.
- The volume and variety of services rise.
- New firms enter the industry, and other firms fail and exit the industry.

The Airline Deregulation Act of 1978 provided these results by changing the structure and business behavior of the airline industry. Although the Federal Aviation Administration (FAA) would still regulate the safety of air service, the CAB was eliminated under this act in 1984, and price competition produced the expected results of lower fares and greater quantity of service. The average passenger price per mile for a flight declined continuously from 1978 to half that rate over the next 30 years on an inflation-adjusted basis, saving consumers billions of dollars in lower fares. Over this same period, the fall in fares contributed to a tripling of passenger miles flown per year.[1]

The airline deregulatory movement is not without criticism. One concern is that lots of airlines went "belly up," and these exits from the industry increased the percentage of all domestic air travel controlled by the industry's largest carriers. Moreover, under the pressure of competition, carriers searched for ways to cut costs, and they created the hub-and-spoke delivery system. This system allows carriers to gather passengers from the "spoke" routes by using smaller, less efficient planes and fly the passengers from the hub in fully occupied, bigger planes at lower cost. Many carriers have gained near monopoly power in "hub" airports. These dominant hub carriers can control access to terminal gates, takeoff time slots, and baggage service, and they can charge smaller airlines high rates for using these airport rights.

Today, deregulation continues to exert downward pressure on fares, and old-guard carriers scramble to compete with low-cost carriers such as Southwest, JetBlue, and Spirit Airlines. Low-fare tickets, cyberfares, and frequent-flier miles are popular. Should the airlines remain deregulated or return to a government-enforced cartel? Critics point to airlines that are in financial trouble. Defenders of deregulation argue that growth of market concentration and its abuses can be controlled by enforcing antitrust laws and allowing global competition.

ANALYZE THE ISSUE Prior to deregulation, critics argued that airline safety would suffer. Instead, although the Federal Aviation Administration's budget was cut following deregulation, the accident rate involving fatalities has fallen. Give a rationale for why the critics' prediction did not come to pass.

---

1. *Statistical Abstract of the United States*, 2014, http://www.census.gov/compendia/statab/ Table 1072.

---

misallocated because they could have been used to produce other goods and services. The solution is for government to prevent companies from making false or deceptive claims by gathering and disseminating accurate information to consumers. This is the rationale for the safety testing of cars, EPA mileage ratings on cars, and warning labels on cigarettes. In extreme cases, a product may be deemed too unsafe, and it is outlawed from sale. Others disagree with this view and argue that the government should only provide information. Once consumers have sufficient information, they should be free to choose.

Key Concepts

Trust

Predatory pricing

Sherman Act of 1890

Clayton Act of 1914

Federal Trade Commission Act of 1914

Robinson–Patman Act of 1936

Celler–Kefauver Act of 1950

Rule of reason

Per se rule

Horizontal merger

Vertical merger

Conglomerate merger

Deregulation

Marginal cost pricing

Summary

- A **trust** is a cartel that places the assets of competing companies in the custody of a board of trustees. During the last decades of the 19th century, trusts engaged in anticompetitive strategies to eliminate competition and raise prices.

- **Predatory pricing** is the anticompetitive practice of one or more firms temporarily reducing prices in order to eliminate competition and then raising prices.

- The **Sherman Act of 1890** and the **Clayton Act of 1914** are the two most important antitrust laws. The Sherman Act marked the first attempt of the U.S. government to outlaw monopolizing behavior. Because this act was vague, the Clayton Act was passed to define anticompetitive behavior more precisely. The Clayton Act prohibited

  - price discrimination

  - exclusive dealing

  - tying contracts

  - stock acquisition of competing companies

  - interlocking directorates

- The **Federal Trade Commission Act of 1914** established the Federal Trade Commission (FTC) to investigate unfair competitive practices of firms.

- The **Robinson–Patman Act of 1936** strengthened the Clayton Act by prohibiting certain forms of price discrimination. This law is called the "Chain Store Act" because it was aimed at large retail chain stores that were obtaining volume discounts.

- The **Celler–Kefauver Act of 1950** strengthened the Clayton Act by declaring illegal the acquisition of the assets of one firm by another firm if the effect is to lessen competition.

- The **rule of reason** and **per se rule** are the two main doctrines the courts have used in interpreting antitrust law. Under the rule of reason, monopolists were not subject to prosecution unless they acted in an anticompetitive manner. The court decision in the Alcoa case of 1945 replaced the rule of reason with the per se rule, which states that the mere existence of monopoly is illegal. Today, the trend is in favor of dominant firms because of global competition.

- A **horizontal merger** is a merger of two competing firms. A **vertical merger** is a merger of two firms in which one produces an input used by the other firm. A **conglomerate merger** is a merger of two firms producing unrelated products.

Marginal Cost Pricing

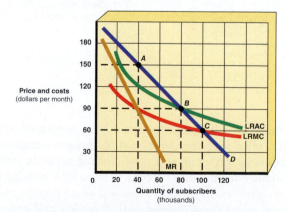

- **Deregulation** is a movement that began in the late 1970s and 1980s to eliminate regulations primarily in the transportation, telecommunications and banking industries. Today, the movement to further deregulate electric utilities is being questioned.

- **Marginal cost pricing** is a pricing strategy for a regulated natural monopoly designed to achieve a competitive production level. Using this approach, regulators set the monopolist's price equal to its marginal cost. Another method is for regulators to establish a fair-return price equal to long-run average cost, and the monopolist earns zero economic profit. Regulation of a natural monopoly is justified on the basis of market failure. Two other economic justifications for regulation based on market failure include externalities and imperfect information.

Summary of Conclusion Statements

- Government regulators can achieve efficiency for a natural monopoly by setting a price ceiling equal to the intersection of the demand and the marginal cost curves, but this policy results in losses. An alternative is to set a price ceiling, called the fair-return price, which yields a normal profit, but is somewhat inefficient.

- Deficient information on unsafe products can cause consumers to overconsume a product.

Study Questions and Problems

Please see Appendix A for answers to the odd-numbered questions. Your instructor has access to the answers for even-numbered questions.

1. Describe the major provisions of the Sherman Act and the Clayton Act. Who is responsible for enforcing these laws?

2. Two business practices outlawed by the Clayton Act are tying contracts and interlocking directorates. Explain the condition required for these two practices to be a violation of this antitrust law.

3. Distinguish between the Robinson–Patman Act of 1936 and the Celler–Kefauver Act of 1950.

4. Using cases presented in the text, explain the issue in the courts' interpretation of "monopoly versus monopolizing."

5. A controversy in many antitrust court cases involves the definition of the relevant market for a firm's product. How would you argue in the Alcoa case that the government's claim of the firm's high market share was in error?

6. In the MIT case, which students are harmed by the Ivy League schools' coordination of scholarship policy? Professional baseball is exempt from antitrust laws. Should colleges and universities also be exempt from antitrust laws?

7. Based on the antitrust laws, how would you expect the federal government to react to the following situations?
   a. A college bookstore deliberately reduces prices until its only rival is driven out of business. The bookstore then raises its prices.
   b. Real estate firms meet in an open meeting and agree to charge a given percent commission on sales.
   c. Microsoft merges with Apple by a stock acquisition.
   d. A small tax preparation company merges with a regional grocery store chain.

8. Based on the cases discussed in the chapter, is the following statement correct? "The antitrust laws in reality deal less with monopolies than with oligopolies."

9. Assume a regulatory agency is given authority over prices and entry conditions for a given industry. Also assume the agency decides to allow

new entry, as the CAB did before deregulation, only when it is proven to be "necessary." Would this condition be expected to favor existing regulated firms, new entrants, or consumers? Explain.

10. Exhibit 6 represents a natural monopolist.
    a. If the monopolist is not regulated, what price will it charge, and what quantity will it produce?
    b. If the monopolist is required to use marginal cost pricing, what price will it charge, and what quantity will it produce? Why will the monopolist stay in business?
    c. Assume regulators set a fair-return price at P_b. Why would the monopolist stay in business?

11. Assume a natural monopolist is required to use marginal cost pricing and a government subsidy covers the loss. What problems might be associated with a public subsidy?

12. Do you agree that "cost does not really matter" as a principle for safety regulation, or do you believe

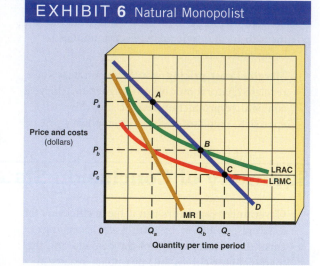

EXHIBIT 6 Natural Monopolist

that the cost of a safety device must be justified on the basis of the value of human life protected from a hazard?

✔ **CHECKPOINT ANSWERS**

Checkpoint: Apple Does It Again! Now It Brings to Life Applications of Artificial Intelligence!

Under the per se rule, the existence of monopoly alone is illegal, regardless of whether or not the monopoly engages in illegal business practices. On the other hand, under the rule of reason antitrust doctrine, Apple would not be found guilty of violating the Sherman Antitrust Act unless it was otherwise engaging in illegal business practices. If you said the courts based their ruling that Apple was not in violation of the law, and, therefore, used the rule of reason in their decision, **YOU ARE CORRECT**.

Checkpoint: Does Price Fixing Improve Your Education?

Accepting the schools' argument that they improve quality by price fixing makes no more sense than allowing General Motors, Ford, DaimlerChrysler, and Japanese automakers to fix prices in order to improve quality. However, there is often a thin line between price fixing and price leadership. Price leadership is not illegal as long as the price followers are not coerced. If you said price leadership is defendable and price fixing is not, **YOU ARE CORRECT**.

Checkpoint: Why Doesn't the Water Company Compete?

Suppose new firms are allowed to compete with the water company, which is a natural monopolist. The concern is that the rivals will be outcompeted. New water companies must build plants, dig up the streets, and lay new water pipes and duplicate other resources in the same neighborhood. Because the competitors cannot produce water at a lower cost, they will leave the industry, and the resources used to compete with the natural monopolist will be wasted. If you said the government is not protecting the natural monopolist from competition so much as it is protecting against inefficient competitors wasting resources, **YOU ARE CORRECT**.

Sample Quiz

Please see Appendix B for answers to Sample Quiz questions.

1. The antitrust law that prohibits firms from combining or conspiring to restrain trade in interstate commerce is the
   a. Federal Trade Commission Act.
   b. Clayton Act.
   c. Sherman Antitrust Act.
   d. Robinson–Patman Act.

2. Price discrimination that tends to lessen competition is outlawed by the
   a. Sherman Act.
   b. Clayton Act and amended by the Robinson–Patman Act.
   c. Federal Trade Commission Act.
   d. Interstate Commerce Act.

3. If a firm has a tying agreement with a distributor which substantially lessens competition, then it is likely to be in violation of the
   a. Clayton Act.
   b. Robinson–Patman Act.
   c. Sherman Antitrust Act.
   d. Federal Trade Commission Act.

4. For many years, AT&T required customers to rent telephones from AT&T in order to receive phone service. This is an example of
   a. price discrimination.
   b. a tying contract.
   c. an interlocking directorate.
   d. exclusive dealing.

5. Interlocking directorates are illegal under the _____ whether or not the effect may be to substantially lessen competition.
   a. Clayton Act
   b. Robinson–Patman Act
   c. Sherman Antitrust Act
   d. Federal Trade Commission Act

6. Which of the following was *not* illegal under the original Clayton Act?
   a. Tying contracts
   b. Interlocking directorates
   c. Merger by purchase of assets with cash
   d. All of the above were illegal under the original Clayton Act.

7. During the last century, court decisions on antitrust have
   a. changed from per se to rule of reason and back to per se.
   b. changed from rule of reason to per se and back to rule of reason.
   c. always emphasized per se.
   d. always emphasized rule of reason.

8. The importance of the Federal Trade Commission Act of 1914 is that it
   a. set up an independent antitrust agency with the power to bring court cases.
   b. strengthened the law against mergers.
   c. strengthened the law against price discrimination.
   d. All of the above answers are correct.

9. The antitrust legislation designed to help small stores survive competition with large retail chains was the
   a. FTC Act.
   b. Sherman Antitrust Act.
   c. Celler–Kefauver Act.
   d. Robinson–Patman Act.

10. What antitrust legislation made it illegal for a firm to pay cash for a competitor's patents, plant, and equipment?
    a. Sherman Antitrust Act
    b. Celler–Kefauver Act
    c. Robinson–Patman Act
    d. Clayton Act

11. The per se rule was introduced in which case?
    a. Standard Oil
    b. IBM
    c. American Tobacco Trust
    d. Alcoa

12. The Interstate Commerce Commission (ICC) was established in 1887 to regulate
    a. banking.
    b. railroads and all surface transportation.
    c. nationwide advertising.
    d. interstate sales of food and drugs.

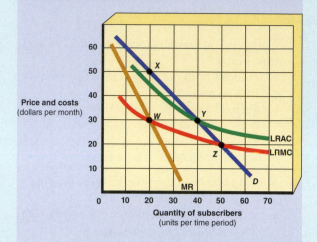

EXHIBIT 7 Public Utility Monopolist

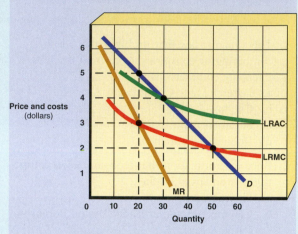

EXHIBIT 8 A Monopolist

13. The Civil Aeronautics Board (CAB) was
    a. established in 1934 and reorganized in 1984.
    b. established in 1938 and eliminated in 1984.
    c. established in 1938 and reorganized in 1991.
    d. never a regulatory agency.

14. As shown in Exhibit 7 an unregulated monopolist would operate at point
    a. W.
    b. Y.
    c. Z.
    d. None of the above answers are correct.

15. In Exhibit 8 if this industry is regulated and the regulatory commission wants no excess profits or losses (normal economic profit) to occur, the proper price and output combination to be set is
    a. price = $5; output = 20.
    b. price = $4; output = 30.
    c. price = $3; output = 20.
    d. price = $2; output = 50.

16. In Exhibit 8 if this industry is regulated and the regulatory commission sets price equal to long run marginal cost (LRMC), then
    a. this firm would earn excess profit.
    b. price would equal LRAC.
    c. the firm would suffer losses.
    d. marginal revenue would just be sufficient to cover marginal costs for all units.

17. Under the Clayton Act, which of the following was illegal, even if it was not shown to lessen competition substantially?
    a. Price discrimination
    b. Tying contracts
    c. Horizontal mergers by stock acquisition
    d. Interlocking directorates

18. Under the Clayton Act,
    a. the same person can not sit on the boards of directors of competing corporations.
    b. mergers are illegal.
    c. monopoly is illegal.
    d. the Sherman Act was repealed.

19. Which of the following is concerned primarily with price discrimination?
    a. Sherman Act
    b. Clayton Act
    c. Robinson–Patman Act
    d. Celler–Kefauver Act

20. Imperfect knowledge about a product can cause
    a. excessive resources devoted to producing a product.
    b. consumers paying too high a price for a product.
    c. overconsumption of a product.
    d. All of the above answers are true.
    e. None of the above answers are true.

CHAPTER 14

Environmental Economics

CHAPTER PREVIEW

Some years ago, the Nobel Prize–winning economist Milton Friedman and his wife Rose wrote *Free to Choose*, in which they put forward the importance of choice in economic as well as personal decisions. Consistent with freedom of economic choices, Americans can select from an almost unlimited number of goods and services. When it comes to transportation, for example, the typical family may drive Minis or Excursions. This same family may own touring bikes, mountain bikes, and hybrid bikes that incorporate features of each. Some U.S. citizens own boats, and others own Jet Skis. Those in colder climates may get around on sleds, snowshoes, or snowmobiles. Some families even own their own planes. The choice of what to buy in the United States is a private decision. I will choose a snowmobile over snowshoes if I want to travel fast and am willing to spend the money. I will choose a Jet Ski over a kayak if I find high-speed travel more exciting than paddling along quietly.

While my choice is private, my decision has consequences for others. My Jet Ski may create waves that threaten to tip your kayak. The noise I make may spoil your desire for peace and quiet. It may also scare wildlife. And the fuel I use to power the Jet Ski not only adds to fuel consumption, but also can contribute to water pollution. Engine exhaust may even make a small contribution to carbon emissions, which may contribute to climate change. The scientific community informs us that climate change is causing melting of the polar ice caps, resulting in rising ocean levels that could create massive flooding of

coastal areas throughout the world, as well as climate shifts that could render today's farms tomorrow's deserts.

The other side of the Friedman call for freedom is the damage that is done when these freedoms are limited by government. Up to this point, the competitive market has been shown to be the best engine to generate what consumers want at the lowest possible price. Yet the unbridled production and use of many of these goods, from Jet Skis and snowmobiles to Coke cans and cigarettes, may not be the best choice for society or the planet. Competitive markets work well when producers and consumers consider *all* costs in their decisions. But for some goods and services, external costs exist, in which decision makers fail to include the cost to others of their decision, such as revving the Jet Ski or snowmobile to the detriment of others or throwing the Coke can or cigarette butt out the car window. Although these are local problems, other problems such as climate change are global in scale.

This chapter will begin by showing why competitive markets may fail to sufficiently protect the environment and why government intervention may improve our well-being. First, we will see that competitive markets result in market failure by producing "too much pollution." Then we will see how we might correct the market failure, including the possibility of government intervention. Finally, the Friedmans would urge us to recognize that while the government has the potential to improve our well-being, there is also the potential for government failure, where government intervention actually worsens the outcome.

IN THIS CHAPTER, YOU WILL LEARN TO SOLVE THESE ECONOMICS PUZZLES:

- Why do competitive markets produce too many hogs and charge too low a price for those hogs?
- How can government legislation, taxes, and permits help society achieve its environmental goals?
- Can government intervention actually reduce environmental quality?

14-1 COMPETITIVE MARKETS AND ENVIRONMENTAL EFFICIENCY

While society values goods and services produced in markets, it also values air, water, and other environmental amenities. Air and water are shared resources that generally are not priced in the marketplace. The result is that markets often treat these resources as if they were free, resulting in their overuse. Competitive markets, which are ideal in efficiently allocating many goods and services, fail to achieve preferred levels of output when they treat valuable resources such as air and water as if they were free.

The competitive market has been shown in earlier chapters to achieve *economic efficiency*. This efficiency exists when the price to consumers, reflecting marginal benefit, equals marginal cost. Consumers, such as Jet Ski buyers, consider purchase price, styling, and performance features, such as speed, when comparing models. Producers choose what type of Jet Ski to make based on their desire to maximize profits. Assuming perfect competition, profit maximization occurs where price equals marginal cost.

Private benefits and costs

Benefits and costs to the decision maker, ignoring benefits and costs to third parties. Third parties are people outside the market transaction who are affected by the product.

However, buyers and sellers consider only their personal or private benefits and costs. **Private benefits and costs** are benefits and costs to the decision maker, ignoring benefits and costs to third parties. Third parties are people outside the market transaction who are affected by the product. As explained in Chapter 4, benefits and costs to third parties are known by a variety of names, including third-party effects, spillovers, and most commonly *external benefits and costs* or *externalities*. Recall that externalities are benefits or costs that are not considered by market buyers and sellers. Noise pollution is an externality that affects third parties not taken into consideration by Jet Ski buyers and sellers.

Other externalities that degrade the environment include sulfur emissions from coal-burning electric power plants and the emission of chlorofluorocarbons (CFCs) associated with aerosol sprays and air conditioners. Sulfur emissions are widely thought to contribute to acid rain, resulting in tree deaths and fish kills. CFCs may be linked to a hole in the atmosphere's ozone layer, which increases the chance of skin cancer from the sun's ultraviolet rays. While CFCs have declined greatly as a result of a worldwide agreement known as the Montreal Protocol, the ozone hole is not expected to disappear before 2050. Automobile emissions contribute to air pollution, which reduces visibility and impairs health. Natural gas prices have fallen to their lowest level in years as a result of a new technology known as hydraulic fracturing, or "fracking," which allows producers to extract more natural gas than they could previously. But with fracking has come reports of contaminated groundwater; small earthquakes; and more controversially, flames coming out of faucets.

Everyday externalities include the secondhand effects of cigarette smoke on the health of nonsmokers, as well as cigarette butts tossed out of car windows, farmers' use of pesticides that wash into soil and water with detrimental health effects, and even noise from your next-door neighbor who is having a loud party while you are trying to study for an economics exam. Externalities can be positive as well as negative. For example you benefit from your classmate's decision to get a flu vaccine.

Social benefits

The sum of benefits to everyone in society, including both private benefits and external benefits. Social costs are the sum of costs to everyone in society, including both private costs and external costs.

When externalities are present, competitive markets are not likely to achieve economic efficiency. In competitive markets, price, which reflects marginal *private* benefit, equals marginal *private* cost. Efficiency for society requires consideration of both private and social benefits and costs. **Social benefits** are the sum of benefits to everyone in society, including both private benefits and external benefits. **Social costs** are the sum of costs to everyone in society, including both private costs and external costs. The condition for economic efficiency occurs when each unit of a good that is produced creates at least as much benefit to society as it does in social costs. As a society, we do not want to produce any units of a good that create more in additional social cost than they create in extra social benefit. In other words, we do not want our scarce resources used up on items that will not enhance our collective well-being. A succinct way of stating this condition for maximizing social welfare is to produce units of any good up to the point where

Marginal social benefit = marginal social cost

Environmental regulations force market participants to include externalities in their decision making. Regulations can take many forms, one of which is a ban. For example, U.S. regulations prohibit the use of CFCs in air conditioners, aerosol cans, and other products. Although regulations such as the ban on CFCs reduce emissions, they are not necessarily the most efficient approach to achieving less pollution. With the dramatic decrease in legal supply, price can rise to the point where some suppliers make the good available illegally. Still, if the side effect is sufficiently dangerous, a ban may be appropriate.

As an alternative to banning an activity, the government can specify the goal, but leave the method up to the firm. Suppose businesses wish to expand the production of goods with high levels of pollution. As an alternative to reducing their own emissions, they can pay another party to reduce its emissions to meet the regulated limited allowable level of pollution. For example, a steel company wishing to expand can buy up old cars and retire them as a way of reducing emissions. It may be cheaper for the company to pay someone else to reduce emissions than to achieve an in-house reduction. While the primary purpose of the government's 2009 Cash for Clunkers program was to stimulate car sales, a secondary purpose was to substitute new, high-mileage, low-polluting vehicles in place of old, low-mileage, high-polluting vehicles. Mexico ran a program from 2009 through 2012 directed at providing an incentive to trade in older refrigerators and air conditioners for newer, more energy-efficient models. We discuss this different approach in more detail later in the chapter in the section on emissions trading.

14-1a **Private and Social Costs**

When a producer of Jet Skis or any other product chooses a production method, the producer is motivated by profit maximization. To maximize profit, the firm must choose the most efficient, least costly production method. Production costs include the costs of capital, labor, natural resources (such as land or energy), and entrepreneurship. External costs to others, such as pollution, are not included in production costs because the firm considers only its private costs. Social costs include private costs and external costs.

14-1b **Competition and External Costs**

Suppose large amounts of carbon emissions are produced by gasoline-powered lawn mowers. To reduce pollution, the manufacturer must redesign the engine. Also, suppose there is a lawn mower manufacturer, GreenAcres, that considers social costs. It will choose a different production method for lower emissions lawn mowers. This production method for lower emissions lawn mowers must have a higher cost than the method used by other, more polluting lawn mowers produced by other firms. If this were not the case, other companies would already be using this method.

In a perfectly competitive market, consumers perceive all products as identical. While there may be exceptions, the typical consumer, as a rational self-interested individual, will pay no more for an environmentally friendly GreenAcres mower than for other lawn mowers. In the short run, GreenAcres will earn less than other firms because its costs are higher. In the long run, GreenAcres will lose money and eventually go out of business. Only the lowest-cost firms will survive in the long run. Because price exactly equals minimum *private* average (and marginal) cost in the long run, average cost for the environmentally conscious company will lie above price, resulting in losses and eventual exit from the industry.

Exhibit 1(a) compares the typical and the "green" lawn mower companies in the short run. Exhibit 1(b) compares the two companies in the long run. The typical company chooses the lowest-cost method of production considering *private cost* only. Its marginal private cost and average private cost are shown as MPC and APC, respectively. The "green" company chooses the production method that has the lowest marginal and average *social cost*, shown as MSC and ASC, respectively. Social costs include the private *plus* external costs. In the short run, MSC lies above MPC, so that the "green" company produces less. In the long run, ASC lies above APC, so the "green" company loses money and eventually exits the industry.

14-1c Competitive Market Inefficiency When Externalities Exist

In competition, only firms that choose the lowest-cost method of production will survive. Firms that choose higher-cost methods will lose money and eventually exit the industry. There is no room for GreenAcres or any other firm that does not minimize cost.

EXHIBIT 1 A Comparison of Costs for Typical and "Green" Firms

A "green" firm has higher costs in both the short run and the long run. The typical firm considers only private costs, as shown by MPC (marginal private cost) in part (a) and APC (average private cost) in part (b). The "green" firm includes both private *and* external costs, as shown by MSC (marginal social cost) in part (a) and ASC (average social cost) in part (b). These curves reflect social costs. In the short run, price in a competitive industry equals marginal private cost. The "green" firm produces a smaller quantity than the competitive firm. In the long run, price equals minimum long-run average private cost in a competitive industry. Minimum cost for the "green" firm is above price, so the "green" firm loses money and eventually leaves the industry.

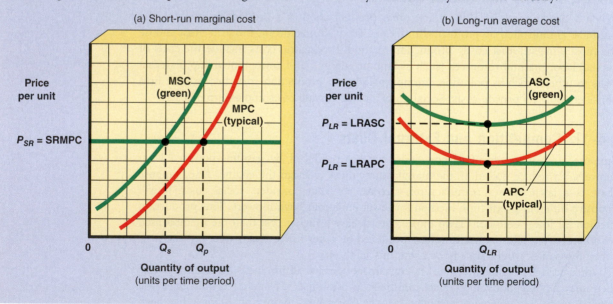

Rewarding firms that ignore externalities while punishing firms that recognize externalities is not socially efficient. Efficiency requires that price reflect marginal *social* benefit and equal marginal *social* cost. A competitive market, on the other hand, results in a price that reflects only marginal private benefit and equals marginal private cost. Efficiency requires that all relevant opportunity costs be included in marginal social cost, while competition forces firms to consider only private costs if they are to survive. If they are allowed to, competitive firms will ignore harmful by-products of their products, such as pollution, climate change, and congestion.

Exhibit 2 shows lawn mower market equilibrium in a competitive market of traditional firms compared to a market of environmentally sensitive "green" firms. Competitive industry supply, S_P, sums the *marginal private costs* of "typical" individual firms that ignore externalities, while "green" industry supply, S_S, sums the *marginal social costs* of GreenAcres and other firms that recognize external costs in their engine design.

When negative externalities are present, competition leads to a lower price and a larger quantity than the socially efficient point (also see Exhibit 8(a) in Chapter 4).

EXHIBIT 2 A Comparison of Equilibriums for Typical Competitive and "Green" Industries

A typical competitive industry operates at price P_c, below the socially efficient price P_s, which would be charged by "green" firms, including all social costs. The competitive industry produces too large a quantity Q_c, compared to the socially efficient quantity Q_s, and charges too low a price, P_c, compared to the socially efficient "green" industry price, P_s.

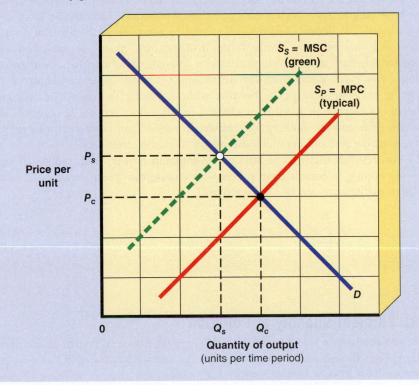

By ignoring external costs, competitive firms produce "too much," and the market equilibrium price is "too low," compared to a socially efficient industry. Competitive markets lead to too many lawn mowers bought and sold because neither the buyers nor the sellers take into account the external cost of lawn mower engines that release emissions when used for mowing. When there are external costs, the efficient point is at the intersection of the demand curve and the social supply curve, S_S.

From society's point of view, the efficient outcome is an equilibrium quantity of Q_s lawn mowers sold at price P_s. Associated with this outcome is a smaller quantity of pollution than the quantity at the competitive market equilibrium. The quantity of pollution associated with quantity Q_s of lawn mowers is the socially efficient quantity of pollution.

If left to the competitive market, profit-maximizing producers would have no reason to reduce emissions. Emissions reductions, if they occurred at all, would be only an unintended by-product of technological change. For example, if manufacturers substitute a smaller engine so as to reduce lawn mower fuel use, the smaller engine would emit fewer pollutants. The emissions reduction is a by-product of the market reward for a more fuel-efficient mower, which consumers want and are willing to pay for. For emissions reduction to be worthwhile in its own right in a competitive market, it is necessary that consumers be willing to pay for a lower emissions mower.

Why won't consumers offer more for a cleaner mower, just as they might for a more fuel-efficient one? First, consider choosing between two mowers that are identical except that one mower uses one gallon of gas per acre, while the other uses two gallons per acre. You will be willing to pay more for the first mower because you will get to keep the full monetary benefit of reduced fuel purchases.

Now suppose you must choose between two identical mowers except that the "green" mower emits only half as much pollution as the other one. The typical consumer will not be willing to pay more for the "green" mower because individually he or she will get only a negligible benefit. Benefits will extend to everyone in the form of cleaner air and reduced global warming. Furthermore, if others buy "green" mowers, you will get the benefits whether or not you purchase a low-emission machine. You are better off being a *free rider*. Recall from the definition of a public good in Chapter 4 that a **free rider** is someone who enjoys benefits without paying the cost. You will get the same benefit of cleaner air whether or not you buy the clean mower. So you will choose to be a free rider and pay nothing for cleaner air, rather than paying extra to get a low-emission machine and still breathing essentially the same cleaner air.

The end result is that no one buys a low-emission mower. Each individual chooses to free-ride hoping to benefit from others who choose the "green" model. Once again, competitive markets are unlikely to be efficient.

Free rider
An individual who enjoys benefits without paying the costs.

CONCLUSION   Unregulated competitive markets will oversupply and underprice products that pollute.

14-1d Efficient Quantity of Pollution

The efficient production level for society is where marginal social benefit equals marginal social cost. The efficient amount of pollution is the amount generated at the socially efficient output level. It is of utmost importance to recognize that the efficient quantity of pollution is not zero. Zero pollution would require zero lawn mowers. Unless society is willing to abandon the American ideal of a neatly trimmed, emerald green lawn, there will continue to be lawn mowers. Nor is it likely that many Americans will return to manual push mowers that do not require fuel, but are slower and take more effort to use than gasoline-engine mowers.

Other alternatives to consider are reduced-emission or emission-free lawn mowers, such as electric mowers. For a parallel situation, consider alternatives to conventional gasoline-engine automobiles. Alternatives include solar and electric vehicles, as well as other transport modes, such as bus, rail, and bicycle. Solar cars, powered by photovoltaic cells, and hydrogen-powered cars are among the virtually emission-free alternatives. But a fundamental concept in economics is that there are tradeoffs. Currently, the cost of solar and hydrogen cars is too high given society's unwillingness to pay for reduced emissions. Performance may suffer as well; solar cars, for example, are slower and less able to climb mountainous terrain compared to gasoline-powered cars. New technologies or changes in society's attitudes toward the environment could change these tradeoffs.

14-2 ACHIEVING ENVIRONMENTAL EFFICIENCY

Competitive markets fail to produce the socially efficient quantity when there are externalities. Externalities are a cause of **market failure**. As explained in Chapter 4, market failure occurs when the private market fails to produce society's preferred outcome.

When there is market failure, we must consider alternatives to the market to achieve efficiency. Government has a potential role when market failure occurs. Just as government can apply antitrust laws when an industry is not competitive, government can apply environmental laws when an industry ignores external costs. Not only are cars required to have catalytic converters, but many states also require annual inspections to make sure the converters are working properly (and to check that consumers have not removed the converters in order to improve gas mileage!).

In the environmental arena, as in other areas of government intervention, there is always the possibility of government failure. **Government failure** occurs when the government fails to correct market failure. Government officials may fail to achieve an efficient outcome either by doing too little about pollution or by doing too much.

Government officials motivated to keep their jobs may be influenced by large campaign contributors as well as by voter desires. A Michigan legislator is likely to be sympathetic to the concerns of the auto industry and will also be aware of the autoworker layoffs and unemployment that accompany reduced car production. The official may be less motivated by externalities that are borne by third parties who do not vote in Michigan. On the other hand, a New York legislator may support an overly strict emissions standard for automobiles. New York voters benefit from cleaner air and are less concerned about auto-industry job losses.

Much of the effort of environmental economists has gone toward improving the odds that government will help, rather than hinder, attempts to reach environmental goals. Economists generally favor incentive-based regulations over command-and-control regulations. **Incentive-based (IB) regulations** set an environmental goal, but are flexible as to how buyers and sellers achieve the goal. Incentive-based regulations can make it profitable for firms to reduce emissions. **Command-and-control regulations (CAC)** set an environmental goal and dictate how the goal will be achieved. Firms unable to meet the goal are penalized, and those that exceed it are not rewarded.

Market failure
A situation in which market equilibrium results in too few or too many resources used in the production of a good or service.

Government failure
Government intervention or lack of intervention that fails to correct market failure.

Incentive-based (IB) regulations
Government regulations that set an environmental goal, but are flexible as to how buyers and sellers achieve the goal.

Command-and-control regulations (CAC)
Government regulations that set an environmental goal and dictate how the goal will be achieved.

The advantage of IB over CAC regulations is comparable to the advantages of a market system over a command system. Market systems are more efficient because they allow gains from comparative advantage. Businesses can pursue activities with low opportunity costs. Similarly, allowing firms to choose how to achieve environmental goals encourages firms that can improve at low cost to reduce emissions more than firms less able to achieve lower emissions.

More efficiency gains are obtainable from IB regulations than from CAC regulations in both the short run and long run. In the short run, allowing firms to choose how they will reduce emissions is more efficient than prescribing a single approach because firms incur different opportunity costs to lower emissions. Over time, firms have an incentive to further reduce emissions by improving their technology. It is possible, although unlikely, that CAC regulations will be as efficient as IB regulations in the short run, just as it is possible, although unlikely, that a command system will happen to choose the lowest cost method of production in the long run; however, command systems do not encourage innovative technology. There is no reward for improving, only a penalty for not meeting the standard. Let's consider how CAC and IB regulations reduce auto emissions.

14-2a Command-and-Control Regulations

In the 1970s, the U.S. government mandated the use of catalytic converters to reduce auto pollutants. The converter results in reduced hydrocarbon emissions associated with the burning of gasoline. While the catalytic converter undoubtedly reduces pollution, it suffers from several inefficiencies.

First, the requirement that cars have catalytic converters is uniform throughout the country. The marginal car in a high-pollution region, such as Los Angeles, has a much higher external cost than the same car driven across the prairies of Kansas. Efficiency calls for stricter regulations in automobile-intensive regions, such as Los Angeles. Second, there may be other technologies that can achieve the same reduced emissions at a lower cost. Finally, automakers have little incentive to invest in better future technology because the regulations require the firm to meet, but not beat, the standard.

A more subtle inefficiency is that CAC regulations may act as a barrier to entry to other firms, both domestic and international. The U.S. auto industry initially resisted environmental controls, knowing that controls would drive up costs. Foreign manufacturers, such as the Japanese automakers, already met the proposed U.S. standards, but achieved their goal with a different technology. Catalytic converters put the Japanese at a temporary cost disadvantage. Japanese cars were required to have catalytic converters even though they already met the air quality standard.

Another example of CAC regulations is the use of Corporate Average Fuel Economy (CAFE) standards. These oft-discussed standards require each automaker to achieve a minimum number of miles per gallon (mpg) for its fleet. For example, Ford's cars might be required to achieve at least 27 mpg. When this standard was imposed, Ford and other manufacturers invented minivans and sport-utility vehicles (SUVs), which were classified as trucks and therefore not subject to the standard. Consumers shifted to minivans and SUVs despite their lower fuel efficiency until gas prices rose, and returned to them when gas prices dropped. In the end, Ford met the higher fuel standard, while the average mpg of its vehicles actually on the road decreased! By 2025, the standard is scheduled to increase to 54.5 mpg. No doubt hybrid and electric cars will be part of the solution. We may be driving cars that run on biofuels, even french fry grease. Only time will tell what ingenuity car companies will display to meet this lofty target.

14-2b **Incentive-Based Regulations**

Effluent Taxes

The simplest type of IB regulation is an effluent tax. An **effluent tax** is a tax on the pollutant. If car manufacturers face a tax that depends on emissions, they can no longer ignore externalities. They must consider the tax based on emissions in addition to private resource costs. Exhibit 3 shows how an effluent tax can achieve efficiency.

Effluent tax
A tax on the pollutant.

EXHIBIT 3 Using an Effluent Tax to Achieve Environmental Efficiency

An effluent tax can achieve efficiency. The tax, t, equals marginal external cost, which is the difference between marginal social cost (MSC) and marginal private cost (MPC) at the socially efficient quantity (Q_s). The firm's production costs now include both its private costs and the effluent tax it must pay, so it makes production decisions as if it considered marginal social cost.

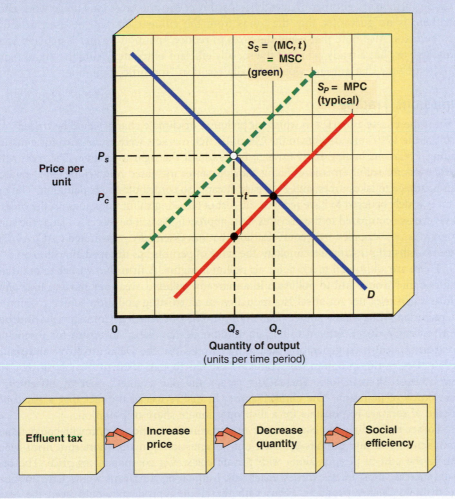

A less direct way of reducing pollutants is a gasoline tax. By increasing the price of gasoline to car owners, the tax results in a smaller quantity demanded of gasoline and, in turn, lower emissions. Over time, consumers faced with high gas prices seek more fuel-efficient cars, lowering emissions even more.

Taxes can achieve efficiency directly or indirectly and can be placed on buyers or sellers. Although the tax approach may appear simple in theory, some important practical difficulties limit the use of pollution taxes. First, how do we measure external cost? There is no market that buys and sells air pollution or climate change. So the tax is at best an approximation of external cost. Second, studies that have attempted to measure external cost find it to be quite large, requiring a substantial tax. It is widely thought that the price of a gallon of gasoline would have to increase by at least $1 to approximate the external costs of auto emissions. Such a tax, added to the approximately 40 cents in state and federal gasoline taxes that are already imposed to pay for roads, would be unpopular with voters and as a consequence would be unattractive to politicians.

Those who favor the effluent tax approach propose that its revenues could be used for a variety of purposes, one of which could be a reduction in income taxes. If so, this approach is referred to as a *double dividend*. Lower pollution is one dividend, and lower taxes on income are another dividend because lower income taxes encourage work effort. But there is no guarantee that the funds from the effluent tax will be used to reduce income taxes. Also note that using the taxes to reduce pollution further is actually inefficient. The tax has already achieved the socially efficient outcome. Using the tax to reduce pollution below that amount would actually result in "too little" pollution.

Emissions Trading

Emissions trading
Firms buying and selling the right to pollute.

What if there were a market in which air pollution or climate change could be traded? As a result of the 1990 amendments to the Clean Air Act, markets were established for emissions trading. **Emissions trading** allow firms to buy and sell the right to pollute. The most active market was for sulfur emissions. Sulfur dioxide causes increased rain acidity. Acid rain can cause damage to lakes, trees, and even cars. It can also contribute to air pollution. The program is widely believed to have reduced the cost of reducing sulfur emissions on the order of 40 percent, as compared to the previous CAC approach. As will be discussed later, the sulfur program is now crippled by a court decision that has essentially reinstituted CAC. As firms must now install prescribed technology, the value of permits has dropped almost to $0.

Offset
A reduction in an existing pollution source to counteract pollution from a new source.

There are additional markets for air pollution rights. A firm that wishes to build new factories that would add to pollution in an already polluted area may have to find *offsets* before it can relocate. An **offset** is a reduction in an existing pollution source to counteract pollution from a new source. For example, U.S. Generating Company, an independent power producer, offered to buy up automobile "clunkers" in return for permission to expand a coal-fired generating facility that would use the Delaware River and pollute the air. Under this program, the company offered to pay $500 to owners of cars that were at least 16 years old. The factory scraps the old clunkers, thereby offsetting its new source of pollution. The clunker approach makes use of the fact that a small percentage of cars are responsible for a disproportionate share of pollution.

To set up trading for lawn mower or car emissions, the government could require manufacturers to buy permits for each unit of emissions. In the short run, firms would include the cost of permits along with private costs as a component of price. The price would increase most for the dirtiest machines. In the long run, firms would have an incentive to build cleaner products. Firms with the cleanest products would need the fewest permits and might even profit by selling permits to companies that cannot improve as quickly. Whereas GreenAcres lawn mowers would go out of business in an unfettered competitive lawn mower industry, the company would now be in a position to succeed.

Alternatively, emissions trading for cars could be attached to CAFE standards. Auto manufacturers would have to possess permits based on gasoline use. This system would allow manufacturers with more fuel-efficient fleets to sell permits to manufacturers relying on larger, less fuel-efficient cars.

A simple example can demonstrate the cost savings of an IB approach, such as emissions trading, compared to a CAC approach. Suppose two coal-fired electric plants each emit 100 tons of sulfur into the air. Plant A can reduce sulfur at a constant cost of $100/ton, while plant B can do so at a cost of $200/ton. The Environmental Protection Agency (EPA) announces that it wishes to cut sulfur emissions in half. Under CAC regulations, each plant will reduce its emissions to 50 tons, a reduction of 100 tons. The cost to plant A is $100/ton × (50 tons) = $5,000. The cost to plant B is $200/ton × (50 tons) = $10,000. The total cost to society of achieving a 100-unit reduction in sulfur emissions is $15,000.

Now suppose the EPA announces that it will give away 100 emissions permits, 50 to plant A and 50 to plant B. Each plant now is allowed to emit 50 units of sulfur. If the two plants do nothing more, each will have to reduce emissions from 100 to 50 tons and each will do so at the same cost as with CAC regulations. However, there is a lower-cost solution. Plant A is willing to sell its 50 permits at any price above $100/ton because it can reduce its emissions in-house for $100/ton. Plant B is willing to buy emissions permits at any price below $200/ton, the marginal cost of reducing its own emissions. Both plants can gain by plant A selling an additional 50 permits to plant B at a price between $100 and $200.

Suppose they agree to a price of $150/ton. Plant A now finds it profitable to eliminate all its emissions. Its marginal cost of reducing emissions is $100/ton. By reducing its emissions to zero, plant A no longer needs any permits. It can sell its 50 permits for $150/ton, making a profit of $50 per ton by reducing its emissions to zero (at a cost of $100/ton) and selling its permits to plant B (at a gain of $150/ton). In turn, plant B finds it cheaper to buy permits for $150/ton than to reduce emissions at a cost of $200/ton.

In sum, the net cost to reduce emissions by 100 tons for plant A is $100/ton × (100 tons) − $150/ton × (50 tons) = $2,500. The cost to plant B, now that it no longer reduces emissions, is $150/ton × (50 tons) = $7,500. The cost to society of achieving a 100-unit reduction in emissions is $10,000, which is $5,000 less than under the original CAC method.

The real world helps us see problems that textbook theory does not always reveal. Emissions trading have the theoretical potential to achieve environmental goals at the lowest cost, but so far, real-world trading has fallen short of efficiency. There are a number of obstacles to efficient trading, some minor and some major.

Taking the factory and clunker example, one minor problem is a new-source bias. A **new-source bias** occurs when regulations provide an incentive to keep assets past the efficient point. A firm faced with the need to find offsets if it builds a new factory may stick with an older and dirtier factory rather than pay for offsets. If there were no offset program, it might have been economical to retire the old factory in favor of a less polluting new factory. But if the new factory cannot meet the air quality standard without offsets, the lowest-cost solution becomes extending the life of the old plant. Electric utilities are also finding it worthwhile to continue to operate old coal-fired plants that are exempt from stringent regulations known as New Source Performance Standards that can only be met by newer technology. There also may be a type of free-rider problem. Car owners

New-source bias
Bias that occurs when regulations provide an incentive to keep assets past the efficient point.

about to junk their 15-year-old clunkers for $500 may keep them another year if a firm or the government is willing to pay, for example, $4,000 for them next year. These minor problems are just growing pains of emissions trading, and future emissions markets will find ways to reduce these undesirable outcomes.

Other growing pains include small numbers of buyers or sellers, imperfect information about the value of a permit, and concerns about permit value in the future. Firms will trade actively only if trading is a better alternative than other choices. Some firms may shut down or perhaps relocate in other countries where permits are not needed. Also, emissions may be higher in regions where electric utilities buy permits rather than reduce emissions, known as the hot spot problem. The **hot spot problem** applies to emissions that do not disperse uniformly, and therefore, emissions may be higher in locations where firms buy permits that allow them to increase emissions. The Tennessee Valley Authority has been a buyer of permits. Not only does Tennessee's air quality suffer, but North Carolina believes its air quality is also compromised as pollution drifts east. The collapse of the sulfur dioxide (SO_2) program came about when North Carolina joined other states to challenge the sulfur trading program on the grounds that it did not account for hot spots. Ironically, studies have suggested that the hot spot problem was not widespread. The latest EPA rule, the Cross-State Air Pollution Rule, has added some limitations on interstate trading to address the effect of pollution by upwind states on downwind states. If all legal challenges are met, there will be two groups of states with separate SO_2 trading markets. States will not be able to use permits from the earlier program to meet the new requirement.

Nevertheless, emissions trading, also referred to as cap and trade, is increasingly accepted. Europe has established a carbon trading system. Such a system was seriously discussed in the United States, but ultimately did not get through the national political process, although there have been some regional initiatives in California and in the Northeast United States. When new programs are initiated, the government may give away permits according to production or pollution over a designated period, or it may sell permits through an auction to the highest bidders. Naturally, businesses prefer a giveaway, and so governments have typically given away permits to get businesses on board. Buyers of permits may be companies such as electric utilities, or they may be environmentalists. Environmentalists can achieve pollution reduction by outbidding utilities for permits and then refusing to sell them to utilities, thereby forcing the utilities to reduce pollution.

The Chicago Board of Trade or "Smog" Exchange was given the initial role to allow trading in pollution permits much like trading on the New York Stock Exchange. Companies are required to own a permit for each unit of emissions. Clean companies need fewer permits and offer to sell their extra permits on the exchange. Dirty companies need additional permits and are buyers on the exchange. They will only buy if the permit price is less than what it would cost them to reduce pollution in-house by one more unit. Sellers of permits will charge at least what it costs them to reduce pollution by one more unit. While U.S. companies are not yet required to pay for carbon emissions, some firms have participated in the Chicago exchange in anticipation that controls may be coming.

Exhibit 4 shows the permit price per ton of sulfur dioxide allowances since trading began in 1994. Over the years, the permit price has fluctuated widely from a high of almost $1,600 after a sharp reduction in permits with the passage by the EPA of the Clean Air Interstate Act on March 10, 2005, to its current low of near $0. The EPA has also introduced a market for the trading of nitrogen oxides NO_X, an emission that contributes to smog. That price has also fluctuated enormously. Initially traded at approximately $800 per ton, it quickly rose to $1,400 but has since fallen to as low as $40.

Hot spot problem
For emissions that do not disperse uniformly, emissions may be higher in locations where firms buy permits that allow them to increase emissions.

EXHIBIT 4 Monthly Average Price of Sulfur Dioxide Allowances under the Acid Rain Program

The Chicago Board of Trade allows trading in pollution permits much like trading on the New York Stock Exchange. This figure shows the sulfur dioxide allowance prices.

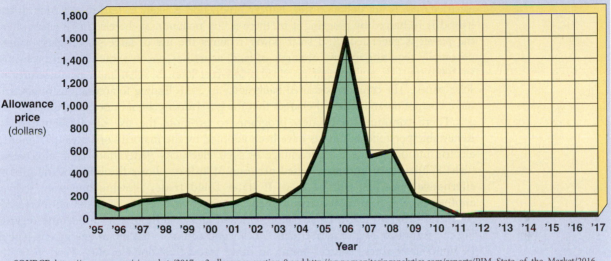

SOURCE: https://www.epa.gov/airmarkets/2017-so2-allowance-auction-0 and http://www.monitoringanalytics.com/reports/PJM_State_of_the_Market/2016/2016q2-som-pjm-sec8.pdf

There is concern that the benefits of emissions trading will be diminished by lack of trading and lingering opposition to the idea of creating a market for pollution rights, especially when permits are given away rather than auctioned, particularly if rights are given away for carbon emissions. There is even a revival of interest in command-and-control regulation. If the government happens to pick the right approach and rewards cleaner technology, some economists favor CAC over the imperfect emissions trading to date. For example, there are supporters of California's approach to reducing auto emissions. California considered a requirement that 10 percent of the cars sold within California must be emissions-free. They anticipated that the mandate would be met with electric vehicles (EVs). However, California then modified the requirement that a similar percentage of cars be hybrids, rather than EVs. The requirement continues to undergo modifications but California's goal has increased to 15 percent of cars sold must be emissions-free by 2025. One of the problems of the CAC approach is trying to second-guess the movements of the market. Just as California assumed electric cars would be a viable alternative, the U.S. government subsidized solar power in the late 1970s. Solar power did not develop as an attractive alternative then. Solar energy now provides a small but rapidly growing amount of electricity, but not for vehicles where other alternatives to the gas combustion engine have instead emerged.

Furthermore, critics of the California approach point out that EVs are not emissions-free if they require electricity from a power plant. Certainly, power plants also pollute, although there may be an advantage to transferring pollution away from the most densely populated areas. EVs powered by photovoltaic cells (PVCs) that use solar energy are closer to being emissions free, but there is still pollution in the PVC production process.

In response to rising gas prices, Toyota and other car manufacturers responded with gas-electric hybrid vehicles. Toyota also has hopes for hydrogen-powered cars in the not-too-distant future. Critics of CAC suggest that the market has a superior ability to innovate, such as a hybrid vehicle with low emissions, as compared to CAC requiring zero emissions that could not be met by a gas-electric hybrid. However, even hybrid electricity use is not pollution free. Battery production is likely to lead to pollution. If the hybrid is recharged by plugging it in, there is still pollution at the electricity plant where the power is generated. And solar power requires the use of large silicon glass panels, potentially requiring massive amounts of land, as well as silicon waste disposal problems. In 2009, the U.S. government provided a low-cost loan to Solyndra, a manufacturer of solar panels. The company declared bankruptcy in 2011, leading to accusations of government corruption and renewed charges that the government should not pick winners.

There continues to be new programs to promote the use of alternative fuels. Renewable portfolio standards have been adopted by the majority of states that require electric utilities to meet a percentage of their electricity generation using alternative fuels. While not an incentive-based program, it at least allows flexibility in the mix of alternative fuels that can be used. If states could trade, allowing one state to pay another state to help meet a requirement, program efficiency could then be increased. A federal program might be still more efficient and could establish uniformity regarding the definition of alternative fuels. Does wood count? What about energy efficiency? In some states, these sources count, in other states they don't qualify. Feed-in tariffs work in a similar way, requiring utilities to purchase alternative fuels at a relatively high price. These types of rates were actually used in the late 1970s, again to promote solar energy.

CONCLUSION   Economist generally believe that incentive-based regulations are more efficient than command-and-control regulations.

Still, much of the public seems more comfortable with controls and rules than with prices and trading. There are a number of possible explanations for the public's view. First, people have difficulty accepting that any pollution is efficient. Nobody wants to think about a higher risk of cancer due to a leak from a nuclear power plant.

Another possible reason for the public's view is a mistrust of experts. People were told by experts that nuclear power would be safe; that hazardous waste disposal sites would not leak; and that people living near Yucca Mountain, Nevada, would accept that location as a safe site for burial of nuclear radioactive wastes. Nevada has since fought off allowing Yucca Mountain to be used as a waste site. The disaster at the Fukushima nuclear plant after the Japanese earthquake and tsunami in March 2011 has been a major setback for nuclear energy, which had been poised for a renaissance by virtue of producing carbon-free electricity. States and cities are debating the wisdom of fracking for natural gas and oil, with Pennsylvania one of the top producers while New York imposes a ban. Even within Texas, the town of Denton voted to ban fracking close to their houses, but lawsuits from powerful oil and gas companies quickly followed and the Texas legislature even passed a law prohibiting any ban on fracking in the state. When outcomes differ from what experts promise, the public favors safety over efficiency. No one wants to take a chance on illness or death if the experts are wrong again. And yet would you give up your car or favor a law that set the speed limit at 20 miles per hour? These laws might increase safety, but they would certainly be inefficient.

14-2c Government and Environmental Efficiency

Market failure exists for products with external costs. To achieve efficiency, buyers and sellers must consider external costs. Government has the power to establish laws, taxes, or permit systems so that market participants pay for external costs.

Although government policy can potentially improve efficiency, there is no guarantee it will. Government can fail to improve a market outcome. This government failure can stem from corruption, ignorance, or politicians succumbing to special-interest group pressure. Consider the countries that emerged from the Soviet Union, where government played a far more dominant role than in the United States. They have environmental problems that dwarf those in the United States. In these countries, air and water quality borders on ecocide, with high rates of illness due to environmental degradation. The Chernobyl disaster, in which a nuclear plant malfunctioned and released radioactivity, has caused thousands of premature deaths. In China, another nation where the government plays a major role in the economy, the Beijing weather report frequently calls for "smoky" skies as well as dust storms blowing in from an expanding desert. Only recently has the Chinese government explicitly recognized their willingness to lower their growth targets in order to improve the environment.

In the United States, large numbers of U.S. Department of Defense sites are among the biggest environmental challenges. Hazardous wastes from the production of weapons resulted in toxic burial sites, including Oak Ridge, Tennessee, and Richland, Washington. The U.S. Forest Service frequently permits lumber companies to harvest trees from national forests at subsidized prices. Government environmental officials have even gone to prison for illegally meeting with industry representatives to weaken environmental regulations. And government has tended to ignore the cost to firms of complying with hundreds of thousands of pages of environmental legislation, a set of regulations more voluminous than the U.S. Tax Code. For all these reasons, as well as the widespread dissatisfaction with government in general, there is concern about the effectiveness of government policy in achieving environmental goals. Government officials may pursue self-interest, which could favor polluting industries over societal interests as a whole, especially if industry executives are major campaign contributors.

The Coase Theorem

Ronald Coase, an economist at the University of Chicago and the winner of the 1991 Nobel Prize in Economics, was among the first to caution against the assumption that government intervention in the environmental arena would improve upon private-sector environmental performance. In his famous 1960 paper "The Problem of Social Cost," he even questioned the fundamental assumption of market failure. According to the **Coase Theorem**, the private sector could achieve social efficiency with minimal government intervention. The role of the government should be limited to the legal establishment of property rights, with environmental disputes resolved with the help of the court. The Coase Theorem is the proposition that private market negotiations can achieve social efficiency regardless of the initial definition of property rights.

Coase Theorem
The proposition that private market negotiations can achieve social efficiency regardless of the initial definition of property rights.

As an example of how the Coase Theorem works, consider a train that throws off sparks and occasionally burns a farmer's crops. Exhibit 5 shows railroad profits increasing and farm profits decreasing as more trains run. Each train has an external cost. Emitted sparks can cause fires, which reduce the farmer's crops. If the railroad ignores external cost, it appears that the railroad would choose to run five trains so as to maximize profit, leaving the farmer with no crops. It also appears that to protect the farmer, there should be a law requiring the railroad to find a spark-free technology. Suppose the

EXHIBIT 5 Choosing the Efficient Amounts of Spark-Emitting Trains and Farm Crops

Number of trains	Total railroad profit	Marginal railroad profit	Number of crops	Total farm profit	Marginal farm profit
0	$0		10.5	$105	
		$20			$ −5
1	20		10	100	
		20			−10
2	40		9	90	
		20			−20
3	60		7	70	
		20			−30
4	80		4	40	
		20			−40
5	100		0	0	

courts establish a law that farmers have the right to spark-free trains. How could the railroad meet this tougher environmental standard? The railroad could change to a new, higher-cost technology. The cost must be higher, or the railroad would have chosen this environmentally friendly technology in the first place. If the cost is too high, the railroad might go out of business or relocate its tracks away from farms. Alternatively, it may be less expensive to offer the farmer money for any burned crops.

If the trains continue to throw off sparks, the first train will reduce the farmer's profits by $5 and will add $20 to the railroad's profits. The two parties will be able to negotiate a deal, with the farmer receiving a payment of between $5 and $20 from the railroad. What about a second train? This train will add another $20 to railroad profits, but will reduce farm profits by $10. Again, the farmer will permit the railroad to run a second train as long as the railroad pays the farmer at least $10. If a third train runs, marginal social benefit will equal marginal social cost. Society will benefit from more train service, but will lose from fewer crops. The third train will be marginally worthwhile, but additional trains will not run. The fourth train will add $20 to railroad profits, but will reduce farm profit by $30. Thus, the railroad will lose money if it runs the fourth train. By clearly establishing the farmer's right to spark-free trains, the number of trains will be decreased from five to three trains.

Notice that the farmer will be better off if he or she allows sparks as long as the railroad compensates the farmer for damage than if the government requires a spark-free technology. The farmer earns $105 when there are no sparks. With sparks, the farmer will earn at least $105, receiving between $5 and $20 for permitting the first train, at least $10 (and possibly as much as $20) for permitting the second train, and another $20 for the third train. With three trains, the farmer will still earn $70 from crops, in addition to a minimum of $35 for allowing trains, for a total of at least $105.

This outcome is similar to the government solutions examined earlier. Efficiency leads to the efficient amount of pollution, which is typically not zero. No sparks may mean no trains. But Coase asks, why assume that society is best served by assuming the railroad is the polluter and the farmer the victim? In the 1800s, sparking engines may have been the best available technology, and an occasional fire may have been a natural consequence.

So consider the outcome if property rights to produce sparks are given to the railroads so that trains are allowed to throw off sparks. If the farmer does nothing, the railroad will run five trains, and the farmer will end up with no crops and no profit. The farmer will increase profit by $40 if only four trains run. Since the fifth train will add only $20 to railroad profit, the farmer can afford to pay as much as $40 (or as little as $20) to stop the fifth train. Similarly, the farmer will gain $30 by stopping the fourth train, more than enough to pay the railroad for forgoing $20 in profit. Once again, negotiations will stop at three trains, the efficient number.

This example demonstrates the Coase Theorem: As long as the courts clearly establish property rights, markets may achieve social efficiency *regardless of the initial assignment of property rights*. Coase's great contribution was to focus attention on property rights, a focus that foreshadowed the emissions-trading approach that allows firms to negotiate by buying and selling the right to pollute. But Coase argues for an even more limited role for government. In his view, the government should establish clearly defined property rights and courts and then let markets negotiate.

Some Limitations on the Coase Theorem

Coase was instrumental in raising concern about government solutions. It might then seem a simple step to accept his claim that private markets would efficiently resolve environmental problems. In actuality, only a small number of environmental problems readily qualify for Coase Theorem solutions.

First, there are no transactions costs in the Coase Theorem. **Transactions costs** are the costs of negotiating and enforcing a contract. Turning to the courts is a costly process, in terms of both time and money. And dealing with the source of the externality has its own costs. Have you ever tried to negotiate with a noisy neighbor at 2 a.m.? However, there are also transactions costs associated with government solutions. So Coasean negotiations may be preferable to government intervention even when there are substantial private transactions costs.

Second, there are no differences in willingness to pay (WTP) and willingness to accept (WTA) in the Coase Theorem. Many studies have found that people's willingness to pay to acquire a property right, such as an improvement in air quality, is less than the compensation they require to give up a property right, such as accepting lower air quality. If the farmer has the right to spark-free air, he or she may require $50 to allow sparks. Alternatively, if the farmer has to buy that right, he or she may be willing to pay only $20. In other words, people may not view giving up an environmental right you already own as equivalent to buying a right you do not currently own.

Third, Coase assumes there are only two parties in the negotiation. Externalities are typically third-party problems, and there may be many third parties. Do all the farmers get together to negotiate with the railroad, and do all the neighbors get together to reduce noise from the party? With many participants, there is once again a free-rider problem. If noise levels decrease, I get the benefit whether or not I contribute to the negotiations. So why contribute? The **free-rider problem** is that if some individuals benefit while others pay, few will be willing to pay for improvement of the environment or other public goods. As a result, these goods are under produced.

Transactions costs
The costs of negotiating and enforcing a contract.

Free-rider problem
The problem that if some individuals benefit, while others pay, few will be willing to pay for improvement of the environment or other public goods. As a result, these goods are under produced.

GLOBAL ECONOMICS

How Should Carbon Emissions Be Reduced: Cap and Trade or Carbon Taxes?

Applicable Concepts: Emissions Trading and Effluent Taxes

With the great success that was enjoyed until recently in sulfur dioxide trading and the more modest success of trading in nitrous oxides, we may eventually turn to emissions trading to reduce carbon emissions in the United States. In fact, Europe has already instituted such an exchange. In 2005, the European Union instituted a carbon permit system for electric utilities and other major emitters such as steel companies. However, smaller emitters such as smaller industries and nonpoint sources such as automobiles are not covered.

In some ways, carbon would seem ideally positioned for emissions trading. To the extent that it contributes to global warming, the effect is the same regardless of where that emission takes place. Whether carbon is emitted in France, Spain, or for that matter the United States or China, its effect on the global atmosphere is the same. In this way, carbon is a better candidate for trading than is sulfur, which has a greater impact in the vicinity of its release.

But there is increasing questioning of whether or not carbon trading is preferable to a tax on carbon. One contributing argument is the initial European experience was disappointing. Early projections anticipated that carbon contracts would trade for about $50/ton, given the high cost to industry of reducing carbon. By mid-2006, the price of contracts had collapsed to €10/ton (approximately $15). The primary factor for the lower-than-expected price was

© Lane V. Erickson/Shutterstock.com

that numerous national governments had issued enough permits that covered producers did not find it necessary to buy permits. In fact, carbon emissions increased in many countries during the first year of the carbon trading regime.

Tragedy of the Commons

Individuals will use an open access resource to the point of exhaustion, basing their use on private benefits while disregarding external costs to others.

A related debate is taking place regarding the "Tragedy of the Commons." **Tragedy of the Commons** occurs when individuals use an open access resource to the point of exhaustion, basing their use on private benefits, while disregarding external costs to others. Ecologist Garrett Hardin maintained that for open access resources, such as fisheries or grazing lands where there are no private property rights, the resources will be overused to the point of collapse. An additional fisher or cattle farmer will consider the private benefit to fishing or grazing, but not the externality of reduced fish or grass to other users of the resource. But political scientist Elinor Ostrom, who was one of the winners of the 2009 Nobel Prize in Economics, found that private parties will design institutions to sustain the resource. The group will define common property rights, rather than allowing open access, where no one has rights. In some circumstances such as the commons, common property may be preferable to open access or private property rights.

Since that time, there have been reforms in the trading system, and prices have risen. While price jumped to €30 by the middle of 2008, it is now back down to €4 (US $6). The possibility that an emissions trading system might not reduce carbon emissions has given impetus to those who argue for a carbon tax.[1]

For those who prefer the tax approach, perhaps the most widespread reason is that the tax will raise revenue. The revenue could provide a double dividend, if it is used to reduce taxes that discourage productive activities, such as the income tax. Of course, the revenues could go toward research and development into carbon-reducing technologies or reduction of the national debt. (Or tax opponents would point out it could simply be wasted on pork barrel projects.) While permits could raise revenue if they were auctioned off, rather than given away, the auction would negate one of the main reasons for favoring permits—that industry is willing to support the permit approach because they do not have to pay for the permits.

Other reasons to favor the tax approach include its ability to be more comprehensive, covering all carbon emissions, rather than being limited primarily to large point sources. It could also be fashioned to include other greenhouse gases, such as methane; farmers, for example, would pay a tax based on the number of cows they owned and perhaps on other animals that emit methane.[2] Some prefer the carbon tax on equity grounds. Particularly if

coupled with a reduction in income taxes, the tax could offer relief to lower-income households. In contrast, the main beneficiaries of giving away permits are stockholders, which may represent wealthier citizens.[3]

The latest twist is that cap and trade has been spurned by the United States with its opponents calling it a disguised tax that will show up in higher prices for all carbon-emitting goods. In a recent court decision, carbon was declared a pollutant, giving the U.S. Environmental Protection Agency the right to regulate carbon emissions. New regulations aimed at carbon will likely mean the end of new coal-fired electric plants. But existing plants will still pour carbon into the air unless there is a program that imposes a cost on all carbon emissions.

ANALYZE THE ISSUE

1. What are the advantages and disadvantages of carbon trading, as compared to sulfur dioxide trading?
2. What are the advantages and disadvantages of a tax system, as compared to carbon trading?
3. If a carbon tax is preferable to a trading system on economic grounds, why might we adopt a trading system anyway?

1. Phil MacDonald, "EU Carbon Price Falls Below €4,"Sandbag Smarter Climate Policy. September 2, 2016. Found at: https://sandbag.org.uk/2016/09/02/eu-carbon-price-falls-below-e4-2/ and http://www.monitoringanalytics.com/reports/PJM_State_of_the_Market/2016/2016q2-som-pjm-sec8.pdf.
2. Jonathan A. Lesser, "Control of Greenhouse Gases Difficult With Cap-and-trade or Tax-and-spend," *Natural Gas and Electricity*, December 2007, Wiley Periodicals Inc., http://www3.interscience.wiley.com/cgi-bin/jhome/105559587.
3. Ian W. H. Parry, "Should We Abandon Cap and Trade in Favor of a CO$_2$ Tax?" *Resources*, Summer 2007, 6–10, Resources for the Future, http://www.rff.org/Publications/Resources/Pages/AbandonCapandTrade.aspx

Ecologists and other physical scientists have taken the issue a step further with calls for **sustainability**. The most common definition is that of the Brundtland Commission (1987) that calls for us to "meet the needs of the present without compromising future needs." Economists have begun to recognize that ecological systems such as the carbon cycle that influences climate must be sustained in order to sustain life. Sustainability is typically a more stringent requirement than social efficiency, as socially efficient solutions are not limited to those that also increase the well-being of future generations. Social efficiency may call for actions to reduce carbon emissions, but sustainability might well call for stronger actions to ensure that future generations are protected from today's decisions. Economists are at the early stages of how to incorporate sustainability into economic analysis.

Sustainability
Meeting the needs of the present generation without compromising the ability of future generations to meet their needs.

GLOBAL ECONOMICS

Why Is the Climate Change Problem So Hard to Solve?

Applicable Concepts: Emissions Trading and Effluent Taxes

The United Nations Framework Convention on Climate Change (UNFCCC) adopted its first treaty on May 9, 1992, and it has adopted several more since then. Its latest is the 2015 Paris Climate Agreement (also known as the Paris Accords).

The central goal of the Paris Climate Agreement, which was adopted by 196 nations, is to prevent the global average temperature from increasing more than 2 degrees Celsius above pre-industrial levels. The global average temperature has already risen about 1 degree Celsius. Unfortunately, the Paris Accords are unlikely to meet its goal since even if every signatory country meets their current pledges to reduce greenhouse emissions, the world is still expected to warm by more than 2 degrees.

The actual reductions in emissions are set to begin in 2020 and then the emissions reduction target will be re-evaluated every 5 years. The deal is supposed to reach zero net emissions by "mid-century." Zero net emissions imply that any greenhouse emissions emitted could be offset by an equivalent amount extracted from the atmosphere by, for example, growing forests that absorb carbon dioxide.

Although developing countries are given some time and leeway in meeting emission reductions, developed countries are expected to reduce their emissions right away. To encourage underdeveloped countries to meet their pledged reduction in emissions, the developed world is expected to provide $100 billion each year to assist them in switching away from less-expensive fossil fuels. The United States has pledged $3 billion per year, the largest total amount pledged and the 11th largest amount pledged per capita.[1]

Although the United States initially signed on during the Obama administration, President Trump withdrew from the Paris Climate Accords on June 1, 2017. This leaves the U.S., Syria, and Nicaragua as the only nations that are not part of the deal (and Nicaragua withdrew because the deal didn't go far enough!). In his address in the Rose Garden, announcing U.S. withdrawal, President

MANDEL NGAN/AFP/Getty Images

Trump argued that the Paris Accords unfairly advantaged foreign nations. Trump said, "China will be able to build hundreds of coal plants. We can't build the plants, but they can, according to this agreement." He asserted the deal placed "draconian" financial burdens on the American people.[2]

As you might expect, this is a hot political issue. Critics of President Trump's withdrawal from the Paris Accords worry about the consequences this may have on the global environment. They also worry that other leaders may follow suit and, as they describe it, "put their own short-term political interests ahead of a long-term global campaign."[3]

The Paris Climate Agreement is not the first attempt at combating climate change. The Kyoto Protocol agreement of 1997 was another attempt; however, it failed perhaps because the United States declined to sign over its concerns that it was a "legally" binding treaty. We will have to wait and see if the Paris Agreement will be able to achieve its goals.

Why is this problem proving so difficult to solve? There has been widespread, although not universal, agreement that human activity is contributing to a warming planet, which could lead to flooding, desertification, weather events such as stronger hurricanes, and the spread of tropical diseases to warming countries.

One of the continuing controversies that has run through many climate change treaties is whether countries, developed and developing, should receive credit for offsets. Brazil, for example, wants credit for slowing or reversing the rate at which it is cutting down its rain forest. Trees store carbon. Countries could receive carbon credits for planting trees or possibly for slowing the rate at which trees are being cut down. Brazil and other developing countries want developed countries to pay them, as they claim they are slowing their own development by growing new forests or slowing the conversion of existing forest to agricultural resources.

Further, there is not even agreement over which countries are still developing. For purposes of avoiding the cost of slowing emissions, never mind reducing them; it is advantageous to claim you are still developing. The argument is that developed countries were able to grow and emit greenhouse gases with impunity; it is only fair that developing countries be able to do the same. Developed countries have benefited from industrialization without having to pay for their emissions, so is it fair that developing countries should do so now?

But perhaps most fundamentally, a viable solution will have to address the problems of externalities and public goods. Consumers and producers of carbon-emitting products, such as coal-burning power plants and gasoline-burning automobiles, will, in the absence of government intervention, ignore emissions. Furthermore, any global agreement to reduce emissions will benefit everyone, whether or not an individual has borne the expense of reducing emissions, a classic example of a public good. Benefits are nonrival and nonexcludable. And agreeing on whether we will actually reduce emissions or simply slow them down will be contentious. Nor is CO_2 the only greenhouse gas. Methane, of which cows are a major emitter, is smaller in volume, but more potent in effect.

So in sum, taking action to slow or stop climate change is one of the most difficult problems humans have faced. There may be some doubt on whether humans have contributed to the problem, and some disagreement on what countries are responsible for paying for the solution, and how to develop a mechanism that can overcome externalities and public goods problems. However, if left unaddressed, we may find ourselves left to adapt to climate change, abandoning low-lying lands, accepting millions of immigrants from those countries, switching to hot weather crops, and losing flora and fauna that cannot adapt, unless we can develop effective approaches to address this challenge.

ANALYZE THE ISSUE

1. Give an example of an equity (fairness) issue that arises in working toward a global agreement to limit greenhouse gas emissions.

2. Give an example of an efficiency (market failure) issue that arises in working toward a global agreement to limit greenhouse gas emissions.

3. Many countries will be able to receive some funding under the Paris Agreement for offsets, such as planting trees. Explain whether the case for offsets is based on efficiency or equity arguments.

4. How can the free-rider problem emerge in efforts to combat climate change?

1. Green Climate Fund. Found at: http://www.greenclimate.fund/partners/contributors/resources-mobilized.
2. https://www.whitehouse.gov/the-press-office/2017/06/01/statement-president-trump-paris-climate-accord
3. Keith Bradsher, "China Looks to Capitalize on Clean Energy as U.S. Retreats," *The New York Times*, June 5, 2017. Found at: https://www.nytimes.com/2017/06/05/business/energy-environment/china-clean-energy-coal-pollution.html

CONCLUSION

Neither government nor markets can be asserted to be the best solution to environmental problems. On balance, though, the effort to work toward improved government solutions seems worthwhile, given the outcome for the environment of purely self-interested markets. But alternatives including private ownership and common-property ownership may be preferable where transactions costs are low enough to allow individual or group negotiations over resource use.

CHECKPOINT

Is It Efficient to Buy Odor-Reducing Technology If You Live Next to a Hog Farm?

You live next door to a hog farm. It is estimated that the smell from the hog farm reduces the value of your home by $7,000. For $5,000, you can purchase technology that reduces the hog smell by half, so your house value would decrease by only $3,500. Assuming the hog farm has the property right to locate next door and that it is not required to reduce the hog smell, what will you do? Will you do nothing or buy the new technology?

Key Concepts

Private benefits and costs

Social benefits and costs

Free rider

Market failure

Government failure

Incentive-based regulations

Command-and-control regulations

Effluent tax

Emissions trading

Offset

New-source bias

Hot spot problem

Coase Theorem

Transactions costs

Free-rider problem

Tragedy of the Commons

Sustainability

Summary

- **Externalities** are benefits or costs that fall on third parties who are neither buyers nor sellers. Pollution is a negative externality or an external cost that is a by-product of many industrial production processes.

- **Market failure** is present when the market produces a socially inefficient outcome (for example, when there are externalities). All firms, including competitive firms, consider private costs, but disregard external costs in making decisions.

- **Government failure** occurs when public-sector actions or lack of actions fail to improve an inefficient market outcome. Government failure stems from corruption, ignorance, or special-interest group pressure. For example, government officials seeking campaign contributions and votes may choose environmental measures that favor wealthy contributors over society's best interests.

- **Command-and-control regulations** occur when the government dictates the approach to achieving an environmental goal. Command-and-control regulations are generally inefficient on three grounds: They do not distinguish between high- and low-pollution areas, they do not allow firms to choose lower-cost technologies that could achieve the environmental standard, and they do not encourage investment in improved technology to lower future emissions.

- **Incentive-based regulations** build on markets to achieve environmental efficiency. **Effluent taxes** are taxes that reflect external costs. **Emissions trading** allows firms to buy and sell the "right to pollute."

- The **hot spot problem** applies to emissions that do not disperse uniformly, and therefore, emissions may be higher in locations where firms buy permits that allow them to increase emissions.

- The **Coase Theorem** maintains that markets can be efficient in the presence of externalities with minimal government intervention. Even in the presence of externalities, markets may produce efficient outcomes so long as property rights are clearly established.

- **Transactions costs**, **income effects**, and **free-rider problems** are obstacles to achieving environmental efficiency through markets. Transactions costs are the costs of negotiating an agreement, income effects are present when limited income prevents one party from being able to afford the efficient solution, and free-rider problems are present when participants are better off hiding than revealing their willingness to pay for an environmental improvement.

- **Tragedy of the Commons** predicts that individuals will use fisheries and grazing areas to exhaustion, as they base their use on their private benefits, disregarding the effects of their use on others. The "tragedy" has been questioned by Elinor Ostrom, who finds individuals will establish institutions converting open access property to common property so that the resource can be sustained over time.

Summary of Conclusion Statements

- Unregulated competitive markets will oversupply and underprice products that pollute.

- Economists generally believe that incentive-based regulations are more efficient than command-and-control regulations.

- Neither government nor markets can be asserted to be the best solution to environmental problems. On balance, though, the effort to work toward improved government solutions seems worthwhile, given the outcome for the environment of purely self-interested markets. But alternatives including private ownership and common-property ownership may be preferable where transactions costs are low enough to allow individual or group negotiations over resource use.

Study Questions and Problems

Please see Appendix A for answers to the odd-numbered questions. Your instructor has access to the answers for even-numbered questions.

1. Compare price and quantity in a competitive industry to those of a "green" industry for a product that generates pollution.

2. Suppose a car sells for $20,000 in a market with no pollution restrictions. Will the car sell for more than $20,000, less than $20,000, or $20,000 when there are pollution restrictions? Explain.

3. You are considering whether to buy one house for $100,000 or another identical house located near high-voltage electric power lines for $90,000. Assume that it has been established that

living near high-voltage lines increases the risk of cancer due to electromagnetic fields (EMFs). If you choose the $90,000 house, is the radiation from EMFs an externality? Explain.

4. Restaurants have observed that large parties (eight or more) leave a lower average tip than smaller parties. Identify the effect, which also makes it more difficult to reach global environmental agreements, responsible for this phenomenon.

5. Suppose your instructor gives eight homework assignments during the semester. She indicates that anyone who does not turn in all eight assignments will automatically fail the course. Is this an example of a command-and-control or an incentive-based regulation? Explain any inefficiencies of your instructor's approach.

   An instructor who automatically flunks students who do not turn in all homework assignments is exhibiting command-and-control regulation. She is dictating the production process for achieving knowledge. The inefficiencies are that students may turn in poorly done assignments or may copy assignments and that some students may understand the material without doing the homework or may have an alternative production method, such as the use of computer software, to achieve knowledge. The instructor's method is particularly inefficient if her assignments are busywork and do not really help the students to achieve knowledge.

6. Environmentalists in Tennessee brought suit against the Champion Paper Company of North Carolina for polluting the Pigeon River, which flows from North Carolina into eastern Tennessee. Tennessee claimed that the coffee-colored water smelled bad and would not support fishing or swimming. Environmentalists requested that the river be restored to its pristine state, whereby water quality is restored to the level before the coming of industry. The Environmental Protection Agency heard the suit and applied an efficiency standard. Is pristine water an efficiency standard? Explain.

7. Draw a graph to demonstrate your answer to question 6.

8. California once proposed legislation that would have required 10 percent of its car fleet to be nearly emissions-free by the year 2003. This mandate spurred electric vehicle research. Such vehicles could be powered by photovoltaic cells or by batteries that are recharged using an electrical outlet. Would you agree that it is correct to conclude that electric vehicles that use electrical outlets are emissions-free? What about electric vehicles powered by photovoltaic cells?

9. Explain why consumers would not be willing to pay the full costs of a less polluting car in the absence of government regulations.

10. Evaluate the following statement: "When products pollute, government solutions are more efficient than market solutions."

11. Provide an example of a market where you think the Coase Theorem applies. Explain why you think the market satisfies assumptions regarding transactions costs, income effects, and free riders.

12. In a study of ranching laws in the 1800s, an economic researcher found that as these laws restricted the ability of cattle to roam freely, agricultural output increased. Does this researcher's findings support the Coase Theorem? Explain.

13. If we are to take action against global warming, we must reduce carbon emissions. Explain how to reduce carbon emissions by using
    a. command-and-control regulation.
    b. an effluent tax.
    c. emissions trading.

14. A global agreement known as the Montreal Protocol led to the phase-out of chlorofluorocarbons (CFCs), chemical compounds found in aerosol cans and refrigerants. CFCs may have contributed to the growing hole in the ozone layer. With a diminished ozone layer, there is an increased chance of skin cancer. Explain the effect of this agreement on the price of deodorants and air-conditioning. Also, is a ban on CFCs an efficient approach to the ozone hole problem?

15. Explain the "Tragedy of the Commons" as described by Garrett Hardin. Why does Elinor Ostrom disagree with Hardin's prediction that fisheries and other "commons" will collapse?

16. Distinguish between the concepts of social efficiency and sustainability. Provide an example to demonstrate the distinction.

✔ CHECKPOINT ANSWERS

Is It Efficient to Buy Odor-Reducing Technology If You Live Next to a Hog Farm?

It is not efficient to purchase the new odor-reducing technology. It would cost $5,000, but would increase your house value by only $3,500. It is not efficient to cut the odor by half if the market will not compensate you sufficiently for reduced hog odors. If your only option is to do nothing or to buy the new technology and you said do nothing, **YOU ARE CORRECT**. (A third option is to pay the hog farm to locate elsewhere. You would be willing to pay up to $7,000 to avoid the $7,000 lost due to the smell of the nearby farm.)

Sample Quiz

Please see Appendix B for answers to Sample Quiz questions.

1. Private costs are
   a. the full resource costs of an economic activity.
   b. always less than social costs.
   c. the costs of an economic activity borne by the producer.
   d. All of the above answers are correct.

2. When negative externalities such as pollution exist, competition leads to
   a. a socially efficient outcome.
   b. too few goods being bought and sold.
   c. a market equilibrium price that is too high.
   d. more production than would be efficient.

3. From an economic viewpoint, the optimal amount of pollution
   a. is zero because all pollution imposes costs on society.
   b. is that amount firms create when they maximize economic profits by setting their marginal private costs equal to market price.
   c. is that amount where the marginal social costs of producing a good precisely equals the price of the good.
   d. Both answers b. and c. are correct.

4. Which of the following provides an example of command-and-control regulation?
   a. Taxing producers based on the external costs created by their pollution, thus internalizing external costs.

   b. Requiring firms to reduce their pollution by 50 percent, thus allowing them to emit 50 percent of their historical emissions, and allowing them to freely buy and sell allowances.
   c. Requiring firms to use a particular type of pollution-control technology, such as smokestack scrubbers or catalytic converters.
   d. Subsidizing firms that exceed their pollution-control targets.

EXHIBIT 6 Private and Social Cost

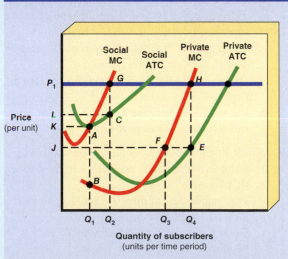

5. The perfectly competitive profit-maximizing firm in Exhibit 6 creates water and air pollution as a consequence of producing its output of pigs. If pollution costs are borne by third parties, the firm will maximize economic profit by choosing to
   a. voluntarily incur costs to reduce its pollution.
   b. produce at output rate Q_3.
   c. produce at output rate Q_2.
   d. produce at output rate Q_4.

6. Use Exhibit 6 to answer the following question. To maximize social welfare, the firm should produce at output rate
   a. Q_1.
   b. Q_2.
   c. Q_3.
   d. Q_4.

7. At the efficient level of pollution, the
   a. total social costs and total social benefits of reduction are equal.
   b. marginal social costs and marginal social benefits are equal.
   c. marginal private costs and marginal private benefits are equal.
   d. total private costs and total private benefits are equal.

8. A government policy that charges coal producers a fee per ton of coal produced (an effluent charge) where the fee is determined by the amount of pollutants discharged into the air or water will lead to
   a. a decrease in the market equilibrium quantity of coal produced.
   b. a decrease in the market equilibrium price of coal.
   c. an increase in the market equilibrium price of coal.
   d. the results in answers a. and b.
   e. the results in answers a. and c.

9. Which of the following is an important lesson from the environmental experience in the former Soviet Union?
   a. Free-market economies are unlikely to have long-run environmental problems.
   b. Government-owned industry tends to be cleaner than privately-owned industry.

   c. Pollution can be worse in a communist system than in a capitalist system.
   d. Pollution can be worse in a capitalist system than in a communist system.

10. According to *most* economists, reducing automobile emissions to zero would be
    a. optimal.
    b. inefficient.
    c. beneficial.
    d. impossible.

11. In a perfectly competitive industry with external costs, which of the following is *true*?
    a. The competitive price is higher and the quantity is higher than the socially efficient point.
    b. The competitive price is higher and the quantity is lower than the socially efficient point.
    c. Since the industry is perfectly competitive, price and quantity are at the socially efficient levels.
    d. The competitive price is lower and the quantity is higher than the socially efficient point.

Each time Orville flies over Wilbur's house, the noise reduces the value of Wilbur's house. Exhibit 7 shows the profits to Orville of each flight and the value of Wilbur's house at each flight.

EXHIBIT 7 Impact of Flights on House Value

Number of flights	Total profits	Marginal profits	Value of Wilbur's house
1	$10,000	$10,000	$100,000
2	18,000	8,000	95,000
3	24,000	6,000	90,000
4	28,000	4,000	85,000
5	30,000	2,000	80,000

12. As shown in Exhibit 7, if Orville has the property right to fly over Wilbur's house but Wilbur is allowed to negotiate with Orville on the number of flights, what will be the number of flights?
    a. 2
    b. 3
    c. 4
    d. 5

13. As shown in Exhibit 7, if Wilbur has the property right to have no planes flying over his house but Orville is allowed to negotiate with Wilbur, what will be the number of flights?
    a. 2
    b. 3
    c. 4
    d. 5

14. As shown in Exhibit 7, at the socially efficient number of flights, what will be the market value of Orville's house?
    a. $100,000
    b. $95,000
    c. $90,000
    d. $85,000

15. According to the Coase Theorem, the private sector can achieve social efficiency if the government
    a. establishes and enforces property rights.
    b. imposes taxes to serve as proxies for external costs.
    c. sets rigorous environmental standards.
    d. encourages competition with antitrust laws.

16. The costs of an economic activity borne by the producers are
    a. always less than social costs.
    b. the full resource costs of an economic activity.
    c. private costs.
    d. All of the above answers are correct.

17. An example of the command-and-control approach to environmental policy is
    a. placing a tax on Freon to reduce its use and the corresponding CFC emissions (which contribute to the ozone hole).
    b. requiring car producers to install new air conditioners that do not use Freon.

c. allowing coal producers to buy and sell permits to allow CFC emissions.
d. allowing individuals to sue Freon producers if CFC emissions exceed a government-set standard.

18. If a good is produced up to the point where marginal social benefit equals marginal social cost,
    a. social welfare is maximized.
    b. the good is overproduced and the market is inefficient.
    c. firms are earning zero profits.
    d. all externalities have been eliminated.

Jack enjoys smoking, while Jill fears that secondhand smoke will shorten her life. Exhibit 8 shows the value Jack places on each cigarette he smokes and the value Jill places on her shortened life. Use the table to answer the following questions.

EXHIBIT 8 Cigarette Smoking Data

Quantity of cigarettes	Total value to Jack of cigarettes	Days of life lost	Total value to Jill of days lost
1	$50	1	$30
2	90	2	60
3	120	3	90
4	140	4	120
5	150	5	150

19. As shown in Exhibit 8, if smokers have the right to smoke as many cigarettes as they want, and nonsmokers have the right to negotiate, how many cigarettes will Jack smoke?
    a. 1
    b. 3
    c. 5
    d. more than 5

20. As shown in Exhibit 8, what is the socially efficient number of cigarettes?
    a. 0
    b. 1
    c. 3
    d. 5

PART 4
Microeconomics Policy Issues

This road map feature helps you tie together material in the part as you travel the Economic Way of Thinking Highway. The following are review questions listed by chapter from the previous part. The key concept in each question is given for emphasis, and each question or set of questions concludes with an interactive game to reinforce the concepts. The correct answers to the multiple choice questions are given in Appendix C. If your instructor has included MindTap in your course, visit MindTap to play the interactive Causation Chain Game.

Chapter 12: Income Distribution, Poverty, and Discrimination

1. Key Concept: Income Distribution

Which of the following *most* closely represents the share of total U.S. income to the poorest 20 percent of all U.S. families?

a. Excessive resources devoted to producing a product
b. 50 percent
c. 25 percent
d. 10 percent
e. 5 percent

2. Key Concept: Lorenz Curve

When the Lorenz curve lies above the diagonal,

a. the poorest 20 percent of the population receive more than 20 percent of income.
b. the richest 20 percent of the population receive more than 20 percent of income.
c. everyone receives the same income.
d. the curve is wrong because the curve is drawn below the diagonal.

3. Key Concept: Comparable Worth

Some people believe that employees should be paid the same wages when their jobs, although different, require similar levels of education, training, experience, and responsibility. This principle is known as

a. the equal-pay-for-equal work doctrine.
b. Lorenz equivalence.
c. marginal productivity theory.
d. comparable worth.

Chapter 13: Antitrust and Regulation

4. Key Concept: Antitrust Laws

Which of the following is concerned primarily with price discrimination?

a. Sherman Act
b. Clayton Act
c. Celler–Kefauver Act
d. Robinson–Patman Act

5. Key Concept: Imperfect Information

Which of the following may be the result of a higher equilibrium price for a product?

a. Advertising
b. Expectations
c. Imperfect information
d. All of the answers are correct
e. None of the answers above are correct

6. Key Concept: Imperfect Information

Deficient information on unsafe products can cause:

a. overconsumption of a product.
b. waste of resources used to produce a product.
c. consumers paying a higher price for a product.
d. All of the answers above are correct.
e. None of the answers above are correct.

 CAUSATION CHAIN GAME
The Impact of Imperfect Information of the Market—Exhibit 5

Chapter 14: Environmental Economics

7. Key Concept: Effluent Tax

Which of the following is *true* about incentive-based regulations?

a. They set an environmental goal, but are flexible on how to achieve the goal.
b. They obtain more efficiency gains than is obtainable from CAC regulations.
c. Effluent taxes are an example of incentive-based regulations.
d. All of the answers are correct.
e. None of the answers above are correct.

8. Key Concept: Effluent Tax

In order to increase society's total welfare (social efficiency), a production process that produces a negative externality should be

a. taxed.
b. provided by the government.
c. ignored.
d. subsidized.

9. Key Concept: Effluent Tax

A government policy that charges coal producers a fee per ton of coal produced (an "effluent charge"), where the fee is determined by the amount of pollutants discharged into the air or water will lead to a(an)

a. decrease in the market equilibrium quantity of coal produced.
b. decrease in the market equilibrium price of coal.
c. increase in the market equilibrium price of coal.
d. Both answers a. and c. are correct.

10. Key Concept: Command-and-Control

An example of the command-and-control approach to environmental policy is

a. requiring electric utilities to install scrubbers to reduce sulfur dioxide emissions (which contribute to acid rain).
b. placing a tax on high-sulfur coal to reduce its use and the corresponding sulfur emissions (which contribute to acid rain).
c. allowing coal producers to buy and sell permits to allow sulfur emissions.
d. allowing individuals to sue coal producers if sulfur emissions exceed government-set standard.

CAUSATION CHAIN GAME
Using an Effluent Tax to Achieve Environmental Efficiency—Exhibit 3

PART 5

The International Economy

The final part of this text is devoted to global topics. The first chapter explains the importance of free trade and the mechanics of trade bookkeeping and exchange rates. Here you will find a feature on the birth of the euro. The second chapter takes a historical look at the theoretical debate over capitalism and the transition of Cuba, Russia, and China toward this system. The final chapter provides comparisons of advanced and developing countries.

CHAPTER 15

International Trade and Finance

CHAPTER PREVIEW

Just imagine your life without world trade. For openers, you could not eat bananas from Honduras or chocolate from Nigerian cocoa beans. Nor could you sip French wine, Colombian coffee, or Indian tea. Also, forget about driving a Japanese motorcycle or automobile. In addition, you could not buy Italian shoes and most DVDs, televisions, fax machines, and personal computers because they are foreign-made. Taking your vacation in London would also be ruled out if there were no world trade. And the list goes on and on, so the point is clear. World trade is important because it gives consumers more power by expanding their choices. Today, the speed of transportation and communication means producers must compete on a global basis for the favor of consumers.

Trade is often highly controversial. Regardless of whether it is a World Trade Organization (WTO) meeting or a G8 summit meeting, trade talks face protesters in the streets complaining that globalization has triggered a crisis in the world, such as global warming, poverty, soaring oil prices, or food shortages. And in the United States, outsourcing jobs to lower-paid workers overseas continues to be a hotly debated issue.

The first part of this chapter explains the theoretical reason why countries should specialize in producing certain goods and then trade them for imports. Also, you will study arguments for and against the United States protecting itself from "unfair" trade practices by other countries. In the second part of the chapter, you will learn how nations pay each other for world trade. Here you will explore international bookkeeping and discover how supply and demand forces determine that, for example, 1 dollar is worth 100 Japanese yen.

IN THIS CHAPTER, YOU WILL LEARN TO SOLVE THESE ECONOMICS PUZZLES:

- How does Babe Ruth's decision not to remain a pitcher illustrate an important principle in global trade?

- Is there a valid argument for trade protectionism?

- Should the United States return to the gold standard?

15-1 WHY NATIONS NEED TRADE

The United States leads the world in imports while also being one of the top exporters in the world. Exhibit 1 reveals which regions are our major trading partners (exports plus imports). Leading the list of nations is China, our largest trading partner, followed by Canada, Mexico, and Japan. Leading U.S. exports are chemicals, machinery, agricultural products, computers, automobiles, and airplanes. Major imports include petroleum, cars, trucks, clothing, and electronics. Why does a nation even bother to trade with the rest of the world? Does it seem strange for the United States to import goods it could produce for itself? Indeed, why doesn't the United States become self-sufficient by growing all its own food, including bananas, sugar, and coffee, making all its own cars, and prohibiting sales of all foreign goods? This section explains why specialization and trade are a nation's keys to a higher standard of living.

15-1a The Production Possibilities Curve Revisited

Consider a world with only two countries—the United States and Japan. To keep the illustration simple, also assume both countries produce only two goods—grain and steel. Accordingly, we can construct in Exhibit 2 a *production possibilities curve* for each

---

EXHIBIT 1 U.S. Trading Partners, 2016

In 2016, Canada, China, Mexico, and Japan accounted for over 40 percent of U.S. trade (exports plus imports).

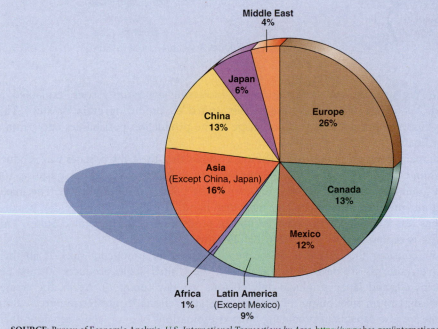

SOURCE: Bureau of Economic Analysis, *U.S. International Transactions by Area*, https://www.bea.gov/international /bp_web/tb_download_type_modern.cfm?list=11&RowID=0, Table 1.3.

EXHIBIT 2 The Benefits of Specialization and Trade

As shown in part (a), assume the United States chooses point *B* on its production possibilities curve, *PPC*~U.S.~ Without trade, the United States produces and consumes 60 tons of grain and 20 tons of steel. In part (b), assume Japan also operates along its production possibilities curve, *PPC*~Japan~, at point *E*. Without trade, Japan produces and consumes 30 tons of grain and 10 tons of steel.

Now assume the United States specializes in producing grain at point *A* and imports 20 tons of Japanese steel in exchange for 30 tons of grain. Through specialization and trade, the United States moves to consumption possibility point *B'*, outside its production possibilities curve. Japan also moves to a higher standard of living at consumption possibility point *E'*, outside its production possibilities curve.

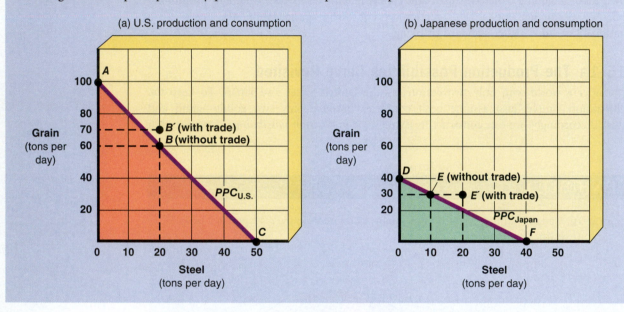

(a) U.S. production and consumption

(b) Japanese production and consumption

country. We will also set aside the *law of increasing opportunity costs*, explained in Chapter 2, and assume workers are equally suited to producing grain or steel. This assumption transforms the bowed-out shape of the production possibilities curve into a straight line.

Comparing parts (a) and (b) of Exhibit 2 shows that the United States can produce more grain than Japan. If the United States devotes all its resources to this purpose, 100 tons of grain are produced per day, represented by point *A* in Exhibit 2(a). The maximum grain production of Japan, on the other hand, is only 40 tons per day because Japan has less labor, land, and other factors of production than the United States. This capability is represented by point *D* in Exhibit 2(b).

Now consider the capacities of the two countries for producing steel. If all their respective resources are devoted to this output, the United States produces 50 tons per day (point *C*), and Japan produces only 40 tons per day (point *F*). Again, the greater potential maximum steel output of the United States reflects its greater resources. Both countries are also capable of producing other combinations of grain and steel along their respective production possibilities curves, such as point *B* for the United States and point *E* for Japan.

15-1b Specialization without Trade

Assuming no world trade, the production possibilities curve for each country also defines its *consumption possibilities*. Stated another way, we assume that both countries are *self-sufficient* because without imports they must consume only the combination chosen along their production possibilities curve. Under the assumption of self-sufficiency, suppose the United States prefers to produce and consume 60 tons of grain and 20 tons of steel per day (point *B*). Also assume Japan chooses to produce and consume 30 tons of grain and 10 tons of steel (point *E*). Exhibit 3 lists data corresponding to points *B* and *E* and shows that the total world output is 90 tons of grain and 30 tons of steel.

Now suppose the United States specializes by producing and consuming at point *A*, rather than point *B*. Suppose also that Japan specializes by producing and consuming at point *F*, rather than point *E*. As shown in Exhibit 3, specialization in each country increases total world output per day by 10 tons of grain and 10 tons of steel. Because this extra world output has the potential for making both countries better off, why wouldn't the United States and Japan specialize and produce at points *A* and *F*, respectively? The reason is that although production at these points is clearly possible, neither country wants to consume these combinations of output. The United States prefers to consume less grain and more steel at point *B* compared to point *A*. Japan, on the other hand, prefers to consume more grain and less steel at point *E*, rather than point *F*.

When countries specialize, total world output increases, and therefore, the potential for greater total world consumption also increases.	**CONCLUSION**

15-1c Specialization with Trade

Now let's return to Exhibit 2 and demonstrate how world trade benefits countries. Suppose the United States agrees to specialize in grain production at point *A* and to import 20 tons of Japanese steel in exchange for 30 tons of its grain output. Does the United

EXHIBIT 3 Effect of Specialization without Trade on World Output

	Grain production (tons per day)	Steel production (tons per day)
Before specialization		
United States (at point *B*)	60	20
Japan (at point *E*)	30	10
Total world output	90	30
After specialization		
United States (at point *A*)	100	0
Japan (at point *F*)	0	40
Total world output	100	40

States gain from trade? The answer is Yes. At point *A*, the United States produces 100 tons of grain per day. Subtracting the 30 tons of grain traded to Japan leaves the United States with 70 tons of its own grain production to consume. In return for grain, Japan unloads 20 tons of steel on U.S. shores. Hence, specialization and trade allow the United States to move from point *A* to point *B'*, which is a consumption possibility *outside* its production possibilities curve in Exhibit 2(a). At point *B'*, the United States consumes the same amount of steel and 10 more tons of grain compared to point *B* (without trade).

Japan also has an incentive to specialize by moving its production mix from point *E* to point *F*. With trade, Japan's consumption will be at point *E'*. At point *E'*, Japan has as much grain to consume as it had at point *E* (30 tons), plus 10 more tons of steel (now having 20 tons). Thus, point *E'* is a consumption possibility that lies *outside* Japan's production possibilities curve.

CONCLUSION | Global trade allows a country to consume a combination of goods that exceeds its production possibilities curve.

15-2 ABSOLUTE AND COMPARATIVE ADVANTAGE

Why did the United States decide to produce and export grain instead of steel? Why did Japan choose to produce and export steel rather than grain? Here you study the economic principles that determine specialization and trade. These concepts are absolute advantage and comparative advantage. **Absolute advantage** is the ability of a country to produce more of a good using the same or fewer resources as another country. **Comparative advantage** is the ability of a country to produce a good at a lower opportunity cost than another country.

Perhaps a noneconomic example will clarify the difference between absolute advantage and comparative advantage. When Babe Ruth played for the New York Yankees, he was the best hitter and the best pitcher not only on the team, but also in all of Major League Baseball. In fact, before Ruth was traded to the Yankees and switched to the outfield, he was the best left-handed pitcher in the American League for a few seasons with the Boston Red Sox. His final record was 94–46. In other words, he had an *absolute advantage* in both hitting and throwing the baseball. Stated differently, Babe Ruth could produce the same home runs as any other teammate with fewer times at bat. The problem was that if he pitched, he would bat fewer times because pitchers need rest after pitching. The coaches decided that the Babe had a *comparative advantage* in hitting. A few pitchers on the team could pitch almost as well as the Babe, but no one could touch his hitting. In terms of opportunity costs, the Yankees would lose fewer games if the Babe specialized in hitting.

15-2a Absolute Advantage

So far in our grain versus steel example, a country's production and trade decisions have not considered how much labor, land, or capital either the United States or Japan uses to produce a ton of grain or steel. For example, Japan might have an absolute advantage in producing *both* grain and steel. In our example, compared to the United States, Japan might use fewer resources per ton to produce grain and steel. Maybe the Japanese work harder or are more skilled. In short, the Japanese may be more productive producers, but

Absolute advantage
The ability of a country to produce a good using the same or fewer resources than another country.

Comparative advantage
The ability of a country to produce a good at a lower opportunity cost than another country.

their absolute advantage does not matter in specialization and world trade decisions. If Japan has a comparative advantage in steel, it should specialize in steel even if, compared to the United States, it can produce both grain and steel with fewer resources.

> Specialization and trade are based on opportunity costs (comparative advantage) and not on absolute advantage.
>
> **CONCLUSION**

15-2b Comparative Advantage

Engaging in world trade permits countries to consume more than they ever could without trade. The decision of the United States to specialize in and export grain and the decision of Japan to specialize in and export steel are based on comparative advantage. Continuing our example from Exhibit 2, we can calculate opportunity costs for the two countries and use comparative advantage to determine which country should specialize in grain and which should specialize in steel. For the United States, the opportunity cost of producing 50 tons of steel is 100 tons of grain not produced, so 1 ton of steel costs 2 tons of grain ($100/50 = 2$). For Japan, the opportunity cost of producing 40 tons of steel is 40 tons of grain, so 1 ton of steel costs 1 ton of grain ($40/40 = 1$). Japan's steel is therefore cheaper in terms of grain forgone. This means Japan has a comparative advantage in steel production because it must give up less grain to produce steel than the United States. Stated differently, the opportunity cost of steel production is lower in Japan than in the United States.

The other side of the coin is to measure the opportunity cost of grain in terms of steel. For the United States, the opportunity cost of producing 100 tons of grain is 50 tons of steel not produced. This means 1 ton of grain costs 1/2 ton of steel ($50/100 = ½$). For Japan, the opportunity cost of producing 40 tons of grain is 40 tons of steel so 1 ton of grain costs 1 ton of steel ($40/40 = 1$). The United States has a comparative advantage in grain because its opportunity cost in terms of steel forgone is lower. Thus, the United States should specialize in grain because it is more efficient in grain production. Japan, on the other hand, is relatively more efficient at producing steel and should specialize in this product.

> Comparative advantage refers to the relative opportunity costs between different countries of producing the same goods. World output and consumption are maximized when each country specializes in producing and trading goods for which it has a comparative advantage.
>
> **CONCLUSION**

Do Nations with an Advantage Always Trade?

Comparing labor productivity, suppose the United States has an absolute advantage over Costa Rica in the production of calculators and towels. In the United States, a worker can produce 4 calculators or 400 towels in 10 hours. In Costa Rica, a worker can produce 1 calculator or 100 towels in the same amount of time. Under these conditions, would Costa Rica specialize in calculators and trade for towels? Would Costa Rica specialize in towels and trade for calculators?

CHECKPOINT

15-3 FREE TRADE VERSUS PROTECTIONISM

Free trade
The flow of goods between countries without restrictions or special taxes.

Protectionism
The government's use of embargoes, tariffs, quotas, and other restrictions to protect domestic producers from foreign competition.

Embargo
A law that bars trade with another country.

Tariff
A tax on an import.

World Trade Organization (WTO)
An international organization of member countries that oversees international trade agreements and rules on trade disputes.

In theory, global trade should be based on comparative advantage and free trade. **Free trade** is the flow of goods between countries without restrictions or special taxes. In practice, despite the advice of economists, to some degree, every nation protects its own domestic producers from foreign competition. Behind these barriers to trade are special interest groups whose members feel that their jobs and incomes are threatened, so they clamor to the government for protectionism. **Protectionism** is the government's use of embargoes, tariffs, quotas, and other trade restrictions to protect domestic producers from foreign competition.

15-3a Embargo

Embargoes are the strongest limit on trade. An **embargo** is a law that bars trade with another country. For example, the communist government in Cuba seized a U.S.-owned oil refinery, prompting the United States to impose an embargo in the 1960s. Although the embargo is still enforced, many travel restrictions have been lifted during the last decade. The United States also maintains embargoes against North Korea, Sudan, and Syria.

15-3b Tariff

Tariffs are the most popular and visible measures used to discourage trade. A **tariff** is a tax on an import. Tariffs are also called customs duties. Suppose the United States imposes a tariff of 2.9 percent on autos. If a foreign car costs $40,000, the amount of the tariff equals $1,160 ($40,000 × 0.029), and the U.S. price, including the tariff, is $41,160. The current U.S. tariff code specifies tariffs on over 6,000 imports. A tariff can be based on weight, volume, or number of units, or it can be *ad valorem* (figured as a percentage of the price). The average U.S. tariff is less than 5 percent, but individual tariffs vary widely, and 22 agricultural products even have tariffs over 100 percent. Tariffs are imposed to reduce imports by raising import prices and to generate revenues for the U.S. Treasury. Exhibit 4 shows the trend of the average tariff rate since 1930.

During the worldwide depression of the 1930s, when one nation raised its tariffs to protect its industries against foreign competition, other nations retaliated by raising their tariffs. Under the Smoot–Hawley tariffs of the 1930s, the average tariff in the United States reached a peak of 20 percent. Durable imports, which were one-third of imports, were subject to an unbelievable tariff rate of 60 percent. In 1947, most of the world's industrialized nations mutually agreed to end the tariff wars by signing the *General Agreement on Tariffs and Trade* (GATT). Since then, GATT nations have met periodically to negotiate lower tariff rates. GATT agreements have significantly reduced tariffs over the years among member nations. In the 1994 *Uruguay Round*, member nations signed a GATT agreement that decreased tariffs and reduced other trade barriers. The most divisive element of this agreement was the creation in 1995 of the Geneva-based **World Trade Organization (WTO)** to enforce rulings in global trade disputes. The WTO currently has 164 members and a standing appellate body to render final decisions regarding disputes between WTO members. Critics fear that the WTO might be far more likely to rule in favor of other countries in their trade disputes with the United States. Some people argue that the WTO is unaccountable, and these critics reject free trade and discount the gains from globalization.

EXHIBIT 4 The Average Tariff Rate, 1930–2015

Under the Smoot–Hawley Act of 1930, the average tariff rate peaked at 20 percent. Since the *General Agreement on Tariffs and Trade (GATT)* in 1947 and other trade agreements, tariffs have declined to less than 5 percent.

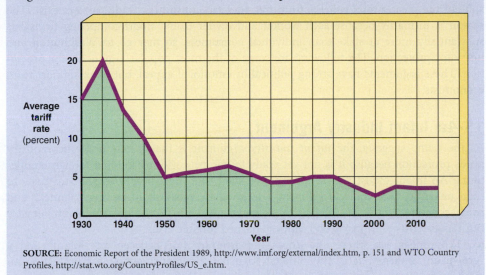

SOURCE: Economic Report of the President 1989, http://www.imf.org/external/index.htm, p. 151 and WTO Country Profiles, http://stat.wto.org/CountryProfiles/US_e.htm.

To illustrate an interesting case, the United States imposed tariffs in 2002 on steel imports to protect jobs in the struggling U.S. steel industry against foreign competition. The WTO ruled these tariffs were illegal, and countries in Europe and Asia prepared a list of retaliatory tariffs. These levies targeted products such as citrus fruit grown in Florida and apparel produced in southern states crucial to President Bush's reelection. Meanwhile, U.S. automakers and other steel-consuming industries complained because the tariffs increased their costs. Facing these complaints and an upcoming Presidential reelection bid in 2004, the United States removed the tariffs on steel imports in 2003.

15-3c Quota

Another way to limit foreign competition is to impose a quota. A **quota** is a limit on the quantity of a good that may be imported in a given time period. For example, the United States may allow 10 million tons of sugar to be imported over a one-year period. After this quantity is reached, no more sugar can be imported for the year. There are import quotas on sugar, dairy products, textiles, steel, and even ice cream. Quotas can limit imports from all foreign suppliers or from specific countries. Critics argue that, like all barriers to trade, quotas invite nations to retaliate with their own measures to restrict trade, and consumers are harmed by higher prices because of the lack of competition from lower-priced imports. In addition to embargoes, tariffs, and quotas, some nations use subtler measures to discourage trade, such as setting up an overwhelming number of bureaucratic steps that must be taken in order to import a product.

Quota
A limit on the quantity of a good that may be imported in a given time period.

15-4 ARGUMENTS FOR PROTECTION

Free trade provides consumers with lower prices and larger quantities of goods from which to choose. Thus, removing import barriers might save each family a few hundred dollars a year. The problem, however, is that imports could cost some workers their jobs and thousands of dollars per year from lost income. Hence, it is no wonder that in spite of the greater total benefits from free trade to consumers, trade barriers exist. The reason is primarily because each worker and owner from import-competing firms has substantially more at stake than individual consumers, so they go to Washington and lobby for protection. The following are some of the most popular arguments for protection. These arguments have strong political or emotional appeal, but weak support from economists.

15-4a Infant Industry Argument

As the name suggests, the *infant industry argument* is that a new domestic industry needs protection because it is not yet ready to compete with established foreign competitors. An infant industry is in a formative stage and must bear high start-up costs to train an entire workforce, develop new technology, establish marketing channels, and reach economies of scale. With time to grow and with protection, an infant industry can reduce costs and "catch up" with established foreign firms.

Economists ask where one draws the arbitrary line between an "infant" and a "grown-up" industry. It is also difficult to make a convincing case for protecting an infant industry in a developed country, such as the United States, where industries are well established. The infant industry argument, however, may have some validity for less-developed countries. Yet, even for these countries, there is a danger. When protection is granted, the new industry will not experience the competitive pressures necessary to encourage reasonably quick growth and participation in world trade. Also, after an industry is given protection, it is difficult to take it away.

15-4b National Security Argument

Another common argument is that defense-related industries must be protected with embargoes, tariffs, and quotas to ensure national security. By protecting critical defense industries, a nation will not be dependent on foreign countries for the essential defense-related goods it needs to defend itself in wartime. The *national defense argument* has been used to protect a long list of industries, including petrochemicals, munitions, steel, and rubber.

This argument gained validity during the War of 1812. Great Britain, the main trading partner of the United States, became an enemy that blockaded our coast. Today, this argument makes less sense for the United States. The government stockpiles missiles, sophisticated electronics, petroleum, and most goods needed in wartime.

15-4c Employment Argument

The *employment argument* suggests that restricting imports increases domestic jobs in protected industries. According to this protectionist argument, the sale of an imported good comes at the expense of its domestically produced counterpart. Lower domestic output therefore leads to higher domestic unemployment than would otherwise be the case.

It is true that protectionism can increase output and save jobs in some industries at home. Ignored, however, are the higher prices paid by consumers because protectionism reduces competition between domestic goods and imported goods. In addition, there are employment reduction effects to consider. For example, suppose a strict quota is imposed on steel imported into our nation. Reduced foreign competition allows U.S. steelmakers to charge higher prices for their steel. As a result, prices rise and sales fall for cars and other products using steel, causing production and employment to fall in these industries. Thus, the import quota on steel may save jobs in the steel industry, but at the expense of more jobs lost in the steel-consuming industries. Also, by selling U.S. imports, foreigners earn dollars that they can use to buy U.S. exports. Import quotas cause foreigners to have fewer dollars to spend on U.S. exports, resulting in a decrease in employment in U.S. export industries. In short, protectionism may cause a net reduction in the nation's total employment.

15-4d Cheap Foreign Labor Argument

Another often-heard popular claim is the *cheap labor argument*. It goes something like this: "How can we compete with such unfair competition? Labor costs $15 an hour in the United States (a hypothetical example), and firms in many developing countries pay only $1 an hour. Without protection against outsourcing our jobs, U.S. wages will be driven down, and our standard of living will fall."

A major flaw in this argument is that it neglects the reason for the difference in the wage rates between countries. A U.S. worker has more education, training, capital, and access to advanced technology. Therefore, if U.S. workers produce more output per hour than workers in another country, U.S. workers will justifiably earn higher wages without a competitive disadvantage. Suppose textile workers in the United States are paid $15 per hour. If a U.S. worker takes 1 hour to produce a rug, the labor cost per rug is $15. Now suppose a worker in India earns $1 per hour, but requires 20 hours to produce a rug on a handloom. In this case, the labor cost per rug is $20. Although the wage rate is 15 times higher in the United States, U.S. productivity is 20 times higher because a U.S. worker can produce 20 rugs in 20 hours, while the worker in India produces only 1 rug in the same amount of time.

Sometimes U.S. companies move their operations to foreign countries where labor is cheaper. Such moves are not always successful because the savings from paying foreign workers a lower wage rate are offset by lower productivity. Other disadvantages of foreign operations include greater transportation costs to U.S. markets and greater uncertainty due to political instability.

15-4e Free-Trade Agreements

The trend in recent years has been for nations to negotiate a reduction in trade barriers. In 1993, Congress approved the *North American Free Trade Agreement (NAFTA)*, which linked the United States to its second- and third-largest trading partners, Canada and Mexico. Under NAFTA, which became effective January 1, 1994, tariffs were phased out, and other impediments to trade and investment were eliminated among the three nations. For example, elimination of trade restrictions allows the United States to supply Mexico with more U.S. goods and to boost U.S. jobs. On the other hand, NAFTA was expected to raise Mexico's wages and standard of living by increasing Mexican exports to the United States. Note that NAFTA made no changes in restrictions on labor

GLOBAL ECONOMICS

World Trade Slips on Banana Peel

Applicable Concept: Protectionism

Growing bananas for European markets was a multibillion-dollar bright spot for Latin America's struggling economies. In fact, about half of this region's banana exports traditionally were sold to Europe. Then, in 1993, the European Union (EU) adopted a package of quotas and tariffs aimed at cutting Europe's banana imports from Latin America. The purpose of these restrictions was to give trade preference to 66 banana-growing former colonies of European nations in Africa, the Caribbean, and the Pacific. Ignored was the fact that growers in Latin America grow higher-quality bananas at half the cost of EU-favored growers because of their low labor costs and flat tropical land near port cities.

In 1999, the World Trade Organization (WTO) ruled that the EU was discriminating in favor of European companies importing the fruit and the WTO imposed $191.4 million per year in punitive tariffs on European goods. This was the first time in the four years the WTO had been in existence that such retaliation had

Jean-Daniel Sudres/Encyclopedia/Corbis

been approved and only the second time going back to its predecessor, the General Agreement on Tariffs and Trade. When the EU failed to comply with the WTO findings, the United States enforced its WTO rights by imposing increased duties on EU imports, including goods ranging from cashmere sweaters and Italian handbags to sheep's milk cheese, British biscuits, and German coffeemakers.

movement, and workers must enter the United States under a limited immigration quota or illegally. The success of NAFTA remains controversial. At the conclusion of this chapter, we will use data to examine its impact. In 2005, the *Central American Free Trade Agreement (CAFTA)* was signed by six additional Central American countries and extended the NAFTA free-trade zone to include Costa Rica, Guatemala, El Salvador, Honduras, Nicaragua, and Dominican Republic.

The United States and other countries are considering other free-trade agreements. In Europe, 27 nations are members of the *European Union (EU)*, which is dedicated to removing all trade barriers within Europe, thereby creating a single European economy almost as large as the U.S. economy. See the Birth of the Euro boxed feature in this chapter.

The *Asia-Pacific Economic Cooperation (APEC)* was formed in 1989 and today has 21 member nations, including China, Hong Kong, Russia, Japan, and Mexico. This organization is based on a nonbinding agreement to reduce trade barriers between member nations. Eleven of APEC's nations negotiated the Trans-Pacific Partnership (TPP) agreement to lower trade tariffs and reduce trade barriers. In 2017, before the agreement went into effect, President Trump withdrew the United States from this deal.

The effect of the U.S. sanctions was to double the wholesale prices of these items. Denmark and the Netherlands were exempt from the U.S. tariffs because they were the only nations that voted against the EU banana rules.

Critics charged that the United States was pushing the case for political reasons. American companies, including Chiquita Brands International and Dole Food Company, grow most of their bananas in Latin America. With America's trade deficit running at a record level, U.S. trade experts also argued that the United States had little choice but to act against the EU for failing to abide by the WTO's ruling. Moreover, with increasing voices in the United States questioning the wisdom of globalization, it was important that the WTO prove that it could arbitrate these disputes.

In 2001, it appeared that the banana dispute might be resolved. The EU agreed to increase market access for U.S. banana distributors, and the United States lifted its retaliatory duties on EU products. The agreement also provided that the United States could reimpose the duties if the EU did not complete its phased-in reductions in restrictions on Latin American banana imports.

But the banana story just kept "slipping along." European Union anti-fraud officials say that illegal banana trafficking is proving more lucrative than that in cocaine. An exposed scheme saw Italian banana importers use false licenses to pay greatly reduced customs duties on non-quota fruit. The fraud netted smugglers hundreds of millions of euros over a two-year period.

In 2004, Latin American growers again complained that the EU was discriminating against their bananas in favor of producers from African, Caribbean, and Pacific countries. Under the 2001 WTO ruling, the EU was compelled to replace its complex quota and tariff system on bananas with a tariff-only regime. So the EU placed a 176-euro tariff per ton on Latin American suppliers to get into the EU market, while bananas from African and Caribbean countries could export up to 775,000 tons duty-free. The banana war continued in 2008 when a WTO dispute panel ruled for the third time that the EU tariff/quota banana regime was unfair. Finally, in 2012 the EU and 11 Latin American countries ended the longest running trade dispute since the 1990s. They reached an agreement to gradually reduce the EU's tariffs on Latin American bananas.

ANALYZE THE ISSUE Make an argument in favor of the European import restrictions. Make an argument against this plan.

Critics are concerned that regional free-trade accords will make global agreements increasingly difficult to achieve. Some fear that trading blocs may erect new barriers, creating "Fortress North America," "Fortress Europe," and similar impediments to the worldwide reduction of trade barriers.

15-5 THE BALANCE OF PAYMENTS

When trade occurs between the United States and other nations, many types of financial transactions are recorded in a summary called the **balance of payments**. The **balance of payments** is a bookkeeping record of all the international transactions between a country and other countries during a given period of time. This summary is the best way to understand interactions between economies because it records the value of a nation's spending inflows and outflows made by individuals, firms, and governments. Exhibit 5 presents a simplified U.S. balance of payments for 2016.

Note the pluses and minuses in the table. A transaction that is a payment to the United States is entered as a positive amount. A payment by the United States to another country is entered with a minus sign. As our discussion unfolds, you will learn that the balance of payments provides much useful information.

Balance of payments
A bookkeeping record of all the international transactions between a country and other countries during a given period of time.

BIRTH OF THE EURO

In 1958, several European nations formed a Common Market to eliminate trade restrictions among member countries. The Common Market called for gradual removal of tariffs and import quotas on goods traded among member nations. Later the name was changed to the *European Economic Community (EEC)*, and it is now called the *European Union (EU)*. This organization established a common system of tariffs for imports from nonmember nations and created common policies for economic matters of joint concern, such as agriculture and transportation. The EU now comprises the 27 nations listed in the following table.

In 1999, 11 European countries, joined later by Greece, followed the United States as an example and united in the *European Economic and Monetary Union (EMU)*. In the United States, 50 states are linked with a common currency, and the Federal Reserve serves as the central bank by conducting monetary policy for the nation. Among the states, trade, labor, and investment enjoy freedom of movement. In 2002, many of the EMU members replaced their national currencies with a single currency, the euro. The objective was to remove exchange rate fluctuations that impede cross-border transactions. This is why the U.S. Congress created a

national currency in 1863 to replace state and private bank currencies.

The EU faces many unanswered questions. Unlike the states of the United States, the EU's member nations do not share a common language or a common government. This makes maintaining common macro policies difficult, and in recent years, Greece and several other members have experienced financial crises. France, for example, might seek to use fiscal or budgetary policies to control inflation, whereas Germany has reducing unemployment as its highest fiscal priority. Coordinating monetary policy among EU

15-5a Current Account

The first section of the balance of payments is the *current account*, which includes trade in goods and services and income receipts and payments. The most widely reported part of the current account is the balance of trade, also called the trade balance. The **balance of trade** is the value of a nation's imports subtracted from its exports, and it can be expressed in terms of goods, services, or goods and services. The balance of trade most often reported is in terms of goods and services. As shown in lines 1–4, the United States had a *balance of trade deficit* of −$501 billion in 2016. A trade deficit occurs when the value of a country's imports exceeds the value of its exports. When a nation has a trade deficit, it is called an *unfavorable balance of trade* because more is spent for imports than is earned from exports. Recall that net exports $(X - M)$ can have a positive (favorable) or negative (unfavorable) effect on GDP $= C + I + G + (X - M)$.

Exhibit 6 charts the annual balance of trade for the United States from 1975 through 2016. Observe that the United States experienced a *balance of trade surplus* in 1975. A trade surplus arises when the value of a country's exports is greater than the value of its imports. This is called a *favorable balance of trade* because the United States earned more from exports than it spent for imports. Since 1975, however, sizable trade deficits have occurred. These trade deficits have attracted much attention because in part they reflect the popularity of foreign goods and the lack of competitiveness of goods "Made in

Balance of trade
The value of a nation's imports subtracted from its exports. Balance of trade can be expressed in terms of goods, services, or goods and services.

nations is also difficult. Although the EU has established the *European Central Bank* headquartered in Frankfurt, Germany, with sole authority over the supply of euros, the central banks of member nations still function. But these national central banks operate similar to the district banks of the Federal Reserve System in the United States. Only time will tell whether EU nations will perform better with a single currency than with separate national currencies. Currently, 19 EU countries have adopted the euro as their national currency.

European Union (EU) members		
Austria	Germany	Poland
Belgium	Greece	Portugal
Bulgaria	Hungary	Romania
Croatia	Ireland	Slovakia
Cyprus	Italy	Slovenia
Czech Republic	Latvia	Spain
Denmark	Lithuania	Sweden
Estonia	Luxembourg	
Finland	Malta	
France	Netherlands	

U.S.A." Between 2005 and 2008, the U.S. trade deficits reached record-breaking levels of about $700 billion due in part to the rising price of oil imports. During this period, the price per barrel grew steadily until it reached a peak in 2008, and the U.S. trade deficit with OPEC countries doubled while our trade deficit with China tripled. After 2008, oil import prices decreased from a high of $125 per barrel in 2008 to $38 per barrel in 2016. As a result, U.S. trade deficits with OPEC countries fell, contributing to the fall in the U.S. balance of trade deficits after 2008.

Lines 3–5 of the current account in Exhibit 5 list ways other than trade of goods that move dollars back and forth between the United States and other countries. Services include insurance, banking, transportation, and tourism. For example, a Japanese tourist who pays a hotel bill in Hawaii buys an export of services, which is a plus, or credit, to our current account (line 3). Similarly, an American visitor to foreign lands buys an import of services, which is a minus, or debit, to our services and therefore a minus to our current account (line 4). As shown on line 5, income flowing back from U.S. investments abroad, such as plants, real estate, and securities, is a payment for use of the services of U.S. capital. Foreign countries also receive income receipts flowing from the services of their capital owned in the United States. This category also includes gifts made by our government, charitable organizations, or private individuals to other governments or private parties elsewhere in the world. For example, this item includes U.S. foreign aid to other nations. Similar unilateral transfers into the United States must be

EXHIBIT 5 U.S. Balance of Payments, 2016 (billions of dollars)

Type of transaction	
Current account	
1. Goods exports	$ + 1,460
2. Goods imports	− 2,210
3. Service exports	+ 752
4. Service imports	− 503
Trade balance (lines 1–4)	− 501
5. Income (net)	+ 19
Current account balance (lines 1–5)	− 482
Capital account	
6. U.S. capital inflow	+ 759
7. U.S. capital outflow	− 331
Capital account balance (lines 6–7)	+ 428
8. Statistical discrepancy	−54
Net balance (lines 1–8)	0

SOURCE: Bureau of Economic Analysis, U.S. International Transactions, https://www.bea.gov/international/bp_web /tb_download_type_modern.cfm?list=1&RowID=1, Table 1.1.

subtracted to determine net income transfers. In 2016, line 5 of the table reports a net income flow of $19 billion to the United States.

Adding lines 1–5 gives the current account balance deficit of −$482 billion in 2016. This deficit means that foreigners sent us more goods, services, and income than we sent to them. Because the current account balance includes more than goods and services, it is a broader measure than the trade balance. Since 1982, the trend in the current account balance has followed the swing into the red shown by the trade balance in Exhibit 6.

15-5b Capital Account

The second section of the balance of payments is the *capital account*, which records payment flows for financial capital, such as real estate, corporate stocks, bonds, government securities, and other debt instruments. For example, when Chinese investors buy U.S. Treasury bills or Japanese investors purchase farmland in Hawaii, there is an inflow of dollars into the United States. As Exhibit 5 shows, foreigners made payments of $759 billion to our capital account (line 6). This exceeded the −$331 billion outflow (line 7) from the United States to purchase foreign-owned financial capital.

An important feature of the capital account is that the United States finances any deficit in its current account through this account. The capital account balance in 2016 was $428 billion. This surplus indicates that there was more foreign investment in U.S. assets than U.S. investment in foreign assets during this year.

EXHIBIT 6 U.S. Balance of Trade, 1975–2016 (billions of dollars)

Since 1975, the United States has experienced trade deficits in which the value of goods and services imported has exceeded the value of goods and services exported. These trade deficits attract much attention because, in part, they reflect the popularity of foreign goods in the United States. During the recession in 2001, the U.S. trade deficit narrowed briefly before continuing an upward trend. The deficit grew to an all-time high of about $700 billion between 2005 and 2008 before declining to $501 billion in 2016.

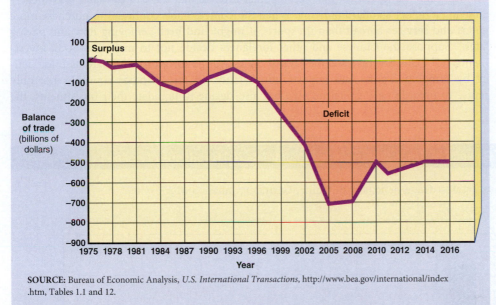

SOURCE: Bureau of Economic Analysis, *U.S. International Transactions*, http://www.bea.gov/international/index .htm, Tables 1.1 and 12.

A current account deficit is financed by a capital account surplus.

CONCLUSION

The current account deficit should equal the capital account surplus, but line 8 in the exhibit reveals that the balance of payments is not perfect. The capital account balance does not exactly offset the current account balance. Hence, a credit or debit amount is simply recorded as a statistical discrepancy; therefore, the balance of payments always balances, or equals zero.

15-5c The International Debt of the United States

If each nation's balance of payments is always zero, why is there so much talk about a U.S. balance-of-payments problem? The problem is with the *composition* of the balance of payments. Suppose the United States runs a $500 billion deficit in its current account. This means that the current account deficit must be financed by a net annual capital inflow in the capital account of $500 billion. That is, foreign lenders, such as banks and businesses, must purchase U.S. assets and grant loans to the United States that on balance equal $500 billion. For example, a Chinese bank could buy U.S. Treasury bonds.

The portion of the national debt owed to lenders outside the United States is called *external debt*.

In 1984, the United States became a net debtor for the first time in about 70 years. This means that investments in the United States accumulated by foreigners—stocks, bonds, real estate, and so forth—exceeded the stock of foreign assets owned by the United States. In fact, during the decade of the 1980s, the United States moved from being the world's largest creditor nation to being the largest debtor nation.

Exhibit 7 shows that the United States has its largest trade deficits with China, Germany, Mexico, and Japan, respectively. The concern over continuing trade deficits and the rising international debt that accompanies them is that the United States is artificially enjoying a higher standard of living. When the United States continues to purchase more goods and services abroad than it exports, it might find itself "enjoying now and paying later." Suppose the Chinese and other foreigners decide not to make new U.S. investments and loans. In this case, the United States will be forced to eliminate its trade deficit by bringing exports and imports into balance. In fact, if other countries not only refuse to provide new capital inflows, but also decide to liquidate their investments, the

---

EXHIBIT 7 U.S. Balance of Trade with Selected Countries, 2016 (billions of dollars)

The United States has its greatest trade deficits with China, Germany, Japan, and Mexico.

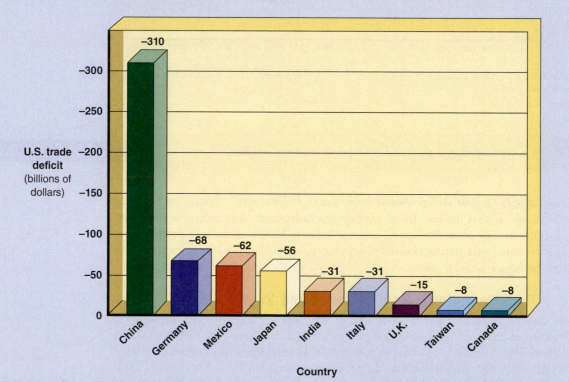

SOURCE: Bureau of Economic Analysis, *U.S. International Transactions by Area*, https://www.bea.gov/international/bp_web/tb_download_type_modern.cfm?list=11&RowID=0, Table 1.3.

United States would be forced to run a trade surplus. Stated differently, we would be forced to tighten our belts and accept a lower standard of living. How a change in foreign willingness to purchase U.S. assets also affects the international value of the dollar is the topic to which we now turn.

CHECKPOINT

Should Everyone Keep a Balance of Payments?
Nations keep balances of payments and calculate accounts such as their trade deficit or surplus. If nations need these accounts, the 50 states should also maintain balances of payments to manage their economies. Or should they? What about cities?

15-6 EXCHANGE RATES

Each transaction recorded in the balance of payments requires an exchange of one country's currency for that of another. Suppose you buy a Japanese car made in Japan, say, a Mazda. Mazda wants to be paid in yen and not dollars, so dollars must be traded for yen. On the other hand, suppose Pink Panther Airline Company in France purchases an airplane from Boeing in the United States. Pink Panther has euros to pay the bill, but Boeing wants dollars. Consequently, euros must be exchanged for dollars.

The critical question for Mazda, Pink Panther, Boeing, and everyone involved in world trade is, "What is the exchange rate?" The **exchange rate** is the number of units of one nation's currency that equals one unit of another nation's currency. For example, assume 1.30 dollars can be exchanged for 1 British pound. This means the exchange rate is 1.30 dollars = 1 pound. Alternatively, the exchange rate can be expressed as a reciprocal. Dividing 1 British pound by 1.30 dollars gives 0.769 pounds per dollar. Now suppose you are visiting England and want to buy a T-shirt with a price tag of 10 pounds. Knowing the exchange rate tells you the T-shirt costs $ 13.00 (10 pounds × $1.30/pound).

Exchange rate
The number of units of one nation's currency that equals one unit of another nation's currency.

An exchange rate can be expressed as a reciprocal.

CONCLUSION

15-6a Supply and Demand for Foreign Exchange

The exchange rate for dollars, or any nation's currency floats, which means it is determined by global forces of supply and demand. For example, consider the exchange rate of yen to dollars, shown in Exhibit 8. Like the price and the quantity of any good traded in markets, the quantity of dollars exchanged is measured on the horizontal axis, and the price per unit is measured on the vertical axis. In this case, the price per unit is the value of the U.S. dollar expressed as the number of yen per dollar.

The demand for dollars in the world currency market comes from Japanese individuals, corporations, and governments that want to buy U.S. exports. Because the Japanese buyers must pay for U.S. exports with dollars, they *demand* to exchange their yen for dollars. As expected, the demand curve for dollars or any foreign currency is downward sloping. A decline in the number of yen per dollar means that one yen buys a larger portion of a dollar. This means U.S. goods and investment opportunities are less expensive to Japanese buyers because they must pay fewer yen for each dollar. Thus, as

EXHIBIT 8 The Supply of and Demand for Dollars

The number of Japanese yen per dollar in the foreign exchange market is determined by the demand for dollars by Japanese citizens and the supply of dollars by U.S. citizens. The equilibrium exchange rate is 100 yen per dollar, and the equilibrium quantity is $300 million per day.

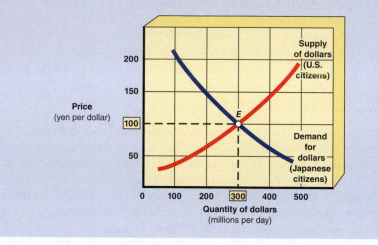

the yen price of dollars decreases, the quantity of dollars demanded by the Japanese to purchase Fords, stocks, land, and other U.S. products and investments increases. For example, suppose a CD recording of the hottest rock group has a $20 price tag. If the exchange rate were 200 yen to the dollar, a Japanese importer would pay 4,000 yen. If the price of dollars to Japanese buyers falls to 100 yen each, the same $20 CD will cost Japanese importers only 2,000 yen. This lower price causes Japanese buyers to increase their orders, which, in turn, increases the quantity of dollars demanded.

The supply curve of dollars is upward sloping. This curve shows the amount of dollars offered for exchange at various yen prices per dollar in the world currency exchange market. Similar to the demand for dollars, the supply of dollars in this market flows from individuals, corporations, and governments in the United States that want to buy Mazdas, stocks, land, and other products and investments from Japan. Because U.S. citizens must pay for the Japanese goods and services in yen, they must exchange dollars for yen. An example will illustrate why the supply curve of dollars slopes upward. Suppose a Nikon camera sells for 100,000 yen in Tokyo and the exchange rate is 100 yen per dollar or 0.01 dollar per yen ($1/100 yen). Therefore, the camera costs an American tourist $1,000. Now assume the exchange rate rises to 250 yen per dollar or 0.004 dollar per yen ($1/250 yen). The camera will now cost the American buyer only $400. Because the prices of the Nikon camera and other Japanese products fall when the number of yen per dollar rises, Americans respond by purchasing more Japanese imports, which, in turn, increases the quantity of dollars supplied.

The foreign exchange market in Exhibit 8 is in equilibrium at an exchange rate of 100 yen for $1. As you learned in Chapter 3, if the exchange rate is above equilibrium, there will be a surplus of dollars in the world currency market. Citizens of the United States are supplying more dollars than the Japanese demand, and the exchange rate falls. On the other hand, below equilibrium, there will be a shortage of dollars in the world currency market. In this case, the Japanese are demanding more dollars than Americans supply, and the exchange rate rises.

15-6b Shifts in Supply and Demand for Foreign Exchange

For most of the years between World War II and 1971, currency exchange rates were *fixed*. Exchange rates were based primarily on gold. For example, the German mark was fixed at about 25 cents. The dollar was worth 1/35 of an ounce of gold, and 4 German marks were worth 1/35 of an ounce of gold. Therefore, 1 dollar equaled 4 marks, or 25 cents equaled 1 mark. In 1971, Western nations agreed to stop fixing their exchange rates and to allow their currencies to *float* according to the forces of supply and demand. Exhibit 9 illustrates that these rates can fluctuate widely. For example, in 1980, 1 dollar was worth about 230 Japanese yen. After gyrating up and down over the years, the exchange rate hit a postwar low of 80 yen per dollar in 2011. In 2016, the rate rose to 109 yen per dollar.

Recall from Chapter 3 that the equilibrium price for products changes in response to shifts in the supply and demand curves. The same supply and demand analysis applies to equilibrium exchange rates for foreign currency. There are four important sources of shifts in the supply and demand curves for foreign exchange. Let's consider each in turn.

Tastes and Preferences

Exhibit 10(a) illustrates one important factor that causes the demand for foreign currencies to shift. Suppose the Japanese lose their "taste" for tobacco, U.S. government bonds, and other U.S. products and investment opportunities. This decline in the popularity of U.S. products in Japan decreases the demand for dollars at each possible exchange rate, and the demand curve shifts leftward from D_1 to D_2. This change causes the equilibrium

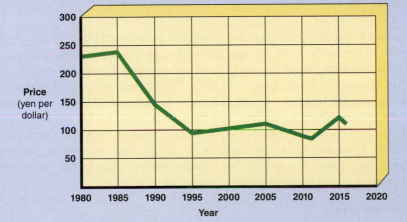

EXHIBIT 9 Changes in the Yen-per-Dollar Exchange Rate, 1980–2016

Today, most economies are on a system of flexible exchange rates. As the demand and supply curves for currencies change, exchange rates change. In 1980, 1 dollar was worth about 230 Japanese yen. By 2011, the exchange rate had dropped to a postwar low of 80 yen per dollar. In 2016, the rate rose to 109 yen per dollar.

SOURCE: Foreign Exchange Rates, http://www.federalreserve.gov/releases/G5A/current/. Japan/U.S. Foreign Exchange, Fred, Federal Reserve Bank of St. Louis.

EXHIBIT 10 Changes in the Supply and Demand Curves for Dollars

In part (a), U.S. exports become less popular in Japan. This change in tastes for U.S. products and investments decreases the demand for dollars, and the demand curve shifts leftward from D_1 to D_2. As a result, the equilibrium exchange rate falls from 150 yen to the dollar at E_1 to 100 yen to the dollar at E_2.

Part (b) assumes U.S. citizens are influenced by the "Buy American" idea. In this case, our demand for Japanese imports decreases, and U.S. citizens supply fewer dollars to the foreign currency market. The result is that the supply curve shifts leftward from S_1, and the equilibrium exchange rate rises from 100 yen per dollar at E_1 to 150 yen per dollar at E_2.

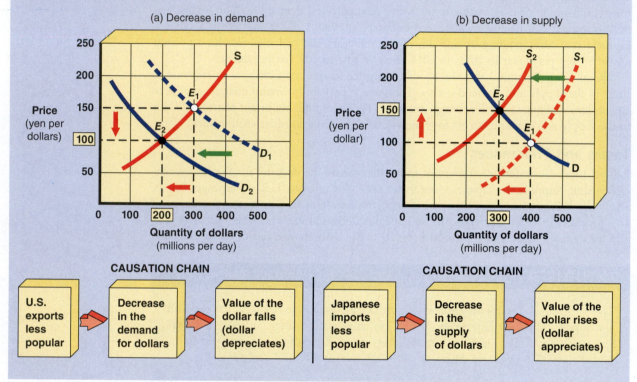

exchange rate to fall from 150 yen to the dollar at E_1 to 100 yen to the dollar at E_2. Because the number of yen to the dollar declines, the dollar is said to *depreciate* or become *weaker*. **Depreciation of currency** is a fall in the price of one currency relative to another.

What happens to the exchange rate if the "Buy American" idea changes our tastes and the demand for Japanese imports decreases? In this case, U.S. citizens supply fewer dollars at any possible exchange rate, and the supply curve in Exhibit 10(b) shifts leftward from S_1 to S_2. As a result, the equilibrium exchange rate rises from 100 yen to the dollar at E_1 to 150 yen to the dollar at E_2. Because the number of yen per dollar rises, the dollar is said to *appreciate* or become *stronger*. **Appreciation of currency** is a rise in the price of one currency relative to another.

Depreciation of currency
A fall in the price of one currency relative to another.

Appreciation of currency
A rise in the price of one currency relative to another.

Relative Incomes

Assume income in the United States rises, while income in Japan remains unchanged. As a result, U.S. citizens buy not only more domestic products and but more Japanese imports as well. The results are a rightward shift in the supply curve for dollars and a decrease in the equilibrium exchange rate. Paradoxically, growth of U.S. income leads to the dollar depreciating, or becoming weaker, against the Japanese yen.

An expansion in relative U.S. income causes a depreciation of the dollar.	**CONCLUSION**

Relative Price Levels

Now we consider a more complex case in which a change in a factor causes a change in both the supply and demand curves for dollars. Assume the foreign exchange rate begins in equilibrium at 100 yen per dollar, as shown at point E_1 in Exhibit 11. Now assume the

EXHIBIT 11   The Impact of Relative Price Level Changes on Exchange Rates

Begin at E_1, with the exchange rate equal to 100 yen per dollar. Assume prices in Japan rise relative to those in the United States. As a result, the demand for dollars increases, and the supply of dollars decreases. The new equilibrium is at E_2 when the dollar appreciates (rises in value) to 200 yen per dollar.

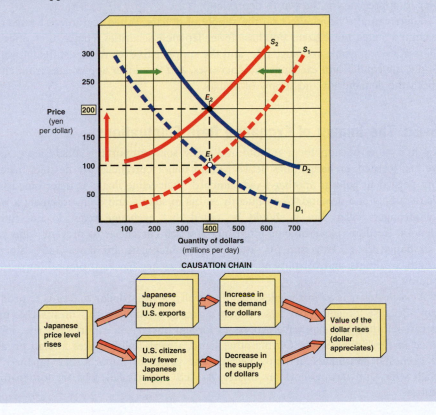

CAUSATION CHAIN

price level increases in Japan, but remains constant in the United States. The Japanese therefore want to buy more U.S. exports because they have become cheaper relative to Japanese products. This willingness of the Japanese to buy U.S. goods and services shifts the demand curve for dollars rightward from D_1 to D_2. In addition, U.S. products are cheaper for U.S. citizens compared to Japanese imports. As a result, the willingness to import from Japan is reduced at each exchange rate, which means the supply curve of dollars decreases from S_1 to S_2. The result of the shifts in both the demand and supply curves for dollars is to establish a new equilibrium at point E_2, and the exchange rate reaches 200 yen per dollar.

CONCLUSION   A rise in a trading partner's relative price level causes the dollar to appreciate.

Relative Real Interest Rates

Changes in relative real (inflation-adjusted) interest rates can have an important effect on the exchange rate. Suppose real interest rates in the United States rise, while those in Japan remain constant. To take advantage of more attractive yields, Japanese investors buy an increased amount of bonds and other interest-bearing securities issued by private and government borrowers in the United States. This change increases the demand for dollars, which increases the equilibrium exchange rate of yen to the dollar, causing the dollar to appreciate (or the yen to depreciate).

There can also be an effect on the supply of dollars. When real interest rates rise in the United States, our citizens purchase fewer Japanese securities. Hence, they offer fewer dollars at each possible exchange rate, and the supply curve for dollars shifts leftward. As a result, the equilibrium exchange rate increases, and the dollar appreciates from changes in both the demand for and supply of dollars.

15-6c The Impact of Exchange Rate Fluctuations

Now it is time to stop for a minute and draw some important conclusions. As you have just learned, exchange rates between most major currencies are flexible. Instead of being pegged to gold or another fixed standard, their value floats as determined by the laws of supply and demand. Consequently, shifts in supply and demand create a weaker or a stronger dollar. But it should be noted that exchange rates do not fluctuate with total freedom. Governments often buy and sell currencies to prevent wide swings in exchange rates. Governments attempt to manipulate exchange rates since the strength, weakness, and volatility of any nation's currency have a profound impact on its economy.

A weak dollar is a "mixed blessing." Ironically, a weak dollar makes U.S. producers happy. Because foreigners pay less of their currency for dollars, this means U.S. producers can sell their less expensive exports to foreign buyers. As export sales rise, jobs are created in the United States. On the other hand, a weak dollar makes foreign producers and domestic consumers unhappy because the prices of imports, like Japanese cars, French wine, and Italian shoes are higher. As U.S. imports fall, jobs are lost in foreign countries.

When the dollar is weak, or depreciates, U.S. goods and services cost foreign consumers less, so they buy more U.S. exports. At the same time, a weak dollar means foreign goods and services cost U.S. consumers more, so they buy fewer imports.

CONCLUSION

A strong dollar is also a "mixed blessing." A strong dollar makes our major trading partners happy. U.S. buyers pay fewer dollars for foreign currency which means the prices of Japanese cars, French wine, and Italian shoes are lower. A strong dollar, contrary to the implication of the term, makes U.S. producers unhappy because their exports are more expensive and related jobs decline. Conversely, a strong dollar makes foreign producers happy because the prices of their goods and services are lower, causing U.S. imports to rise. Exhibit 12 summarizes the weak versus strong dollar effects.

When the dollar is strong, or appreciates, U.S. goods and services cost foreign consumers more, so they buy fewer U.S. exports. At the same time, a strong dollar means foreign goods and services cost U.S. consumers less, so they buy more foreign imports.

CONCLUSION

EXHIBIT 12 Effects of a Strong or Weak Dollar on U.S. Trade

A strong dollar leads to a decrease in exports and an increase in imports. A weak dollar leads to an increase in exports and a decrease in imports.

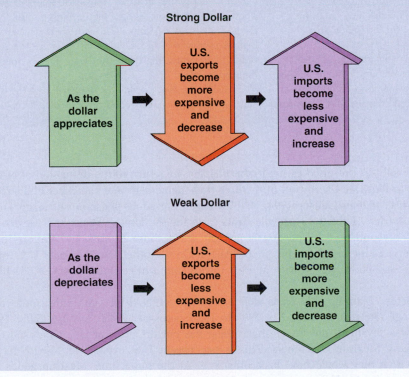

GLOBAL ECONOMICS

Return to the Yellow Brick Road?

Applicable Concept: Exchange Rates

Gold is always a fascinating story. *The Wonderful Wizard of Oz* was first published in 1900, and this children's tale has been interpreted as an allegory for political and economic events of the 1890s. For example, the Yellow Brick Road represents the gold standard, Oz in the title is an abbreviation for ounce, Dorothy is the naive public, Emerald City symbolizes Washington, D.C., the Tin Woodman represents the industrial worker, the Scarecrow is the farmer, and the Cyclone is a metaphor for a political revolution. In the end, Dorothy discovers magical powers in her *silver* shoes (changed to ruby in the 1939 film) to find her way home and not the fallacy of the Yellow Brick Road. Although the author of the story, L. Frank Baum, never stated it was his intention, it can be argued that the issue of the story concerns the election of 1896. Democratic presidential nominee William Jennings Bryan (the Cowardly Lion) supported fixing the value of the dollar to both gold and silver (bimetallism), but Republican William McKinley (the Wicked Witch) advocated using only the gold standard. Since McKinley won, the United States remained on the Yellow Brick Road.[1]

The United States adopted the gold standard in 1873, and until the 1930s, most industrial countries were on the gold standard. The gold standard served as an international monetary system in which currencies were defined or pegged in terms of gold. Under the gold standard, a nation with a balance of payments deficit was required to ship gold to other nations to finance the deficit. Hence, a large excess of imports over exports meant a corresponding outflow of gold from a nation. As a result, that nation's money supply decreased, which, in turn, reduced the aggregate demand for goods and services. Lower domestic demand led to falling prices, lower production, and fewer jobs. In contrast, a nation with a balance of payments surplus would experience an inflow of gold and the opposite effects. In this case, the nation's money supply increased, and its aggregate demand for goods and services rose. Higher aggregate spending, in turn, boosted employment and the price level. In short, the gold standard meant that governments could not control their money supplies to conduct monetary policy.

The gold standard worked fairly well as a fixed exchange rate system so long as nations did not face sudden or severe swings in flows from their stocks of gold. The Great Depression marked the beginning of the end of the gold standard. Nations faced with trade deficits and high unemployment began going off the gold standard, rather than contracting their money supplies by following the gold standard.

In 1933, President Franklin D. Roosevelt took the United States off the gold standard and ordered all 1933 gold

Finally, as promised earlier in this chapter, we return to the discussion of NAFTA in order to illustrate the impact of this free-trade agreement and the effect of a strong dollar. Recall that in January 1994, NAFTA began a gradual phase-out of tariffs and other trade barriers. Exhibit 13 provides trade data for the United States and Mexico for the years surrounding NAFTA. As the exhibit shows, both exports and imports of goods and services increased sharply after NAFTA. On the other hand, a small U.S. trade surplus of $4 billion with Mexico in 1993 turned into a huge trade deficit of $62 billion in 2016.

Before blaming this trade deficit entirely on NAFTA, you must note that the exchange rate rose from 3.12 in 1993 to 18.67 pesos per dollar in 2016. Since 1995, the peso was devalued, and the stronger dollar has put the price of U.S. goods out of reach for many Mexican consumers. This is one reason U.S. exports to Mexico have been lower than they would have been otherwise. At the same time, Mexican goods became less expensive for U.S. consumers, so U.S. imports from Mexico have risen.

double eagle coins already manufactured to be melted down and not circulated. Through a long twisted story worthy of a Sherlock Holmes mystery novel involving the Smithsonian Institution, the former king of Egypt, the Treasury Department, the Justice Department, the U.S. Mint, and a long list of intriguing supporting characters, one 1933 double eagle surfaced and was sold for $7.59 million in 2002. This was double the previous record for a coin.

Once the Allies felt certain they would win World War II, the finance ministers of Western nations met in 1944 at Bretton Woods, New Hampshire, to establish a new international monetary system. The new system was based on fixed exchange rates and an international central bank called the *International Monetary Fund (IMF)*. The IMF makes loans to countries faced with short-term balance-of-payments problems. Under this system, nations were expected to maintain fixed exchange rates within a narrow range. In the 1960s and early 1970s, the Bretton Woods system became strained as conditions changed. In the 1960s, inflation rates in the United States rose relative to those in other countries, causing U.S. exports to become more expensive and U.S. imports to become less expensive. This situation increased the supply of dollars abroad and caused an increasing surplus of dollars, thus putting downward pressure on the exchange rate. Monetary authorities in the United States worried that central banks would demand gold for their dollars, the U.S. gold stock would diminish sharply, and the declining money supply would adversely affect the economy.

Something had to give, and it did. In August 1971, President Richard Nixon announced that the United States would no longer honor its obligation to sell gold at $35 an ounce. By 1973, the gold standard was dead, and most of our trading partners were letting the forces of supply and demand determine exchange rates.

Today, some people advocate returning to the gold standard. These gold buffs do not trust the government to control the money supply without the discipline of a gold standard. They argue that if governments have the freedom to print money, political pressures will sooner or later cause them to increase the money supply too much and let inflation rage.

One argument against the gold standard is that no one can control the supply of gold. Big gold discoveries can cause inflation and have done so in the past. On the other hand, slow growth in the stock of mined gold can lead to slow economic growth and a loss of jobs. Governments, therefore, are unlikely to return to the gold standard because it would mean turning monetary policy over to uncontrollable swings in the stock of gold.

ANALYZE THE ISSUE Return to Exhibit 8, and assume the equilibrium exchange rate is 150 yen per dollar and the equilibrium quantity is $300 million. Redraw this figure, and place a horizontal line through the equilibrium exchange rate to represent a fixed exchange rate. Now use this figure to explain why a country would abandon the gold standard.

---

1. Bradley A. Hansen, "The Fable of the Allegory," *Journal of Economic Education*, Summer 2002, pp. 254–264.

EXHIBIT 13 U.S. Trade Balances with Mexico, Selected Years

Year	U.S. exports to Mexico (billions of dollars)	U.S. imports from Mexico (billions of dollars)	Exchange rate (pesos per dollar)	U.S. trade surplus (+) or deficit (−) (billions of dollars)
1993	$52	$48	3.12	$4
1995	55	71	6.45	−16
2000	127	148	9.46	−21
2005	143	188	10.89	−45
2010	188	247	12.62	−59
2016	262	324	18.67	−62

SOURCES: Bureau of Economic Analysis, *U.S. International Transactions by Area*, http://www.bea.gov/international/index.htm, Table 1.3, and Mexico/U.S. Foreign Exchange Rate, FRED, Federal Reserve Bank of St. Louis.

Key Concepts

Absolute advantage

Comparative advantage

Free trade

Protectionism

Embargo

Tariff

World Trade
Organization (WTO)

Quota

Balance of payments

Balance of trade

Exchange rate

Depreciation of currency

Appreciation of
currency

Summary

- **Absolute Advantage** is the ability of a country to produce more of a good using the same or fewer resources as another country.

- **Comparative advantage** is a principle that allows nations to gain from trade. Comparative advantage means that each nation *specializes* in a product for which its opportunity cost is lower in terms of the production of another product, and then nations trade. When nations follow this principle, they gain. The reason is that world output increases, and each nation ends up with a higher standard of living by consuming more goods and services than would be possible without specialization and trade.

Comparative Advantage

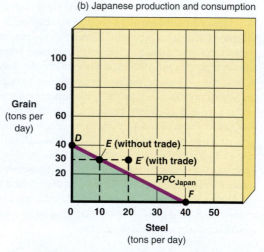

(b) Japanese production and consumption

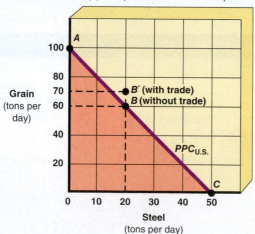

(a) U.S. production and consumption

- **Free trade** benefits a nation as a whole, but individuals may lose jobs and incomes because of the competition from foreign goods and services.

- **Protectionism** is a government's use of embargoes, tariffs, quotas, and other methods to impose barriers intended to both reduce imports and protect particular domestic industries. *Embargoes* prohibit the import or export of particular goods. *Tariffs* discourage imports by making them more expensive. *Quotas* limit the quantity of imports or exports of certain goods. These trade barriers often result primarily from domestic groups that exert political pressure on government in order to gain from these barriers.

- The **balance of payments** is a summary bookkeeping record of all the international transactions a country makes during a year. It is divided into different accounts, including the *current account*, the *capital account*, and the *statistical discrepancy*. The current account summarizes all transactions in currently produced goods and services. The overall balance of payments is always zero after an adjustment for the statistical discrepancy.

- The **balance of trade** is the value of a nation's imports subtracted from its exports. A balance of trade can be in deficit or in surplus. The balance of trade is the most widely reported and largest part of the current account. Since 1975, the United States has experienced balance of trade deficits.

Balance of Trade

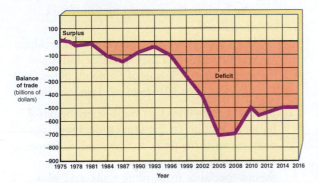

- An **exchange rate** is the price of one nation's currency in terms of another nation's currency. Foreigners who wish to purchase U.S. goods, services, and financial assets demand dollars. The supply of dollars reflects the desire of U.S. citizens to purchase foreign goods, services, and financial assets. The intersection of the supply

and demand curves for dollars determines the number of units of a foreign currency per dollar.

Exchange Rate

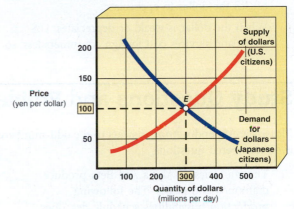

- **Shifts in supply and demand for foreign exchange** result from changes in such factors as tastes, relative price levels, relative real interest rates, and relative income levels.

- **Depreciation of currency** occurs when one currency becomes worth fewer units of another currency. If a currency depreciates, it becomes weaker. Depreciation of a nation's currency increases its exports and decreases its imports.

- **Appreciation of currency** occurs when one currency becomes worth more units of another currency. If a currency appreciates, it becomes stronger. Appreciation of a nation's currency decreases its exports and increases its imports.

Summary of Conclusion Statements

- When countries specialize, total world output increases, and therefore, the potential for greater total world consumption also increases.

- Global trade allows a country to consume a combination of goods that exceeds its production possibilities curve.

- Specialization and trade are based on opportunity costs (comparative advantage) and not on absolute advantage.

- Comparative advantage refers to the relative opportunity costs between different countries of producing the same goods. World output and consumption are maximized when each country specializes in producing and trading goods for which it has a comparative advantage.

- A current account deficit is financed by a capital account surplus.

- An exchange rate can be expressed as a reciprocal.
- An expansion in relative U.S. income causes a depreciation of the dollar.
- A rise in a trading partner's relative price level causes the dollar to appreciate.
- When the dollar is weak, or depreciates, U.S. goods and services cost foreign consumers less, so

they buy more U.S. exports. At the same time, a weak dollar means foreign goods and services cost U.S. consumers more, so they buy fewer imports.

- When the dollar is strong, or appreciates, U.S. goods and services cost foreign consumers more, so they buy fewer U.S. exports. At the same time, a strong dollar means foreign goods and services cost U.S. consumers less, so they buy more foreign imports.

Study Questions and Problems

Please see Appendix A for answers to the odd-numbered questions. Your instructor has access to the answers for even-numbered questions.

1. The countries of Alpha and Beta produce diamonds and pearls. The following production possibilities schedule describes their potential output in tons per year:

Points on production possibilities curve	Alpha		Beta	
	Diamonds	Pearls	Diamonds	Pearls
A	150	0	90	0
B	100	25	60	60
C	50	50	30	120
D	0	75	0	180

Using the data in the table, answer the following questions:
a. What is the opportunity cost of diamonds for each country?
b. What is the opportunity cost of pearls for each country?
c. In which good does Alpha have a comparative advantage?
d. In which good does Beta have a comparative advantage?
e. Suppose Alpha is producing and consuming at point B on its production possibilities curve and Beta is producing and consuming at point C on its production possibilities

curve. Use a table such as Exhibit 3 to explain why both nations would benefit if they specialized.
f. Draw a graph, and use it to explain how Alpha and Beta benefit if they specialize and Alpha agrees to trade 50 tons of diamonds to Beta and Alpha receives 50 tons of pearls in exchange.

2. Bill can paint either two walls or one window frame in 1 hour. In the same time, Frank can paint either three walls or two window frames. To minimize the time spent painting, who should specialize in painting walls, and who should specialize in painting window frames?

3. Consider this statement: "The principles of specialization and trade according to comparative advantage among nations also apply to states in the United States." Do you agree or disagree? Explain.

4. Would the U.S. government gain any advantage from using tariffs or quotas to restrict imports?

5. Suppose the United States passed a law stating that we would not purchase imports from any country that imposed any trade restrictions on our exports. Who would benefit and who would lose from such retaliation?

6. Now consider Question 5 in terms of the law's impact on domestic producers that export goods. Does this policy adversely affect domestic producers that export goods?

7. Consider this statement: "Unrestricted foreign trade costs domestic jobs." Do you agree or disagree? Explain.

8. Do you support a constitutional amendment to prohibit the federal government from imposing any trade barriers, such as tariffs and quotas, except in case of war or national emergency? Why or why not?

9. Discuss this statement: "Because each nation's balance of payments equals zero, it follows that there is actually no significance to a balance of payments deficit or surplus."

10. For each of the following situations, indicate the direction of the shift in the supply curve or the demand curve for dollars, the factor causing the change, and the resulting movement of the equilibrium exchange rate for the dollar in terms of foreign currency:
    a. American-made cars become more popular overseas.
    b. The United States experiences a recession, while other nations enjoy economic growth.
    c. Inflation rates accelerate in the United States, while inflation rates remain constant in other nations.

d. Real interest rates in the United States rise, while real interest rates abroad remain constant.
e. The Japanese put quotas and high tariffs on all imports from the United States.
f. Tourism from the United States increases sharply because of a fare war among airlines.

11. The following table summarizes the supply and the demand for euros:

	U.S. Dollars per Euro				
	$0.05	**$0.10**	**$0.15**	**$0.20**	**$0.25**
Quantity demanded (per day)	500	400	300	200	100
Quantity supplied (per day)	100	200	300	400	500

Using the previous table:
a. Graph the supply and demand curves for euros.
b. Determine the equilibrium exchange rate.
c. Determine what the effect of a fixed exchange rate at $0.10 per euro would be.

 CHECKPOINT ANSWERS

Checkpoint: Do Nations with an Advantage Always Trade?

In the United States, the opportunity cost of producing 1 calculator is 100 towels. In Costa Rica, the opportunity cost of producing 1 calculator is 100 towels. If you said because the opportunity cost is the same for each nation, specialization and trade would not boost total output and therefore these countries would not trade these products, **YOU ARE CORRECT**.

Checkpoint: Should Everyone Keep a Balance of Payments?

The principal purpose of the balance of payments is to keep track of payments of national currencies. Because states and cities within the same nation use the same national currency, payments for goods and services traded between these parties do not represent a loss (outflow) or gain (inflow). If you said only nations need to use the balance of payments to account for flows of foreign currency across national boundaries, **YOU ARE CORRECT**.

Sample Quiz

Please see Appendix B for answers to Sample Quiz questions.

1. The theory of comparative advantage suggests that a (an)
   a. industrialized country should not import.
   b. country that is not competitive should import everything.
   c. country specialize in producing goods or services for which it has a lower opportunity cost.
   d. None of the above answers are correct.

2. Assume the United States can use a given amount of its resources to produce either 20 airplanes or 8 automobiles and Japan can employ the same amount of its resources to produce either 20 airplanes or 10 automobiles. The United States should specialize in
   a. airplanes.
   b. automobiles.
   c. both goods.
   d. neither good.

EXHIBIT 14 Potatoes and Wheat Output (tons per hour)

Country	Potatoes	Wheat
United States	4	2
Ireland	3	1

3. In Exhibit 14, the United States has an absolute advantage in producing
   a. potatoes.
   b. wheat.
   c. both potatoes and wheat.
   d. neither potatoes nor wheat.

4. In Exhibit 14, Ireland's opportunity cost of producing one unit of wheat is
   a. 1/3 ton of potatoes.
   b. 3 tons of potatoes.
   c. either a or b.
   d. neither a nor b.

5. In Exhibit 14, the United States has a comparative advantage in producing
   a. potatoes.
   b. wheat.
   c. both potatoes and wheat.
   d. neither potatoes nor wheat.

6. If each nation in Exhibit 14, specializes in producing the good for which it has a comparative advantage, then
   a. Ireland would produce neither potatoes nor wheat.
   b. the United States would produce both potatoes and wheat.
   c. the United States would produce potatoes.
   d. Ireland would produce potatoes.

7. A tariff is a
   a. tax on an exported product.
   b. limit on the number of goods that can be exported.
   c. limit on the number of goods that can be imported.
   d. tax on an imported product.
   e. subsidy on an imported product.

8. The principal objective of the WTO is to
   a. reduce the level of all tariffs.
   b. establish fair prices for all goods traded internationally.
   c. prevent the trading of services across nations' borders.
   d. encourage countries to establish quotas.

9. Which of the following is *not* an argument used in favor of protectionism?
   a. to protect an "infant" industry
   b. to protect domestic jobs
   c. to preserve national security
   d. to protect against "unfair" competition because of cheap foreign labor
   e. to reduce prices paid by domestic consumers

10. The main explanation for why the cheap foreign labor argument is a poor reason for restricting international trade is that
    a. workers who get paid less tend to have lower productivity than those who get paid more.

b. all firms and workers gain when there are no restrictions on international trade.

c. infant industries such as steel and automobiles need to be protected.

d. specialization and free trade usually raise the prices of all the traded goods, so that the workers can get paid more.

11. The account that records a nation's foreign economic transactions is called the
   a. trade account.
   b. T account.
   c. exchange market.
   d. balance of payments.

12. Expenditures for services such as tourism, income for foreign investment, and foreign gifts are tabulated in the
   a. current account.
   b. capital account.
   c. official reserve account.
   d. goods account.

13. Suppose a German bank purchases a U.S. Treasury bond. This transaction would be recorded in the
   a. capital account.
   b. current account.
   c. goods trade balance.
   d. unilateral transfers.

14. Exhibit 15 shows a situation in which
   a. both the dollar and the pound have depreciated.
   b. both the dollar and the pound have appreciated.
   c. the dollar has depreciated and the pound has appreciated.
   d. the dollar has appreciated and the pound has depreciated.

15. Which of the following could cause the dollar-pound exchange rate to change as shown in Exhibit 15?
   a. American goods become more popular in Great Britain.
   b. British incomes rise, while U.S. incomes remain unchanged.
   c. The U.S. price level rises, while the British price level remains unchanged.
   d. The U.S. real interest rate rises, while the British real interest rate remains unchanged.

16. A country that has a lower opportunity cost of producing a good
   a. has a comparative advantage.
   b. can produce the good using fewer resources than another country.
   c. requires fewer labor hours to produce the good.
   d. All of the above answers are correct.

17. If one country can produce a good with fewer resources than another country, this is called
   a. specialization.
   b. geographic advantage.
   c. comparative advantage.
   d. absolute advantage.

18. One big difference between tariffs and quotas is that tariffs
   a. raise the price of a good while quotas lower it.
   b. generate tax revenues while quotas do not.
   c. stimulate international trade while quotas inhibit it.
   d. hurt domestic producers while quotas help them.

EXHIBIT 15 Foreign Exchange Market for U.S. Dollars and British Pounds

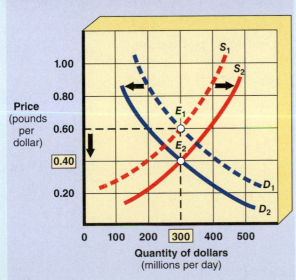

19. Which of the following is *not* included in the current account?
    a. exports of goods
    b. imports of goods
    c. U.S. capital inflow and outflow
    d. unilateral transfers

20. A shift of the U.S. demand curve for Mexican pesos to the left and a decrease in the peso price per dollar would result from

a. an increase in the U.S. inflation rate relative to the rate in Mexico.
b. a change in U.S. consumers' tastes away from Mexican products and toward products made in South Korea, India, and Taiwan.
c. U.S. buyers perceiving that domestically - produced products are of a lower quality than products made in Mexico.
d. all of the above answers are correct.

CHAPTER 16

Economies in Transition

CHAPTER PREVIEW

The inherent vice of capitalism is the unequal sharing of blessings. The inherent virtue of communism is the equal sharing of miseries.

—**Winston Churchill**

The emergence of the market system in Russia, China, and other countries continues while leaders of these countries who were devoted followers of Marxist ideology now say they believe that capitalism, private property, and profit are ideas superior to the communist system. The failure of communism and the transformation toward a market system is personified by the success of McDonald's in Russia and Walmart in China. Today, Russia and other countries continue to experience economic problems during their restructuring, but the commitment to free-market reforms remains. In contrast, in 2009, the media reported the news

that the United States was nationalizing banks and General Motors. And in 2011 and 2012, a protest movement called Occupy Wall Street spread across the United States. The anticapitalist slogan of the protests was "We are the 99 percent." The main issues protested were inequity between the wealthiest 1 percent and the rest of the population and corrupt influence of corporations on government. What caused these astonishing turn of events?

To understand how the pieces of the global economic puzzle fit together, this chapter begins with a discussion of the three basic types of economies. Then you will examine the pros and cons of the "isms"—capitalism, socialism, and communism. Here you will explore the worldwide clash between the ideas of Adam Smith and Karl Marx and study their current influence on economic systems. Finally, you will examine economic reforms in Cuba, Russia, and China.

IN THIS CHAPTER, YOU WILL LEARN TO SOLVE THESE ECONOMICS PUZZLES:

- Why did drivers in the former Soviet Union remove the windshield wipers and side mirrors whenever they parked their cars?

- What did Adam Smith mean when he said that an "invisible hand" promotes the public interest?

- If the Soviet Union was foolish to run its economy on five-year plans, why do universities, businesses, and governments in a capitalistic economy bother to plan?

16-1 BASIC TYPES OF ECONOMIC SYSTEMS

Economic system
The organizations and methods used to determine what goods and services are produced, how they are produced, and for whom they are produced.

North Korea and South Korea share the same language and historical background. However, South Korea today is a modern economy and people starve in North Korea. This difference relates to their differing economic systems. An **economic system** consists of the organizations and methods used to determine what goods and services are produced, how they are produced, and for whom they are produced. As explained earlier in Chapter 2, scarcity forces each economic system to decide what combination of goods to produce, how to produce such goods, and who gets the output once it is produced. The decision-making process involves interaction among many aspects of a nation's culture, such as its laws, form of government, ethics, religions, and customs. Each economic system can be classified into one of three basic types: (1) Traditional, (2) Command, or (3) Market.

16-1a The Traditional Economy

Traditional economy
An economic system that answers the What, How, and For Whom questions the way they have always have been answered.

Why does England have a king or queen? Tradition is the answer. Historically, the traditional economy has been a common system for making economic decisions. The **traditional economy** is a system that answers the What, How, and For Whom questions the way they have always been answered. People in this type of society learn that copying the previous generation allows them to feel accepted. Anyone who changes ways of doing things asks for trouble from others. This is because people in such a society believe that what was good yesterday, and years ago, must still be a good idea today.

Although most traditional economies have changed to keep pace with modern economic trends, traditional systems are used today, for example, by the Ainu of Canada, the native people of Brazil's rain forest, and the Amish of Pennsylvania. In these societies, the way past generations decided what crops are planted, how they are harvested, and to whom they are distributed remains unchanged over time. People perform their jobs in the manner established by their ancestors. The Amish are well known for rejecting tractors and using horse-drawn plows. Interestingly, the Amish reject Social Security because their society voluntarily redistributes wealth to members who are needy.

16-1b The Traditional Economy's Strengths and Weaknesses

The benefit of the traditional approach is that it minimizes friction among members because relatively little is disputed. Consequently, people in this system may cooperate more freely with one another. In today's industrial world, the Amish and other traditional economies appear very satisfied with their relatively uncomplicated systems. However, critics argue that the traditional system restricts individual initiative and therefore does not lead to the production of advanced goods, new technology, and economic growth.

16-1c The Command Economy

Command economy
An economic system that answers the What, How, and For Whom questions by a dictator or central authority.

In a **command economy**, a dictator or group of central planners makes economic decisions for society. In this system, the What, How, and For Whom questions are answered by a dictator or planners with central authority. The former Soviet Union in the past and Cuba and North Korea today are examples of nations with command economies using national economic plans implemented through powerful government committees.

Politically selected committees decide on everything, including the number, color, size, quality, and price of autos, brooms, sweaters, and tanks. The state owns the factors of production and dictates answers to the three basic economic questions. The authorities might decide to produce modern weapons instead of schools, or they might decide to devote resources to building huge monuments like the pyramids, built by the rulers of ancient Egypt to honor their dead kings and queens.

In the old Soviet economy, for example, the three basic economic questions were answered by a central planning agency called the *Gosplan*. Following the policies of the political authority (the Politburo), the Gosplan set production quotas and prices for farms, factories, mines, housing construction, medical care, and other producing units. What should the cows be fed? If it is hay, how much land can be used to grow it? How much milk should the cows give? How many people will be dairy farmers? What wages should a dairy farmer earn? Should milk be given to everyone, to a few, or to people chosen by the leaders? If there was a shortage of goods in the shops, then goods would be rationed through queuing. The Gosplan tried to make all these decisions. Today, in Russia and the other former Soviet republics, the Gosplan is a distant memory of the discarded Soviet command system.

The pyramid shown in Exhibit 1 represents the command economy. At the top of the pyramid is a supremely powerful group of central planners, such as the old Soviet Gosplan. That agency established production targets and prices for goods and services.

EXHIBIT 1 The Command Economy Pyramid

The principal feature of a command economy is the central planning board at the top, which transmits economic decisions down to the various producing and consuming units below. This process begins with an overall plan from a supreme planning board, such as the old Soviet Gosplan. The Gosplan established production targets and was the ultimate authority over a layer of specialized planning agencies, which authorized capital expansion, raw material purchases, prices, wages, and all other production decisions for individual producing units. Finally, the factories, farms, mines, and other producers distributed the specified output to consumers according to the approved master plan.

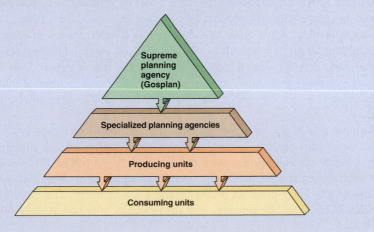

Then the Gosplan transmitted this information to a second layer of specialized state planning agencies. One of these specialized government bureaucracies purchased raw materials, another agency established fashion trends, another set prices, and another government bureaucracy made decisions based on employment and wages.

Production objectives were transmitted from the upper authority layers to the individual producing units, represented by the third layer of the pyramid in Exhibit 1. These producers supplied goods and services to the consumers, as commanded by the central authorities. The bottom portion of the pyramid illustrates the distribution, according to the master plan, of output to consuming units of individuals and households.

16-1d The Command Economy's Strengths and Weaknesses

Believe it or not, the command system can be defended. Proponents argue that economic change occurs much faster in a command system than in a traditional economy. This is one reason those dissatisfied with a traditional society might advocate establishment of a command system. The central authorities can ignore custom and order new ways of doing things. Another reason for adopting a command economy is the controversial belief that the government will provide economic security and equity. It is alleged that central authorities ensure that everyone is provided food, clothing, shelter, and medical care regardless of their ability to contribute to society.

The absolute power of central authorities to make right decisions is also the power to be absolutely wrong. Often the planners do not set production goals accurately, and either shortages or surpluses of goods and services are the result. For example, at one point, the planners miscalculated and produced too few windshield wipers and side mirrors for Soviet cars. Faced with shortages of these parts, Soviet drivers removed windshield wipers and side mirrors whenever they parked their cars to prevent theft. On the other hand, the Gosplan allocated some collective farms far more fertilizer than they could use. To receive the same amount of fertilizer again the next year, farmers simply burned the excess fertilizer. As a result of such decision-making errors, people waited in long lines or stole goods. How does any decision-making group really know how many windshield wipers to produce each year and how much workers making them should earn?

Because profit is not the motive of producers in a command economy, quality and variety of goods also suffer. If the Gosplan ordered a state enterprise to produce 400,000 side mirrors for cars, for example, producers had little incentive to make the extra effort required to create a quality product in a variety of styles. The easiest way to meet the goal was to produce a low-quality product in one style regardless of consumer demand.

Exhibit 2 illustrates how the pricing policy of central planners causes shortages. The demand curve for side mirrors conforms to the law of demand. At lower prices in rubles, the quantity demanded increases. The supply curve is fixed at 400,000 side mirrors because it is set by the central planners and is therefore unresponsive to price variations.

Suppose one of the principal goals of the command economy is to keep the price low. To reach this goal, the central planners set the price of side mirrors at 20 rubles, which is below the equilibrium price of 40 rubles. At 20 rubles, more people can afford a side mirror than at the equilibrium price set by an uncontrolled marketplace. The consequence of this lower price set by the planners is a shortage. The quantity demanded at 20 rubles is 800,000 side mirrors, and the quantity supplied is only 400,000 mirrors.

EXHIBIT 2 Central Planners Fixing Prices

The central planners' goal is to keep prices low, so they set the price of a side mirror for a car at 20 rubles, which is below the market-determined equilibrium price of 40 rubles. At the set price, however, the quantity demanded is 800,000 side mirrors per year. Also set by the planners, the quantity supplied is 400,000 per year. Thus, the shortage at the government-established price is 400,000 side mirrors per year. As a result, long lines form to buy side mirrors, and black markets appear.

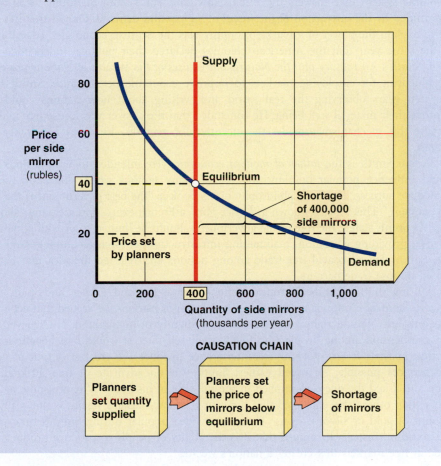

Thus, the model explains why side mirrors disappeared from stores long before many willing buyers could purchase them.

The same graphical analysis applies to centrally planned rental prices for apartments. The central planners in the former Soviet Union set rents below the equilibrium rental prices for apartments. As the model predicts, low rents resulted in a shortage of housing. Meanwhile, the planners promised that improvements in housing would come in time.

CONCLUSION	When central planners set prices below equilibrium for goods and services, they create shortages, which mean long lines, empty shelves, and black markets.[1]

16-1e The Market Economy and the Ideas of Adam Smith

Market economy
An economic system that answers the What, How, and For Whom questions using prices determined by the interaction of the forces of supply and demand.

In a market economy, neither customs nor a single person or group of central planners answers the three basic economic questions facing society. **The market economy** is an economic system that answers the What, How, and For Whom questions using prices determined by the interaction of the forces of supply and demand. One of the first people to explain the power of a market economy was the Scottish economist Adam Smith. In the same year that the American colonies declared their political independence in 1776, Smith's *An Inquiry into the Nature and Causes of the Wealth of Nations* presented the blueprint for employing markets to improve economic performance. Smith spent over ten years observing the real world and writing about how nations could best improve their material well-being. He concluded that the answer was to use free markets because this mechanism provides the incentive for everyone to follow his or her *self-interest*.

Adam Smith is the *father of modern economics*. He intended to write a book that would influence popular opinion, and unlike many famous works, his book was an immediate success. The basic philosophy of his book is "the best government is the least government." This belief is known as *laissez-faire*, a French expression meaning "allow to act." As Smith stated, the role of the government should be limited to providing national defense, providing education, maintaining infrastructure, enforcing contracts, and little else. Smith also advocated free trade among nations and rejected the idea that nations should impose trade barriers.

During Smith's lifetime, European nations such as England, France, and Spain intervened to control economic activities. In *The Wealth of Nations*, he argued that economic freedoms are "natural rights" necessary for the dignity of humankind. He believed that free competition among people who follow their self-interest would best benefit society because markets free of government interference produce the greatest output of goods and services possible. As noted earlier, Smith was an advocate of free international trade and asked the question implied in the full title of his book: Why are some nations richer than others? He explained that the source of any nation's wealth is not really the amount of gold or silver it owns. This was an idea popular during Smith's time called *mercantilism*. Instead, he argued that it is the ability of people to produce products and trade in free markets that creates a nation's wealth.

The importance of markets is that they harness the power of self-interest to answer the What, How, and For Whom questions. Without central planning, markets coordinate the actions of millions of consumers and producers. Smith said that the market economy seemed to be controlled by an *invisible hand*. The **invisible hand** is a phrase that expresses the belief that the best interests of a society are served when individual consumers and producers compete to achieve their own private interests. Guided by an invisible hand, producers must compete with one another to win consumers' money. The

Invisible hand
A phrase that expresses the belief that the best interests of a society are served when individual consumers and producers compete to achieve their own private interests.

---

[1]Recall from Exhibit 5 in Chapter 4 that a black market is an illegal market that emerges when a price ceiling is imposed in a free market.

profit motive in a competitive marketplace provides profits as a reward for efficient producers, while losses punish inefficient producers. Smith saw profit as the necessary driving force in an individualistic market system. The profit motive leads the butcher, the baker, and other producers to answer the What, How, and For Whom questions at the lowest prices. Consumers also compete with one another to purchase the best goods at the lowest price. Competition automatically regulates the economy and provides more goods and services than a system in which government attempts to accomplish the same task in the *public interest*. In Smith's own words:

> *Every individual necessarily labours to render the annual revenue of the society as great as he can. He generally, indeed, neither intends to promote the public interest, nor knows how much he is promoting it. By … directing that industry in such a manner as its produce may be of the greatest value, he intends only his own gain, and he is in this, as in many other cases, led by an invisible hand to promote an end which was no part of his intention. Nor is it always the worse for the society that it was no part of it. By pursuing his own interest he frequently promotes that of the society more effectually than when he really intends to promote it.[2]*

16-1f The Market Economy's Strengths and Weaknesses

In a market system, if consumers want Sudoku puzzles, they can buy them because sellers seek to profit from the sale of Sudoku puzzles. No single person or central planning board makes a formal decision to shift resources and tells firms how to produce what many might view as a frivolous product. Because no central body or set of customs interferes, the market system provides a wide variety of goods and services that buyers and sellers exchange at the lowest prices.

> A market economy answers the What to produce and How to produce questions very effectively.   **CONCLUSION**

Those who attack the market economy point out the market failure problems of lack of competition, externalities, lack of public goods, and income inequality, discussed in Chapter 4. For example, critics contend that competition among buyers and sellers results in people who are very wealthy and people who are very poor. In a market economy, output is divided in favor of people who earn higher incomes and own property. Some people will dine on caviar in fine restaurants, while others will wander the streets and beg for food and shelter. Supporters of the market system argue that this inequality of income must exist to give people incentives or rewards for the value of their contributions to others.

16-1g The Mixed Economy

In the real world, no nation is a pure traditional, command, or market economy. Even primitive tribes employ a few markets in their system. For example, members of a tribe may exchange shells for animal skins. In China, the government allows many private shops and farms to operate in free markets. Although the United States is best described

---

[2]Adam Smith, *An Inquiry into the Nature and Causes of the Wealth of Nations* (1776; reprint, New York: Random House, 1937), p. 423.

as a market economy, it is also a blend of the other two systems. As mentioned earlier, the Amish operate a well-known traditional economy in our nation. The draft during wartime is an example of a command economy in which the government obtains involuntary labor. In addition, taxes "commanded" from taxpayers fund government programs, such as national defense and Social Security. If the economic systems of most nations do not perfectly fit one of the basic definitions, what term best describes their economies? A more appropriate description is that most countries employ a blend of the basic types of economic systems, broadly called a mixed economy. A **mixed economy** is a system that answers the What, How, and For Whom questions through a mixture of traditional, command, and market systems.

The traditional, command, and market economies can exist in a wide variety of political situations. For instance, the United States and Japan are politically "free" societies in which the market system flourishes. But China uses the market system to a limited degree in spite of its lack of political freedom. Moreover, some of the Western democracies engage in central economic planning. French officials representing government, business, and labor meet annually to discuss economic goals for industry for the next five-year period, but compliance is voluntary. In Japan, a government agency called the *Ministry of Economy, Trade and Industry (METI)* engages in long-term planning. One of the goals of the METI is to encourage exports so that Japan can earn the foreign currencies it needs to pay for oil and other resources.

> **Mixed economy**
> An economic system that answers the What, How, and For Whom questions through a mixture of traditional, command, and market systems.

16-2 THE "ISMS"

What type of economic system will a society choose to answer the What, How, and For Whom questions? We could call most economies "mixed," but this would be too imprecise. In the real world, economic systems are labeled with various forms of the popular "isms"—capitalism, socialism, and communism, which are based on the basic types of systems.

16-2a Capitalism

The popular term for the market economy discussed previously is capitalism. **Capitalism** is an economic system characterized by private ownership of resources and markets. *Capitalism* is also called the *free enterprise system*. Regardless of its political system, a capitalist economic system must possess two characteristics: private ownership of resources, and decentralized decision making using markets.

> **Capitalism**
> An economic system characterized by private ownership of resources and markets.

Private Ownership

Ownership of resources determines to a great degree who makes the What, How, and For Whom decisions. In a capitalist system, resources are primarily *privately* owned and controlled by individuals and firms, rather than having property rights be *publicly* held by government on behalf of society. In the United States, most capital resources are privately owned, but the term *capitalism* is somewhat confusing because it stresses private ownership of factories, raw materials, farms, and other forms of *capital* even though public ownership of land exists as well.

Decentralized Decision Making

This characteristic of capitalism allows buyers and sellers to exchange goods in markets without government involvement. A capitalist system operates on the principle of consumer sovereignty. **Consumer sovereignty** is the freedom of consumers to cast their dollar votes to buy, or not to buy, at prices determined in competitive markets. As a result, consumer spending determines what goods and services firms produce. In a capitalist system, most allocative decisions are coordinated by consumers and producers interacting through markets and making their own decisions guided by Adam Smith's "invisible hand." Friedrich Hayek, an Austrian economist who was a 1974 recipient of the Nobel Prize and author of *The Road to Serfdom*, argued that political and economic freedoms are inseparable.

In the real world, many U.S. markets are not perfectly open or free markets with the consumer as sovereign. For example, consumers cannot buy illegal drugs or body organs. In Chapter 4, you learned that the U.S. government has set minimum prices (support prices) for wheat, milk, cheese, and other products. These markets are free only if the market price is above the support price. Similarly, the minimum wage law forces employers to pay a wage above some dollar amount per hour regardless of market conditions.

Consumer sovereignty
The freedom of consumers to cast their dollar votes to buy, or not to buy, at prices determined in competitive markets.

No nation in the world precisely fits the two criteria for capitalism; however, the United States comes close.

CONCLUSION

16-2b **Capitalism's Strengths and Weaknesses**

One of the major strengths of capitalism is its capacity to achieve *economic efficiency* because competition and the profit motive force production at the lowest cost. Another strength of pure capitalism is *economic freedom* because economic power is widely dispersed. Individual consumers, producers, and workers are free to make decisions based on their own self-interest. Economist Milton Friedman makes a related point: Private ownership limits the power of government to deny goods, services, or jobs to its adversaries.

Critics of capitalism cite several shortcomings. First, capitalism tends toward an unequal distribution of income. This inequality of income among citizens results for several reasons. Private ownership of capital and the other factors of production can cause these factors to become concentrated in the hands of a few individuals or firms. Also, people do not have equal labor skills, and the marketplace rewards those with greater skills. These inequalities may be perpetuated because the rich can provide better education, legal aid, political platforms, and wealth to their heirs. Second, private markets can fail to provide an adequate amount of public goods, like roads and national defense. Third, some critics believe capitalism inevitably leads to macroeconomic instability that can result in severe recessions or even depressions. Finally, pure capitalism is criticized for its failure to protect the environment. The pursuit of profit and self-interest can take precedence over damage or pollution to the air, rivers, lakes, and streams. Recall the graphical model used in Chapter 4 to illustrate the socially unacceptable impact of producers who pollute the environment.

16-2c **Socialism**

The idea of socialism has existed for thousands of years. Its basis is the command system. **Socialism** is an economic system characterized by government ownership of resources and centralized decision making. Socialism is also called *command socialism*. Under a socialist economy, a command system owns and controls in the *public interest* the major industries, such as steel, electricity, and agriculture. However, some free markets can exist in farming, retail trade, and certain service areas. Just as no pure capitalist system

Socialism
An economic system characterized by government ownership of resources and centralized decision making.

exists in the real world, none of the socialist countries in the world today practices pure socialism. In fact, there are as many variants of socialism as there are countries called socialist. Even in the United States, there are some elements of socialism. For example, the federal government owns and operates the Tennessee Valley Authority (TVA), the National Aeronautics and Space Administration (NASA), and the U.S. Postal Service, while at the same time allowing private utilities and mail service firms to operate.

Advocates of socialism believe that the market failures in a capitalist system create so much economic hardship that a country is better off using socialism to organize its production; however, because it is impossible to objectively measure the extent to which these market failures exist, reasonable people often disagree over the degree to which the government should intervene to try to correct for these problems. On the other side of the issue, critics of socialism argue that the government may fail to improve on these market outcomes. Or worse yet, government intervention may make matters worse. These critics believe that socialism produces poor economic results mostly because some government officials are corrupt, ignorant, or succumb to special-interest-group political pressure.

Before discussing socialism further, you must realize that socialism is an economic system, and political systems should not be confused with economic systems. Socialist economies may be controlled by any number of political systems ranging from a dictatorship to a democracy. Generally, socialist economies run by non-democratic governments are referred to as *communist* nations today. On the other hand, *democratic socialism* exists when the government is a freely and fairly elected democracy. The degree of socialism, or government influence over economic affairs, can vary dramatically among nations. And, it is difficult to say when a country has become a "socialist" state. Nevertheless, there are elements of socialism in every nation. For example, Great Britain, France, Italy, and the Scandinavian nations of Norway, Sweden, and Denmark all have representative democracies, but many of their major industries (such as railroads and coal mining) are or have been nationalized.

16-2d The Ideas of Karl Marx

Despite the transition toward more capitalist systems in Russia and Eastern Europe, China, Cuba, and many less-developed countries are still primarily socialist. The theory for socialism and *communism* can be traced to Karl Marx. Marx was a nineteenth-century German philosopher, revolutionary, and economist. Unlike other economists of the time who followed Adam Smith, Marx rejected the concept of a society operating through private interest and profit.

Karl Marx was born in Germany, the son of a lawyer. In 1841, after receiving a doctorate in philosophy from Berlin University, he turned to journalism and became interested in radical politics. In 1843, Marx married the daughter of a wealthy family and moved to Paris, but his political activities forced him to leave Paris for England. From the age of 31, he lived and wrote his books in London. In London, Marx lived an impoverished life while he and his lifelong friend Friedrich Engels wrote *The Communist Manifesto* published in 1848. A massive work followed, titled *Das Kapital*, which was published in three volumes between 1867 and 1894. These two works made Karl Marx the most influential economist in the history of socialism. In fact, he devoted his entire life to a revolt against capitalism. As Marx read *The Wealth of Nations*, he saw profits as unjust payments to owners of firms—the capitalists. Marx predicted that the market system would destroy itself because wealthy owners would go too far and exploit workers because unrelenting greed for profits would lead the owners to pay starvation wages. Moreover, the owners would force laborers to work in unsafe conditions, and many would not have a job at all.

Karl Marx (1818–1883)
His criticism of capitalism advanced communism.
He wrote *The Communist Manifesto and Das Kapital.*

Photos.com/Getty Images Plus/Getty Images

Marx believed that private ownership and exploitation would produce a nation driven by a class struggle between a few "haves" and many "have-nots." As he stated in *The Communist Manifesto*, "The history of all existing society is the history of class struggle. Freeman and slave, patrician and plebeian, lord and serf, guildmaster and journeyman, in a word, oppressor and oppressed."[3] In Marx's vision, capitalists were the modern-day oppressors, and the workers were the oppressed proletariat. Someday, Marx predicted, the workers would rise up in a spontaneous bloody revolution against a system benefiting only the owners of capital. Marx believed communism to be the ideal system, which would evolve in stages from capitalism through socialism. **Communism** is a stateless, classless economic system in which all the factors of production are owned by the workers and people share in production according to their needs. This is the highest form of socialism toward which the revolution should strive.

Under communism, no private property exists to encourage self-interest. There is no struggle between classes of people, and everyone cooperates. In fact, there is no reason to commit crime, and police, lawyers, and courts are unnecessary. Strangely, Marx surpassed Adam Smith in advocating a system with little central government. Marx believed that those who work hard, or are more skilled, will be public spirited. Any "haves" will give voluntarily to "have-nots." In Marx's own words, people would be motivated by the principle "from each according to his ability, to each according to his need." World peace would evolve as nation after nation accepted cooperation and rejected profits and competition. Under the idealized society of communism, there would be no state. No central authority would be necessary to pursue the interests of the people.

Today, we call the economic systems that existed in the former Soviet Union and Eastern Europe, and still exist in Cuba and other countries, *communist*. However, the definition of *socialism* given in this chapter more accurately describes their real-world economic systems. Actually, no nation has achieved the ideal communist society described by Marx, nor has capitalism self-destructed as he predicted. The 1917 communist revolution in Russia did not fit Marx's theory. At that time, Russia was an underdeveloped country, rather than an industrial country filled with greedy capitalists who exploited workers.

Communism
A stateless, classless economic system in which all the factors of production are owned by the workers and people share in production according to their needs. In Marx's view, this is the highest form of socialism toward which the revolution should strive.

16-2e **Characteristics of Socialism**

Regardless of a society's political system, a socialist economy has two basic characteristics: public ownership, and centralized decision making.

Public Ownership

Under socialism, the government owns most of the factors of production, including factories, farms, mines, and natural resources. Agriculture in the old Soviet Union illustrates how even this real-world socialist country deviated from total public ownership. In the Soviet Union, there were three rather distinct forms of agriculture: state farms, collective farms, and private plots. In both the state farm and collective farm sectors, central planning authorities determined prices and outputs. In contrast, the government allowed those holding small private plots on peasant farms to operate primarily in free markets that determined price and output levels. Reforms allowed farmers to buy land, tractors, trucks, and other resources from the state, and dramatically end the collectivization of agriculture begun under Josef Stalin.

Centralized Decision Making

Instead of the pursuit of *private interest*, the motivation of pure socialism is the *public interest* of the whole society. For instance, a factory manager cannot decide to raise or

---

[3]Karl Marx and Friedrich Engels, The Communist Manifesto (New York: International Press, 1848), p. 31.

lower prices to obtain maximum profits for the factory. Regardless of inventory levels or the opportunity to raise prices, the planners will not permit this action. Instead of exploiting the ups and downs of the market, the goal of the socialist system is to make centralized decisions that protect workers and consumers from decentralized market decisions. Critics argue that the main objective of this centralization is to perpetuate the personal dictatorships of leaders such as Stalin in the old Soviet Union and Raul Castro in Cuba.

Before the open market reforms, Soviet planners altered earnings to attract workers into certain occupations and achieve planned goals. For example, if space projects needed more engineers, then the state raised the earnings of engineers until the target number of people entered the engineering profession. As shown earlier in Exhibit 2, central planners in the Soviet Union also manipulated consumer prices. If consumers desired more cars than were available, the authorities increased the price of cars. If people wished to purchase less of an item than was available, planners lowered prices. The problem was that this decision process took time. And while the market awaited its orders from the Soviet planners, excess inventories of some items accumulated, and consumers stood in line for cheap products that never seemed to be available. There was an old Soviet saying, "If you see a line, get in it. Whatever it is, it's scarce, and you will not see it tomorrow."

The Soviet factory system did not adhere completely to the command system. The government rewarded successful managers with bonuses that could be substantial. Better apartments, nice vacations, and medals were incentives for outstanding performance. Under economic reforms, plant managers now make decisions based on profitability instead of centralized controls.

CHECKPOINT

To Plan or Not to Plan—That Is the Question
You make plans. You planned to go to college. You plan which career to follow. You plan to get married, and so on. Businesses plan to hire employees, expand their plants, increase profits, and so forth. Because individuals and businesses plan in a market economy, there is really no difference between our system and a command economy. Or is there?

16-2f Socialism's Strengths and Weaknesses

Proponents of the socialism model argue that this system is superior in achieving an equitable distribution of income. This is because government ownership of capital and other resources prevents a few individuals or groups from acquiring a disproportionate share of the nation's wealth. Also, supporters argue that rapid economic growth is achieved when planners have the power to direct more resources to producing capital goods and fewer resources to producing consumer goods (see Exhibit 5 in Chapter 2).

National goals may seem to be easily formulated and pursued under state directives, but there are problems. For example, proponents of such an economy can claim there is no unemployment because the government assigns all workers a job and allocates resources to complete their production goals. However, economic inefficiency results because the government often uses many workers to perform work requiring only one or two workers. Critics also point out that the absence of the profit motive discourages entrepreneurship and innovation and thus suppresses economic growth.

Socialism is particularly vulnerable to the charge that it ignores the goal of economic freedom and instead creates a privileged class of government bureaucrats who assume the role of "capitalists." Central planners are the key translators of information about consumer preferences and production capabilities flowing to millions of economic units. This complex and cumbersome process is subject to errors and is unresponsive to the wants of the majority of the population. Critics also question whether the distribution of income under socialism is more equitable than under capitalism. In the socialist system, "perks" for government officials, nepotism, and the illegal use of markets create disparities in income.

16-2g Comparing Economic Systems

In reality, all nations operate economic systems that blend capitalism and socialism. Exhibit 3 presents a continuum that attempts to place countries between the two extremes of pure socialism on the left and pure capitalism on the right. Economies characterized by a high degree of both private ownership and market allocation are closest to pure capitalism. Hong Kong, Japan, the United States, and Canada fall at the capitalism end of the line. Conversely, economies characterized by much government ownership of resources and central planning are closest to pure socialism. North Korea and Cuba fall close to the pure socialism end of the spectrum, with China and Russia further away from pure socialism.

16-3 ECONOMIES IN TRANSITION

By the early 1990s, the centrally planned economies in the old Soviet Union and Eastern Europe had collapsed. After more than 70 years in the Soviet Union and over 40 years in Eastern Europe and China, the failed communist economies made a startling switch to embrace capitalism. Faced with severe shortages of food, housing, cars, and other consumer goods, communism could no longer claim better living standards for its citizens. The following is a brief discussion of reforms aimed at introducing market power into the economic systems of Cuba, Russia, and China.

16-3a Cuba

Cuba is a landscape of crumbling once-elegant buildings that often experiences daily power blackouts, fuel shortages, housing shortages, food shortages, and other economic hardships. But regardless of its economic woes, Cuba remains wedded to the communist

---

EXHIBIT 3 A Classification of Economic Systems

No nation has an economic system that is pure socialism or pure capitalism. All nations mix government ownership and reliance on markets. North Korea and Cuba are closest to pure socialism, while Hong Kong comes closest to pure capitalism. Other real-world economies are placed between these two extremes on the basis of their use of government ownership versus markets.

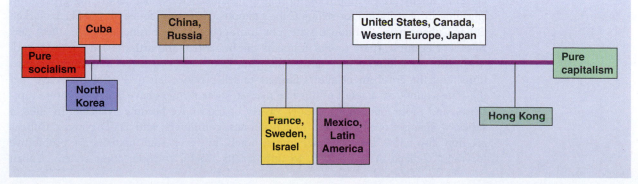

The Unrealistic Path to Communism

Marx believed that capitalism would create a class of rich business owners and a class of poor workers, which would wage class warfare when workers realized that they were being exploited. Marx also believed that the working class would win this struggle because, as he put it, capitalism will "sow the seeds of its own destruction." In Marx's view, wealth would become increasingly concentrated in a capitalist society, adding to the number of people in the working class, eliminating the middle class, and reducing the ranks of the rich class. As the working class became larger, they would become more successful in the struggle between the classes and eventually win, eliminating the classes in society. In the early 1900s, many European intellectuals felt that the injustices of their day could be traced to capitalism, and they grew impatient for change. The intellectuals wanted to move things along. In Russia, Vladimir Lenin led a revolution that established a socialist government, with its ability to make rapid decisions informed by experts. Lenin believed that socialism would enable Russia to industrialize rapidly, allowing the country to more quickly transition to communism. Lenin also believed his government was a "vanguard state," and necessary only for a short period of time until "the state could wither away" and the communist ideal of a classless society could be attained. In Lenin's vision, the state's rulers had the purest of motives, and they did what they thought was best for the people.[1]

Vladimir Lenin and James Buchanan

Library of Congress Prints and Photographs Division Washington, D.C. 20540 USA http://hdl.loc.gov/loc.pnp/pp.print/LC-DIG-ds-04387

MIKE THEILER/AFP/Getty Images

Lenin's vision of the path to a utopian communist state has come under attack from several different quarters, one being from academia. For example, Nobel Laureate James Buchanan and his co-author Gordon Tullock argued that it was unrealistic to believe that people, who are motivated by self-interest in a market setting, would act benevolently when they made decisions in their capacity as government officials. They believed that human action can best be

system. Nevertheless, the collapse of Soviet bloc aid, coupled with the effects of the U.S. trade embargo forced the late Fidel Castro and the country's new leader, Raul Castro, die-hard Marxists, to reluctantly adopt limited free market reforms. To earn foreign exchange, the dollar has been legalized, and the Cuban government has poured capital into tourism by building several new state-owned hotels and restoring historic sections of Havana. Interestingly, Cuba operates special medical tourist hospitals that treat foreigners and diplomats while excluding Cubans. Cuba has also set up quasi-state enterprises that accept only hard currency. Because few Cubans have dollars or other hard currency, many are earning it by turning to illegal schemes, such as driving gypsy cabs, engaging in prostitution, or selling Cuba's famous cigars and coffee on the black market. Other Cubans have abandoned state jobs and opened small businesses under these new rules. For example, spare rooms in houses can be rented, and artisans can sell their work to tourists. In addition, state farm enterprises have been organized into worker-owned units, and the government allows farmers to sell produce left over after they have met the state's quota. As a result of this free market, some farmers have become venture capitalists, and more food, and a greater variety of food have become available. In 2008, a series of changes opened access to cell phones, computers, and DVD players. Cubans are now also allowed to patronize tourist hotels; however, such luxuries are prohibitive for most Cubans. And in 2009, to improve its woeful transportation system, Cuban explained by assuming people are motivated by their own self-interests regardless of the environment in which they find themselves.[2]

Another major criticism of Lenin's vision came from a socialist leader who helped lead one of these vanguard governments. Milovan Djilas, who was second in charge of Yugoslavia, a country in the old Soviet bloc, leveled a devastating criticism against the vanguard state. Djilas wrote in a time when the governments of the Soviet Union (Russia) and many of the Eastern European countries were ruled by vanguard states that claimed to be moving their countries toward the ideal stateless communist society. These governments claimed that they had eliminated all classes, so that there were not rich people and poor people. Basically, these governments asserted that they were forcing a classless society on their citizens until the people were willing to form them on their own. Djilas started his critique by agreeing with Marx's argument that in capitalist societies, capital owners form a rich class and workers form a poorer class. However, Djilas did not believe that the vanguard states in Eastern Europe had eliminated classes. Djilas argued these governments just changed who were in the classes. In these countries, the government officials were rich and made up one class, while everyone else was poor and made up the other class. Djilas revealed that government officials used their positions to benefit themselves. They spent resources enhancing their own lifestyles rather than using these resources to help the workers.[3]

Djilas, Buchanan, and Tullock all point to the pitfalls of trusting leaders of a socialist government to act for society's benefit rather than their own. Even within a primarily capitalist country like the United States, a similar lesson applies. The founding fathers realized that we were a nation governed by men and not by angels. Consequently, they set up democratic institutions that could produce good results even though our leaders are self-interested rather than angelic. Our democratic government's system of checks and balances is an attempt to create a system that works for how people are really motivated, rather than how we wish they were motivated.

ANALYZE THE ISSUE

1. Aside from the government, what other institutions have leaders who claim that they do not act in their own self-interest?

2. In the institutions that you named in the previous question, do you think the leaders are self-interested as Buchanan and Tullock might predict, or do they have a different motivation? Explain.

1. V.I. Lenin, State and Revolution (New York: International Publishers, 1943).
2. James Buchanan and Gordon Tullock, The Calculus of Consent: Logical Foundations of Constitutional Democracy (Ann Arbor: University of Michigan Press, 1962).
3. Milovan Djilas, The New Class: An Analysis of the Communist System (New York: Praeger, 1957).

owners of classic American cars were recruited by the government to apply for taxi licenses and set their own fares subject to price floors. And in 2014, a new law allows Cubans to buy cars from the government. However, few were able to buy the cars because of heavy taxes designed to redistribute money from the very rich. A joke is that "if you buy a car, the next day the police show up and ask where you got the money."

In spite of the private enterprise reforms, Cuba remains essentially a communist system. Workers receive free education, housing, health care, low state salaries in pesos, and rations of staples, such as a monthly allowance of rice, beans, and milk. Profits from hotels and shops go directly into the central bank and help finance Castro's government. The state also discourages private enterprises by taxing them heavily on expected earnings, rather than on actual sales. In addition, there are highly restrictive regulations. For example, restaurants in Havana are limited to 12 seats and cannot expand regardless of demand. And Cuba has halted new licenses for some types of self-employment, including jewelers, mousetrap makers, and magicians or clowns.

In 2014 the United States announced sweeping changes. Diplomatic relations with Cuba were restored and an embassy was set up. The United States also loosen restrictions on travel and trade with Cuba. For example, the export of certain goods, such as telecommunications equipment and medicine, is now permitted. However, these moves stop short of lifting the economic embargo against Cuba.

GLOBAL ECONOMICS

Shining Light on a Debate

Applicable Concept: Comparative Economic Systems

For a long time, economists have argued whether socialism or capitalism is better equipped to produce rapid rates of economic growth. This issue is not as easy to resolve as you might imagine. It is not enough to say a country like Great Britain is capitalist and rich and another country like Sudan is socialist and poor, so capitalism is a better economic system. Great Britain may be rich for reasons that have nothing to do with its economic system. It may have abundant natural resources, or a hard-working educated workforce. Sudan may be poor for reasons that have nothing to do with its economic system. It may have suffered the hardships of long wars that put investments at such risk that people failed to build new plants and equipment.

The best way to determine which economic system is most effective is to have two identical areas that differ only in their economic systems. This type of controlled experiment is commonplace in a chemistry lab, but not an option open to economists. The closest economists can come to the laboratory setting is when a natural experiment occurs (a real world event that approximates the controls available in a laboratory). The Korean experience may approximate such a natural experiment.

After World War II, the Soviet Union and the United States split up Korea. The Soviet Union and China extended their influences into North Korea, and South Korea became aligned with the United States. At the time of the split, these two Koreas were similar. They had people with similar work habits and education. They had similar access to natural resources and roughly the same amount of per-capita income. Actually, in the 1950s North Korea was a bit richer than South Korea.[1] Although a natural experiment is never perfect, the story of the two Koreas remains enlightening.

In the first few years after the split, it would have been hard to determine which economic system was better at creating wealth. However, 80 years after Korea was divided, the differences are dramatic. South Korea has

NASA

become a nation as rich as some European countries. North Korea has remained poor. Perhaps the old adage "a picture is worth a 1,000 words" can shed some light on the huge impact an economic system can make to a country's standard of living. See the satellite picture of the Korean Peninsula at night. Notice that South Korea is lit up with bright lights. The socialist North Korea, on the other hand, is dark. Not enough of its residents can turn on lights for the light to show up in pictures. Lights, which we take for granted in most capitalist countries, are not widely available to North Koreans.

ANALYZE THE ISSUE

1. Beyond the amount of light that can be visible from a satellite at night, what might be some other relatively easy ways to measure the differences in the standards of living between the two Koreas?

2. Suppose that North Korea eventually decided to join South Korea and live under South Korea's political and economic system. After this union, what would happen to the distribution of light in the night-time satellite picture?

---

1. Key Points in Developments in East Asia: 20th Century, Asia for Educators Columbia University, http://afe.easia.columbia.edu/main_pop/kpct/kp_korea1945.htm.

16-3b Russia

In 1991, communist rule ended in Russia. To function efficiently, markets must offer incentives, so workers, the public, and even foreign investors were permitted to buy state property. This meant individuals could own the factors of production and earn profits. Such market incentives were a dagger thrust into the heart of a system previously devoted to rejecting capitalism. A key reform for Russia was to allow supply and demand to set higher prices for basic consumer goods. As shown earlier in Exhibit 2, without central planners, when prices rise to their equilibrium level, the quantity supplied increases and the quantity demanded decreases. At the beginning of 1992, the Russian government removed direct government price controls on most market goods. As the model predicts, average prices rose, leaping 1,735 percent in 1992, and a greater variety of goods started appearing on the shelves. Although workers had to pay more for basic consumer goods, they could at least find goods to buy.

Since 1992, Russia has established an independent central bank and implemented anti-inflationary monetary policies. Cities throughout Russia now have restaurants, megamalls, decent hotels, and streets choked with foreign cars. Russian entrepreneurial spirit and acceptance of it in society is in an embryonic stage, and corruption, including in the legal system, is a frequent way of life. Although Russia is far from a successful market economy, the nation is struggling to achieve an amazing economic transition. Russian privatization plans have been implemented, and steps are continuing to create an economy embracing capitalism. And *Forbes* magazine reports that 77 billionaires reside in Russia.

16-3c The People's Republic of China

Unlike Russia, China has sought economic reform under the direction of its Communist Party. Fundamental economic reforms began in China after the death of Mao Zedong in 1976. Much of this reform was due to the leadership of Deng Xiaoping. Mao was devoted to the egalitarian ideal of communist ideology. Under his rule, thoughts of self-interest were counterrevolutionary, and photographs of Marx, Lenin, and Mao hung on every street corner and in every office and factory. Deng shifted priorities by increasing production of consumer goods and steering China toward becoming a global economic power. And the results have been dramatic. International trade expanded from less than 1 percent of U.S. trade in 1975 to 15 percent in 2016, and the label "Made in China" is common throughout the world. China joined the WTO in 2001 and agreed to open some markets closed to foreigners. China's real GDP growth rate averaged 9.5 percent between 2005 and 2016, making it the world's fastest-growing economy.

To make China an industrial power in the twenty-first century, Chinese planners introduced a two-tier system for industry and agriculture in 1978. Each farm and state enterprise was given a contract to produce a quota. Any amount produced over the quota could be sold in an open market. The Chinese government also encouraged the formation of nonstate enterprises owned jointly by managers and their workforces and special economic zones open to foreign investment. In other words, a blend of capitalism and socialism would provide the incentives needed to increase output. As Deng Xiaoping explained, "It doesn't matter whether the cat is black or white as long as it catches mice." These reforms worked, leading to huge increases in farm and industrial output in the 1980s. In fact, some peasant farmers became the wealthiest people in China. After Deng's death in the mid-1990s, leadership of China passed to leaders who continued the policy of free market reforms. Today, forests of glossy skyscrapers, expressways, upscale apartments, and enormous shopping malls in Beijing, Shanghai, and other cities attest to the market-oriented reforms begun years ago. And life in China's fast lane now includes the opportunity of dining at Kentucky

Fried Chicken and McDonald's restaurants located in cities throughout the country. Disney opened its theme park in 2016, and China is estimated to overtake the United States in total theme park visits by 2020. Also, despite government censorship, China has the largest number of Internet users in the world. Today, China is a huge nation transforming itself swiftly into a powerful player in the global economy. U.S. exporters are overjoyed at the prospect of selling products to over a billion Chinese consumers. For example, swarms of bicyclists once synonymous with urban China are being pushed off the road by consumers who now can afford cars and trucks. Rolls-Royce and Bentley, the ultra-luxury cars, have expanded into China, and it is estimated that by 2030, China will have more cars on the road than the United States. Also, more Chinese are traveling by air. Consequently, the Chinese are buying more Boeing airplanes and American-made cars. The other side of the coin is the threat of what goods the industrious Chinese workers, with increasing training and foreign investment, might produce and sell abroad. For example, China manufactures most of the world's copiers, microwave ovens, Blu-ray players, and shoes. A ballooning U.S. trade deficit with China is often cited as evidence that China is not playing fair, and the political rhetoric has intensified on both sides of the issue. Other countries fear that China will eliminate their export business with the United States. Moreover, there is concern that lowering trade barriers under free trade agreements will increase Chinese imports into domestic markets and eliminate jobs. In 2007, one Chinese-made product after another was removed from U.S. shelves, for example, lethal pet food, toxic toothpaste, and other contaminated products. This prompted calls for more stringent safety regulations for imports.

China's economic growth has caused some problems. There is discontent over labor issues, pollution, and income inequality. While some people dig through trash bins, there are now wealthy private business owners. Despite the unease, China remains a market of great profit and promise and a target for protectionists as it continues its transition from a communist command economy to capitalism. And the debate continues over whether China, a socialist economy, is a strategic trading partner or an emerging economic colossus that will dominate the world economy.

16-3d Privatization versus Nationalization

Privatization
The process of turning a government enterprise into a private enterprise.

The previous discussions of Cuba, Russia, and China provide examples of privatization. **Privatization** is the process of turning a government enterprise into a private enterprise. It is the opposite of **nationalization**, which is the act of transforming a private enterprise's assets into government ownership. The motives for nationalization are political as well as economic. Proponents believe that government ownership enables the state on behalf of the people to exercise more effective control and equitable redistribution of wealth and income. Critics argue that government ownership suppresses incentives, entrepreneurship, and private investment that are essential for an enterprise to prosper. During a financial crisis, the argument in favor of nationalization is that a brief period of nationalization is needed to prevent the largest corporations and banks from a downward spiral that affects the entire economy. This is the "too big to fail" argument.

Nationalization
The act of transforming a private enterprise's assets into a government enterprise.

The United States has a history of nationalization—most of which was temporary. But one that has endured: Amtrak is a government-owned corporation created in 1971 after railroads had petitioned repeatedly to abandon unprofitable passenger service. The Resolution Trust Corporation (RTC) was established in 1989 to take over more than 1,000 failed savings and loans institutions (S&Ls) with bad loans and foreclosed homes. After fulfilling its mission to sell the assets of these S&Ls, the RTC was closed in 1995. The financial crisis of the Great Recession generated several nationalizations and General Motors (GM) provides a prime case. With GM facing bankruptcy in 2009, the U.S. government replaced the CEO and took a 60 percent controlling share, with Canada taking a 12.5 percent share, the United Auto Workers (UAW) taking a 17.5 percent share, and bondholders ending up with the remaining 10 percent. Existing stockholders were given zero shares. However, by 2015 the U.S. and Canadian governments had sold all of their shares of GM stock, and by 2017 the UAW had sold about half of their shares.

Key Concepts

Economic system	Market economy	Capitalism	Communism
Traditional economy	Invisible hand	Consumer sovereignty	Privatization
Command economy	Mixed economy	Socialism	Nationalization

Summary

- An **economic system** is the set of established procedures by which a society answers the What, How, and For Whom to produce questions.

- **Three basic types of economic systems** are the traditional, command, and market systems. The **traditional system** makes decisions according to custom, and the **command system**, shown in the figure below, answers the three economic questions through some powerful central authority. In contrast, the **market system** uses the impersonal mechanism of the interaction of buyers and sellers in markets to answer the What, How, and For Whom questions.

Command Economy

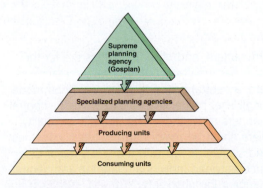

- **Capitalism** is an economic system in which the factors of production are privately owned and economic choices are made by consumers and firms in markets. As prescribed by Adam Smith, government plays an extremely limited role, and self-interest is the driving force, held in check, or regulated, by competition.

- **Consumer sovereignty** is the freedom of consumers to determine the types and quantities of products that are produced in an economy by choosing to buy or not to buy.

- **Socialism** is an economic system in which the government owns the factors of production. The central authorities make the myriad of society's economic decisions according to a national plan. The collective good, or public interest, is the intended guiding force behind the central planners' decisions.

- **Communism** is an economic system envisioned by Karl Marx to be an ideal society in which the workers own all the factors of production. Marx believed that workers who work hard will be public spirited and voluntarily redistribute income to those who are less productive. Such a communist nation described by Marx has never existed.

- **Privatization** is the process of turning a government enterprise into a private enterprise. It is the opposite of **nationalization**, which is the act of transforming a private enterprise's assets into government ownership.

Summary of Conclusion Statements

- When central planners set prices below equilibrium for goods and services, they create shortages, which mean long lines, empty shelves, and black markets.

- A market economy answers the What to produce and How to produce questions very effectively.

- No nation in the world precisely fits the two criteria for capitalism; however, the United States comes close.

Study Questions and Problems

Please see Appendix A for answers to the odd-numbered questions. Your instructor has access to the answers for even-numbered questions.

1. Give an example of how a nation's culture affects its economic system.

2. Explain the advantages and disadvantages of any two of the three basic types of economic systems.

3. Suppose a national program of free housing for the elderly is paid for by a sizable increase in income taxes. Explain a trade-off that might occur between economic security and efficiency.

4. "The schools are not in the business of pleasing parents and students, and they cannot be allowed to set their own agendas. Their agendas are set by politicians, administrators, and various constituencies that hold the keys to political power. The public system is built to see to it that the schools do what their government wants them to do—that they conform to the higher-order values their governors seek to impose."[4] Relate this statement to Exhibit 1.

5. Suppose you are a farmer. Explain why you would be motivated to work in traditional, command, and market economies.

6. Karl Marx believed the market system was doomed. Why do you think he was right or wrong?

7. If all real-world economies are mixed economies, why is the U.S. economy described as capitalist, while the Cuban economy is described as communist?

8. Suppose you are a factory manager. Describe how you might reach production goals under a system of pure capitalism and under a system of pure socialism.

✓ CHECKPOINT ANSWERS

To Plan or Not to Plan—That Is the Question

When an individual or a business plans in a market economy, other individuals are free to make and follow their own plans. Suppose Hewlett-Packard decides to produce *X* number of laser printers and sell them at a certain price. The decision does not prohibit IBM from producing *Y* number of laser printers and selling them for less than Hewlett-Packard's printers. If either firm makes a mistake, only that firm suffers, and other industries are for the most part unaffected. Under a command system, a central economic plan would be made for all laser printer manufacturers. If the central planners order the wrong quantity or quality, there could be major harm to other industries and society. If you said there is a major difference between individual planning and central planning for all society, **YOU ARE CORRECT**.

---

[4]John Chubb and Terry More, Politics, Markets, and the Nation's Public Schools (Washington, D.C.: Brookings Institution, 1990), p. 38.

Sample Quiz

Please see Appendix B for answers to Sample Quiz questions.

1. An economic system is the organizations and methods used to determine
   a. what goods and services are produced.
   b. how goods and services are produced.
   c. for whom goods and services are produced.
   d. All of the above answers are correct.

2. In a command economy, the basic economic questions are answered by
   a. central authority.
   b. individual buyers and sellers.
   c. traditional methods.
   d. None of the above answers are correct.

3. Adam Smith was an advocate of
   a. mercantilism.
   b. a nation maximizing its stock of gold.
   c. unrestricted or free trade.
   d. the "visible hand" of public interest.

4. In Adam Smith's competitive market economy, the question of what goods to produce is determined by the
   a. "invisible hand" of the price system.
   b. "invisible hand" of government.
   c. "invisible hand" of public interest.
   d. "visible hand" of laws and regulations.

5. Adam Smith wrote that the
   a. economic problems of eighteenth-century England were caused by free markets.
   b. government should control the economy.
   c. pursuit of private self-interest promotes the public interest in a market economy.
   d. public or collective interest is not promoted by people pursuing their self-interest.

6. Which of the following is a criticism of capitalism?
   a. Unequal distribution of income
   b. Failure to protect the environment
   c. Exploitation of workers
   d. All of the above answers are correct.

7. Which of the following statements is true?
   a. The doctrine of *laissez-faire* advocates an economic system with extensive government intervention and little individual decision making.
   b. In capitalism, income is distributed on the basis of need.
   c. Adam Smith was the father of socialism.
   d. Most real-world economies are mixed economic systems.

8. Which of the following is a strength of a command-based economic system?
   a. Goods can be allocated based on need rather than willingness and ability to pay.
   b. Producers have strong incentives to innovate because successful innovators are rewarded with higher profit.
   c. Consumers can transmit their preference for product quality and variety by way of their "dollar votes" cast in the marketplace.
   d. Because price is freely set based on supply and demand, there are few shortages or surpluses.

9. The term *socialism* refers to which of the following?
   a. A religion centered on community interaction
   b. An economic system characterized by private ownership of resources and decentralized market-price allocation
   c. An economic system characterized by government ownership of resources and centralized allocation
   d. An economic system characterized by voluntary allocation

10. Karl Marx was a (an)
    a. nineteenth-century German philosopher.
    b. eighteenth-century Russian economist.
    c. fourteenth-century Polish banker.
    d. nineteenth-century Russian journalist.

11. Karl Marx published
    a. *Das Kapital*.
    b. *General Theory of Communism*.
    c. *The Wealth of Nations*.
    d. *The Capitalist Manifesto*.

12. In Marx's ideal communist society, the state
    a. actively promotes income incentives.
    b. follows the doctrine of *laissez-faire*.
    c. owns resources and conducts planning.
    d. does not exist.

13. According to Adam Smith, the "invisible hand" refers to which of the following?
    a. The "best interests of society" (public interest) will occur as an outcome of the market process coordinating the self-interested interactions of buyers and sellers (private interest).
    b. Government interference in markets to prevent greed.
    c. Bribes and graft that interfere with the market process.
    d. The "best interest of society" (public interest) will occur as an outcome of careful guidance by government authorities in allocating scarce good and services according to private interest.

14. A principal feature of a command economy is that _____.
    a. production decisions are made by profit-maximizing firms.
    b. there is a central planning board at the top, which transmits economic decisions down to the various producing and consuming units below.
    c. consumers are allowed to determine that is produced based on their demand for goods and services.
    d. regulatory agencies constrain the most egregious forms of market power in a market system of allocation.

15. Which nation achieved the ideal communist society as described by Marx?
    a. Castro's Cuba
    b. Mao's China
    c. Stalin's Soviet Union
    d. No nation has achieved Marx's vision of a communist society.

16. Adam Smith's book, *Wealth of Nations* was published at the time of the
    a. War of 1812.
    b. U.S. Declaration of Independence.
    c. U.S. Civil War.
    d. Great Depression.

17. Which of the following economies is an example of a mixed system?
    a. United States
    b. United Kingdom
    c. Sweden
    d. All of the above answers are correct.

18. Property rights allowing individuals to own goods, services, and factors of production are *most* important in
    a. socialistic economies.
    b. planned economies.
    c. capitalist economies.
    d. command economies.

19. Which of the following is a correct characterization of socialism?
    a. Tradition answers the basic economic questions.
    b. Markets are used exclusively to answer the basic economic questions.
    c. Central planning is used to answer the basic economic questions.
    d. Government ownership of many resources and centralized decision-making answers the basic economic questions.

20. Which of the following statements is *true*?
    a. The United States today comes closer to the socialist form of economic organization than it does to capitalism.
    b. When central planners set prices above equilibrium for goods and services, they create shortages.
    c. According to Karl Marx, under capitalism, workers would be exploited and would revolt against the owners of capital.
    d. Adam Smith argued that government's role in society would be to do absolutely nothing.

CHAPTER 17

Growth and the Less-Developed Countries

CHAPTER PREVIEW

How would your life be different if you lived in Rwanda or Haiti instead of the United States? It is unlikely that anyone in your family would have a telephone or a car. You surely would not own a personal computer or an iPad. You would not have new clothes or be enrolled in a college or university studying economics. You would not be going out to restaurants or movies. You would be fortunate to have shoes and one full meal each day. You would receive little or no medical care and live in unsanitary surroundings. Hunger, disease, and squalor would engulf you. In fact, the World Bank estimates that hundreds of millions of people survive on at or below $1.90 per day. It is exceedingly difficult for Americans to grasp that one-fifth of the world's population lives at such a meager

subsistence level. This chapter's important task is unraveling the secrets of economic growth and development. Why do some countries prosper while others decline?

At different times in history, Egypt, China, Italy, and Greece were highly developed by the standards of their time. On the other hand, at one time the United States was a struggling, relatively poor country on the path to becoming a rich country. Its growth came in three stages: First, was the agricultural stage. Then came the manufacturing stage when industries such as railroads, steel, and automobiles were driving forces toward economic growth. And, finally, there has been a shift toward service industries. This is the U.S. success story, but it is not the only road countries can follow to lift themselves from the misery of poverty.

IN THIS CHAPTER, YOU WILL LEARN TO SOLVE THESE ECONOMICS PUZZLES:

- Is there a difference between economic growth and economic development?

- Why are some countries rich and others poor?

- Is trade a better "engine of growth" than foreign aid and loans?

17-1 COMPARING DEVELOPED AND LESS-DEVELOPED COUNTRIES

Income disparity exists not only among families within the United States, but also among nations. In this section, the great inequality of income between the families of nations will be used to classify nations as rich or poor.

17-1a Classifying Countries by GDP per Capita

GDP per capita
The value of final goods produced (GDP) divided by the total population.

Industrially advanced countries (IACs)
High-income nations that have market economies based on large stocks of technologically advanced capital and well-educated labor. The United States, Canada, Australia, New Zealand, Japan, and most of the countries of Western Europe are IACs.

Less-developed countries (LDCs)
Nations without large stocks of technologically advanced capital and without well educated labor. LDCs are economies based on agriculture, such as most countries of Africa, Asia, and Latin America.

There are about 195 countries in the world. Exhibit 1 shows a ranking of selected countries from high to low GDP per capita. **GDP per capita** is the value of final goods produced (GDP) divided by the total population. Although any system of defining rich versus poor countries is arbitrary, GDP per capita or average GDP is a fundamental measure of a country's economic well-being. At the top of the income ladder are 39 developed countries called the industrially advanced countries. **Industrially advanced countries (IACs)** are high-income nations that have market economies based on large stocks of technologically advanced capital and well-educated labor. The United States, Canada, Australia, New Zealand, Japan, and most of the countries of Western Europe are IACs. Excluded from the IACs are countries with high incomes whose economies are based on oil under the sand, and not on widespread industrial development. The United Arab Emirates is an example of such a country.

Countries of the world other than IACs are classified as underdeveloped or less-developed countries. **Less-developed countries (LDCs)** are nations without large stocks of technologically advanced capital and without well-educated labor. Their economies are based on agriculture, as in most countries of Africa, Asia, and Latin America. Most of the world's population live in LDCs and share widespread poverty.

A closer examination of Exhibit 1 reveals that the differences in living standards between the IACs and LDCs are enormous. For example, the GDP per capita in the United States was $57,436, which is much greater than the average income of $795 in Ethiopia. Stated differently, the 2016 average income in the United States was about 72 times larger than the average income in Ethiopia. What a difference! Imagine trying to live on only $795 a year in the United States. You probably would not survive.

Exhibit 2 compares GDP per capita for IACs to LDCs by regions of the world for 2016. The average citizen in the IACs enjoyed an income of $47,383, which was 12 times that of the average citizen in Sub-Saharan Africa. Sub-Saharan Africa includes countries such as Nigeria, Angola, Congo, Sudan, and Zimbabwe. The exhibit also reveals that the greatest concentrations of world poverty are located in the rural areas of Sub-Saharan Africa and Asia. These regions have many countries characterized by bleak and pervasive poverty, but there are notable exceptions, nicknamed the "Four Tigers" of East Asia—Hong Kong, Singapore, South Korea, and Taiwan. These Pacific Rim countries are newly industrialized economies.

17-1b Problems with GDP per Capita Comparisons

Several problems are associated with using GDP per capita to compare rich versus poor countries. First, there is a measurement problem because countries tabulate GDP with differing degrees of accuracy. LDCs in general do not use sophisticated methods of gathering and processing GDP and population data. For example, in countries whose economies are based largely on agriculture, a family is more likely to produce goods and services outside

EXHIBIT 1 Annual GDP per Capita for Selected Countries, 2016

Country	GDP per capita	Country	GDP per capita
Industrially Advanced Countries (IACs)			
Luxembourg	$103,199	Germany	41,902
Switzerland	79,242	Belgium	41,283
Norway	70,392	United Kingdom	40,096
Ireland	62,562	Japan	38,917
United States	57,436	New Zealand	38,345
Denmark	53,744	France	38,128
Singapore	52,961	Israel	37,262
Australia	51,850	Italy	30,507
Sweden	51,165	South Korea	27,539
Netherlands	45,283	Spain	26,609
Austria	44,498	Taiwan	22,453
Hong Kong	43,528	Portugal	19,832
Finland	43,169	Greece	17,901
Canada	42,210		
Less-Developed Countries (LDCs)			
Panama	13,654	Georgia	3,842
Chile	13,576	Egypt	3,685
Turkey	10,743	Indonesia	3,604
Romania	9,465	Ukraine	2,194
Venezuela	9,258	Vietnam	2,173
Russia	8,929	India	1,723
Brazil	8,727	Pakistan	1,468
Mexico	8,555	Bangladesh	1,411
China	8,113	Ethiopia	795
Thailand	5,899	Haiti	761
South Africa	5,261	Rwanda	729
Iran	4,683	Mozambique	392
Iraq	4,631		

SOURCE: International Monetary Fund, World Economic Outlook Database April 2017, http://www.imf.org
/externalpubs/ft/weo/2017/01.

EXHIBIT 2 Average GDP per Capita for IACs and LDCs by Region, 2016

This exhibit shows average GDP per capita by regions of the world for 2016. The differences between the rich, industrially advanced countries (IACs) and the poor, less-developed countries (LDCs) in the various regions of the world are enormous. For example, the average citizen in the IACs had an income 12 times that of the average citizen in the LDCs of Sub-Saharan Africa.

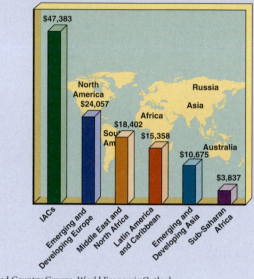

SOURCE: IMF, Selected Country Groups, World Economic Outlook

the price system. In LDCs, families often grow their own food, make their own clothes, and build their own homes. Estimating the value of this output at market prices is difficult.

CONCLUSION   LDCs' GDP per capita is subject to greater measurement errors than data for IACs.

Second, GDP per capita comparisons among countries can be misleading because they ignore the relative income distribution. Some countries have very high per capita incomes, yet most of the income goes to just a few wealthy families. The United Arab Emirates' GDP per capita is higher than that of several IACs. However, the UAE earns its income from oil exports, and its income is actually distributed disproportionately to a relatively small number of wealthy families.

CONCLUSION   GDP per capita comparisons among nations can be misleading because GDP per capita does not measure income distribution.

Third, GDP per capita comparisons between nations are subject to conversion problems. Making these data comparisons requires converting one nation's currency, say,

Japan's yen, into a common currency, the U.S. dollar. Because, as explained in the chapter on international trade and finance, the value of a country's currency can rise or fall for many reasons, the true value of a nation's output can be distorted. For example, during a given year, one government might maintain an artificially high exchange rate and another government might not.

A conversion problem may widen or narrow the GDP per capita gap between nations because the fluctuations in exchange rates do not reflect actual differences in the value of goods and services produced.	**CONCLUSION**

17-1c Quality-of-Life Measures of Development

GDP per capita measures market transactions, but this measure does not give a complete picture of differences in living standards among nations. Exhibit 3 presents other selected socioeconomic indicators of the quality of life. These are variables such as life expectancy at birth, infant mortality rate, literacy rate, per capita electricity consumption, and economic freedom ranking. Take a close look at the statistics in Exhibit 3. These data reflect the dimensions of poverty in many of the LDCs. For example, a person born in Japan has a life expectancy that is much longer than a person born in Mozambique, and the infant mortality rate is dramatically higher in Mozambique. Per capita electricity consumption measures the use of nonhuman energy to perform work. In IACs, most work is done by machines, and in LDCs, virtually all work is done by people. For example, the average American uses 12,973 kilowatts of electricity per year, while the average person

EXHIBIT 3 Quality-of-Life Indicators for Selected Countries, 2015

Country	(1) GDP per capita	(2) Life expectancy at birth (years)	(3) Infant mortality rate[1]	(4) Literacy rate[2]	(5) Per capita electricity consumption[3]	(6) Economic freedom rank[4]
United States	$57,436	79	6	99%	12,973	17
Japan	38,917	84	2	99	7,829	40
Mexico	8,555	77	11	95	2,071	70
China	8,113	76	9	96	3,927	111
India	1,723	68	38	72	805	143
Bangladesh	1,411	72	31	61	311	128
Mozambique	392	55	57	59	463	158

[1]Per 1,000 live births

[2]Percentage age 15 and over who can read and write

[3]Kilowatts per capita

[4]The Heritage Foundation

SOURCES: World Bank, http://www.worldbank.org/en/country and The Heritage Foundation, http://www.heritage.org/index/. Per capita GDP is for 2016, electricity consumption is for 2014, the remaining data is from 2015.

in Mozambique uses only 463 kilowatts. Finally, it is interesting to note that GDP per capita and other quality-of-life indicators are related to the ranking in economic freedom.

How good an indicator of the quality of life is GDP per capita? Exhibit 3 reflects the principle that GDP per capita is highly correlated with alternative measures of the quality of life.

CONCLUSION   In general, GDP per capita is highly correlated with alternative measures of quality of life.

17-2 ECONOMIC GROWTH AND DEVELOPMENT AROUND THE WORLD

Economic growth and development are major goals of IACs and LDCs. People all over the world strive for a higher quality of life for their generation and future generations. However, growth is closer to a life-or-death situation for many LDCs, such as Bangladesh and Mozambique.

Economic growth and economic development are somewhat different, but related, concepts. As shown in Exhibit 4, recall from Chapter 2 that economic growth is the ability of an economy to produce greater levels of output, represented by an outward shift of its production possibilities curve (PPC). Thus, economic growth is defined on a *quantitative* basis using the percentage change in GDP per capita. When a nation's GDP rises more rapidly than its population, GDP per capita rises, and the nation experiences a higher average absolute standard of living. Conversely, if GDP expands less than the population of a nation, GDP per capita falls, and the nation experiences a lower average standard of living.

Economic development is a broader concept that is more *qualitative* in nature. Economic development encompasses improvement in the quality of life, including economic growth in the production of goods and services. In short, continuous economic growth is necessary for economic development, but economic growth is not the only consideration. For example, as explained earlier, GDP per capita does not measure the distribution of income or the political environment that provides the legal, monetary, education, and transportation structures necessary for economic development, which can impact the quality of life.

Economic growth and development involve a complex process that is determined by several interrelated factors. Like the performance of an NBA basketball team, success depends on the joint effort of team players, and one or two weak players can greatly reduce overall performance. However, there is no precise formula for winning. If your team has a player like NBA great LeBron James, it can win even with a few weak players. The remainder of this section examines the key factors, or players, that operate together to produce a nation's economic well-being.

17-2a Endowment of Natural Resources

Most of the LDCs have comparatively limited bases of natural resources, including mineral deposits and arable land resources. In these countries, most of the available land is

EXHIBIT 4 Economic Growth

The economy begins with the capacity to produce combinations along production possibilities curve PPC$_1$. Growth in the resource base or a technological advance shifts the production possibilities curve outward from PPC$_1$ to PPC$_2$. Points along PPC$_2$ represent new production possibilities that were previously impossible. The distance that the curve shifts represents an increase in the nation's productive capacity.

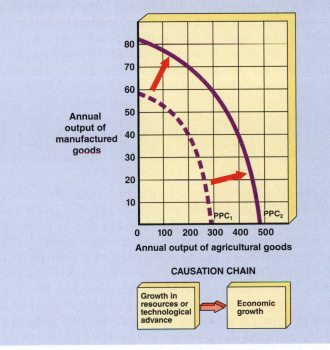

used for agricultural production, and clearing tropical forests to obtain more land can cause soil erosion. Also, tropical climates prevail in Central and South America, Africa, the Indian subcontinent, and Southeast Asia. The hot, humid climate in these regions is conducive to weed and insect infestations that plague agriculture.

Although a narrow base of resources does pose a barrier to economic growth and development, no single conclusion can be drawn. For example, how have Hong Kong, Japan, and Israel achieved high standards of living in spite of limited natural resource bases? Each has practically no minerals, little fertile land, and no domestic sources of energy. Nonetheless, these economies have become prosperous. In contrast, Argentina and Venezuela have abundant fertile land and minerals. Yet these and other countries have been growing slowly or not at all. Venezuela, for example, is one of the most oil-rich countries in the world. Ghana, Kenya, and Bolivia are also resource-rich countries that are poor, with little or no economic growth.

Natural resource endowment can promote economic growth, but a country can develop without a large natural resource base.

CONCLUSION

17-2b Investment in Human Resources

A low level of human capital can also present a barrier to economic growth and development. Recall that human capital is the education, training, experience, and health that improve the knowledge and skills of workers to produce goods and services. In most of the LDCs, investment in human capital is much less than in the IACs. Look back at column (4) in Exhibit 3. Consider how low the literacy rate is for the poorer countries. A country with a lower literacy rate has less ability to educate its labor force and create a basic foundation for economic growth. In fact, often the skills of workers in the poor countries are suited primarily to agriculture, rather than being appropriate for a wide range of industries and economic growth. Further complicating matters is a "brain drain" problem because the best educated and trained workers of poor countries often leave to pursue careers in richer countries. Column (2) of Exhibit 3 also gives a measure of health among countries with varying levels of GDP per capita. As the GDP per capita falls, the life expectancy at birth falls. Thus, richer countries have the advantage of a better educated and healthier workforce.

CONCLUSION   Investment in human capital generally results in increases in GDP per capita.

Thus far, the discussion has been about the quality of labor. We must also talk about the quantity of labor because productivity is related to both the quality and quantity of labor. Overpopulation is a problem for LDCs. In a nutshell, here is why: Other factors held constant, population (labor force) growth can increase a country's GDP. Yet rapid population growth can convert an expanding GDP into a GDP per capita that is stagnant, slow growing, or negative. Stated another way, there is no gain to the output available to the average person if an increase in output is more than matched by an increase in the number of mouths that must be fed. Suppose the GDP of an LDC grows at, say, 3 percent per year. If there is no growth in population, GDP per capita also grows at 3 percent per year. But what if the population also grows at 3 percent per year? The result is that GDP per capita remains unchanged. If population growth is instead only 1 percent per year, GDP per capita rises 2 percent per year. Obstacles to population control are great and include strong religious and sociocultural arguments against birth control programs.

CONCLUSION   Rapid population growth combined with low human capital investment explains why many countries are LDCs.

CHECKPOINT

Does Rapid Growth Mean a Country Is Catching Up?
Suppose country Alpha has a production possibilities curve closer to the origin than the curve for country Beta. Now assume Alpha experiences a 3 percent growth rate in GDP for ten years and Beta experiences a 6 percent growth rate in GDP for ten years. At the end of five years, which of the following is the best prediction for the standard of living? (1) Alpha's residents are better off. (2) Beta's residents are better off. (3) Which country's residents are better off cannot be determined.

17-2c **Accumulation of Capital**

It did not take long for Robinson Crusoe stranded on a deserted island to invest in a net in order to catch more fish than he could catch with his hands. Similarly, farmers working with modern tractors can cultivate more acres than farmers working with horse-drawn plows. Recall from Chapter 1 that capital in economics means factories, tractors, trucks, roads, computers, irrigation systems, electricity-generating facilities, and other human-made goods used to produce goods and services.

LDCs suffer from a critical shortage of capital. A family in Somalia owns little in the way of tools except a wooden plow. To make matters worse, roads are terrible, there are few plants generating electricity, and telephone lines are scarce. As shown in Exhibit 5, recall from Chapter 2 that a high-investment country can shift its production possibilities curve outward, but investment in capital goods is not a "free lunch." When more resources are used to produce more factories and machines, there is an opportunity cost of fewer resources available for the production of current consumer goods. This means that LDCs are often caught in a vicious circle of poverty. A **vicious circle of poverty** is the trap in which countries are poor and cannot afford to save. And low savings translate into low investment. Low investment results in low productivity, which, in turn, keeps incomes low. Any savings that do exist among higher-income persons in poor LDCs are often invested in IACs. This phenomenon is often called "capital flight." These wealthy individuals are afraid to save in their own countries because they fear that their governments may be overthrown and their savings could be lost.

Vicious circle of poverty
The trap in which countries are poor because they cannot afford to save and invest, but they cannot save and invest because they are poor.

EXHIBIT 5 Alpha's and Beta's Present and Future Production Possibilities Curves

In part (a), each year Alpha produces only enough capital (K_a) to replace existing capital that is worn out. Without greater capital and assuming other resources remain fixed, Alpha is unable to shift its production possibilities curve outward. In part (b), each year Beta produces K_a capital, which is more than the amount required to replenish its depreciated capital. In 2018, this expanded capital provides Beta with the extra production capacity to shift its production possibilities curve to the right. If Beta chooses point B on its curve, it has the production capacity to increase the amount of consumer goods from C_b to C_c without producing fewer capital goods.

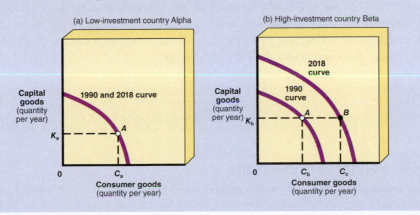

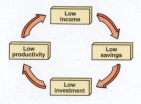

The United States and other nations have attempted to provide LDCs with foreign aid so that they might grow. These countries desperately need more factories and infrastructure. **Infrastructure** is capital goods usually provided by the government, including highways, bridges, waste and water systems, and airports. Unfortunately, the amount of foreign aid provided to the LDCs for capital improvements is relatively small, and as explained earlier, workers in the LDCs lack the skills necessary to use the most modern forms of capital. More specifically, LDCs face a major obstacle to capital accumulation because of the lack of entrepreneurs to assume the risks of capital formation.

| CONCLUSION | There is a significant positive relationship between investment and economic growth and development. |

Infrastructure
Capital goods usually provided by the government, including highways, bridges, waste and water systems, and airports.

17-2d Technological Progress

As explained earlier in Chapter 2, holding natural resources, labor, and capital constant, advancing the body of knowledge applied to production shifts the production possibilities curve of a country. In fact, technological advances have been at the heart of economic growth and development in recent history. During the last 250 years, brainpower has invented new power-driven machines, advanced communication devices, new energy sources, and countless ways to produce more output with the same resources. How have innovative products improved your productivity? Consider, to name just a few products, the impact of personal computers, word processing software, cell phone photography, the iPhone, and the Internet. In contrast, in many poor countries, waterwheels still bring water to the surface, cloth is woven on handlooms, and oxcarts are the major means of transportation. Consequently, large inputs of human effort are used relative to capital resources.

The United States and other IACs have provided the world with an abundant accumulation of technological knowledge that might be adopted by those LDCs without the resources to undertake the required cost of research and development. However, the results of this transfer process have been mixed. For example, countries such as China, Hong Kong, Singapore, Taiwan, South Korea, and Japan have surely achieved rapid growth in part from the benefit of technological borrowing. The other side of the coin is that much available technology is not well-suited to LDCs. The old saying "You need to learn to walk before you can run" often applies to the LDCs. For example, small farms of most LDCs are not well-suited for much of the agricultural technology developed for IACs' large farms. And how many factories in the LDCs are ready to use the most modern robotics in the production process? Stated differently, LDCs need appropriate technology, rather than necessarily the latest technology.

| CONCLUSION | Many LDCs continue to experience low growth rates even though IACs have developed advanced technologies that the world can utilize. |

17-2e Political Environment

The preceding discussion leads to the generalization that in order for LDCs to achieve economic growth and development, they must wisely use natural resources, invest in human and physical capital, and adopt advanced technology. This list of policies is not complete. LDC governments must also create a political environment favorable to economic growth. All too often a large part of the problem in poor countries is that resources are wasted as a result of war and political instability. Political leaders must not be corrupt and/or incompetent. Instead of following policies that favor a small elite ruling class, LDC governments must adopt appropriate domestic and international economic policies, discussed under the following three headings of law and order, infrastructure, and international trade.

Law and Order

A basic governmental function is to establish domestic law and order. This function includes many areas, such as a stable legal system, stable money and prices, competitive markets, and private ownership of property. In particular, expropriation of private property rights among LDCs is a barrier to growth. Well-defined private property rights have fostered economic growth in the IACs because this institutional policy has encouraged an entrepreneurial class. Private ownership provides individuals with the incentive to save money and invest in businesses. A stable political environment that ensures private ownership of profits also provides an incentive for individuals in other countries to invest in developing poor countries.

Infrastructure

Assuming an LDC government maintains law and order and the price system is used to allocate goods and services, it is vital that wise decisions be made concerning infrastructure. Indeed, inadequate infrastructure is one of the greatest problems of LDCs. Without such public goods as roads, schools, bridges, and public health and sanitation services, poor countries are unable to generate the substantial external benefits that are an important ingredient in economic growth and development. From the viewpoint of individual firms, government must provide infrastructure because these public goods projects are too costly for a firm to undertake.

International Trade

In general, LDCs can benefit from an expanding volume of trade. This is the theory behind the North American Free Trade Agreement (NAFTA), the General Agreement on Tariffs and Trade (GATT), and the World Trade Organization (WTO) discussed in the chapter on international trade and finance. As explained earlier in this chapter, policies such as tariffs and quotas restrain international trade and thereby inhibit economic growth and development. These trade policies are antigrowth because they restrict the ability of people in one country to trade with people in other countries. Similarly, a country that fixes the exchange rate of its own currency above the market-determined exchange rate makes that country's exports less attractive to foreigners. This means, in turn, that domestic citizens sell less of their goods to foreigners and earn less foreign currency with which to buy imports.

By fixing its exchange rates and by imposing trade barriers, a country will lower its economic growth rate.

CONCLUSION

Exhibit 6 summarizes the key factors explained earlier that determine the economic growth and development of countries. Analysis of this exhibit reveals that economic growth and development are the result of a multidimensional process. This means that

GLOBAL ECONOMICS

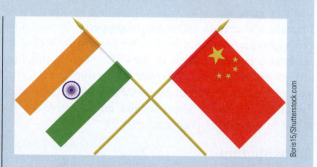

India and China's Economic Growth: An Updated Version of Aesop's Tale

Applicable Concept: Sustaining Growth

The most famous footrace ever held occurred in the pages of a book and is a fictional tale involving two animals. As the story unfolds, a rabbit gets off to a fast start, but he does not keep up this pace, and instead takes a nap, halting his progress. A tortoise, on the other hand, starts slow but maintains his pace, eventually overtaking the rabbit to win the race. Some economists have argued that India and China are in an economic development race that shares many characteristics of the race between the tortoise and the hare.

Before the race began in 1978, China and India were both very poor. When the starting gun fired, China, playing the role of the rabbit in our analogy, began running with dazzling speed as a result of a series of reforms that allowed it to use its factors of production more productively. First, China reformed its agricultural sector. Before the reforms, 70 percent of the Chinese labor force worked in agriculture, and yet the country was still unable to provide its people with even the United Nations' minimum recommended daily intake of 2,300 calories a day.[1] China's new leader Deng Xiaoping inherited a system where farmers had to meet production quotas and sell all their output to the government at official prices, which were so low that farmers had no incentive to produce beyond their quotas. Under Deng's reforms, farmers were still required to produce their quotas and to sell this amount of grain to the government at the mandated prices; however, Deng allowed farmers to sell any extra output they produced beyond their

mandated quotas and receive market prices in return. Market prices were high enough to encourage more production, and to encourage farmers to discover more efficient ways to grow their crops. In just six years agricultural output in China increased by 47 percent.

Farm workers became more productive, so fewer workers were needed to produce crops. Over the next 30 years, the share of the labor force in agriculture dropped to 26 percent—less than half of what it had been. With fewer workers needed on farms, these workers could move to cities and work in industry. In cities, workers were exposed to advanced capital-intensive production processes, which elevated their productivity. In 1978 nonfarm workers were six times more productive than farm workers, so simply getting workers off the farm, where they are relatively unproductive, and into cities, where they are much more

it is difficult for countries to break the poverty barrier because they must improve many factors in order to increase their economic well-being. But it is important to remember that lack of one or more key factors, such as natural resources, does not necessarily keep an LDC in the trap of underdevelopment.

CONCLUSION There is no single strategy for economic growth and development.

productive, enabled very robust economic growth in China.

In the 1990s, China initiated another round of reforms. It began to allow government-owned enterprises to shrink and even to fail. Between 1995 and 2001, the state-run sector of the economy went from employing 17 percent to employing 12 percent of the workforce. These newly mobile workers needed some place to go, and China's next policy found such a place. China allowed foreign countries to build factories within its borders. This foreign investment allowed China to move even more of its labor force into its productive manufacturing sector.

Whereas China got off to a quick start, India did not even leave the starting blocks until 1991, when it opened up its economy in three important ways.[2] First, India reduced trade barriers, slashing tariffs in half within 4 years. The increased foreign competition forced Indian firms to become more efficient. Second, India removed a requirement that had prevented foreigners from owning a majority ownership stake in Indian firms. As a result, large amounts of foreign investment flowed into India, giving Indian workers access to better technology and enabling them to work in firms that were larger and more efficient. Finally, the country moved away from a reliance on inefficient bureaucratic government planning and toward a greater reliance on market forces to direct the economy. All three reforms increased India's economic growth by encouraging self-interested market participants to use resources more efficiently.

Both countries are still growing rapidly; however, economist Jagdish Bhagwati contends that India is more likely than China to sustain its high growth rates.[3]

He believes India's democracy gives it an important advantage over China. In a democracy, when people are displeased, they can channel their energies into an election, making them feel that they have some influence over government policy. Democratic governments are also good at coming up with compromises that no one loves, but that everyone can live with. In short, democracies provide a pressure release valve that prevents unrest from creating enough political uncertainty to derail economic growth. China, on the other hand, does not possess democratic institutions; therefore, if the Chinese people are unhappy, they may challenge the government directly, causing enough political unrest to threaten the government's survival. The accompanying uncertainty will discourage investments and cause Chinese economic growth to come to a screeching halt. If Professor Bhagwati is correct, India is like the tortoise in the famous race. India got off to a slow start, but because it is more likely to sustain its economic growth, it may eventually become a richer country than China.

ANALYZE THE ISSUE

1. What have been the ingredients for economic growth and development that China and India share? What have been their differences?
2. How important do you think democracy is for economic growth and development? What political reforms would you recommend for China? How likely are these recommendations to be implemented in China?

---

1. The data about and the discussion of China in this passage come from the following source. Xiaodong Zhu, "Understanding China's Growth: Past, Present, and Future," *Journal of Economic Perspectives* 26, 4 (Fall 2012), pp. 103–124.
2. The discussion on India's economic growth is derived from the following source. Montek S. Ahluwalia, "Economic reforms in India Since 1991: Has Gradualism Worked," *Journal of Economic Perspectives* 16, 3 (Summer 2002): pp. 67–88.
3. Jagdish Bhagwati, "Indian Lessons," *Wall Street Journal*, February 28, 2006, p. A16.

17-3 THE HELPING HAND OF ADVANCED COUNTRIES

How can poor countries escape the vicious circle of poverty? Low GDP per capita leads to low savings and investment, which lead, in turn, to low growth. Although there is no easy way for poor countries to become richer, the United States and other advanced countries can be an instrument of growth. The necessary funds can come from the LDCs' own domestic savings, or it can come from external sources that include foreign private investment, foreign aid, and foreign loans.

EXHIBIT 6 Key Categories That Determine Economic Growth and Development

There are five basic categories that interact to determine the economic growth and development of countries: natural resources, human resources, capital, technological progress, and the political environment. The exhibit also indicates important factors that influence the five factors. LDCs are faced with a formidable task. Because economic growth and development are multidimensional, LDCs must improve many factors in order to achieve economic progress.

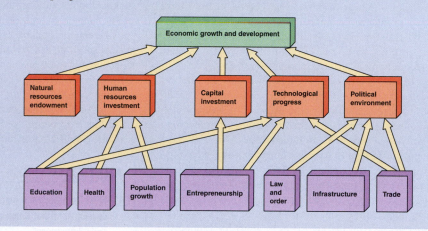

Exhibit 7 illustrates how external funds can shift a country's production possibilities curve outward. Here you should look back and review Exhibit 5. Suppose country Alpha is trapped in poverty and produces only enough capital (K_a) to replace the existing capital being worn out. Alpha's consumption level is at C_a, corresponding to point A on production possibilities curve PPC$_1$. Because C_a is at the subsistence level, Alpha cannot save and invest by substituting capital for current consumption and move upward along PPC$_1$. This inability to increase capital means Alpha cannot use internal sources of funds to increase its production possibilities curve in the future. There is a way out of the trap using external sources. Now assume Alpha receives an inflow of funds from abroad and buys capital goods that increase its rate of investment from K_a to K_b. At K_b, the rate of capital formation exceeds the value of capital depreciated, and Alpha's production possibilities curve shifts rightward to PPC$_1$. Economic growth made possible by external investment means Alpha can improve its standard of living by increasing its consumption level from C_a at point A on PPC$_1$ to C_b at point B on PPC$_2$.

17-3a Foreign Private Investment

Many countries' development benefits from private-sector foreign investment from private investors. For example, Microsoft might finance construction of a plant in the Philippines to manufacture software, or Bank of America may make loans to the

EXHIBIT 7 The Effect of External Financing on an LDC's Production Possibilities Curve

The poor country of Alpha is initially operating at point A on production possibilities curve PPC$_1$, with only enough capital (K_a) to replace depreciation. If C_a is the consumption level of subsistence, Alpha's economy cannot grow by reducing consumption. An inflow of external funds from abroad permits the LDC to increase its capital from K_a to K_b and its production possibilities curve shifts outward to PPC$_2$. At PPC$_2$, Alpha is able to increase its production of consumer goods from C_a to C_b.

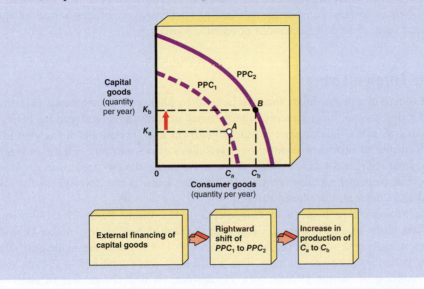

government of Haiti. These large multinational corporations and commercial banks supply scarce capital to the LDCs. A multinational corporation is a firm with headquarters in one country and one or more branch or plants in other countries. Multinational firms often seek new investment opportunities in LDCs because these poor countries offer abundant supplies of low-wage labor and raw materials. But the political environment in the LDCs must be conducive to investment. Multinational corporations often become the largest employers, largest taxpayers, and largest exporters in the LDCs.

17-3b **Foreign Aid**

About 1 percent of the U.S. federal budget is spent on foreign aid. **Foreign aid** is the transfer of money or resources from one government to another with no repayment required. These transfers may be made as outright grants, technical assistance, or food supplies. Foreign aid flows from country to country through governments and voluntary agencies, such as the Red Cross, CARE, and Church World Relief. The United States distributes most of its official development assistance through the Agency for International Development, established in 1961. The **Agency for International Development (AID)** is the agency of the U.S. State Department that is in charge of U.S. aid to foreign countries.

One reason that countries such as the United States provide foreign aid to LDCs is the belief that it is a moral responsibility of richer countries to share their wealth with

Foreign aid
The transfer of money or resources from one government to another with no repayment required.

Agency for International Development (AID)
The agency of the U.S. State Department that is in charge of U.S. aid to foreign countries.

poorer countries. A second reason is that it is in the best economic interest of the IACs to help the LDCs. When these countries become more prosperous, the IACs have more markets for their exports, and thereby all countries benefit from trade.

The LDCs often complain that foreign aid comes with too many economic and political strings attached. The aid is often offered on a take-it-or-leave-it basis, tied to policies other than basic trade policies, such as human rights, politics, or the military. Consequently, many LDCs argue for "trade, not aid." If the IACs would simply buy more goods from the LDCs, the LDCs could use their gains in export earnings to purchase more capital and to invest in other ingredients needed for growth. Many people in the United States believe that most foreign aid is a waste of money because it is misused by the recipient countries. This belief has caused Congress to grow increasingly reluctant to send taxpayers' money abroad except in the clearest cases of need or for reasons of national security.

17-3c **Foreign Loans**

A third source of external funds that can be used to finance LDCs' domestic investment is loans from abroad. Governments, international organizations, and private banks all make loans to LDCs. Like foreign private investment and foreign aid, loans give LDCs the opportunity to shift their production possibilities curves outward. There are various types of loan sources for LDCs. Bilateral loans are made directly from one country to another. The principal agent for official U.S. bilateral loans is the U.S. Agency for International Development, introduced earlier.

World Bank
The lending agency that makes long-term low interest loans and provides technical assistance to less developed countries.

One prominent multilateral lending agency is the World Bank. The 189-member **World Bank** is the lending agency affiliated with the United Nations that makes long-term low-interest loans and provides technical assistance to LDCs. Loans are made only after a planning period lasting a year or more. The World Bank was established in 1944 by major nations meeting in Bretton Woods, New Hampshire. Its first charge was to assist with reconstruction after World War II. Today, the World Bank is located in Washington, D.C., and its main purpose is to channel funds from rich countries to poor countries. Voting shares are in proportion to the money provided by the members. The World Bank makes "last resort" loans to LDCs that are limited to financing basic infrastructure projects, such as schools, health centers, dams, irrigation systems, and transportation facilities, for which private financing is not available. In addition, the World Bank helps LDCs get loans from private lenders by insuring the loans. Thus, the poor countries are able to complete projects and use the economic returns to pay off the lender with interest.

International Monetary Fund (IMF)
The lending agency that makes short-term conditional low-interest loans to developing countries.

The World Bank is not the only multilateral lending agency making loans to LDCs. The World Bank's partner institution is the International Monetary Fund. The **International Monetary Fund (IMF)** is the lending agency that makes short-term conditional low-interest loans to developing countries. The IMF was also established at Bretton Woods in 1944. Its purpose is to help countries overcome short-run financial difficulties. Typically, the IMF makes conditional loans that require the debtor countries to implement fiscal and monetary policies that will alleviate balance-of-payments deficit problems and promote noninflationary economic growth. The 189-member IMF is not a charitable institution. It operates like a credit union with funding quotas that earn interest on the loans. The United States is the IMF's largest shareholder and thus has effective veto power over IMF decisions.

The IMF has performed a major role in providing short-term loans to developing countries and to economies making the transition to capitalism. In the late 1990s, the IMF provided multibillion-dollar bailouts to Russia, several Asian countries, Brazil, and other countries experiencing economic turmoil. In recent years, the IMF and some of the

EU countries made rescue loans to debt-plagued Greece with the condition of deep cut-backs in government spending and tax hikes. Critics argue that as long as governments believe the IMF will bail them out, they will fail to correct their own problems. IMF supporters counter that if the IMF does not intervene, troubled economies will default on outstanding loans and cause a worldwide financial ripple effect. Critics respond that a flood of low-cost short-term loans from the IMF encourages bad government policies and excessive risk taking by banks. Consequently, a bailout in a crisis generates new financial crises and reduces world economic growth.

Is the Minimum Wage an Antipoverty Solution for Poor Countries?
Imagine you are an economic adviser to the president of a poor LDC. The president is seeking policies to promote economic growth and a higher standard of living for citizens of this country. You are asked whether adopting a minimum wage equal to the average of the IACs' average hourly wages would achieve these goals. Recall the discussion of the minimum wage from Chapter 4 and evaluate this policy.

CHECKPOINT

Key Concepts

GDP per capita

Industrially advanced
   countries (IACs)

Less-developed
   countries (LDCs)

Vicious circle of poverty

Infrastructure

Foreign aid

Agency for International
   Development (AID)

World Bank

International Monetary
   Fund (IMF)

Summary

- **GDP per capita** provides a general index of a country's standard of living. Countries with low GDP per capita and slow growth in GDP per capita are less able to satisfy basic needs for food, shelter, clothing, education, and health.

- **Industrially advanced countries (IACs)** are countries with high GDP per capita, and output is produced by technologically advanced capital. Countries that have high incomes without widespread industrial development, such as the oil-rich Arab countries, are not included in the IAC list.

- **Less-developed countries (LDCs)** are countries with low production per person. In these countries, output is produced without large amounts of technologically advanced capital and without

well-educated labor. The LDCs account for about three-fourths of the world's population.

- The *Four Tigers of the Pacific Rim* are Hong Kong, Singapore, South Korea, and Taiwan. These recently industrialized countries have achieved high growth rates and standards of living.

- **GDP per capita comparisons** are subject to three problems: (1) the accuracy of LDC data is questionable, (2) GDP per capita ignores income distribution, (3) fluctuations in exchange rates affect GDP per capita gaps between countries.

- **Economic growth** and **economic development** are related, but somewhat different, concepts. Economic growth is measured *quantitatively* by

GDP per capita, while economic development is a broader concept that includes *qualitative* factors. In addition to GDP per capita, economic development includes quality-of-life measures, such as life expectancy at birth, adult literacy rate, and per capita energy consumption. Economic growth and development are the result of a complex process that is determined by five major factors: (1) natural resources, (2) human resources, (3) capital, (4) technological progress, and (5) the political environment. There is no single correct strategy for economic development and a lack of strength in one or more of the five areas does not prevent growth.

- The **vicious circle of poverty** is a trap in which an LDC is too poor to save and therefore it cannot invest and shift its production possibilities curve outward. As a result, the LDC remains poor. One way for a poor country to gain savings, invest, and grow is to use funds from external sources such as foreign private investment, foreign aid, and foreign loans.

Summary of Conclusion Statements

- LDCs' GDP per capita is subject to greater measurement errors than data for IACs.

- GDP per capita comparisons among nations can be misleading because GDP per capita does not measure income distribution.

- A conversion problem may widen or narrow the GDP per capita gap between nations because the fluctuations in exchange rates do not reflect actual differences in the value of goods and services produced.

- In general, GDP per capita is highly correlated with alternative measures of quality of life.

- Natural resource endowment can promote economic growth, but a country can develop without a large natural resource base.

- Investment in human capital generally results in increases in GDP per capita.

- Rapid population growth combined with low human capital investment explains why many countries are LDCs.

- There is a significant positive relationship between investment and economic growth and development.

- Many LDCs continue to experience low growth rates even though IACs have developed advanced technologies that the world can utilize.

- By fixing its exchange rates and by imposing trade barriers, a country will lower its economic growth rate.

- There is no single strategy for economic growth and development.

Study Questions and Problems

Please see Appendix A for answers to the odd-numbered questions. Your instructor has access to the answers for even-numbered questions.

1. What is the difference between industrially advanced countries (IACs) and less-developed countries (LDCs)? List five IACs and five LDCs.

2. Explain why GDP per capita comparisons among nations are not a perfect measure of differences in economic well-being.

3. Assume you are given the following data for country Alpha and country Beta:

Country	GDP per capita
Alpha	$25,000
Beta	15,000

a. Based on the GDP per capita data given here, in which country would you prefer to live?
b. Now assume you are given the following additional quality-of-life data. In which country would you prefer to reside?

Country	Life expectancy at birth (years)	Daily per capita calorie supply	Per capita energy consumption*
Alpha	65	2,500	3,000
Beta	70	3,000	4,000

*Kilograms of oil equivalent.

4. What is the difference between economic development and economic growth? Give examples of how each of these concepts can be measured.

5. Do you agree with the argument that the rich nations are getting richer and the poor nations are getting poorer? Is this an oversimplification? Explain.

6. Explain why it is so difficult for poor LDCs to generate investment in capital in order to increase productivity and growth and, therefore, improve their standard of living.

7. Why is the quest for economic growth and development complicated?

8. Indicate whether each of the following is associated with a high or low level of economic growth and development:

	High	Low
a. Overpopulation	___	___
b. Highly skilled labor	___	___
c. High savings rate	___	___
d. Political stability	___	___
e. Low capital accumulation	___	___
f. Advanced technology	___	___
g. Highly developed infrastructure	___	___
h. High proportion of agriculture	___	___
i. High degree of income inequality	___	___

9. Without external financing from foreign private investment, foreign aid, and foreign loans, poor countries are caught in the vicious circle of poverty. Explain. How does external financing help poor countries achieve economic growth and development?

10. What are some of the problems for LDCs of accepting foreign aid?

11. Why would an LDC argue for "trade, not aid"?

12. Explain the differences among the Agency for International Development (AID), the World Bank, and the International Monetary Fund (IMF).

✔ CHECKPOINT ANSWERS

Does Rapid Growth Mean a Country Is Catching Up?

GDP growth alone does not measure the standard of living. You must also consider population. Even though Beta experienced a greater GDP growth rate, its GDP per capita might be less than Alpha's because its population growth rate is greater. Of course, the reverse is also possible, but without population data, we cannot say. If you said which country's people are better off cannot be determined because the GDP must be divided by the population to measure the average standard of living, **YOU ARE CORRECT**.

Is the Minimum Wage an Antipoverty Solution for Poor Countries?

An important source of foreign investment for LDCs is multinational corporations that locate plants and other facilities in these countries. LDCs compete with each other for the economic growth and development benefits that these multinational corporations can provide. For an LDC to win the competition, it must offer political stability, adequate infrastructure, a favorable business climate, and a cheap labor force. If you said you would not support the president's proposal to raise the minimum wage because it would

place the LDC at a competitive disadvantage in the labor market, thereby reducing foreign private investment and growth, **YOU ARE CORRECT**.

Sample Quiz

Please see Appendix B for answers to Sample Quiz questions.

1. Which of the following is a problem when comparing GDP per capita between nations?
    a. GDP per capita fails to measure income distribution.
    b. Fluctuations in exchange rates affect differences in GDP per capita.
    c. GDP per capita is subject to greater measurement errors for LDCs compared to IACs.
    d. All of the above answers are correct.

2. GDP per capita is a relatively good measurement of
    a. the distribution of income.
    b. purchasing power.
    c. household production.
    d. the standard of living.

3. Which of the following is infrastructure?
    a. Police
    b. Training and education
    c. Highways
    d. All of the answers above answers are correct.

4. Which of the following statements explains the vicious circle of poverty?
    a. By investing in education and infrastructure at the same time, the country can overcome the problems of poverty.
    b. Poverty arises out of the lack of investment, but countries cannot invest because they are poor.
    c. A nation can shift its production possibilities curve inward by shifting more resources into the production of capital goods.
    d. A nation can shift its production possibilities curve outward by shifting more resources into the production of consumer goods.

5. Which of the following is not a characteristic of most less-developed countries?

    a. Inadequate human capital
    b. Inadequate capital goods
    c. High population growth rate
    d. Inadequate water supplies
    e. High productivity

6. Compared to IACs, LDCs are often characterized by
    a. lower life expectancy.
    b. lower adult literacy.
    c. lower per capita energy consumption.
    d. All of the above answers are correct.

7. Real GDP per capita and other alternative measures of the quality of life are
    a. independent.
    b. directly correlated.
    c. poorly correlated.
    d. inversely related.

8. Economic development encompasses which of the following measures?
    a. Economic growth
    b. The political environment
    c. Education
    d. All of the above answers are correct.

9. Which of the following is a characteristic of an LDC?
    a. Capital flight
    b. Vicious circle of poverty
    c. Lack of entrepreneurs
    d. All of the answers are correct.

10. Economic growth and development in LDCs are low because many of them lack
    a. savings.
    b. infrastructure.

c. a political environment favorable to growth.

d. All of the answers are correct.

11. Which of the following is a *true* statement?
    a. The LDC classification is of questionable accuracy.
    b. GDP per capita ignores the degree of income distribution.
    c. GDP per capita is affected by exchange rate changes.
    d. GDP per capita does not account for the difference in the cost of living among nations.
    e. All of the answers are correct.

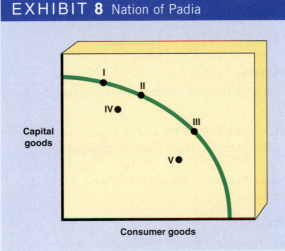

EXHIBIT **8** Nation of Padia

12. Exhibit 8 shows the production possibilities curve of the nation of Padia. Based only on this information, which point would produce the highest rate of growth?
    a. I
    b. II
    c. III
    d. IV
    e. V

13. Exhibit 8 shows the production possibilities curve of the nation of Padia. Based only on this information, the point which would produce the lowest rate of growth would be
    a. I
    b. II
    c. III
    d. IV
    e. V

14. Which of the following is in charge of U.S. aid to foreign countries?
    a. Agency for International Development (AID)
    b. World Bank
    c. International Monetary Fund (IMF)
    d. New International Economic Order (NIEO)

15. Which of the following makes long-term low-interest loans to LDCs?
    a. Agency for International Development (AID)
    b. World Bank
    c. International Monetary Fund (IMF)
    d. New International Economic Order (NIEO)

16. Which of the following makes short-term conditional low-interest loans to LDCs?
    a. World Bank
    b. Agency for International Development (AID)
    c. Agency for International Finance (AIF)
    d. International Monetary Fund (IMF)

17. Which of the following is *not* an example of a country's infrastructure?
    a. Transportation system
    b. Communications system
    c. Political system
    d. Educational system

18. Which of the following *best* defines the vicious circle of poverty?
    a. Countries are poor because they cannot afford to save and invest.
    b. Countries are poor because of high population growth.
    c. Countries are poor because of lack of education and training for workers.
    d. Countries are poor because of poor international credit.

19. If a country's population grows at the same rate as its real GDP, then real per capita GDP
    a. grows at an increasing rate.
    b. grows at a constant rate.
    c. doesn't change.
    d. decreases at a decreasing rate.

20. In order for Ethiopia to increase its future economic growth, it must choose a point that is
    a. below its production possibilities curve.
    b. further along on its production possibilities curve toward the capital goods axis.
    c. further along on its production possibilities curve toward the consumption goods axis.
    d. above its production possibilities curve.

PART 5
The International Economy

This road map feature helps you tie together material in the part as you travel the Economic Way of Thinking Highway. The following are review questions listed by chapter from the previous part. The key concept in each question is given for emphasis, and each question or set of questions concludes with an interactive game to reinforce the concepts. The correct answers to the multiple choice questions are given in Appendix C. If your instructor has included MindTap in your course, visit MindTap to play the interactive Causation Chain Game.

Chapter 15: International Trade and Finance

1. Key Concept: Exchange rate changes

Which of the following would cause the U.S. demand curve for Japanese yen to shift to the right?

a. An increase in the U.S. inflation rate compared to the rate in Japan.
b. A higher real rate of interest on investments in Japan than on investments in the United States.
c. The popularity of Japanese products increases in the United States.
d. All of the answers above are correct.

2. Key Concept: Exchange rate changes

In the foreign exchange market, where Japanese Yen and United States dollars are traded, which of the following would cause the supply of dollars curve to shift to the right?

a. Japanese imports become less popular.
b. The value of the dollar falls.
c. The supply of dollars decreases.
d. Japanese imports become more popular.

CAUSATION CHAIN GAME
Changes in the Supply and Demand Curves for Dollars—Exhibit 10

3. Key Concept: Impact of relative price level changes

An increase in inflation in the United States relative to the rate in France would make

a. U.S. goods relatively less expensive in the United States and in France.
b. French goods relatively less expensive in the United States, and U.S. goods relatively more expensive in France.

c. French goods relatively more expensive in the United States and in France.
d. French goods relatively more expensive in the United States, and U.S. goods relatively less expensive in France.

4. Key Concept: Impact of relative price level changes

If the Japanese price level falls relative to the price level in the United States, then

a. Japanese buy U.S. exports.
b. the demand for dollars decreases.
c. the supply of dollars increases.
d. the value of the dollar falls.
e. All of the answers above are correct.

CAUSATION CHAIN GAME
The Impact of Relative Price Level Changes on Exchange Rates—Exhibit 11

Chapter 16: Economies in Transition

5. Key Concept: Command economy

Which of the following statements is *true* about a command economy?

a. Shortages occur because of complexities in the planning process.
b. Planners determine what, how many, and for whom goods and services are to be produced.
c. Planners often allocate goods and services using a rationing system.
d. The quality of produced goods and services tends to be inferior.
e. All of the answers are correct.

6. Key Concept: Command economy

Which of the following statements *best* describes the role played by prices in a command economy such as the former Soviet Union?

a. Prices were used to allocate resources.
b. Prices played the same role as in a market economy.
c. Prices and queuing were used to ration final goods and services.
d. None of the statements are true.

CAUSATION CHAIN GAME
Central Planners Fixing Prices—Exhibit 2

Chapter 17: Growth and the Less-Developed Countries

7. Key Concept: Economic growth

An outward shift of an economy's production possibilities curve is caused by an

a. increase in capital.
b. increase in labor.

c. advance in technology.
d. All of the answers are correct.

8. Key Concept: Economic growth

Which of the following statements are *correct*?

a. Economic development is more quantitative than economic growth.
b. A country cannot achieve economic growth with a limited base of natural resources.
c. Infrastructure is capital provided by the private sector.
d. All of the above are correct.
e. All of the above are incorrect.

 CAUSATION CHAIN GAME
Economic Growth—Exhibit 4

9. Key Concept: Achieving economic growth

Which of the following can be a barrier to an LDC's economic growth and development?

a. Low population growth
b. A low level of human capital
c. Faster capital accumulation
d. More infrastructure

10. Key Concept: Economic growth and development

To grow and prosper, less-developed countries must *not*

a. invest in human capital.
b. build a strong infrastructure.
c. shift resources out of the production of consumer goods and into the production of capital goods.
d. shift resources out of the production of capital goods and into the production of consumer goods.
e. improve the quality of the water supply.

CAUSATION CHAIN GAME
The Effect of External Financing on an LDC's Production Possibilities Curve—Exhibit 7

Answers to Odd-Numbered Study Questions and Problems*

CHAPTER 1
INTRODUCING THE ECONOMIC WAY OF THINKING

1. A poor nation with many people who lack food, clothing, and shelter certainly experiences wants beyond the availability of goods and services to satisfy these unfulfilled wants. On the other hand, no wealthy nation has all the resources necessary to produce everything everyone in the nation wants to have. Even if you had $1 million and were completely satisfied with your share of goods and services, other desires would be unfulfilled. There is never enough time to accomplish all the things that you can imagine would be worthwhile.

3. Macroeconomics applies an overview perspective to an economy by examining economy-wide variables, such as inflation, unemployment, and growth of the economy. Microeconomics examines individual economic units, such as the market for corn, gasoline, or ostrich eggs.

5. The real world is full of complexities that make it difficult to understand and predict the relationships between variables. For example, the relationship between changes in the price of gasoline and changes in consumption of gasoline requires abstraction from the reality that variables such as weather and the fuel economy of cars often change at the same time as the price of gasoline.

7. The two events are associated because the first event (cut in military spending) is followed by the second event (higher unemployment in the defense industry). The point is that association does not necessarily mean causation, but it might. For example, the economy could be in recession.

APPENDIX TO CHAPTER 1
APPLYING GRAPHS TO ECONOMICS

1. a. The probability of living is *inversely* related to age. This model could be affected by improvements in diet, better health care, reductions in hazards to health in the workplace, or changes in the speed limit.

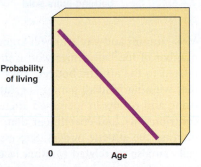

b. Annual income and years of formal education are *directly* related. This relationship might be influenced by changes in such human characteristics as intelligence, motivation, ability, and family background. An example of an institutional change that could affect this relationship over a number of years is the draft.

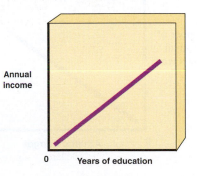

*Note: Answers to even-numbered questions are in the Instructor's Manual.

c. Inches of snow and sales of bathing suits are *inversely* related. The weather forecast and the price of travel to sunny vacation spots can affect this relationship.

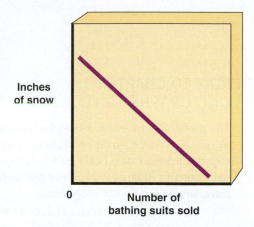

d. Most alumni and students will argue that the number of football games won is *directly* related to the athletic budget. They reason that winning football games is great advertising and results in increased attendance, contributions, and enrollment that, in turn, increase the athletic budget. Success in football can also be related to other factors, such as school size, age and type of institution, number and income of alumni, and quality of the faculty and administrators.

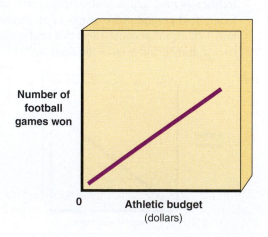

CHAPTER 2
PRODUCTION POSSIBILITIES, OPPORTUNITY COST, AND ECONOMIC GROWTH

1. Because the wants of individuals and society exceed the goods and services available to satisfy these desires, choices must be made. The consumption possibilities of an individual with a fixed income are limited, and as a result, additional consumption of one item necessarily precludes an expenditure on another next-best choice. The forgone alternative is called the opportunity cost, and this concept also applies to societal decisions. If society allocates resources to the production of guns, then those same resources cannot be used at the same time to make butter.

3. Regardless of the price of a lunch, economic resources—land, labor, and capital—are used to produce the lunch. These scarce resources are no longer available to produce other goods and services.

5. Using marginal analysis, students weigh the benefits of attending college against the costs. There is an incentive to attend college when the benefits (improved job opportunities, income, improvement, social life, and so on) outweigh the opportunity costs.

7.

Flower boxes	Opportunity cost (pies forgone)
0	—
1	4 (30 − 26)
2	5 (26 − 21)
3	6 (21 − 15)
4	7 (15 − 8)
5	8 (8 − 0)

9. Movements along the curve are efficient points and conform to the well-known "free lunch" statement. However, points inside the curve are exceptions because it is possible to produce more of one output without producing less of another output.

11.

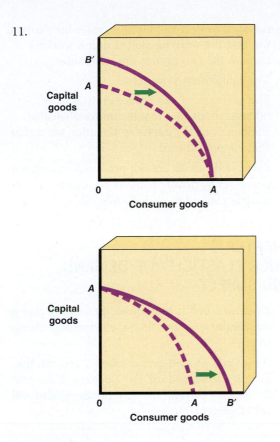

5. One reason that the demand curve for word processing software shifted to the right might be that people desire new, higher-quality output features. The supply curve can shift to the right when new technology makes it possible to offer more software for sale at different prices.

7. a. Demand shifts to the right.
    b. Supply shifts to the left.
    c. Supply shifts to the right.
    d. Demand shifts to the right.
    e. Demand shifts to the right.
    f. Supply of cotton shifts to the right.

9. a. The supply of Blu-ray players shifts rightward.
    b. The demand for Blu-ray players is unaffected.
    c. The equilibrium price falls, and the equilibrium quantity increases.
    d. The demand for Blu-ray discs increases because of the fall in the price of Blu-ray players (a complementary good).

11. The number of seats (quantity supplied) remains constant, but the demand curve shifts because tastes and preferences change according to the importance of each game. Although demand changes, the price is a fixed amount, and to manage a shortage, colleges and universities use amount of contributions, number of years as a contributor, or some other rationing device.

CHAPTER 3
MARKET DEMAND AND SUPPLY

1. If people buy a good or service because they associate higher quality with higher price, this is a violation of the ceteris paribus assumption. An increase in the quantity demanded results only from a decrease in price. Quality and other nonprice determinants of demand, such as tastes and preferences and the price of related goods, are held constant in the model.

3. a. Demand for cars decreases; oil and cars are *complements*.
    b. Demand for insulation increases; oil and home insulation are *substitutes*.
    c. Demand for coal increases; oil and coal are *substitutes*.
    d. Demand for tires decreases; oil and tires are *complements*.

APPENDIX TO CHAPTER 3
CONSUMER SURPLUS, PRODUCER SURPLUS, AND MARKET EFFICIENCY

1. $50

3.

Price	$30	$15
Consumer surplus	$50	$105
Producer surplus	$25	$5
Total surplus	$75	$110

The lower price results in higher total surplus because in this case the rise in consumer surplus exceeds fall in producer surplus.

CHAPTER 4
MARKETS IN ACTION

1.

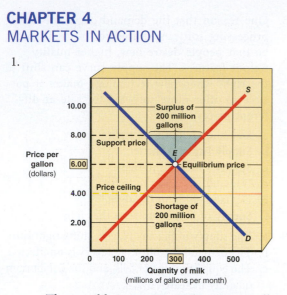

a. The equilibrium price is $6.00 per gallon, and the equilibrium quantity is 300 million gallons per month. The price system will restore the market's $6.00 per gallon price because a surplus will either drive prices down or a shortage will drive prices up.

b. The support price results in a persistent surplus of 200 million gallons of milk per month, which the government purchases with taxpayers' money. Consequently, taxpayers who do not drink milk are still paying for milk. The purpose of the support price is to bolster the incomes of dairy farmers.

c. The ceiling price will result in a persistent shortage of 200 million gallons of milk per month, but 200 million gallons are purchased by consumers at the low price of $4.00 per gallon. The shortage places a burden on the government to ration milk in order to be fair and to prevent black markets. The government's goal is to keep the price of milk below the equilibrium price of $6.00 per gallon, which would be set by a free market.

3. The labor market can be divided into two separate markets, one for skilled union workers and one for unskilled workers. If the minimum wage is above the equilibrium wage rate and is raised, the effect will be to increase the demand for, and the wage of, skilled union workers because the two groups are substitutes.

5. The equilibrium price rises.

7. The government can reduce emissions by (a) regulations that require smoke-abatement equipment or (b) imposing pollution taxes that shift supply leftward.

9. Pure public goods are not produced in sufficient quantities by private markets because there is no feasible method to exclude free riders.

CHAPTER 5
PRICE ELASTICITY OF DEMAND AND SUPPLY

1. Demand is elastic because the percentage change in quantity is greater than the percentage change in price.

3. If the price of used cars is raised 1 percent, the quantity demanded will fall 3 percent. If the price is raised 10 percent, the quantity demanded will fall 30 percent.

5.

$$E_d = \frac{\%\Delta Q}{\%\Delta P} = \frac{\dfrac{4,500 - 5,000}{5,000 + 4,500}}{\dfrac{3,500 - 3,000}{3,000 + 3,500}} = \frac{\dfrac{1}{19}}{\dfrac{1}{13}} = 0.68$$

The price elasticity of demand for the university is inelastic.

7. Demand for popcorn is perfectly inelastic, and total revenue will increase.

9. a. Sunkist oranges
   b. Cars
   c. Foreign travel in the long run

11. Furniture sales fall by 30 percent and physician services by only 3 percent. Thus, the demand for physician services is much less responsive to a reduction in income than the demand for furniture.

13. The negative number tells you car tires are complements. If the price of cars rises by 10 percent, the quantity demanded of car tires falls by 20 percent.

15. As the demand for a product becomes more inelastic, the greater the amount of a tax on this product that sellers can pass on to consumers by raising the product's price.

CHAPTER 6
CONSUMER CHOICE THEORY

1. Utility is a subjective concept, and, therefore, this statement may or may not be true.

3. Marginal utility is 10 utils. When you attend the fourth party, total utility will increase, but marginal utility will be less than 10 utils.

5. In consumer equilibrium, the marginal utility ratio is 3/4, which is equal to the price ratio.

7. As people consume more of any product, eventually the satisfaction per unit decreases. Since the marginal utility from additional units falls, people will not buy a greater quantity unless the price falls.

9. The initial consumer equilibrium is as follows:

$$\frac{\text{MU of steak meal}}{\text{Price of steak meal}} = \frac{\text{MU of hamburger meal}}{\text{Price of hamburger meal}}$$

$$\frac{12\text{utils}}{\$10} = \frac{6\text{utils}}{\$5}$$

The marginal utility per dollar for each good equals 1.2. If the price of a hamburger meal falls to $2, this equality no longer holds. Now the marginal utility per dollar for a hamburger meal becomes higher at 3 (6 utils/$2). James can now increase his total utility by purchasing more hamburger meals per month. Given the law of diminishing returns, the marginal utility of hamburger meals falls until consumer equilibrium is restored.

APPENDIX TO CHAPTER 6
INDIFFERENCE CURVE ANALYSIS

1. MRS = 3 (3 slices of pizza per Coke), but the ratio of prices is 1/2 ($1.00 per Coke/$2.00 per slice of pizza). Since MRS > slope (the ratio of prices), the consumer is not maximizing total utility. Therefore, the consumer should consume less pizza and more Coke in order to maximize total utility by moving downward along the consumer's indifference curve until

consumer equilibrium is achieved where MRS = price ratio = 1/2.

3. a. and b.

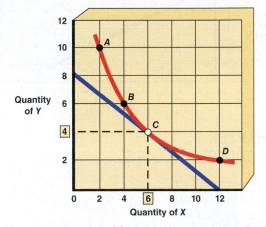

c. Consumer equilibrium occurs at point C with 6 units of X and 4 units of Y purchased.

d. $\text{MRS} = P_x/P_y = \frac{\$1}{\$1.50} = \frac{2}{3}$

e. Hold the price of Y constant at $1.50, and decrease the price of X from $1.00 to $0.50. The new budget line will shift northeastward from the Y axis intercept point of 8 units. Now draw a new indifference curve, and determine the new equilibrium point. Finally, draw a graph with various prices of X on the vertical axis and the quantity of X on the horizontal axis. Connecting the two consumer equilibrium points will allow you to draw a downward sloping demand curve.

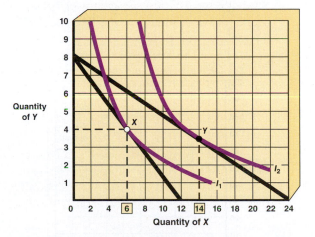

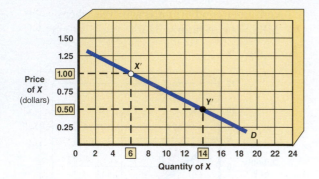

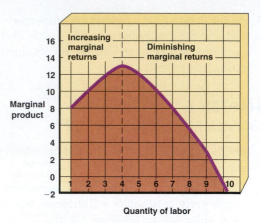

Quantity of labor

CHAPTER 7
PRODUCTION COSTS

1. a. explicit cost
   b. explicit cost
   c. implicit cost
   d. implicit cost
   e. explicit cost
   f. implicit cost

3. a.

Labor	Marginal product
1	8
2	10
3	12
4	13
5	12
6	10
7	8
8	6
9	3
10	−2

b.

5. None. The position of a firm's short-run average total cost curve is not related to the demand curve.

7. The *ATC* and *AVC* curves converge as output expands because $ATC = AVC + AFC$. As output increases, *AFC* declines, so most of *ATC* is therefore *AVC*.

9. The average total cost-marginal cost rule states that when the marginal cost is below the average total cost, the addition to total cost is below the average total cost, and the average total cost falls. When the marginal cost is greater than the average total cost, the average total cost rises. In this case, the average total cost is at a minimum because it is equal to the marginal cost.

11. The marginal product for any number of workers is the slope of the total output curve. The marginal product is the derivative of the total output curve dTO/dQ, where *TO* is the total output and *Q* is the number of workers.

CHAPTER 8
PERFECT COMPETITION

1. A perfectly competitive firm will not advertise. Because all firms in the industry sell the same product, there is no reason for ads to influence customers into buying one firm's product rather than another firm's product.

3.

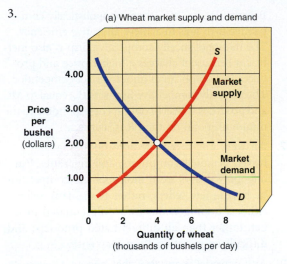

(a) Wheat market supply and demand

Price per bushel (dollars)

Quantity of wheat (thousands of bushels per day)

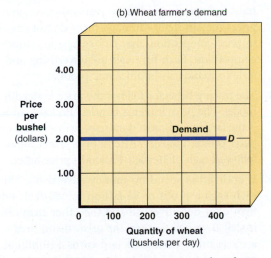

(b) Wheat farmer's demand

Price per bushel (dollars)

Quantity of wheat (bushels per day)

A single wheat farmer is a price taker facing a perfectly elastic demand curve because in perfect competition one seller has no control over its price. The reason is that each wheat farmer is one among many, sells a homogeneous product, and must compete with any new farmer entering the wheat market.

5. At a price of $150, the firm produces 4 units and earns an economic profit of $70 ($TR - TC = 600 - 530$). The firm breaks even at an output of 2 units.

7. This statement is incorrect. A firm can earn maximum profit (or minimum loss) when marginal revenue equals marginal cost. The confusion is between the "marginal" and the "total" concepts. Marginal cost is the change in total cost from one additional unit of output, and marginal revenue is the change in total revenue from one additional unit of output.

9. The statement is incorrect. The perfectly competitive firm must consider both its marginal revenue and its marginal cost. Instead of trying to sell all the quantity of output possible, the firm will sell the quantity where $MR = MC$ because beyond this level of output the firm earns less profit.

11. Advise the residential contractor to shut down because the market price does not exceed the average variable cost, and the firm cannot cover its operating costs.

CHAPTER 9
MONOPOLY

1. Each market is served by a single firm providing a unique product. There are no close substitutes for local water service, a newly invented cancer drug with patent protection, and first-class mail service. A government franchise imposes a legal barrier to potential competitors in the water and first-class mail services. Patent protection also grants monopoly power to the maker of that new drug.

3. The reason may be that the hospital has monopoly power because it is the only hospital in the area and patients have no choice. On the other hand, there may be many drugstores competing to sell drugs, and this keeps prices lower than those charged by the hospital.

5. In a natural monopoly, a single seller can produce electricity at a lower cost because the $LRAC$ curve declines. One firm can therefore sell electricity at a cheaper price and drive its competitor out of business over time. Another possibility would be for two competing firms to merge and earn greater profit by lowering cost further.

7. In this special case, sales maximization and profit maximization are the same. The monopolist should charge $2.50 per unit, produce 5 units of output, and earn $12.50 in profit. When the marginal cost curve is not equal to zero, the monopolist's $MR = MC$ output is less than 5 units, the price is higher than $2.50 per unit, and profit is below $12.50.

9. a. increase output
   b. decrease output

11. a. not price discrimination
    b. price discrimination
    c. price discrimination

13. Answers vary with students.

CHAPTER 10
MONOPOLISTIC COMPETITION AND OLIGOPOLY

1. The monopolistically competitive firm's demand curve is less elastic (steeper) than a perfectly competitive firm's demand curve, but more elastic (flatter) than a monopolist's demand curve.

3. a. P_1
   b. Q_1
   c. Q_3
   d. greater than the marginal cost ($B > A$)

5.

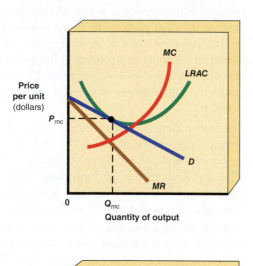

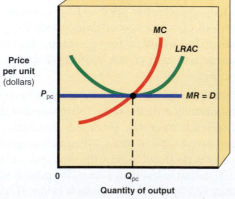

Because $P_{mc} > MC$, the monopolistically competitive firm fails to achieve allocative efficiency. The monopolistically competitive firm is also inefficient because it charges a higher price and produces less output than under perfect competition. The perfectly competitive firm sets P_{pc} equal to MC and produces a level of output corresponding to the minimum point on the $LRAC$ curve.

7. Answers might include automobiles, airline travel, personal computers, and cigarettes. An oligopoly differs from monopolistic competition by having few sellers, rather than many sellers; either a homogeneous or a differentiated product, rather than all differentiated products; and difficult entry rather than easy entry.

9. Any maverick jeans firm that raises or lowers its price will earn less profits. Therefore, firms in the jeans industry face a kinked demand curve, and prices remain rigid. Although firms do not engage in price competition, they can engage in nonprice competition. Each firm can use advertising and style to market its brand-name product.

11. The pricing behavior follows the price leadership model. The price leader is Hewlett-Packard, which is the largest and most dominant firm in the computer printer industry. After a price war, Canon followed each of Hewlett-Packard's price hikes.

13. If both firms spend no money advertising, they each earn a profit of $8 billion in cell A. If one firm does not advertise and the other firm does in cell B or cell C, then the advertising firm attracts more customers and earns $10 billion compared to a $2 billion loss for the rival without ads. This outcome forces both firms to advertise and reduce mutual profits at cell D. As a result of both firms spending large budgets on advertising, their mutual profits are reduced to $5 billion. If the government bans all cigarette advertising, the result is that both firms will move to the mutually high profit cell A.

CHAPTER 11
LABOR MARKETS

1. This statement is incorrect. Workers supply their labor to employers. Demand refers to the quantity of labor employers hire at various wage rates based on the marginal revenue product of labor.

3. The MRP of the second worker is this person's contribution to total revenue, which is $50 ($150 − $100). Because $MRP = P \times MP$ and $MP = MRP/P$, the second worker's marginal product (MP) is 10 ($50/$5).

5. The firm in a perfectly competitive labor market is a price taker. Because a single firm buys the labor of a relatively small portion of workers in an industry, it can hire additional workers and not drive up the wage rate. For the industry, however, all firms must offer higher wages to attract workers from other industries.

7. Students investing in education are increasing their human capital. As a student's human capital increases, his or her marginal product and MRP increase as well. At a given product price, firms find it profitable to hire the better-educated worker and pay higher wages.

9. At a wage rate of $90 per day, Zippy Paper Company hires 3 workers because each worker's MRP exceeds or equals the wage rate. Setting the wage rate at $100 per day causes Zippy Paper Company to cut employment from 3 to 2 workers because the third worker's MRP is $10 below the union-caused wage rate of $100 per day.

11. As shown in the following exhibit, for a monopsony, the optimum quantity of labor is 3 quarterbacks, determined at point A, where the MFC curve intersects the MRP curve. However, the team can attract and hire 3 quarterbacks for an annual salary of $300,000 each at point B on the supply of labor curve, rather than paying a quarterback's contribution to the team's revenues (MRP), which is $500,000 per year at point A. In a competitive labor market, the Jacksonville Jaguars hire 4 quarterbacks and pay each $400,000 per year.

CHAPTER 12
INCOME DISTRIBUTION, POVERTY, AND DISCRIMINATION

1. a.

| | Alpha | | Beta | |
Percentage of families	Percent-age share	Cumula-tive share	Percent-age share	Cumula-tive share
Lowest fifth	17.7%	17.7%	9.0%	9.0%
Second-lowest fifth	19.9	37.6	14.2	23.2
Middle fifth	20.4	58.0	17.5	40.7
Second-highest fifth	20.7	78.7	21.9	62.6
Highest fifth	21.3	100.0	37.4	100.0

b.

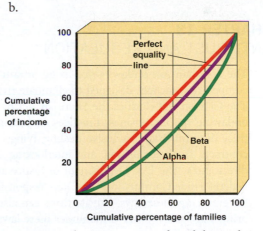

c. Because the Lorenz curve for Alpha is closest to the perfect equality line, Alpha's distribution of income is more equal compared to Beta.

3. Absolute poverty is defined as a dollar figure that represents some level of income per year required to purchase some minimum amount of goods and services essential to meeting a person's or a family's basic needs. Relative poverty is defined as a level of income required to place a person or family in, say, the lowest 20 percent among all persons or families receiving incomes. The poverty line is based on the absolute definition.

5. In-kind transfers are payments in the form of goods and services rather than cash. Examples include such government programs as food stamps, Medicaid, and housing. Noncash income is not counted in a family's income to determine whether the family's income is below the poverty line.

7. The percentage of families in the United States classified as poor was about 14 percent. Poor families are more likely to live in the South. The age, race, and education of the head of the family are also important characteristics of poor families.

9. The three major criticisms are that welfare: (1) reduces the work incentive, (2) is inefficient because the programs cost too much to administer, and (3) treats poor persons with the same needs unequally because the states pay different benefits.

11. This is an opinion question. To agree, you assume that markets are perfectly competitive and discrimination is therefore unprofitable. To disagree, you can argue that in reality labor markets will never be perfectly competitive and the government must therefore address the institutional causes of poverty.

CHAPTER 13
ANTITRUST AND REGULATION

1. The Sherman Act outlaws price-fixing or anti-competitive practices designed to eliminate rivals. The Clayton Act clarifies the Sherman Act by outlawing specific business practices, including price discrimination, exclusive dealing, tying contracts, stock acquisition, and interlocking directorates. The U.S. Department of Justice and Federal Trade Commission (FTC) are responsible for enforcing these laws. Private firms can also bring suit against other firms under these laws.

3. Both the Robinson–Patman Act and the Celler–Kefauver Act were amendments to close loopholes in the Clayton Act. The Robinson–Patman Act expanded the list of illegal price discrimination practices to include quantity discounting, free advertising, and promotional allowances offered that "substantially lessen competition or tend to create a monopoly." The Celler–Kefauver Act closed the loophole in the Clayton Act whereby competing firms could merge by asset acquisition (not outlawed in the Clayton Act), rather than by acquiring stock (outlawed in the Clayton Act).

5. In fact, Alcoa argued that metals such as copper and steel are substitutes for aluminum; therefore, the relevant industry to compute market share was the metals industry and not the aluminum industry. If the court had chosen the U.S. metals industry as the relevant industry, Alcoa would not have a monopoly.

7. a. The federal government will charge the bookstore with predatory pricing in order to monopolize its college market for books, which is a violation of the Sherman Act.
   b. The federal government will charge the real estate firms with collusion to fix prices, which is a violation of the Sherman Act.
   c. The federal government will charge a violation of the Clayton Act because the combined market share of this horizontal merger would substantially lessen competition in the personal computer market.
   d. The federal government will not charge a violation because this is a conglomerate merger between firms in unrelated industries.

9. The "necessary" condition would be expected to favor existing regulated firms by eliminating or greatly restricting competition and raising prices. The existing regulated firms are better organized politically than either new competitors or consumers. While consumers favor competition and lower prices, regulators would be expected to interpret "necessary" to mean that the service provided by existing firms is sufficient without new firms.

11. Although a public subsidy achieves efficiency, marginal-cost pricing is usually unpopular with voters, who must provide the monopolist with public funds. Moreover, a public subsidy gives the monopolist a disincentive to minimize costs.

CHAPTER 14
ENVIRONMENTAL ECONOMICS

1. A competitive industry selling a pollution-generating product will charge a lower price and sell a larger quantity than would be the case for a "green" industry. The competitive industry has lower costs because it fails to include external costs. Lower costs allow a lower price.

A lower price leads to a larger quantity demanded and sold.

3. If you choose the $90,000 house, the EMF radiation is *not* an externality. An externality is a third-party effect, whereby buyers and sellers of a product ignore the spillover effects of their transaction. In this case, the market reflects the risk of cancer, with the seller accepting a lower price and the buyer saving $10,000 to reflect the cancer risk.

   Houses have many characteristics that influence their price, including number of rooms, location, nearby schools, and environmental amenities. If you are willing to buy a house near a nuclear plant, or near EMFs, you the buyer, not a third party, bear the consequences.

5. An instructor who automatically flunks students who do not turn in all homework assignments is exhibiting command-and-control regulation. She is dictating the production process for achieving knowledge. The inefficiencies are that students may turn in poorly done assignments or may copy assignments and that some students may understand the material without doing the homework or may have an alternative production method, such as the use of computer software, to achieve knowledge. The instructor's method is particularly inefficient if her assignments are busywork and do not really help the students achieve knowledge.

7.

Paper industry

At Q_p, pollution from paper production leads to coffee-colored rivers. At socially efficient Q_s, there is less pollution, and rivers are less polluted. The rivers are unlikely to be pristine, which requires no production at all.

9. Consumers will share in the benefits of cleaner air if any individual buys a less polluting car. Since they enjoy the same benefit whether they pay extra or their neighbor pays extra for a cleaner car, they will let the neighbor buy the cleaner car. Of course, because their neighbor uses the same reasoning, no one ends up paying extra to buy a cleaner car.

11. Convincing examples should be sent to the author of the text. It is very difficult to find markets where the transaction costs of reaching an agreement are near zero. It is also difficult to find two-party situations, because most pollution spills over to many individuals. With many individuals involved, the free-rider problem arises, as a given individual wants to benefit from pollution agreements, but let others bear the cost. There can often be income effects, as fighting pollution may take a large amount of one's income. Candidates for markets where the Coase Theorem might apply include convincing your neighbor to leash her dog (you might help finance invisible fencing), enforcing laws concerning the fencing of cattle (see question 12 for further discussion), and settling disputes when one builder interferes with the views of existing homes.

13. a. Command-and-control regulation would dictate the use of an alternative technology with lower carbon emissions.
    b. An effluent tax would place a tax on carbon emissions so that firms could no longer ignore these costs. In turn, prices of carbon-emitting products would increase, and quantities would decrease.
    c. Permits would be issued giving the right to emit carbon. The number of permits would equal the socially efficient emissions level. Firms would be allowed to buy or sell these permits. Firms with higher marginal costs of emissions abatement would buy permits,

whereas firms that could reduce emissions at a lower cost would profit from selling permits.

15. According to Garrett Hardin, individuals will use a common property resource as long as their marginal benefits exceed their marginal costs. They will disregard the external costs to others if additional fishing or grazing subtracts from the fish or grass available to others using the common. As all users of the common will behave in this way, the commons will be used beyond the efficient point, and potentially to the point of exhaustion, where the availability of the commons will collapse.

Elinor Ostrom has studied fisheries and other commons and finds that those who are using the resource will attempt to establish institutions that will lead to optimal use. Rather than leave the commons as open access, they will convert it to common property. They will limit who can access the property and limit its use, so that the commons will not be fished or grazed into exhaustion.

CHAPTER 15
INTERNATIONAL TRADE AND FINANCE

1. a. In Alpha, the opportunity cost of producing 1 ton of diamonds is 1/2 ton of pearls. In Beta, the opportunity cost of producing 1 ton of diamonds is 2 tons of pearls.
   b. In Alpha, the opportunity cost of producing 1 ton of pearls is 2 tons of diamonds. In Beta, the opportunity cost of producing 1 ton of pearls is 1/2 ton of diamonds.
   c. Because Alpha can produce diamonds at a lower opportunity cost than Beta can, Alpha has a comparative advantage in the production of diamonds.
   d. Because Beta can produce pearls at a lower opportunity cost than Alpha can, Beta has a comparative advantage in the production of pearls.

e.

	Diamonds (tons per year)	Pearls (tons per year)
Before specialization		
Alpha (at point B)	100	25
Beta (at point C)	30	120
Total output	130	145
After specialization		
Alpha (at point A)	150	0
Beta (at point D)	0	180
Total output	150	180

As shown in the previous table, specialization in each country increases total world output per year by 20 tons of diamonds and 35 tons of pearls.

f.

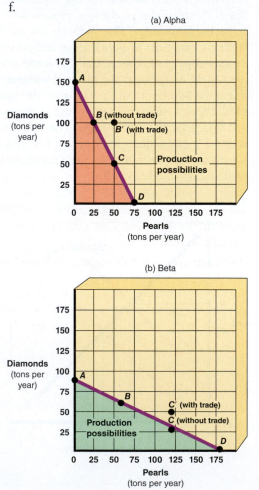

Without trade, Alpha produces and consumes 100 tons of diamonds and 25 tons of pearls at point *B* on its production possibilities curve. Without trade, Beta produces and consumes 30 tons of diamonds and 120 tons of pearls (point *C*). Now assume Alpha specializes in producing diamonds at point *A* and imports 50 tons of pearls in exchange for 50 tons of diamonds. Through specialization and trade, Alpha moves its consumption possibility to point *B′*, outside its production possibilities curve.

3. The principle of specialization and trade according to comparative advantage applies to both nations and states in the United States. For example, Florida grows oranges, and Idaho grows potatoes. Trade between these states, just like trade between nations, increases the consumption possibilities.

5. U.S. industries (and their workers) that compete with restricted imports would benefit. Consumers would lose from the reduced supply of imported goods from which to choose and from higher prices for domestic products, resulting from lack of competition from imports.

7. Although some domestic jobs may be lost, new ones are created by international trade. Stated differently, the economy as a whole gains when nations specialize and trade according to the law of comparative advantage, but imports will cost jobs in some specific industries.

9. Although each nation's balance of payments equals zero, its current and capital account balances usually do not equal zero. For example, a current account deficit means a nation purchased more in imports than it sold in exports. On the other hand, this nation's capital account must have a surplus to offset the current account deficit. This means that foreigners are buying more domestic capital (capital inflow) than domestic citizens are buying foreign capital (capital outflow). Thus, net ownership of domestic capital stock is in favor of foreigners.

11. a.

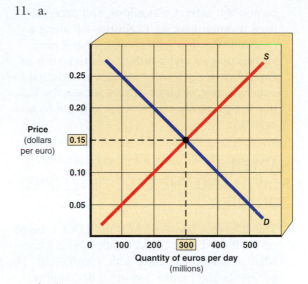

b. $0.15 per euro

c. An excess quantity of 200 million euros would be demanded.

CHAPTER 16
ECONOMIES IN TRANSITION

1. Americans prefer large cars and canned soup. Europeans predominantly buy small cars and dry soup. The role of women and minorities in the workplace is an excellent example of how culture relates to the labor factor of production.

3. Such a program would provide additional economic security for the elderly, but higher taxes could reduce the incentive to work, and economic efficiency might be reduced.

5. In a traditional agricultural system, a benefit would be that members of society would cooperate by helping to build barns, harvest, and so on. Under the command system, worrying about errors and crop failures would be minimized because the state makes the decisions and everyone in society has a basic income. In a market economy, a bumper crop would mean large profits and the capacity to improve one's standard of living.

7. Because most economies are mixed systems, this term is too broad to be very descriptive. The terms *capitalism* and *communism* are more definitive concerning the role of private

ownership, market allocations, and decentralized decision making. Countries fall along a spectrum that has pure capitalism and pure socialism as its end points. Countries, such as Cuba, that are primarily socialist are referred to as communist, while countries, such as the U.S., that are primarily capitalist are referred to as capitalist.

CHAPTER 17
GROWTH AND THE LESS-DEVELOPED COUNTRIES

1. The difference between IACs and LDCs is based on GDP per capita. This classification is somewhat arbitrary. A country with a high GDP per capita and narrow industrial development based on oil, such as the United Arab Emirates, is excluded from the IAC list. There are 27 economies listed in the text as IACs, including Switzerland, Japan, the United States, Singapore, and Hong Kong. The following countries are considered to be LDCs: Argentina, Sudan, South Africa, Jordan, and Bangladesh.

3. a. Based only on GDP per capita, you would conclude that Alpha is a better place to live because this country produces a greater output of goods and services per person.
   b. Based on the additional evidence, you would change your mind and prefer to live in Beta because the quality-of-life data indicate a higher standard of living in this country.

5. The average growth rate of GDP per capita for IACs exceeds the GDP per capita growth rate for LDCs. This evidence is consistent with the argument. The argument is oversimplified because there is considerable diversity among the LDCs. In a given year, a LDC may have a GDP per capita growth rate greater than many IACs.

7. Economic growth and development are complicated because there is no single prescription that a country can follow. The chapter presents a multidimensional model with five basic categories: natural resources, human resources, capital, technological progress, and political environment. Because an LDC is weak in one or more of the key factors, such as natural resources, does not necessarily mean that the LDC cannot achieve economic success.

9. Because they are poor countries with low GDP per capita, they lack domestic savings to invest in capital; and lacking investment, they remain poor. The rich in these poor countries often put their savings abroad because of the fear of political instability. An inflow of external funds from abroad permits the LDC to increase its capital without reducing its consumption and to shift its production possibilities curve outward.

11. Poor countries are too poor to save enough to finance domestic capital formation. International trade is a way LDCs can generate savings from abroad. Exports provide the LDCs with foreign exchange to pay for imports of capital stock that is necessary for economic growth and development. LDCs often prefer trade to aid since they feel that aid comes with too many political and economic strings attached.

Answers to Sample Quizzes

Chapter 1 Introducing the Economic Way of Thinking

1. d   2. c   3. a   4. c   5. b   6. d   7. d   8. d   9. b
10. d   11. a   12. c   13. a   14. b   15. c   16. d
17. d   18. b   19. a   20. d

Appendix 1 Applying Graphs to Economics

1. d   2. d   3. b   4. c   5. a   6. a   7. d   8. c
9. a   10. c   11. d   12. a. 13. b   14. d   15. d   16. c
17. c   18. c   19. d   20. c

Chapter 2 Production Possibilities, Opportunity Cost, and Economic Growth

1. d   2. b   3. a   4. c   5. c   6. e   7. b   8. a   9. c
10. d   11. d   12. b   13. a   14. b   15. a   16. a
17. a   18. d   19. a   20. c

Chapter 3 Market Demand and Supply

1. b   2. a   3. d   4. c   5. d   6. c   7. c   8. d
9. b   10. a   11. b   12. e   13. d   14. a   15. b
16. c   17. d   18. a   19. a   20. b   21. c   22. e
23. d   24. a   25. e

Appendix to Chapter 3 Consumer Surplus, Producer Surplus and Market Efficiency

1. c   2. c   3. c   4. d   5. e   6. d   7. d   8. d
9. a   10. d   11. d   12. d   13. a   14. b   15. d
16. a   17. b   18. d   19. d   20. d

Chapter 4 Markets in Action

1. b   2. c   3. a   4. c   5. b   6. b   7. a   8. d
9. b   10. a   11. b   12. b   13. b   14. c   15. a
16. a   17. b   18. c   19. d   20. c

Chapter 5 Price Elasticity of Demand and Supply

1. d   2. b   3. a   4. c   5. b   6. a   7. b   8. b
9. b   10. c   11. c   12. a   13. c   14. a   15. d
16. a   17. a   18. b   19. a   20. a   21. d   22. c
23. d   24. c   25. b

Chapter 6 Consumer Choice Theory

1. e   2. a   3. d   4. b   5. d   6. b   7. a   8. c
9. b   10. c   11. c   12. d   13. b   14. d   15. d

16. a   17. c   18. d   19. c   20. a   21. b   22. a
23. d   24. c   25. c

Appendix to Chapter 6 Indifference Curve Analysis

1. d   2. a   3. c   4. d   5. a   6. d   7. a   8. a
9. d   10. d   11. a   12. c   13. d   14. c   15. b

Chapter 7 Production Costs

1. d   2. a   3. c   4. c   5. c   6. d   7. b   8. e
9. b   10. b   11. c   12. d   13. e   14. c   15. b
16. c   17. c   18. b   19. a   20. a   21. c   22. c
23. b   24. a   25. c

Chapter 8 Perfect Competition

1. e   2. d   3. c   4. c   5. a   6. e   7. c   8. d   9. d
10. b   11. d   12. c   13. a   14. d   15. d   16. b
17. d   18. b   19. d   20. c

Chapter 9 Monopoly

1. c   2. a   3. b   4. b   5. d   6. c   7. d   8. c
9. d   10. d   11. e   12. c   13. d   14. d   15. b
16. d   17. b   18. c   19. b   20. b

Chapter 10 Monopolistic Competition and Oligopoly

1. c   2. b   3. b   4. a   5. c   6. d   7. c   8. b
9. a   10. d   11. c   12. a   13. d   14. c   15. d
16. d   17. a   18. b   19. c   20. b

Chapter 11 Labor Markets

1. b   2. a   3. c   4. d   5. d   6. a   7. c   8. c   9. c
10. d   11. d   12. c   13. e   14. b   15. e   16. b
17. c   18. d   19. c   20. c

Chapter 12 Income Distribution, Poverty, and Discrimination

1. c   2. d   3. b   4. c   5. c   6. d   7. b   8. a
9. c   10. d   11. c   12. b   13. d   14. b   15. d
16. c   17. c   18. d   19. a   20. c

Chapter 13 Antitrust and Regulation

1. c 2. b 3. a 4. b 5. a 6. c 7. b 8. a
9. d 10. b 11. d 12. b 13. b 14. a 15. b
16. c 17. d 18. a 19. c 20. d

Chapter 14 Environmental Economics

1. c 2. d 3. c 4. c 5. d 6. b 7. b 8. e
9. c 10. b 11. d 12. b 13. b 14. c 15. a
16. c 17. b 18. a 19. b 20. c

Chapter 15 International Trade and Finance

1. c 2. a 3. c 4. b 5. b 6. d 7. d 8. a
9. e 10. a 11. d 12. a 13. a 14. c 15. c
16. a 17. d 18. b 19. c 20. b

Chapter 16 Economies in Transition

1. d 2. a 3. c 4. a 5. c 6. d 7. d 8. a
9. c 10. a 11. a 12. d 13. a 14. b 15. d
16. b 17. d 18. c 19. d 20. c

Chapter 17 Growth and the Less-Developed Countries

1. d 2. d 3. c 4. b 5. e 6. d 7. b 8. d
9. d 10. d 11. e 12. a 13. e 14. a 15. b
16. d 17. c 18. a 19. c 20. b

Answers to Road Map Questions

Part 1 Introduction to Economics

1. e 2. c 3. c 4. d 5. a 6. e 7. d 8. d
9. d 10. b

Part 2 Microeconomics Fundamentals

1. b 2. c 3. a 4. a 5. d 6. d 7. d 8. c
9. c 10. c 11. b 12. a 13. c

Part 3 Market Structures

1. c 2. e 3. c 4. b 5. a 6. a 7. b 8. c 9. d
10. b 11. d

Part 4 Microeconomics Policy
Issues

1. e 2. d 3. d 4. d 5. d 6. d 7. d 8. a
9. d 10. a

Part 5 The International Economy

1. d 2. d 3. b 4. e 5. e 6. c 7. d 8. e
9. b 10. d

GLOSSARY

A

Ability-to-pay principle The concept that those who have higher incomes can afford to pay a greater proportion of their income in taxes, regardless of benefits received.

Absolute advantage The ability of a country to produce a good using the same or fewer resources than another country.

Adaptive expectations theory The concept that people believe the best indicator of the future is recent information. As a result, people persistently underestimate inflation when it is accelerating and overestimate it while it is slowing down.

Adjustable-rate mortgage (ARM) A home loan that adjusts the nominal interest rate to changes in an index rate, such as rates on Treasury securities that reflect changes in inflation.

Agency for International Development (AID) The agency of the U.S. State Department that is in charge of U.S. aid to foreign countries.

Aggregate demand curve (AD) The curve that shows the level of real GDP purchased by households, businesses, government, and foreigners (net exports) at different possible price levels during a time period, ceteris paribus.

Aggregate expenditures function (AE) The total spending in an economy at different levels of real GDP.

Aggregate expenditures model The model that determines the equilibrium level of real GDP by the intersection of the aggregate expenditures and aggregate output and income (real GDP) curves.

Aggregate supply curve (AS) The curve that shows the level of real GDP produced at different possible price levels during a time period, ceteris paribus.

Appreciation of currency A rise in the price of one currency relative to another.

Arbitrage The practice of earning a profit by buying a good at a low price and reselling the good at a higher price.

Automatic stabilizers Federal expenditures and tax revenues that automatically change levels in order to stabilize an economic expansion or contraction; sometimes referred to as nondiscretionary fiscal policy.

Autonomous consumption Consumption spending that is independent of the level of real disposable income.

Autonomous expenditure Spending that does not vary with the level of real disposable income.

Average fixed cost (AFC) Total fixed cost divided by the quantity of output produced.

Average tax rate The tax divided by the income.

Average total cost (ATC) Total cost divided by the quantity of output produced.

Average variable cost (AVC) Total variable cost divided by the quantity of output produced.

B

Balance of payments A bookkeeping record of all the international transactions between a country and other countries during a given period of time.

Balance of trade The value of a nation's imports subtracted from its exports. Balance of trade can be expressed in terms of goods, services, or goods and services.

Balanced budget multiplier An equal change in government spending and taxes, which changes aggregate demand by the amount of the change in government spending.

Barrier to entry Any obstacle that makes it difficult for a new firm to enter a market.

Barter The direct exchange of one good or service for another good or service, rather than for money.

Base year A year chosen as a reference point for comparison with some earlier or later year.

Benefit-cost analysis The comparison of the additional rewards and costs of an economic alternative.

Benefits-received principle The concept that those who benefit from government expenditures should pay the taxes that finance their benefits.

Board of Governors of the Federal Reserve System The seven members appointed by the president and confirmed by the U.S. Senate who serve for one nonrenewable 14-year term. Their responsibility is to supervise and control the money supply and the banking system of the United States.

Budget deficit A budget in which government expenditures exceed government revenues in a given time period.

Budget line A line that shows the different combinations of two goods a consumer can purchase with a given amount of money and at given prices.

Budget surplus A budget in which government revenues exceed government expenditures in a given time period.

Business cycle Alternating periods of economic growth and contraction, which can be measured by changes in real GDP.

C

Capital A human-made good used to produce other goods and services.

Capitalism An economic system characterized by private ownership of resources and markets.

Cartel A group of firms that formally agree to reduce competition by coordinating the price and output of a product.

Celler–Kefauver Act of 1950 An amendment to the Clayton Act that prohibits one firm from merging with a competitor by purchasing its physical assets if the effect is to substantially lessen competition.

Ceteris paribus A Latin phrase that means while certain variables change, all other things remain unchanged.

Change in demand An increase or a decrease in the quantity demanded at each possible price. An increase in demand is a rightward shift in the entire demand curve. A decrease in demand is a leftward shift in the entire demand curve.

Change in quantity demanded A movement between points along a stationary demand curve, ceteris paribus.

Change in quantity supplied A movement between points along a stationary supply curve, ceteris paribus.

Change in supply An increase or a decrease in the quantity supplied at each possible price. An increase in supply is a rightward shift in the entire supply curve. A decrease in supply is a leftward shift in the entire supply curve.

Checkable deposits The total money in financial institutions that can be withdrawn on demand by writing a check.

Circular flow model A diagram showing the exchange of money, products, and resources between households and businesses.

Civilian labor force The number of people 16 years of age and older who are employed or who are actively seeking a job, excluding armed forces, homemakers, discouraged workers, and other persons not in the labor force.

Classical economics The theory that free markets will restore full employment without government intervention.

Classical economists A group of economists whose theory dominated economic thinking from the 1770s to the Great Depression. They believed recessions would naturally cure themselves because the price system would automatically restore full employment.

Classical range The vertical segment of the aggregate supply curve, which represents an economy at full-employment output.

Clayton Act of 1914 An amendment that strengthens the Sherman Act by making it illegal for firms to engage in certain anticompetitive business practices.

Coase Theorem The proposition that private market negotiations can achieve social efficiency regardless of the initial definition of property rights.

Coincident indicators Variables that change at the same time real GDP changes.

Collective bargaining The process of negotiating labor contracts between the union and management concerning wages and working conditions.

Command economy An economic system that answers the What, How, and For Whom questions by a dictator or central authority.

Command-and-control regulations Government regulations that set an environmental goal and dictate how the goal will be achieved.

Commodity money Anything that serves as money while having market value based on the material from which it is made.

Communism A stateless, classless economic system in which all the factors of production are owned by the workers and people share in production according to their needs. In Marx's view, this is the highest form of socialism toward which the revolution should strive.

Comparable worth The principle that employees who work for the same employer must be paid the same wage when their jobs, even if different, require similar levels of education, training, experience, and responsibility. A nonmarket wage-setting process is used to evaluate and compensate jobs according to point scores assigned.

Comparative advantage The ability of a country to produce a good at a lower opportunity cost than another country.

Complementary good A good that is jointly consumed with another good. As a result, there is an inverse relationship between a price change for one good and the demand for its "go together" good.

Conglomerate merger A merger between firms in unrelated markets.

Constant returns to scale A situation in which the long-run average cost curve does not change as the firm increases output.

Constant-cost industry An industry in which the expansion of industry output by the entry of new firms has no effect on the individual firm's average total cost curve.

Consumer equilibrium A condition in which total utility cannot increase by spending more of a given budget on one good and spending less on another good.

Consumer Financial Protection Bureau (CFPB) An independent bureau within the Federal Reserve that helps consumers make financial decisions.

Consumer price index (CPI) An index that measures changes in the average prices of consumer goods and services.

Consumer sovereignty The freedom of consumers to cast their dollar votes to buy, or not to buy, at prices determined in competitive markets.

Consumer surplus The value of the difference between the price consumers are willing to pay for a product on the demand curve and the price actually paid for it.

Consumption function The graph or table that shows the amount households spend for goods and services at different levels of real disposable income.

Cost-push inflation An increase in the general price level resulting from an increase in the cost of production, and illustrated by a leftward shift of the aggregate supply curve.

Cross-elasticity of demand The ratio of the percentage change in the quantity demanded of a good or service to a given percentage change in the price of another good or service.

Crowding-in effect An increase in private-sector spending as a result of federal budget deficits financed by U.S. Treasury borrowing. At less than full employment, consumers hold more Treasury securities, and this additional wealth causes them to spend more. Business investment spending increases because of optimistic profit expectations.

Crowding-out effect A reduction in private-sector spending as a result of federal budget deficits financed by U.S. Treasury borrowing. When federal government borrowing increases interest rates, the result is lower consumption spending by households and lower investment spending by businesses.

Currency Money, including coins and paper money.

Cyclical unemployment Unemployment caused by the lack of jobs during a recession.

D

Deadweight loss The net loss of consumer and producer surplus from underproduction or overproduction of a product.

Debt ceiling A legislated legal limit on the national debt.

Decreasing-cost industry An industry in which the expansion of industry output by the entry of new firms decreases the individual firm's average total cost curve (cost curve shifts downward).

Deflation A decrease in the general (average) price level of goods and services in the economy.

Demand curve for labor A curve showing the different quantities of labor employers are willing to hire at different wage rates in a given time period, ceteris paribus. It is equal to the marginal revenue product of labor.

Demand for money curve A curve representing the quantity of money that people hold at different possible interest rates, ceteris paribus.

Demand A curve or schedule showing the various quantities of product consumers are willing to purchase at possible prices during a specified period of time, ceteris paribus.

Demand-pull inflation A rise in the general price level resulting from an excess of total spending (demand); illustrated by a rightward shift of the aggregate demand curve.

Depreciation of currency A fall in the price of one currency relative to another.

Deregulation The elimination or phasing out of government restrictions on economic activity.

Derived demand The demand for labor and other factors of production that depends on the consumer demand for the final goods and services the factors produce.

Direct relationship A positive association between two variables. When one variable increases, the other variable increases, and when one variable decreases, the other variable decreases.

Discount rate The interest rate the Fed charges on loans of reserves to banks.

Discouraged worker A person who wants to work, but who has given up searching for work because he or she believes there will be no job offers.

Discretionary fiscal policy The deliberate use of changes in government spending or taxes to alter aggregate demand and stabilize the economy.

Diseconomies of scale A situation in which the long-run average cost curve rises as the firm increases output.

Disinflation A reduction in the rate of inflation.

Disposable personal income (DI) The amount of income that households actually have to spend or save after payment of personal taxes.

Dissaving The amount by which real personal consumption expenditures exceed real disposable income.

E

Economic growth The ability of an economy to produce greater levels of output, represented by an outward shift of its production possibilities curve. An expansion in national output measured by the annual percentage increase in a nation's real GDP.

Economic profit Total revenue minus explicit and implicit costs.

Economic system The organizations and methods used to determine what goods and services are produced, how they are produced, and for whom they are produced.

Economics The study of how society chooses to allocate its scarce resources to the production of goods and services to satisfy unlimited wants.

Economies of scale A situation in which the long-run average cost curve declines as the firm increases output.

Effluent tax A tax on the pollutant.

Elastic demand A condition in which the percentage change in quantity demanded is greater than the percentage change in price.

Embargo A law that bars trade with another country.

Emissions trading Firms buying and selling the right to pollute.

Entrepreneurship The creative ability of individuals to seek profits by taking risks and combining resources to produce innovative products.

Equation of exchange An accounting identity that states the money supply times the velocity of money equals total spending.

Equilibrium A market condition that occurs at any price and quantity at which the quantity demanded and the quantity supplied are equal.

Excess reserves Potential loan balances held in vault cash or on deposit with the Fed in excess of required reserves.

Exchange rate The number of units of one nation's currency that equals one unit of another nation's currency.

Expansion An upturn in the business cycle during which real GDP rises. Also called a recovery.

Expenditure approach The national income accounting method that measures GDP by adding all the spending for final goods during a period of time.

Explicit costs Payments to nonowners of a firm for their resources.

External national debt The portion of the national debt owed to foreign citizens.

Externality A cost or benefit imposed on people other than the consumers and producers of a good or service.

F

Federal Deposit Insurance Corporation (FDIC) A government agency established in 1933 to insure customer deposits up to a limit if a bank fails.

Federal funds market A private market in which banks lend reserves to each other for less than 24 hours.

Federal funds rate The interest rate banks charge for overnight loans of reserves to other banks.

Federal Open Market Committee (FOMC) The Federal Reserve's committee that directs the buying and selling of U.S. government securities, which are major instruments for controlling the money supply. The FOMC consists of the 7 members of the Federal Reserve's Board of Governors, the president of the New York Federal Reserve Bank, and the presidents of 4 other Federal Reserve District Banks.

Federal Reserve System The central bank of the United States that consists of 12 Federal Reserve District Banks that service banks and other financial institutions within each of the Federal Reserve districts; popularly called the Fed.

Federal Trade Commission Act of 1914 The federal act that in 1914 established the Federal Trade Commission (FTC) to investigate unfair competitive practices of firms.

Fiat money Money accepted by law and not because of its redeemability or intrinsic value.

Final goods Finished goods and services produced for the ultimate user.

Fiscal policy The use of government spending and taxes to influence the nation's output, employment, and price level.

Fixed input Any resource for which the quantity cannot change during the period of time under consideration.

Flow A rate of change in a quantity during a given time period, such as dollars per year. For example, income and consumption are flows that occur per week, per month, or per year.

Foreign aid The transfer of money or resources from one government to another with no repayment required.

Fractional reserve banking A system in which banks keep only a percentage of their deposits on reserve as vault cash and deposits at the Fed.

Free rider An individual who enjoys benefits without paying the costs.

Free trade The flow of goods between countries without restrictions or special taxes.

Free-rider problem The problem that if some individuals benefit, while others pay, few will be willing to pay for improvement of the environment or other public goods. As a result, these goods are under produced.

Frictional unemployment Temporary unemployment caused by the time required of workers to move from one job to another.

Full employment The situation in which an economy operates at an unemployment rate equal to the sum of the frictional and structural unemployment rates. Also called the natural rate of unemployment.

G

Game Theory A model of the strategic moves and countermoves of rivals.

GDP chain price index A measure that compares changes in the prices of all final goods during a given time period relative to the prices of those goods in a base year. This index is also called GDP price index or simply GDP deflator.

GDP gap The difference between actual real GDP and potential or full-employment real GDP.

GDP per capita The value of final goods produced (GDP) divided by the total population.

Government expenditures Federal, state, and local government outlays for goods and services, including transfer payments.

Government failure Government intervention or lack of intervention that fails to correct market failure.

Gross domestic product (GDP) The market value of all final goods and services produced in a nation during a period of time, usually a year.

H

Homogeneous product A good or service that is identical regardless of which firm produces it.

Horizontal merger A merger of firms that compete in the same market.

Hot spot problem For emissions that do not disperse uniformly, emissions may be higher in locations where firms buy permits that allow them to increase emissions.

Human capital The accumulation of education, training, experience, and the level of good health that enables a worker to enter an occupation and be productive.

Hyperinflation An extremely rapid rise in the general price level.

I

Implicit costs The opportunity costs of using resources owned by a firm.

Incentive-based regulations Government regulations that set an environmental goal, but are flexible as to how buyers and sellers achieve the goal.

Income approach The national income accounting method that measures GDP by adding all incomes during a period of time, including compensation of employees, rents, net interest, and profits.

Income effect The change in quantity demanded of a good or service caused by a change in real income (purchasing power).

Income elasticity of demand The ratio of the percentage change in the quantity demanded of a good or service to a given percentage change in income.

Incomes policies Federal government policies designed to affect the real incomes of workers by controlling nominal wages and prices. Such policies include presidential jawboning, wage–price guidelines, and wage–price controls.

Increasing-cost industry An industry in which the expansion of industry output by the entry of new firms increases the individual firm's average total cost curve (cost curve shifts upward).

Independent relationship A zero association between two variables. When one variable changes, the other variable remains unchanged.

Indifference curve A curve showing the different combinations of two products that yield the same satisfaction or total utility to a consumer.

Indifference map A selection of indifference curves with each curve representing a different level of satisfaction or total utility.

Indirect business taxes Taxes levied as a percentage of the prices of goods sold and therefore collected as part of the firm's revenue. Firms treat such taxes as production costs. Examples include general sales taxes, excise taxes, and customs duties.

Industrially advanced countries (IACs) High-income nations that have market economies based on large stocks of technologically advanced capital and well-educated labor. The United States, Canada, Australia, New Zealand, Japan, and most of the countries of Western Europe are IACs.

Inelastic demand A condition in which the percentage change in quantity demanded is less than the percentage change in price.

Inferior good Any good for which there is an inverse relationship between changes in income and its demand curve.

Inflation An increase in the general (average) price level of goods and services in the economy.

Inflationary gap The amount by which the aggregate expenditures exceed the amount required to achieve full-employment equilibrium.

Infrastructure Capital goods usually provided by the government, including highways, bridges, waste and water systems, and airports.

In-kind transfers Government payments in the form of goods and services, rather than cash, including such government programs as food stamps, Medicaid, and housing.

Interest-rate effect The impact on total spending (and therefore real GDP) caused by the direct relationship between the price level and the interest rate.

Intermediate goods Goods and services used as inputs for the production of final goods.

Intermediate range The rising segment of the aggregate supply curve, which represents an economy as it approaches full employment output.

Internal national debt The portion of the national debt owed to a nation's own citizens.

International Monetary Fund (IMF) The lending agency that makes short-term conditional low-interest loans to developing countries.

Inverse relationship A negative association between two variables. When one variable increases, the other variable decreases, and when one variable decreases, the other variable increases.

Investment demand curve The curve that shows the amount businesses spend for investment goods at different possible rates of interest.

Investment The accumulation of capital, such as factories, machines, and inventories, used to produce goods and services.

Invisible hand A phrase that expresses the belief that the best interests of a society are served when individual consumers and producers compete to achieve their own private interests.

J

Jawboning Oratory intended to pressure unions and businesses to reduce wage and price increases.

K

Keynesian economics The theory, first advanced by John Maynard Keynes, that the role of the federal government is to increase or decrease aggregate demand to achieve economic goals.

Keynesian range The horizontal segment of the aggregate supply curve, which represents an economy in a severe recession.

Kinked demand curve A demand curve facing an oligopolist that assumes rivals will match a price decrease, but ignore a price increase.

L

Labor The mental and physical capacity of workers to produce goods and services.

Laffer curve A graph depicting the relationship between tax rates and total tax revenues.

Lagging indicators Variables that change after real GDP changes.

Land Any natural resource provided by nature that is used to produce a good or service.

Law of demand The principle that there is an inverse relationship between the price of a good and the quantity buyers are willing to purchase in a defined time period, ceteris paribus.

Law of diminishing marginal utility The principle that the extra satisfaction provided by a good or service declines as people consume more in a given period.

Law of diminishing returns The principle that beyond some point the marginal product decreases as additional units of a variable factor are added to a fixed factor.

Law of increasing opportunity costs The principle that the opportunity cost increases as production of one output expands.

Law of supply The principle that there is a direct relationship between the price of a good and the quantity sellers are willing to offer for sale in a defined time period, ceteris paribus.

Leading indicators Variables that change before real GDP changes.

Less-developed countries (LDCs) Nations without large stocks of technologically advanced capital and without well-educated labor. LDCs are economies based on agriculture, such as most countries of Africa, Asia, and Latin America.

Long run A period of time so long that all inputs are variable.

Long-run aggregate supply curve (LRAS) The curve that shows the level of real GDP produced at different possible price levels during a time period in which nominal incomes change by the same percentage as the price level changes.

Long-run average cost curve (LRAC) The curve that traces the lowest cost per unit at which a firm can produce any level of output when the firm can build any desired plant size.

Lorenz curve A graph of the actual cumulative distribution of income compared to a perfectly equal cumulative distribution of income.

M

M1 The narrowest definition of the money supply. It includes currency and checkable deposits.

M2 The definition of the money supply that equals M1 plus near monies, such as savings deposits and small time deposits of less than $100,000.

Macroeconomics The branch of economics that studies decision making for the economy as a whole.

Marginal analysis An examination of the effects of additions to or subtractions from a current situation.

Marginal cost (MC) The change in total cost when one additional unit of output is produced.

Marginal cost pricing A system of pricing in which the price charged equals the marginal cost of the last unit produced.

Marginal factor cost (MFC) The additional total cost resulting from a one-unit increase in the quantity of a factor.

Marginal product The change in total output produced by adding one unit of a variable input, with all other inputs used being held constant.

Marginal propensity to consume (MPC) The change in consumption resulting from a given change in real disposable income.

Marginal propensity to save (MPS) The change in saving resulting from a given change in real disposable income.

Marginal rate of substitution (MRS) The rate at which a consumer is willing to substitute one good for another without a change in total utility. The MRS equals the slope of the indifference curve at any point on the curve.

Marginal revenue (MR) The change in total revenue from the sale of one additional unit of output.

Marginal revenue product (MRP) The increase in a firm's total revenue resulting from hiring an additional unit of labor or other variable resource.

Marginal tax rate The fraction of additional income paid in taxes.

Marginal utility The change in total utility from one additional unit of a good or service.

Marginal-average rule The rule that states when marginal cost is below average cost, average cost falls. When marginal cost is above average cost, average cost rises. When marginal cost equals average cost, average cost is at its minimum point.

Market economy An economic system that answers the What, How, and For Whom questions using prices determined by the interaction of the forces of supply and demand.

Market failure A situation in which market equilibrium results in too few or too many resources being used in the production of a good or service. This inefficiency may justify government intervention.

Market structure A classification system for the key traits of a market, including the number of firms, the similarity of the products they sell, and the ease of entry into and exit from the market.

Market Any arrangement in which buyers and sellers interact to determine the price and quantity of goods and services exchanged.

Means test A requirement that a family's income not exceed a certain level to be eligible for public assistance.

Medium of exchange The primary function of money to be widely accepted in exchange for goods and services.

Microeconomics The branch of economics that studies decision making by a single individual, household, firm, industry, or level of government.

Mixed economy An economic system that answers the What, How, and For Whom questions through a mixture of traditional, command, and market systems.

Model A simplified description of reality used to understand and predict the relationship between variables.

Monetarism The theory that changes in the money supply directly determine changes in prices, real GDP, and employment.

Monetary Control Act A law, formally titled the Depository Institutions Deregulation and Monetary Control Act of 1980, that gave the Federal Reserve System greater control over nonmember banks and made all financial institutions more competitive.

Monetary policy The Federal Reserve's use of open market operations, changes in the discount rate, and changes in the required reserve ratio to change the money supply (M1).

Money multiplier The maximum change in the money supply (checkable deposits) due to an initial change in the excess reserves held by banks. The money multiplier is equal to 1 divided by the required reserve ratio.

Money Anything that serves as a medium of exchange, unit of account, and store of value.

Monopolistic competition A market structure characterized by many small sellers, a differentiated product, and easy market entry and exit.

Monopoly A market structure characterized by a single seller, a unique product, and impossible entry into the market.

Monopsony A labor market in which a single firm hires labor.

Mutual interdependence A condition in which an action by one firm may cause a reaction from other firms.

N

National debt The total amount owed by the federal government to owners of government securities.

National income (NI) The total income earned by resource owners, including wages, rents, interest, and profits. NI is calculated as gross domestic product minus depreciation of the capital worn out in producing output.

Nationalization The act of transforming a private enterprise's assets into a government enterprise.

Natural monopoly An industry in which the long-run average cost of production declines throughout the entire market. As a result, a single firm can supply the entire market demand at a lower cost than two or more smaller firms.

Natural rate hypothesis The concept that argues that the economy will self-correct to the natural rate of unemployment. The long-run Phillips curve is therefore a vertical line at the natural rate of unemployment.

Negative income tax (NIT) A plan under which families below a certain breakeven level of income would receive cash payments that decrease as their incomes increase.

Net exports effect The impact on total spending (and therefore real GDP) caused by the inverse relationship between the price level and the net exports of an economy.

Net public debt National debt minus all government interagency borrowing.

Network good A good that increases in value to each user as the total number of users increases. As a result, a firm can achieve economies of scale. Examples include Facebook and Match.com.

New-source bias Bias that occurs when regulations provide an incentive to keep assets past the efficient point.

Nominal GDP The value of all final goods based on the prices existing during the time period of production.

Nominal income The actual number of dollars received over a period of time.

Nominal interest rate The actual rate of interest without adjustment for the inflation rate.

Nonprice competition The situation in which a firm competes using advertising, packaging, product development, better quality, and better service, rather than lower prices.

Normal good Any good for which there is a direct relationship between changes in income and its demand curve.

Normal profit The minimum profit necessary to keep a firm in operation. A firm that earns normal profits earns total revenue equal to its total opportunity cost.

Normative economics An analysis based on subjective value judgments.

O

Offset A reduction in an existing pollution source to counteract pollution from a new source.

Offshoring The practice of work for a company performed by the company's employees located in another country.

Oligopoly A market structure characterized by few large sellers, either a homogeneous or a differentiated product, and difficult market entry.

Open market operations The buying and selling of government securities by the Federal Reserve System.

Opportunity cost The best alternative sacrificed for a chosen alternative.

Outsourcing The practice of a company having its work done by another company in another country.

P

Peak The phase of the business cycle in which real GDP reaches its maximum after rising during a recovery.

Per se rule The antitrust doctrine that the existence of monopoly alone is illegal, regardless of whether or not the monopoly engages in illegal business practices.

Perfect competition A market structure characterized by a large number of small firms; a homogeneous product; and very easy entry into or exit from the market. Perfect competition is also referred to as pure competition.

Perfectly competitive firm's short-run supply curve A firm's marginal cost curve above the minimum point on its average variable cost curve.

Perfectly competitive industry's long-run supply curve The curve that shows the quantities supplied by the industry at different equilibrium prices after firms complete their entry and exit.

Perfectly competitive industry's short-run supply curve The supply curve derived from horizontal summation of the marginal cost curves of all firms in the industry above the minimum point of each firm's average variable cost curve.

Perfectly elastic demand A condition in which a small percentage change in price brings about an infinite percentage change in quantity demanded.

Perfectly inelastic demand A condition in which the quantity demanded does not change as the price changes.

Personal income (PI) The total income received by households that is available for consumption, saving, and payment of personal taxes.

Phillips curve A curve showing an inverse relationship between the inflation rate and the unemployment rate.

Political business cycle A business cycle caused by policymakers to improve politicians' reelection chances.

Positive economics An analysis limited to statements that are verifiable.

Poverty line The level of income below which a person or a family is considered to be poor.

Precautionary demand for money The stock of money people hold to pay unpredictable expenses.

Predatory pricing The practice of one or more firms temporarily reducing prices in order to eliminate competition and then raising prices.

Price ceiling A legally established maximum price a seller can charge.

Price discrimination The practice of a seller charging different prices for the same product that are not justified by cost differences.

Price elasticity of demand The ratio of the percentage change in the quantity demanded of a product to a percentage change in its price.

Price elasticity of supply The ratio of the percentage change in the quantity supplied of a product to the percentage change in its price.

Price floor A legally established minimum price a seller can be paid.

Price leadership A pricing strategy in which a dominant firm sets the price for an industry and the other firms follow.

Price maker A firm that faces a downward-sloping demand curve, and therefore it can choose among price and output combinations along the demand curve.

Price system A mechanism that uses the forces of supply and demand to create an equilibrium through rising and falling prices.

Price taker A seller that has no control over the price of the product it sells.

Private benefits and costs Benefits and costs to the decision maker, ignoring benefits and costs to third parties. Third parties are people outside the market transaction who are affected by the product.

Privatization The process of turning a government enterprise into a private enterprise.

Producer surplus The value of the difference between the actual selling price of a product and the price producers are willing to sell it for on the supply curve.

Product differentiation The process of creating real or apparent differences between goods and services.

Production function The relationship between the maximum amounts of output a firm can produce and various quantities of inputs.

Production possibilities curve A curve that shows the maximum combinations of two outputs an economy can produce in a given period of time with its available resources and technology.

Progressive tax A tax that charges a higher percentage of income as income rises.

Proportional tax A tax that charges the same percentage of income, regardless of the size of income. Also called a flat tax rate or simply a flat tax.

Protectionism The government's use of embargoes, tariffs, quotas, and other trade restrictions to protect domestic producers from foreign competition.

Public choice theory The analysis of the government's decision-making process for allocating resources.

Public good A good or service with two properties: users collectively consume benefits; and there is no way to bar people who do not pay (free riders) from consuming the good or service.

Q

Quantity theory of money The theory that changes in the money supply are directly related to changes in the price level.

Quota A limit on the quantity of a good that may be imported in a given time period.

R

Rational expectations theory The belief that people use all available information to predict the future, including the future impact of predictable expansionary monetary and fiscal policies. Predictable expansionary macroeconomic policies can therefore be negated by immediately flexible wages and prices when businesses and workers anticipate the effects of these policies on the economy.

Rational ignorance The voter's choice to remain uninformed because the marginal cost of obtaining information is higher than the marginal benefit from knowing it.

Real balances effect The impact on total spending (and therefore real GDP) caused by the inverse relationship between the price level and the real value of financial assets with fixed nominal value.

Real GDP The value of all final goods produced during a given time period based on the prices existing in a selected base year.

Real income The actual number of dollars received (nominal income) adjusted for changes in the CPI.

Real interest rate The nominal rate of interest minus the inflation rate.

Recession A downturn in the business cycle during which real GDP declines, and the unemployment rate rises. Also called a contraction.

Recessionary gap The amount by which the aggregate expenditures fall short of the amount required to achieve full-employment equilibrium.

Regressive tax A tax that charges a lower percentage of income as income rises.

Required reserve ratio The percentage of deposits that the Fed requires a bank to hold in vault cash or on deposit with the Fed rather than being loaned.

Required reserves The minimum balance that the Fed requires a bank to hold in vault cash or on deposit with the Fed.

Resources The basic categories of inputs used to produce goods and services. Resources are also called factors of production. Economists divide resources into three categories: land, labor, and capital.

Robinson—Patman Act of 1936 An amendment to the Clayton Act that strengthens the Clayton Act's provision against price discrimination.

Rule of reason The antitrust doctrine that the existence of monopoly alone is not illegal unless the monopoly engages in illegal business practices.

S

Saving The part of disposable income households do not spend for consumer goods and services.

Say's Law The theory that supply creates its own demand.

Scarcity The condition in which human wants are forever greater than the available supply of time, goods, and resources.

Sherman Act of 1890 The federal antitrust law enacted that prohibits monopolization and conspiracies to restrain trade.

Short run A period of time so short that there is at least one fixed input.

Shortage A market condition existing at any price at where the quantity supplied is less than the quantity demanded.

Short-run aggregate supply curve (SRAS) The curve that shows the level of real GDP produced at different possible price levels during a time period in which nominal incomes do not change in response to changes in the price level.

Slope The ratio of the change in the variable on the vertical axis (the rise or fall) to the change in the variable on the horizontal axis (the run).

Social benefits and costs The sum of benefits to everyone in society, including both private benefits and external benefits. Social costs are the sum of costs to everyone in society, including both private costs and external costs.

Socialism An economic system characterized by government ownership of resources and centralized decision making.

Speculative demand for money The stock of money people hold to take advantage of expected future changes in the price of bonds, stocks, or other nonmoney financial assets.

Spending multiplier (SM) The change in aggregate demand (total spending) resulting from an initial change in any component of aggregate expenditures, including consumption, investment, government spending, and net exports. As a formula, spending multiplier equals $1/(1 - MPC)$ or $1/MPS$.

Stagflation The condition that occurs when an economy experiences the twin maladies of high unemployment and rapid inflation simultaneously.

Stock A quantity measured at one point in time. For example, an inventory of goods or the amount of money in a checking account

Store of value The ability of money to hold value over time.

Structural unemployment Unemployment caused by a mismatch of the skills of workers out of work and the skills required for existing job opportunities.

Subprime mortgage loan A home loan made to borrowers with poor or less than ideal credit scores.

Substitute good A good that competes with another good for consumer purchases. As a result, there is a direct relationship between a price change for one good and the demand for its competitor good.

Substitution effect The change in quantity demanded of a good or service caused by a change in its price relative to substitutes.

Supply curve of labor A curve showing the different quantities of labor workers are willing to offer employers at different wage rates in a given time period, ceteris paribus.

Supply A curve or schedule showing the various quantities of a product sellers are willing to produce and offer for sale at possible prices during a specified period of time, ceteris paribus.

Supply-side fiscal policy A fiscal policy that emphasizes government policies that increase aggregate supply in order to achieve long-run growth in real output, full employment, and a lower price level.

Surplus A market condition existing at any price where the quantity supplied is greater than the quantity demanded.

Sustainability Meeting the needs of the present generation without compromising the ability of future generations to meet their needs.

T

Tariffs A tax on an import.

Tax incidence The share of a tax ultimately paid by consumers and sellers.

Tax multiplier The change in aggregate expenditures (total spending) resulting from an initial change in taxes. As a formula, the tax multiplier equals 1 – spending multiplier.

Technology The body of knowledge applied to how goods are produced.

Total cost (TC) The sum of total fixed cost and total variable cost at each level of output.

Total fixed cost (TFC) Costs that do not vary as output varies and that must be paid even if output is zero. These are payments that the firm must make in the short run, regardless of the level of output.

Total revenue (TR) The total number of dollars a firm earns from the sale of a good or service, which is equal to its price multiplied by the quantity demanded.

Total utility The amount of satisfaction received from all the units of a good or service consumed.

Total variable cost (TVC) Costs that are zero when output is zero and vary as output varies.

Traditional economy An economic system that answers the What, How, and For Whom questions the way they have always have been answered.

Tragedy of the Commons Individuals will use an open access resource to the point of exhaustion, basing their use on private benefits while disregarding external costs to others.

Transactions costs The costs of negotiating and enforcing a contract.

Transactions demand for money The stock of money people hold to pay everyday predictable expenses.

Transfer payment A government payment to individuals not in exchange for goods or services currently produced.

Trough The phase of the business cycle in which real GDP reaches its minimum after falling during a recession.

Trust A combination or cartel consisting of firms that place their assets in the custody of a board of trustees.

U

Unemployment compensation The government insurance program that pays income for a short time period to unemployed workers.

Unemployment rate The percentage of people in the civilian labor force who are without jobs and are actively seeking jobs.

Unit of account The function of money to provide a common measurement of the relative value of goods and services.

Unitary elastic demand A condition in which the percentage change in quantity demanded is equal to the percentage change in price.

Utility The satisfaction, or pleasure, that people receive from consuming a good or service.

V

Variable input Any resource for which the quantity can change during the period of time under consideration.

Velocity of money The average number of times per year a dollar of the money supply is spent on final goods and services.

Vertical merger A merger of a firm with its suppliers.

Vicious circle of poverty The trap in which countries are poor because they cannot afford to save and invest, and they cannot save and invest because they are poor.

W

Wage and price controls Legal restrictions on wage and price increases. Violations can result in fines and imprisonment.

Wage and price guidelines Voluntary standards set by the government for permissible wage and price increases.

Wage-price spiral A situation that occurs when increases in nominal wage rates are passed on in higher prices, which, in turn, result in even higher nominal wage rates and prices.

Wealth effect A shift in the consumption function caused by a change in the value of real and financial assets.

Wealth The value of the stock of assets owned at some point in time.

World Bank The lending agency affiliated with the United Nations that makes long-term low-interest loans and provides technical assistance to less developed countries.

World Trade Organization (WTO) An international organization of member countries that oversees international trade agreements and rules on trade disputes.

INDEX